Come with us to the French-speaking world!

Allez, viens!

—a fully integrated French program—makes it possible for you to accomplish all your teaching objectives as never before! *Allez, viens!* ensures development of language proficiency in French and builds students' language skills, so they can communicate effectively and express themselves with confidence.

- The **FOUR LANGUAGE SKILLS**—listening, speaking, reading, and writing—plus **CULTURE**, are all interwoven throughout the program.

- Strong **GRAMMAR** support lays an invaluable foundation for proficiency.

- All three levels of *Allez, viens!* are **PACED** so that you can finish each text within the year. And because the first two chapters of the Levels 2 and 3 *Pupil's Editions* are review, the program provides an easy transition from level to level.

- Designed for **LEARNERS OF ALL TYPES**, *Allez, viens!* is the program of choice for every one of your students.

- **VIDEO CORRELATIONS** and **ON-PAGE BARCODES** let you easily integrate video and videodisc segments into your instruction.

- A **COMPLETE AUDIO PROGRAM**—available on audiocassettes or compact discs—reinforces the text material and gives students another learning option.

- Constant **SPIRALING** and **RE-ENTRY** of material from earlier chapters provide consistent reinforcement and review.

See and hear native speakers in authentic locations around the francophone world!

CHAPITRE 4

Allez, viens à Québec

Québec

Capitale de la province du Québec
Population : plus de 574 400
Points d'intérêt : le château Frontenac, l'université de Laval, la terrasse Dufferin, le musée du Québec, les fortifications de Québec, les chutes Montmorency, le mont Sainte-Anne, Québec Expérience
Personnes célèbres : Samuel de Champlain, François de Montmorency-Laval, le marquis de Montcalm
Ressources et industries : produits de papier, de cuir et d'érable; tourisme
Spécialités : ragoût de boulettes, tourtière, cretons, soupe aux pois, tarte au sucre, tarte à la farlouche

Where Will We Go?

Each Location Opener introduces your students to the diversity of French-speaking countries. The *Video Program, Expanded Video Program,* and *Videodisc Program* target the same locations so your students see, hear, understand—and use—the language and culture.

CHAPITRE

5
On va au café?

① On va au café?

124 *cent vingt-quatre*

Where are your favorite places to meet and relax with your friends? In France, people of all ages meet at cafés to talk, have a snack, or just watch the people go by!

In this chapter you will learn
- to make suggestions; to make excuses; to make a recommendation
- to get someone's attention; to order food and beverages
- to inquire about and express likes and dislikes; to pay the check

And you will
- listen to people ordering in a café
- read a café menu
- write about your food and drink preferences
- find out about French cafés

② L'addition, s'il vous plaît.

cent vingt-cinq 125

How Will We Get There?

Chapter Openers serve as advance organizers, identifying learner outcomes and stimulating interest.

Mise en train

Un petit service

Do you ever run errands for your family? What kinds of things do you have to do? Look at the pictures below and see if you can figure out what Lucien's mother, father, and sister are asking him to do.

Lucien · Lisette · La mère
Le père · Une voisine

Maman, je vais en ville. J'ai rendez-vous avec Mireille. On va passer la journée à Fort-de-France. Je vais lui faire visiter le fort Saint-Louis.

Avant de rentrer, passe au marché et prends de l'ananas, des oranges et des caramboles.

Ah, tu peux rendre ces livres à la bibliothèque aussi, s'il te plaît? Et en échange, tu me prends trois autres livres. Voilà ma carte.

Est-ce que tu peux aller à la poste et envoyer ce paquet?

Je ne sais pas si je vais avoir le temps.

Je vais d'abord au fort Saint-Louis, puis je dois aller au marché et ensuite...

C'est important...

Bon.

Tu peux passer chez le disquaire? J'ai commandé un disque-compact.

Bien. C'est tout?

Au retour, tu peux aller à la boulangerie? Prends deux baguettes.

Tiens, voilà 5 francs. Prends-moi aussi le journal.

Bon, ça suffit pour aujourd'hui!

Merci, Lucien. C'est sympa.

Tu vas voir, c'est très intéressant, le fort Saint-Louis.

Bonjour. Est-ce que par hasard vous allez en ville aujourd'hui?

Au secours!

CHAPITRE 12 En ville

MISE EN TRAIN

Authentic Locations & Language

Mise en train features introduce the functions, vocabulary, and grammar targeted in the chapter and are reproduced in both the video and audio programs.

Your Building Blocks to Proficiency

The function, grammar, and vocabulary features in each chapter of *Allez, viens!* are linked to give your students the building blocks they need to develop complete language proficiency.

The *Grammaire* presentation provides strong grammar support for the function-driven base of *Allez, viens!*, the perfect combination to help your students develop their French proficiency.

The *Vocabulaire* found in each chapter relates to the theme and language function, and is presented visually whenever possible.

In this function-driven program, each *Comment dit-on?* presentation equips your students for specific language tasks appropriate to the chapter theme.

An Abundance of Activities

Throughout *Allez, viens!*, activities flow from controlled and structured through transitional to open-ended, communicative activities. Plenty of activities are contained within the program to build competency in each of the four language skills. Types of activities included in each chapter are:

- Contextualized listening activities
- Pair and group work
- Journal writing activities (can be used as portfolio assessment activities)
- Reading, writing, and role-playing activities
- Discovery questions and discussions of culture topics

Critical Thinking Through
Multicultural Awareness

The *Panorama Culturel* is designed to give your students a chance to meet people from around the French-speaking world who share their views, opinions, and thoughts on a variety of topics that are thematically related to the chapters in *Allez, viens!*. Filmed on location, authentic interviews with native speakers can be found in the text, on the *Video Program,* the *Expanded Video Program,* the *Audio Program*, and the *Videodisc Program.* The result: total video, audio, and text integration for complete language development. The *Panorama Culturel* also contains critical-thinking activities that expand upon what students learn from the interviews.

An Encounter
of Cultures

Do you ever wonder how you can make your students "walk in someone else's shoes?" With *Allez, viens!*'s *Rencontre Culturelle,* you can do just that! This unique presentation introduces your students to customs in French-speaking cultures that may be unfamiliar to them, but are a way of life in those cultures. They'll also learn what people in the target cultures may find unfamiliar about Americans, and follow up what they've learned with critical-thinking questions. This expands your students' horizons beyond their own backyard. They'll realize that diverse viewpoints and different ways of doing similar things enrich our global community.

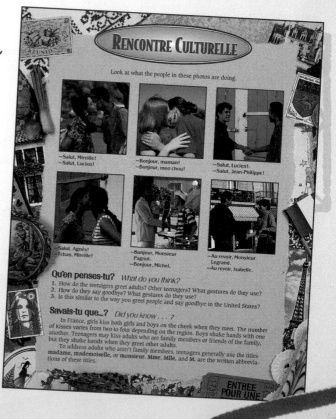

Allez, viens!

Holt French
Level 2

ANNOTATED
TEACHER'S EDITION

HOLT, RINEHART AND WINSTON

Harcourt Brace & Company

Austin • New York • Orlando • Atlanta • San Francisco • Boston • Dallas • Toronto • London

In the *Annotated Teacher's Edition:*

Photography Credits
Abbreviations used: (t) top, (c) center, (b) bottom, (l) left, (r) right.
Front Matter: Page T23(bl), HRW Photo by Marty Granger/Edge Productions; T23(br), Joe Viesti/Viesti Associates; T24(b), HRW Photo by Marty Granger/Edge Productions; T32(br), HRW Photo by Marty Granger/Edge Productions; T33(all), HRW Photo by Marty Granger/Edge Productions; T37(b), HRW Photo by Marty Granger/Edge Productions; T45(bl), HRW Photo by Michelle Bridwell; T47(bl), HRW Photo by Lance Shriner; T47(br), HRW Photo. **Chapter One:** Page 3D(b), Emmanuel Rongiéras d'Usseau; 3D(cr), Ulrike Welsch/PhotoEdit; 3E, HBJ Photo by Capretz; 3F(c), HRW Photo by May Polycarpe; 3F(cl), (cr), (r), HRW Photo by Marty Granger/Edge Productions; 3F(l), Walter Chandoha. **Chapter Two:** Page 27D(bl), IPA/The Image Works; 27D(cr), HRW Photo; 27D(tl), HRW Photo by John Langford; 27D (all remaining), HRW Photo by Marty Granger/Edge Productions. **Chapter Four:** Page 81C(b), HRW Photo by Marty Granger/Edge Productions; 81C(c), Robert Fried; 81C(t), Allan Philiba; 81E(all), HRW Photo by Marty Granger/Edge Productions. **Chapter Six:** Page 135E(t), Paul Barton/The Stock Market; 135E(b), T. Mogi/SuperStock; 135F(b), Image Works Archive; 135F(c), Culver Pictures; 135F(t), The Bettmann Archive. **Chapter Eight:** Page 189F(both), HRW Photo by Sam Dudgeon. **Chapter Ten:** Page 243D(c), HRW Photo by May Polycarpe; 243D(br), HRW Photo by Daniel Aubry. **Chapter Eleven:** Page 267E (all), HRW Photo by Sam Dudgeon; 267F(bc), Francois Duhamel/Fotos International/Archive Photos; 267F(all remaining), Motion Picture and TV Photo Archive.

Illustration Credits
Front Matter: Page T49(b), Jocelyne Bouchard. **Chapter Two:** Page 27F(br), Janet Brooks. **Chapter Three:** Page 51E(r), Doug La Rue. **Chapter Four:** Page 81D(b), Anne Stanley; 81F(all), Anne de Masson. **Chapter Five:** Page 111C(all), Marie Gillis Baur; 111E(all), Bruce Roberts; 111F(all), Marie Gillis Baur. **Chapter Seven:** Page 159F(b), Bruce Roberts. **Chapter Eight:** Page 189D(all), Gilbert Gnangbel. **Chapter Nine:** Page 219F(all), Jocelyne Bouchard. **Chapter Ten:** Page 243C(all), Jocelyne Bouchard; 243D, 243F(b), Janet Brooks. **Chapter Twelve:** Page 297C(b), Anne Stanley; 297D(all), Jocelyne Bouchard; 297F(all), Marie Gillis Baur.

ACKNOWLEDGMENTS
For permission to reprint copyrighted material, grateful acknowledgement is made to the following sources:

Camping Granby: Advertisement, "Camping Granby," from *Camping/Caravaning 1993.*

City Lights Books and Izis Bidermanas: Cover of *Paroles: Selected Poems* by Jaques Prévert, translated by Lawrence Ferlinghetti. Translation copyright © 1958 by Lawrence Ferlinghetti.

Editions J'ai Lu: Cover of *Les années metalliques* by Michael Demuth. Copyright © 1977 by Éditions Robert Laffont, S.A.

Editions J.M. Fuzeau: Cover of "Lycée Alfred Kastler: Carnet de correspondance."

Groupement E. Leclerc: Nine photographs of fruits and vegetables and logo from *Grande Fraicheur à petits prix,* October 13-23, 1993.

Parc Bromont: Advertisement, "Parc Bromont," from *Camping/Caravaning '93.*

Présence Africaine: Cover of *La tragédie du Roi Christophe* by Aimé Césaire. Copyright © 1963 by Présence Africaine.

Sony Music France: Cover and side 2 of CD from *Tékit izi* by Kassav'. Copyright © 1992 by Sony Music Entertainment (France) S. A./Saligna Production.

Sony Tunes: Lyrics from "An Sél Zouk" from *Tékit izi* by Kassav'. Copyright © 1992 by Sony Music Entertainment (France) S. A./Saligna Production.

In the *Pupil's Edition:*

A l'Escargot d'Or: Advertisement, "A l'Escargot d'Or," from *Chartres: Ville d'Art.*

Association de Promotion du Tourisme Fluvial sur le Bassin du Maine: Advertisement, "Tourisme Fluvial dans les pays de la Loire" from *Évasions.*

Au Plaisir d'offrir: Advertisement, "Au Plaisir d'offrir," from *Chartres: Ville d'Art.*

Bayard Presse Jeune: "Etes-vous un bon copain?" from *Okapi,* October 15-31, 1989. Copyright © 1989 by Okapi. From "12 Sports à la Carte" from *Okapi,* no. 507, January 1-15, 1993. Copyright © 1993 by Okapi. Text from "Les enfants du paradis," text from "2001, l'Odyssée de l'espace," text from "Il était une fois dans l'ouest," text from "Le cercle des poètes disparus," text from "Cyrano de Bergerac," and text from "Terminator 2" from "10 Films Qui Ont Fait Date" from *Okapi: Cinéma mon plaisir.* Copyright © by Okapi. Text from "La leçon, la cantatrice chauve by Eugène Ionesco" by Rémy Lillet from *Phosphore,* no. 94, November 1988. Copyright © 1988 by Bayard Presse Jeune. Text from *"Daïren* by Alain Paris" by Denis Guiot from *Phosphore,* no. 97, February 1989. Copyright © 1989 by Bayard Presse Jeune.

ACKNOWLEDGMENTS continued on page 387, which is an extension of the copyright page.

Annotated Teacher's Edition

CONTRIBUTING WRITERS

Gail Corder
Trinity Valley School
Fort Worth, TX
Ms. Corder was the principal writer of the
Level 2 *Annotated Teacher's Edition.*

Judith Ryser
San Marcos High School
San Marcos, TX
Ms. Ryser wrote teaching suggestions
and notes for the reading selections of the
Level 2 *Annotated Teacher's Edition.*

Véronique Dupont
Westwood High School
Austin, TX
Ms. Dupont wrote answers to activities
of the Level 2 *Annotated Teacher's Edition.*

Jayne Abrate
The University of Missouri
Rolla, MO
Ms. Abrate wrote teaching suggestions
and notes for the Location Openers for
the Level 2 *Annotated Teacher's Edition.*

FIELD TEST PARTICIPANTS

Marie Allison
New Hanover High School
Wilmington, NC

Gabrielle Applequist
Capital High School
Boise, ID

Jana Brinton
Bingham High School
Riverton, UT

Nancy J. Cook
Sam Houston High School
Lake Charles, LA

Rachael Gray
Williams High School
Plano, TX

Priscilla Koch
Troxell Junior High School
Allentown, PA

Katherine Kohler
Nathan Hale Middle School
Norwalk, CT

Nancy Mirsky
Museum Junior High School
Yonkers, NY

Myrna S. Nie
Whetstone High School
Columbus, OH

Jacqueline Reid
Union High School
Tulsa, OK

Judith Ryser
San Marcos High School
San Marcos, TX

Erin Hahn Sass
Lincoln Southeast High School
Lincoln, NE

Linda Sherwin
Sandy Creek High School
Tyrone, GA

Norma Joplin Sivers
Arlington Heights High School
Fort Worth, TX

Lorabeth Stroup
Lovejoy High School
Lovejoy, GA

Robert Vizena
W.W. Lewis Middle School
Sulphur, LA

Gladys Wade
New Hanover High School
Wilmington, NC

Kathy White
Grimsley High School
Greensboro, NC

REVIEWERS

John Billus
Weston High School
Weston, CT

Eugène Blé
Consultant
Austin, TX

Betty Clough
McCallum High School
Austin, TX

Jennifer Jones
U.S. Peace Corps volunteer
Côte d'Ivoire 1991-1993
Austin, TX

Audrey O'Keefe
David Starr Jordan High School
Los Angeles, CA

Agathe Norman
Consultant
Austin, TX

Mayanne Wright
Consultant
Burnet, TX

Jo Anne S. Wilson
Consultant
Glen Arbor, MI

PROFESSIONAL ESSAYS

*Standards for Foreign
Language Education*
Robert La Bouve
Board of National Standards in
Foreign Language Education
Austin, TX

Multi-Level Classrooms
Dr. Joan H. Manley
The University of Texas
El Paso, TX

Teaching Culture
Nancy A. Humbach
The Miami University
Oxford, OH

Dorothea Brushke
Parkway School District
Chesterfield, MO

*Learning Styles and
Multi-Modality Teaching*
Mary B. McGehee
Louisiana State University
Baton Rouge, LA

Higher-Order Thinking Skills
Audrey L. Heining-Boynton
The University of North Carolina
Chapel Hill, NC

*Using Portfolios in the Foreign
Language Classroom*
Jo Anne S. Wilson
J. Wilson Associates
Glen Arbor, MI

Pupil's Edition

Authors

Emmanuel Rongiéras d'Usseau
Le Kremlin-Bicêtre, France

Mr. Rongiéras d'Usseau contributed to the development of the scope and sequence for the chapters, created the basic material and listening scripts, selected realia, and wrote activities.

John DeMado
Washington, CT

Mr. DeMado helped form the general philosphy of the French program and wrote activities to practice basic material, functions, grammar, and vocabulary.

Contributing Writers

Jayne Abrate
The University of Missouri
Rolla, MO

Jill Beede
Educational writer
Tahoma, CA

Judith Ryser
San Marcos High School
San Marcos, TX

Reviewers

Jeannette Caviness
Mount Tabor High School
Winston-Salem, NC

Jennie Bowser Chao
Consultant
East Lansing, MI

Gail Corder
Trinity Valley School
Ft. Worth, TX

Jennifer Jones
U. S. Peace Corps volunteer
Côte d'Ivoire 1991–1993
Austin, TX

Joan H. Manley
The University of Texas at El Paso
El Paso, TX

Marie Line McGhee
Consultant
Austin, TX

Gail Montgomery
Foreign Language Program
Administrator
Greenwich, CT Public Schools

Agathe Norman
Consultant
Austin, TX

Marc Prévost
Austin Community College
Austin, TX

Norbert Rouquet
Consultant
La Roche-sur-Yon, France

Robert Trottier
St. Johnsbury Academy
Saint Johnsbury, VT

Michèle Viard
The Dalton School
New York, NY

Jack Yerby
Farmington High School
Farmington, NM

Field Test Participants

Marie Allison
New Hanover High School
Wilmington, NC

Gabrielle Applequist
Capital High School
Boise, ID

Jana Brinton
Bingham High School
Riverton, UT

Nancy J. Cook
Sam Houston High School
Lake Charles, LA

Rachael Gray
Williams High School
Plano, TX

Priscilla Koch
Troxell Junior High School
Allentown, PA

Katherine Kohler
Nathan Hale Middle School
Norwalk, CT

Nancy Mirsky
Museum Junior High School
Yonkers, NY

Myrna S. Nie
Whetstone High School
Columbus, OH

Jacqueline Reid
Union High School
Tulsa, OK

Judith Ryser
San Marcos High School
San Marcos, TX

Erin Hahn Sass
Lincoln Southeast High School
Lincoln, NE

Linda Sherwin
Sandy Creek High School
Tyrone, GA

Norma Joplin Sivers
Arlington Heights High School
Fort Worth, TX

Lorabeth Stroup
Lovejoy High School
Lovejoy, GA

Robert Vizena
W.W. Lewis Middle School
Sulphur, LA

Gladys Wade
New Hanover High School
Wilmington, NC

Kathy White
Grimsley High School
Greensboro, NC

To the Student

*Some people have the opportunity to learn a new language by living in another country.
Most of us, however, begin learning another language and getting acquainted with a foreign
culture in a classroom with the help of a teacher, classmates, and a book.
To use your book effectively, you need to know how it works.*

Allez, viens! *(Come along!)* takes you to six different French-speaking locations. Each location is introduced with photos and information on four special pages called Location Openers.

There are twelve chapters in the book, and each one follows the same pattern.

The two Chapter Opener pages announce the chapter theme and list the objectives. These objectives set goals that you can achieve by the end of the chapter.

Mise en train *(Getting started)* The next part of the chapter is an illustrated story that shows you French-speaking people in real-life situations, using the language you'll be learning in the chapter. You'll also have fun watching this story on video.

Première, Deuxième, Troisième Etape *(First, Second, Third Part)* Following the opening story, the chapter is divided into three parts, called **étapes.** At the beginning of each **étape** there's a reminder of the objective(s) you'll be aiming for in this part. In order to communicate, you'll need the French expressions listed in boxes called **Comment dit-on... ?** *(How do you say . . . ?).* You'll also need vocabulary; look for new words under the heading **Vocabulaire.** You won't have trouble finding grammar, for you're sure to recognize the headings **Grammaire** and **Note de Grammaire.** Now all you need is plenty of practice. In each **étape** there are listening, speaking, reading, and writing activities for you to do individually, with a partner, or in groups. By the end of the **étape,** you'll have achieved your objective(s).

This book will also help you get to know the cultures of the people who speak French.

Panorama Culturel *(Cultural Panorama)* On this page of the chapter you'll read interviews with French-speaking people around the world. They'll talk about themselves and their lives, and you can compare their culture to yours. You'll watch these interviews on video or listen to them on audiocassette or CD.

Note Culturelle *(Culture Note)* These notes provide a lot of interesting cultural information.

Rencontre Culturelle *(Cultural Encounter)* This page in six of the chapters offers a firsthand encounter with French-speaking cultures.

Lisons! *(Let's read!)* After the three **étapes,** one or more reading selections related to the chapter theme will help you develop your reading skills.

Mise en pratique *(Putting into practice)* A variety of activities gives you opportunities to put into practice what you've learned in the chapter in new situations. You'll improve your listening skills and practice communicating with others orally and in writing.

Que sais-je? *(What do I know?)* On this page at the end of the chapter, a series of questions and short activities will help you decide how well you can do on your own.

Vocabulaire *(Vocabulary)* On the last page of the chapter, you'll find a French-English vocabulary list. The words are grouped by **étape** and listed under the objectives they support. You'll need to know these words and expressions for the Chapter Test!

Throughout the book, you'll get a lot of help.

De bons conseils *(Good advice)* Check out the helpful study hints in these boxes.

Tu te rappelles? *(Do you remember?)* Along the way, these notes will remind you of things you might have forgotten.

A la française *(The French way)* Be on the lookout for these boxes, too. They'll give you additional language tips to help you sound more like a native speaker.

Vocabulaire à la carte *(Your choice of vocabulary)* From these lists, you'll be able to choose extra words and expressions you might want to use when you talk about yourself and your interests.

At the end of your book, you'll find more helpful material, including a list of the communicative expressions you'll need, a summary of the grammar you've studied, supplementary vocabulary, and French-English, English-French vocabulary lists with the words you'll need to know in bold type.

Allez, viens! Come along on an exciting trip to a new culture and a new language.

Bon voyage!

ANNOTATED TEACHER'S EDITION

Contents

ALLEZ, VIENS
aux environs de Paris!

VISIT THE REGION AROUND PARIS AND—

Imagine what you'd do if you were an exchange student • CHAPITRE 1
Find out what French homes and towns are like • CHAPITRE 2
Shop for a meal and gifts for special occasions • CHAPITRE 3

CHAPITRE 1

Bon séjour! 4

CHAPITRE 2

Bienvenue à Chartres! 28

CHAPITRE 2

Bienvenue à Chartres! 28

ALLEZ, VIENS
aux environs de Paris!

Bon séjour! 4

CHAPITRE 3

Un repas à la française 52

ALLEZ, VIENS

en Touraine!

VISIT THE TOURAINE REGION OF FRANCE AND—

Find out what it's like to attend a **lycée** in France • CHAPITRE 5
Learn about châteaux and how to travel in France • CHAPITRE 6
Talk about health and ways to stay healthy • CHAPITRE 7

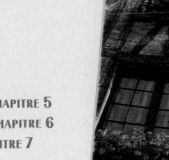

CHAPITRE 5

Quelle journée! 112

CHAPITRE 6

A nous les châteaux! 136

CHAPITRE 7

En pleine forme 160

ALLEZ, VIENS

en Côte d'Ivoire

LOCATION • CHAPITRE 8 186

VISIT THE COUNTRY OF COTE D'IVOIRE AND—

Learn about life in Ivorian
cities and villages • CHAPITRE 8

CHAPITRE 8

C'était comme ça 190

M. et Mme kouamé
BP. 31

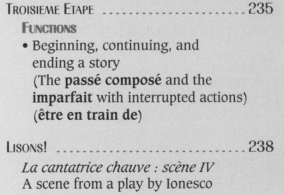

T19

CHAPITRE 10

Je peux te parler? 244

C'est

L'ANNIVERSAIRE

de *Manu* !

S... ous voulez faire ...

... avec nous, ven...

SURPRISE ...

que nou... ...isons!

...edi 14 avril

DATE ...9... HEURES

...rine Morel

...e 26, rue V. Hugo

CHAPITRE 11

Chacun ses goûts 268

ALLEZ, VIENS

au Québec!

T22

Cultural References

Page numbers referring to material in the Pupil's Edition *appear in regular type. When the material referenced is located in the* Annotated Teacher's Edition, *page numbers appear in* **boldface type.** ◆

T25

Maps

La France

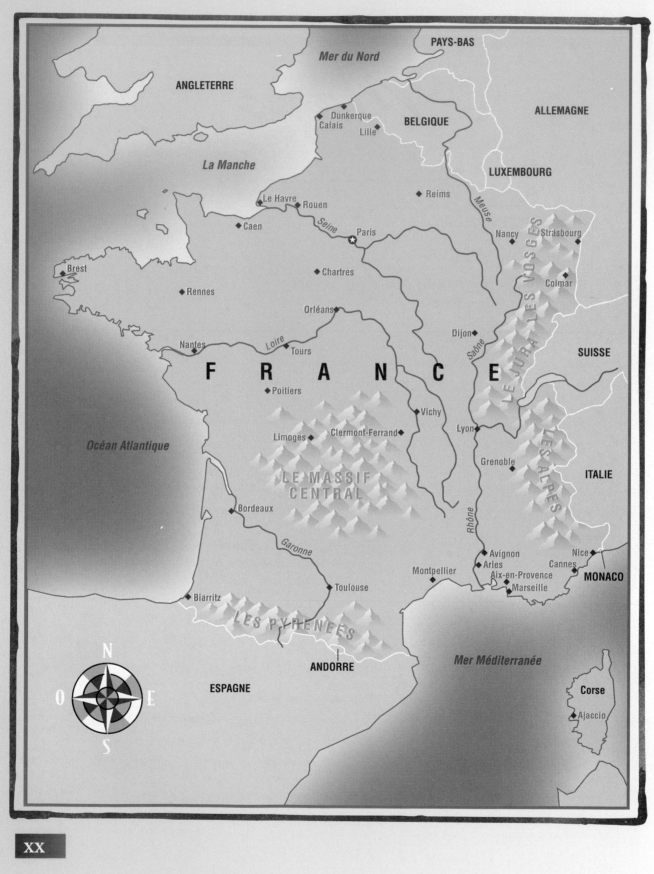

L'Afrique francophone

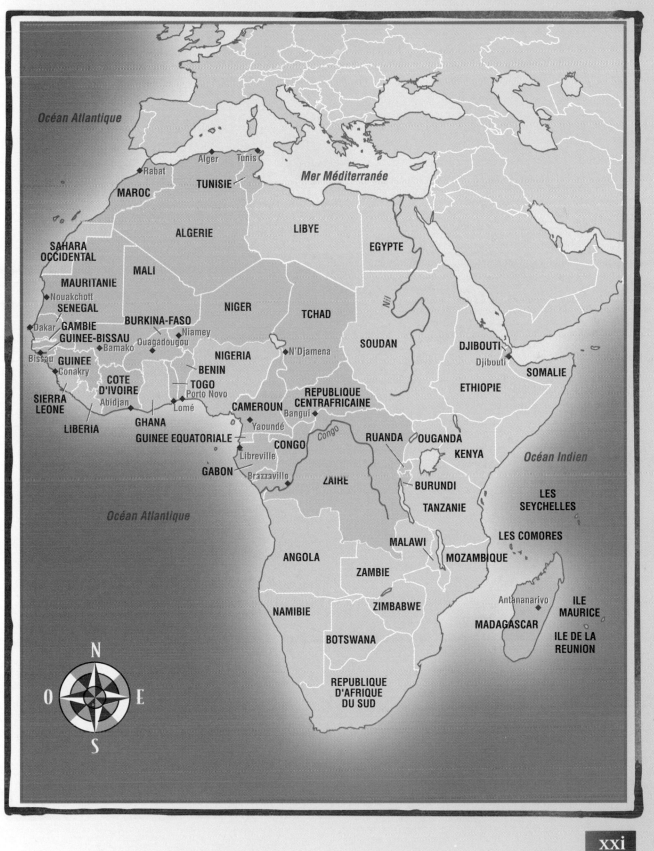

Océan Atlantique

Mer Méditerranée

Rabat
MAROC
Alger
TUNISIE
Tunis

ALGERIE

LIBYE

EGYPTE

SAHARA OCCIDENTAL

MALI

MAURITANIE
Nouakchott
SENEGAL

NIGER

TCHAD

SOUDAN

Nil

DJIBOUTI
Djibouti

Dakar
GAMBIE
GUINEE-BISSAU
Bissau
GUINEE
Conakry

BURKINA-FASO
Niamey
Ouagadougou
Bamako

N'Djamena

SOMALIE

ETHIOPIE

NIGERIA
BENIN

COTE D'IVOIRE
TOGO
Porto Novo

REPUBLIQUE CENTRAFRICAINE

SIERRA LEONE
Abidjan
Lomé

CAMEROUN
Banguí

LIBERIA
GHANA

Yaoundé

RUANDA
OUGANDA

Océan Indien

GUINEE EQUATORIALE

CONGO

Congo

KENYA

Libreville

BURUNDI

GABON
Brazzaville

ZAIRE

TANZANIE

LES SEYCHELLES

MALAWI

LES COMORES

ANGOLA

MOZAMBIQUE

ZAMBIE

Antananarivo
ILE MAURICE

NAMIBIE

ZIMBABWE

MADAGASCAR
ILE DE LA REUNION

Océan Atlantique

BOTSWANA

REPUBLIQUE D'AFRIQUE DU SUD

N
O E
S

xxi

T29

L'Amérique francophone

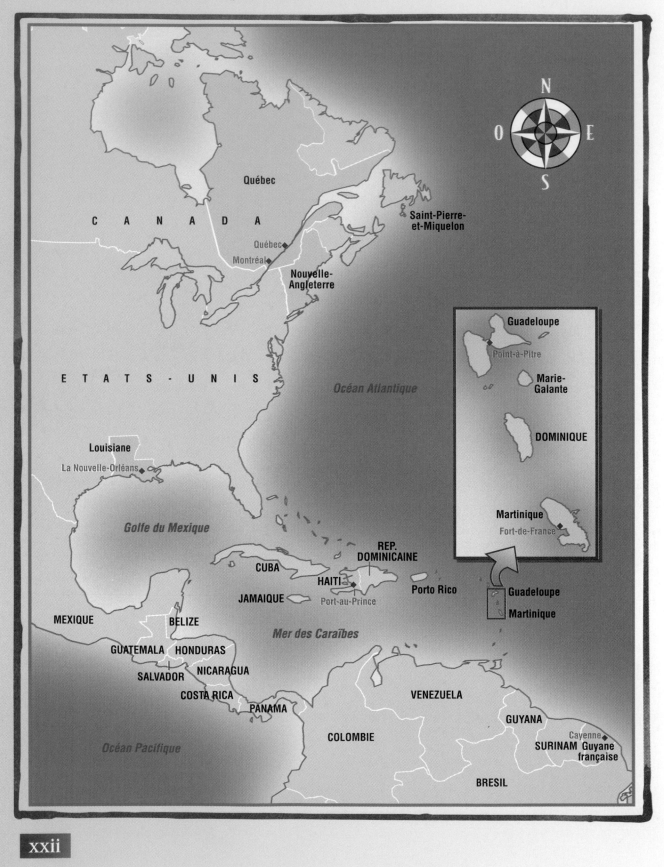

Le Monde francophone

*S*ince the early eighties, we have seen significant advances in modern foreign language curriculum practices:

(1) a redefinition of the objectives of foreign language study involving a commitment to the development of proficiency in the four skills and in cultural awareness;

(2) a recognition of the need for longer sequences of study;

(3) a new student-centered approach that redefines the role of the teacher as facilitator and encourages students to take a more active role in their learning;

(4) the inclusion of students of all learning abilities.

The new Holt, Rinehart and Winston foreign language programs take into account not only these advances in the field of foreign language education, but also the input of teachers and students around the country. ◆

PRINCIPLES AND PRACTICES

As nations become increasingly interdependent, the need for effective communication and sensitivity to other cultures becomes more important. Today's youth must be culturally and linguistically prepared to participate in a global society. At Holt, Rinehart and Winston, we believe that proficiency in more than one language is essential to meeting this need.

The primary goal of the Holt, Rinehart and Winston foreign language programs is to help students develop linguistic proficiency and cultural sensitivity. By interweaving language and culture, our programs seek to broaden students' communication skills while at the same time deepening their appreciation of other cultures.

◆◆

We believe that all students can benefit from foreign language instruction. We recognize that not everyone learns at the same rate or in the same way; nevertheless, we believe that all students should have the opportunity to acquire language proficiency to a degree commensurate with their individual abilities.

Holt, Rinehart and Winston's foreign language programs are designed to accommodate all students by appealing to a variety of learning styles.

◆◆

We believe that effective language programs should motivate students. Students deserve an answer to the question they often ask: "Why are we doing this?" They need to have goals that are interesting, practical, clearly stated, and attainable.

Holt, Rinehart and Winston's foreign language programs promote success. They present relevant content in manageable increments that encourage students to attain achievable functional objectives.

We believe that proficiency in a foreign language is best nurtured by programs that encourage students to think critically and to take risks when expressing themselves in the language. We also recognize that students should strive for accuracy in communication. While it is imperative that students have a knowledge of the basic structures of the language, it is also important that they go beyond the simple manipulation of forms.

Holt, Rinehart and Winston's foreign language program reflects a careful progression of activities that guides students from comprehensible input of authentic language through structured practice to creative, personalized expression. This progression, accompanied by consistent re-entry and spiraling of functions, vocabulary, and structures, provides students with the tools and the confidence to express themselves in their new language.

◆◆

Finally, we believe that a complete program of language instruction should take into account the needs of teachers in today's increasingly demanding classrooms.

At Holt, Rinehart and Winston, we have designed programs that offer practical teacher support and provide resources to meet individual learning and teaching styles.

Using the Pupil's Edition of Allez, viens!

A llez, viens! *offers an integrated approach to language learning. Presentation and practice of functional expressions, vocabulary, and grammar structures are interwoven with cultural information, language learning tips, and realia to facilitate both learning and teaching. The technology, audiovisual materials, and additional print resources integrated throughout each chapter allow instruction to be adapted to a variety of teaching and learning styles.* ◆

A LLEZ, VIENS! LEVEL 2

Allez, viens! Level 2 consists of twelve instructional chapters. To ensure successful completion of the book and to facilitate articulation from one level to the next, Chapters 1 and 12 are review chapters and Chapters 2 and 11 introduce minimal new material.

Following is a description of the various features in *Allez, viens!* and suggestions on how to use them in the classroom. While it is not crucial for students to cover all material and

do all activities to achieve the goals listed at the beginning of each chapter, the material within each chapter has been carefully sequenced to enable students to progress steadily at a realistic pace to the ultimate goal of linguistic and cultural proficiency. You, the teacher, as presenter, facilitator, and guide, will determine the precise depth of coverage, taking into account the individual needs of each class and the amount and type of alternative instructional material to be used from the *Allez, viens!* program.

S TARTING OUT...

In *Allez, viens!,* chapters are arranged by location. Each new location is introduced by a **Location Opener,** four pages of colorful photos and background information that can be used to introduce the region and help motivate students.

The two-page **Chapter Opener** is intended to pique students' interest and focus their attention on the task at hand. It is a visual introduction to the theme of the chapter and includes a brief description of the topic and situations students will encounter, as well as a list of objectives they will be expected to achieve.

S ETTING THE SCENE...

Language instruction begins with the **Mise en train,** the comprehensible input that models language in a culturally authentic setting. Whether presented on video or as a reading accompanied by the audiocassette or compact disc recording, the highly visual presentation—frequently in **roman-photo** format in the textbook—ensures success as students practice their receptive skills and begin to recognize some of the new functions and vocabulary they will encounter in the chapter. Following the **Mise en train** is a series of activities that can be used to help guide students through the story and check comprehension.

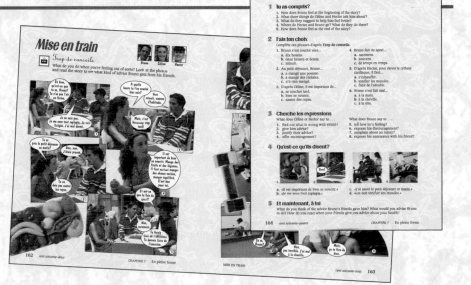

Building Proficiency Step by Step...

Première, Deuxième, and **Troisième étape** are the three core instructional sections where the greater part of language acquisition will take place. The communicative goals in each chapter center on the functional expressions presented in **Comment dit-on... ?** boxes. These expressions are supported and expanded by material in the **Vocabulaire, Grammaire,** and **Note de grammaire** sections. Activities immediately following the above features are designed to practice recognition or to provide closed-ended practice with the new material. Activities then progress from controlled to open-ended practice where students are able to express themselves in meaningful communication. Depending on class size, general ability level, and class dynamics, you may wish to proceed sequentially through all activities in a chapter, supplementing presentation or practice at various points with additional materials from *Allez, viens!,* or to proceed more quickly to open-ended pair and group work.

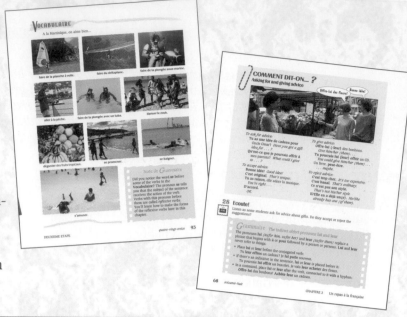

Discovering the People and the Culture...

Cultural information has been incorporated into activities wherever possible. There are also two major cultural features to help students develop an appreciation and understanding of the cultures of French-speaking countries.

Panorama Culturel presents spontaneous interviews conducted in various countries in the French-speaking world on a topic related to the chapter theme. The interviews may be presented on video or done as a reading supplemented by the audiocassette or compact disc recording. Culminating activities on this page may be used to verify comprehension and encourage students to think critically about the target culture as well as their own.

Rencontre Culturelle presents a cultural encounter that invites students to compare and contrast the foreign culture with their own.

Note Culturelle provides tidbits of both "big C" and "little c" culture that can be used to enrich and enliven activities and presentations at various places throughout each chapter.

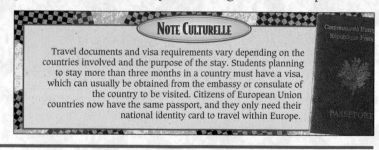

Understanding Authentic Documents...

Lisons! presents reading strategies that help students understand authentic French documents. The reading selections vary from advertisements to letters to short stories in order to accommodate different interests and familiarize students with different styles and formats. The accompanying activities progress from prereading to reading to postreading tasks and are designed to develop students' overall reading skills and challenge their critical thinking abilities.

TARGETING STUDENTS' NEEDS...

In each **étape** several special features may be used to enhance language learning and cultural appreciation.

De bons conseils suggests effective ways for students to learn a foreign language.

A la française provides students with tips for speaking more natural-sounding French.

Vocabulaire à la carte presents optional vocabulary related to the chapter theme. These words are provided to help students personalize activities; students will not be required to produce this vocabulary on the Chapter Quizzes and Test.

Tu te rappelles? is a re-entry feature that lists and briefly explains previously-learned vocabulary, functions, and grammar that students might need to review at the moment.

Si tu as oublié... is a handy page reference to either an earlier chapter where material was presented or to a reference section in the back of the book that includes such aids as the Summary of Functions and the Grammar Summary.

WRAPPING IT ALL UP...

Mise en pratique, at the end of each chapter, gives students the opportunity to review what they have learned and to apply their skills in new communicative contexts. Focusing on all four language skills as well as cultural awareness, the **Mise en pratique** can help you determine whether students are ready for the Chapter Test.

Que sais-je? follows the **Mise en pratique** and is a checklist that students can use on their own to see if they have achieved the goals stated on the Chapter Opener. Each communicative function is paired with one or more activities for students to use as a self-check. Page references are given for students who need to return to the chapter for review.

Vocabulaire presents the chapter vocabulary grouped by **étape** and arranged according to communicative function or theme. This list represents the active words and expressions that students will be expected to know for the Chapter Quizzes and Test.

The Annotated Teacher's Edition

The **Allez, viens!** Annotated Teacher's Edition *is designed to help you meet the increasingly varied needs of today's students by providing an abundance of suggestions and strategies. The* Annotated Teacher's Edition *includes the reduced pages of the* Pupil's Edition *with teacher annotations, wrap-around teacher text with video references and bar codes, notes, suggestions, answers, and additional activities, as well as interleafed pages of scripts, projects, and games before each chapter.* ◆

USING THE LOCATION OPENER

Each reduced student page is wrapped with background information for you about the photographs and settings. In addition, teaching suggestions help you motivate students to learn more about the history, geography, and culture of French-speaking countries.

USING THE CHAPTER INTERLEAF

The chapter interleaf includes a chapter overview correlation chart for teaching resources, *Pupil's Edition* listening scripts, and suggestions for projects and games.

The **Chapter Overview** chart outlines at a glance the functions, grammar, culture, and re-entry items featured in each **étape**. A list of corresponding print and audiovisual resource materials for each section of the chapter is provided to help integrate video and ancillaries into your lessons. The reading and review features for each chapter are also referenced, as well as a variety of assessment and portfolio options.

Textbook Listening Activities Scripts provide the scripts of the chapter listening activities for reference or for use in class. The answers to each activity are provided below each script for easy reference.

Projects propose extended four-skills activities based on the chapter theme and content. **Projects** suggestions are provided to give students the opportunity to personalize the information they've learned in the chapter. Individual projects offer students the chance to explore topics related to the chapter theme that are of personal interest to them. Group and cooperative learning projects encourage students to work together to apply what they've learned in the chapter by creating a poster, brochure, or report, often accompanied by an oral presentation.

Games provide students with informal, entertaining activities in which they can apply and reinforce the functions, structures, vocabulary, and culture of the chapter. **Games** appeal to a variety of learners and encourage teamwork and cooperation among students of different levels and learning styles.

USING THE WRAP-AROUND TEACHER TEXT

Wrap-around teacher text gives point-of-use suggestions and information to help you make the most of class time. The wrap-around style of the *Annotated Teacher's Edition* conveniently presents bar codes, video references, teacher notes, suggestions, and activity answers together on the same page with the reduced *Pupil's Edition* page.

TEACHING CYCLE

For each **étape,** a logical instructional sequence includes the following steps to enable you to:

- **Jump Start!** your students with an individual writing activity that focuses their attention on previously-learned material while they wait for class to begin.
- **Motivate** students by introducing the topic in a personalized and contextualized way.
- **Teach** the functions, vocabulary, structures, and culture with a variety of approaches.
- **Close** each **étape** with activities that review and confirm the communicative goals.
- **Assess** students' progress with a quiz and/or performance assessment activity. **Performance Assessment** suggestions provide an alternative to pen and paper tests and give you the option of evaluating students' progress by

having them perform communicative, competency-based tasks. These may include teacher-student interviews, conversations, dialogues, or skits that students perform for the entire class. These tasks can also be recorded or videotaped for evaluation at a later time.

Portfolio icons signal activities that are appropriate for students' oral or written portfolios. They may include lists, posters, letters, journal entries, or taped conversations or skits. A variety of suggestions are provided within each chapter so that you can work with your students to select the activities that would best document their strengths and progress in the language. Portfolio information, including checklists and suggestions for evaluation, is provided in the *Assessment Guide,* pages 2–13. On pages 14–25 of the *Assessment Guide,* there are suggestions for the expansion of the two designated portfolio activities from the *Pupil's Edition.* In each chapter overview, these two activities (one written and one oral) are listed under "Portfolio Assessment." The portfolio suggestions will help students to further develop their oral and written language skills, often in the context of real-life situations. For a discussion of portfolio creation and use, see *Using Portfolios in the Foreign Language Classroom,* page T52.

FOR INDIVIDUAL NEEDS

Suggestions under the following categories provide alternate approaches to help you address students' diverse learning styles.

- **Visual, Auditory, Tactile, and Kinesthetic Learners** benefit from activities that accommodate their unique learning styles.
- **Slower Pace** provides ideas for presenting material in smaller steps to facilitate comprehension.

- **Challenge** extends activities into more challenging tasks that encourage students to expand their communicative skills.

Making Connections

To help students appreciate their membership in a global society, suggestions for linking French with other disciplines, their community, and other cultures appear under the following categories:

- **Math...Geography...Health...Science ...History...Language Arts Links** relate the chapter topic to other subject areas, making French relevant to the students' overall academic experience.
- **Multicultural Links** provide students the opportunity to compare and contrast their language and culture with those of French-speaking countries and other parts of the world.
- **Community...Family Links** encourage students to seek opportunities for learning outside of the classroom by interacting with neighbors and family members. These suggestions also call on students to share their learning with their family and community.

Developing Thinking Skills

Thinking Critically helps students develop their higher-order thinking skills.

Drawing Inferences, Comparing and Contrasting, Analyzing, Observing, and Synthesizing offer suggestions to extend activities beyond an informational level. They increase comprehension of language and culture, and they help students exercise and develop higher-order thinking skills.

Establishing Collaborative Learning

Cooperative Learning allows students to work together in small groups to attain common goals by sharing responsibilities. Students are accountable for setting the group objectives, completing the assignment, and ensuring that all group members master the material. Working together in cooperative groups allows students to take an active role in the classroom, to develop more self-esteem as they contribute to the success of the group, and to experience less anxiety by working in small groups. Cooperative learning enables students to improve interpersonal communication skills by encouraging them to listen to and respect other opinions, and to share their own.

Total Physical Response (TPR) techniques visually and kinesthetically reinforce structures and vocabulary. They are active learning exercises that encourage students to focus on class interaction while learning French.

Teaching Lisons!

Teacher's notes and suggestions in **Lisons!** offer prereading, reading, and postreading activities to help students develop reading skills. Background information and useful terms related to the reading are provided as well.

Allez, viens! *Video*

Allez, viens! *Video Program and* Allez, viens! *Expanded Video Program bring the textbook to life and introduce your students to people they will encounter in every chapter of the* Pupil's Edition. *Filmed entirely on location in French-speaking countries around the world, these video programs feature native speakers of French in realistic, interesting situations.*

Video is an ideal medium for providing authentic input needed to increase proficiency in French. Both informative and entertaining, the episodes of the **Video Program** *and* **Expanded Video Program** *provide rich visual clues to aid comprehension and motivate students to learn more.* ◆

*A*LLEZ, VIENS! VIDEO PROGRAM

The video program is fully integrated and correlates directly with the *Allez, viens! Pupil's Edition:*

MISE EN TRAIN The introductory dialogue or story in each chapter is a videotaped dramatic episode based on the chapter theme. It introduces the targeted functions, vocabulary, and grammar of the chapter, in addition to re-entering material from previous chapters in new contexts. Since this video episode corresponds directly with the **Mise en train** and the chapter, it can be used as a general introduction to the chapter, as a chapter review, and as a visual support for presenting the elements of the lesson.

PANORAMA CULTUREL Authentic interviews with native speakers of French bring the French-speaking world to life as real people talk about themselves, their country, and their way of life. Each interview topic is thematically related to the chapter.

*A*LLEZ, VIENS! EXPANDED VIDEO PROGRAM

The **Expanded Video Program** includes all of the material provided in the **Video Program,** plus additional materials designed to extend and enrich students' learning experience through additional authentic input. Included in the **Expanded Video Program** are the following:

LOCATION OPENER A narrated collage of images from regions of French-speaking countries expands students' acquaintance with the geography and people of the places presented in each Location Opener.

MISE EN TRAIN (see **Video Program**)

MISE EN TRAIN (SUITE) These continuations of the dramatic episodes provide high-interest input that helps motivate students and offers additional opportunities to expand on what they've learned. The **Mise en train (suite)** continues the story and resolves the dramatic conflict that was created in the **Mise en train.** Designed to facilitate proficiency by providing additional comprehensible input, this episode offers an

extended presentation of the chapter material as well as re-entering functions, vocabulary, and structures from previous chapters.

PANORAMA CULTUREL Additional authentic interviews are offered in the **Expanded Video Program.** They feature a wide variety of native speakers from around the world and introduce students to regional variations in speech, cultural diversity, and varying points of view. This assortment of interviews from around the French-speaking world enriches students' appreciation of French-speaking cultures and helps them better understand their own.

VIDÉOCLIPS Students will enjoy the authentic footage from French television: music videos, commercials, and more. These short segments of video give students confidence as they realize that they can understand and enjoy material that was produced for native speakers of French!

*A*LLEZ, VIENS! VIDEO GUIDE

Allez, viens! **Video Guide** provides background information together with suggestions for presentation and pre- and post-viewing activities for all portions of the **Video Program** and the **Expanded Video Program.** In addition, the **Video Guide** contains a transcript and synopsis of each episode, supplementary vocabulary lists, and reproducible student activity sheets.

*A*LLEZ, VIENS! VIDEODISC PROGRAM AND GUIDE

Allez, viens! **Videodisc Program** presents in videodisc format all the authentic footage, interviews, and dramatic episodes presented in the **Expanded Video Program,** plus additional cultural and geographic material to further enrich your students' experience. Bar codes provide instant access to all material and facilitate efficient integration of video resources into each lesson. Key bar codes are provided in the *Annotated Teacher's Edition.* Teaching suggestions, activity masters, and a complete bar-code directory are provided in the **Videodisc Guide.**

Allez, viens! *Ancillaries*

*The **Allez, viens!** French program offers a state-of-the-art ancillary package that addresses the concerns of today's teachers. Because foreign language teachers are working with all types of students, the activities in our ancillaries accommodate all learning styles. The activities provided in the **Allez, viens!** ancillary materials are both innovative and relevant to students' experiences.* ◆

TEACHING RESOURCES WITH PROFESSIONAL ORGANIZER

Holt, Rinehart and Winston has taken an innovative approach to organizing our teaching resources. The *Allez, viens!* ancillaries are conveniently packaged in time-saving **Chapter Teaching Resources** booklets with a tri-fold **Professional Organizer**. Each **Chapter Teaching Resources** booklet puts a wealth of resources at your fingertips!

CHAPTER TEACHING RESOURCES, BOOKS 1-3

Oral communication is the language skill that is most challenging to develop and test. The *Allez, viens!* **Situation Cards** and **Communicative Activities** help students develop their speaking skills and give them opportunities to communicate in a variety of situations.

Additional **Listening Activities**, in combination with the **Audiocassette** and **Audio CD Program,** provide students with a unique opportunity to actively develop their listening skills in a variety of authentic contexts.

The *Allez, viens!* **Realia** reproduce real documents to provide your students with additional reading and language practice using culturally authentic material. Included with the **Realia** are teacher suggestions and student activities.

The **Student Response Forms** are provided for your convenience. These copying masters can be reproduced and used as answer forms for all the textbook listening activities.

The **Assessment Program** responds to your requests for a method of evaluation that is fair to all students and that encourages students to work towards realistic, communicative goals. The

Assessment Program includes the following components:

- Three **Quizzes** per chapter (one per **étape**)
- One **Chapter Test** per chapter; each **Chapter Test** includes listening, reading, writing, and culture sections and a score sheet for easy grading. Part of each test can be corrected on ScanTron®.
- **Speaking tests,** provided in the **Assessment Guide.**

Also included in the **Chapter Teaching Resources:**

- **Answer Key** for the **Practice and Activity Book**
- **Teaching Transparency Masters** and suggestions for use in a variety of activities
- **Listening Scripts** and **Answers** for the **Additional Listening Activities, Quizzes,** and **Chapter Tests.**

ASSESSMENT GUIDE

The **Assessment Guide** describes various testing and scoring methods. This guide also includes:

- **Portfolio Assessment** suggestions and rubrics
- **Speaking Tests** to be used separately or as part of the **Chapter Test**
- A cumulative **Midterm Exam** with scripts and answers
- A comprehensive **Final Exam** with scripts and answers.

PROFESSIONAL ORGANIZER

A tri-fold binder helps you organize the ancillaries for each chapter.

TEACHING TRANSPARENCIES

The **Teaching Transparencies** benefit all students, and the visual learner in particular. These colorful transparencies add variety and focus to your daily lesson plans. Suggestions for using the transparencies can be found in the **Chapter Teaching Resources** books.

AUDIO PROGRAM

All recorded material is available in either the **Audiocassette Program** or the **Audio CD Program.** The listening activities, pronunciation activities, interviews, and dialogues help students further develop their listening and pronunciation skills by providing opportunities to hear native speakers of French in a variety of authentic situations.

PRACTICE AND ACTIVITY BOOK

The **Practice and Activity Book** is filled with a variety of activities that provide further practice with the functions, grammar, and vocabulary presented in each **étape.** Additional reading, culture, and journal activities for each chapter give students the opportunity to apply the reading and writing strategies they've learned in relevant, personalized contexts.

TEST GENERATOR

The **Test Generator** is a user-friendly software program that enables you to create customized worksheets, quizzes, and tests for each chapter in *Allez, viens!* The **Test Generator** is available for IBM® PC and Compatibles and Macintosh® computers.

Chapter 4 Sample Lesson Plan

The following lesson plan suggests how the material in Chapter 4 may be distributed over twelve days. You may choose to prepare similar plans to guide you through the other chapters of **Allez, viens!**, adjusting the daily schedule and selecting appropriate activities and ancillary material that best suit your individual needs and those of your students. (Page numbers set in **boldface** type refer to activities in the Annotated Teacher's Edition.)

CHAPITRE 4 : SOUS LES TROPIQUES

DAILY PLANS		RESOURCES
DAY 1 — OBJECTIVE: To find out what there is to see and do in Martinique		

Location Opener, pp. 78–81
Chapter Opener, pp. 82–83
  Motivating Activity, **p. 82**
  Focusing on Outcomes, **p. 83**
Mise en train, pp. 84–86
  Motivating Activity, **p. 84**
	Presentation: **Un concours photographique, p. 85**
	  Activities 1–4, p. 86
	Close: Activity 5, p. 86
	Assignment: Activities 1–2, *Practice and Activity Book*, p. 37
		Textbook Audiocassette 2B/Audio CD 4
		Practice and Activity Book, p. 37
		Video Program OR Expanded Video Program, Videocassette 2
		Videodisc Program, Videodisc 2B

DAY 2 — OBJECTIVE: To describe the features of Martinique		
Review Assignment from Day 1 **Première étape**, p. 87 Jump Start!, **p. 87** Motivate, **p. 87** Activity 6, p. 87 Option: **Note Culturelle**, p. 87 Option: For Individual Needs, **p. 87** Presentation: **Vocabulaire, p. 88**	Activity 7, p. 88 Option: For Individual Needs, **p. 88** Activity 8, p. 89 Close: Teaching Suggestion, **p. 88** Assignment: Activity 9, p. 89; Activities 3–4, *Practice and Activity Book*, p. 38	*Textbook Audiocassette 2B/Audio CD 4* *Practice and Activity Book, pp. 38–40* *Chapter Teaching Resources, Book 1* *Teaching Transparency 4-1, pp. 175, 178* *Videodisc Program, Videodisc 2B*
DAY 3 — OBJECTIVE: To ask for information and describe a place; to find out about tourist attractions in francophone countries		

Review Assignment from Day 2
  Activities 10–11, p. 89
Presentation:
Comment dit-on... ?, p. 90
  Activities 12–13, p. 90
Panorama Culturel, p. 91
  Motivating Activity, **p. 91**
	Presentation:
	Panorama Culturel, p. 91
	Questions, p. 91
	Close: Question 3, p. 91
	Assignment: Activity 14, p. 90; Activities 6–7, *Practice and Activity Book*, p. 39
		Textbook Audiocassette 2B/Audio CD 4
		Practice and Activity Book, pp. 38–40
		Chapter Teaching Resources, Book 1
		  Teaching Transparency 4-1, pp. 175, 178
		Video Program OR Expanded Video Program, Videocassette 2
		Videodisc Program, Videodisc 2B

DAY 4 — OBJECTIVE: To talk about popular sports activities in Martinique		

Review Assignment from Day 3
  Activity 15, p. 90
  Teaching Transparency 4-1
Quiz 4-1
Assessment: Performance Assessment, **p. 90**
Deuxième étape, p. 92
	Jump Start!, **p. 92**
	Motivate, **p. 92**
	Activity 16, p. 92
	  Presentation: **Vocabulaire, p. 93**
	Close: Thinking Critically, p. 93
	Assignment: Activities 8–9, *Practice and Activity Book*, pp. 40–41
		Practice and Activity Book, pp. 38–43
		Chapter Teaching Resources, Book 1
		  Teaching Transparency 4-1, pp. 175, 178
		  Quiz 4-1, pp. 191–192
		Assessment Items
		  Audiocassette 7B/Audio CD 4
		Videodisc Program, Videodisc 2B

DAY 5 — OBJECTIVE: To ask for and make suggestions		
Review assignment from Day 4 TPR, **p. 93** Activities 17–18, p. 94 Presentation: **Comment dit-on... ?, p. 94** **Note Culturelle**, p. 94	Activities 19–21, p. 95 Close: Activity 11, *Practice and Activity Book*, p. 42 Assignment: Activities 10–13, *Practice and Activity Book*, pp. 41–42	*Textbook Audiocassette 2B/Audio CD 4* *Practice and Activity Book, pp. 41–43* *Chapter Teaching Resources, Book 1* *Teaching Transparency 4-2, pp. 176, 178* *Videodisc Program, Videodisc 2B*

DAY 6   **OBJECTIVE: To emphasize likes and dislikes; to learn about Carnaval in Martinique**

Review Assignment from Day 5
Presentation:
Comment dit-on... ?, p. 96
Activities 22–23, p. 96
Note de grammaire, p. 96
Rencontre Culturelle, p. 97
Motivating Activity, **p. 97**
	Presentation:
	Rencontre Culturelle, p. 97
	Option: Culture Note, **p. 97**
	Close: Close, **p. 96**
	Assignment: Activity 24, p. 96;
	  Activities 14–15, *Practice and Activity Book*, p. 43
		Textbook Audiocassette 2B/Audio CD 4
		Practice and Activity Book, pp. 41–43
		Chapter Teaching Resources, Book 1
		  Teaching Transparency 4-2, pp. 176, 178
		Videodisc Program, Videodisc 2B

DAY 7   **OBJECTIVE: To relate a series of events**

Review Assignment from Day 6
  Activity 16, *Practice and Activity Book*, p. 43
  Teaching Transparency 4-2
Quiz 4-2
Assessment: Performance
Assessment, **p. 96**
Troisième étape, p. 98
  Jump Start!, **p. 98**
  Motivate, **p. 98**
	Activity 25, p. 98
	Option: **Note Culturelle**, p. 98
	Presentation: **Vocabulaire/Comment dit-on... ?, p. 99**
	Activity 26, p. 99
	Close: TPR, **p. 99**
	Assignment: Activity 27, p. 100;
	  Activities 17–19, *Practice and Activity Book*, p. 44
		Textbook Audiocassette 2B/Audio CD 4
		Practice and Activity Book, pp. 41–46
		Chapter Teaching Resources, Book 1
		  Teaching Transparency 4-2, pp. 176, 178
		  Quiz 4-2, pp. 193–194
		Assessment Items
		  Audiocassette 7B/Audio CD 4

DAY 8   **OBJECTIVE: To talk about your daily routine**

Review Assignment from Day 7
  Presentation: **Grammaire, p. 100**
  Building on Previous Skills, **p. 100**
  Activity 28, p. 100
  Game, **p. 100**
  Activities 29-30, p. 101
	Close: Close, **p. 101**
	Assignment: Activity 31, p. 101;
	  Activities 20–22, *Practice and Activity Book*, pp. 45–46
		Textbook Audiocassette 2B/Audio CD 4
		Practice and Activity Book, pp. 44–46
		Chapter Teaching Resources, Book 1
		  Teaching Transparency 4-3, pp. 177, 178
		Videodisc Program, Videodisc 2B

DAY 9   **OBJECTIVE: To extend what you've learned**

Review Assignment from Day 8
  Cooperative Learning, **p. 101**
  Teaching Transparency 4-3
Quiz 4-3
Assessment: Performance
Assessment, **p. 101**
	Option: Projects, **p. 81E**
	Assignment: Activities 1-8,
	Que sais-je?, p. 106; *Practice and Activity Book*, Activities 27–28, p. 47
		Textbook Audiocassette 28/Audio CD 4
		Practice and Activity Book, pp. 44–47
		Chapter Teaching Resources, Book 1
		  Teaching Transparency 4-3,
		  pp. 177, 178
		Videodisc Program, Videodisc 28

DAY 10   **OBJECTIVE: To read the lyrics of a zouk song**

Lisons!, pp. 102–103
  Motivating Activity, **p. 102**
  Option: Multicultural Link, **p. 102**
  Activities A-D, p. 102
  Activities E-G, p. 103
	Close: Activity H, p. 103
	Assignment: Activity I, p. 103; Activities 25–26, *Practice and Activity Book*, p. 47
		Textbook Audiocassette 2B/Audio CD 4
		Practice and Activity Book, p. 47
		Chapter Teaching Resources, Book 1

DAY 11   **OBJECTIVE: To use what you have learned; to prepare for Chapter Test**

Review Assignments from Days 9
and 10
Mise en pratique, pp. 104–105
  Activites 1-3, p. 105
  Activities 5-6, p. 105
	Option: Games, **p. 81F**
	Assignment: Activity 4, p. 105;
	Mon journal, *Practice and Activity Book*, p. 148
		Textbook Audiocassette 2B/Audio CD 4
		Chapter Teaching Resources, Book 1
		Video Program OR Expanded Video Program, Videocassette 2
		Videodisc Program, Videodisc 2B

DAY 12   **OBJECTIVE: To assess progress**

Chapitre 4 Chapter Test		*Chapter Teaching Resources, Book 1,*
		pp. 197–202
		Assessment Guide
		  Speaking Test, p. 29
		  Portfolio Assessment, pp. 2–13, 17
		Assessment Items
		  Audiocassette 7B/Audio CD 4

Standards for Foreign Language Education

BY ROBERT LABOUVE

STANDARDS AND SCHOOL REFORM

In 1989 educational reform in the United States took on an entirely different look when state and national leaders reached consensus on six national educational goals for public schools. In 1994 a new law, *Goals 2000: Educate America Act,* endorsed these six goals and added two more. The most important national goal in the law for foreign language educators is Goal Three, which establishes a core curriculum and places foreign languages in that core. As a result of this consensus on national goals, the Federal government encouraged the development of high standards in the core disciplines. While the Federal government does not have the authority to mandate the implementation of foreign language standards locally, it will encourage their use through leadership and projects funded by the U.S. Department of Education.

We must first define "standards" in order to fully understand the rationale for their development. Content standards ask: What should students know and be able to do? Content standards are currently under development by foreign language professionals. Performance standards ask: How good is good enough? Opportunity-to-learn standards ask: Did the school prepare all students to perform well? There is a growing consensus that states and local districts should address the last two types of standards.

PROGRESS TOWARD FOREIGN LANGUAGE STANDARDS

A task force of foreign language educators began work on the standards in 1993 by establishing specific foreign language goals. They then set content standards for each goal. The task force sought feedback from the foreign language profession through an extensive dissemination program and produced a draft of the standards document for introduction at a number of sites around the United States during the 1994–1995 school year.

The target publication date for a final document is late 1995. The final version will incorporate suggestions from the sites where the standards were introduced and reaction from volunteer reviewers and the field in general. While the standards should be world class, they must also be realistic and attainable by most students. The task force also realizes that the general set of goals and standards will have to be made language specific in a curriculum development process and that continuing staff development will be essential.

PROPOSED FOREIGN LANGUAGE STANDARDS

Goal One	Communicate in languages other than English	**Standard 1.1**	Students engage in conversations, provide and obtain information, express feelings and emotions, and exchange opinions.
		Standard 1.2	Students understand and interpret written and spoken language on a variety of topics.
		Standard 1.3	Students present information, concepts, and ideas to an audience of listeners or readers on a variety of topics.
Goal Two	Gain knowledge and understanding of other cultures	**Standard 2.1**	Students demonstrate knowledge and understanding of the traditions, institutions, ideas and perspectives, the literary and artistic expressions, and other components of the cultures being studied.
Goal Three	Connect with other disciplines and acquire information	**Standard 3.1**	Students reinforce and further their knowledge of other disciplines through the foreign language.
		Standard 3.2	Students gain access to information and perspectives that are only available through the foreign language and within culture.
Goal Four	Develop insight into own language and culture	**Standard 4.1**	Students recognize that different languages use different patterns to express meaning and can apply this knowledge to their own language.
		Standard 4.2	Students recognize that cultures develop different patterns of interaction and can apply this knowledge to their own culture.
Goal Five	Participate in multilingual communities and global society	**Standard 5.1**	Students use the language both within and beyond the school setting.
		Standard 5.2	Students use the language for leisure and personal enrichment.

PROPOSED FOREIGN LANGUAGE GOALS AND STANDARDS

The proposed goals and standards in the draft document describe a K–12 foreign language program for *all* students, presenting languages, both modern and classical, as part of the core curriculum for every student, including those whose native language is not English. Broad goals establish the basic framework of the language program. The proposed content standards set for these goals describe what students should know and be able to do in a language. The chart on page T42 shows how the standards are arrayed alongside the goals.

The first two goals in this expanded language program describe today's typical school language program. The last three are often identified by teachers as important, but are not always implemented. The standards-based program moves beyond an emphasis on skills to a redefinition of the content of a language program itself.

Sample benchmark tasks will be provided for Grades 4, 8, and 12 as examples of what students can do to meet the standards and accomplish the goals of the language program. A higher level of performance will be expected as students progress from one benchmark grade to another. For example, Standard 1.1 at Grade 4 suggests that students can "describe various objects and people in their everyday environment at home and in school," but Standard 1.1 at Grade 12 suggests that students can "exchange opinions and individual perspectives on a variety of topics including issues that are of contemporary and historical interest in the foreign culture and in their own."

IMPACT OF THE STANDARDS

While there is an assumption that foreign language goals and standards will have a great impact upon the states and local districts, the standards themselves are voluntary. Clearly, standards will influence instruction and curriculum development in districts that choose to align their language programs with the national standards. Assessment programs will most likely begin to reflect the influence of the standards. The standards will also have an impact on the preparation of future teachers and on staff development for teachers now in the classroom.

A curriculum based on the standards will encourage students to take responsibility for their learning by making the language curriculum coherent and transparent to them. Students will know from the beginning what they should be able to do when they exit the program and they will be able to judge for themselves how they are progressing, especially at established benchmarks, i.e., Grades 4, 8, and 12.

The standards will direct instruction in the classroom by providing curriculum developers and teachers with a broad framework upon which to construct the expanded language program. Standards for each goal will ensure that no goal is treated informally or left to chance. Teachers who use the content standards should play a critical role in their district by deciding how good is good enough for students who exit the program.

The standards will also have a significant impact on the demand for sequential, cross-disciplinary instructional materials for a K–12 language program. Another challenge will be the development of new technologies that increase learning in order to meet high standards.

Probably the greatest benefit that national standards may bring will be in the area of making possible articulation that is horizontal (linking languages to other disciplines) and vertical (grade to grade, school to school, and school to college). Language teachers will join their English and social studies colleagues in helping students become language-competent, literate citizens of the world. A language program that is at once coherent and transparent to students and others will provide all language educators a basis for reaching consensus about their expectations on what students should know and do. To those of us who feel that foreign language education is basic education for all students, the national standards document will become a strong advocate for languages in the curriculum of every school and for the extended sequences of study presented by the goals and standards. The standards document will make it easier for language educators to present a solid rationale for foreign languages in the curriculum.

The standards document is still in draft form and some changes are expected before the official document is published. To receive the most up-to-date version, please contact the project office:

National Standards Project
c/o ACTFL
6 Executive Plaza
Yonkers, NY 10701
(914) 963–8830

Allez, viens!

supports the proposed Foreign Language Goals and Standards in the following ways:

THE PUPIL'S EDITION

- Encourages students to take responsibility for their learning by providing clearly defined objectives at the beginning of each chapter.

- Provides a variety of pair- and group-work activities to give students an opportunity to use the target language in a wide range of settings and contexts.

- Offers culture-related activities and poses questions that develop students' insight and encourage them to develop observational and analytical skills.

THE ANNOTATED TEACHER'S EDITION

- Provides a broad framework for developing a foreign language program and offers specific classroom suggestions for reaching students with various learning styles.

- Offers ideas for multicultural and multidisciplinary projects as well as community and family links that encourage students to gain access to information both at school and in the community.

THE ANCILLARY PROGRAM

- Provides students with on-location video footage of native speakers interacting in their own cultural and geographic context.

- Includes multiple options for practicing new skills and assessing performance, including situation cards, portfolio suggestions, speaking tests, and other alternatives.

- Familiarizes students with the types of tasks they will be expected to perform on exit exams.

Multi-Level Classrooms

BY JOAN H. MANLEY

So you have just heard that your third-period class is going to include both Levels 2 and 3! While this is never the best news for a foreign language teacher, there are positive ways, both psychological and pedagogical, to make this situation work for you and your students. ◆

There are positive ways, both psychological and pedagogical, to make this situation work for you and your students.

RELIEVING STUDENT ANXIETIES

Initially, in a multi-level class environment, it is important to relieve students' anxiety by orienting them to their new situation. From the outset, let all students know that just because they "did" things the previous year, such as learn how to conjugate certain verbs, they may not yet be able to use them in a meaningful way. Students should not feel that it is demeaning or a waste of time to recycle activities or to share knowledge and skills with fellow students. Second-year students need to know they are not second-class citizens and that they can benefit from their classmates' greater experience with the language. Third-year students may achieve a great deal of satisfaction and become more confident in their own language skills when they have opportunities to help or teach their second-year classmates. It is important to reassure third-year students that you will devote time to them and challenge them with different assignments.

EASING YOUR OWN APPREHENSION

When you are faced with both Levels 2 and 3 in your classroom, remind yourself that you teach students of different levels in the same classroom every year, although not officially. After one year of classroom instruction, your Level 2 class will never be a truly homogeneous group. Despite being made up of students with the same amount of "seat time," the class comprises multiple layers of language skills, knowledge, motivation, and ability. Therefore, you are constantly called upon to make a positive experience out of a potentially negative one.

Your apprehension will gradually diminish to the extent that you are able to . . .

- make students less dependent on you for the successful completion of their activities.
- place more responsibility for learning on the students.
- implement creative group, pair, and individual activities.

How can you do this? Good organization will help. Lessons will need to be especially well-planned for the multi-level class. The following lesson plan is an example of how to treat the same topic with students of two different levels.

TEACHING A LESSON IN A MULTI-LEVEL CLASSROOM

LESSON OBJECTIVES

Relate an incident in the past that you regret.
Level 2: Express surprise and sympathy.
Level 3: Offer encouragement and make suggestions.

LESSON PLAN

1. **Review and/or teach the past tense.** Present the formation of the past tense. Model its use for the entire class or call upon Level 3 students to give examples.
2. **Practice the past tense.** Have Level 3 students who have mastered the past tense teach it to Level 2 students in pairs or small groups. Provide the Level 3 student instructors with several drill and practice activities they may use for this purpose.
3. **Relate your own regrettable past experience.** Recount a personal regrettable incident—real or imaginary—to the entire class as a model. For example, you may have left your automobile lights on, and when you came out of school, the battery was dead and you couldn't start your car. Or you

may have scolded a student for not doing the homework and later discovered the student had a legitimate reason for not completing the assignment.

4. **Prepare and practice written and oral narratives.** Have Level 2 students pair off with Level 3 students. Each individual writes about his or her experience, the Level 3 partner serving as a resource for the Level 2 student. Partners then edit each other's work and listen to each other's oral delivery. You might choose to have students record their oral narratives.

5. **Present communicative functions.**
   A. Ask for a volunteer to recount his or her own regrettable incident for the entire class.
   B. Model reactions to the volunteer's narrative.
      (1) Express surprise and sympathy (for Level 2): "Really! That's too bad!"
      (2) Offer encouragement and make suggestions (for Level 3): "Don't worry. You can still..."

6. **Read narratives and practice communicative functions.** Have Level 2 students work together in one group or in small groups, listening to classmates' stories and reacting with the prescribed communicative function. Have Level 3 students do the same among themselves. Circulate among the groups, listening, helping, and assessing.

7. **Assess progress.** Repeat your personal account for the entire class and elicit reactions from students according to their level. Challenge students to respond with communicative functions expected of the other level if they can.

Every part of the above lesson plan is important. Both levels have been accommodated. The teacher has not dominated the lesson. Students have worked together in pairs and small groups, while Level 3 students have helped their Level 2 classmates. Individual groups still feel accountable, both within their level and across levels.

Any lesson can be adapted in this way. It takes time and effort, but the result is a student-centered classroom where students share and grow, and the teacher is the facilitator.

Teaching Culture

BY NANCY HUMBACH AND DOROTHEA BRUSCHKE

Ask students what they like best about studying a foreign language. Chances are that learning about culture, the way people live, is one of their favorite aspects. Years after language study has ended, adults remember with fondness the customs of the target culture, even pictures in their language texts. It is this interest in the people and their way of life that is the great motivator and helps us sustain students' interest in language study.

We must integrate culture and language in a way that encourages curiosity, stimulates analysis, and teaches students to hypothesize and seek answers to questions about the people whose language they are studying. Teaching isolated facts about how people in other cultures live is not enough. This information is soon dated and quickly forgotten. We must go a step beyond and teach students that all behavior, values, and traditions exist because of certain aspects of history, geography, and socio-economic conditions.

There are many ways to help students become culturally knowledgeable and to assist them in developing an awareness of differences and similarities between the target culture and their own. Two of these approaches involve critical thinking, that is, trying to find reasons for a certain behavior through observation and analysis, and putting individual observations into larger cultural patterns. ◆

> We must integrate culture and language in a way that encourages curiosity, stimulates analysis, and teaches students to hypothesize.

FIRST APPROACH: QUESTIONING

The first approach involves questioning as the key strategy. At the earliest stages of language learning, students begin to learn ways to greet peers, elders, and strangers, as well as the use of **tu** and **vous.** Students need to consider questions such as: "How do French-speaking people greet each other? Are there different levels of formality? Who initiates a handshake? When is a handshake or kisses on the cheeks **(la bise)** appropriate?" Each of these questions leads students to think about the values that are expressed through word and gesture. They start to "feel" the other culture, and at the same time, understand how much of their own behavior is rooted in their cultural background.

Magazines, newspapers, advertisements, and television commercials are all excellent sources of cultural material. For example, browsing through a French magazine, one finds a number of advertisements for food items and bottled water. Could this indicate a great interest in eating and preparing healthy food? Reading advertisements can be followed up with viewing videos and films, or with interviewing native speakers or people who have lived in French-speaking countries to learn about customs involving food selection and preparation.

Students might want to find answers to questions such as: "How much time do French people spend shopping for and preparing a meal? How long does a typical meal **en famille** last? What types of food and beverages does it involve?" This type of questioning might lead students to discover different attitudes toward food and mealtimes.

An advertisement for a refrigerator or a picture of a French kitchen can provide an insight into practices of shopping for food. Students first need to think about the refrigerator at home, take an inventory of what is kept in it, and consider when and where their family shops. Next, students should look closely at a French refrigerator. What is its size? What could that mean? (Shopping takes place more often, stores are within walking distance, and people eat more fresh foods.)

Food wrappers and containers also provide good clues to cultural insight. For example, since bread is often purchased fresh from a **boulangerie,** it is usually carried in one's hand or tote bag, with no packaging at all. Since most people shop daily and carry their own groceries home, heavier items like sodas often come in bottles no larger than one and one-half litres.

SECOND APPROACH: ASSOCIATING WORDS WITH IMAGES

The second approach for developing cultural understanding involves forming associations of words with the cultural images they suggest. Language and culture are so closely related that one might actually say that language *is* culture. Most words, especially nouns, carry a cultural connotation. Knowing the literal equivalent of a word in another language is of little use to students in understanding this connotation. For example, **ami** cannot be translated simply as *friend*, **pain** as *bread*, or **rue** as *street*. The French word **pain**, for instance, carries with it the image of a small local bakery stocked with twenty or thirty different varieties of freshly-baked bread, all warm from a brick oven. At breakfast, bread is sliced, covered with butter and jam, and eaten as a **tartine;** it is eaten throughout the afternoon and evening meals, in particular as an accompaniment to the cheese course. In French-speaking countries, "bread" is more than a grocery item; it is an essential part of every meal.

When students have acquired some sense of the cultural connotation of words —not only through teachers' explanations but, more importantly, through observation of visual images—they start to discover the larger underlying cultural themes, or what is often called deep culture.

These larger cultural themes serve as organizing categories into which individual cultural phenomena fit to form a pattern. Students might discover, for example, that French speakers, because they live in much more crowded conditions, have a great need for privacy (cultural theme), as reflected in such phenomena as closed doors, fences or walls around property, and sheers on windows. Students might also discover that love of nature and the outdoors is an important cultural theme, as indicated by such phenomena as flower boxes and planters in public places—even on small traffic islands—well-kept public parks in every town, and people going for a walk or going hiking.

As we teach culture, students learn not only to recognize elements of the target culture but also of their American cultural heritage. They see how elements of culture reflect larger themes or patterns. Learning what constitutes American culture and how that information relates to other people throughout the world can be an exciting journey for a young person.

As language teachers, we are able to facilitate that journey into another culture and into our own, to find our similarities as well as our differences from others. We do not encourage value judgments about others and their culture, nor do we recommend adopting other ways. We simply say to students, "Other ways exist. They exist for many reasons, just as our ways exist due to what our ancestors have bequeathed us through history, traditions, values, and geography."

Allez, viens!

develops cultural understanding and awareness in the following ways:

THE PUPIL'S EDITION

- Informs students about francophone countries through photo essays, maps, almanac boxes, and **Notes Culturelles** that invite comparison with the students' own cultural experiences.

- Engages students in analysis and comparison of live, personal interviews with native speakers in the **Panorama Culturel** sections.

- Uses the **Rencontre Culturelle** section to expose students to cross-cultural situations that require observation, analysis, and problem-solving.

- Helps students integrate the language with its cultural connotations through a wealth of authentic documents.

THE ANNOTATED TEACHER'S EDITION

- Provides teachers with additional culture, history, and language notes, background information on photos and almanac boxes, and multicultural links.

- Suggests problem-solving activities and critical thinking questions that allow students to hypothesize, analyze, and discover larger underlying cultural themes.

THE ANCILLARY PROGRAM

- Includes additional realia to develop cultural insight by serving as a catalyst for questioning and direct discovery.

- Offers activities that require students to compare and contrast cultures.

- Provides songs, short readings, and poems, as well as many opportunities for students to experience regional variation and idioms in the video and audio programs.

Learning Styles and Multi-Modality Teaching

BY MARY B. MCGEHEE

The larger and broader population of students who are enrolling in foreign language classes brings a new challenge to foreign language educators, calling forth an evolution in teaching methods to enhance learning for all our students. Educational experts now recognize that every student has a preferred sense for learning and retrieving information: visual, auditory, or kinesthetic. Incorporating a greater variety of activities to accommodate the learning styles of all students can make the difference between struggle and pleasure in the foreign language classroom. ◆

Incorporating a greater variety of activities to accommodate the learning styles of all students can make the difference between struggle and pleasure in the foreign language classroom.

ACCOMMODATING DIFFERENT LEARNING STYLES

A modified arrangement of the classroom is one way to provide more effective and enjoyable learning for all students. Rows of chairs and desks must give way at times to circles, semicircles, or small clusters. Students may be grouped in fours or in pairs for cooperative work or peer teaching. It is important to find a balance of arrangements, thereby providing the most comfort in varied situations.

Since visual, auditory, and kinesthetic learners will be in the class, and because every student's learning will be enhanced by a multi-sensory approach, lessons must be directed toward all three learning styles. Any language lesson content may be presented visually, aurally, and kinesthetically.

Visual presentations and practice may include the chalkboard, charts, posters, television, overhead projectors, books, magazines, picture diagrams, flashcards, bulletin boards, films, slides, or videos. Visual learners need to see what they are to learn. Lest the teacher think he or she will never have the time to prepare all those visuals, Dickel and Slak (1983) found that visual aids generated by students are more effective than ready-made ones.

Auditory presentations and practice may include stating aloud the requirements of the lesson, oral questions and answers, paired or group work on a progression of oral exercises from repetition to communication, tapes, CDs, dialogues, and role-playing. Jingles, catchy stories, and memory devices using songs and rhymes are good learning aids. Having students record themselves and then listen as they play back the cassette allows them to practice in the auditory mode.

Kinesthetic presentations entail the students' use of manipulatives, chart materials, gestures, signals, typing, songs, games, and role-playing. These lead the students to associate sentence constructions with meaningful movements.

A SAMPLE LESSON USING MULTI-MODALITY TEACHING

A multi-sensory presentation on greetings might proceed as follows.

FOR VISUAL LEARNERS

As the teacher begins oral presentation of greetings and introductions, he or she simultaneously shows the written forms on transparencies, with the formal expressions marked with an adult's hat, and the informal expressions marked with a baseball cap.

The teacher then distributes cards with the hat and cap symbols representing the formal or informal expressions. As the students hear taped mini-dialogues, they hold up the appropriate card to indicate whether the dialogues are formal or informal. On the next listening, the students repeat the sentences they hear.

FOR AUDITORY LEARNERS

A longer taped dialogue follows, allowing the students to hear the new expressions a number of times. They write from dictation several sentences containing the new expressions. They may work in pairs, correcting each other's work as they "test" their own understanding of the lesson at hand. Finally, students respond to simple questions using the appropriate formal and informal responses cued by the cards they hold.

FOR KINESTHETIC LEARNERS

For additional kinesthetic input, members of the class come to the front of the room, each holding a hat or cap symbol. As the teacher calls out situations, the students play the roles, using gestures and props appropriate to the age group they are portraying. Non-cued, communicative role-playing with props further enables the students to "feel" the differences between formal and informal expressions.

HELPING STUDENTS LEARN HOW TO USE THEIR PREFERRED MODE

Since we require all students to perform in all language skills, part of the assistance we must render is to help them develop strategies within their preferred learning modes to carry out an assignment in another mode. For example, visual students hear the teacher assign an oral exercise and visualize what they must do. They must see themselves carrying out the assignment, in effect watching themselves as if there were a movie going on in their heads. Only then can they also hear themselves saying the right things. Thus, this assignment will be much easier for the visual learners who have been taught this process, if they have not already figured it out for themselves. Likewise, true auditory students, confronted with a reading/writing assignment, must talk themselves through it, converting the entire process into sound as they plan and prepare their work. Kinesthetic students presented with a visual or auditory task must first break the assignment into tasks and then work their way through them.

Students who experience difficulty because of a strong preference for one mode of learning are often unaware of the degree of preference. In working with these students, I prefer the simple and direct assessment of learning styles offered by Richard Bandler and John Grinder in their book *Frogs into Princes*, which allows the teacher and student to quickly determine how the student learns. In an interview with the student, I follow the assessment with certain specific recommendations of techniques to make the student's study time more effective.

It is important to note here that teaching students to maximize their study does not require that the teacher give each student an individualized assignment. It does require that each student who needs it be taught how to prepare the assignment using his or her own talents and strengths. This communication between teacher and student, combined with teaching techniques that reinforce learning in all modes, can only maximize pleasure and success in learning a foreign language.

▶ REFERENCES

Dickel, M.J. and S. Slak. "Imaging Vividness and Memory for Verbal Material." *Journal of Mental Imagery* 7, i (1983):121–6.

Bandler, Richard, and John Grinder. *Frogs into Princes*. Real People Press, Moab, UT. 1978.

Allez, viens!

accommodates different learning styles in the following ways:

THE PUPIL'S EDITION

- Presents basic material in audio, video, and print formats.
- Includes role-playing activities and a variety of multi-modal activities, including an extensive listening strand and many art-based activities.

THE ANNOTATED TEACHER'S EDITION

- Provides suggested activities for visual, auditory, and kinesthetic learners, as well as suggestions for slower-paced learning and challenge activities.
- Includes Total Physical Response activities.

THE ANCILLARY PROGRAM

- Provides additional reinforcement activites for a variety of learning styles.
- Presents a rich blend of audiovisual input through the video program, audio program, transparencies, and blackline masters.

The following is an example of an art-based activity from *Allez, viens!*

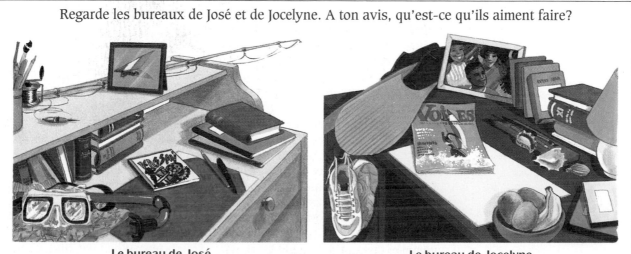

Regarde les bureaux de José et de Jocelyne. A ton avis, qu'est-ce qu'ils aiment faire?

Le bureau de José

Le bureau de Jocelyne

Higher-Order Thinking Skills

BY AUDREY L. HEINING-BOYNTON

Our profession loves acronyms! TPR, ALM, OBI, and now the HOTS! HOTS stands for higher-order thinking skills. These thinking skills help our students listen, speak, write, and learn about culture in a creative, meaningful way, while providing them with necessary life skills. ◆

Introduce students to the life skills they need to become successful, productive citizens in our society.

WHAT ARE HIGHER-ORDER THINKING SKILLS?

Higher-order thinking skills are not a new phenomenon on the educational scene. In 1956, Benjamin Bloom published a book that listed a taxonomy of educational objectives in the form of a pyramid similar to the one in the following illustration:

Bloom's Taxonomy of Educational Objectives

EVALUATION
SYNTHESIS
ANALYSIS
APPLICATION
COMPREHENSION
KNOWLEDGE

Knowledge is the simplest level of educational objectives, and is not considered a higher-order thinking skill. It requires the learner to remember information without having to fully understand it. Tasks that students perform to demonstrate knowledge are recalling, identifying, recognizing, citing, labeling, listing, reciting, and stating.

Comprehension is not considered a higher-order thinking skill either. Learners demonstrate comprehension when they paraphrase, describe, summarize, illustrate, restate, or translate.

Foreign language teachers tend to focus the most on knowledge and comprehension. The tasks performed at these levels are important because they provide a solid foundation for the more complex tasks at the higher levels of Bloom's pyramid. However, offering our students the opportunity to perform at still higher cognitive levels provides them with more meaningful contexts in which to use the target language.

When teachers incorporate **application, analysis, synthesis,** and **evaluation** as objectives, they allow students to utilize **higher-order thinking skills.**

- **Application** involves solving, transforming, determining, demonstrating, and preparing.

- **Analysis** includes classifying, comparing, making associations, verifying, seeing cause-and-effect relationships, and determining sequences, patterns, and consequences.

- **Synthesis** requires generalizing, predicting, imagining, creating, making inferences, hypothesizing, making decisions, and drawing conclusions.

- Finally, **evaluation** involves assessing, persuading, determining value, judging, validating, and solving problems.

Most foreign language classes focus little on higher-order thinking skills. Some foreign language educators mistakenly think that all higher-order thinking skills require an advanced level of language ability. Not so! Students can demonstrate these skills by using very simple language available even to beginning students. Also, higher-order thinking tasks about the target culture or language can be conducted in English. The use of some English in the foreign language class in order to utilize higher cognitive skills does not jeopardize progress in the target language.

Higher-order thinking skills prepare our students for more than using a foreign language. They introduce students to the life skills they need to become successful, productive citizens in our society. When we think about it, that *is* the underlying purpose of education.

WHY TEACH HIGHER-ORDER THINKING SKILLS?

There is already so much to cover and so little time that some teachers may question the worth of adding these types of activities to an already full schedule. Yet we know from experience that simply "covering" the material does not help our students acquire another language. Incorporating higher-order thinking skills in the foreign language classroom can help guide students toward language acquisition by providing meaningful experiences in a setting that can otherwise often feel artificial.

Also, we now know that employing higher-order thinking skills assists all students, including those who are at risk of failing. In the past, we felt that at-risk students were incapable of higher-order thinking, but we have since discovered that we have been denying them the opportunity to experience what they are capable of doing and what they need to do in order to be successful adults.

SAMPLE ACTIVITIES EMPLOYING HIGHER-ORDER THINKING SKILLS

There are no limitations to incorporating higher-order thinking skills in the foreign language classroom. What follows are a few sample activities, some of which you might already be familiar with. Use *your* higher-order thinking skills to develop other possibilities!

▶ LISTENING

HOTS:	Analysis
TASKS:	Patterning and sequencing
VOCABULARY NEEDED:	Three colors
MATERIALS REQUIRED:	Three colored-paper squares for each student

After reviewing the colors, call out a pattern of colors and have the students show their comprehension by arranging their colored pieces of paper from left to right in the order you give. Then have them finish the pattern for you. For example, you say: **rouge, vert, bleu, rouge, vert, bleu...** now what color follows? And then what color?

This is not only a HOTS activity; it also crosses disciplines. It reviews the mathematical concept of patterning and sequencing. You can have the students form patterns and sequences using any type of vocabulary.

▶ READING

HOTS:	Synthesis
TASKS:	Hypothesizing and imagining
VOCABULARY NEEDED:	Determined by level of students
MATERIALS REQUIRED:	Legend or short story

After the students have read the first part of the story, have them imagine how the story would end, based on the values of the target culture.

▶ SPEAKING

HOTS:	Evaluation
TASKS:	Assessing and determining value
VOCABULARY NEEDED:	Numbers 0-25, five objects students would need for school
MATERIALS REQUIRED:	Visuals of five school-related objects with prices beneath them

Tell students that they each have twenty-five dollars to spend on back-to-school supplies. They each need to tell you what they would buy with their money.

▶ WRITING

HOTS:	Analysis
TASKS:	Classifying
VOCABULARY NEEDED:	Leisure activities
MATERIALS REQUIRED:	Drawings of leisure activities on a handout

From the list of activities they have before them, students should write the ones that they like to do on the weekend. Then they should write those that a family member likes to do. Finally, students should write a comparison of the two lists.

COMMITMENT TO HIGHER-ORDER THINKING SKILLS

Teaching higher-order thinking skills takes no extra time from classroom instruction since language skills are reinforced during thinking skills activities. What teaching higher-order thinking skills does require of teachers is a commitment to classroom activities that go beyond the objectives of Bloom's knowledge and comprehension levels. Having students name objects and recite verb forms is not enough. Employing HOTS gives students the opportunity to experience a second language as a useful device for meaningful communication.

▶ REFERENCES

Bloom, Benjamin. *Taxonomy of Educational Objectives. Handbook 1: Cognitive Domain.* New York: David McKay Company, 1956.

Allez, viens!

encourages higher-order thinking skills in the following ways:

THE PUPIL'S EDITION

• Develops critical thinking skills through a variety of activities, including interpretation of the visually-presented **Mise en train**, journal writing, interviews, **Rencontre Culturelle** presentations, application of reading strategies, and situational role-plays.

THE ANNOTATED TEACHER'S EDITION

• Includes Thinking Critically and Multicultural Links features that provide the teacher with suggestions for activities requiring students to draw inferences, compare and contrast, evaluate, and synthesize.

THE ANCILLARY PROGRAM

• Incorporates higher-order thinking skills in Communicative Activities, Additional Listening Activities, and the chapter-related realia. In the *Practice and Activity Book,* students are guided carefully from structured practice to open-ended tasks that require higher-order thinking.

Using Portfolios in the Foreign Language Classroom

BY JO ANNE S. WILSON

The communicative, whole-language approach of today's foreign language instruction requires assessment methods that parallel the teaching and learning strategies in the proficiency-oriented classroom. We know that language acquisition is a process. Portfolios are designed to assess the steps in that process. ◆

Portfolios offer a more realistic and accurate way to assess the process of language teaching and learning.

WHAT IS A PORTFOLIO?

A portfolio is a purposeful, systematic collection of a student's work. A useful tool in developing a student profile, the portfolio shows the student's efforts, progress, and achievements for a given period of time. It may be used for periodic evaluation, as the basis for overall evaluation, or for placement. It may also be used to enhance or provide alternatives to traditional assessment measures, such as formal tests, quizzes, class participation, and homework.

WHY USE PORTFOLIOS?

Portfolios benefit both students and teachers because they

- **Are ongoing and systematic.** A portfolio reflects the real-world process of production, assessment, revision, and reassessment. It parallels the natural rhythm of learning.

- **Offer an incentive to learn.** Students have a vested interest in creating the portfolios through which they can showcase their ongoing efforts and tangible achievements. Students select the works to be included and have a chance to revise, improve, evaluate, and explain the contents.

- **Are sensitive to individual needs.** Language learners bring varied abilities to the classroom and do not acquire skills in a uniformly neat and orderly fashion. The personalized, individualized assessment offered by portfolios responds to this diversity.

- **Provide documentation of language development.** The material in a portfolio is evidence of student progress in the language learning process. The contents of the portfolio make it easier to discuss student progress with the students as well as with parents and others interested in the student's progress.

- **Offer multiple sources of information.** A portfolio presents a way to collect and analyze information from multiple sources that reflect a student's efforts, progress, and achievements in the language.

PORTFOLIO COMPONENTS

The foreign language portfolio should include both oral and written work, student self-evaluation, and teacher observation, usually in the form of brief, non-evaluative comments about various aspects of the student's performance.

THE ORAL COMPONENT

The oral component of a portfolio might be an audio- or videocassette. It may contain both rehearsed and extemporaneous monologues and conversations. For a rehearsed speaking activity, give a specific communicative task that students can personalize according to their individual interests (for example, ordering a favorite meal in a restaurant). If the speaking activity is extemporaneous, first acquaint students with possible topics for discussion or even the specific task they will be expected to perform. (For example, tell them they will be asked to discuss a picture showing a sports activity or a restaurant scene.)

THE WRITTEN COMPONENT

Portfolios are excellent tools for incorporating process writing strategies into the foreign language classroom. Documentation of various stages of the writing process—brainstorming, multiple drafts, and peer comments—may be included with the finished product.

Involve students in selecting writing tasks for the portfolio. At the beginning levels, the tasks might include some structured writing, such as labeling or listing. As students become more profiicient, journals, letters, and other more complicated writing tasks are valuable ways for them to monitor their progress in using the written language.

STUDENT SELF-EVALUATION

Students should be actively involved in critiquing and evaluating their portfolios and monitoring their own progress. The process and procedure for student self-evaluation should be considered in planning the contents of the portfolio. Students should work with you and their peers to design the exact format. Self-evaluation encourages them to think about what they are learning (content), how they learn (process), why they are learning (purpose), and where they are going in their learning (goals).

TEACHER OBSERVATION

Systematic, regular, and ongoing observations should be placed in the portfolio after they have been discussed with the student. These observations provide feedback on the student's progress in the language learning process.

Teacher observations should be based on an established set of criteria that has been developed earlier with input from the student. Observation techniques may include the following:

- Jotting notes in a journal to be discussed with the student and then placed in the portfolio
- Using a checklist of observable behaviors, such as the willingness to take risks when using the target language or staying on task during the lesson
- Making observations on adhesive notes that can be placed in folders
- Recording anecdotal comments, during or after class, using a cassette recorder.

Knowledge of the criteria you use in your observations gives students a framework for their performance.

HOW ARE PORTFOLIOS EVALUATED?

The portfolio should reflect the process of student learning over a specific period of time. At the beginning of that time period, determine the criteria by which you will assess the final product and convey them to the students. Make this evaluation a collaborative effort by seeking students' input as you formulate these criteria and your instructional goals.

Students need to understand that evaluation based on a predetermined standard is but one phase of the assessment process; demonstrated effort and growth are just as important. As you consider correctness and accuracy in both oral and written work, also consider the organization, creativity, and improvement revealed by the student's portfolio over the time period. The portfolio provides a way to monitor the growth of a student's knowledge, skills, and attitudes, and shows the student's efforts, progress, and achievements.

HOW TO IMPLEMENT PORTFOLIOS

Teacher-teacher collaboration is as important to the implementation of portfolios as teacher-student collaboration. Confer with your colleagues to determine, for example, what kinds of information you want to see in the student portfolio, how the information will be presented, the purpose of the portfolio, the intended purposes (grading, placement, or a combination of the two), and criteria for evaluating the portfolio. Conferring among colleagues helps foster a departmental cohesiveness and consistency that will ultimately benefit the students.

THE PROMISE OF PORTFOLIOS

The high degree of student involvement in developing portfolios and deciding how they will be used generally results in renewed student enthusiasm for learning and improved achievement. As students compare portfolio pieces done early in the year with work produced later, they can take pride in the progress as well as reassess their motivation and work habits.

Portfolios also provide a framework for periodic assessment of teaching strategies, programs, and instruction. They offer schools a tool to help solve the problem of vertical articulation and accurate student placement. The more realistic and accurate assessment of the language learning process that is provided by portfolios is congruent with the strategies that should be used in the proficiency-oriented classroom.

Allez, viens!
supports the use of portfolios in the following ways:

THE PUPIL'S EDITION

- Includes numerous oral and written activities that can be easily adapted for student portfolios, such as **Mon journal** and the more global review activities in the **Mise en pratique.**

THE ANNOTATED TEACHER'S EDITION

- Suggests activities in the Portfolio Assessment feature that may serve as portfolio items.

THE ANCILLARY PROGRAM

- Includes criteria in the *Assessment Guide* for evaluating portfolios, as well as Speaking Tests for each chapter that can be adapted for use as portfolio assessment items.

This section provides information about several resources that can enrich your French class. Included are addresses of government offices of francophone countries, pen pal organizations, subscription agencies, and many others. Since addresses change frequently, you may want to verify them before you send your requests. ◆

CULTURAL AGENCIES

For historic and tourist information about France and francophone countries, contact:

French Cultural Services
972 Fifth Ave.
New York, NY 10021
(212) 439-1400

French Cultural Services
540 Buth St.
San Francisco, CA 94108
(415) 397-4330

TOURIST OFFICES

Maison de la France
1007 Slocum St.
Dallas, TX 75027
(214) 742-1222

Délégation du Québec
53 State Street
Exchange Place Bldg., 19th floor
Boston, MA 02109
(617) 723-3366

Caribbean Tourism Association
20 E. 46th St., 4th floor
New York, NY 10017
(212) 682-0435

INTERCULTURAL EXCHANGE

American Field Service
220 East 42nd St.
New York, NY 10017
(212) 949-4242

CIEE Student Travel Services
205 East 42nd St.
New York, NY 10017
(212) 661-1414

PEN PAL ORGANIZATIONS

For the names of pen pal groups other than those listed below, contact your local chapter of AATF. There are fees involved, so be sure to write for information.

Student Letter Exchange (League of Friendship)
630 Third Avenue
New York, NY 10017
(212) 557-3312

World Pen Pals
1694 Como Avenue
St. Paul, MN 55108
(612) 647-0191

PERIODICALS

Subscriptions to the following cultural materials are available directly from the publishers. See also the section on Subscription Services.

- *Phosphore* is a monthly magazine for high school students.
- *Okapi* is a bimonthly environmentally-oriented magazine for younger teenagers in France.
- *Vidéo-Presse* is a monthly magazine, aimed at 9- to 16-year-olds in Quebec schools.
- *Le Monde* is the major daily newspaper in France.
- *Le Figaro* is an important newspaper in France. Daily or Saturday editions are available by subscription.
- *Elle* is a weekly fashion magazine for women.
- *Paris Match* is a general interest weekly magazine.
- *Le Point* is a current events weekly magazine.
- *L'Express* is a current events weekly magazine.

SUBSCRIPTION SERVICES

French-language magazines can be obtained through subscription agencies in the United States. The following companies are among the many that can provide your school with subscriptions.

EBSCO Subscription Services
P. O. Box 1943
Birmingham, AL 35201-1943
(205) 991-6600

Continental Book Company
8000 Cooper Ave., Bldg. 29
Glendale, NY 11385
(718) 326-0572

PROFESSIONAL ORGANIZATIONS

The two major organizations for French teachers at the secondary-school level are:

The American Council on the Teaching of Foreign Languages (ACTFL)
6 Executive Blvd.
Upper Level
Yonkers, NY 10701
(914) 963-8830

The American Association of Teachers of French (AATF)
57 East Armory Ave.
Champaign, IL 61820
(217) 333-2842

A Bibliography for the French Teacher

This bibliography is a compilation of several resources available for professional enrichment. ◆

SELECTED AND ANNOTATED LIST OF READINGS

▶ I. METHODS AND APPROACHES

Cohen, Andrew D. *Assessing Language Ability in the Classroom,* 2/e. Boston, MA: Heinle, 1994.
• Assessment processes, oral interviews, role-playing situations, dictation, and portfolio assessment.

Hadley, Alice Omaggio. *Teaching Language in Context,* 2/e. Boston, MA: Heinle, 1993.
• Language acquisition theories and models and adult second language proficiency.

Krashen, Stephen, and Tracy D. Terrell. *The Natural Approach: Language Acquisition in the Classroom.* New York: Pergamon, 1983.
• Optimal Input Theory: listening, oral communication development, and testing.

Oller, John W., Jr. *Methods That Work: Ideas for Language Teachers,* 2/e. Boston, MA: Heinle, 1993.
• Literacy in multicultural settings, cooperative learning, peer teaching, and CAI.

Shrum, Judith L., and Eileen W. Glisan. *Teacher's Handbook: Contextualized Language Instruction.* Boston, MA: Heinle, 1993.
• Grammar, testing, using video texts, microteaching, case studies, and daily plans.

▶ II. SECOND LANGUAGE THEORY

Krashen, Stephen. *The Power of Reading.* New York: McGraw, 1994.
• Updates Optimal Input Theory by incorporating the reading of authentic texts.

Liskin-Gasparro, Judith. *A Guide to Testing and Teaching for Oral Proficiency.* Boston, MA: Heinle, 1990.
• Oral proficiency through interview techniques and speech samples.

Rubin, Joan, and Irene Thompson. *How To Be a More Successful Language Learner,* 2/e. Boston, MA: Heinle, 1993.
• Psychological, linguistic, and practical matters of second language learning.

▶ III. VIDEO AND CAI

Altmann, Rick. *The Video Connection: Integrating Video into Language Teaching.* Boston, MA: Houghton, 1989.
• Diverse strategies for using video texts to support second language learning.

Dunkel, Patricia A. *Computer-Assisted Language Learning and Testing.* Boston, MA: Heinle, 1992.
• CAI and computer-assisted language learning (CALL) in the foreign language classroom.

Kenning, M. J., and M.M. Kenning. *Computers and Language Learning: Current Theory and Practice.* New York, NY: E. Horwood, 1990.
• Theoretical discussions and practical suggestions for CAI in second language development.

▶ IV. PROFESSIONAL JOURNALS

Calico
(Published by Duke University, Charlotte, N.C.)
• Dedicated to the intersection of modern language learning and high technology. Research articles on videodiscs, using computer-assisted language learning, how-to articles, and courseware reviews.

The Foreign Language Annals
(Published by the American Council on the Teaching of Foreign Languages)
• Consists of research and how-to-teach articles.

The French Review
(Published by the American Association of Teachers of French)
• Articles on French-language literature.

The IALL Journal of Language Learning Technologies
(Published by the International Association for Learning Laboratories)
• Research articles as well as practical discussions pertaining to technology and language instruction.

The Modern Language Journal
• Primarily features research articles.

Scope and Sequence: French Level 1

CHAPITRE PRELIMINAIRE : ALLEZ, VIENS!

Functions
- Introducing yourself
- Spelling
- Counting
- Understanding classroom instructions

Grammar
- French alphabet
- French accent marks

Culture
- The French-speaking world
- Famous French-speaking people
- The importance of learning French
- French gestures for counting

CHAPITRE 1 : FAISONS CONNAISSANCE!
Location: Poitiers

Functions
- Greeting people and saying goodbye
- Asking how people are and telling how you are
- Asking someone's name and age and giving yours
- Expressing likes, dislikes, and preferences about things
- Expressing likes, dislikes, and preferences about activities

Grammar
- ne... pas
- The definite articles le, la, l', and les and the gender of nouns
- The connectors et and mais
- Subject pronouns
- -er verbs

Culture
- Greetings and goodbyes
- Hand gestures
- Leisure-time activities

Re-entry
- Introductions
- Numbers 0–20
- Expressing likes, dislikes, and preferences about things

CHAPITRE 2 : VIVE L'ECOLE!
Location: Poitiers

Functions
- Agreeing and disagreeing
- Asking for and giving information
- Telling when you have class
- Asking for and expressing opinions

Grammar
- Using si instead of oui to contradict a negative statement
- The verb avoir

Culture
- The French educational system/le bac
- L'heure officielle
- Curriculum in French schools
- The French grading system

Re-entry
- Greetings
- The verb aimer
- Numbers for telling time

CHAPITRE 3 : TOUT POUR LA RENTREE
Location: Poitiers

Functions
- Making and responding to requests
- Asking others what they need and telling what you need
- Telling what you'd like and what you'd like to do
- Getting someone's attention
- Asking for information
- Expressing thanks

Grammar
- The indefinite articles un, une, and des
- The demonstrative adjectives ce, cet, cette, and ces
- Adjective agreement and placement

Culture
- Bagging your own purchases
- Buying school supplies in French-speaking countries
- French currency

Re-entry
- The verb avoir
- Expressing likes and dislikes
- Numbers

CHAPITRE 4 : SPORTS ET PASSE-TEMPS
Location: Quebec

Functions
- Telling how much you like or dislike something
- Exchanging information
- Making, accepting, and turning down suggestions

Grammar
- Contractions with à and de
- Question formation
- de after a negative verb

- The verb faire
- Adverbs of frequency

Culture
- Old and new in Quebec City
- Celsius and Fahrenheit
- Sports in francophone countries
- Maison des jeunes et de la culture

Re-entry
- Expressing likes and dislikes
- The verb aimer; regular -er verbs
- Agreeing and disagreeing

CHAPITRE 5 : ON VA AU CAFE?
Location: Paris

Functions
- Making suggestions and excuses
- Making a recommendation
- Getting somone's attention
- Ordering food and beverages
- Inquiring about and expressing likes and dislikes
- Paying the check

Grammar
- The verb prendre
- The imperative

Culture
- Food served in a café
- Waitpersons as professionals
- La litote
- Tipping

Re-entry
- Accepting and turning down a suggestion
- Expressing likes and dislikes
- Numbers 20–100

CHAPITRE 6 : AMUSONS-NOUS!
Location: Paris

Functions
- Making plans
- Extending and responding to invitations
- Arranging to meet someone

Grammar
- Using le with days of the week
- The verb aller and aller + infinitive
- The verb vouloir
- Information questions

Culture
- Going out
- Dating in France
- Conversational time

Re-entry
- Expressing likes and dislikes
- Contractions with **à**
- Making, accepting, and turning down suggestions
- **L'heure officielle**

CHAPITRE 7 : LA FAMILLE
Location: Paris

Functions
- Identifying people
- Introducing people
- Describing and characterizing people
- Asking for, giving, and refusing permission

Grammar
- Possession with **de**
- Possessive adjectives
- Adjective agreement
- The verb **être**

Culture
- Family life
- Pets in France

Re-entry
- Asking for and giving people's names and ages
- Adjective agreement

CHAPITRE 8 : AU MARCHE
Location: Abidjan

Functions
- Expressing need
- Making, accepting, and declining requests
- Telling someone what to do
- Offering, accepting, or refusing food

Grammar
- The partitive articles **du, de la, de l'**, and **des**
- **avoir besoin de**
- The verb **pouvoir**
- **de** with expressions of quantity
- The pronoun **en**

Culture
- The Ivorian market
- Shopping for groceries in francophone countries
- The metric system
- Foods of Côte d'Ivoire
- Mealtimes in francophone countries

Re-entry
- Food vocabulary
- Activities
- Making purchases

CHAPITRE 9 : AU TELEPHONE
Location: Arles

Functions
- Asking for and expressing opinions
- Inquiring about and relating past events
- Making and answering a phone call
- Sharing confidences and consoling others
- Asking for and giving advice

Grammar
- The **passé composé** with **avoir**
- Placement of adverbs with the **passé composé**
- The -**re** verbs: **répondre**
- The object pronouns **le, la, les, lui**, and **leur**

Culture
- History of Arles
- The French telephone system
- Telephone habits of French-speaking teenagers

Re-entry
- Chores
- Asking for, giving, and refusing permission
- **aller** + infinitive

CHAPITRE 10 : DANS UN MAGASIN DE VETEMENTS
Location: Arles

Functions
- Asking for and giving advice
- Expressing need; inquiring
- Asking for an opinion; paying a compliment; criticizing
- Hesitating; making a decision

Grammar
- The verbs **mettre** and **porter**
- Adjectives used as nouns
- The -**ir** verbs: **choisir**
- The direct object pronouns **le, la**, and **les**
- **c'est** versus **il/elle est**

Culture
- Clothing sizes
- Fashion in francophone countries
- Responding to compliments

Re-entry
- The future with **aller**
- Colors
- Likes and dislikes

CHAPITRE 11 : VIVE LES VACANCES!
Location: Arles

Functions
- Inquiring about and sharing future plans
- Expressing indecision; expressing wishes
- Asking for advice; making, accepting, and refusing suggestions
- Reminding; reassuring
- Seeing someone off
- Asking for and expressing opinions
- Inquiring about and relating past events

Grammar
- The prepositions **à** and **en**
- The -**ir** verbs: **partir**

Culture
- **Colonies de vacances**
- Vacations

Re-entry
- **aller** + infinitive
- Asking for advice
- Clothing vocabulary
- The imperative
- Weather expressions
- The **passé composé**
- The verb **vouloir**

CHAPITRE 12 : EN VILLE
Location: Fort-de-France
(Review)

Functions
- Pointing out places and things
- Making and responding to requests
- Asking for advice and making suggestions
- Asking for and giving directions

Grammar
- The pronoun **y**

Culture
- Store hours in France and Martinique
- Making "small talk" in francophone countries
- Getting a driver's license in francophone countries
- **DOMs** and **TOMs**
- Public areas downtown

Re-entry
- Contractions with **à**
- The partitive
- Contractions with **de**
- Family vocabulary
- Possessive adjectives
- The **passé composé**
- Expressing need
- Making excuses
- Inviting

CHAPITRE 1 : BON SEJOUR!
Location: Paris region (Review)

Functions
- Describing and characterizing yourself and others
- Expressing likes, dislikes, and preferences
- Asking for information
- Asking for and giving advice
- Asking for, making, and responding to suggestions
- Relating a series of events

Grammar
- Adjective agreement
- The imperative
- The future with **aller**

Culture
- Travel documents for foreign countries
- Ethnic restaurants
- Studying abroad

Re-entry
- Adjectives to characterize people
- Pronunciation: **liaison**
- Family vocabulary
- Clothing and colors
- Weather expressions and seasons
- Telling time

CHAPITRE 2 : BIENVENUE A CHARTRES!
Location: Paris region (Review)

Functions
- Welcoming someone and responding to someone's welcome
- Asking how someone is feeling and telling how you're feeling
- Pointing out where things are
- Paying and responding to compliments
- Asking for and giving directions

Grammar
- Irregular adjectives
- Contractions with **à**

Culture
- Paying and receiving compliments
- Teenagers' bedrooms in France
- **Notre-Dame-de-Chartres**
- Houses in francophone countries

Re-entry
- Use of **tu** versus **vous**

- Pronunciation: intonation
- Prepositions of location
- Contractions with **de**
- Making suggestions

CHAPITRE 3 : UN REPAS A LA FRANÇAISE
Location: Paris region

Functions
- Making purchases
- Asking for, offering, accepting, and refusing food
- Paying and responding to compliments
- Asking for and giving advice
- Extending good wishes

Grammar
- The object pronoun **en**
- The partitive articles
- The indirect object pronouns **lui** and **leur**

Culture
- Neighborhood stores
- Typical meals in the francophone world
- Courses of a meal
- Polite behavior for a guest
- Special occasions

Re-entry
- Giving prices
- Expressions of quantity
- Food vocabulary

CHAPITRE 4 : SOUS LES TROPIQUES
Location: Martinique

Functions
- Asking for information and describing a place
- Asking for and making suggestions
- Emphasizing likes and dislikes
- Relating a series of events

Grammar
- The use of **de** before a plural adjective and noun
- Recognizing reflexive verbs
- The reflexive verbs **se coucher** and **se lever**
- The present tense of reflexive verbs

Culture
- **La ville de Saint-Pierre**
- Places to visit in different regions
- **Yoles rondes**
- The **créole** language
- **Carnaval**
- Music and dance in Martinique

Re-entry
- Connectors for sequencing events
- Adverbs of frequency
- Pronunciation: **e muet**
- Sports vocabulary

CHAPITRE 5 : QUELLE JOURNEE!
Location: Touraine

Functions
- Expressing concern for someone
- Inquiring; expressing satisfaction and frustration
- Sympathizing with and consoling someone
- Giving reasons and making excuses
- Congratulating and reprimanding someone

Grammar
- The **passé composé** with **avoir**
- Introduction to verbs that use **être** in the **passé composé**

Culture
- **Carnet de correspondance**
- Meals at school
- French grades and report cards
- School life in francophone countries

Re-entry
- Connector words
- Sports and leisure activities
- Pronunciation: the nasal sound [ɛ̃]
- Question words
- Reflexive verbs

CHAPITRE 6 : A NOUS LES CHATEAUX!
Location: Touraine

Functions
- Asking for opinions; expressing enthusiasm, indifference, and dissatisfaction
- Expressing disbelief and doubt
- Asking for and giving information

Grammar
- The phrase **c'était**
- The **passé composé** with **être**
- Formal and informal phrasing of questions
- The verb **ouvrir**

Culture
- Types of châteaux in France
- Buses and trains in France
- Historical figures of Chenonceau
- Studying historical figures in school

Re-entry
- Pronunciation: [y] versus [u]

- The **passé composé** with **avoir**
- Expressing satisfaction and frustration
- Telling time

CHAPITRE 7 : EN PLEINE FORME
Location: Touraine
Functions
- Expressing concern for someone and complaining
- Giving advice; accepting and rejecting advice
- Expressing discouragement and offering encouragement
- Justifying your recommendations; advising against something

Grammar
- Reflexive verbs in the **passé composé**
- The pronoun **en** with activities
- The verb **se nourrir**

Culture
- Pharmacies in France
- Figures of speech
- Teenagers' exercise habits
- Staying healthy
- Mineral water

Re-entry
- Expressing doubt
- Telling how often you do something
- Pronunciation: the [r] sound
- Sports activities

CHAPITRE 8 : C'ETAIT COMME ÇA
Location: Côte d'Ivoire
Functions
- Telling what or whom you miss; reassuring someone
- Asking and telling what things were like
- Reminiscing
- Making and responding to suggestions

Grammar
- Introduction to the **imparfait**
- Formation of the **imparfait**
- **si on** + the **imparfait**

Culture
- Village life in Côte d'Ivoire
- Ethnic groups in West Africa
- High school in Côte d'Ivoire
- Félix Houphouët-Boigny
- Abidjan
- City living versus country living

Re-entry
- Pronunciation: the [ɛ] sound
- Adjectives of personality
- Chores
- Places in a city

CHAPITRE 9 : TU CONNAIS LA NOUVELLE?
Location: Provence
Functions
- Wondering what happened; offering possible explanations
- Accepting and rejecting explanations
- Breaking some news; showing interest
- Beginning, continuing, and ending a story

Grammar
- **avoir l'air** + adjective
- The **passé composé** vs. the **imparfait**
- The **passé composé** and the **imparfait** with interrupted actions
- **être en train de**

Culture
- The Cours Mirabeau, Aix-en-Provence
- **Histoires marseillaises**
- Friendship

Re-entry
- School-related mishaps
- The **passé composé** of reflexive verbs
- Accidents and injuries
- Explanations and apologies

CHAPITRE 10 : JE PEUX TE PARLER?
Location: Provence
Functions
- Sharing a confidence
- Asking for and giving advice
- Asking for and granting a favor; making excuses
- Apologizing and accepting an apology; reproaching someone

Grammar
- Object pronouns and their placement
- Direct object pronouns with the **passé composé**
- Object pronouns before an infinitive

Culture
- Paul Cézanne
- Roman ruins in Aix-en-Provence
- Provençale cuisine
- Talking about personal problems

Re-entry
- Accepting and refusing advice
- Personal happenings
- Pronunciation: the nasal sound [ã]
- Making excuses

CHAPITRE 11 : CHACUN SES GOUTS
Location: Provence
Functions
- Identifying people and things
- Asking for and giving information
- Giving opinions
- Summarizing

Grammar
- The verb **connaître**
- **c'est** versus **il/elle est**
- The relative pronouns **qui** and **que**

Culture
- **La Fête de la musique**
- Musical tastes
- Movie theaters in France
- The **Minitel**

Re-entry
- Emphasizing likes and dislikes
- Making and responding to suggestions

CHAPITRE 12 : A LA BELLE ETOILE
Location: Quebec
(Review)
Functions
- Asking for and giving information; giving directions
- Complaining; expressing discouragement and offering encouragement
- Asking for and giving advice
- Relating a series of events; describing people and places

Grammar
- The verb **emporter**
- The **passé composé** and the **imparfait**

Culture
- **Le parc de la Jacques-Cartier**
- Ecology in Canada
- Endangered animals
- French-Canadian expressions

Re-entry
- Sports and activities
- Clothing vocabulary
- Making and responding to suggestions

Scope and Sequence: French Level 3

CHAPITRE 1 : FRANCE, LES REGIONS
Location: France
(Review)

Functions
- Renewing old acquaintances
- Inquiring; expressing enthusiasm and dissatisfaction
- Exchanging information
- Expressing indecision
- Making recommendations
- Ordering and asking for details

Grammar
- The passé composé

Culture
- Traditional regional clothing
- Regional specialties
- Eating out in France
- Regional foods

Re-entry
- Food vocabulary
- Question formation

CHAPITRE 2 : BELGIQUE, NOUS VOILA!
Location: Belgium
(Review)

Functions
- Asking for and giving directions
- Expressing impatience
- Reassuring someone
- Expressing enthusiasm and boredom
- Asking and telling where things are

Grammar
- The verb conduire

Culture
- Languages in Belgium
- Favorite comic book characters
- Overview of Belgium

Re-entry
- Extending invitations
- The imperative
- Direct and indirect object pronouns
- The forms of the imperfect
- Making, accepting, and refusing suggestions

CHAPITRE 3 : SOYONS RESPONSABLES!
Location: Switzerland

Functions
- Asking for, granting, and refusing permission
- Expressing obligation
- Forbidding
- Reproaching
- Justifying your actions and rejecting others' excuses

Grammar
- The verb devoir
- The subjunctive
- ne... pas + infinitive

Culture
- Swiss work ethic
- Switzerland's neutrality
- Overview of Switzerland
- Environmental issues
- La minuterie

Re-entry
- Complaining
- Chores

CHAPITRE 4 : DES GOUTS ET DES COULEURS
Location: France

Functions
- Asking for and giving opinions
- Asking which one(s)
- Pointing out and identifying people and things
- Paying and responding to compliments
- Reassuring someone

Grammar
- The interrogative and demonstrative pronouns
- The causative faire

Culture
- French clothing stores
- Fashion and personal style
- French sense of fashion

Re-entry
- Clothing vocabulary
- Adjectives referring to clothing
- Family vocabulary
- Chores

CHAPITRE 5 : C'EST NOTRE AVENIR
Location: Senegal

Functions
- Asking about and expressing intentions
- Expressing conditions and possibilities
- Asking about future plans
- Expressing wishes
- Expressing indecision
- Giving advice
- Requesting information
- Writing a formal letter

Grammar
- The future
- The conditional

Culture
- Careers and education in Senegal
- Overview of Senegal
- Planning for a career
- The apprenticeship system

Re-entry
- The subjunctive
- Giving advice

CHAPITRE 6 : MA FAMILLE, MES COPAINS ET MOI
Location: Morocco

Functions
- Making, accepting, and refusing suggestions
- Making arrangements
- Making and accepting apologies
- Showing and responding to hospitality
- Expressing and responding to thanks
- Quarreling

Grammar
- Reciprocal verbs
- The past infinitive

Culture
- Bargaining in North Africa
- Values of francophone teenagers
- Overview of Morocco
- Hospitality in Morocco

Re-entry
- Reflexive verbs
- Family vocabulary

CHAPITRE 7 : UN SAFARI-PHOTO
Location: Central African Republic

Functions
- Making suppositions
- Expressing doubt and certainty
- Asking for and giving advice
- Expressing astonishment
- Cautioning someone
- Expressing fear
- Reassuring someone
- Expressing relief

Grammar
- Structures that take the subjunctive
- Using the subjunctive
- Irregular subjunctive forms

Culture
- Overview of the Central African Republic

- Animal conservation in the Central African Republic
- Stereotypical impressions of francophone regions

Re-entry
- The subjunctive
- The conditional

CHAPITRE 8 : LA TUNISIE, PAYS DE CONTRASTES
Location: Tunisia

Functions
- Asking someone to convey good wishes
- Closing a letter
- Expressing hopes or wishes
- Giving advice
- Complaining
- Expressing annoyance
- Making comparisons

Grammar
- **Si** clauses
- The comparative

Culture
- Overview of Tunisia
- Traditional and modern life in Tunisia
- Carthage
- Modernization in francophone countries
- Traditional and modern styles of dress in Tunisia

Re-entry
- The imperfect
- Formation of the conditional
- Making requests

CHAPITRE 9 : C'EST L'FUN!
Location: Canada

Functions
- Agreeing and disagreeing
- Expressing indifference
- Making requests
- Asking for and making judgments
- Asking for and making recommendations
- Asking about and summarizing a story

Grammar
- Negative expressions
- The relative pronouns **qui, que,** and **dont**

Culture
- Multilingual broadcasting in Canada
- Overview of Montreal
- Favorite types of movies

- The Canadian film industry

Re-entry
- Expressing opinions
- Quarreling
- Types of films

CHAPITRE 10 : RENCONTRES AU SOLEIL
Location: Guadeloupe

Functions
- Bragging
- Flattering
- Teasing
- Breaking some news
- Showing interest
- Expressing disbelief
- Telling a joke

Grammar
- The superlative
- The past perfect

Culture
- Climate and natural assets of Guadeloupe
- Overview of Guadeloupe
- **La fête des cuisinières**
- Daily routines of francophone teenagers
- Greetings in Guadeloupe

Re-entry
- Forms of the comparative
- The **passé composé**

CHAPITRE 11 : LAISSEZ LES BONS TEMPS ROULER!
Location: Louisiana

Functions
- Asking for confirmation
- Asking for and giving opinions
- Agreeing and disagreeing
- Asking for explanations
- Making observations
- Giving impressions

Grammar
- The relative pronouns **ce qui** and **ce que**

Culture
- **Mardi Gras** and festivals in Louisiana
- Cajun French
- Cajun music
- History of Louisiana
- Parties and celebrations in francophone countries

Re-entry
- Renewing old acquaintances
- Food vocabulary
- Making suggestions

CHAPITRE 12 : ECHANGES SPORTIFS ET CULTURELS
Location: Worldwide (Review)

Functions
- Expressing anticipation
- Making suppositions
- Expressing certainty and doubt
- Inquiring
- Expressing excitement and disappointment

Grammar
- The future after **quand** and **dès que**

Culture
- International sporting events in francophone countries
- Stereotypes of people in francophone countries

Re-entry
- Sports vocabulary
- Prepositions with countries
- Adjectives of nationality

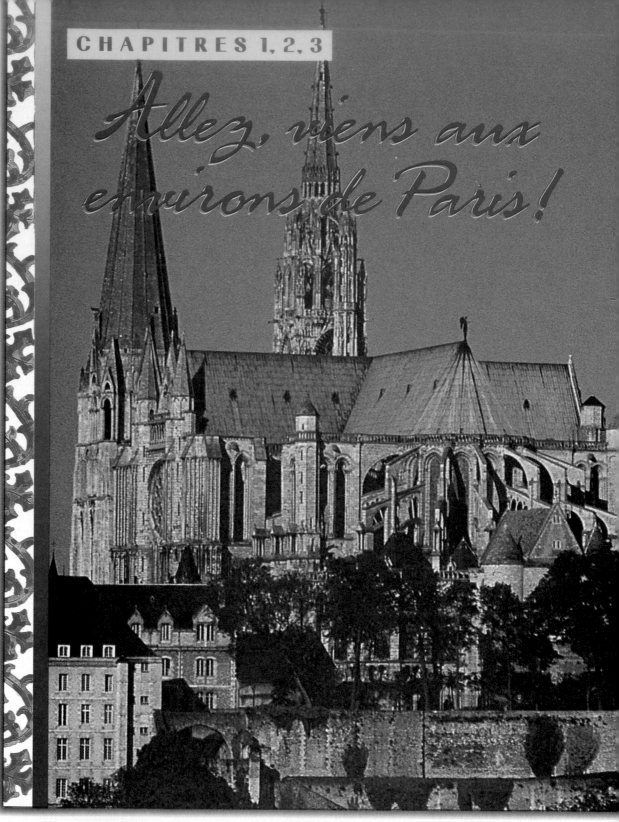

EXPANDED VIDEO PROGRAM, *Videocassette 1* 01:23–04:11

OR *VIDEODISC PROGRAM,* *Videodisc 1A*

Search 2456, Play To 7540

Motivating Activity

Ask students to recall what they already know about Paris: the monuments, cathedrals, museums, gardens, transportation, and any other aspects. Then, ask them if they can name any cities or attractions in the area around Paris. You might refer students to the map of France on pupil page xx or the smaller map on page 1. You might also project *Map Transparency 1.* Have students compare what they know with the photos on pupil pages xxiv-3.

Background Information

The area surrounding Paris has been central to the political and economic life of France for centuries. The region, known as **Ile-de-France,** is composed of seven **départements.** The gently rolling countryside surrounding Paris is indented with many valleys. Numerous churches and **châteaux** are located in the region. The wooded areas encircling the city are well-known, the most famous being the **bois de Vincennes** and the **bois de Boulogne.** As the city of Paris has grown, the suburbs (**la banlieue**) have extended outward, engulfing older towns and giving rise to new ones.

CHAPITRES 1, 2, 3

Allez, viens aux environs de Paris!

History Link

La cathédrale de Notre-Dame-de-Chartres, dedicated to the Virgin Mary, is famous for its differing towers, beautiful stained-glass windows with over 5,000 characters, and more than 4,000 impressive sculptures. The foundation and the Gothic facade of the church, built between 1140 and 1160, survived a series of fires, but the remainder of the church had to be rebuilt. Beginning in 1195, the reconstruction project was both a cooperative effort and a demonstration of Christian unity as the rich donated money and joined other citizens in providing the manual labor to rebuild the cathedral. It was finally consecrated in 1260. Built in only 25 years, its architecture is remarkably homogeneous and has survived all of the wars that have been fought since.

Les environs de Paris

Population : plus de 11.000.000

Villes : Paris, Chartres, Chantilly, Provins, Rambouillet, Barbizon, Malmaison, Compiègne

Châteaux : Vaux-le-Vicomte, Versailles, Fontainebleau

Points d'intérêt : le Parc Astérix, la cathédrale de Notre Dame-de-Chartres, le centre Georges Pompidou

Parcs et jardins : le bois de Vincennes, le bois de Boulogne, le parc des bords de l'Eure

Ressources et industries : agriculture, tourisme, transports

Personnages célèbres : Claude Monet, George Sand, Simone de Beauvoir, Marcel Proust

La cathédrale de Notre-Dame-de-Chartres

Using the Almanac and Map

Terms in the Almanac

- **Chartres** is the capital of **la Beauce**, a region known as the breadbasket of France.
- **Chantilly** is located just north of Paris. Products associated with Chantilly are lace, china, and whipped cream (**crème Chantilly**).
- Since 1897, the **château de Rambouillet** has been an official residence of the President of the Republic.
- **Barbizon**, located south of Paris, is famous for its school of painting, started by a group of nineteenth-century painters, including Bazille, Renoir, Sisley, and Monet.
- **Versailles** was the showpiece of King Louis XIV. It satisfied his desire for grandeur and his wish to remove the court from Paris.
- Situated east of Paris, **le bois de Vincennes** was once a royal forest. It now houses the Paris zoo and the parc floral de Paris.
- **Claude Monet** (1840–1926) gave the name to the impressionist movement with his painting *Impression: soleil levant.*
- **George Sand** (1804–1876), the pen name of Aurore Dupin, was a Romantic novelist, whose inspiration came from her love of the countryside and sympathy for the poor. Her works include *Indiana* (1832) and *Lélia* (1833).
- **Simone de Beauvoir** (1908–1986) was a writer known for her existential themes (*L'invitée,* 1943), her treatment of feminist issues (*Le deuxième sexe,* 1949), and her concern for the aged (*Une mort très douce,* 1964).
- **Marcel Proust** (1871–1922) is famous for his seven-volume work, *A la recherche du temps perdu.*

Using the Map

Ask students where Paris is located in relation to the rest of France. Ask them to think of reasons why the city, which is located so far to the north and has long been the heart of French political and economic life, has gained such a position of prominence. (Possible reasons might include its position both on the Seine River and on the route from Italy, Spain, and Germany towards England.)

Geography Link

Ask students to think of American and Canadian cities that have become prominent because of their location on rivers or other trade routes. (Students might mention cities such as Chicago or Duluth, MN on the Great Lakes, New Orleans on the Mississippi, steel and manufacturing towns in Ohio or Pennsylvania, and Quebec City and Montreal on the St. Lawrence River.)

Using the Photo Essay

① **Ile de la Cité** is the oldest part of Paris, and in fact, the city's ancient name, **Lutèce,** means *inhabitants in the middle of the water.* In the Middle Ages, however, the population outgrew the confines of the island and spread to the river banks: **la rive droite** to the north and **la rive gauche** to the south. Together with **Ile Saint-Louis,** it is now an elegant residential area. King Louis-Philippe and Emperor Napoléon III had much of **Ile de la Cité** razed in the nineteenth century to make way for new and expanded administrative buildings, such as the palais de Justice. The **bateaux-mouches,** pictured in the photo, are a popular way to view Paris as early river travelers must have seen it. Notre-Dame, Sainte-Chapelle, and La Conciergerie are located on the island.

② This painting by **Georges Seurat** is called *Le dimanche d'été à la Grande Jatte.* It shows a mixed crowd of people enjoying a Sunday afternoon on an island in the Seine River. The painting shows individuals engaged in a variety of activities: walking, sitting under trees, fishing, and boating. However, Seurat has given the painting an overall feeling of stillness and suspended motion. He concentrated mainly on the observation of light and color rather than on texture or facial detail.

③ The impressionist painter, **Claude Monet,** lived in the small village of **Giverny** from 1882 until his death in 1926 and is buried there. He was a brilliant innovator who excelled in presenting the effects of light at different times of the day. His paintings of the Rouen cathedral, water lilies, and haystacks at all times of the day are a few of his masterpieces.

Les environs de Paris

Avec ses nombreux châteaux au milieu des forêts, ses cathédrales gothiques et sa merveilleuse campagne immortalisée par les peintres impressionnistes, la région parisienne est le cœur historique et culturel de la France.

① C'est à partir de **l'île de la Cité** que la ville de Paris s'est développée petit à petit.

② En 1886, quand Georges Seurat a peint ce tableau, **l'île de la grande Jatte** n'était encore qu'une banlieue où les Parisiens aimaient aller se détendre.

③ Le jardin de Claude Monet à **Giverny**

History Link

① The sister island of **Ile de la Cité** is **Ile Saint-Louis,** which was formed between 1614 and 1630 from two smaller islands. Among its former residents are Marie Curie, writers Charles Baudelaire and François Voltaire, and painter Honoré Daumier. On the island are aristocratic, seventeenth-century townhouses, mansions, and courtyards.

Art Link

② **Georges Seurat** painted in the nineteenth-century neo-impressionist style. His technique of portraying light by using tiny brushstrokes of contrasting colors was known as *pointillism.* The colors tend to blend when observed from a distance. In addition to *Le dimanche d'été à la Grande Jatte* (seen on this page) another of Seurat's masterpieces is *Baignade à Asnières.*

④ La modernité du **centre Georges Pompidou,** grande structure mi-métal, mi-verre, attire de nombreux visiteurs à l'intérieur comme à l'extérieur.

Dans les chapitres suivants, tu vas faire la connaissance d'une élève américaine et de la famille chez qui elle va faire un séjour. Ils habitent à Chartres, à 180 kilomètres au sud-ouest de Paris. C'est dans la Beauce, une grande région agricole que l'on a surnommée «le grenier à grain» de la France.

④ **Le centre Georges Pompidou,** the most visited attraction in Paris, was named after former French president Pompidou (1911–1974). It was completed in 1977. Because of its modernistic steel and glass construction, Parisians often refer to it as "the refinery." The escalators located outside the structure in glass tubes offer a panoramic view of Paris. It is often called the **centre Beaubourg** because of its location on the Beaubourg plateau.

⑤ Une vue pittoresque de **la ville de Chartres** et sa belle cathédrale

⑤ The two towers of the **cathédrale de Notre-Dame-de-Chartres** were constructed at different times during the twelfth century. **Le Clocher vieux** on the left is the older of the two, while **le Clocher neuf** was constructed about 20 years later. The cathedral is a masterpiece of Gothic architecture, although it still shows evidence of Romanesque influence. It is the largest of all French cathedrals.

⑥ Les grandes eaux, ou fontaines, du **château de Versailles** consomment 3,8 millions de litres d'eau par heure.

⑥ The gardens at **Versailles,** covering 250 acres, were designed by André le Nôtre. The famous Hall of Mirrors (**la galerie des Glaces**) overlooking the grounds, is lined with windows and mirrors that reflect both the light and the view. **Le Grand Canal** allowed Louis XV to take gondola rides with his courtiers and imagine he was in Venice. The thousands of fountains throughout the park are turned on for the public on summer weekends during **Les Grandes Eaux.** Also located on the grounds are **le Grand Trianon,** a small pink marble palace built by Louis XIV and **le Petit Trianon,** a favorite retreat of Marie-Antoinette.

⑦ Astérix le Gaulois est devenu le sujet d'un parc d'attractions, **le Parc Astérix,** qui se trouve à moins d'une heure de Paris.

trois 3

⑦ The French have their own famous amusement park, **le Parc Astérix,** located near Roissy Airport. The theme park is inspired by the adventures of **Astérix,** the famous Gallic warrior of the **bandes dessinées** by Uderzo and Goscinny. **Astérix's** village includes the recreation of different periods of French history, as well as many of the places featured in the different **Astérix** stories. There are also arenas (**arènes**), where bumbling gladiators engage in mock combat for the spectators.

Chapitre 1 : Bon séjour!
Chapter Overview

Mise en train pp. 6–8	Une méprise		Practice and Activity Book, p. 1		Video Guide OR Videodisc Guide

	FUNCTIONS	GRAMMAR	CULTURE	RE-ENTRY
Première étape pp. 9–12	• Describing and characterizing yourself and others, p. 10 *Review* • Expressing likes, dislikes, and preferences, p. 11 • Asking for information, p. 12	*Review* Adjective agreement, p. 11		• Pronunciation: **liaison** • Adjectives to characterize people • Family vocabulary
Deuxième étape pp. 13–17	*Review* Asking for and giving advice, p. 15	*Review* The imperative, p. 15	• **Note Culturelle,** Travel documents for foreign countries, p. 14 • **Panorama Culturel,** Studying abroad, p. 17	• Weather expressions and seasons • Clothing and colors
Troisième étape pp. 18–21	*Review* • Asking for, making, and responding to suggestions, p. 18 • Relating a series of events, p. 20	*Review* The future with **aller,** p. 21	• Realia: **Les restaurateurs de la rue de la Porte-Morard,** p. 19 • **Note Culturelle,** Ethnic restaurants, p. 19 • Realia: TV listings from **Télé 7 Jours,** p. 21	How to tell time

Lisons! pp. 22–23	Une année scolaire aux USA	**Reading Strategy:** Previewing and skimming

Review pp. 24–27	Mise en pratique, pp. 24–25	Que sais-je? p. 26	Vocabulaire, p. 27

Assessment Options	**Etape Quizzes** • *Chapter Teaching Resources, Book 1* **Première étape,** Quiz 1-1, pp. 23–24 **Deuxième étape,** Quiz 1-2, pp. 25–26 **Troisième étape,** Quiz 1-3, pp. 27–28 • *Assessment Items, Audiocassette 7A/Audio CD 1*	**Chapter Test** • *Chapter Teaching Resources, Book 1,* pp. 29–34 • *Assessment Guide,* Speaking Test, p. 28 • *Assessment Items, Audiocassette 7A/Audio CD 1* **Test Generator, Chapter 1**

Video Program OR *Expanded Video Program, Videocassette 1*
OR *Videodisc Program, Videodisc 1A*

Textbook Audiocassette 1A/Audio CD 1

RESOURCES: Print	**RESOURCES: Audiovisual**

Textbook Audiocassette 1A/Audio CD 1

Practice and Activity Book, pp. 2–4
Chapter Teaching Resources, Book 1
* Teaching Transparency Master 1-1, pp. 7, 10 . . . . *Teaching Transparency 1-1*
* Additional Listening Activities 1-1, 1-2, p. 11 . . . . *Additional Listening Activities, Audiocassette 9A/Audio CD 1*
* Realia 1-1, pp. 15, 17
* Situation Cards 1-1, pp. 18–19
* Student Response Forms, pp. 20–22
* Quiz 1-1, pp. 23–24 . . . . *Assessment Items, Audiocassette 7A/Audio CD 1*
Videodisc Guide . . . . *Videodisc Program, Videodisc 1A*

Textbook Audiocassette 1A/Audio CD 1

Practice and Activity Book, pp. 5–7
Chapter Teaching Resources, Book 1
* Communicative Activity 1-1, pp. 3–4
* Teaching Transparency Master 1-2, pp. 8, 10 . . . . *Teaching Transparency 1-2*
* Additional Listening Activities 1-3, 1-4, p. 12 . . . . *Additional Listening Activities, Audiocassette 9A/Audio CD 1*
* Realia 1-2, pp. 16, 17
* Situation Cards 1-2, pp. 18–19
* Student Response Forms, pp. 20–22
* Quiz 1-2, pp. 25–26 . . . . *Assessment Items, Audiocassette 7A/Audio CD 1*
Video Guide . . . . *Video Program* OR *Expanded Video Program, Videocassette 1*
Videodisc Guide . . . . *Videodisc Program, Videodisc 1A*

Textbook Audiocassette 1A/Audio CD 1

Practice and Activity Book, pp. 8–10
Chapter Teaching Resources, Book 1
* Communicative Activity 1-2, pp. 5–6
* Teaching Transparency Master 1-3, pp. 9, 10 . . . . *Teaching Transparency 1-3*
* Additional Listening Activities 1-5, 1-6, p. 13 . . . . *Additional Listening Activities, Audiocassette 9A/Audio CD 1*
* Realia 1-2, pp. 16, 17
* Situation Cards 1-3, pp. 18–19
* Student Response Forms, pp. 20–22
* Quiz 1-3, pp. 27–28 . . . . *Assessment Items, Audiocassette 7A/Audio CD 1*
Videodisc Guide . . . . *Videodisc Program, Videodisc 1A*

Practice and Activity Book, p. 11

Video Guide . . . . *Video Program* OR *Expanded Video Program, Videocassette 1*
Videodisc Guide . . . . *Videodisc Program, Videodisc 1A*

Alternative Assessment
* Performance Assessment
  Première étape, p. 12
  Deuxième étape, p. 16
  Troisième étape, p. 21
* Portfolio Assessment
  Written: **Mise en pratique,** Activity 2, *Pupil's Edition,* p. 25
    Assessment Guide, p. 14
  Oral: **Mise en pratique,** Activity 4, *Pupil's Edition,* p. 25
    Assessment Guide, p. 14

For Student Response Forms, see *Chapter Teaching Resources, Book 1*, pp. 20–22.

Première étape

5 Ecoute! p. 9

1. Pour lui, le sport est très important. Il a dix-sept ans, et il est très sympa.

2. Il s'appelle Félix, et il est très gros.

3. Elle a trente-neuf ans, mais elle est très jeune de caractère.

4. Elle aime les magasins, le cinéma et la musique.

5. Il a quarante-deux ans, et il travaille dans un bureau d'informatique.

Answers to Activity 5
1. c   2. a   3. d   4. e   5. b

6 Ecoute! p. 10

1. Vanessa Paradis, une chanteuse célèbre, est grande et mince. Elle a les cheveux longs et châtain et les yeux marron. Elle est aussi actrice de cinéma.

2. MC Solaar, alias Claude M'Barali, est rappeur. Il a les cheveux noirs et les yeux marron. Il est très populaire en France.

3. Elsa, une française d'origine italienne, aime chanter et faire du cinéma. Belle et mince, elle a les cheveux bruns et bouclés. Ses yeux sont bleus.

4. Patrick Bruel est chanteur et acteur de cinéma. Il est grand. Il a les cheveux bruns, bouclés et assez longs.

Answers to Activity 6
1. a   2. d   3. b   4. c

9 Ecoute! p. 12

Bon, mon cousin Eric, il est très sympa. Il adore la musique, surtout la musique classique. Il va souvent aux concerts. Il aime aussi sortir avec des copains et jouer au basket-ball. Il adore aller se promener à la campagne avec son chien.

Ma cousine Caroline est très sociable; elle est toujours au téléphone. Elle adore sortir. Elle aime aller manger des hamburgers avec ses copains parce qu'elle est très gourmande. Caroline est aussi très sportive: elle joue souvent au tennis et au foot.

Answer to Activity 9
Caroline

Deuxième étape

16 Ecoute! p. 15

1. — Qu'est-ce que je dois prendre?
   — Pense à prendre des lunettes de soleil, un short et un tee-shirt. Prends aussi des sandales et un maillot de bain. Bon voyage!

2. — Voyons... qu'est-ce qu'il faut prendre?
   — Prends des pulls et des bottes; oh, un anorak, bien sûr. Et prends ton bonnet, ton écharpe et tes gants. Et pense à prendre tes lunettes de soleil.

3. — Alors... je dois prendre des jeans, des pulls et mes baskets. Quoi d'autre?
   — Ben, n'oublie pas ton passeport! C'est essentiel pour aller aux Etats-Unis!

Answers to Activity 16
1. b   2. d   3. c

Troisième étape

22 Ecoute! p. 19

SANDRA   Où est-ce qu'on pourrait bien aller manger ce soir? Je n'ai pas très envie de faire la cuisine. Et toi?

ETIENNE   Moi non plus. Regardons dans le journal. Il y a une liste de bons restaurants. On pourrait aller dans un restaurant indien. Ça nous changerait.

SANDRA   Ah, non, je n'aime pas la cuisine épicée. Il n'y a pas autre chose? Un restaurant traditionnel, peut-être?

ETIENNE   Si, mais nous n'allons pas au restaurant pour manger de la cuisine traditionnelle. Maman prépare ça tous les jours.

SANDRA   Si tu veux, on peut aller à "La Cave." J'adore le fromage!

ETIENNE   Non, je préfère le restaurant indochinois.

SANDRA   Pas question!

ETIENNE   Alors? Qu'est-ce qu'on fait?

SANDRA   Et une pizza, ça te dit?

ETIENNE   Bonne idée, mais il n'y a pas de pizzeria dans le journal.

SANDRA   Ne t'inquiète pas. J'en connais une très bonne pas loin d'ici.

ETIENNE   D'accord. Allons-y.

Answers to Activity 22
Etienne: an Indian or Indochinese restaurant
Sandra: a traditional restaurant, "La Cave"
They decide to go to a pizzeria.

25 Ecoute! p. 20

Tiens, j'ai beaucoup de projets pour samedi! D'abord, le matin, je vais faire de la natation. Ensuite, je vais faire un pique-nique au parc avec des copains. On va prendre des sandwiches et des fruits. Puis, on va faire du vélo ensemble. Du vélo en plein air, c'est génial! Enfin, le soir, on va aller voir un film au cinéma. Ça va être une journée super!

Answers to Activity 25
b, c, a, d

Mise en pratique

3 p. 25

Ça y est. J'ai enfin mon billet. J'arrive jeudi à dix-huit heures. C'est le vol Air France cinquante-cinq. J'ai oublié de t'envoyer une photo de moi! Alors, j'ai les cheveux bruns, je suis de taille moyenne et je vais mettre un pull rouge. Mais vous allez me reconnaître facilement, je suis le plus beau!

Answers to Mise en pratique Activity 3
He's arriving Thursday at 6:00 p.m. on Air France flight 55. He has dark hair, is of average height, and will be wearing a red sweater.

Projects

Mon/Ma correspondant(e)
(Individual Project)

ASSIGNMENT

Students will invent an exchange student from a franco-phone country who is coming to stay with them for a year. The project will include a letter from and pictures of the student and his or her family, as well as a postcard he or she writes to a friend or family member after arriving in the United States. Students will introduce their exchange students to the class by means of the letter, the pictures, and the postcard.

MATERIALS

✂ **Students may need**

- Magazines
- Old photographs
- Scissors
- Paper
- Postcards
- Posterboard
- Pencil or pen
- Colored markers

SUGGESTED SEQUENCE

1. Each student imagines a French-speaking exchange student and family. Have students use the map on page xxiii **(Le Monde francophone)** and choose a French-speaking country and city. Students might research the country and city they choose in order to tell about the family members' lives.

2. Students find pictures on which to base the descriptions in their letters. The pictures may be photographs (of people their classmates won't recognize), magazine pictures cut to look like photographs, or drawings. The pictures must be labeled with the names, ages, and interests of the people in the pictures.

3. Students write a letter from the imaginary exchange student to themselves. The letter should include the following:
   - a description of the exchange student, including some of his or her likes and dislikes;
   - descriptions of his or her family members;
   - questions about the host student;
   - a few things the exchange student would like to do upon arrival.
   Note: Remind students that the descriptions should match their pictures.

4. After students have proofread their letters, form groups for peer editing. Each student in the group should proofread every letter, making note of any errors as well as suggestions for improving the letters. Afterwards, have students rewrite their letters.

5. Students write postcards from the exchange student to someone back home. The cards may be purchased or homemade, but should reflect your city or state. The text of the postcards should include the following:
   - a statement saying how the student is enjoying his or her stay;
   - a short paragraph stating four things that he or she and the host student are going to do this week, using **aller + infinitive** and the expressions **d'abord, puis, ensuite,** and **enfin.**

6. Repeat the peer editing process with the postcards.

7. Students display the letter, the pictures, and the postcards on a sheet of posterboard.

8. Have each student introduce his or her exchange student to the class by describing the person and telling about the pictures, rather than reading the letter and postcard to the class.

GRADING THE PROJECT

You might want to grade students on the written and oral parts of their project. The writing grade should be based on the content (including all the required functions), accuracy of the language, and presentation of the project. The oral grade should be based on comprehensibility and presentation.

Suggested Point Distribution: (total = 100 points)

Writing

Content . . . . 20 points

Language use . . . . 20 points

Overall presentation . . . . 20 points

Oral

Comprehensibility . . . . 20 points

Presentation . . . . 20 points

JE VAIS EN FRANCE

In this game, students will practice the vocabulary for clothing and travel items.

Procedure One student starts the game by saying **Je vais en France et je vais prendre...** completing the sentence with an article of clothing or accessory. The next student repeats the first item and adds another item to the list. A student who cannot correctly repeat everything that was said is out, but may remain involved by keeping an accurate list of what is said in case of a dispute.

NI OUI NI NON

In this game, students will practice asking yes-no questions and using alternate expressions for **oui** *and* **non.**

Procedure
1. Distribute five playing cards to each student.
2. Students circulate and ask one another *yes-no* questions, trying to trick one another into answering **oui** or **non. (Tu as quinze ans? Tu as les yeux bleus? Tu aimes danser? Madame Dupont est très gentille, n'est-ce pas?)**
3. Students try to avoid answering **oui** or **non** when their classmates ask them a question (**C'est vrai... , C'est pas vrai... , C'est ça... , Tu as raison... , Pas du tout... , Peut-être, mais... , Je ne suis pas sûr(e)...**).
4. A student who answers **oui** or **non** must award a card to the person who asked the question.
5. The student with the most playing cards after a specified amount of time wins.

VINGT QUESTIONS

In this game, students will practice using descriptive adjectives and asking questions.

Procedure A student secretly chooses one character or person mentioned in the chapter, such as Sandra's brother or MC Solaar. The other students try to guess who it is by asking *yes-no* questions about the person. They may ask up to twenty questions, but may only make three guesses as to the identity of the person. Whoever guesses correctly chooses the next secret identity.

JE ME SOUVIENS

In this game, students will practice asking questions and using the vocabulary and functions from this chapter.

Procedure Gather magazine or catalogue pictures of people doing various activities. Form groups of nine and divide each group into two teams of four and one scorekeeper. Distribute one picture to each team and tell them to study it for three minutes. Then, call time and have the two teams exchange pictures. Team A makes true-false statements about the picture they have received from Team B. Team B must respond to the statements according to what they remember of the picture they studied. Then, team B does the same. (**La fille a les yeux bleus. Elle joue au tennis. Le garçon porte un tee-shirt blanc.**) Any incorrect responses count against the team.

Chapitre 1
Bon séjour!
pp. 4–27

𝒰sing the Chapter Opener

Motivating Activity

Explain the difference between **Bon séjour!** (refers to a stay) and **Bon voyage!** (refers to a trip). Ask students what the people in the photographs are doing and why. Then, ask the following questions:

• If you were going to spend a year with a family in a foreign country, what would you like them to know about you?

• Would it be difficult to pack for a year abroad? Why or why not? What would you need to know about the country and the family in order to pack well?

• What would you want to do once you arrived?

Photo Flash!

① Pamela and Sandra are walking on a street in Chartres, a city of about 28,000 located 96 kilometers southwest of Paris, just an hour train ride from there. Chartres is best known for its cathedral, a masterpiece of Gothic architecture with exquisite stained-glass windows.

Teaching Suggestion

① Ask students if they know the significance of the cross over the store (indicating a pharmacy) and the street sign with a white bar on a red circle (one-way street, do not enter).

CHAPITRE
1 Bon séjour!

① Tu as envie de voir la France? Allez, viens!

4 *quatre*

🌍 **Culture Note**
Point out that French and other European teenagers tend to spend more time visiting historical sites and monuments than American teenagers. Since most of them grow up among buildings and streets that are many hundreds of years old, history has more of an immediate presence in their lives. Therefore, it is not unusual for French teenagers to ride their bicycles or mopeds to a neighboring town on the weekend for some sightseeing.

Teacher Note
Some activities suggested in the Annotated Teacher's Edition ask students to contact various people, businesses, and organizations in the community. Before assigning these activities, it is advisable to request parental permission. In some cases, you may also want to obtain permission from the parties the students will be asked to contact.

Many students experience other cultures as exchange students. One day you might have the opportunity to visit another country and live with a family. What would you do to get ready? You'd exchange letters with your family, decide what to pack, make plans for your stay . . . and be prepared for anything to happen!

In this chapter you will review and practice

- describing and characterizing yourself and others; expressing likes, dislikes, and preferences; asking for information
- asking for and giving advice
- asking for, making, and responding to suggestions; relating a series of events

And you will

- listen to people talk about their families
- read about French exchange students who've come to the United States
- write a description of yourself
- find out what it's like to be an exchange student in a francophone country

② *J'aime bien faire des photos… et j'adore Paris!*

③ Qu'est-ce que je dois prendre?

MOORE

DE / from
HOUSTON

A / to
PARIS/C GAULLE

VOL / Flight   CLASSE   DATE   DEPAR

035   Y   13MAR

Culture Note

During the school year at French high schools, one- and two-week exchanges are often arranged with schools in neighboring countries, especially in Germany and England. French high school students have the opportunity to participate in exchanges because of the French **lycée** vacation schedule. During the school year, **lycéens** look forward to several breaks: **les vacances de la Toussaint** (one week around October 31), **les vacances de Noël** (two weeks at Christmas), **les vacances d'hiver** (two weeks beginning in February), and **les vacances de printemps** (two weeks around Easter). Summer vacation at a French **lycée** begins during the first or second week in July and ends with **la rentrée** *(the first day of school)* at the end of the first or second week in September.

Focusing on Outcomes

Have students determine which chapter outcome is represented by each photo. Then, have them think of English expressions or other French expressions they may have learned that accomplish the functions listed. Have one student compile a list on the board of the various suggestions. NOTE: You may want to use the video to support the objectives. The self-check activities in **Que sais-je?** on page 26 help students assess their achievement of the objectives.

Photo Flash!

② Pamela is taking a picture of Sandra during their ride on a **bateau-mouche** on the Seine River in Paris. Taking the sightseeing boat is a popular tourist excursion. The Seine offers a good view of many famous sights, such as the cathedral of Notre Dame and the Eiffel Tower. The excursions are often accompanied by a recorded commentary in three or four different languages. Many people prefer to take the tour at night when the famous sites are illuminated.

Teacher Note

Call students' attention to the ticket in the lower right-hand corner of the page. Explain that "PARIS/C GAULLE" refers to the Roissy-Charles-de-Gaulle airport in Paris. Two other airports service Paris: **le Bourget** and **Orly**.

Culture Note

② The Eiffel Tower (**la tour Eiffel**), designed by Gustave Eiffel, was built for the Centennial Exposition of 1889 to commemorate the French Revolution. Standing at 984 feet, it was the tallest structure in the world until the completion of the Chrysler Building in New York City in 1930.

VIDEO PROGRAM
OR EXPANDED VIDEO
PROGRAM,
Videocassette 1
04:12–07:59

OR VIDEODISC PROGRAM,
VIDEODISC 1A

Search 7540, Play To 14375

Video Synopsis

In this segment of the video, Sandra and her parents are about to leave to pick up Pamela, an American student who will be their guest. Sandra describes Pamela to her parents. When they arrive at the airport, Sandra and her mother go inside to look for Pamela. Mr. Lepic, who stays in the van, notices a girl who fits Pamela's description. He greets the girl, Patricia, and puts her suitcase in the back of the van. Sandra, her mother, and Pamela arrive back at the van. Mr. Lepic realizes his mistake and apologizes to Patricia. Just then, Patricia's French host arrives. Everyone says goodbye and the Lepics leave. Suddenly, Patricia and her friend notice that they have the wrong suitcase!

Motivating Activity

Have students suggest some problems that might occur if they were to pick up an exchange student at the airport. Then, ask them what problems they think they might have upon arrival in a foreign country.

Mise en train

Sandra   M. Lepic   Mme Lepic

Une méprise

The Lepic family is going to pick up their exchange student at the airport, but they're having a few problems. Can you guess what these problems might be from looking at the photos?

> Pamela arrive à l'aéroport à dix heures vingt. Dépêchez-vous!

> N'oublie pas que d'abord elle va récupérer ses bagages et puis passer à la douane. Alors, comment est-elle? Brune? Blonde? Grande? Petite?

> Elle a 16 ans. Elle est grande et elle a les cheveux bruns. D'après sa lettre, elle va porter une jupe rouge et elle aura une valise noire.

Chez la famille Lepic à Chartres : Il est 9 h du matin et on est en retard.

①

②

Si tu veux, je peux vous retrouver ici..

A l'aéroport...

> D'accord. Bonne idée.

> Bien. Allez-y!

③

Quelques minutes plus tard...

Ah, c'est elle. Brune, une jupe rouge, une valise noire...

④

> Bonjour! Tu n'as pas vu ma femme et ma fille?

⑤

6   six

CHAPITRE 1   Bon séjour!

RESOURCES FOR MISE EN TRAIN
Textbook Audiocassette 1A/Audio CD 1
Practice and Activity Book, p. 1
Video Guide
   Video Program
   Expanded Video Program, Videocassette 1
Videodisc Guide
   Videodisc Program, Videodisc 1A

Culture Note

Passer à la douane means *to go through customs.* Passengers arriving in France on international flights must show their passports to customs officials (**les douaniers**) before claiming their luggage.

Presentation

Have students view the video of the **Mise en train** with their books closed. Afterwards, ask them to name the characters in the story and their relationships to one another. Tell them to open their books and look at the title of the **Mise en train**. Have them try to deduce the meaning of the word **méprise** from what they saw in the video. Then, ask them to look at the photos on page 6 and tell what mistakes are made. Then, form groups and have the members choose a role and read the story aloud. Finally, do the comprehension activities on page 8.

For Individual Needs

Visual Learners Trace the **Mise en train** photos without the dialogue in the speech bubbles, number the empty speech bubbles, and give each student a copy. Project the various lines of speech in random order on the overhead projector and have students give the number of the corresponding speech bubble.

Auditory Learners Do the same as above, but read the lines aloud as you project them on the transparency.

Teaching Suggestion

Ask students to guess the English equivalent of **Tout est bien qui finit bien.** *(All's well that ends well.)*

Video Integration

- **EXPANDED VIDEO PROGRAM,**
  Videocassette 1, 08:00–12:25
- **VIDEODISC PROGRAM,**
  Videodisc 1A

Search 14375, Play To 22320

You may choose to continue with **Une méprise (suite)** at this time or wait until later in the chapter. When the story continues, Patricia and Bertrand manage to stop the Lepics, and they exchange suitcases. The Lepics then take Pamela on a tour of Paris by **bateau mouche** before returning to Chartres.

1 Tu as compris? See answers below.

1. Why does Sandra tell her family to hurry?
2. How does Sandra describe her friend?
3. When they arrive at the airport, what do Sandra and Mrs. Lepic do?
4. What's Mr. Lepic's first mistake? Why does he make it?
5. What happens at the end of **Une méprise?**

2 Arrange la scène

Choisis la photo qui correspond à chaque phrase. Ensuite, mets les phrases en ordre d'après **Une méprise.** 5, 4, 2, 1, 3, 6

1. Pamela arrive à la voiture avec Mme Lepic et Sandra. f
2. Mme Lepic, Pamela et Sandra sortent de l'aéroport. e
3. Bertrand arrive à la voiture. d
4. M. Lepic voit Patricia. a
5. La famille Lepic arrive à l'aéroport. c
6. Patricia a la valise de Pamela. b

a.   b.   c.

d.   e.   f.

3 Cherche les expressions

According to **Une méprise,** how do you . . . See answers below.

1. tell what time it is?
2. ask what someone looks like?
3. ask how someone's trip was?
4. express concern for someone?
5. introduce someone?
6. apologize for your mistake?

4 Et maintenant, à toi

With a partner, talk about what might happen next in **Une méprise.**

Answers

1 1. They're late picking up the exchange student.
2. sixteen, tall, brown hair, red skirt, black suitcase
3. go to look for Pamela
4. He thinks Patricia is Pamela; She fits Pamela's description.
5. Bertrand finds Patricia, and Mr. Lepic drives off with Patricia's suitcase.

3 1. Il est neuf heures du matin...
2. ... comment est-elle?
3. ... tu as fait bon voyage?
4. Ça va? Pas trop fatiguée?
5. Je te présente...
6. ... excusez-moi...

PREMIERE ETAPE

Describing and characterizing yourself and others; expressing likes, dislikes, and preferences; asking for information

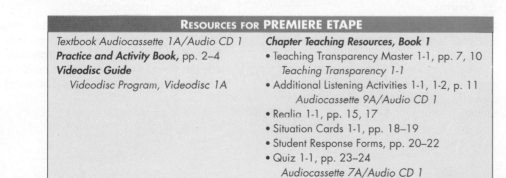

Chartres, le 30 juillet

Chère Pamela,

La dame qui s'occupe des échanges franco-américains a téléphoné hier pour nous annoncer la bonne nouvelle. Tu vas donc venir passer un an avec nous. J'espère que tu vas te plaire ici.

Voilà, je m'appelle Sandra. J'ai quinze ans. Je suis brune, plutôt moyenne, j'ai les yeux marron Et toi? Tu es comment? Envoie-moi vite une photo.

Dans notre famille, nous sommes quatre, enfin cinq avec notre chat. Il s'appelle Félix et il est très gros. Mon père travaille dans un bureau d'informatique et ma mère travaille à mi-temps dans une boutique de souvenirs près de la cathédrale. Mon père a quarante-deux ans et ma mère trente-neuf. Ils sont très jeunes de caractère.

Mon frère Etienne a dix-sept ans. Je l'aime bien, il est sympa. Pour l'instant, il va au lycée au Texas dans le cadre d'un échange. Lui, il adore le sport. Moi, mon truc, c'est plutôt le cinéma ou les magasins. En sport, je suis nulle. Je peux rester des heures dans ma chambre à écouter de la musique. Et toi, quels sont tes groupes préférés? J'ai tellement de questions à te poser sur ta vie aux Etats-Unis, ta famille, tes amis, l'école... Qu'est-ce que tu aimes faire?

5 Ecoute!

Ecoute Sandra qui parle de sa famille. De quelle photo est-ce qu'elle parle? **1.** c **2.** a **3.** d **4.** e **5.** b

a.

b.

c.

d.

e.

PREMIERE ETAPE

RESOURCES FOR PREMIERE ETAPE

Textbook Audiocassette 1A/Audio CD 1
Practice and Activity Book, pp. 2–4
Videodisc Guide
  Videodisc Program, Videodisc 1A

Chapter Teaching Resources, Book 1
• Teaching Transparency Master 1-1, pp. 7, 10
  Teaching Transparency 1-1
• Additional Listening Activities 1-1, 1-2, p. 11
  Audiocassette 9A/Audio CD 1
• Realia 1-1, pp. 15, 17
• Situation Cards 1-1, pp. 18–19
• Student Response Forms, pp. 20–22
• Quiz 1-1, pp. 23–24
  Audiocassette 7A/Audio CD 1

---

*J*ump Start!

Write the following scrambled sentences from the **Mise en train** on the board or on a transparency. Students should unscramble and rewrite the sentences.
1. bon as alors voyage tu fait?
2. grande les bruns elle cheveux elle et est a.
3. vu fille tu et ma n'as femme pas ma?
4. vingt l'aéroport arrive à Pamela dix à heures.
5. est qui bien finit tout bien.

MOTIVATE

Have students imagine they are going to spend a year in France as exchange students. Have them make a list in French of five qualities the ideal **correspondant(e)** would have. What activities would he or she like? Have students list five things they would tell their **correspondant(e)** about themselves in a letter before their arrival. Have students save these lists for possible use in their projects (see the projects on page 3E).

TEACH

For Individual Needs

Slower Pace Read the letter from Sandra aloud. Stop after each paragraph to ask simple comprehension questions. For example, after the first paragraph, ask **Qui a téléphoné hier? Pourquoi?** (la dame qui s'occupe des échanges franco-américains; pour annoncer la nouvelle) Write some questions on the board or on a transparency for visual learners.

5 Slower Pace Before you play the recording, have students look back at the **Mise en train** to identify the animal and the people in the photos.

Presentation

Comment dit-on... ?

• To present hair and eye color and age, use magazine pictures of people whose hair and eye color are obvious. Tape a card with the person's age written on it to the picture. Then, describe the people. **(Elle a les cheveux bruns. Elle a 17 ans.)** Afterwards, ask either-or questions about each picture. **(Elle a les cheveux blonds ou les cheveux bruns?)**

• To present height and recycle the expressions above, choose students of varying heights and have them stand in front of the class (avoiding making anyone feel self-conscious). Describe their height to the class. **(Voilà Marie, elle est petite.)** Then, ask either-or questions. **(Marie est grande ou elle est petite?)** Ask questions about hair and eye color and age as well (students might hold cards representing their age).

For videodisc application, see *Videodisc Guide.*

Additional Practice

To practice the **je** and **tu** forms of the expressions, describe yourself. Then, ask individuals **Tu as les yeux bleus ou les yeux marron?** to elicit **J'ai les yeux marron.** Finally, ask students to describe themselves or others.

Language Note

Châtain is the French word for a hair color that is between brunette and blonde. Point out that you can say **Elle est blonde, Il est brun,** and **Elles sont rousses,** but you must say **Elle a les cheveux noirs, Il a les cheveux gris,** and **Ils ont les cheveux châtain.**

COMMENT DIT-ON... ?

Describing and characterizing yourself and others

Je m'appelle Catherine et j'ai quinze ans. J'ai les yeux bleus et les cheveux châtain. Je suis de taille moyenne. J'adore les bandes dessinées.

Voilà Astérix. Il a les yeux noirs et les cheveux blonds et courts. Il est petit. Il est beau? Pas vraiment, mais il est brave et toujours prêt à partir pour une nouvelle aventure.

Et voici Obélix. Il a les yeux verts? marron? On ne sait pas, ils sont si petits. Il a les cheveux roux et longs. Il est très grand, très fort et très gourmand. C'est le meilleur ami d'Astérix.

To describe yourself:
> **J'ai** quinze **ans.**
> **J'ai les yeux** bleus.
> *I have . . . eyes.*
> **J'ai les cheveux** courts.
> *I have . . . hair.*
> **Je suis** grand(e).

To characterize yourself:
> **Je suis** gourmand(e)!

To describe others:
> **Elle a** sept **ans.**
> **Elles ont les yeux** marron.
> **Ils ont les cheveux** bruns.
> **Elle est** petite.
> **Ils sont de taille moyenne.**
> *They're of medium height.*

To characterize others:
> **Il est** intelligent.
> **Elles sont** sympa.

6 Ecoute!

Match the descriptions of these stars with their photos. **1.** a **2.** d **3.** b **4.** c

a.

b.

c.

d.

Tu te rappelles ?

Do you remember how to make **liaisons?** You pronounce the final consonant of one word when the following word begins with a vowel sound, as in **les yeux** and **ils ont.**

CHAPITRE 1   Bon séjour!

Game

6 C'EST QUI? Have each student write a brief description of a celebrity or a TV or comic book character, using the listening activity as a model. Then, have students read their descriptions aloud. The first person to correctly guess whom they are describing earns a point.

Teaching Suggestion

Tu te rappelles? Have students reread the letter on page 9 and find all the examples of liaison (des échanges, nous annoncer, un an, les yeux, dans un, dans une, deux ans, des heures, aux Etats-Unis, les amis).

*G*rammaire Adjective agreement

As you remember, you often change the forms of adjectives in French to match the nouns they describe.

- You add an **e** to the masculine form of most adjectives to describe feminine nouns or pronouns.

  Il est **intelligent.** Elle est **intelligente.**

- You don't have to change singular adjectives that already end in a silent **e**.

  Il est **jeune.** Elle est **jeune.**

- You add an **s** to adjectives when you're describing plural nouns, unless the adjectives end in **s** or **x**.

  Ils sont **jeunes.** Elle a les cheveux **gris.** Ils sont **heureux.**

- Remember that some adjectives have irregular feminine forms.

  Il est **beau.** Elle est **belle.**
  Il est **gentil.** Elle est **gentille.**
  Il est **sportif.** Elle est **sportive.**

- You don't have to change the form of some adjectives. How many of these can you find in **Comment dit-on... ?** on page 10?*

7 Jeu de portraits

Take on the identity of a cartoon or TV character and describe yourself to your group. The person who guesses who you are takes the next turn.

8 Mon Journal

Décris-toi, ainsi que ta famille réelle ou imaginaire, dans ton journal.

Si tu as oublié **family vocabulary** *va à la page 340.*

Tu te rappelles ?

Here are some more adjectives to help you characterize people:
méchant(e)
gentil (gentille)
amusant(e)
pénible
mignon (mignonne)
embêtant(e)

COMMENT DIT-ON... ?
Expressing likes, dislikes, and preferences

To tell what you like:
J'adore le sport.
J'aime bien faire des photos.

To tell what you dislike:
Je n'aime pas le tennis.

To tell what you prefer:
Je préfère jouer au foot.
J'aime mieux faire de la vidéo.

---

* **marron, sympa,** and **châtain**

📖 Mon journal

8 For an additional journal entry suggestion for Chapter 1, see *Practice and Activity Book,* page 145. Refer students to the Supplementary Vocabulary on page 341 for additional adjectives.

Additional Practice

Have students gather magazine or catalogue pictures that represent their likes and dislikes and create a collage on posterboard. Then, have students explain their visual representations of themselves to the class. (**J'adore danser et écouter de la musique.**) To keep the class involved, have students volunteer facts about the presenter. (**Il/Elle aime danser.**)

~~~~~~~~~~~~

Presentation

Grammaire Prepare sets of large cards. On the first set of four cards, write **il, elle, ils,** and **elles.** On the second set of two, write **est** and **sont.** On the third set of several cards write adjectives in their masculine singular form. On the fourth set write **-e, -s, -es, -le, -ve,** and **-x.** Have four students each take one set of cards. Student #1 chooses and shows a subject card. Student #2 then selects and shows the appropriate verb form. Student #3 holds up any adjective. Student #4 must choose the correct ending for the adjective.

❖ For Individual Needs

Kinesthetic Learners Prepare sentences using third person pronouns and various adjectives. (**Il est beau. Elles sont intelligentes.**) Seat four students in front of the room in groups of two: two boys and two girls. Read a sentence and have the students in the chairs stand to represent its structure. For example, for the first sentence above, one boy stands. For the second sentence, both girls stand. Have students repeat each sentence while their classmates in front of the class are still standing in order to provide an audio-visual connection for auditory and visual learners or slower-paced learners.

~~~~~~~~~~~

Presentation

Comment dit-on... ? Show pictures of various activities and tell which activities you like or dislike. Then, ask students about their preferences as you show the pictures again. (**Tu aimes jouer au tennis, Jean?**)

Portfolio

10 Written You might have students include their self-portraits in their written portfolios. For portfolio information, see *Assessment Guide*, pages 2–13.

Presentation

Comment dit-on... ? Ask students **Qu'est-ce que tu aimes faire?** If necessary, prompt with additional questions, such as **Tu aimes écouter de la musique? Tu aimes aller à la plage?** When students have heard several responses, ask them what other students like to do. **(Qu'est-ce que Paul aime faire?)** Repeat the process for each question in the function box, re-entering the first questions as you go.

Language Note

Point out that **Qu'est-ce que** is followed by a subject and verb, **Quel est** by a thing, and **Qui est** by a person.

CLOSE

To close this **étape,** put the names of all the students in a box. Have them draw names and give three sentences describing the person and telling what he or she likes.

ASSESS

Quiz 1-1, *Chapter Teaching Resources, Book 1,* pp. 23–24

Assessment Items, Audiocassette 7A/Audio CD 1

Performance Assessment

Have groups write and perform a skit about meeting francophone students. The people involved should get to know one another and ask about the others' likes and dislikes.

---

9 Ecoute!

Listen to Etienne describe his cousins Eric and Caroline. Look at his self-portrait below and decide which cousin has more in common with him. *Caroline*

10 Un auto-portrait

Make a self-portrait like Etienne's. Use the categories he used, some of those suggested below, or some of your own.

- livre préféré
- musique préférée
- groupe préféré
- jeu préféré
- acteur/actrice préféré(e)
- couleur préférée

Nom :	LEPIC
Prénom :	Etienne
Né(e) le :	10 mai
A :	Dijon
Résidence :	Chartres
Animaux domestiques :	un chat et deux poissons rouges
Sports pratiqués :	le tennis, le vélo, le foot
Lieu(x) de vacances préféré(s) :	la plage, l'Italie
Plats préférés :	les hamburgers et le bœuf bourguignon
Passions :	le sport, la musique rock, les copains, la lecture
Ambition :	participer au Tour de France

COMMENT DIT-ON... ?
Asking for information

Qu'est-ce que tu aimes faire?
Qu'est-ce que tu fais comme sport?
Qu'est-ce que tu aimes comme musique?
Quel est ton groupe/film/cours/plat **préféré**? *What is your favorite . . . ?*
Qui est ton acteur/actrice **préféré(e)**? *Who is your favorite . . . ?*

11 Sondage

Using the questions in **Comment dit-on... ?** and the self-portrait you made in Activity 10, interview three classmates to find the person whose interests most closely match yours.

12 Jeu de rôle

Choose a famous person you and your partner are interested in and stage an interview. One of you is the famous person; the other is the interviewer. When you present your interview to the class, use props, costumes, or music to entertain your audience.

12   *douze*   CHAPITRE 1   Bon séjour!

Family Link

Have students teach a family member to describe himself or herself and to say what he or she likes in French. When assigning Family Link activities, keep in mind that some students and families may consider family matters private.

Culture Note

10 Etienne was born in Dijon, the capital of Burgundy **(la Bourgogne),** in east central France. Dijon is known for its mustard, its vinegar, and its gingerbread. One of Etienne's favorite dishes is **bœuf Bourgignon,** a specialty of the region, which is made by marinating beef cubes in flour, red wine, thyme, and bay leaves before cooking.

DEUXIEME ETAPE

Asking for and giving advice

Ici, le climat est assez douce. Apporte quand même un manteau et deux ou trois gros pulls; il peut faire froid en hiver. Prends aussi un imperméable et des bottes parce qu'il pleut souvent. L'été, il fait chaud mais pas trop. Pense à prendre un maillot de bain. Quand il fait beau, on peut aller se baigner au lac. Pour l'école, on y va le plus souvent en jean et en tee-shirt. Apporte une tenue pour sortir aussi.

13 Pense à prendre...

D'après la lettre de Sandra, quels vêtements est-ce que Pamela doit mettre...

1. en hiver? **d** 2. quand il pleut? **e, f** 3. pour se baigner au lac? **a** 4. pour l'école? **b, c**

a.   b.   c.   d.   e.   f.

De bons conseils

Do you recall everything you learned last year? It's easy to forget your French when you don't use it for a while. Here are some tips.

- Use the flashcards you've made to review vocabulary. Make new ones for verbs or phrases that you use frequently.

- If you can't remember how to say something in French, look in the glossary or ask someone **Comment dit-on... ?** You can also try using words you do know or gestures to explain what you mean.

- Don't be afraid to speak out. Attempting to speak will sometimes jog your memory. Even if you make a mistake, you're still communicating.

DEUXIEME ETAPE   *treize*   **13**

*J*ump Start!

Have students rewrite the following paragraph, changing the underlined items to describe their best friend or an imaginary friend.

   <u>Ma</u> meilleur<u>e</u> ami<u>e</u> a <u>quinze</u> ans, et <u>elle</u> est <u>très petite</u>. <u>Elle</u> a les cheveux <u>noirs</u> et les yeux <u>bleus</u>. <u>Elle</u> adore <u>jouer au tennis</u> et <u>faire du vélo</u>.

MOTIVATE

Ask students what kinds of clothes they wear in each season and what they wear for different occasions. Ask them what Pamela needs to know in order to pack wisely for a year in France.

TEACH

For Individual Needs

Slower Pace Have students scan the letter and list the different weather conditions that are mentioned. Then, have them list the clothing Sandra asks Pamela to bring for each weather condition.

Challenge Have students name as many additional types of clothing as they can for each of the weather conditions mentioned.

Auditory Learners Read the letter aloud while students listen with their books closed. Each time students hear an expression about the weather they should raise one hand. Each time they hear an article of clothing mentioned, they should raise both hands.

Visual/Auditory Learners Draw simple representations of all the clothes and weather mentioned in the letter in random order. Distribute copies to students who will number the drawings in the order they hear them as you read the letter aloud.

Presentation

Vocabulaire Try to bring to class a suitcase and all the items in the **Vocabulaire**. Identify the items in French as you place them around the room where students will be able to see them. Tell them you are going to spend a year in France and you need to get organized before you pack. On the board, write **A prendre**. Underneath, list all the items you have placed around the room. Then, as you start to pack, pretend you can't find anything. Ask **Est-ce que quelqu'un a vu mon imperméable?** If a student hands you the wrong item, say **Merci, mais ce n'est pas mon imperméable, c'est mon écharpe.** You may give clues, such as **Je porte mon imperméable quand il pleut,** and mime holding an umbrella in the rain. When a student holds up the correct item, ask other students **Qu'est-ce que Michel a trouvé?**

 For videodisc application, see *Videodisc Guide.*

Additional Practice

Have one student name a vocabulary item in French. A partner will draw an illustration. Partners should take turns and check to see if the drawing accurately represents the item named.

♜ Game

 PICTIONNAIRE Distribute sheets of butcher paper to small groups. Have each group write all the vocabulary words on slips of paper. Then, have a student draw a slip and sketch an illustration representing that word. The first student to say the French word for that drawing scores a point. Students take turns drawing.

VOCABULAIRE

Pour mon voyage, il me faut...

des baskets · une écharpe · un sweat · mon passeport · un imperméable · deux pulls · un anorak · des bottes · deux tee-shirts · des gants · mon billet d'avion · deux jeans · mon appareil-photo · des chèques de voyage

14 Que mettre?

Qu'est-ce que tu mets... *See answers below.*

Si tu as oublié clothing and colors va à la page 340.

1. pour aller dans un restaurant chic?
2. pour aller à l'école?
3. pour aller à la plage?
4. pour faire du ski?
5. pour aller à un concert de ton groupe préféré?

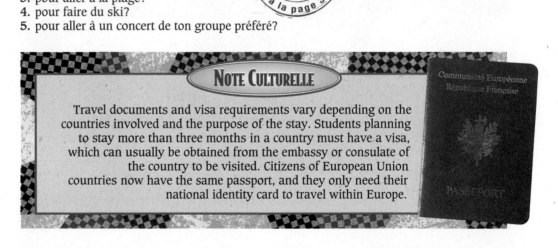

NOTE CULTURELLE

Travel documents and visa requirements vary depending on the countries involved and the purpose of the stay. Students planning to stay more than three months in a country must have a visa, which can usually be obtained from the embassy or consulate of the country to be visited. Citizens of European Union countries now have the same passport, and they only need their national identity card to travel within Europe.

Teaching Suggestion

14 As a variation of this activity, have pairs of students add to the list of possible occasions. Then, one partner describes the clothes he or she is going to wear, without mentioning the destination. The other partner guesses where he or she is going.

Possible answers

14 1. une robe, un pantalon, une cravate, une chemise, des chaussures
2. un jean, un tee-shirt, des baskets
3. un maillot de bain, des sandales
4. des gants, une écharpe, un anorak, un pantalon, des lunettes de soleil
5. un jean, un tee-shirt, des baskets

15 Devinons!

Write down three activities that you'd like to do. Choose one of the activities. Then, tell your group what you're going to wear for the activity. The person who guesses what you're going to do takes the next turn.

—Je vais mettre un jean et un gros pull, un anorak, des gants et des bottes.
—Tu vas faire du ski!

COMMENT DIT-ON...?
Asking for and giving advice

To ask for advice:
Qu'est-ce que je dois prendre?
What should I . . . ?

To give advice:
Pense à prendre ton passeport.
Remember to take . . .
Prends un dictionnaire bilingue.
N'oublie pas tes bottes.

Note de *Grammaire*

One way to give advice is to use commands.

- When you're talking with a friend, use the **tu** form of the verb without **tu**: **Prends ton maillot de bain.**

- Don't forget to drop the **s** when you're using the **tu** form of an **-er** verb as a command: **Pense à moi!**

- To make a command negative, put **ne... pas** around the verb: **N'oublie pas ton billet!**

16 Ecoute!

D'après ces conversations, où est-ce que ces gens vont pour les vacances?   1. b   2. d   3. c

a. à Paris   **b.** à la plage   **c.** à New York   **d.** à la montagne pour faire du ski

17 A mon avis

Possible answers: Joseph: Prends des jeans, un tee-shirt et un maillot de bain.
Marie-Claire: Prends des jeans, une écharpe et un manteau.

Your friends Joseph and Marie-Claire are packing for their vacations, but they've forgotten a few things. Give them advice on what else they should bring.

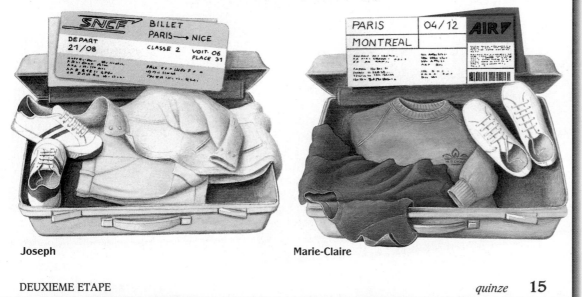

Joseph   Marie-Claire

DEUXIEME ETAPE   *quinze*   **15**

Building on Previous Skills

Gather pictures of different weather conditions. Hold them up and ask either-or questions, such as **Il fait froid ou il fait chaud?** In addition, post several weather expressions on a bulletin board. Ask students to bring magazine pictures of outfits suitable for each kind of weather and display them under the appropriate expression.

Culture Note

17 Call attention to the dates on the train and airline tickets in the drawing. Explain that in France, the day is written before the month when writing dates. Therefore, it is important to understand that the date **04/12** written on the plane ticket means *the fourth of December* and not *the twelfth of April.*

For Individual Needs

15 Visual Learners
Assign each student a particular activity (**aller à l'école**) or type of weather (**Il neige**). Have them design and draw an outfit for that activity or weather condition, label it, and describe it to the class.

Presentation

Comment dit-on... ? First, ask students to recall the items they helped you "pack" (see Presentation on page 14). They might add others. Then, write the expressions **Pense à prendre...** , **Prends...** , and **N'oublie pas...** on the board. Tell students once again that you're going to France and ask **Qu'est-ce que je dois prendre?** Have students suggest items, using the expressions on the board. Mention specific activities (**Je vais faire du ski**) or types of weather (**Il pleut là-bas**) to prompt students.

TPR **Note de grammaire**
To review the imperative, write several commands on index cards using the **tu**, **nous**, and **vous** forms. They must be instructions that can easily be acted out, such as **Allez à la porte** or **Dessine un chat.** Select a leader to stand in front of the class. The other students stand by their desks. The leader reads the commands, addressing them either to one person, using the **tu** form, to all the others, using the **vous** form, or to everyone, using the **nous** form.

CLOSE

Game

One student tells another what he or she is going to do. (**Je vais faire du ski.**) You might write suggestions on the board for students to refer to, such as **visiter Londres, faire de la natation,** and **aller au match de football américain.** The other student must give some appropriate advice. (**Prends des gants.**) The second student then tells a third student what he or she is going to do. The third student gives advice, and so on. A student who cannot give an appropriate suggestion is out, but can get back in the game by helping another student who cannot respond.

ASSESS

Quiz 1-2, *Chapter Teaching Resources, Book 1,* pp. 25–26.

Assessment Items, Audiocassette 7A/Audio CD 1

Performance Assessment

Copy the situations below on separate slips of paper and distribute one slip of paper to each group of two to four. Have each group create a conversation based on their situation.

• A friend is going to an elegant restaurant on a special occasion and asks for advice on what to wear.
• A new student asks for advice on what type of clothes to wear to school.
• A neighbor is spending the weekend at the beach and asks for advice on what to pack.
• A classmate is planning a ski trip during winter break. Tell him or her what to pack.
• You and some friends are going to a birthday party. Ask and advise each other what to bring and what to buy for a present.

---

18 Qu'est-ce que je dois faire?

A lot can happen when you travel. What would you do if you found yourself in the situations pictured below? With a partner, take turns asking and giving advice about what to do next.

Achète... Va... Mets... Parle à...
Prends... Invite...
Téléphone à... Trouve...

19 Qu'est-ce qu'on prend?

Ton ami(e) français(e) va passer une année chez toi. Il/Elle te téléphone pour savoir quoi prendre comme vêtements pour chaque saison. Joue la scène avec un(e) camarade.

—Qu'est-ce que je prends pour l'été?
—Bon... Il fait très chaud ici. Pense à prendre un short et un tee-shirt.

Si tu as oublié weather expressions and seasons va à la page 340.

20 Des cartes postales

Imagine you're spending some time in one of the places shown on these postcards. A friend is going to join you later. Write a message for the postcard advising your friend what to bring.

Possible answers: Prends des bottes, un anorak, des pantalons et des gros pulls.

QUÉBEC

Martinique

Possible answers: Prends un maillot de bain, des sandales, des shorts et des tee-shirts.

16 *seize*

CHAPITRE 1   Bon séjour!

Teaching Suggestion

20 Ask students to choose a place to go for vacation. Then, have them write short letters, telling where they are going, what they are going to do there, and asking for advice on what to pack. Have them sign their letters with a pen name. Collect the letters, redistribute them randomly, and have each student answer the letter on a separate sheet of paper, also signing a pen name. Collect the letters and responses from one group, shuffle them, and pass them to another group. Have that group match the responses to the letters.

PANORAMA CULTUREL

Yvette • Côte d'Ivoire

Jean-Christophe • France

Onélia • France

VIDEO PROGRAM
OR EXPANDED VIDEO
PROGRAM,
Videocassette 1
12:26–17:13

OR *VIDEODISC PROGRAM,*
VIDEODISC 1A

Search 22320, Play To 25540

We talked to some francophone students about traveling and studying abroad. We asked them for advice for students planning to study in their countries. Here's what they had to say.

Quels conseils donnerais-tu à un élève américain qui arrive dans ton pays?

«Si cet élève vient en Côte d'Ivoire pour faire ses études, je lui dirais de bien apprendre le français, de ne pas se décourager. C'est un peu difficile. En tout cas, d'être patient, sérieux, tout ça parce que c'est pas facile.»

—Yvette

«Un conseil que je donnerais à un étudiant américain arrivant en France... ce serait de s'incorporer dans une famille pour bien s'habituer à leurs manières, pour travailler avec eux, pour voir comment nous vivons et de sortir parce que les jeunes Français savent s'amuser.»

—Jean-Christophe

«La France est très différente des Etats-Unis. Aux Etats-Unis, on n'a pas le droit de sortir [en boîte] avant 21 ans... [La France,] c'est un peu plus libéral que les Etats-Unis, donc, [il] faut faire attention. [Il ne] faut pas non plus abuser de l'alcool par exemple, ou du tabac quand on arrive en France. Donc, voilà. C'est les conseils que je pourrais donner aux Américains.»

—Onélia

Qu'en penses-tu?

1. Are there any exchange students in your school? Where are they from? What languages do they speak?
2. If you were to study in a francophone country, how might things be different for you? What kinds of problems might you have adjusting to life in a foreign country?
3. What advice do you have for foreign students who want to study in your area?

Questions

1. D'après Yvette, qu'est-ce qu'il faut bien apprendre? (le français)
2. Selon Jean-Christophe, pourquoi est-il important de s'incorporer dans une famille? (pour bien s'habituer à leurs manières, pour travailler avec eux, pour voir comment ils vivent)
3. D'après Onélia, quelle est la différence entre la France et les Etats-Unis? (La France est plus libérale.)

Multicultural Link

If there are any exchange students in your school, have your students interview them, asking the following questions:
• What surprised you the most about American life?
• What do you like best about American life?
• What problems have you had because of language or cultural differences?
• What advice would you give to a student planning to spend time abroad?

Teacher Notes

• See *Video Guide, Videodisc Guide,* and *Practice and Activity Book* for activities related to the **Panorama Culturel.**
• Remind students that cultural material may be included in the Chapter Quizzes and Test.
• The interviewees' language represents informal, unrehearsed speech. Occasionally, edits have been made for clarification.

Motivating Activity

Ask students to imagine an exchange student is coming to stay with them. Ask them what advice they would give this student.

Presentation

On the board or on a transparency, write the following paraphrases of the advice given by the interviewees. As students view the video, have them write the numbers in the order in which they hear the advice.
1. Il faut s'incorporer dans une famille.
2. Il ne faut pas abuser de l'alcool et du tabac en France.
3. Il faut être patient et sérieux.
4. Il faut sortir parce que les jeunes français savent s'amuser.
5. Il faut bien apprendre le français.
(Answers: 5, 3, 1, 4, 2)

TROISIEME ETAPE

Asking for, making, and responding to suggestions; relating a series of events

J'ai beaucoup de projets pour cette année avec toi. D'abord, je voudrais te présenter tous mes amis. Ils sont super sympa. Ensuite, tu vas voir Chartres; c'est une très jolie ville et il y a des tas de choses à faire. Si tu veux, on peut aller voir la cathédrale, aller au cinéma, écouter de la musique française, manger de la cuisine française... Tu n'as pas envie de manger du bon pain français?... Et pendant les vacances de Noël, on pourrait aller faire du ski avec mes cousins! Ecris-nous vite. Pose toutes les questions que tu veux. Vivement ton arrivée! On va bien s'amuser!
Sincères amitiés et à bientôt. Bises,

Sandra

21 Que faire?

What are some of the things Sandra plans to do when Pamela arrives? What would you like to do if you were visiting France?

introduce her to friends, visit Chartres, go to the cathedral, go to the movies, listen to French music, eat French food, go skiing; Answers will vary.

COMMENT DIT-ON... ?
Asking for, making, and responding to suggestions

To ask for suggestions:
   Qu'est-ce qu'on fait? *What should we do?*

To make suggestions:
   Si tu veux, on peut jouer au foot.
      If you like, we can . . .
   On pourrait aller au fast-food.
      We could . . .
   Tu as envie de faire les magasins?
      Do you feel like . . . ?
   Ça te dit de manger du couscous?
      Does . . . sound good to you?

To respond to suggestions:
   D'accord.
   C'est une bonne/excellente idée.
      That's a good/excellent idea.
   Je veux bien.
   Je ne peux pas.
   Ça ne me dit rien.
   Non, je préfère... *No, I'd rather . . .*
   Pas question!

22 Ecoute!

Sandra et Etienne vont manger au restaurant ce soir. D'abord, lis ces descriptions de restaurants. Ensuite, écoute Sandra et Etienne. Où est-ce qu'Etienne veut aller? Et Sandra? Qu'est-ce qu'ils décident de faire? Answers on p. 3D.

Les restaurateurs de la rue de la Porte-Morard

Au cœur du Secteur Sauvegardé, en prolongement du pont St-Hilaire qui offre un beau panorama sur la rivière et la Cathédrale, les cinq restaurants de la rue de la Porte-Morard vous proposent cinq façons différentes d'apprécier une bonne table :

au n°6 **LE MAHARADJA** - Spécialités indiennes et pakistanaises - Tél. 37 31 45 06.

au n°14 **LE CHENE FLEURI** - Hôtel-restaurant avec grande terrasse en saison - Cuisine traditionnelle - Tél. 37 35 25 70.

au n°24 **LA CAVE** - Restaurant de fromages, une autre façon de déguster la richesse de la cuisine française - Tél. 37 30 18 64.

au n°25 **LE P'TIT MORARD** - Cuisine traditionnelle dans un cadre rustique - Tél. 37 34 15 89.

au n°28 **LE TEMPLE D'ANGKOR** - Restaurant indochinois, spécialités du Sud-Est Asiatique - Tél. 37 30 01 66.

Parking gratuit proche, place Morard.

NOTE CULTURELLE

As you know, French is spoken in many countries outside of France. People from all over the world come to France to study or work, bringing with them the unique aspects of their culture. In many French cities, it is common to find restaurants offering diverse ethnic specialties.

23 Qu'est-ce qu'on mange?

Tu es à Paris avec ton ami(e). Vous choisissez un restaurant, mais ce n'est pas facile!

—Tu as envie d'aller dans un restaurant chinois?
—Non, ça ne me dit rien. Je préfère un restaurant...

marocain   indonésien
cambodgien   mexicain
russe   vietnamien
    français traditionnel
indien
    libanais   grec
thaïlandais   antillais

24 Qu'est-ce qu'on fait?

You, your friends, and a French guest are spending Saturday together. Decide on three things you want to do.

faire la cuisine
aller danser à...   faire les magasins
aller au cinéma pour voir...
aller au match de...   déjeuner au restaurant
faire du roller en ligne
faire un pique-nique au parc

TROISIEME ETAPE

dix-neuf **19**

Presentation

Comment dit-on... ? Write the following activities on the board and tell in what order you plan to do some of them, using **d'abord, ensuite, puis,** and **enfin.**
• trouver un bon emploi
• finir mes études du lycée
• acheter une grande maison
• aller à l'université
• acheter une mobylette
• trouver un petit boulot *(job)*
• me marier
• économiser mon argent
• gagner de l'argent
• avoir des enfants
• voyager partout en Europe
• avoir mon diplôme à l'université

Do this a couple of times and ask students what you are doing and what words you are using to do this. Then, read the function box with students. Have them close their books and do as you did, selecting some activities from the list on the board and telling in what order they are going to do them.

Thinking Critically

Analyzing Have students read the story in **Comment dit-on... ?** and pick out the words that link the parts of the story together (**d'abord, ensuite, puis, enfin**). Ask students why these words are important. (They link ideas together, making communication easier.)

◆ For Individual Needs

25 Challenge Have students say as much as they can in French about each picture before completing the listening activity.

Teaching Suggestion

26 You might have partners volunteer to read their vacation plans to the class, who will guess where they are going.

20 **TROISIEME ETAPE** **CHAPITRE 1**

COMMENT DIT-ON... ?
Relating a series of events

QU'EST-CE QUE TU VAS FAIRE EN FRANCE?

D'ABORD, JE VAIS VISITER LA TOUR EIFFEL.

ENSUITE, JE VAIS PRENDRE DES ESCARGOTS DANS UN BON RESTAURANT.

PUIS, JE VAIS VOIR LA JOCONDE AU LOUVRE.

ENFIN, JE VAIS FAIRE LA CONNAISSANCE D'UNE JEUNE FILLE FRANÇAISE.

25 Ecoute!

Tarek raconte ses projets pour samedi. Mets les images en ordre.   b, c, a, d

a.   b.   c.   d.

26 Les vacances de mes rêves

Choose a vacation destination and tell your partner what you're going to do there. Can your partner guess where you're going?

| D'abord, Ensuite, Puis, Enfin, | je vais je voudrais | manger... visiter... faire la connaissance de... voir... acheter... faire... aller à... |

Culture Notes

• By law, French employees are entitled to five weeks of vacation per working year, whereas American employees can look forward to only two weeks of vacation in a year. Generally, most French families take advantage of their vacation during the month of August when school is out. Tourists visiting France at this time might witness a mass exodus from Paris and the northern part of France to the south of France!

• The *Mona Lisa,* or *La Joconde* in French, is located in the Louvre museum in Paris. It is a masterpiece by Leonardo da Vinci, painted in the early sixteenth century, and is known for the mysterious smile of the woman in the portrait. Prior to this masterpiece, portrait artists had always shown only the face and the upper chest of the model. Da Vinci broke the pattern by including the arms and hands of the model, which gave a more natural disposition to the portrait.

MERCREDI

TF1

13.00 LE JOURNAL DE LA UNE
avec LA METEO, LA BOURSE,
et LA METEO DES PLAGES.
13.35 LES FEUX DE L'AMOUR
Feuilleton américain
Nikki.........................Melody Thomas Scott
Ashley.............................Brenda Epperson
Jessica..............................Rebecca Street
14.30 MEDECIN A HONOLULU ↗
I CARE
Daniel Kulani..............Richard Chamberlain
Nana Kulani ....Betty Carvalho
Caitlin McGrath...........................Carol Huston
15.20 ®HAWAI, POLICE D'ETAT ↗
HOROSCOPE POUR UN MEURTRE
McGarrett.....................................Jack Lord
Danny Williams..................James McArthur
16.15 UNE FAMILLE EN OR
16.45 CLUB DOROTHEE VACANCES ⓙ
ARNOLD ET WILLY
CHARLES S'EN CHARGE
LES JEUX
18.00 ®CHIPS ↗
SUR LE TOURBILLON
Jon..Larry Wilcox
Ponch.....................................Erik Estrada

2

13.00 JOURNAL
présenté par Laurence Piquet et Gérard
Morin
13.05 METEO
13.40 INC
13.45 TATORT
Téléfilm allemand
15.30 LES DEUX FONT LA PAIRE
LE FILM DE SCOTTI
16.15 ®DES CHIFFRES ET DES LETTRES
16.45 ®L'EQUIPEE DU PONEY EXPRESS
UNE AUTRE VIE

Ty Miller

Le Kid...Ty Miller
James Butler Hickok...............Josh Brolin

3

13.00 MISS MARPLE
LE MANOIR DE L'ILLUSION
14.00 DYNASTIE ↗
UN AVENIR MOINS SOMBRE

14.45 LES LOUPS BLANCS DE L'ARCTIQUE
15.40 LA CROISIERE S'AMUSE
MONNAIE DE SINGE
16.30 40° A L'OMBRE
En direct d'Antibes
Avec Johnigo et Claude Barzotti
18.25 QUESTIONS POUR UN CHAMPION
Par Julien Lepers

---

27 **Le petit écran**

Tu es malade et tu dois rester chez toi tout l'après-midi. Fais
une liste des émissions que tu vas regarder et à quelle heure. Ensuite,
compare ta liste avec la liste de ton ami(e).

> D'abord, je vais regarder Miss Marple à 13h, puis Médecin à
> Honolulu à 14h30. Ensuite,... Enfin,...

Si tu as oublié how to tell time va à la page 340.

28 **Qu'est-ce que tu vas faire samedi?**

Make a list of four things you're going to
do Saturday and at what time you plan to
do them. Then, find someone to do them
with by asking some classmates what they
plan to do and at what time.

29 **Mon journal**

You probably have lots of plans for what
you're going to do—and not do!—this
school year. Make at least five resolutions.

Note de Grammaire

Use the appropriate form of **aller**
followed by an infinitive to say that
you're going to do something:

— Tu **vas sortir** ce soir?
— Oui, je **vais manger** au
restaurant.

To say that you aren't going to do
something, put **ne... pas** around the
form of **aller**.

Je **ne vais pas** sortir ce soir.

Presentation

Note de grammaire
Conjugate the verb **aller** on the
board. Then, form five or six
groups around the classroom.
Give each group a card with an
activity written on it in large
letters (**aller au cinéma**).
Move around the room, pointing to different groups and
asking questions. Students will
answer your questions according to their cards. For example,
hold up the card of one group
and ask **Qu'est-ce qu'ils vont
faire ce week-end? Ils vont
jouer au tennis ou ils vont
faire du vélo? Et Alain,**
(holding up another group's
card and pointing to one student in the group) **qu'est-ce
qu'il va faire? Il va au parc
ou il va aller au cinéma? Et
nous?** (including yourself in
the group and asking only
your group). **Et vous?** (pointing to a group). **Et moi, je
vais faire les magasins** (holding up your own card). **Et toi?**
and so on.

Teaching Suggestions

27 Use the TV schedule for
additional listening practice.
Call out times and channels at
random and have students
write down the appropriate
programs, or call out a program and have them write the
channel and time.

28 You might refer students
to the Supplementary Vocabulary on page 342 for additional
activities.

CLOSE

To close this **étape,** have students list in French five activities they plan to do this week-
end and mime them for the
class. Classmates should tell
what the student is going to do
this weekend, using **d'abord,
puis, ensuite,** and **enfin.**

ASSESS

Quiz 1-3, *Chapter Teaching Resources,
Book 1,* pp. 27–28
*Assessment Items, Audiocassette 7A
Audio CD 1*

Performance Assessment

In groups of four, have students act out a discussion in which they plan a day of activities.

Each student in the group takes on a different
persona: **un sportif/une sportive, un
studieux/une studieuse, un paresseux/une
paresseuse, un musicien/une musicienne.**
One student starts the conversation by asking
what the group should do. (**Qu'est-ce qu'on
fait?**) Each student must suggest activities
suitable to his or her persona. For example,
the musician might say **On pourrait aller au
concert ou écouter des disques.**

LISONS!

READING STRATEGY

Previewing and skimming

Teacher Note

For an additional reading, see *Practice and Activity Book,* page 11.

PREREADING
Activity A

Teacher Note

Talk about some of the features of the French **lycée** and how it differs from the typical American high school. For example, **lycéens** do not have organized sports in school. There is no prom or yearbook at the end of the school year. French high school students typically have Wednesday afternoons free, but they often go to school on Saturday mornings.

Thinking Critically

Comparing and Contrasting

Ask students to list three ways in which they think French students might resemble American students. French teenagers, too, have a desire to dress fashionably, be with friends, and enjoy music. However, the two cultures often differ. For example, unlike American teenagers, French teenagers usually do not have after-school jobs, they don't have cars, and they can't get their driver's license until they are 18 years old.

READING
Activities B-G

Teaching Suggestion

Challenge students to read carefully so that they will be able to judge how accurately these French students perceive the American high school.

DE BONS CONSEILS

What are the first two things you should do when faced with a new text? A good reader *previews* the reading and then *skims* it. To *preview*, glance quickly at the layout of a reading to understand how it is organized. Next *skim* the sections of the text by reading the headings, captions, and the first sentences of paragraphs or blocks of text. Ask yourself: What is the reading about? Who was it written for? Where is it set? Why was it written?

A. Preview the article. What kind of text do you think it is?

  a. a pamphlet
  b. a pen pal letter
  c. an essay

B. Skim the reading to answer the *W* questions.

  1. Read the major headings. *What* is the article about?

    a. a scholar
    b. an academic year in a high school
    c. a year in France

  2. Look at the photos. *Where* and *why* do you think they were taken?   See answers below.

  3. The major headings talk about **votre année** and the school year being **pour vous.** The headings of the first two paragraphs say "Live the American dream" and "Welcome to the United States." Look at the captions under Guillaume and Sonia's names. *Who* are the intended readers?   students in France

---

STUDENT TRAVEL SCHOOLS

Une année scolaire aux USA

Une année scolaire à l'étranger pour vous qui avez entre 15-18 ans

Vous serez rapidement la mascotte de l'école, tout le monde viendra vous poser des questions sur la France.

Vivez le "rêve américain"

"The American Dream" est un idéal de liberté, de bonheur et la possibilité de décider de son propre avenir. Une année dans une High School est pour vous l'occasion de découvrir "le pays où tout est possible". Celle-ci sera l'une des plus belles de votre vie! Profitez de cette occasion unique pour devenir américain pendant un an. Ce sera passionnant et vous en tirerez le plus grand profit.

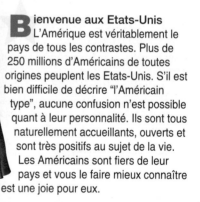

Bienvenue aux Etats-Unis

L'Amérique est véritablement le pays de tous les contrastes. Plus de 250 millions d'Américains de toutes origines peuplent les Etats-Unis. S'il est bien difficile de décrire "l'Américain type", aucune confusion n'est possible quant à leur personnalité. Ils sont tous naturellement accueillants, ouverts et sont très positifs au sujet de la vie. Les Américains sont fiers de leur pays et vous le faire mieux connaître est une joie pour eux.

Participez au bal de la High School, le "Prom".

Language Notes

- Remind students of the definition of a cognate. Use **un idéal** as an example. Have students work in small groups to find as many cognates as they can in two minutes.
- Assure students they will not know every word or verb form, but encourage them to look for what they do know and to make guesses about unfamiliar words based on the context.

Answers

B 2. *Where:* U.S.A.
    Why: to show different aspects of an American high school

STUDENT TRAVEL SCHOOLS

Votre année en High School aux USA

La fête de la "Graduation" restera un jour mémorable dans votre vie.

GUILLAUME   **S**ONIA

"20 août à l'aéroport d'Orly. Ma destination était Binghamton, petit point sur la carte de l'état de New-York. C'était le début d'une merveilleuse aventure. J'allais avoir 18 ans; j'aurais dû entrer en terminale et je découvrais une autre vie. J'étais le fils de ma famille d'accueil. L'école était comme dans les films américains: des profs très proches des élèves, des copains sûrs faisant tout pour m'aider, et ce jour inoubliable de la graduation avec ma robe de "gradué" et mon bonnet carré. Aujourd'hui je crois que j'ai rêvé mais les rêves sont peut-être ce qu'il y a de plus vrai."

"Le Michigan est devenu, après mon année en high school, ma deuxième maison. Avec les amis que je m'y suis faits, j'ai vécu les meilleurs moments de mon année: la graduation, le "bal de prom", les matchs de foot-ball. En cas de problème, les professeurs, devenus eux aussi des amis, étaient toujours là. J'ai également découvert lors de cette année un "nouveau monde", les U.S. mais aussi celui des exchange students. Ils venaient de tous les pays: de la Colombie à l'Australie en passant par les pays scandinaves... Je vous souhaite donc à tous de vivre la même expérience extraordinaire."

4. *Why* was this text written?
   a. to show American students how their schools differ from French schools.
   b. to describe the average American high school.
   c. <u>to persuade a French student to consider a year abroad in an American high school.</u>

Vivez le "Rêve Américain"

C. What are some phrases used to describe "The American Dream"? Do you agree?   See answers below.

Bienvenue aux Etats-Unis

D. If **accueillir** means *to welcome*, someone who is **accueillant** is __1__.   welcoming

If **ouvrir** means *to open*,   open someone who is **ouvert** is __2__.

If **la fierté** is *pride*, someone who is **fier** is __3__.   proud

E. Are Americans described favorably? Are all Americans like this? Are you?   Yes; Answers will vary.

Guillaume Fabry

F. Guillaume says his host school is like schools he's seen in American movies. In what way? Did Guillaume have a good time as an exchange student? How do you know?   See answers below.

Sonia Gabor   G. See answers below.

G. How does Sonia describe her experience in the States?

H. If you were a French student, would you want to come to the United States after reading this article? Why or why not?

I. Make a pamphlet describing your school to attract French-speaking exchange students. Include events and distinctive features. Add photos or drawings with captions to your pamphlet.

vingt-trois **23**

Culture Note

Discuss the notions of the "American Dream" and the American stereotype described in **Bienvenue aux Etats-Unis.** Remind students that many French and European teenagers know their American counterparts only through their exposure to American television shows that air in Europe. What stereotypes about American teenagers might these shows perpetuate among Europeans?

POSTREADING
Activities H-I

For Individual Needs

Slower Pace Have students work in pairs. For each of the three major photographs, have students reduce the photo caption to one or two words that convey the gist of the whole caption.

Cooperative Learning

I. Have students work in groups of four to make the pamphlets. Assign the roles of leader, writer, proofreader, and artist. The leader heads a discussion of what to include in the pamphlet, group members dictate the text to the writer, the proofreader checks for errors, and the artist collects and arranges the art and layout of the pamphlet.

Teaching Suggestion

I. Have students add to their brochures mock interviews of what visiting students might say about their school. They might also want to include the interviews in their oral portfolios.

Terms in Lisons!

Students may want to know the following terms from **Une année scolaire aux USA:**
véritablement *(truly)*
accueillants *(friendly)*
un pays *(a country)*
vous le faire mieux connaître *(to show (their country) to you)*
J'allais avoir 18 ans. *(I was almost 18)*
J'aurais dû entrer en terminale. *(I would have been in my last year of school.)*
une famille d'accueil *(a host family)*
que je m'y suis faits *(that I made)*
lors *(at the time of)*
souhaiter *(to wish)*

MISE EN PRATIQUE

The Mise en pratique reviews and integrates all four skills and culture in preparation for the Chapter Test.

Teaching Suggestion

Have partners make up questions about Patrick's letter and take turns asking them to each other.

For Individual Needs

Slower Pace   Have students look at the photo and describe Patrick's family. Then, have them guess what Patrick might say in his letter. To read the letter, have students read only one paragraph at a time. Remind them that they do not have to understand every word to get the general meaning of the letter. Ask simple comprehension questions about each paragraph before going on to the next. For example, after the first paragraph, ask **Patrick a quel âge? Où habite-t-il? Où va-t-il passer un an?** What is the first paragraph mostly about? The second? The third? Finally, ask the comprehension questions in Activity 1 on page 25.

Tactile Learners   Write the sentences of the letter on a piece of paper. Make copies and cut the papers into strips, with one sentence per strip. Mix up the strips and pass them out to groups of students. With the students reading along, read the letter aloud and ask simple comprehension questions. Then, have students close their books and arrange the strips from memory in the proper sequence as best they can. When they've finished, they may check the text for accuracy. Circulate around the room and praise students for putting the strips in a logical order, even if they do not match the text exactly.

After a year of studying French, you're going to host a French exchange student in your home! He writes to you and sends a photo of his family to introduce himself.

Bonjour,

Super! J'ai reçu une bonne nouvelle. Je vais aller passer un an en Amérique. Je suis fou de joie. J'ai plein de questions, trop. Mais d'abord, je me présente. Je m'appelle Patrick, j'ai 15 ans, et j'habite à Poitiers avec mes parents et mon petit frère. On a aussi un chien de chasse.

Je voudrais te demander ce que je pourrais acheter comme cadeau pour tes parents. Et pour toi? Qu'est-ce que tu aimes comme musique? Dis-moi aussi ce qu'il faut prendre comme vêtements. Pour aller au lycée, un pantalon, une chemise, et un pull, ça va? Je m'inquiète aussi pour les profs. Ils sont sévères? Mon anglais n'est pas très bon.

Est-ce que tu fais du sport? À ton avis, j'apporte ma raquette de tennis ou non? Il y a un stade près de chez toi? Est-ce qu'on peut jouer au foot? Qu'est-ce que vous faites après l'école? J'attends avec impatience une réponse. Si tu peux, envoie-moi une photo de ta maison et de ta famille.

Amicalement,
Patrick

24   *vingt-quatre*

CHAPITRE 1   Bon séjour!

Culture Note

In 1985, the French government launched a public service advertising campaign to encourage families to have more children. At that time, families were having on average one less child per family than they were twenty years before. A government agency calculated that families needed to have more children in order to maintain the population growth. Today, the government continues to encourage families to have children by offering monetary incentives to large families to help with education and other expenses.

1 How would you describe Patrick? Where is he from? Who does he live with? What is he worried about? Can you figure out what his favorite sports are? *See answers below.*

2 Answer Patrick's letter. Write about yourself and your family. Don't forget to answer his questions.

3 There's a message on your answering machine from Patrick to let you know when he's arriving, at what time, and on what flight. He also describes himself so you'll recognize him. Jot down the necessary information. *Answers on p. 3D.*

4 What are some of the activities Patrick should do in the coming school year that would really show him what life is like where you live? With a partner, decide on four or five things to do when Patrick arrives.

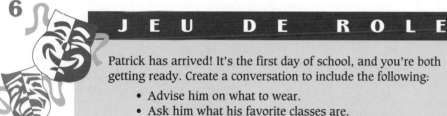

Si Patrick veut, on peut...   C'est barbant!

Non, je préfère...   Bof!   Pas question!

On pourrait...   C'est une bonne idée.   Chouette!

5 From what you know about life in France and what exchange students expect to find in the United States, what do you think Patrick might have trouble adjusting to? What might surprise him about your home and your school?

6

JEU DE ROLE

Patrick has arrived! It's the first day of school, and you're both getting ready. Create a conversation to include the following:

- Advise him on what to wear.
- Ask him what his favorite classes are.
- Describe your principal and your favorite teacher.
- Talk about what you're going to do after school.

MISE EN PRATIQUE

vingt-cinq **25**

Answers

1 fifteen, enthusiastic, full of questions; Poitiers; his parents, little brother, and dog; He worries about what to bring as a gift, his teachers, what to wear; tennis and soccer

Multicultural Link

5 Have groups create conversations in English, with one person playing the role of Patrick and the others playing his new American friends. The conversations should reflect the cultural differences between American and French lifestyles. For each topic, such as breakfast or what to wear, Patrick should express surprise and tell how things are done differently in France.

Group Work

2 Have students work in groups of four or five to peer edit their letters. Assign each member of a group a different area to check, such as spelling and accents, verbs, nouns and adjectives, and correct use of vocabulary. Every member should read each letter and suggest corrections and/or improvements.

For Individual Needs

3 **Slower Pace** Form small groups and make each group responsible for retrieving only one piece of information (when, what time, what flight, how Patrick is dressed) as they listen to the recording. Then, have students from each group report their findings. Write the information on the board and play the recording again.

Portfolio

2 **Written** This activity is appropriate for students' written portfolios.

4 **Oral** This activity is appropriate for students' oral portfolios. For portfolio suggestions, see *Assessment Guide*, page 14.

Video Wrap-Up

- *VIDEO PROGRAM*
- *EXPANDED VIDEO PROGRAM*, Videocassette 1, 04:12–19:05
- *VIDEODISC PROGRAM*, Videodisc 1A

At this time, you might want to use the video resources for additional review and enrichment. See *Video Guide* or *Videodisc Guide* for suggestions regarding the following:
- **Une méprise** (Dramatic episode)
- **Panorama Culturel** (Interviews)
- **Vidéoclips** (Authentic footage)

This page is intended to help students prepare for the test. It is a brief checklist of the major points covered in the chapter. The students should be reminded that this is only a checklist and does not necessarily include everything that will appear on the test.

♜ Game

Sur la sellette (The Hot Seat) Choose one student to sit in a chair in front of the class (the "hot seat"). The student answers questions asked by his or her classmates. When three questions have been answered correctly, the student chooses another classmate to sit in the "hot seat." Students might use the **Que sais-je?** section for their questions, or they might select their questions from any part of the chapter.

QUE SAIS-JE?

Can you describe and characterize yourself and others? p. 10

Can you express likes and dislikes? p. 11

Can you ask for information? p. 12

Can you ask for and give advice? p. 15

Can you ask for, make, and respond to suggestions? p. 18

Can you relate a series of events? p. 20

Can you use what you've learned in this chapter?

1 How would you describe and characterize . . .
1. yourself?   2. your best friend?   3. a family member?

2 How would you say that you like the following things? How would you say that you dislike them? That you prefer something else? See answers below.

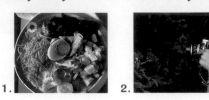 1.    2.   3.

3 How would you ask someone . . .   See answers below.
1. what he or she likes to do?   3. what type of music he or she likes?
2. what sport he or she plays?   4. what his or her favorite film is?

4 How would you ask what to take on a trip?   Qu'est-ce que je dois prendre?

5 What would you advise a friend to bring to...   See answers below.
1. the beach?   2. the mountains in the winter?   3. Chicago in the spring?

6 How would you . . .
1. ask a friend what to do?
2. suggest that you can go shopping if your friend wants to?
3. suggest that you could play soccer?   On pourrait jouer au football.
4. ask your friend if he or she would like to go to the movies?
   Tu as envie d'aller au cinéma? Ça te dit d'aller au cinéma?

   1. Qu'est-ce qu'on fait?
   2. Si tu veux, on peut aller faire les magasins.

7 How would you respond to the following suggestions if you agreed? If you disagreed? If you preferred to do something else?   See answers below.
1. On pourrait faire les magasins.
2. Tu as envie de regarder la télévision?

8 How would your friend tell you that she is going to do these activities in this order?   See answers below.

 1.   2.   3.

CHAPITRE 1   Bon séjour!

Answers

2 1. *Like:* J'adore la salade. J'aime bien la salade. *Dislike:* Je n'aime pas la salade. *Prefer:* Je préfère... ; J'aime mieux...
2. *Like:* J'adore faire des photos. J'aime bien faire des photos. *Dislike:* Je n'aime pas faire des photos. *Prefer:* Je préfère... ; J'aime mieux...
3. *Like:* J'adore faire du roller en ligne. J'aime bien faire du roller en ligne. *Dislike:* Je n'aime pas faire du roller en ligne. *Prefer:* Je préfère... ; J'aime mieux...

3 1. Qu'est-ce que tu aimes faire?
2. Qu'est-ce que tu fais comme sport?
3. Qu'est-ce que tu aimes comme musique?
4. Quel est ton film préféré?

5 *Possible answers:* Pense à prendre... ; Prends... ; N'oublie pas...
1. un maillot de bain, des sandales et des lunettes de soleil.
2. des bottes, des pantalons, des pulls, un manteau et des gants.
3. un imperméable, des jeans, des tee-shirts et des baskets.

7 *Agree:* D'accord. C'est une bonne (excellente) idée. Je veux bien.
Disagree: Je ne peux pas. Ça ne me dit rien. Pas question.
Prefer to do something else: Non, je préfère...

8 1. D'abord, je vais faire de l'équitation.
2. Ensuite, je vais faire mes devoirs.
3. Enfin, je vais regarder la télévision.

PREMIERE ETAPE

Describing and characterizing yourself and others

avoir... ans   *to be . . . years old*
J'ai...   *I have . . .*
Il/Elle a...   *He/She has . . .*
Ils/Elles ont...   *They have . . .*
les yeux marron   *brown eyes*
　　bleus   *blue*
　　verts   *green*
　　noirs   *black*
les cheveux blonds   *blond hair*
　　bruns   *dark brown*
　　châtain   *brown*
　　courts   *short*
　　longs   *long*
　　noirs   *black*
　　roux   *red*
Je suis...   *I am . . .*
Il/Elle est...   *He/She is . . .*
Ils/Elles sont...   *They are . . .*

amusant(e)   *funny*
beau (belle)   *handsome (beautiful)*
brave   *brave*
de taille moyenne   *of medium height*
embêtant(e)   *annoying*
fort(e)   *strong*
gentil (gentille)   *nice*
gourmand(e)   *someone who loves to eat*
grand(e)   *tall, big*
intelligent(e)   *smart*
jeune   *young*
méchant(e)   *mean*
mignon (mignonne)   *cute*
petit(e)   *short, small*
pénible   *a pain*
sportif (sportive)   *athletic*
sympa   *nice*

Expressing likes, dislikes, and preferences

J'adore...   *I love . . .*
J'aime bien...   *I like . . .*
Je n'aime pas...   *I don't like . . .*
J'aime mieux...   *I prefer . . .*
Je préfère...   *I prefer . . .*

Asking for information

Qu'est-ce que tu aimes faire?   *What do you like to do?*
Qu'est-ce que tu fais comme sport?   *What sports do you play?*
Qu'est-ce que tu aimes comme musique?   *What music do you like?*
Quel(le) est ton/ta... préféré(e)?   *What is your favorite . . . ?*
Qui est ton/ta... préféré(e)?   *Who is your favorite . . . ?*

DEUXIEME ETAPE

Asking for and giving advice

Qu'est-ce que je dois... ?   *What should I . . . ?*
Pense à prendre...   *Remember to take . . .*
Prends...   *Take . . .*
N'oublie pas...   *Don't forget . . .*

Clothing and travel items

un imperméable   *a raincoat*
un jean   *a pair of jeans*
un tee-shirt   *a T-shirt*
des bottes (f.)   *a pair of boots*
des baskets (f.)   *a pair of sneakers*
un anorak   *a ski jacket*

un pull   *a sweater*
un sweat   *a sweatshirt*
une écharpe   *a scarf*
des gants (m.)   *a pair of gloves*
un appareil-photo   *a camera*
un passeport   *a passport*
un billet d'avion   *a plane ticket*
des chèques (m.) de voyage   *traveler's checks*

TROISIEME ETAPE

Asking for, making, and responding to suggestions

Qu'est-ce qu'on fait?   *What should we do?*
Si tu veux, on peut...   *If you like, we can . . .*
On pourrait...   *We could . . .*
Tu as envie de... ?   *Do you feel like . . . ?*
Ça te dit de... ?   *Does . . . sound good to you?*

D'accord.   *OK.*
C'est une bonne/excellente idée.   *That's a good/excellent idea.*
Je veux bien.   *I'd like to.*
Je ne peux pas.   *I can't.*
Ça ne me dit rien.   *That doesn't interest me.*
Non, je préfère...   *No, I'd rather . . .*
Pas question!   *No way!*

Relating a series of events

Qu'est-ce que tu vas faire... ?   *What are you going to do . . . ?*
D'abord, je vais...   *First, I'm going to . . .*
Ensuite,...   *Next, . . .*
Puis,...   *Then, . . .*
Enfin,...   *Finally, . . .*

To review vocabulary, have students select two photos of people from this chapter and write a description of them and what they're wearing.

CHAPTER 1 ASSESSMENT

CHAPTER TEST
- *Chapter Teaching Resources, Book 1*, pp. 29–34
- *Assessment Guide,* Speaking Test, p. 28
- *Assessment Items,* Audiocassette 7A Audio CD 1

TEST GENERATOR, CHAPTER 1

ALTERNATIVE ASSESSMENT
Performance Assessment
You might want to use the **Jeu de rôle** (p. 25) as a cumulative performance assessment activity.

Portfolio Assessment
- **Written: Mise en pratique,** Activity 2, *Pupil's Edition,* p. 25
  Assessment Guide, p. 14
- **Oral: Mise en pratique,** Activity 4, *Pupil's Edition,* p. 25
  Assessment Guide, p. 14

Game

J'EN DOUTE Form two teams. Students from one team call out a word from the vocabulary list, which a student from the opposing team must use in a sentence. The sentence must clearly illustrate the meaning of the word in order to receive a point. For example, **J'ai un imperméable** would not count. An acceptable answer might be **Je prends mon imperméable parce qu'il pleut.** If a student does not know the meaning of the word, he or she can try to bluff the other team by making up a sentence. The other team can call his or her bluff, however, by saying **J'en doute.** If they are right, and the player doesn't know the word, they receive two points. If they are wrong, and the player did know the word, they lose a point.

Chapitre 2 : Bienvenue à Chartres!
Chapter Overview

Mise en train pp. 30–32	**Une nouvelle vie**	*Practice and Activity Book, p. 13*	*Video Guide* OR *Videodisc Guide*

	FUNCTIONS	GRAMMAR	CULTURE	RE-ENTRY
Première étape pp. 33–35	• Welcoming someone; responding to someone's welcome, p. 33 • Asking how someone is feeling and telling how you are feeling, p. 34			• Use of **tu** vs. **vous** • Pronunciation: intonation
Deuxième étape pp. 36–41	• Pointing out where things are, p. 39 • Paying and responding to compliments, p. 40	Irregular adjectives, p. 39	• **Note Culturelle,** Teens' bedrooms in France, p. 38 • **Note Culturelle,** Paying and receiving compliments, p. 40 • **Panorama Culturel,** Houses in francophone countries, p. 41	Contractions with **de**
Troisième étape pp. 42–45	Asking for and giving directions, p. 45	Contractions with **à,** p. 44	**Note Culturelle,** Notre-Dame-de-Chartres, p. 44	• Asking for and giving directions • Making suggestions • Places in town

Lisons! pp. 46–47	**Passez une journée à Chartres**	**Reading Strategy:** Scanning

Review pp. 48–51	**Mise en pratique,** pp. 48–49	**Que sais-je?** p. 50	**Vocabulaire,** p. 51

Assessment Options

Etape Quizzes
• *Chapter Teaching Resources, Book 1*
  Première étape, Quiz 2-1, pp. 79–80
  Deuxième étape, Quiz 2-2, pp. 81–82
  Troisième étape, Quiz 2-3, pp. 83–84
• *Assessment Items, Audiocassette 7A/Audio CD 2*

Chapter Test
• *Chapter Teaching Resources, Book 1,* pp. 85–90
• *Assessment Guide,* Speaking Test, p. 28
• *Assessment Items, Audiocassette 7A/Audio CD 2*

Test Generator, Chapter 2

Video Program OR Expanded Video Program, Videocassette 1
OR Videodisc Program, Videodisc 1B

Textbook Audiocassette 1B/Audio CD 2

RESOURCES: Print	RESOURCES: Audiovisual

Textbook Audiocassette 1B/Audio CD 2

Practice and Activity Book, pp. 14–15
Chapter Teaching Resources, Book 1
• Teaching Transparency Master 2-1, pp. 63, 66. . . . . Teaching Transparency 2-1
• Additional Listening Activities 2-1, 2-2, p. 67 . . . . Additional Listening Activities, Audiocassette 9A/Audio CD 2
• Realia 2-1, pp. 71, 73
• Situation Cards 2-1, pp. 74–75
• Student Response Forms, pp. 76–78
• Quiz 2-1, pp. 79–80. . . . . Assessment Items, Audiocassette 7A/Audio CD 2
Videodisc Guide . . . . Videodisc Program, Videodisc 1B

Textbook Audiocassette 1B/Audio CD 2

Practice and Activity Book, pp. 16–19
Chapter Teaching Resources, Book 1
• Communicative Activity 2-1, pp. 59–60
• Teaching Transparency Master 2-2, pp. 64, 66. . . . . Teaching Transparency 2-2
• Additional Listening Activities 2-3, 2-4, p. 68 . . . . Additional Listening Activities, Audiocassette 9A/Audio CD 2
• Realia 2-2, pp. 72, 73
• Situation Cards 2-2, pp. 74–75
• Student Response Forms, pp. 76–78
• Quiz 2-2, pp. 81–82. . . . . Assessment Items, Audiocassette 7A/Audio CD 2
Video Guide. . . . . Video Program OR Expanded Video Program, Videocassette 1
Videodisc Guide. . . . . Videodisc Program, Videodisc 1B

Textbook Audiocassette 1B/Audio CD 2

Practice and Activity Book, pp. 20–22
Chapter Teaching Resources, Book 1
• Communicative Activity 2-2, pp. 61–62
• Teaching Transparency Master 2-3, pp. 65, 66. . . . . Teaching Transparency 2-3
• Additional Listening Activities 2-5, 2-6, p. 69 . . . . Additional Listening Activities, Audiocassette 9A/Audio CD 2
• Realia 2-2, pp. 72, 73
• Situation Cards 2-3, pp. 74–75
• Student Response Forms, pp. 76–78
• Quiz 2-3, pp. 83–84. . . . . Assessment Items, Audiocassette 7A/Audio CD 2
Videodisc Guide. . . . . Videodisc Program, Videodisc 1B

Practice and Activity Book, p. 23

Video Guide. . . . . Video Program OR Expanded Video Program, Videocassette 1
Videodisc Guide. . . . . Videodisc Program, Videodisc 1B

Alternative Assessment
• Performance Assessment   • Portfolio Assessment
  Première étape, p. 35   Written: **Mise en pratique,** Activity 2, Pupil's Edition, p. 48
  Deuxième étape, p. 40   Assessment Guide, p. 15
  Troisième étape, p. 45   Oral: Activity 33, Pupil's Edition, p. 45
                  Assessment Guide, p. 15

Chapitre 2 : Bienvenue à Chartres!
Textbook Listening Activities Scripts

For Student Response Forms, see *Chapter Teaching Resources, Book 1,* pp. 76–78

Première étape

7 Ecoute! p. 34

1. — Bienvenue chez moi, Maryse!
— Merci.
— Fais comme chez toi.
— C'est gentil de ta part.
— Tu as fait bon voyage?
— C'était fatigant!

2. — Bienvenue à la maison, monsieur!
— Merci.
— Faites comme chez vous.
— C'est gentil.
— Vous avez fait bon voyage?
— Oh, ça a été, mais je suis très fatigué!

3. — Bienvenue chez nous, Tante Monique!
— Merci.
— Tu as fait bon voyage?
— Excellent!

Answers to Activity 7
1. tiring   2. tiring   3. good

10 Ecoute! p. 35

1. — Bienvenue, Stéphanie. Tu as fait bon voyage?
— Oui, excellent.
— Alors, entre... Fais comme chez toi.
— C'est gentil de ta part.
— Dis, tu n'as pas faim?
— Si, un peu.
— Alors, on passe à table?

2. — Bonjour, madame. Bienvenue à Chartres!
— Oh, merci. Tu es gentil.
— Vous avez fait bon voyage?
— Oui, mais c'était fatigant.
— Alors, entrez. Vous n'avez pas soif?
— Si, un peu.
— Tenez, voilà un verre d'eau.

3. — Salut, Ginette. Tu as fait bon voyage?
— Oui, excellent.
— Alors, entre... fais comme chez toi. Il est déjà midi. Tu n'as pas faim?
— Non, ça va.

Answers to Activity 10
1. b   2. c   3. a

Deuxième étape

15 Ecoute! p. 38

1. Mettez-le dans le salon, s'il vous plaît.
2. Ça, ça va dans la salle à manger.
3. Mettez tout ça dans le jardin.
4. Mettez-le dans la cuisine, s'il vous plaît.
5. Oh, il va dans la chambre d'Antoine.

Answers to Activity 15
1. d   2. a   3. e   4. b   5. c

18 Ecoute! p. 39

1. Le salon est au premier étage.
2. Les toilettes sont à côté de la salle de bains.
3. Les Morel ont un jardin et un balcon.
4. La salle à manger est au rez-de-chaussée, près de la cuisine.
5. La chambre des parents a un balcon.
6. Dans la chambre d'Antoine, il y a deux lits et un joli tapis rouge.

Answers to Activity 18
1. false   3. true   5. true
2. false   4. true   6. false

22 Ecoute! p. 40

1. SOLANGE   Bon, ici, c'est le salon.
   ARNAUD   Oh, j'adore le tapis.
   SOLANGE   Vraiment?

2. SOLANGE   Ensuite, il y a le bureau de maman. Elle aime y travailler le soir.
   ARNAUD   Dis donc, elle a un super ordinateur, ta mère.
   SOLANGE   Tu trouves?

3. SOLANGE   Et enfin, voilà ma chambre. Entre.
   ARNAUD   Merci. Tiens, j'aime beaucoup ce poster.
   SOLANGE   C'est vrai?
   ARNAUD   Oui, et tu sais, Céline Dion est ma chanteuse préférée.

4. ARNAUD   Elle est chouette, ta chambre.
   SOLANGE   C'est gentil!

Answers to Activity 22
1. a rug   3. a poster
2. a computer   4. a bedroom

*T*roisième étape

26 Ecoute! p. 43

PATRICK   Qu'est-ce qu'on va faire aujourd'hui?

CHANTAL   On va visiter la cathédrale, bien sûr! Les vitraux sont magnifiques!

PATRICK   D'accord... mais j'ai besoin d'aller à la poste. J'ai des cartes postales à envoyer.

CHANTAL   D'accord, on va d'abord à la poste, puis à la cathédrale.

PATRICK   Tu as envie d'aller au Musée des Beaux-Arts?

CHANTAL   Oui, pourquoi pas?

PATRICK   D'accord, alors on va au musée après la cathédrale. Et ensuite?

CHANTAL   Tu sais, c'est déjà beaucoup!

PATRICK   Si on allait se reposer au parc? On pourrait faire un pique-nique.

CHANTAL   Non, je n'ai pas très envie d'aller au parc. Si on allait à la piscine?

PATRICK   A la piscine? C'est une bonne idée.

CHANTAL   Alors c'est décidé. On y va!

Answers to Activity 26

— la poste, la cathédrale, le Musée des Beaux-Arts, la piscine

— e, b, a; f

29 Ecoute! p. 45

1. Bon, prenez le boulevard Chasles à droite. Traversez la Place Pasteur. C'est sur la droite, juste avant la rue des Bas-Bourgs.

2. Oh, ça, c'est facile. C'est tout près d'ici. Prenez la rue M. Violette. Vous ne pouvez pas la manquer, c'est le grand bâtiment sur la gauche.

3. Attendez... prenez le boulevard de la Résistance. Tournez à droite dans la rue Charles-de-Gaulle. Ne la ratez pas, c'est une toute petite rue. Vous verrez, c'est sur la droite, après la rue Famin.

Answers to Activity 29

1. à la piscine
2. à la poste
3. à l'église Saint-Foy

*M*ise en pratique

4 p. 49

Ah, le musée? C'est simple. Voyons... Vous êtes sur la place Saint-Michel. Prenez le boulevard Saint-Michel jusqu'au boulevard Saint-Germain. Tournez à droite. Allez tout droit. Prenez à droite, rue du Bac. Allez tout droit jusqu'au quai Voltaire. Le musée est là, à gauche.

Answers to Mise en pratique Activity 4

le Musée d'Orsay

Chapitre 2 : Bienvenue à Chartres!
Projects

Ma ville
(Group Project)

ASSIGNMENT

Students will create a map of a town on the classroom floor with masking tape. Afterwards, they will conduct a tour of their town, using the map to give and follow directions. This may be done as a joint project by all class sections of the same level throughout the day.

MATERIALS
✄ **Teacher and students may need**
• Masking tape
• Overhead projector
• Transparency of any town map

SUGGESTED SEQUENCE

1. On the transparency of the map, overlay a nine-square grid. Then, make a similar grid on the floor with masking tape. The floor map will have to be large enough so that students can walk comfortably on the streets.

2. Project the map on the overhead and assign two or three students to each section of the grid. They must then reproduce their section of the map on the corresponding section on the floor with masking tape, making sure that their section joins the others correctly. If the class is large, you may wish to have some students plan where to put the buildings. NOTE: The streets are delineated by masking tape on both sides. To label the streets, have students write the names of the streets on sheets of construction paper and tape them to the middle of the streets.

3. When the streets have been laid out and labeled, add the buildings. The map should have ten to twelve buildings, a park, and a swimming pool. The buildings do not have to be placed as they are on the transparency. Let students plan the town. To label the buildings, have students write the French names of the buildings on construction paper and tape them to the map.

4. When the map is completed, carefully remove the grid of masking tape without disturbing the streets and buildings.

5. The students responsible for each section will now conduct a tour of their section. They should point out the streets and buildings and tell where each building is in relation to another building. (**A côté de la bibliothèque, il y a le musée.**)

6. Next, form two groups: residents and tourists. Have one student from each group come to the map. The resident gives the directions, and the tourist follows them. The resident should indicate a starting point for the tourist and choose a secret destination. Have the resident whisper the secret destination to you or write it on a slip of paper. He or she then directs the tourist to the destination. The directions may be direct or circuitous. If the tourist does not arrive at the intended destination, the resident should continue giving directions until the destination is reached. Continue this activity with other pairs of students until everyone has had a chance to participate.

GRADING THE PROJECT

Give an oral grade to the resident based on accuracy and comprehensibility, and an aural grade to the tourist based on comprehension. Both participants should be graded on overall participation and effort in the creation of the town. If you wish to give a written grade for the project, you might assign students to write a letter to a friend describing their town. It should include the names and locations of at least six buildings or sites and should be graded on the inclusion of the required elements, accuracy, and variety of vocabulary.

Suggested Point Distribution (total = 100 points)

Oral

The resident:

Language use......................25 points
Comprehensibility ....25 points
Participation/effort ....50 points

The tourist:

Comprehension ....50 points
Participation/effort ....50 points

Written

Required elements.................25 points
Language use......................50 points
Variety of vocabulary ....25 points

🨖 *Games*

JEU D'OBSTACLE

In this game, students will practice giving directions.

Procedure To prepare for the game, create an obstacle course in the classroom by rearranging chairs, desks, and tables. Choose a finish line and two starting points equidistant from it. Form two teams. Choose one player from each team, blindfold them, and station them at their respective starting points. Have a member from the oppos-

ing team spin each blindfolded player around four or five times, then quickly call out **Allez!** The teammates of each blindfolded player must call out directions in French to get him or her safely to the finish line without hitting any of the obstacles. If the player hits an obstacle, he or she must stand in place for five seconds. The team whose player is first to reach the finish line wins. Repeat the process several times so that other team members may play.

MEMOIRE

In this game, students will practice the vocabulary for rooms of a house or places in a town.

Materials

✂ **Teacher may need**
• 30 to 40 index cards
• 40 library circulation-card pockets
• 2 sheets of posterboard
• Cardboard or foam board
• Glue

This game is similar to Concentration®. To make the game board:

1. Glue twenty card pockets in five rows of four to each of the two posterboards.

2. Number the pockets on each posterboard from 1-20.

3. If possible, laminate each board for durability and cut open the pockets.

4. Make a hinge by folding the cardboard or foam board in half. Fasten one posterboard to each half so that the boards stand side by side. The Concentration board should now be freestanding and ready to be used repeatedly.

Procedure Choose 20 vocabulary words for rooms of a house (**le salon**) or places in a town (**la gare**). For each room or place, write a short sentence telling what one does there. (**On regarde la télé. On prend le train.**) Write the words and their corresponding sentences on separate index cards. Hold the card vertically and write the word near the bottom of the card. Make sure there is only one word that corresponds to each sentence. Put the word cards in random order in the pockets of one side of the Concentration board, and the sentence cards in the pockets on the other side. (If you do not have a Concentration board, number

the backs of the cards and tape them to the blackboard.) Form three or four teams. The teams take turns matching words and sentences from the two sides of the board. For example, a team member might call out **à gauche, treize et à droite, deux**. Pull out the two cards to see if they correspond to each other. If a match is made, the student must make a new sentence combining the two elements to receive credit for the match. (**Je vais à la gare pour prendre le train.**) If the sentence is correct, take the two cards out and mark a point for that team.

Students on each team take turns guessing. If a team scores a point, they get another turn, but a team may not take more than three turns in a row. If no match is made, the next team takes a turn. When all the matches are found, the team with the most points wins.

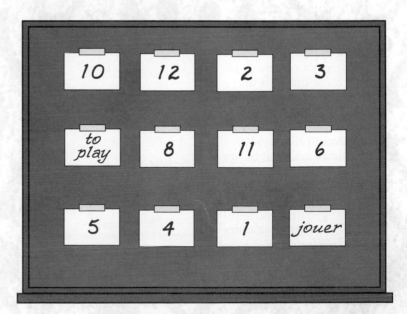

CHAPITRE

2
Bienvenue à Chartres!

① Bienvenue chez nous!

28 *vingt-huit*

Chapitre 2 Bienvenue à Chartres!

pp. 28–51

*U*sing the Chapter Opener

Motivating Activity

If any of your students have participated in a foreign exchange program, have them describe some of the differences they found in family life or in the home where they stayed. If students have ever hosted an exchange student, have them tell what the visitor found different. If no one has had one of these experiences, share one of your own or ask students to imagine the adjustments they would have to make in these situations.

Photo Flash!

① This photo shows a living room (**le salon, la salle de séjour**) in a French home. Many French homes are furnished with beautiful antiques rich with history. Some common styles of furniture are Louis XIV (**Louis quatorze**) from the seventeenth century; Louis XVI (**Louis seize**) from the eighteenth century; **le style empire** and **le style second empire,** dating from the reigns of Napoléon I and III in the nineteenth century; and Louis Philippe from the nineteenth century. Many country homes have furniture in **le style rustique** (fashioned in a traditional, provincial style, which is simple, heavy, and unrefined).

Culture Notes

• France has had a serious shortage of housing since 1945. The problem is due in part to the antiquity of existing structures, and also to the destruction of property by two world wars. From 1945 to 1974, France constructed more than 7 million new housing units, but gained more than 12 million new residents. As of 1990, there were esti-mated to be 26 million living accommodations in France.

• In 1962, only 41% of homes had indoor toilets (**des W.–C.**), as compared to 94% in 1990. Only 29% had a shower or bathtub (**une douche, une baignoire**) in 1962, as compared to 94% in 1990, and only 11% had telephones. Even in 1990, only 76% of homes had a phone.

Living with a new family in a foreign country . . . what a change! What do you think you might see in a French home that would be different from your home? How would a French town differ from your town? The contrasts and the similarities might surprise you!

In this chapter you will review and practice

- welcoming someone; responding to someone's welcome; asking how someone is feeling and telling how you are feeling
- pointing out where things are; paying and responding to compliments
- asking for and giving directions

And you will

- listen to people give directions
- read about what you can do in Chartres
- write a description of your room and how to get to your home
- find out about types of homes in the francophone world

② Où est la cathédrale?

③ Il est génial, ce poster.

🌐 Culture Notes

- Call attention to the street sign in Photo 2. Signs that indicate the names of the streets in France are generally blue with a green border, and the letters are white. They are usually posted on the sides of buildings, rather than on poles, as they commonly are in the United States.

- France Gall (pictured in the poster on the wall in Photo 3) has been a popular singer in France for 25 years. She was well-known for her children's songs and later became a pop singer.

Focusing on Outcomes

Have students match each of the photos with the outcomes listed. Ask them to recall expressions they've already learned to accomplish these functions. NOTE: You may want to use the video to support the objectives. The self-check activities in **Que sais-je?** on page 50 help students assess their achievement of the objectives.

Photo Flash!

② Sandra and Pamela are going to visit the Notre-Dame cathedral in Chartres. Originally a Romanesque cathedral, Notre-Dame is known today as one of the greatest High Gothic cathedrals and the first to use flying buttresses. The cathedral's stained-glass windows are outstanding, in particular the twelfth-century **Vierge de la belle verrière** *(Our Lady of the Beautiful Window).*

Teaching Suggestion

Encourage students to say as much as they can in French about the photos. Descriptions may be as simple as **deux filles.** If necessary, prompt students with the following questions: **Il y a combien de tables sur la première photo? C'est un salon français ou américain sur la première photo? Sur la deuxième photo, combien de filles voyez-vous? Où sont-elles? En ville ou à la maison? Elles sont en France ou aux Etats-Unis? Que porte la fille sur la gauche? Que font les deux filles sur la troisième photo? De quelle couleur est le pull? Et le tee-shirt?**

VIDEO PROGRAM
OR EXPANDED VIDEO
PROGRAM,
Videocassette 1
19:21–23:04

OR **VIDEODISC PROGRAM,**
Videodisc 1B

Search 1, Play To 6665

Video Synopsis

The Lepic family arrives in Chartres with Pamela and welcomes her to their home. Sandra gives Pamela a tour of the house, showing her the living room, dining room, kitchen, bathroom, toilet, and bedrooms. Sandra assumes that Pamela is exhausted and wants to rest, but Pamela says she wants to go visit the cathedral. Sandra leaves Pamela to unpack. Later, when Sandra goes to get her, she discovers Pamela asleep on the bed.

Motivating Activity

Ask students to imagine themselves arriving at a host family's home in a foreign country. What are some of the things they would need to be able to say or ask in the first 30 minutes? On the first day? On later occasions?

Presentation

Before showing the video, ask students to look at the photos and identify the characters. Ask them what they remember about the characters from Chapter 1 and what they can tell you about this story based on the photos. Then, have students view the video. Ask the questions in **Tu as compris?** on page 32. Then, you might have small groups act out scenes from **Une nouvelle vie.**

Mise en train

Une nouvelle vie

Look at the photos. How is this house different from those where you live?

Sandra   Pamela   M. Lepic

Mme Lepic

30 *trente*   CHAPITRE 2   Bienvenue à Chartres!

RESOURCES FOR MISE EN TRAIN

Textbook Audiocassette 1B/Audio CD 2
Practice and Activity Book, p. 13
Video Guide
    Video Program
    Expanded Video Program, Videocassette 1
Videodisc Guide
    Videodisc Program, Videodisc 1B

For Individual Needs

Slower Pace   On the board or on a transparency, list in random order the rooms of the house that are introduced in the **Mise en train** and number them. Then, have students view the video and number the rooms as Sandra shows them to Pamela during the tour of the house.

Visual/Tactile Learners On a transparency, draw the photos of the **Mise en train** using stick figures. Do not include the speech bubbles. Draw and fill in the speech bubbles on small pieces of transparency and place them at random above the drawings on the overhead projector. Have individual students come up one at a time to place a speech bubble in the proper place.

Auditory Learners   Draw the photos of the **Mise en train** using stick figures without the speech bubbles and give a copy to each student. Then, in random order, call out the utterances, each preceded by a number. Have students write the number of the sentence above the appropriate character.

Language Note

The top floor of many French homes is often directly under the pointed, steep roof. Therefore, rooms on the top floor with slanted interior walls (see Photo 7) are quite common. They are called **des chambres mansardes**.

MISE EN TRAIN

trente et un **31**

📺 **Video Integration**

- **Expanded Video Program,** Videocassette 1, 23:05–29:48
- **Videodisc Program,** Videodisc 1B

Search 6665, Play To 18765

You may choose to continue with **Une nouvelle vie (suite)** at this time or wait until later in the chapter. When the story continues, Sandra and Pamela are in Chartres. Pamela changes money, buys a tourist guide, and she and Sandra visit the cathedral. Then, they walk around the old section of town (**le Vieux Chartres**). Sandra keeps expecting Pamela to get tired, but she is full of energy!

Additional Practice

2 To extend this activity, have students work in pairs. One student repeats a sentence from the **Mise en train,** and the other, without looking in the book, tells who is speaking. They should take turns.

Building on Previous Skills

3 Ask students to recall as many expressions as possible for asking how someone is feeling and responding. (**Ça va? Comment ça va? Ça va bien. Très bien. Pas mal.**) Ask them if they remember how to express a desire for something (**Je voudrais...**).

For Individual Needs

4 Auditory Learners For listening comprehension, randomly call out the rooms of the house represented in these illustrations and have students write down the letters of the appropriate pictures.

4 Tactile/Visual Learners Have students pair off and take turns pointing out the rooms. (**Ça, c'est la salle à manger.**) Have them touch the photo as they and their partners say the names of the rooms.

For videodisc application, see *Videodisc Guide.*

Culture Note Point out the difference between **les toilettes** and **la salle de bains. La salle de bains** is used only for washing and bathing. For this reason, one never refers to a public restroom as **la salle de bains.** It is called **les toilettes** or **les W.-C.**

1 Tu as compris? See answers below.

1. Which rooms of the Lepic house does Pamela see?
2. What would Pamela like to do?
3. Why don't the girls visit the cathedral?

2 Qui...

1. trouve la maison sympa?   Pamela
2. montre la maison à Pamela?   Sandra
3. aimerait bien visiter la cathédrale?   Pamela
4. explique comment aller à la cathédrale?   Sandra

3 Cherche les expressions   See answers below.

1. How does . . .

  a. Sandra welcome Pamela?
  b. Mrs. Lepic respond to a compliment?
  c. Sandra ask how Pamela's feeling?
  d. Sandra tell her to make herself at home?

2. How does Pamela . . .

  a. pay compliments?
  b. say how she's feeling?
  c. express a desire to do something?

4 C'est quelle pièce?

Qu'est-ce que Sandra dit pour montrer chaque pièce?

1. Ce sont nos toilettes.   **2.** Notre salle de bains est à côté.   **3.** Et voilà ta chambre.

4. Ça, c'est la salle à manger.   **5.** Et voilà la cuisine.

5 Et maintenant, à toi

If you had just arrived in a town in France, what would you want to do?

32 *trente-deux*   CHAPITRE 2   Bienvenue à Chartres!

Answers

1 1. entrance hallway, living room, dining room, kitchen, toilets, bathroom, Pamela's bedroom
2. visit the cathedral
3. Pamela falls asleep.

3 1. a. Bienvenue chez nous.
  b. Tu trouves?
  c. Pas trop fatiguée?
  d. Fais comme chez toi.
2. a. C'est sympa ici.
  b. Non, ça va.
  c. J'ai envie de visiter la cathédrale.

PREMIERE ETAPE

Welcoming someone; responding to someone's welcome; asking how someone is feeling and telling how you are feeling

6 Qu'en penses-tu?

How does the guest in the cartoon act? How should he act?

Possible answers: He acts as if he is at his own home; with more respect and consideration

COMMENT DIT-ON... ?

Welcoming someone; responding to someone's welcome

To welcome someone:

Bienvenue chez moi (chez nous).
Welcome to my home (our home).
Faites comme chez vous.
Fais comme chez toi.
Make yourself at home.
Vous avez fait bon voyage?
Tu as fait bon voyage?
Did you have a good trip?

To respond:

Merci.
Thank you.
C'est gentil de votre part.
C'est gentil de ta part.
That's nice of you.
Oui, excellent. *Yes, excellent.*
C'était fatigant! *It was tiring!*

PREMIERE ETAPE

trente-trois **33**

RESOURCES FOR PREMIERE ETAPE

Textbook Audiocassette 1B/Audio CD 2
Practice and Activity Book, pp. 14–15
Videodisc Guide
  Videodisc Program, Videodisc 1B

Chapter Teaching Resources, Book 1
• Teaching Transparency Master 2-1, pp. 63, 66
  Teaching Transparency 2-1
• Additional Listening Activities 2-1, 2-2, p. 67
  Audiocassette 9A/Audio CD 2
• Realia 2-1, pp. 71, 73
• Situation Cards 2-1, pp. 74–75
• Student Response Forms, pp. 76–78
• Quiz 2-1, pp. 79–80
  Audiocassette 7A/Audio CD 2

Jump Start!

Have students complete the following sentence fragments with the appropriate room of the house:

1. **On prépare le dîner dans...**
2. **On prend un bain dans...**
3. **On mange dans...**
4. **On dort dans...**
5. **On regarde la télé dans...**
6. **Après la porte principale, on est dans...**

(Answers: 1. **la cuisine** 2. **la salle de bains** 3. **la salle à manger** 4. **la chambre** 5. **le salon** 6. **l'entrée)**

MOTIVATE

Have students improvise in English the arrival of an exchange student at the home of a host family. Point out that knowing what to say is important in order to make a good impression and to avoid awkward silences after the first **Bonjour.**

TEACH

Presentation

Comment dit-on... ? Write the new expressions on individual strips of transparency. Arrange some of the pieces on the projector to create a formal conversation and present each sentence. For example, draw a house on the board and point to it as you say **Bienvenue chez nous!** and gesture as if welcoming someone. Then, have two students create another informal conversation with the remaining expressions, using yours as an example. Afterwards, have students act out the conversations for the class.

For videodisc application, see *Videodisc Guide.*

Teaching Suggestion

8 Students might work in pairs, taking turns being the host and the guest. You might also have individuals write out dialogues for each photo.

Presentation

Comment dit-on... ? Write the words **fatigué, faim, soif, un peu, crevé,** and **meurs** on the board. Act out their meanings, saying **Je suis fatigué(e), J'ai faim,** and so on. Then, have students repeat the expressions, acting them out with you. Have individuals come to the front of the class to mime the various expressions for their classmates to guess. Have students tell you what is being mimed. (**Elle a soif. Il meurt de faim.**)

TPR Tell students that they feel a certain way (**Vous avez faim!**) and have them act out your instructions to demonstrate their comprehension.

Language Notes

• You may want to point out that the French often use the negative form of a verb to be more polite. For example, they might say **Tu n'as pas un stylo?** just as we might similarly say in English *You wouldn't have a pen (I could borrow), would you?*

• Remind students that **si** is used to answer *yes* to a negative question. (**Tu n'as pas un stylo? Si, j'ai un stylo.**)

For Individual Needs

9 Tactile/Visual Learners Have students write the questions, comments, and responses on separate strips of paper. Then, have them arrange the strips to make a conversation.

---

7 Ecoute!

Listen to the following dialogues in which people are being welcomed. Did they have a good trip or a tiring trip?
Answers on p. 27C.

8 Bienvenue!

How would you welcome the following people to your home and ask about their trip? What would they answer? See answers below.

Mme Ducharme

Sandra

Thierry

M. Belleau

Tu te rappelles?
Do you remember when to use **tu** and when to use **vous**? Use **tu** when you talk to people your age or younger, but when you talk to people older than you, use **vous**. After a while, they might suggest using the **tu** form: *Alors, on se tutoie?* Don't let worries about using **tu** or **vous** keep you from speaking. Follow the lead of the people you're with.

COMMENT DIT-ON... ?
Asking how someone is feeling and telling how you are feeling

To ask how someone is feeling:
Pas trop fatigué(e)?
(You're) not too tired?
Vous n'avez pas faim?
Tu n'as pas faim?
Aren't you hungry?
Vous n'avez pas soif?
Tu n'as pas soif?
Aren't you thirsty?

To tell how you are feeling:
Non, ça va. *No, I'm fine.*
Si, je suis crevé(e).
Yes, I'm exhausted.
Si, un peu. *Yes, a little.*
Si, j'ai très faim/soif!
Yes, I'm very hungry/thirsty!
Si, je meurs de faim/soif!
Yes, I'm dying of hunger/thirst!

9 Les deux font la paire

Match the question or comment with the appropriate response. Then, arrange the exchanges to make a conversation.

1. Tu as fait bon voyage? f
2. Tu n'as pas soif? b
3. Fais comme chez toi. d
4. Bienvenue! c
5. Pas trop fatiguée? a
6. Tu n'as pas faim? e

a. Non, ça va.
b. Si, j'ai très soif.
c. Merci.
d. C'est gentil de ta part.
e. Si, je meurs de faim!
f. Oui, excellent.

Possible answer
—Bienvenue! —Merci.
—Tu as fait bon voyage? —Oui, excellent.
—Fais comme chez toi. —C'est gentil de ta part.
—Pas trop fatiguée? —Non, ça va.
—Tu n'as pas soif? —Si, j'ai très soif.
—Tu n'as pas faim? —Si, je meurs de faim.

Tu te rappelles?
Do you remember the *intonation,* or the way your voice rises and falls, for yes-or-no questions? Your voice falls at the end of statements and most questions, but when you ask a question like **Tu as fait bon voyage?** or **Tu n'as pas faim?**, you raise your voice at the end.

34 *trente-quatre*   CHAPITRE 2   Bienvenue à Chartres!

Multicultural Link

Tu te rappelles? Have students interview foreign exchange students, students of a different culture, relatives, or acquaintances to find out if there are both formal and familiar ways of saying *you* in their language. If so, have them find out if and when one may use the familiar form with certain people.

Possible answers

8 Mme Ducharme: Faites comme chez vous. Vous avez fait bon voyage?; Oui, excellent.
Sandra: Fais comme chez toi. Tu as fait bon voyage?; C'était fatigant.
Thierry: Bienvenue chez moi. Tu as fait bon voyage?; Oui, excellent.
M. Belleau: Faites comme chez vous. Vous avez fait bon voyage?; Non, c'était fatigant.

10 Écoute!

Il y a beaucoup de visiteurs chez Robert. Écoute les conversations et choisis la scène qui représente chaque conversation. 1. b 2. c 3. a

a.

b.

c.

11 Ça ne va pas très bien!

How would you ask these people how they're feeling? How would they answer?
See answers below.

Caroline

Roberto

Mme Prévost

12 Jeu de rôle

An exchange student from Morocco arrives at your home. Welcome the student, ask about the trip, and find out how he or she is feeling. The student should respond appropriately. Continue the conversation. Act out the scene with a partner. Then, change roles.

13 Une bande dessinée

Using magazine cutouts or your own drawings, create a cartoon about a visitor who is very difficult to please. Write what is being said in speech bubbles or in captions below the pictures.

À la française

There are many colorful expressions you can use to sound like a native speaker of French. When you're talking with friends, try saying **J'ai une faim de loup!** *(I'm as hungry as a wolf!)* when you're very hungry and **Je boirais la mer!** *(I could drink the sea!)* when you're very thirsty.

PREMIERE ETAPE

trente-cinq 35

ASSESS

Quiz 2-1, *Chapter Teaching Resources, Book 1,* pp. 79–80

Assessment Items, Audiocassette 7A Audio CD 2

Performance Assessment

Have students form two lines: a "guest" and a "host" line. The first students of each line approach each other. The "host" welcomes the "guest," asks how he or she is feeling, and the "guest" responds appropriately. Then, each student goes to the end of the opposite line, and the next two in line conduct the same dialogue, varying the expressions. Continue until everyone has played both roles.

PREMIERE ETAPE
CHAPITRE 2

Building on Previous Skills

10 Before students begin the listening activity, review the rooms in a house by asking **Où sont-ils?** for each illustration.

Teaching Suggestions

11 Working in small groups, have students take turns asking and telling each other how they feel.

13 Students might assume the roles of the cartoon characters and present the cartoon to the class as a skit.

CLOSE

To close this **étape,** prepare three sets of index cards. For the first and second sets, write on separate cards **un jeune garçon, un homme, une femme, une jeune fille,** and **un couple.** For the third set, write on separate cards *very tired, starving, energetic, but hungry, very excited,* and *happy, but a little tired.* Title the three sets of cards *Host, Guest(s),* and *Condition of the Guest(s).* Have pairs of students draw a card from each stack, copy the information, and write a conversation to correspond to the situation represented on the three cards. For example, if students draw **une jeune fille, un jeune garçon,** and *happy but a little tired,* they should write a conversation about a teen girl welcoming a teen boy who is happy, but a little tired. You might have students perform the conversations for the class.

Possible answers

11 Caroline: Pas trop fatiguée? Tu n'as pas soif?; Si, je suis crevée, et j'ai très soif.
Roberto: Tu n'as pas faim?; Si, je meurs de faim.
Mme Prévost: Vous êtes fatiguée? Vous n'avez pas faim?; Si, je suis très fatiguée, et j'ai un peu faim.

DEUXIEME ETAPE

Pointing out where things are; paying and responding to compliments

*J*ump Start!

Write the following questions and responses on the board or on a transparency and have students rearrange them to make a conversation.
Si, un peu./C'était fatigant./ Vous avez fait bon voyage?/ Vous n'avez pas faim?/ Bienvenue chez nous./Faites comme chez vous./C'est gentil de votre part./Merci.

MOTIVATE

Ask students what might make them uncomfortable if they were staying in someone else's home (not knowing where things are or finding some things different). Then, ask them what they would do to make a guest feel at home.

TEACH

◆ For Individual Needs

Challenge Read Pamela's journal entry aloud as students listen with their books closed. Have them jot down either in English or in French what they were able to understand. Then, on the board or on a transparency, compile a list of everything students wrote down. Finally, distribute copies of the letter you've typed and have students underline in the journal entry the facts listed on the board.

Language Note

You may wish to point out the expression **une drôle de forme**. Using this expression, ask students to point out other things pictured in the chapter that look *funny* or different to them.

---

le 2 septembre

Cher journal,
Quelle journée! C'est aujourd'hui mon premier jour en France. La famille Lepic est super gentille.
Sandra m'a fait voir la maison. Elle est jolie, mais un peu bizarre. Ce n'est pas comme aux Etats-Unis. D'abord, quand on entre dans la maison, on n'est pas au premier étage, on est au rez-de-chaussée. Quand on monte l'escalier, on n'est pas au deuxième étage, on est au premier étage.

En plus, la salle de bains, c'est juste pour se laver. Les toilettes sont à part, de l'autre côté du couloir.
J'ai remarqué que les portes des chambres sont toujours fermées et qu'il faut frapper avant d'entrer. Dans ma chambre, mon lit est très confortable mais un des oreillers a une drôle de forme. Il est aussi large que mon lit. Ils appellent ça un traversin. Il n'y a pas de placard, mais une armoire pour les vêtements.

En tout cas, j'aime beaucoup la vie ici. C'est différent, mais c'est bien.

14 Ce n'est pas comme aux Etats-Unis!

Pamela a pris des photos pour illustrer son journal. Quelle photo correspond à ce qu'elle a écrit?

1. c'est juste pour se laver. b
2. Quand on monte l'escalier, on n'est pas au deuxième étage, on est au premier étage. c
3. mon lit est très confortable a
4. Il n'y a pas de placard, mais une armoire pour les vêtements. d

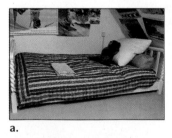
a.

b.

c.

d.

RESOURCES FOR **DEUXIEME ETAPE**

Textbook Audiocassette 1B/Audio CD 2
Practice and Activity Book, pp. 16–19
Video Guide
  Video Program
  Expanded Video Program, Videocassette 1
Videodisc Guide
  Videodisc Program, Videodisc 1B

Chapter Teaching Resources, Book 1
• Communicative Activity 2-1, pp. 59–60
• Teaching Transparency Master 2-2, pp. 64, 66
  Teaching Transparency 2-2
• Additional Listening Activities 2-3, 2-4, p. 68
  Audiocassette 9A/Audio CD 2
• Realia 2-2, pp. 72, 73
• Situation Cards 2-2, pp. 74–75
• Student Response Forms, pp. 76–78
• Quiz 2-2, pp. 81–82
  Audiocassette 7A/Audio CD 2

VOCABULAIRE

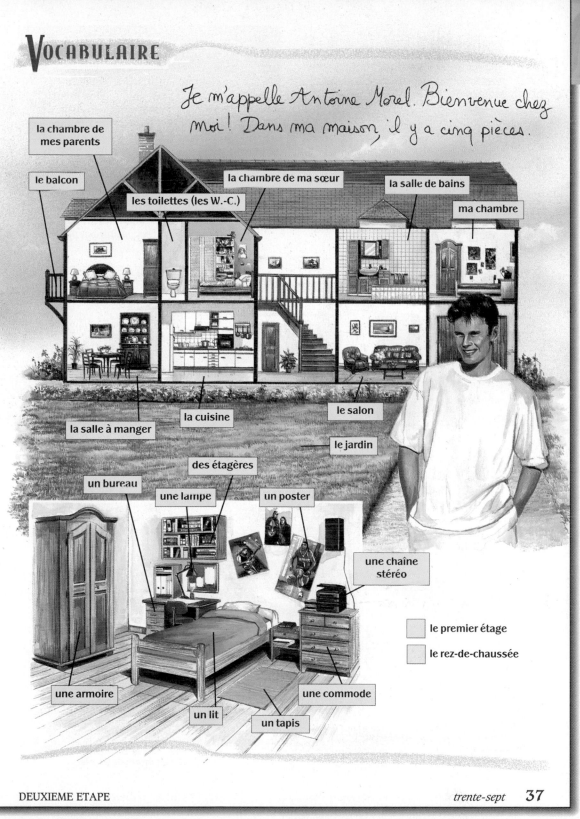

Je m'appelle Antoine Morel. Bienvenue chez moi! Dans ma maison, il y a cinq pièces.

la chambre de mes parents

le balcon

les toilettes (les W.-C.)

la chambre de ma sœur

la salle de bains

ma chambre

la salle à manger

la cuisine

le salon

le jardin

des étagères

un bureau

une lampe

un poster

une chaîne stéréo

une armoire

un lit

un tapis

une commode

le premier étage

le rez-de-chaussée

Presentation

Vocabulaire Show *Teaching Transparency 2-2* to teach the new words, having students repeat after you. Then, point to the items and ask either-or questions, such as **C'est le salon ou la cuisine?** Ask as many questions as possible until students are able to identify all of the vocabulary items. Then, ask for volunteers to come up to the projector and point out items suggested by their classmates.

For videodisc application, see *Videodisc Guide.*

Additional Practice

Vocabulaire Make a drawing similar to the one in the **Vocabulaire** on a transparency, but alter it by omitting certain items, adding others, or moving some around. Have students compare your drawing to the one in the book. (**Dans le livre, il y a un lit dans la chambre, mais sur le transparent, il y a deux lits. Dans le livre, les toilettes sont loin de la salle de bains, mais sur le transparent, les toilettes sont à côté de la salle de bains.**)

Building on Previous Skills

To review ordinal numbers, draw a picture of a tall apartment building on the board and have students name the floors: **le rez-de-chaussée, le premier étage, le deuxième étage,** and so on.

History Link

The word **armoire** was first used in the sixteenth century, and sometimes denoted a cupboard set into the paneling of a room. These cupboards later evolved into free-standing wardrobes, which were originally used to store arms. The cabinetmaker of Louis XIV, André-Charles Boulle, designed **armoires** that became examples of some of the most ornate, imposing pieces of Western furniture.

Culture Notes

• Most French houses in the city are adjoining and have no front or side yard. The backyard is often a courtyard shared by several houses.

• This house has five rooms (**cinq pièces**). Point out that the French do not count the kitchen, bathroom, or W.-C. when counting rooms.

For Individual Needs

15 Challenge Students might present humorous skits about the movers putting everything in the wrong place. They might express surprise at finding certain pieces of furniture in inappropriate places (**Le lit est dans la cuisine!**) and instruct the movers to put the item in another room. (**Mais non, mettez le lit dans la chambre!**)

Group Work

Form groups of three to five. Give each group a large sheet of butcher paper and have students draw an imaginary floor plan and label it. Then, have them cut out pieces of furniture from magazines to furnish the house and label them. Circulate around the room as they work and ask **Qu'est-ce que c'est?**, pointing to rooms or pieces of furniture in order to elicit the vocabulary. Do not have students glue or tape the furniture to the floor plan, however, as both can be used for other activities. Refer students to the Supplementary Vocabulary on page 341 for additional house furnishings.

 Form groups of three to five. Each group should have a floor plan that another group has made and some pieces of furniture cut from magazines (see Group Work above). Have students take turns giving commands to their group members, such as **Mets la lampe dans le salon.**

Additional Practice

16 Have pairs of students point out things in the drawings to one another, asking **Qu'est-ce que c'est?** A partner will respond. (**C'est un lit.**)

---

15 Ecoute! 1. d 2. a 3. e 4. b 5. c

The Morels are moving into their new home. Match the furniture with Mrs. Morel's instructions to the movers.

a.

b.

c.

d.

e.

16 Vive la différence!

Julie and Nicole have some of the same things in their rooms and some different things. Can you name them? Which room is more likely an American teenager's room? Why? See answers below.

La chambre de Julie   **La chambre de Nicole**

Math Link

Ask students to measure the length, width, and height of a room in their house (bedroom, living room) or a room at school (cafeteria, classroom) and convert feet and inches to meters and centimeters. Then, ask them to tell you the area of this room in square meters. They might even calculate the volume of the room in cubic meters.

Possible answers

16 Same things: bed, desk, stereo, chest of drawers, lamp

Different things: traversin/pillow, closet door, blinds, bulletin board, doors, bookcase, poster, telephone, ceiling fan

Julie's bedroom; because of the blinds, wall-to-wall carpet, homecoming corsage, telephone, and pillow.

17 Dessiner, c'est gagné!

Draw a part of a house, a piece of furniture, or a room decoration from the **Vocabulaire** on page 37. The first person in your group to call out the French word makes the next drawing. The group that guesses the most words in five minutes wins.

COMMENT DIT-ON...?
Pointing out where things are

Là, c'est la cuisine.
Here/There is . . .

A côté de la cuisine, **il y a** la salle à manger.
Next to . . .   there is . . .

Ça, c'est la chambre des parents **en face des** toilettes.
This is . . .   across from . . .

---

18 Ecoute!

Look at the **Vocabulaire** on page 37 as you listen to a description of the Morel house. Is each statement true or false? Listen again and write down each statement, correcting those that are false.
Answers on p. 27C.

19 C'est toi, le prof

Write as many statements as you can about the Morel house, some true and some false. Read your statements to a partner, who will guess whether they are **vrai** or **faux**.

Tu le rappelles?

To indicate where things are, you might also want to use **à gauche de** *(to the left of)*, **à droite de** *(to the right of)*, or **près de** *(near)*. Don't forget that after these prepositions, **de** becomes **du** before masculine nouns, and **des** before plural nouns. It doesn't change before feminine nouns or nouns that begin with a vowel.
A gauche **du** salon...
A droite **des** toilettes...
Près **de la** cuisine...
A côté **de l'**étagère...

20 Fais-moi un dessin

How good are you at descriptions? Draw two floor plans of a home you'd like to have and label the rooms on one of the plans. Hand the blank plan to a partner. As you describe the plan, your partner will try to label the rooms correctly.

Quand tu entres dans l'appartement, le salon est à gauche. A côté du salon, il y a la salle à manger. En face de la salle à manger, il y a...

Note de Grammaire

To describe, you can use adjectives like **beau, joli, grand,** and **petit.** Remember that they go before the nouns they describe. The feminine form of **beau** is **belle.** Before a masculine noun that begins with a vowel, **beau** changes to **bel.** Two other adjectives that follow this pattern are **vieux** *(old)* and **nouveau** *(new)*. Their feminine forms are **vieille** and **nouvelle,** and in front of a masculine noun that begins with a vowel, they change to **vieil** and **nouvel.**

21 Mon journal

Imagine la chambre idéale. Fais-en une description dans ton journal. N'oublie pas les couleurs! Tu peux aussi faire un dessin.

DEUXIEME ETAPE
trente-neuf **39**

DEUXIEME ETAPE
CHAPITRE 2

Presentation

Comment dit-on... ? Show a floor plan on a transparency. Point out the rooms and give their locations in reference to other rooms. Then, make some true-false statements about the plan you've just described and have students reply **vrai** or **faux.** Next, ask questions, such as **Qu'est-ce qu'il y a en face de la chambre? C'est où, la salle de bains?** Finally, have individuals present their own plans to the rest of the class, using the expressions from **Comment dit-on... ?**

Teaching Suggestions

19 As an alternative writing activity, have students write sentences in a column labeled **Chez les Morel,** stating where rooms are in relation to one another in the Morel house. Then, in a second column, have them give the locations of the same rooms in their own or an imaginary home.

Note de grammaire On a sheet of paper, use the adjectives in sentences. **(Elles sont belles. C'est un vieil homme.)** Photocopy one sheet for each pair of students, cut apart the words, shuffle them, and distribute to partners, who will rearrange the sentences.

Mon journal

21 Encourage students to use as many adjectives from the **Note de grammaire** as possible in their journal entries. Refer students to the Supplementary Vocabulary on page 341 for additional furnishings and adjectives. For an additional journal entry suggestion for Chapter 2, see *Practice and Activity Book,* page 146.

Teaching Suggestion

To help students remember six useful prepositions, teach them this **chanson de gestes** used in Canadian schools. It is sung to the tune of "London Bridge."

Sur, sous, dans, devant, derrière,
Devant, derrière,
Devant, derrière,
Sur, sous, dans, devant, derrière,
A côté de.

While singing, students should place their hands in the appropriate positions in relation to their desks. As they sing **à côté de,** students should swing their hands by their sides.

Motivating Activity

Ask students what they usually say when they see someone's house or room for the first time. Have them discuss why it is important to pay the host compliments.

Presentation

Comment dit-on... ? Walk around the room, complimenting things that students have. Have students repeat the expressions after you. Then, have students work in pairs, complimenting each other and responding. You might have students read the **Note Culturelle** before complimenting each other.

CLOSE

To close this **étape**, have students imagine they are French students staying with an American family and write a journal entry similar to Pamela's on page 36. They should include a brief description of the house, a brief description of the room in which they are staying, and two compliments. The journal entry should also point out at least two differences between their French home and the American home.

COMMENT DIT-ON... ?
Paying and responding to compliments

To pay a compliment:

Elle est vraiment bien, ta chambre.
Your . . . is really great.
Elle est cool, ta chaîne stéréo.
Il est beau, ton poster.
    génial(e) *great*
    chouette *very cool*

To respond:

Tu trouves?
Do you think so?
C'est vrai? (Vraiment?)
Really?
C'est gentil!
That's nice of you.

22 Ecoute!

Listen as Solange gives Arnaud a tour of her home. What does Arnaud compliment?
Answers on p. 27C.

23 Des compliments

Give your group a "tour" of your ideal room by reading the description you wrote for Activity 21 on page 39. Each person will compliment something. Take turns until everyone has given a tour of his or her ideal room.

24 Elle est géniale, ta chambre!

Suppose Nicole sent you a sketch of her room (see Activity 16 on page 38). Write her a note complimenting some things in the room. Then, describe what you have in your room and how it's similar or different.

NOTE CULTURELLE

When you compliment a French person's home or possessions, the response will be the same as if you complimented the person's clothing or appearance. **Tu trouves? C'est vrai? Vraiment?** or **C'est gentil!** are standard responses to compliments. Remember that **Merci** is not the only appropriate response.

De bons conseils

If a writing task seems too complicated, start off by making a list of words and phrases that you might want to use. Then, add adjectives and connectors like **et** and **mais** to make sentences. You don't have to use all the words on your list; you might even think of others while you're writing. Using connectors will make you sound more sophisticated in French . . . and in your native language.

ASSESS

Quiz 2-2, *Chapter Teaching Resources, Book 1,* pp. 81–82

Assessment Items, Audiocassette 7A Audio CD 2

Performance Assessment

Have students describe their own homes, using the floor plans they drew for Activity 20. They should tell where several rooms are located in relation to others. Grades should be based on accuracy and comprehensibility. Allow students to describe a dream home if they prefer.

PANORAMA CULTUREL

 Geneviève • Québec

Sandrine • Martinique

Adèle • Cameroun

VIDEO PROGRAM
OR EXPANDED VIDEO
PROGRAM,
Videocassette 1
29:49–34:19

OR VIDEODISC PROGRAM,
Videodisc 1B

Search 18765, Play To 21585

We asked some young people to describe their homes. Here's what they said.

Comment est ta maison?

«Il y a le salon, la cuisine. Il y a une salle de jeux. Mon frère a une chambre. J'en ai une. Euh... on a une salle pour nos bureaux. Après ça, il y a la salle de bains, la salle de lavage.»

—Geneviève

«J'habite dans un appartement. Alors, il est assez petit. Il y a une salle à manger, un salon, ma chambre, celle de ma mère, une salle de bains, bien sûr. Et puis la cuisine et un balcon aussi.»

Comment est ta chambre?
«Je pense qu'elle ressemble à la chambre à peu près de toutes les filles de mon âge. Il y a des posters. J'ai une chaîne hi-fi aussi. Voilà.»

—Sandrine

«Ma chambre, je dirais d'abord qu'elle est assez belle. Ce sont mes goûts. Les murs sont blancs et on a fait des décorations en bleu parce que j'adore le bleu et le rose. Donc, j'ai assez de bleu et de rose dans ma chambre. J'ai d'abord comme meuble... j'ai une commode, mon bureau et c'est presque tout. Il n'y a pas grand-chose.»

—Adèle

Qu'en penses-tu?

They are similar to those in the interviews.

1. How do homes in the United States differ from those described in the interviews?
2. What was not mentioned that is commonly found in American teenagers' rooms?

Possible answers: telephone, television, computer

Savais-tu que...?

Homes in France are built of stone or cement blocks. In Quebec, houses are similar to American ones—often made of wood and painted in bright colors. Homes in Martinique and Guadeloupe can be large plantation-style houses or small cement-block houses. The porch is the central gathering place, and kitchens are sometimes separate to keep the rest of the house cool. In Côte d'Ivoire, villages are known for specific kinds of houses: some of clay, some of bamboo, and some built on stilts over lagoons. In cities, you'll see modern houses and apartments.

Multicultural Link

Ask students to find pictures of homes in different countries, provinces, or departments and to explain how the environment influenced the construction and design.

Questions

1. **Qu'est-ce qu'il y a dans la chambre de Sandrine?** (des posters, une chaîne hi-fi)
2. **Qui a une salle de lavage dans sa maison?** (Geneviève)
3. **Les murs sont de quelle couleur dans la chambre d'Adèle?** (blancs)
4. **Adèle aime quelles couleurs?** (le bleu et le rose)

TROISIEME ETAPE

Asking for and giving directions

Jump Start!

Write the following scrambled
words on the board:
**înache-orésté/machber
arimero/rauube/strope**
Have students unscramble
the words. Then, ask them to
imagine the items belong to a
friend and write a compliment
to their friend for each item.
(Answers: **chaîne-stéréo,
chambre, armoire, bureau,
poster**)

MOTIVATE

Ask students to name some
of the places they might need
directions to (such as the post
office) if they were visiting a
foreign country. Have them
think of ways they already
know in French to ask for
directions. (**Pardon, monsieur. Je cherche la poste,
s'il vous plaît.**)

TEACH

For Individual Needs

Auditory/Tactile Learners
Have pairs of students look at
the map in their books as you
describe the location of various
buildings in relation to others,
using **près de, à côté de,
dans,** and **en face de.** Have
partners point to the items on
the map as you mention them.
Then, ask students to complete
sentences about the locations
of the buildings. (**La bibliothèque est en face...**)

Culture Note

Students may notice
from the map of Chartres on
page 42 that the town is not
constructed on a north-south
grid, thus forming city blocks
as in the United States. Rather,
French cities are generally
built around a cathedral with
the streets spiraling out from
this central point.

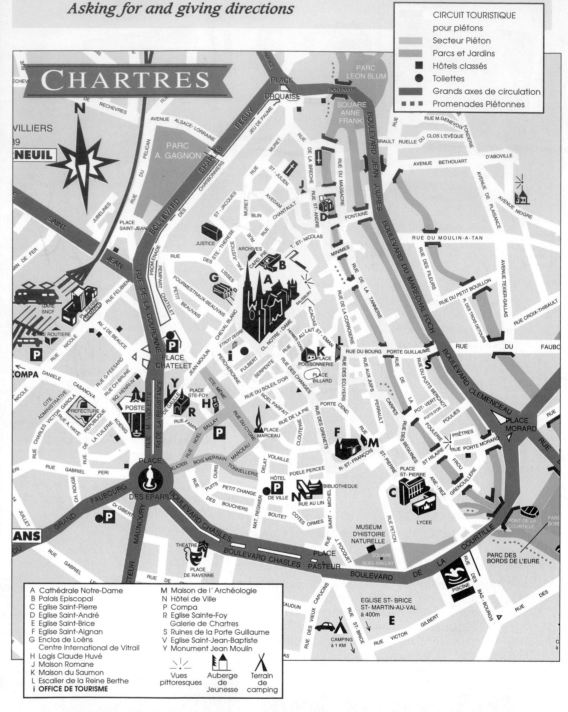

A Cathédrale Notre-Dame
B Palais Episcopal
C Eglise Saint-Pierre
D Eglise Saint-André
E Eglise Saint-Brice
F Eglise Saint-Aignan
G Enclos de Loëns
   Centre International de Vitrail
H Logis Claude Huvé
J Maison Romane
K Maison du Saumon
L Escalier de la Reine Berthe
i OFFICE DE TOURISME

M Maison de l'Archéologie
N Hôtel de Ville
P Compa
R Eglise Sainte-Foy
   Galerie de Chartres
S Ruines de la Porte Guillaume
V Eglise Saint-Jean-Baptiste
Y Monument Jean Moulin

Vues pittoresques
Auberge de Jeunesse
Terrain de camping

CIRCUIT TOURISTIQUE
pour piétons
Secteur Piéton
Parcs et Jardins
Hôtels classés
Toilettes
Grands axes de circulation
Promenades Piétonnes

CHAPITRE 2   Bienvenue à Chartres!

RESOURCES FOR TROISIEME ETAPE

Textbook Audiocassette 1B/Audio CD 2
Practice and Activity Book, pp. 20–22
Videodisc Guide
   Videodisc Program, Videodisc 1B

Chapter Teaching Resources, Book 1
• Communicative Activity 2-2, pp. 61–62
• Teaching Transparency Master 2-3, pp. 65, 66
   Teaching Transparency 2-3
• Additional Listening Activities 2-5, 2-6, p. 69
   Audiocassette 9A/Audio CD 2
• Realia 2-2, pp. 72, 73
• Situation Cards 2-3, pp. 74–75
• Student Response Forms, pp. 76–78
• Quiz 2-3, pp. 83–84
   Audiocassette 7A/Audio CD 2

25 Vrai ou faux?

1. La bibliothèque est à côté de la cathédrale.
2. La gare est près du parc des Bords de l'Eure. *faux*
3. La poste est dans la rue M. Violette. *vrai*

4. La piscine est près de la cathédrale. *faux*
5. Le lycée est à côté de l'église Saint-Pierre. *vrai*

(1. *faux*)

VOCABULAIRE

Est-ce que tu peux trouver les endroits suivants sur le plan de Chartres?

un terrain de camping

une gare

une église

une piscine

une poste

un office de tourisme

une cathédrale	*a cathedral*
un musée	*a museum*
un parc	*a park*

un lycée	*a high school*
une auberge de jeunesse	*a youth hostel*
une bibliothèque	*a library*
un théâtre	*a theater*

26 Ecoute!

Listen to Patrick and Chantal discuss what they're going to do today. First, choose the places they decide to visit. Then, listen again, and put those places in the order in which they'll visit them. *Answers on p. 27D.*

a. le Musée des Beaux-Arts
b. la cathédrale

c. le parc
d. l'office de tourisme

e. la poste
f. la piscine

TROISIEME ETAPE

quarante-trois **43**

History Link

Point out the contrast between the medieval church and the modern train station in the photos. Tell students that European towns exhibit both styles because of their ancient history. You might try to find pictures of well-preserved medieval towns, such as Carcassonne in the south of France, Dinan in Bretagne, and the village of Eguisheim in Alsace, all of which clearly illustrate the contrast between medieval and modern architecture.

Additional Practice

25 Have students create additional true-false statements for a partner to answer.

Presentation

Vocabulaire Gather or draw pictures of the places mentioned here to teach the words, having students repeat after you. Then, mention two places and have students give the location of one in relation to the other, according to the map on page 42. Finally, ask individual students to give a location without naming the building. (**C'est en face de la poste.**) Have other students try to guess what the place is.

Teaching Suggestions

• Have students write "clues" for each vocabulary word. For example, students might write **On y fait de la natation** for **la piscine.** Have students take turns reading their clues and having their classmates try to guess the places.

• Ask students if each of the places in the **Vocabulaire** exists in their town or neighborhood. If so, ask them what is next to it or across from it. (**Il y a une bibliothèque dans ta ville/ton quartier? Qu'est-ce qu'il y a en face de la bibliothèque?**)

Thinking Critically

Comparing and Contrasting
Ask students to imagine why the street in the photo of the church is so narrow. (When the majority of French streets were constructed, they were built to accommodate pedestrians, horses, and carriages.) Ask them to think about the wide streets in the United States, particularly in the West, and how most of them were developed after the invention of the car.

Presentation

Note de grammaire Using the pictures you gathered for the **Vocabulaire** presentation on page 43, mount them on colored construction paper or attach colored index cards to them. Attach paper of one color to pictures of feminine nouns, a second color to pictures of masculine nouns, and a third color to pictures of nouns that begin with a vowel sound. Tape them around the room. Walk from picture to picture, telling students **Je vais à la gare** or **Je vais au parc.** Afterwards, ask students to deduce why you used **à la** or **au.** Have them read the **Note de grammaire** to see if they've guessed correctly.

 Using the pictures from the Presentation above, have students tell each other where to go around the classroom. Have students walk to the places taped around the room as their classmates suggest **Va au lycée** or **Va à l'auberge de jeunesse.**

For Individual Needs

Slower Pace Go through the **Vocabulaire** on page 43, giving the appropriate preposition and contraction for each place (**au terrain de camping, à la gare, à l'église**). Have students write in their notebooks the names of the places with the prepositions.

Answers

27 1. à la poste
    2. au camping
    3. au parc
    4. à la gare
    5. à la piscine
    6. au Musée des Beaux-Arts
    7. à l'office de tourisme
    8. à la bibliothèque
    9. au théâtre
    10. au musée

---

27   Où vas-tu pour...   See answers below.

1. envoyer une lettre?
2. faire du camping?
3. faire un pique-nique?
4. prendre le train?
5. nager?
6. admirer des œuvres d'art?
7. trouver un plan de la ville?
8. emprunter des livres?
9. voir des acteurs et des actrices?
10. admirer des sculptures?

Note de *Grammaire*

When you're talking about going *to* a place, use **au** before masculine nouns, **à la** before feminine nouns, **à l'** before singular nouns that start with a vowel or an *h,* and **aux** before all plural nouns.

28   Que faire?

Ton ami(e) et toi, vous arrivez à Chartres. Qu'est-ce que vous voulez faire le premier jour de votre visite? Choisissez trois choses.

Si tu as oublié — making suggestions — va à la page 18.

—Tu as envie d'aller au parc des Bords de l'Eure?
—Non, ça ne me dit rien. Je préfère aller à la cathédrale.
—D'accord. Et après, on pourrait aller au théâtre sur la place de Ravenne.

NOTE CULTURELLE

Notre-Dame-de-Chartres, one of the most famous Gothic cathedrals, was built in the thirteenth century on a site where a cathedral had stood since the sixth century. The cathedral can easily be recognized by its different towers — the plain Romanesque tower on the left and the more ornate Gothic tower on the right in the photo below. Spared in all major wars and conflicts, Chartres still has most of its original stained-glass windows, famous for their rich colors. The cathedral's flying buttresses, its great size, and its light-filled interior clearly illustrate the genius of Gothic construction.

History Link

Note Culturelle Ask students to imagine why the two towers are different. When the cathedral was destroyed by fire in 1194, only the south tower and the façade were left standing. The north tower was rebuilt in the later, High Gothic style. During World War II, the stained glass was dismantled and removed until the end of the war.

Architecture Link

The vaulted (pointed) arches of the Gothic cathedral support a great deal more weight than the rounded ones in earlier Romanesque architecture, allowing the walls to be thinner and the ceilings higher. Along with the wing-like exterior supports called *flying buttresses,* the Gothic arch allowed for much larger openings in the walls for stained-glass windows, and a much more open and airy atmosphere.

COMMENT DIT-ON... ?

Asking for and giving directions

To ask for directions:

Où est la gare, **s'il vous plaît?**

To give directions:

Traversez la place Châtelet et **prenez** la rue de la Couronne.
Cross . . .   take . . .

Puis, tournez à gauche sur le boulevard de la Courtille.
Then, turn left on . . .

Allez/Continuez tout droit. La gare est **sur la droite** dans la rue Félibien.
Go/keep going straight ahead.   on the right . . .

29 Ecoute!

Look at the map of Chartres on page 42. Imagine you're at the **place des Epars.** Listen to the following directions and figure out where they lead. Answers on p. 27D.

à la cathédrale	à la piscine
à la poste	au lycée
à l'église Sainte-Foy	au parc Gagnon

30 Quelle route?

M. Dupont est à Chartres devant la cathédrale. Il veut aller au théâtre sur la place de Ravenne. Complète les directions.

Tournez ___1___ dans la rue Perchcronne. Ensuite, tournez ___2___ dans la rue du Soleil d'Or. Continuez ___3___. A la place des Epars, tournez à gauche sur ___4___. Le théâtre est ___5___.

1. à gauche   **2.** à droite   **3.** tout droit
4. le boulevard Chasles   **5.** à droite

31 Où va-t-on?

With a partner, decide on a starting point on the map of Chartres. Then, give your partner directions to a place you have in mind. Does your partner end up in that place? Take turns.

32 Viens chez moi!

You've invited the French-speaking exchange student at your school to come to your home. Write a note telling him or her how to get there from school.

33 Jeu de rôle

You've just arrived at the train station in Chartres and can't wait to visit the town. Choose two places you'd like to go. Ask directions from people, who might not always send you the correct way! Act out a humorous scene. Use the map on page 42.

Vocabulaire *à la carte*

Zut!	*Darn!*
Oh là là!	*Oh my goodness!*
Où je suis?	*Where am I?*
Qu'est-ce qui se passe?	*What's going on?*
Et alors?	*So what?*

TROISIEME ETAPE

quarante-cinq **45**

TROISIEME ETAPE
CHAPITRE 2

Presentation

Comment dit-on... ? Show *Teaching Transparency 2-3* to present the expressions as students listen with their books closed. First, present the vocabulary as a conversation, asking where a place is and giving the directions. Trace the route with your finger on the transparency as you speak. Next, have students repeat each expression after you as you retrace the route on the map. Finally, ask students, **Où est... , s'il vous plaît?** and have individual students give you each part of the directions.

For videodisc application, see *Videodisc Guide.*

Language Notes

• Call attention to the fact that you say **sur le boulevard** and **sur l'avenue** but **dans la rue.**

32 Other useful vocabulary items are: **au coin** *(at the corner)*; **au feu** *(at the stoplight)*; **au carrefour** *(at the intersection).*

• Another acceptable way of expressing frustration is **Mince!** *(Darn!)*

Portfolio

33 Oral This activity is appropriate for students' oral portfolios. For portfolio suggestions, see *Assessment Guide,* page 15.

ASSESS

Quiz 2-3, *Chapter Teaching Resources, Book 1,* pp. 83–84

Assessment Items, Audiocassette 7A Audio CD 2

Performance Assessment

Have students look at the map of Chartres on page 42. Choose five sets of starting points and destinations. Have students number their papers from one to five. For the first four sets, give students the starting point and call out a set of directions. When you have finished, they should write down the destination. For the last set, give the starting point and destination. Students must write out directions to get to the destination.

CLOSE

Have students write and perform skits in which they give their classmates a tour of their town. In their conversation, they should re-enter expressions for asking how a student is feeling, such as **Pas trop fatigué?** He or she might respond **Non, ça va.**

READING STRATEGY

Scanning

Teacher Note

For an additional reading, see *Practice and Activity Book,* page 23.

PREREADING
Activity A

Motivating Activity

Ask students what kinds of things interest them most when visiting a town or city.

Teaching Suggestion

Ask students what the function of a brochure is. (A brochure is designed to give as much information as possible on a subject in a very condensed form.) Have students suggest what kinds of information they would expect to find in a travel brochure and write their suggestions on the board or on a transparency.

READING
Activities B–F

Thinking Critically

Drawing Inferences
Encourage students to skim each entry to determine what type of establishment is being discussed.

For Individual Needs

B.–F. Slower Pace These activities are suited to students who need small tasks of manageable scope and length.

Building on Previous Skills

Remind students of the French method of writing calendar dates using numerals. (The day is followed by the month. For example, the date **1/06** is read **le premier juin**.) Have students read aloud the dates in the brochures.

LISONS!

𝒲hat would you like to do in Chartres?

DE BONS CONSEILS

In Chapter 1 you reviewed the first two steps in reading a new selection: previewing and skimming. What should you do next? *Scan* to look for specific information. When you scan, you should look for key words to guide you to the specific information you want to find.

A. What kind of brochure do you see on this page? What does the title mean? What kind of photos and art do you see? What would you do with a brochure like this?   See answers below.

B. Scan each section of the brochure briefly. Match the title of each section to the key word(s) that tell you what the section is about.

e1. **La Passacaille**   a. les tours, découvrir
d2. **Le Musée des**   b. cuisine
   Beaux-Arts   traditionnelle
c3. **Au Plaisir d'Offrir** c. cadeaux
b4. **A l'Escargot d'Or**   d. peintures,
a5. **Les Tours de**   sculptures, art
   la Cathédrale   e. pizzeria

C. Now that you have some key words in mind, scan the brochure again to figure out where you would go to . . . See answers below.
1. take a tour of Chartres.
2. see a house covered with pieces of pottery and glass.
3. learn about making stained-glass windows.

46 *quarante-six*

PASSEZ UNE JOURNEE
A CHARTRES...
VILLE D'ART

LE MUSEE DES BEAUX-ARTS
29, cloître Notre-Dame - 28000 CHARTRES
Tél. 37 36 41 39

Etabli dans l'ancien Palais Episcopal, le Musée des Beaux-Arts présente des collections conjuguant richesse et diversité : peintures (Holbein, Zurbaran, Chardin, une importante collection Vlaminck), sculptures, tapisseries, mobilier, émaux (XVIe s.), clavecins, arts décoratifs, art primitif océanien.

Du 1/06 au 5/10 : exposition temporaire. L'ART DES INCAS dans les collections des Musées de CUZCO (Pérou).

Accès : au chevet de la Cathédrale dans les jardins (secteur piétonnier).

Tous les jours sauf mardi 10 h - 18 h du 1/04 au 31/10; 10 h - 12 h et 14 h - 18 h du 1/11 au 31/03.

Plein tarif musée : 7 FF. Tarif réduit : 3.50 FF

Plein tarif exposition : 20 FF. Tarif réduit exposition : 10 FF.

·R·E·S·T·A·U·R·A·N·T·
Au Chat qui Court
8 rue de la Couronne — Chartres — Tél. 37 28 55 10

UNE PROMENADE INSOLITE, SANS FATIGUE

Départ place de la Cathédrale. Circuit commenté de 35 minutes de 10 h à 19 h dans le Vieux Chartres

de Pâques
à
Octobre

Nocturnes en été

Prix :
25 FF adultes
15 FF enfants

Réservations groupes :

PROMOTRAIN
131, rue de Clignancourt
75018 PARIS - Tél. (1) 42 62 24 03 - Fax (1) 42 62 50 32

A l'Escargot d'Or   Bar - Restaurant
Cuisine traditionnelle de qualité - Produits frais cuisinés maison
Groupes - Repas d'affaires - Service rapide
13, rue du Soleil d'Or - Tél. 37 21 73 53
50 m de la cathédrale
Carte traduite en 4 langues
GB - ALL - ESP - FR

Culture Note

The numeral "1" in parentheses in front of the telephone numbers in the **Promotrain** brochure indicate that they are in Paris. There are two telecommunication regions in France: Paris and the provinces. To reach the provinces, you dial 16 followed by the eight-digit number. To call Paris from anywhere else in France, you must dial 16-1 plus the phone number. When phoning from abroad, Paris is the only place in France that requires the regional code "1" after the country code.

Answers

A a tourist brochure; spend a day in Chartres, city of art; advertisements for tourist attractions in Chartres; use it to plan a day in Chartres

C 1. Promotrain
   2. Maison Picassiette
   3. Centre International du Vitrail

La Passacaille
PIZZERIA
Salle climatisée
ouvert tous les jours
Pendant l'été
service non-stop 11 h 30 - 22 h 30

30, rue Sainte-Même
entre la Place Chatelet
et la Cathédrale
Tél. 37 21 52 10

LA MAISON PICASSIETTE

22, rue du Repos - 28000
CHARTRES - Tél. 37 34 10 76

Un univers surprenant : pas un centimètre de mur, pas un meuble qui ne soit tapissé d'éclats de vaisselle, faïence et verre divers. Un témoignage exceptionnel d'art populaire (classé Monument Historique).

Accès : entre la route de Paris et la route d'Orléans, proche du cimetière de Chartres.

Tous les jours saut mardi 10 h - 12 h et 14 h - 18 h du 1/04 au 31/10.

Plein tarif : 6 FF.
Tarif réduit : 3 FF.

Au Plaisir d'offrir
Cadeaux - Souvenirs - Change - Toilettes
28, place Jean Moulin - Chartres

LE CENTRE INTERNATIONAL DU VITRAIL (C.I.V.)
5, rue du Cardinal Pie - 28000 CHARTRES - Tél. 38 21 65 72

Le Centre International du Vitrail a pour mission de promouvoir l'art du vitrail, il offre au grand public les moyens de connaître et d'apprécier un art ancien que notre temps renouvelle. Il présente des expositions de vitraux de tous pays.

Accès : côté gauche rue parallèle à la Cathédrale.

Tous les jours 9 h 30 - 19 h du 1/04 au 30/09; 10 h - 12 h 30 et 13 h 30 - 18 h du 1/10 au 31/03.

LES TOURS DE LA CATHEDRALE

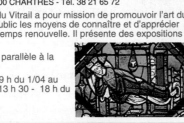

Découvrir Chartres et ses environs des tours de la cathédrale, base du "Clocher vieux" 800 ans d'âge, 103 m de haut et du "Clocher Neuf" élevé à 112 m au 16e s. par Jehan de Beauce.

Amateurs de photos, n'hésitez pas !

Accès : à l'intérieur de la Cathédrale près du portail nord (gauche).

Tous les jours excepté les matinées des dimanches et fêtes religieuses et durant certains offices et les 1/05, 1/11, 11/11, 25/12.

9 h 30 - 11 h 30, 14 h - 17 h 30 du 1/04 au 30/09

10 h 30 - 11 h 30, 14 h - 16 h du 1/10 au 31/03

Plein tarif: 20 FF.
Tarif réduit: 12 FF.

D. Read more closely for the answers to these questions.

1. Could you order a pizza at 11 P.M. at **La Passacaille?**   No
2. If you spoke only Spanish, where would you go to get a meal?   l'Escargot d'Or
3. If you were an amateur photographer, would you be allowed to take pictures on the cathedral tours?   Yes
4. If you plan to visit Chartres in July, will the train tour of Old Chartres run at night?   Yes
5. Would you find the **Musée des Beaux-Arts** open on Tuesday?   No

E. Choose activities that you can do on a Wednesday at 9:30 A.M., noon, 2 P.M., 5 P.M., and 7:30 P.M.   See answers below.

F. You and your friend Héloïse took photos of your day in Chartres. Complete these captions with information you scan from the brochure.

1. Me voilà à l'Escargot d'Or. C'est la première fois que je mange...
2. Nous voilà au Musée des Beaux-Arts. Héloïse regarde...
3. C'est Héloïse et moi devant la cathédrale. On va...
4. C'est moi au Plaisir d'Offrir. Si tu veux, on peut...

G. Create a travel brochure for French-speaking tourists about your town, city, or area. Draw and label pictures of places you think they would like to visit, or use photos from the newspaper. Be sure to include important information, such as times and days the places are open, the entrance fees, the type of food available, and so on. Before you make your final brochure, write a rough draft and have two classmates proofread it.

POSTREADING
Activity G

Cooperative Learning

G. Have students do this project as a group. Have the auditory learners survey the group and list the possible sights and activities from which the group will choose the contents of the brochure. Assign the visual/verbal learners the actual writing of the text. Kinesthetic learners will enjoy gathering and creating graphics for the brochure. Allow tactile learners to cut, paste, and arrange the brochure in its final form.

Culture Notes

• Some of the most beautiful stained-glass windows in the world can be found in Paris, not in Notre-Dame, but in Sainte-Chapelle, a tiny chapel built by Louis XI in the Palais de Justice on the Ile de la Cité. This chapel was built in the twelfth century to house a relic believed to be Jesus' Crown of Thorns.

• La Maison Picassiette was the home of Raymond Isidore. In 1928, he was employed as the caretaker of the Chartres cemetery, near which he built his home. He began collecting glass and pottery shards and eventually decided to use them to mosaic the walls of his home. He started with the interior of his home, covering the walls, floors, and some furniture with mosaic. His work spread to the exterior walls of his home and to the surfaces of his yard. In 1952, his work was complete after more than 29,000 hours of work.

Language Note

Point out the word **change** in the ad for **Au Plaisir d'offrir** and have students try to guess what it means. (Tourists can exchange their foreign currency for local currency.)

Answers

E 9:30 A.M. — Le Centre International du Vitrail, tour de la cathédrale

noon — Le Centre International du Vitrail, La Maison Picassiette, pizzeria, visite de Chartres en train, Le Musée des Beaux-Arts

2 P.M. — tour de la cathédrale, le Musée des Beaux-Arts, visite de Chartres en train, La Maison Picassiette, Le Centre International du Vitrail

5 P.M. — Le Musée des Beaux-Arts, visite en train de Chartres, pizzeria, tour de la cathédrale, Le Centre International du Vitrail

7:30 P.M. — pizzeria

Science Link

Point out that the colors of the stained-glass windows (**les vitraux**) in the Gothic cathedrals were made by adding metal to the molten glass. Since different metals absorb light of different frequencies, the color of the glass varies according to the metal it contains. Copper was used for red, cobalt for blue, antimony for yellow, manganese for purple, and iron for green.

MISE EN PRATIQUE

The **Mise en pratique** reviews and integrates all four skills and culture in preparation for the Chapter Test.

Teaching Suggestions

To familiarize students with the newspaper ad, ask the following questions: **A Paris, l'immeuble a combien de pièces? (cinq) Combien de chambres y a-t-il? (trois) Quel est le numéro de téléphone de l'immeuble à Paris (45.15.92.83) Qu'est-ce qu'on peut faire à Brides les Bains? (du ski, du surf, du monoski) En quelle saison? (en hiver) Il y a combien de kilomètres de pistes de ski à Brides les Bains? (1.200) Qu'est-ce qu'on peut voir de la villa à la Côte d'Azur? (la mer) Quand est-ce que cette villa est disponible? (au mois de juillet)**

• You might write the following vocabulary words on the board for students to refer to as they do Activity 1: **l'ascenseur** *(elevator)*; **une vue** *(a view)*; **un chalet** *(a mountain cottage)*; **en bois** *(made of wood)*; **une télécabine** *(a cable car)*; **une piste de ski** *(ski slope)*; **du surf/du surf sur neige** *(snowboarding)*; **contre** *(a synonym for pour)*; **équipée** *(equipped)*; **une ferme** *(farm)*; **une cheminée** *(fireplace)*.

For Individual Needs

Challenge/Auditory Learners Have students imagine they are employees at the newspaper who take the ads over the phone. "Phone in" one or two of the ads and let them take dictation.

Portfolio

2 Written This activity is appropriate for students' written portfolios. For portfolio suggestions, see *Assessment Guide,* page 15.

Echanges Location

Paris, Ile Saint-Louis: bel immeuble ancien, 5 pièces, meublé, au 4e étage, ascenseur, terrasse vue Seine et Notre-Dame, 3 chambres, 1 bain, 2 W.-C. Disponible fin juin - mi-août contre logement en Californie.
45.15.92.38

Alpes, Brides les Bains—*Village Olympique 92:* chalet en bois, 2 chambres, salon - coin cuisine, près télécabine de l'Olympe aux Trois Vallées (1.200 km de pistes de ski, surf, monoski), disponible hiver contre logement en Floride.
79.55.24.37

Côte d'Azur, Le Lavandou: villa, 7 pièces, cuisine équipée, piscine, jardin, 3 chambres, 1er étage vue mer, 2 bains, 2 W.-C., juillet contre logement côte Est des Etats-Unis de préférence.
94.05.89.63

Franche-Comté, Marigny: ancienne ferme près du Lac Chalain, 5 pièces, style rustique, cuisine moderne, 2 cheminées, grand jardin, recherche logement dans le Mid-West.
84.25.74.47

Loire, Blois: Maison moderne 10 minutes centre-ville, cuisine, salon-salle à manger, 3 chambres, 1 bain-WC, jardin. Visitez les grands châteaux de la Loire. Contre logement en Louisiane de préférence.
54.74.27.25

1 French people who would like to exchange homes with people in the United States placed the ads above.

1. In what order is the following information given?
   a. type of home 2
   b. where the family would like to exchange 4
   c. phone number 5
   d. list of rooms 3
   e. location of home 1

2. Which home(s) would be the best choice for you if . . . See answers below.
   a. you liked to swim?
   b. you lived in California?
   c. you preferred country living?
   d. you liked newer homes?
   e. you had a large family?
   f. you liked to ski?

3. Which house would you like to stay in and why?

 2 Imagine you're an adult with your own home. You'd like to exchange houses with a French family, so you're going to place an ad in a French newspaper. First, make a list of the features of your home: where it's located, the rooms you have, when it's available, and a brief description. Then, write an ad to encourage people to choose your home.

3 Suppose your family has exchanged homes with the Parisian family who placed the first ad above. It's your first day in Paris, and you decide to sightsee! With a partner, decide on three places you'll visit together.

48 *quarante-huit*   CHAPITRE 2   Bienvenue à Chartres!

Language Notes

• Point out that **location** is a **faux ami.** It means *rental,* not *location.* The verb *to rent* is **louer.**
• You might remind students that in France, telephone numbers are read as four sets of two-digit numbers. For example, the first telephone number in the **Echanges Location** is read **quarante-cinq, quinze, quatre-vingt-douze, trente-huit.**

Answers

1 2. a. Côte d'Azur, le Lavandou
      b. Paris, Ile St-Louis
      c. Franche-Comté, Marigny
      d. Loire, Blois
      e. Côte d'Azur, Le Lavandou
      f. Alpes, Brides les Bains

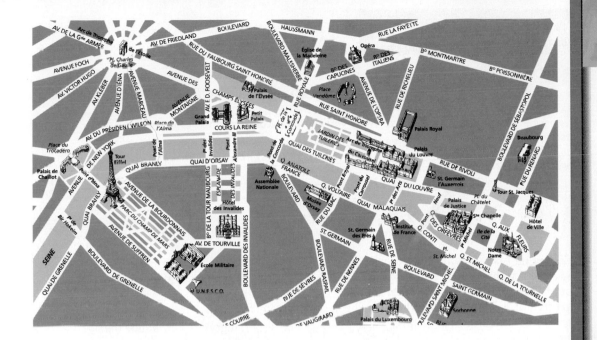

 4 Look at the map above. You're at the **place St-Michel** in the **Quartier latin** and you're trying to find the museum at the **centre Georges Pompidou.** You ask a passerby who, unfortunately, gives you the wrong directions. Listen to the directions and figure out where they would actually lead you. *le musée d'Orsay*

 5 Using the map, direct your classmates from a place in Paris to a final destination. The first person to tell where the directions lead takes the next turn.

6

JEU DE ROLE

An American family has arranged to exchange homes with a French family. The Americans arrive at the French home before the French family leaves for the airport. Play the roles of the two families.

The French family should:
- welcome the American family.
- ask about their trip and how everyone is feeling.
- show the American family around their home.

The American family should:
- respond appropriately to the French family's welcome.
- tell how they are feeling.
- compliment the French family on their home and furnishings.

For Individual Needs

4 Slower Pace Before you play the recording, have students locate the square and the streets on the map that they will hear in the recording (**la place Saint-Michel, le boulevard Saint-Michel, le boulevard Saint-Germain,** and **la rue du Bac**).

Teaching Suggestions

4 Have students give the correct directions from the **place Saint-Michel** to the **centre Pompidou.**

5 Using the map of Paris, have students choose some of the sights that they would like to visit. Have them tell a partner which places they would like to visit and why. (**J'aimerais visiter le Musée d'Orsay parce que j'adore l'impressionisme.**) If possible, you might obtain some travel books such as *Let's Go France* (Saint Martin's Press) or *Frommer's Comprehensive Travel Guide* (Prentice Hall Travel), so that students can read about some of the places shown on the map.

Video Wrap-Up

- **VIDEO PROGRAM**
- **EXPANDED VIDEO PROGRAM,** Videocassette 1, 19:21–35:21
- **VIDEODISC PROGRAM,** Videodisc 1B

At this time, you might want to use the video resources for additional review and enrichment. See *Video Guide* or *Videodisc Guide* for suggestions regarding the following:
- **Une nouvelle vie** (Dramatic episode)
- **Panorama Culturel** (Interviews)
- **Vidéoclips** (Authentic footage)

This page is intended to help students prepare for the test. It is a brief checklist of the major points covered in the chapter. The students should be reminded that this is only a checklist and does not necessarily include everything that will appear on the test.

♜ Game

C'EST À TOI! Form two teams and have the members of each team number themselves. Player one of Team A asks a question from **Que sais-je?** to player one of Team B. If the player answers correctly, Team B receives a point. If not, Team A may "steal" the point by answering the question correctly. Then, player two of Team B asks player two of Team A a question, and so on. Players may also make up additional questions based on the material in the chapter. Original questions are worth two points if answered correctly. Play for a predetermined length of time. The team with the most points at the end of play wins.

QUE SAIS-JE?

Can you use what you've learned in the chapter?

Can you welcome someone and respond to someone's welcome? p. 33

1 What would you say to welcome . . . *Possible answers:*

1. your pen pal Jean-Louis? Bienvenue chez moi. Fais comme chez toi.
2. your mother's friend? Bienvenue chez nous. Faites comme chez vous.

2 How would you respond to your friend's father, who says . . . *Possible answers:*

1. Bienvenue chez nous. Merci.
2. Fais comme chez toi. C'est gentil de votre part.
3. Tu as fait bon voyage? Oui, excellent. C'était fatigant.

Can you ask how someone is feeling and tell how you are feeling? p. 34

3 How would you ask Etienne if he's . . .

1. really tired? Pas trop fatigué?
2. hungry? Tu n'as pas faim?
3. thirsty? Tu n'as pas soif?

4 How would you say that you're . . .

1. not very tired? Non, ça va.
2. very hungry? J'ai très faim.
3. a little thirsty? J'ai un peu soif.

Can you point out where things are? p. 39

5 When you're showing someone your home, how would you point out . . .

1. your room?
2. the bathroom?
3. the kitchen? See answers below.

Can you pay and respond to compliments? p. 40

6 How would you compliment someone on . . . ? See answers below.

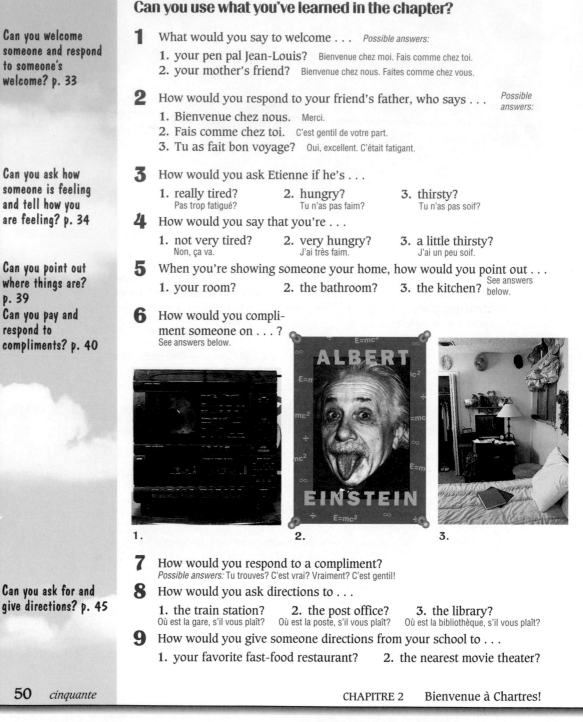

1. 2. 3.

7 How would you respond to a compliment? *Possible answers:* Tu trouves? C'est vrai? Vraiment? C'est gentil!

Can you ask for and give directions? p. 45

8 How would you ask directions to . . .

1. the train station? Où est la gare, s'il vous plaît?
2. the post office? Où est la poste, s'il vous plaît?
3. the library? Où est la bibliothèque, s'il vous plaît?

9 How would you give someone directions from your school to . . .

1. your favorite fast-food restaurant?
2. the nearest movie theater?

50 *cinquante*   CHAPITRE 2   Bienvenue à Chartres!

Possible answers

5 1. Là, c'est ma chambre.
Ça, c'est ma chambre.
2. Là, ce sont les toilettes.
3. Là, c'est la cuisine.
Ça, c'est la cuisine.
6 1. Elle est vraiment bien, ta chaîne stéréo.
2. Il est génial, ton poster.
3. Elle est cool, ta chambre.

PREMIERE ETAPE

Welcoming someone; responding to someone's welcome

Bienvenue chez moi (chez nous). *Welcome to my home (our home).*
Faites/Fais comme chez vous (chez toi). *Make yourself at home.*
Vous avez (Tu as) fait bon voyage? *Did you have a good trip?*
Merci. *Thank you.*

C'est gentil de votre/ta part. *That's nice of you.*
Oui, excellent. *Yes, excellent.*
C'était fatigant! *It was tiring!*

Asking how someone is feeling and telling how you are feeling

Pas trop fatigué(e)? *(You're) not too tired?*
Vous n'avez pas (Tu n'as pas) faim? *Aren't you hungry?*

Vous n'avez pas (Tu n'as pas) soif? *Aren't you thirsty?*
Non, ça va. *No, I'm fine.*
Si, je suis crevé(e). *Yes, I'm exhausted.*
Si, un peu. *Yes, a little.*
Si, j'ai très faim/soif! *Yes, I'm very hungry/thirsty.*
Si, je meurs de faim/soif! *Yes, I'm dying of hunger/thirst!*

DEUXIEME ETAPE

Pointing out where things are

Là, c'est... *Here/There is . . .*
A côté de... *Next to . . .*
Il y a... *There is . . .*
Ça, c'est... *This is . . .*
en face de *across from*
à gauche de *to the left of*
à droite de *to the right of*
près de *near*

Paying and responding to compliments

Il/Elle est vraiment bien, ton/ta... *Your . . . is really great.*

cool *cool*
beau (belle) *beautiful*
génial(e) *great*
chouette *very cool*
Tu trouves? *Do you think so?*
C'est vrai? (Vraiment?) *Really?*
C'est gentil! *That's nice of you.*

Furniture and rooms

l'armoire (f.) *armoire, wardrobe*
le balcon *balcony*
le bureau *desk*
la chaîne stéréo *stereo*
la chambre *bedroom*
la commode *chest of drawers*
la cuisine *kitchen*
les étagères (f.) *shelves*

le jardin *yard*
la lampe *lamp*
le lit *bed*
la pièce *room (of a house)*
le poster *poster*
le premier étage *second floor*
le rez-de-chaussée *first (ground) floor*
la salle à manger *dining room*
la salle de bains *bathroom*
le salon *living room*
le tapis *rug*
les toilettes (f.) (les W.-C.) *toilet, restroom*
beau (bel) (belle) *beautiful*
nouveau (nouvel) (nouvelle) *new*
vieux (vieil) (vieille) *old*

TROISIEME ETAPE

Asking for and giving directions

Où est..., s'il vous plaît? *Where is . . . , please?*
Traversez... *Cross . . .*
Prenez... *Take . . .*
Puis, tournez à gauche dans/sur... *Then, turn left on . . .*
Allez/Continuez tout droit. *Go/Keep going straight ahead.*

sur la droite/gauche *on the right/left*

Places in town

l'auberge (f.) de jeunesse *youth hostel*
la bibliothèque *library*
la cathédrale *cathedral*
l'église (f.) *church*
la gare *train station*

le lycée *high school*
le musée *museum*
l'office (m.) de tourisme *tourist information office*
le parc *park*
la piscine *pool*
la poste *post office*
le terrain de camping *campground*
le théâtre *theater*

VOCABULAIRE

cinquante et un **51**

Game

CATÉGORIES DE VOCABULAIRE Form two teams. Call out a category, such as *pointing out where things are* or *furniture and house vocabulary*. Teams take turns naming items or expressions in the category. When one team can no longer answer, the other team has a chance to "steal" a point if they can name another item from the category. Continue by choosing a new category. The last team to score a point must start the new category. When all the categories have been covered, the team with the most points wins.

Game

PICTIONNAIRE Form small groups and distribute a large sheet of butcher paper to each one. Have each group write all the vocabulary words under *Furniture and house* and *Places in town* on separate, small slips of paper and place them in a box. Then, have one student draw a slip of paper and draw an illustration representing the vocabulary word written on the slip of paper. The first student to say the French word for the drawing scores a point. Have students take turns drawing. After a specified amount of time, the student with the most points wins.

CHAPTER 2 ASSESSMENT

CHAPTER TEST

- *Chapter Teaching Resources, Book 1*, pp. 85–90
- *Assessment Guide,* Speaking Test, p. 28
- *Assessment Items, Audiocassette 7A Audio CD 2*

TEST GENERATOR, CHAPTER 2

ALTERNATIVE ASSESSMENT

Performance Assessment

You might want to use the **Jeu de rôle** (p. 49) as a cumulative performance assessment activity.

Portfolio Assessment

- **Written: Mise en pratique,** Activity 2, *Pupil's Edition,* p. 48
  Assessment Guide, p. 15
- **Oral:** Activity 33, *Pupil's Edition,* p. 45
  Assessment Guide, p. 15

Mise en train pp. 54–56	Une spécialité française		*Practice and Activity Book, p. 25*	*Video Guide* OR *Videodisc Guide*

	FUNCTIONS	GRAMMAR	CULTURE	RE-ENTRY
Première étape pp. 57–60	Making purchases, p. 58	The object pronoun **en,** p. 58	• Realia: Grocery ad, p. 57 • **Note Culturelle,** Neighborhood stores, p. 58	• Giving prices • Expressions of quantity • Food items • Numbers
Deuxième étape pp. 61–65	Asking for, offering, accepting, and refusing food; paying and responding to compliments, p. 64	The partitive articles, p. 65	• **Panorama Culturel,** Typical meals in the francophone world, p. 61 • **Note Culturelle,** French meals, p. 62 • Realia: Menu from **Le Lion d'Or,** p. 62 • Realia: School lunch menus from Martinique, p. 64	• Paying and responding to compliments • Days of the week
Troisième étape pp. 66–71	• Asking for and giving advice, p. 68 • Extending good wishes, p. 71	The indirect object pronouns **lui** and **leur,** p. 68	• **Rencontre Culturelle,** Polite behavior for a guest, p. 66 • **Note Culturelle,** Meals for special occasions, p. 67 • Realia: Greeting cards, p. 71	Asking for and giving advice

Lisons! pp. 72–73	**Le bel âge**		**Reading Strategy:** Guessing meaning from visual clues and context

Review pp. 74–77	**Mise en pratique,** pp. 74–75	**Que sais-je?** p. 76	**Vocabulaire,** p. 77

Assessment Options	**Etape Quizzes**
	 • *Chapter Teaching Resources, Book 1*
	   Première étape, Quiz 3-1, pp. 135–136
	   Deuxième étape, Quiz 3-2, pp. 137–138
	   Troisième étape, Quiz 3-3, pp. 139–140
	 • *Assessment Items, Audiocassette 7A Audio CD 3*
		Chapter Test
		 • *Chapter Teaching Resources, Book 1,* pp. 141–146
		 • *Assessment Guide,* Speaking Test, p. 29
		 • *Assessment Items, Audiocassette 7A/Audio CD 3*
		
		 Test Generator, Chapter 3

Video Program OR Expanded Video Program, Videocassette 1   Textbook Audiocassette 2A/Audio CD 3
OR Videodisc Program, Videodisc 2A

RESOURCES: Print	RESOURCES: Audiovisual
	Textbook Audiocassette 2A/Audio CD 3
Practice and Activity Book, pp. 26–28	
Chapter Teaching Resources, Book 1	
• Teaching Transparency Master 3-1, pp. 119, 122	*Teaching Transparency 3-1*
• Additional Listening Activities 3-1, 3-2, p. 123	*Additional Listening Activities, Audiocassette 9A/Audio CD 3*
• Realia 3-1, pp. 127, 129	
• Situation Cards 3-1, pp. 130–131	
• Student Response Forms, pp. 132–134	
• Quiz 3-1, pp. 135–136	*Assessment Items, Audiocassette 7A/Audio CD 3*
Videodisc Guide	*Videodisc Program, Videodisc 2A*
	Textbook Audiocassette 2A/Audio CD 3
Practice and Activity Book, pp. 29–31	
• *Chapter Teaching Resources, Book 1*	
• Communicative Activity 3-1, pp. 115–116	
• Teaching Transparency Master 3-2, pp. 120, 122	*Teaching Transparency 3-2*
• Additional Listening Activities 3-3, 3-4, p. 124	*Additional Listening Activities, Audiocassette 9A/Audio CD 3*
• Realia 3-2, pp. 128, 129	
• Situation Cards 3-2, pp. 130–131	
• Student Response Forms, pp. 132–134	
• Quiz 3-2, pp. 137–138	*Assessment Items, Audiocassette 7A/Audio CD 3*
Video Guide	*Video Program* OR *Expanded Video Program, Videocassette 1*
Videodisk Guide	*Videodisc Program, Videodisc 2A*
	Textbook Audiocassette 2A/Audio CD 3
Practice and Activity Book, pp. 32–34	
Chapter Teaching Resources, Book 1	
• Communicative Activity 3-2, pp. 117–118	
• Teaching Transparency Master 3-3, pp. 121, 122	*Teaching Transparency 3-3*
• Additional Listening Activities 3-5, 3-6, p. 125	*Additional Listening Activities, Audiocassette 9A/Audio CD 3*
• Realia 3-2, pp. 128, 129	
• Situation Cards 3-3, pp. 130–131	
• Student Response Forms, pp. 132–134	
• Quiz 3-3, pp. 139–140	*Assessment Items, Audiocassette 7A/Audio CD 3*
Videodisc Guide	*Videodisc Program, Videodisc 2A*
Practice and Activity Book, p. 35	
Video Guide	*Video Program* OR *Expanded Video Program, Videocassette 1*
Videodisc Guide	*Videodisc Program, Videodisc 2A*

Alternative Assessment
- Performance Assessment
  Première étape, p. 60
  Deuxième étape, p. 65
  Troisième étape, p. 71
- Portfolio Assessment
  Written: Activity 25, *Pupil's Edition,* p. 65
    Assessment Guide, p. 16
  Oral: Activity 26, *Pupil's Edition,* p. 65
    Assessment Guide, p. 16

For Student Response Forms, see *Chapter Teaching Resources, Book 1,* pp. 132–134

Première étape

8 Ecoute! p. 58

1. — Pardon, vous avez des bananes?
   — Oui, monsieur. Combien en voulez-vous?
   — Un kilo, s'il vous plaît. Ça fait combien?

2. — Bonjour, monsieur. Je voudrais un kilo d'oranges, s'il vous plaît.
   — Oui, bien sûr.
   — Ça fait combien?

3. — Bonjour, madame. Il me faut des tomates et des pommes.
   — Bon. Combien en voulez-vous?
   — Je voudrais un kilo de tomates et un kilo de pommes Golden. Ça fait combien?

Answers to Activity 8
1. bananas   2. oranges   3. tomatoes, apples; 1 kilo of each;   1. 5F90
2. 4F95   3. 9F70

11 Ecoute! p. 60

1. — Maman, je vais en ville. Qu'est-ce que j'achète?
   — J'ai besoin de lait et de beurre.
   — D'accord.

2. — Marine, tu vas me chercher deux baguettes et un kilo de crevettes.
   — Oui, papa, j'y vais.

3. — Oh là là! J'ai oublié le pâté et la tarte! Vincent, tu peux aller les chercher pour moi?
   — Bien sûr, maman.

4. — Il faut m'acheter des œufs, un petit rôti de porc et trois douzaines d'escargots, s'il te plaît.
   — Bon. Allez, au revoir.

Answers to Activity 11
1. e   2. b, a   3. d, f   4. e, c, a

Deuxième étape

18 Ecoute! p. 63

1. — Oh, papa! Tu as acheté des croissants!
   — Oui, et j'ai fait aussi du chocolat pour toi.
   — Youpi!

2. — Maman, il y a du lait dans le frigo?
   — Bien sûr.
   — Je ne trouve pas les œufs!
   — Ah! Je crois que je sais ce que tu vas nous préparer!
   — Et où est le fromage?
   — Attends, je vais t'aider.

3. — C'était délicieux, Michel. J'adore le poulet préparé comme ça. Et ta quiche est toujours très bonne.
   — C'est gentil. Tu veux encore de la mousse au chocolat?
   — Merci, ça va.

4. — Oui, monsieur?
   — Je voudrais un grand café, s'il vous plaît.
   — Et avec ça?
   — Des tartines à la confiture.

Answers to Activity 18
1. petit déjeuner   3. déjeuner ou dîner
2. dîner   4. petit déjeuner

20 Ecoute! p. 64

1. — Qu'est-ce qu'on sert à la cantine aujourd'hui?
   — Du poisson avec des haricots verts et des carottes.
   — Bof. Et comme dessert?
   — Comme dessert, il y a du yaourt.
   — Et ben, ce n'est pas la cantine des gourmets ici!

2. — Qu'est-ce qu'il y a à la cantine?
   — Euh... il y a du poisson.
   — Toujours du poisson! Il y a un dessert intéressant au moins?
   — Euh, non, c'est un fruit.
   — Berk! Cette cantine est vraiment infecte.

3. — Tu aimes la salade de concombres?
   — C'est pas mauvais. Il y en a aujourd'hui?
   — Oui. Et du poisson, bien sûr...
   — Encore?
   — Oui, mais il y a de la glace au dessert!

Answers to Activity 20
1. Vauclin; jeudi   2. Rivière-Salée; mardi   3. Rivière-Salée; lundi

22 Ecoute! p. 65

1. — Encore de la salade?
   — Merci, ça va.

2. — C'est vraiment bon! J'aime beaucoup ta tarte aux fraises!
   — C'est gentil.

3. — Je pourrais avoir du pain, s'il te plaît?
   — Voilà.

4. — Tu veux du pâté?
   — Oui, je veux bien.

5. — C'était délicieux!
   — Oh, ce n'est pas grand-chose.

6. — Tu pourrais me passer les haricots verts?
   — Tiens.

Answers to Activity 22
1. offering food   4. offering food
2. paying a compliment   5. paying a compliment
3. asking for food   6. asking for food

*T*roisième étape

28 Ecoute! p. 68

1. — Eh bien, maman, tu as une idée de cadeau pour Stéphane?
   — Tu pourrais lui offrir des chaussettes. Il en a toujours besoin, j'en suis sûre!
   — Des chaussettes? Oh maman, c'est vraiment banal!

2. — Eh, Sabine! J'ai un petit problème. Je ne sais pas quoi offrir à Jean-Luc pour son anniversaire.
   — Euh, ça, c'est dur. Un portefeuille, peut-être.
   — Non, il en a déjà un.

3. — Salut, Karim. Dis, tu as une idée de cadeau pour ma sœur? C'est son anniversaire demain.
   — Offre-lui un livre.
   — Bonne idée. Elle aime beaucoup lire.

4. — Tu as une idée de cadeau pour Pierre? C'est son anniversaire demain.
   — Ben, je ne sais pas. Il a peut-être besoin d'une cravate?
   — Euh, non, ce n'est pas son style.

5. — Anne, qu'est-ce que je pourrais offrir à Rachida?
   — Offre-lui un disque-compact.
   — Oui, tu as raison! Il adore la musique!

Answers to Activity 28

1. reject	3. accept	5. accept
2. reject	4. reject	

30 Ecoute! p. 70

1. — Oh, des fleurs! Merci, Pamela, c'est gentil.

2. — Oh, Etienne! Quel joli cadre!

3. — Tiens, un foulard! Qu'est-ce qu'il est chic! Bonne idée, Lionel!

4. — Oh, qu'il est beau, ce sac à main! Merci, Sandra.

Answers to Activity 30

1. e   2. d   3. a   4. b

*M*ise en pratique

2 p. 75

1. — Bonjour, monsieur.
   — Bonjour, madame. Qu'est-ce que vous prenez aujourd'hui?
   — Je voudrais un kilo de bifteck, s'il vous plaît.
   — Voilà. Et avec ça?
   — C'est tout.

2. — Papa! Qu'est-ce qu'on mange ce soir?
   — Euh, je ne sais pas. Qu'est-ce que tu veux?
   — J'ai envie de quelque chose aux bleuets.
   — Tu veux que je te prépare une petite surprise?
   — Ouais... je veux bien.

3. — Au revoir, maman.
   — Tu vas en ville?
   — Oui... qu'est-ce que tu veux?
   — J'ai besoin de lait, de beurre et de quelques bananes. Tu peux les acheter?
   — Bon, d'accord.

Answers to Mise en pratique Activity 2

1. steak au poivre
2. pouding au pain et aux bleuets
3. gratin de bananes jaunes

Les menus du monde
(Cooperative Learning Project)

ASSIGNMENT

Students will create a menu for a restaurant in a francophone country.

MATERIALS

✂ **Students may need**
- Posterboard or construction paper
- Markers
- Scissors
- Glue
- Magazine pictures

SUGGESTED SEQUENCE

Form groups of four and assign the roles of organizer, writer, proofreader, and artist. Each group must choose a francophone country and create a restaurant menu that reflects the local cuisine. The menu should include:
- the French name, address, and logo of the restaurant
- at least four **à la carte** items under each of these categories: **entrées, plats principaux, salades, fruits, fromages, desserts,** and **boissons**
- a description of each dish, including the ingredients
- prices in francs
- some artwork, either original or cut from magazines
- at least one house specialty
- **un menu à prix fixe**

GRADING THE PROJECT

When the menu has been completed, each group member must present a part of it to the class, describing some of the dishes and explaining how they represent the cuisine of the country. The group members should receive a collective grade for completion of requirements, accuracy of written work, and overall appearance of the project. Each member should receive an individual grade for his or her oral presentation, taking into account effort and participation.

Suggested Point Distribution (total = 100 points)

Completion of requirements	20 points
Accuracy of written work	20 points
Overall appearance	20 points
Accuracy of oral presentation	20 points
Effort/participation	20 points

LE LION D'OR

Entrées

Pâté de campagne	20 F
Saucisson sec pur porc	20 F
Sardines à l'huile	20 F
Carottes râpées	20 F
Œuf dur mayonnaise	20 F

Viandes–Volaille

Filet de bœuf	65 F
Carré d'agneau	65 F
Steak au poivre	60 F
Poulet garni	45 F
Daube de lapin	70 F
Filet de canard à l'orange	62 F
Tartare (préparé à la commande)	56 F

**Tous nos plats sont accompagnés de frites
ou de salade verte ou de haricots verts**

Fromages

Camembert, Gruyère	19 F
Yaourt	10 F

Fromages Fermiers Sélectionnés

St.-Nectaire	22 F
Roquefort Papillon (Carte Noire)	25 F
Chèvre	27 F

Desserts

Crème de marrons	12 F
Mont-Blanc	16 F
Tarte aux fruits	26 F
Crème caramel	22 F
Mousse au chocolat	24 F

Boissons

Limonade	20 F
Eau minérale	22 F
Jus de fruits	24 F
Thé ou café glacé	26 F
Cidre	24 F
Milk shake	30 F

Au petit déjeuner

Croissant	12 F
Tartine	9 F
Gâteau Breton	9 F

Petit déjeuner complet à . . . . 50 F
Double express ou crème ou chocolat ou thé,
1 croissant, 1 tartine, 1 orange pressée,
confiture, beurre, miel

LOTO!

In this game, students will practice the names of food and drink items and expressions for offering, accepting, or refusing them.

Each student draws a grid with four squares across and four squares down. In each of the 16 squares, students draw a different food or drink. Then, students circulate around the room "offering" the foods and drinks on their cards to their classmates. (**Tu veux des fraises?**) If a particular student has drawn that item on his or her card, he or she must refuse. (**Merci, ça va.**) If the item is not on the student's card, then he or she must accept it. (**Oui, je veux bien.**) In this case, the student who offered the food crosses out that food on his or her card and writes in that square the name of the classmate who accepted it. The first person to write four names in a row, vertically, horizontally, or diagonally, calls out **Loto!** and then names the four foods he or she "offered" and the students who accepted them.

QUE SUIS-JE?

In this game, students will practice the vocabulary for food and drink items and descriptive adjectives.

Gather magazine pictures of food and drink items, one for each student in the class. Without letting students see the pictures, pin or tape them on their backs. Students then circulate around the classroom, asking one another questions to determine their identity. (**Je suis un légume? Je suis jaune?**) The other students can only answer **Oui** or **Non.** Continue until all have discovered their identity.

Chapitre 3
Un repas à la française

pp. 52–77

𝒰sing the Chapter Opener

Motivating Activity

Have students look at the chapter title. Ask if they can guess the meaning of the word **repas** based on the photos and the introductory paragraph on page 53. You might ask them if they have seen or heard the English word *repast,* meaning *meal.* Next, ask students if they know the expression **à la française.** Point out that **à la française** is short for **à la mode** or **à la manière française,** meaning *in the French style.*

Teaching Suggestion

First, have students look at the photos and tell what they see in French. Ask them to pay attention to detail. If they need prompting, ask questions, such as **Sur la première photo, il y a combien de personnes à table? Qu'est-ce que vous voyez sur la table? Sur la troisième photo, les fleurs sont de quelles couleurs?** Finally, ask them what rules they must follow at the table. Ask them what they do differently when they have a meal at someone else's house or at a nice restaurant.

Photo Flash!

① In France, meals are served in separate courses and may last from one to three hours. If you're invited to dinner, it's customary to bring a small gift for the host. It is important to compliment the host on the meal.

CHAPITRE 3
Un repas à la française

① C'est vraiment bon !

52 *cinquante-deux*

Culture Note

Point out the position of Sandra's hands as she is cutting her piece of pie. The French hold the fork in the left hand and the knife in the right at all times while eating. They don't switch the utensils from the left to the right hand as Americans do. The French use the knife not only for cutting, but to scoop food onto the fork as well.

Language Note

Ask students if they know why the nationality in **à la française** is in the feminine form. (The French words **la mode** and **la manière** in the expressions **à la mode** and **à la manière française** are feminine nouns.)

Buying, preparing, eating, and sharing food are an essential part of life in every culture, and each culture has its own distinct customs concerning food. At your house, are there any special rules you have to follow when you're at the table? When you're a guest at someone's house, what should you do?

In this chapter you will learn

- to make purchases
- to ask for, offer, accept, and refuse food; to pay and respond to compliments
- to ask for and give advice; to extend good wishes

And you will

- listen to people at the grocery store and at the table
- read food ads and a comic strip
- write some menus and a card for a special occasion
- find out about typical meals and the behavior of guests in francophone countries

② C'est combien, une tartelette?

③ Je pourrais leur offrir des fleurs.

Multicultural Link

Ask if any students are familiar with table manners in other cultures. If so, ask them how they differ from American table manners. Students might recall from Level 1 that people in Côte d'Ivoire, especially those in the villages, and in much of Africa, often eat with their right hand out of a large bowl that is shared among those eating the meal.

Focusing on Outcomes

Ask students to read the outcomes and match them with the photos. Then, write the following sentences on the board or on a transparency and have students match each one to an outcome:

   C'est combien, les tomates?
   La salade est délicieuse.
   Encore du café?
   Bon anniversaire!
   Offre-lui des bonbons.
   Tu es très gentil.

NOTE: You may want to use the video to support the objectives. The self-check activities in **Que sais-je?** on page 76 help students assess their achievement of the objectives.

Photo Flash!

② A **pâtisserie** may be a separate shop or combined with a **boulangerie. Pâtisseries** sometimes have a tea room where you can sit and enjoy coffee or tea and a pastry.

③ When you're invited to dinner, flowers are an appropriate gift for the hosts. You can buy them at a florist (**chez le fleuriste**) or an open-air market (**au marché aux fleurs**), such as the one pictured in this photo.

Building on Previous Skills

Distribute large sheets of paper to small groups and have them label four columns **Boissons, Fruits, Légumes,** and **Viandes.** Give each group thirty seconds to list in the first column as many drinks as they can recall. The group with the most entries wins. Repeat the procedure for the other categories. You might display the lists in the classroom.

OR VIDEODISC PROGRAM,
Videodisc 2A

Search 1, Play To 8000

Video Synopsis

In this segment of the video, Sandra, Pamela, and Mrs. Lepic are shopping for lunch. Mrs. Lepic decides she will surprise Pamela with something typically French. Sandra and Pamela leave Mrs. Lepic and go to buy bread. As they are walking, they see a tray of **escargots** in the window of a **charcuterie-traiteur.** Pamela does not find them appetizing at all. She wants to buy a gift for Mrs. Lepic and asks Sandra's advice. Sandra suggests flowers, so Pamela buys a bouquet of carnations. Later, Pamela offers the flowers to Mrs. Lepic who is happy to receive them. At lunch, Mrs. Lepic brings out the surprise: **escargots!** Pamela trys to appear enthusiastic.

Motivating Activity

Ask students what specialty from their region they would want to serve a foreign guest.

Presentation

Ask students to study the photos in the **Mise en train** for 30 seconds. Then, have them write briefly in English what they think the story is about. Next, show the video. Finally, as individuals read their original ideas, have the class decide if they were correct.

Mise en train

Une spécialité française

What French specialties do you see in these photos?

54   *cinquante-quatre*   CHAPITRE 3   Un repas à la française

RESOURCES FOR **MISE EN TRAIN**

Textbook Audiocassette 2A/Audio CD 3
Practice and Activity Book, p. 25
Video Guide
   Video Program
   Expanded Video Program, Videocassette 1
Videodisc Guide
   Videodisc Program, Videodisc 2A

Plus tard chez les Lepic...

For Individual Needs

Visual Learners On a transparency, draw the photos from the **Mise en train**, using stick figures. Do not include the speech bubbles. Write the text of the speech bubbles for the photos on small pieces of transparency and place them at random on the overhead. Have students write the sentences in the correct order on a sheet of paper.

Slower Pace On the board or on a transparency, write the following sentences. Have students rewrite them in the proper order to summarize the action of the story.
1. **Pamela offre des fleurs a Madame Lepic.**
2. **Pamela voudrait manger une specialité française.**
3. **Sandra offre Pamela du pain.**
4. **Madame Lepic sert des escargots.**
5. **Pamela achète des fleurs.**
6. **Sandra et Pamela regarde les pâtisseries.**
(*Answers:* 2, 6, 5, 1, 3, 4)

Challenge Have students write a caption for each photo, summarizing the action.

Language Note

Ask students to find the expression Sandra uses to say the pastries look good. (**Elles ont l'air bonnes.**) Point out that the expression **avoir l'air** can be used for people as well. (**Il a l'air fatigué.**) To compliment someone who looks nice today, however, one says **Tu es très beau/belle aujourd'hui.**

MISE EN TRAIN

cinquante-cinq 55

Video Integration

- *EXPANDED VIDEO PROGRAM,*
  Videocassette 1, 40:00–43:59
- *VIDEODISC PROGRAM,*
  Videodisc 2A

Search 8000, Play To 15185

You may choose to continue with **Une spécialité française (suite)** or wait until later in the chapter. When the story continues, Pamela tries the **escargots.** Mrs. Lepic offers her more, but she politely refuses. Mrs. Lepic serves the main course, and after that, salad. With each course, Mrs. Lepic offers Pamela more food, but she refuses because she is full. After the salad, Mrs. Lepic brings out a plate of cheese, and then the dessert. At the end of the meal, Pamela offers to make an American dish for the Lepics.

For Individual Needs

2 Challenge Scramble the statements and write them on the board or on a transparency. Have students unscramble them, and then decide whether they are true or false. Have students correct the false statements.

2 Challenge Have students write some of their own true-false statements and read them to a partner. If the statements are false, have students explain why.

For videodisc application, see *Videodisc Guide*.

Additional Practice

3 For additional listening practice, name the items pictured in random order and have students write the numbers of the corresponding pictures.

For Individual Needs

4 Slower Pace Write the missing words from Pamela's journal on the board or on a transparency in random order for students to choose from. You might also sketch illustrations of the nouns needed to complete the journal entry on the board in random order and label them **A** through **E**. Have students complete the journal entry with the letters that correspond to the pictures.

4 Challenge Have students rewrite the letter from Sandra's point of view.

Teaching Suggestion

5 Once students have identified the expressions, have partners use them in two-line dialogues.

1 Tu as compris?

1. Where are Mrs. Lepic, Sandra, and Pamela at the beginning of **Une spécialité française?** on the street
2. What errand do Pamela and Sandra do for Mrs. Lepic? buy bread
3. What does Pamela buy? Why? flowers; as a gift for Mme Lepic
4. What is Mrs. Lepic's surprise? snails (**escargots**) for lunch

2 Vrai ou faux?

1. Pamela est allée chez le fleuriste pour acheter du pain. faux
2. Pamela et Sandra décident d'acheter des pâtisseries. faux
3. Mme Lepic achète du pain. faux
4. Le bouquet d'œillets coûte 30 francs. vrai
5. En France, on mange des escargots. vrai

3 C'est qui?

Qui a acheté les choses suivantes? Mme Lepic? Sandra ou Pamela? Personne *(Nobody)*?

1. Pamela   2. Sandra et Pamela   3. Mme Lepic   4. Personne

4 Une journée intéressante

Pamela is writing about her day in her journal, but she forgets a few things. Can you help her?   1. Sandra   3. pâtisseries   5. escargots   2. pain   4. fleurs

> Aujourd'hui, je suis allée en ville avec Mme Lepic et __1__. On a acheté du __2__ à la boulangerie-pâtisserie, mais on n'a pas acheté de __3__ parce que ça coupe l'appétit. J'ai acheté des __4__ pour offrir à Mme Lepic. Elle était très contente. On a eu une surprise pour le déjeuner. Des __5__!

5 Cherche les expressions

What do people in **Une spécialité française** say to . . . See answers below.

1. ask for advice?
2. make a suggestion?
3. accept a suggestion?
4. ask for a price?
5. offer food?
6. accept food?

6 Et maintenant, à toi

If you were a guest, what would you do if you were offered something you didn't think you'd like?

56   *cinquante-six*   CHAPITRE 3   Un repas à la française

Answers
5 1. Qu'est-ce que je pourrais lui offrir?
   2. Pourquoi est-ce que tu ne lui achètes pas des fleurs?
   3. Bonne idée!
   4. C'est combien?
   5. Tu veux du pain? Allez, sers-toi.
   6. Oui, je veux bien.

PREMIERE ETAPE

Making purchases

E.LECLERC

4F90 CAROTTES le sachet de 2 kg soit le kg 2,45 F

4F80 RAISINS Italie, Sicile, le kg

5F90 BANANES le kg

6F90 ENDIVES le sachet de 1 kg

10F00 CHOUX-FLEURS les 2

4F95 TOMATES le kg

10F00 ANANAS cat. B, les 2

9F50 POMMES GOLDEN le sachet de 2 kg soit le kg 4,75 F

9F90 ORANGES le sachet de 2 kg soit le kg 4,95

2. 1 or 2 kilos; the bag

7 Les fruits et les légumes

1. Which fruits and vegetables do you recognize in this ad? Are there any you haven't seen before?

2. In what quantity are most of the fruits and vegetables sold? Can you guess what **le sachet** means?

3. If you had 25 francs and you had to make a fruit salad to take to a party, which fruits would you buy?

Tu te rappelles ?

Do you remember how items are sold in French-speaking countries? Fruits and vegetables are priced by the pound (**une livre**≈**500 grammes**) or the kilogram (**un kilo**≈**2 livres ou 1.000 grammes**). To give a price in French, say the amount of francs first, then the centimes: 7F80= **sept francs quatre-vingts.** To review numbers, practice counting by tens from 10 to 100: **dix, vingt, trente, quarante, cinquante, soixante, soixante-dix, quatre-vingts, quatre-vingt-dix, cent.**

PREMIERE ETAPE

cinquante-sept **57**

Presentation

Comment dit-on... ? Bring real or plastic fruits and vegetables to class and attach prices to them. Have a student play the role of the **vendeur (vendeuse)** while you play the role of the **client(e)**. Write on the board under **vendeur (vendeuse)**: **C'est 5 francs le kilo** and **Combien en voulez-vous?** Then, ask for prices and quantities of various items, prompting students' responses by pointing at the board. Next, write on the board what a customer might say and have another student play that role. Finally, have students assume both roles.

Note de grammaire Briefly explain the meaning, function, and position of the pronoun **en** in a sentence. Write the following sentence starters on the board: **J'en ai... , Vous en avez... , Il/Elle en a...** Hold up six pens, ask **J'ai combien de stylos?**, and answer **J'en ai six.** Repeat using other objects. Prompt students to answer using **vous.**

Teaching Suggestion

Ask questions about things students have. (**Marc a combien de cahiers?**) Prompt **Il en a deux.** Finally, ask individuals **Tu as combien de crayons?**

COMMENT DIT-ON... ?
Making purchases

To ask for a price:
C'est combien, s'il vous plaît?
Combien coûtent les pommes?
How much are . . . ?

To ask what quantity someone wants:
Combien en voulez-vous?
How many/much do you want?

To ask for a certain quantity of something:
Je voudrais une livre de tomates.
Je vais prendre un kilo de bananes.
Des pommes? **Je vais en prendre** deux kilos. *I'll take . . . (of them).*

To ask for the total cost:
Ça fait combien?

Note de Grammaire

The object pronoun **en** means *of them.* You use it to replace the phrase **de + a thing or things.**

—Vous voulez **des fraises?**
—Oui, je vais **en** prendre une livre.
—Et avec ça?
—**Des bananes,** s'il vous plaît.
—Combien **en** voulez-vous?
—Un kilo, s'il vous plaît.

8 Ecoute!

Listen to the following conversations to find out what the people are buying at the supermarket. Then, listen a second time for how much they're buying. According to the ad on page 57, how much would each customer pay? Answers on p. 51C.

9 Méli-mélo!

Unscramble the following conversation between a grocer and a customer. Act it out with a partner, exchanging roles. Then, repeat the conversation, substituting different foods at different prices.

5
—Une livre de haricots verts. Ça fait combien?

4
—Et avec ça?

2
—2 F le kilo. Combien en voulez-vous?

1
—C'est combien, les pommes de terre?

3
—Je vais en prendre trois kilos, s'il vous plaît.

6
—Ça fait 9 F.

10 A vos caddies

Your vegetarian friends are coming to lunch. Make a list of the fruits and vegetables you need and shop at **E. Leclerc.** Act out the scene with a partner. Then, change roles.

NOTE CULTURELLE

In France and in many French-speaking countries, people often do their grocery shopping in small neighborhood stores. Although convenience and lower prices are making supermarkets more popular, many people still prefer specialty shops for fresh food of high quality.

Math Link

To practice listening to and saying numbers, have students dictate simple addition and subtraction problems to each other. For example, have one student dictate a problem to another student at the board. (**Quinze et trente-deux font... ?**) The student at the board writes the problem, solves it, and reads it. (**Quinze et trente-deux font quarante-sept.**) Then, he or she chooses another student to go to the board and dictates the next problem. (**Soixante moins deux font... ?**)

VOCABULAIRE

Où est-ce qu'on va pour acheter à manger?

À **la charcuterie**, on trouve...
- du pâté
- des saucissons
- du jambon

À **la boulangerie**, on achète...
- des pains au chocolat
- des baguettes
- des croissants

À **la crémerie**, on vend...
- des œufs
- du beurre
- du fromage
- du lait

À **la pâtisserie**, on se régale avec...
- une tarte aux pommes
- des religieuses[1]
- des mille-feuilles[2]

À **la boucherie**, on peut acheter **de la viande** ou **de la volaille**.
- un bifteck
- un rôti de bœuf
- un poulet

À **la poissonnerie**, on trouve du poisson et **des fruits de mer**.
- des escargots
- des crevettes
- des huîtres
- du poisson

1. pastries made of two iced cream puffs filled with chocolate or coffee cream
2. rectangular pastries made of thin layers of puff pastry and cream filling

PREMIERE ETAPE
cinquante-neuf **59**

Teacher Note

You may point out that live **escargots** are found at the **poissonnerie**, while cooked and prepared **escargots** are found at the **charcuterie-traiteur**, where foods are already prepared for take-out.

♖ Game

Loto! Have each student choose twenty-five vocabulary cards (see TPR activity above) and arrange five rows of five cards on his or her desk. Put one set of cards in a box for yourself and begin a bingo game. Draw cards from the box, call out the vocabulary items, and have students turn over the cards on their desks that correspond to the words you call. A student who turns over five cards in a row calls out **Loto!** and calls out the items in French.

Presentation

Vocabulaire Before presenting this vocabulary, ask each student to draw one of the food items on construction paper and use their illustrations to teach the vocabulary. Then, draw six storefronts on the board and write in the names of the stores. Show the pictures and ask where the items can be bought. (**Où est-ce qu'on achète du lait?**) As students answer **On achète du lait à la crémerie**, have one student tape the picture to the board under the appropriate storefront. When you have used all the pictures in this manner, ask what is sold in each store. (**Qu'est-ce qu'on vend à la crémerie?**) Have students name all of the items available at each store. (**On vend du lait, du fromage, des œufs et du beurre à la crémerie.**)

For videodisc application, see *Videodisc Guide*.

TPR Choose some of the students' drawings (see Presentation above), reduce their size on a photocopier, and photocopy sets of the vocabulary items that students can cut apart into "cards." Have students lay out the vocabulary cards on their desks and arrange them according to your instructions. (**Montrez-moi le pâté. Mettez le pain à côté du poulet.**)

Language Note

Remind students that the -**f** is pronounced in the French word **un œuf**, but that it is not pronounced in **des œufs**.

For Individual Needs

11 Slower Pace Before playing the recording, have students name all the food items that can be bought at each store mentioned in the activity.

13 Challenge Have students make up menus for each meal on the calendar. As an alternative activity, have students plan a menu for a friend or family member, taking into account that person's preferences.

CLOSE

To close this **étape,** have small groups write and perform the conversations in Activity 14 as skits.

ASSESS

Quiz 3-1, *Chapter Teaching Resources, Book 1,* pp. 135–136

Assessment Items, Audiocassette 7A/Audio CD 3

Performance Assessment

On slips of paper, write the names of the foods from the **Vocabulaire** on page 59. Then, write the six store names on the board and have six students act as merchants. The remaining students draw slips of paper. One student at a time purchases the item from the appropriate merchant. The customer and the merchant will ask for and give the price of the item, using the pronoun **en** in their conversation. Example:
— **C'est combien, les bananes?**
— **Quatre francs le kilo.**
— **Je vais en prendre deux kilos, s'il vous plaît.**

---

11 Ecoute!

Listen as some parents tell their children what to buy for dinner. Which store(s) will they have to visit? **1.** e **2.** b, a **3.** d, f **4.** e, c, a

a. la poissonnerie **c.** la boucherie **e.** la crémerie
b. la boulangerie **d.** la charcuterie **f.** la pâtisserie

12 L'intrus

Which item does not belong in each group of words? Can you explain why? See answers below.

1	2	3	4	5
du fromage du lait du pâté du beurre	une religieuse un gâteau une tarte un rôti	la volaille la charcuterie la poissonnerie la pâtisserie	des saucissons des crevettes du jambon du pâté	des huîtres du poisson du poulet des escargots

13 Un cordon bleu attentionné

Toute la semaine, M. Lepic fait la cuisine! Qu'est-ce qu'il peut préparer pour les personnes suivantes? Qu'est-ce qu'il ne devrait pas préparer?

LUN 12: 072 sᵉ Justine 294 — DÉJEUNER = JEAN (aime la viande) 11

MAR 13: 073 s Rodrigue 293

MER 14: 074 sᵉ Mathilde 292 — Pauline et son mari viennent dîner (n'aiment pas les fruits de mer)

JEU 15: 075 sᵉ Louise 291 — DÉJEUNER avec Louis (végétarien)

VEN 16: 076 sᵉ Bénédic. 290

SAM 17: 077 s Patrice 289 — DÎNER pour Christophe (au régime)

DIM 18: 078 s Cyrille 288 — Sandrine et Emilie (aiment les pâtisseries)

14 Vous en voulez combien?

You and a friend are going shopping for Mrs. Lepic this afternoon. With a partner, take turns acting out the roles of vendor and shopper at the various stores. Make sure you get the right quantity and buy everything on her list.

une douzaine d'œufs
deux baguettes
un poulet
500 grammes de crevettes
2 litres de lait
1 kilo de pommes de terre
une tarte aux pommes
500 grammes de jambon

15 Une publicité

Pick a specific kind of food store and make your own ad. Cut pictures from a magazine or newspaper or draw your own pictures. Advertise at least six items and remember to include prices.

60 *soixante* CHAPITRE 3 Un repas à la française

Game

C'EST LOGIQUE! Have each student make up six false statements about where one goes to buy something. (**On achète du lait à la boucherie.**) Then, form two teams. Have the first player from Team A read his or her sentence; the first player from Team B must correct it in order to score a point. (**Mais non, on achète du lait à la crémerie.**) If the sentence is not corrected appropriately, Team A scores a point.

Answers

12 1. pâté; not found at crémerie
2. rôti; not found at pâtisserie
3. volaille; not a store
4. crevettes; not found at charcuterie
5. poulet; not found at poissonnerie

Panorama Culturel

Chantal • Martinique

Emmanuel • France

Sandrine • Martinique

VIDEO PROGRAM OR EXPANDED VIDEO PROGRAM, Videocassette 1 44:00–47:31

OR **VIDEODISC PROGRAM,** Videodisc 2A

Search 15185, Play To 18420

What's a typical breakfast, lunch, or dinner where you live? We talked to francophone people around the world about their meals. Here's what they told us.

Qu'est-ce qu'un petit déjeuner typique ici?

«Au petit déjeuner, je prends du chocolat, un jus de fruit. Je ne mange pas beaucoup, donc c'est tout ce que je prends.»

Quel est ton repas principal?

«Le déjeuner, soit à la cantine, soit chez moi, si je ne suis pas au lycée.»

Qu'est-ce que tu prends?

«D'habitude, eh bien c'est varié, ça peut être des pâtes... Je ne sais pas... des pâtes, du riz, enfin c'est très varié. Il n'y a pas de trucs précis.»

—Chantal

«Typiquement? Un déjeuner typiquement français, c'est en général [un] chocolat chaud avec des croissants. C'est tout différent des Américains. C'est... avec des croissants, des toasts, du pain, du beurre, de la confiture... Voilà.»

—Emmanuel

«Au petit déjeuner, des tartines. Je prends des tartines au petit déjeuner, avec du chocolat.»

Quel est ton repas principal?

«Pour le repas principal, c'est celui du midi.»

Qu'est-ce que tu prends?

«Le midi? C'est très varié, le midi. Je peux prendre du poisson, de la viande, du riz, des légumes du pays aussi.»

—Sandrine

Qu'en penses-tu? See answers below.

1. In what ways are these responses different or similar?
2. How do typical American meals compare with those mentioned in the interviews?
3. How might the area in which people live influence their eating habits?

Possible answers

1. *Different:* For breakfast, Chantal doesn't eat much. Emmanuel has **croissants.** Sandrine has **tartines.** *Same:* Each has hot chocolate for breakfast.
2. Answers will vary.
3. The cuisine of a region is influenced by the products and ingredients available in that area and its local customs.

Questions

1. **Qu'est-ce que Chantal prend d'habitude au déjeuner?** (c'est très varié, des pâtes ou du riz)
2. **D'après Emmanuel, qu'est-ce que c'est qu'un petit déjeuner typiquement français?** (un chocolat chaud, des croissants, des toasts, du pain, du beurre, de la confiture)
3. **Quel est le repas principal de Sandrine?** (celui de midi)

Teacher Notes

• See *Video Guide, Videodisc Guide,* and *Practice and Activity Book* for activities related to the **Panorama Culturel.**
• Remind students that cultural material may be included in the Chapter Quizzes and Test.
• The interviewees' language represents informal, unrehearsed speech. Occasionally, edits have been made for clarification.

Motivating Activity

Ask students how they would describe a typical American breakfast and what they would consider to be their main meal of the day.

Presentation

On a sheet of paper, have students label two columns *Food* and *Beverages.* Have them view the video and list the food and drink items they hear mentioned in the appropriate columns. Show the video a second time and have students add more to their lists. Finally, ask the **Questions** below and have students choose the information listed that answers each question.

DEUXIEME ETAPE

Asking for, offering, accepting, and refusing food; paying and responding to compliments

*J*ump Start!

Write the names of the following stores on the board or on a transparency: **la boulangerie, la pâtisserie, la boucherie, la charcuterie, la crémerie,** and **la poissonnerie.** Have students name two food items that can be purchased at each store.

MOTIVATE

Ask students what expressions they would need to know if they were dinner guests of a French family. Then, ask them why table manners are important. Ask them what table manners are traditionally expected in the United States and if they think there are similar expectations in French homes.

TEACH

Teaching Suggestion

Have students read the menu and ask about items they don't understand. (**Qu'est-ce que c'est «pâté de campagne?»**) Answer in French using gestures and/or drawings as you explain the item. For a listening and reading activity, ask several questions about the menu. (**C'est combien, le poulet garni?** or **Quel dessert coûte douze francs? Qu'est-ce qu'on peut avoir au petit déjeuner?**)

Math Link

Have students convert the prices listed in the menu from French francs to American dollars. The current rate of exchange can be found in the business section of the newspaper.

Answers

16 6 categories; appetizer, meat and fowl, cheese, dessert, drinks, breakfast; *Answers will vary; Possible answers:* appetizer, main course, dessert

---

16 Au Lion d'Or

Look at the menu for **Le Lion d'Or.** How many categories do you see? What are they? When you go to a restaurant, how many courses do you order? What do you call them?
See answers below.

17 Et au petit déjeuner?

What do people where you live usually have for breakfast? Is it similar to or different from the breakfast at **Le Lion d'Or?**

NOTE CULTURELLE

Meals occupy a central place in French family and social life. Lunch and dinner usually consist of several courses: an appetizer, the main course, a simple green salad, cheese, and dessert. A special meal might have as many as nine courses! As an appetizer, the French might eat cold cuts, vegetables in a vinaigrette sauce, or soup. The main course consists of meat or seafood. The French eat a wide variety of meats, fowl, and game such as duck, goose, guinea hen, and rabbit. Potatoes are very common, and you may be served a variety of vegetables like turnips, endive, eggplant, or leeks. For dessert, fresh fruit is often served. Pastries or ice cream are usually reserved for special occasions. The evening meal is generally lighter and often meatless. Eggs are eaten at dinner, but rarely at breakfast.

LE LION D'OR

Entrées

Pâté de campagne	20 F
Saucisson sec pur porc	20 F
Sardines à l'huile	20 F
Carottes râpées	20 F
Œuf dur mayonnaise	20 F

Viandes-Volaille

Filet de bœuf	65 F
Carré d'agneau	65 F
Steak au poivre	60 F
Poulet garni	45 F
Daube de lapin	70 F
Filet de canard à l'orange	62 F
Tartare (préparé à la commande)	56 F

Tous nos plats sont accompagnés de frites ou de salade verte ou de haricots verts

Fromages

Camembert, Gruyère	19 F
Yaourt	10 F

Fromages Fermiers Sélectionnés

St.-Nectaire	22 F
Roquefort Papillon (Carte Noire)	25 F
Chèvre	27 F

Desserts

Crème de marrons	12 F
Mont-Blanc	16 F
Tarte aux fruits	26 F
Crème caramel	22 F
Mousse au chocolat	24 F

Boissons

Limonade	20 F
Eau minérale	22 F
Jus de fruits	24 F
Thé ou café glacé	26 F
Cidre	24 F
Milk shake	30 F

Au petit déjeuner

Croissant	12 F
Tartine	9 F
Gâteau Breton	9 F

Petit déjeuner complet à . . . . **50 F**
Double express ou crème ou chocolat ou thé,
1 croissant, 1 tartine, 1 orange pressée,
confiture, beurre, miel

62 *soixante-deux*   CHAPITRE 3   Un repas à la française

RESOURCES FOR DEUXIEME ETAPE

Textbook Audiocassette 2A/Audio CD 3
Practice and Activity Book, pp. 29–31
Video Guide
  Video Program
  Expanded Video Program, Videocassette 1
Videodisc Guide
  Videodisc Program, Videodisc 2A

Chapter Teaching Resources, Book 1
• Communicative Activity 3-1, pp. 115–116
• Teaching Transparency Master 3-2, pp. 120, 122
  Teaching Transparency 3-2
Additional Listening Activities 3-3, 3-4, p. 124
  Audiocassette 9A/Audio CD 3
• Realia 3-2, pp. 128, 129
• Situation Cards 3-2, pp. 130–131
• Student Response Forms, pp. 132–134
• Quiz 3-2, pp. 137–138
  Audiocassette 7A/Audio CD 3

VOCABULAIRE

des tartines

un chocolat chaud

Pour le petit déjeuner, on prend un café au lait ou un chocolat chaud avec des tartines ou des croissants. Quelquefois, on prend des céréales.

des céréales

un café au lait

la salade

le plat principal

le fromage

l'entrée

le dessert

Pour le déjeuner et pour le dîner, on commence par une entrée. Ensuite, on sert le plat principal suivi d'une salade verte. A la fin du repas, on passe le plateau de fromages. Et pour terminer, on prend un dessert ou un fruit.

18 Ecoute!

Ecoute ces conversations. Est-ce qu'on parle du petit déjeuner, du déjeuner ou du dîner?
Answers on p. 51C.

19 A la carte

Tu vas au **Lion d'Or** pour le déjeuner. Qu'est-ce que tu commandes? Joue la scène avec un(e) camarade.

—Qu'est-ce que vous prenez comme entrée?
—Je voudrais le pâté de campagne, s'il vous plaît.

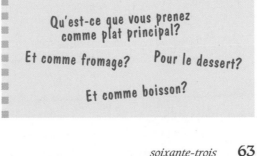

Qu'est-ce que vous prenez comme plat principal?

Et comme fromage?   Pour le dessert?

Et comme boisson?

Presentation

Vocabulaire Use the pictures students drew for the **Vocabulaire** on page 59 and create others to teach this vocabulary. Then, draw three columns on the board and label them **Petit déjeuner, Déjeuner,** and **Dîner.** Under **Déjeuner** and **Dîner,** write **entrée, plat principal, salade, fromage,** and **dessert.** Next, show a picture, ask **Quand est-ce qu'on prend une tartine?** and tape the picture to the board where students suggest. After all the pictures have been taped to the board, ask individuals **Qu'est-ce que tu voudrais manger comme entrée?** and so on.

For Individual Needs

Slower Pace Referring to the display on the board (see Presentation), ask several either-or questions about what one eats for meals or various courses. Write the word next to each picture and ask **Quand est-ce qu'on mange de la salade? Au petit déjeuner ou au déjeuner? Qu'est-ce qu'on mange comme entrée? Une tarte aux pommes ou du pâté?**

Language Note

Point out that in French, **l'entrée** is the appetizer, while in English, *entrée* refers to the main dish. The main course in French is **le plat principal.**

Culture Note

In a French restaurant, if you order **un café,** you will be served **un express:** very strong coffee in a small cup. For something not as strong, people drink coffee with steamed milk (**un café-crème**), served in a large cup. In the morning at home, people will drink coffee with hot milk (**un café au lait**) in a large bowl.

Health Links

• French meals are planned to facilitate digestion. The **entrée** wakes up the palate, and the **plat principal** is the main part of the meal. Next, the **salade,** made with an acidic dressing, help digest the meat. The **fromages** and **fruits** that follow contain enzymes that also aid digestion.

• Obtain a chart from a health teacher that illustrates healthy meals. Use this to practice the vocabulary.

Multicultural Link

Have students interview people from several ethnic or cultural backgrounds different from their own. Have them ask the people to describe a typical breakfast, lunch, or dinner in their culture. Have students work in groups to share and compile their findings.

Teaching Suggestion

20 Have students work in pairs. One student calls out the name of a town and a day of the week (**Vauclin, jeudi; Rivière-Salée, vendredi**). The other student reads the menu and then, based on personal preferences, decides whether he or she would like to eat at the **cantine** that day. (**Oui, parce que j'adore le poisson. Non, parce que je n'aime pas les sardines.**) Then, have students make a similar menu for a week at their school.

Presentation

Comment dit-on... ? Use the pictures students drew for the **Vocabulaire** on page 59 and create others to teach these expressions. Play the role of someone at a dinner table. Choose a volunteer and ask him or her to respond **Tenez** or **Voilà** after everything you ask. You might ask **Je pourrais avoir du sel, s'il te plaît?** Prompt the student to respond **Tenez** or **Voilà** and pass you the picture of that item. Take the picture and say **Merci.** Repeat with the other items. Then, distribute some pictures to students, asking **Tu pourrais me passer le beurre, s'il te plaît?** to elicit the appropriate response as they pass the items back to you. Begin a similar process to teach offering and accepting food. Write the responses for accepting or refusing food on the board before modeling the conversation and circulating in the classroom to offer "food" to students.

For Videodisc application, see *Videodisc Guide.*

---

20 Ecoute!

Read this list of school menus from Martinique. Then, listen to some students talking about lunch. Which town are the speakers from? Which day's menu they are talking about? Answers on p. 51C.

21 Une cantine quatre étoiles

If you were planning meals for a "Francophone Awareness Week" at your school, what would you serve? Write the menus for the week.

LUNDI Entrée :
Plat Principal :
Légume :
Fromage/Dessert :

CANTINES SCOLAIRES
Les menus de la semaine

VAUCLIN :
Lundi: fromage, lapin chasseur, haricots rosés, mandarines.
Mardi: melon, couscous au mouton, lait gélifié.
Jeudi: salade de laitue, poisson au four, haricots verts et carottes, yaourt.
Vendredi: salade de concombres, steak haché au four, chou vert sauce blanche, cocktail de fruits.

RIVIERE-SALEE :
Lundi: salade de concombres, haricots rosés, poisson grillé, glace.
Mardi: fromage, salade de haricots verts, poisson au four, fruit.
Jeudi: salade de carottes, riz blanc, colombo de cabri, glaces.
Vendredi: salade de tomates, sardines, pâté en pot, île au caramel.

COMMENT DIT-ON... ?

Asking for, offering, accepting, and refusing food; paying and responding to compliments

To ask for food:
Je pourrais avoir du pain, **s'il vous plaît (s'il te plaît)?**
  May I have some . . . , please?
Vous pourriez (Tu pourrais) me passer le sel?
  Would you pass me . . . ?

To offer food or drink:
Vous voulez (Tu veux) de la salade?

Encore du gâteau? *Some more . . . ?*

To pay a compliment about food:
C'est vraiment bon!
  This is really good!
C'était délicieux!
  That was delicious!

To respond:
Voilà. *Here it is.*

Tenez (Tiens). *Here you are.*

To accept:
Oui, je veux bien.

To refuse:
Merci, ça va. *Thank you, I've had enough.*
Je n'ai plus faim/soif. *I'm not hungry/thirsty anymore.*

To respond:
Ce n'est pas grand-chose.
  It's nothing special.
C'est gentil!

Teaching Suggestion

Have students present humorous skits about a family at the dinner table. Have them use most of the expressions in Comment dit-on...?

Language Note

Point out that **Tiens!** is also used as an interjection meaning *Hey!* as in **Tiens, voilà Marie!** *(Hey, there's Marie!)*

Culture Note

20 Ask students why there is no menu listed for **mercredi**. Remind them that in many parts of France, Martinique, and Guadeloupe, **collège** and **lycée** students go to school only in the morning on Wednesdays. Most students also go to school on Saturday mornings.

22 Ecoute!

Listen to the following conversations at the table. Is the first speaker asking for food, offering food, or paying a compliment?

Answers on p. 51C.

23 Les deux font la paire

Choisis la bonne réponse.

1. Tu veux encore du poulet? d
2. C'était délicieux! a
3. Je pourrais avoir du brie, s'il te plaît? e
4. Encore de l'eau? c
5. Vous pourriez me passer le pain? b

a. C'est gentil!
b. Tenez.
c. Non, je n'ai plus soif.
d. Merci, ça va.
e. Tiens.

24 La politesse

Accepte ou refuse ces plats. Si tu reprends quelque chose, fais aussi un compliment!

See answers below.

Encore des escargots?

Tu veux du pâté?

Tu veux de la mousse au chocolat?

Encore du poisson?

Tu veux du jus de carotte?

25 Un menu pour des amis

You've invited some friends for a French lunch. Decide what you're going to serve for each course and write out the menu.

26 Jeu de rôle

The guests you've invited in Activity 25 have arrived. Greet and welcome them, and make sure that they have everything they want. The guests should respond politely, compliment your cooking, and ask for seconds if they want them.

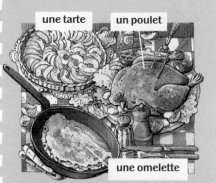

une tarte   un poulet

une omelette

de l'omelette

de la tarte   du poulet

Note de Grammaire

- When you're talking about a whole item, use the article **un** or **une** *(a, an)* before the noun.
- When you're talking about a portion of an item, use the partitive articles **du, de la,** or **de l'** *(some)* before the noun.

À la française

If you'd like to try eating a meal the French way . . .

- wish everyone **Bon appétit!** before you start to eat.
- keep your hands on or above the table.
- place your bread next to your plate.
- after cutting a piece of meat, keep your fork in your left hand.
- eat French fries, pizza, and fruit with a knife and fork, not with your hands.
- ask for something politely and never point.
- eat slowly and enjoy the conversation.

Possible answers

24 *Accept:* Oui, je veux bien.
   Refuse: Merci, ça va. Je n'ai plus faim/soif.
   Compliment: C'est vraiment bon! C'était délicieux!

Presentation

Note de grammaire Bring to class a cake, cookies, orange juice, and individual serving cartons of apple juice. Demonstrate the difference between **un gâteau** (showing the cake) and **du gâteau** (cutting the cake). Do the same for the juice. Count the cookies (**un biscuit, deux biscuits...**). Then, tell them they may ask for some orange juice (**du jus d'orange**), an (individual serving of) apple juice (**un jus de pomme**), some cake (**du gâteau**), or a cookie (**un biscuit**). Have students raise their hands and ask politely for something to eat or drink. (**Je voudrais du gâteau, s'il vous plaît.**)

Portfolio

25 Written This activity is appropriate for students' written portfolios.

26 Oral This activity is appropriate for students' oral portfolios. For portfolio suggestions, see *Assessment Guide,* page 16.

Close

To close this **étape**, distribute to each student an index card on which you've written one expression from **Comment dit-on... ?** on page 64 (asking for or offering food, paying a compliment about food). Then, have students stand in two lines facing one another. Each student reads his or her card aloud and within ten seconds, the person opposite him or her should respond appropriately. At your signal, one line moves down one student, the person at the end of the line moves to the front, and each student has a new player facing him or her. Repeat the process and continue until the original players are facing one another again.

Assess

Quiz 3-2, *Chapter Teaching Resources, Book 1,* pp. 137–138

Assessment Items, Audiocassette 7A Audio CD 3

Performance Assessment

Assign Activity 26 to be written and performed as a humorous skit.

RENCONTRE CULTURELLE

Look at the illustrations below. What's going on in each situation?

Qu'en penses-tu?

1. When you're invited to eat at someone's house, do you or your parents bring a gift? If so, what kind of gift? What gifts are not appropriate?
2. What is considered good or bad manners where you live?
3. What conversation topics are socially acceptable? What topics are too personal? How is this different in France?

Savais-tu que... ?

A guest invited to dinner in a French home is expected to bring a gift. Candy or flowers are always acceptable. However, you should never offer chrysanthemums; they're associated with death and mourning because they bloom around November 1, All Saints Day **(la Toussaint)**. Food or drink items other than candy are best avoided, unless you know the hosts very well. What you choose might not fit with what the host or hostess has planned to serve. Guests aren't expected to arrive exactly on time, and dinner won't be served immediately. A guest who isn't a family member shouldn't enter other areas of the house uninvited.

In polite conversation, certain topics are considered taboo. Asking about someone's profession is almost as rude as asking about the person's salary. Of course, asking an adult's age is considered rude. While politics is a popular conversation topic in France, you shouldn't directly ask what political party someone belongs to. It's best to ask people what they think about a certain event or situation. They will probably be glad to give their personal opinion.

 Culture Note

One traditional meal that the French often celebrate with friends is New Year's Eve dinner, which is planned to end at midnight when friends welcome in the new year together. The meal might begin at nine o'clock in the evening with an elaborate spread of appetizers, including oysters **(des huîtres)**, liver pâté **(du fois gras)**, and smoked salmon **(du saumon fumé)**. The meat served for the main course is usually turkey **(de la dinde)**, goose **(de l'oie)**, or duck **(du canard)**. A similar meal is eaten for Christmas dinner, but a special Yule log cake **(une bûche de Noël)** is prepared for dessert.

TROISIEME ETAPE

Asking for and giving advice; extending good wishes

Salut,
Juste un petit mot pour te demander de venir manger à la maison samedi soir. J'ai invité Jérôme et Béatrice aussi! On va faire une fondue. Ça te dit? Viens vers les sept heures. Tu n'es pas obligé d'apporter quelque chose, mais si tu y tiens, amène un dessert ou quelque chose à boire.
A bientôt!

Sylvie

On fait une petite fête pour l'anniversaire de Gilles dimanche après-midi au parc de la Victoire. Ça va être une surprise, alors surtout ne lui dis rien! On s'occupe du gâteau et des bougies. J'espère que tu vas pouvoir venir. Plus on est de fous, plus on rit. A plus tard.

Jean-Pierre
Céline

1. un cadeau
2. une fête pour l'anniversaire de Gilles
3. dimanche après-midi
4. du gâteau
5. au parc de la Victoire
6. avec Céline et Jean-Pierre

1. un dessert ou une boisson 2. un dîner 3. samedi soir à sept heures

27 Tu es invité(e)
4. une fondue 5. chez Sylvie
6. avec Jérôme, Béatrice et Sylvie

Quelles sont les informations données dans chaque invitation?

1 Qu'est-ce qu'on apporte?
2 Quoi?
3 Quand?
5 Où?
6 Avec qui?
4 Qu'est-ce qu'on va manger?

NOTE CULTURELLE

In France, a meal is often a way to celebrate friendship or a special occasion. The New Year's dinner is usually spent with friends, while birthday and Christmas dinners are traditionally family celebrations when people exchange gifts and cards. Young people often receive a small gift on their saint's day as well.

RESOURCES FOR TROISIEME ETAPE

Textbook Audiocassette 2A/Audio CD 3
Practice and Activity Book, pp. 32–34
Videodisc Guide
 Videodisc Program, Videodisc 2A

Chapter Teaching Resources, Book 1
• Communicative Activity 3-2, pp. 117–118
• Teaching Transparency Master 3-3, pp. 121, 122
  Teaching Transparency 3-3
• Additional Listening Activities 3-5, 3-6, p. 125
  Audiocassette 9A/Audio CD 3
• Realia 3-2, pp. 128, 129
• Situation Cards 3-3, pp. 130–131
• Student Response Forms, pp. 132–134
• Quiz 3-3, pp. 139–140
  Audiocassette 7A/Audio CD 3

Jump Start!

Write the following words on the board or on a transparency: **fromage, salade, entrée, fruits,** and **plat principal.** Have students write the courses in the proper order and add an appropriate food item for each one.

MOTIVATE

Ask students these questions:
1. When you're invited to a party for someone, what must you consider? (choosing a gift or card and what to wear)
2. Do you ever ask advice about what gift to choose or what to wear?
3. What kind of card do you prefer to give — serious or humorous?

TEACH

Teaching Suggestions

• Before students read the letters, pretend you have just received an invitation. Open an envelope that contains an invitation similar to the ones on this page and read it. Have students tell you who sent the invitation, where you are invited, and so on.

27 Have students work in pairs to answer the questions. Then, have them call out the answers and have another pair call out the questions they answer. For example, one pair might call out **un dessert** and another pair would say **Qu'est-ce qu'on apporte?**

For Individual Needs

27 Challenge Have students imagine they are giving a dinner or birthday party, and then write an invitation, using those in the activity as models.

Presentation

Comment dit-on... ? Write on a transparency several questions about what to give people as gifts. **(Tu as une idée de cadeau pour le président des Etats-Unis?)** Next to each question, give two choices: **a. Offre-lui un disque de rock. b. Offre-lui un livre sur l'histoire mondiale.** For each question, have students choose a response: **Offre-lui un livre sur l'histoire mondiale!** Finally, ask **Qu'est-ce que tu en penses? C'est une bonne idée, ou c'est banal?**

Grammaire Explain the use of **lui** and **leur** and give examples. Then, distribute one index card to each student. One half of the cards should contain a question. **(Qu'est-ce que tu offres à Paul?)** The other half should contain the corresponding answers. **(Je lui offre un livre.)** Without showing their cards, students circulate around the room to try to find the answer to their question or vice-versa.

For videodisc application, see *Videodisc Guide.*

◆ For Individual Needs

Slower Pace/Visual Learners On large cards, write questions containing indirect objects underlined in different colored ink. **(Tu offres un cadeau à tes parents?)** Show each card and have students respond, using an indirect object pronoun. **(Je leur offre un cadeau.)** Show the correct response you've written on the opposite side of the card, with the pronoun underlined.

Offre-lui des fleurs!

Bonne idée!

COMMENT DIT-ON... ?
Asking for and giving advice

To ask for advice:

Tu as une idée de cadeau pour Oncle Omar? *Have you got a gift idea for . . . ?*

Qu'est-ce que je pourrais offrir à mes parents? *What could I give to . . . ?*

To accept advice:

Bonne idée! *Good idea!*
C'est original. *That's unique.*
Tu as raison, elle adore la musique. *You're right . . .*
D'accord.
OK.

To give advice:

Offre-lui (-leur) des bonbons.
Give him/her (them). . .
Tu pourrais lui (leur) offrir un CD.
You could give him/her (them) . . .
Un livre, peut-être.
. . . maybe.

To reject advice:

C'est trop cher. *It's too expensive.*
C'est banal. *That's ordinary.*
Ce n'est pas son style.
That's not his/her style.
Il/Elle en a déjà un(e). *He/She already has one (of them).*

28 Ecoute!

Listen as some students ask for advice about gifts. Do they accept or reject the suggestions? Answers on p. 51D.

> *G*rammaire The indirect object pronouns **lui** and **leur**
>
> The pronouns **lui** *(to/for him, to/for her)* and **leur** *(to/for them)* replace a phrase that begins with **à** or **pour** followed by a person or persons. **Lui** and **leur** never refer to things.
>
> - Place **lui** or **leur** before the conjugated verb:
>   Tu **leur offres** un cadeau? Je **lui parle** souvent.
> - If there's an infinitive in the sentence, **lui** or **leur** is placed before it:
>   Tu pourrais **lui offrir** un bracelet. Je vais **leur acheter** des fleurs.
> - In a command, place **lui** or **leur** after the verb, connected to it with a hyphen:
>   **Offre-lui** des bonbons! **Achète-leur** un cadeau.

68 *soixante-huit*   CHAPITRE 3   Un repas à la française

Additional Practice

For additional listening and speaking practice, ask questions containing indirect objects. **(Tu parles souvent à tes copains?)** Challenge volunteers to respond, using an indirect object pronoun. **(Oui, je leur parle souvent.)** You might also ask questions containing infinitives **(Tu vas offrir des fleurs à ton professeur de français?)** and questions to elicit the imperative. **(Qu'est-ce que je pourrais offrir à ma tante?)**

29 Donne des conseils

Ton ami(e) ne sait pas quels cadeaux offrir à ces gens. Donne-lui des idées. *See answers below.*

1. Iman et Sylvie sont toujours à la dernière mode.
2. Catherine fait toujours des photos.
3. Vincent et Paul aiment bien manger.
4. Marc joue au foot tous les jours.
5. Il y a toujours des fleurs sur la table chez tante Marie.
6. Eric va étudier l'allemand à l'université.

un dictionnaire
un joli album de photos
des boucles d'oreilles
des chocolats
des baskets
un vase

Offre-lui...
Tu pourrais lui offrir...
Offre-leur...
Tu pourrais leur offrir...

VOCABULAIRE

Oh, là là, c'est l'anniversaire de maman. Il me faut des idées de cadeaux...

Des bonbons?
Une boîte de chocolats?

Des fleurs?

Un cadre?
Un vase?

Un foulard?
Un portefeuille?
Un sac à main?

Answers

29 1. Offre-leur des boucles d'oreilles.
2. Offre-lui un joli album de photos.
3. Offre-leur des chocolats.
4. Tu pourrais lui offrir des baskets.
5. Tu pourrais lui offrir un vase.
6. Offre-lui un dictionnaire.

🌐 **Culture Note**

Although department stores (**les grands magasins**) are popular in France, there are many small specialty shops, such as **la papeterie** *(a stationery or paper goods store)*, **la carterie** *(a postcard shop)*, **la parfumerie** *(a perfume store)*, **la bijouterie** *(a jewelry store)*, and **le disquaire** *(a CD/music store)*. You might give students some words (**parfum, bijou, carte**) and have them guess the shop's name.

Teaching Suggestion

29 Have students write two sentences describing their friends. They should write one sentence about one friend and another about two friends. Have students read their sentences and have others suggest gifts, using the pronouns **lui** and **leur**.

Building on Previous Skills

29 Ask students to recall the expressions they learned in Chapter 1 for giving advice and making suggestions, and to use them in the context of buying a gift. (**Tu peux lui offrir un CD. Pense à lui acheter un livre.**)

Presentation

Vocabulaire Use pictures or objects to teach the words, having students repeat after you. Then, write the names of the stores on the board. Show an item (**des bonbons**) and ask **Qu'est-ce que c'est?** When students have answered, tell them where the item can be bought. (**On achète des bonbons à la confiserie.**) Then, tape the picture of that item to the board under the appropriate shop. Next, ask questions such as **Qu'est-ce qu'on achète à la confiserie?** Finally, have students ask questions and tape the items to the board.

Building on Previous Skills

Re-enter the expressions used to ask someone to do something for you. (**Tu peux aller... ? Tu me rapportes... ?**) Tell students you are going to a certain store. (**Je vais à la maroquinerie.**) Have them ask you to buy something for them. (**Tu me rapportes un portefeuille?**)

30 Slower Pace Before playing the recording, call out the names of these items and have students jot down the letters of the appropriate illustrations.

31 Slower Pace You might write descriptions of several people and distribute them to groups to use in their conversations.

32 Visual/Auditory Learners For additional writing, speaking, and listening practice, have students write sentences telling what they are going to buy for six to eight people and for which occasions. **(Je vais acheter un portefeuille pour Papa pour la fête des Pères.)** Then, on a separate sheet of paper, have students label three columns: **cadeau, pour qui,** and **la fête.** Have them sketch the gifts they are going to buy in the first column, scramble the order and list the names of the people for whom they are going to buy gifts in the second column, and scramble the order and list the occasions they have chosen in the third column. Then, have them pass the sheet of paper to a partner. The partner will draw lines from the gifts to the appropriate names and occasions as the student reads his or her sentences.

🌐 Culture Note

In French department stores browsing is appropriate. In smaller specialty shops, however, it's better to have a specific idea in mind of what you want before you enter the store. In clothing boutiques, you should only try something on if you're very interested. Small boutiques have limited space, so merchants appreciate serious customers.

30 Ecoute!

Qu'est-ce que chaque personne offre à Mme Lepic pour son anniversaire?
1. e 2. d 3. a 4. b

a.　　　　b.　　　　c.　　　　d.　　　　e.

31 Cadeau d'anniversaire

Mardi prochain, c'est l'anniversaire de ton meilleur ami (ta meilleure amie). Fais une description de ton ami(e), puis demande des conseils à tes camarades.

— Patrick aime la musique et le tennis. Qu'est-ce que je pourrais lui offrir?
— Offre-lui des baskets!
— Non, c'est trop cher.
— Tu pourrais lui offrir...

32 Au grand magasin

You and a friend are shopping at a department store, and you each have 500 francs to spend. Make a list of four people to shop for. Then, suggest some gifts for the people on your lists.

🌐 Culture Note

32 In their dialogues, students may wish to include special occasions, other than birthdays, for which they are buying gifts, such as Kwanzaa or Hanukkah. Kwanzaa is a week-long celebration and reaffirmation of the African-American cultural heritage, beginning on December 26. Created in 1966 by Dr. Maulana Karenga, a leading Black movement theorist, Kwanzaa is based on the harvest festivals of African tribes, and in Swahili means "first fruits of the harvest." Hanukkah, celebrated also in December, commemorates the second century B.C. victory of a small group of Jews against the armed forces of King Antioch. This group of Jews succeeded in the rededication of a Jewish temple in Jerusalem, which had been defiled by the King's army.

COMMENT DIT-ON... ?
Extending good wishes

Bonne fête! *Happy holiday! (Happy saint's day!)*
Joyeux (Bon) anniversaire! *Happy birthday!*
Bonne fête de Hanoukka! *Happy Hanukkah!*
Joyeux Noël! *Merry Christmas!*
Bonne année! *Happy New Year!*
Meilleurs vœux! *Best wishes!*
Félicitations! *Congratulations!*
Bon voyage! *Have a good trip! (by plane, ship)*
Bonne route! *Have a good trip! (by car)*
Bon rétablissement! *Get well soon!*

33 Qu'est-ce que tu dis? See answers below.

1. C'est l'anniversaire de ton ami(e).
2. C'est le vingt-cinq décembre.
3. Ton professeur est malade.
4. On allume la menora.
5. C'est la fête des Pères.
6. C'est le premier janvier.
7. Ton ami(e) part pour la Côte d'Ivoire.
8. C'est le jour du mariage de ta cousine.
9. Tes parents vont faire du camping.
10. Ta mère a une promotion.

34 Les cartes de vœux

Fais une carte de vœux *(greeting card)* humoristique ou sérieuse pour quelqu'un.

35 Mon journal

Choose a couple of special occasions, such as Mother's Day **(la fête des Mères)**, someone's birthday, Kwanzaa, Hanukkah, or Christmas, and write about what you eat, what gifts you give, and what activities you do on that occasion.

Presentation

Comment dit-on... ? Say these expressions and have students repeat after you as they read along in their book. Then, have students illustrate each expression on a separate piece of paper. Display some of their illustrations on the bulletin board under headings you've prepared.

Teaching Suggestion

Students might hold up the dates of certain holidays **(25 décembre)** or illustrations representing them (a birthday cake), to which a partner would respond with the appropriate expression. **(Joyeux Noël! Bon anniversaire!)**

For Individual Needs

33 Auditory/Tactile Learners For listening practice, call out these or other sentences in random order. **(Ton père part pour la France.)** Have students hold up an appropriate illustration from among those they made (see Presentation above) and call out the appropriate expression. **(Bon voyage!)**

Mon journal

35 For an additional journal entry suggestion for Chapter 3, see *Practice and Activity Book,* page 147.

CLOSE

Cooperative Learning

Form groups of four. Within each group, assign a leader, a secretary, a proofreader, and a spokesperson. Using Activity 35, have each group discuss one special occasion and make a report to the class.

ASSESS

Quiz 3-3, *Chapter Teaching Resources, Book 1,* pp. 139–140

Assessment Items, Audiocassette 7A
Audio CD 3

Performance Assessment

Have students bring in priced "gift" items and homemade greeting cards. As students shop in pairs for a gift and card for a friend's birthday, they should ask for and give advice about a gift, accept or refuse advice, mention two items and their prices, and discuss one greeting card.

Answers

33 1. Joyeux anniversaire!   2. Joyeux Noël!   3. Bon rétablissement! 4. Bonne fête de Hanoukka! 5. Bonne fête, papa! 6. Bonne année! 7. Bon voyage! 8. Meilleurs vœux! 9. Bonne route! 10. Félicitations!

LISONS!

READING STRATEGY

Guessing meaning from visual clues and context

Teacher Note

For an additional reading, see *Practice and Activity Book,* page 35.

PREREADING
Activities A–C

Motivating Activity

Have students suggest comics in which children are featured. Then, ask if they are familiar with the American comic strip *Calvin and Hobbes.* Ask them if they know Calvin's age (six years old) and what the comic strip is about. (Calvin is a mischievous boy who wants to be independent, but his parents constantly tell him what to do.) Ask them if they can relate to Calvin even though he is only six years old, and why.

Thinking Critically

Comparing and Contrasting
Have students look at the drawings and ask what similarities they see between this character and Calvin of *Calvin and Hobbes.* (The boy seems to be the same age as Calvin.) Have them skim the captions and look at the pictures. Ask them how they think the text might be similar to *Calvin and Hobbes.* (Adults are telling this boy what to do or what not to do.)

Drawing Inferences Ask students whose age the title **Le bel âge** refers to. Ask them if they think that French children always appreciate suggestions from adults, judging from this cartoon.

When you were younger, did adults always tell you what to do? What did they say?

DE BONS CONSEILS

Become a great guesser! Learn to use visual clues and context to help you guess the meaning of unfamiliar vocabulary. You should try to anticipate the meaning of words, and think about how they fit into the situation you're reading about.

See answers below.

A. Take a moment to preview the pictures and captions. What type of reading is this? Now, skim through the reading. At the beginning, who is saying **Ça commence le matin vers 8 heures... ?** Who is speaking in the other pictures?

B. Before you read the captions, list five "don'ts" that adults usually say to children. After you read the captions, check your list to see how many of your "don'ts" were mentioned.

C. With a partner, cover the captions and look at the drawings in order. What do you think the boy is thinking or doing in each picture?

D. Read the captions to the first row of pictures. Why does the speaker always use the **tu** form of the verb?   An adult is speaking to a child.

Answers
A cartoon; little boy; parents/adults

... ne joue pas avec le pain !

.. finis ta soupe !

... finis ta viande !

... finis tes pâtes !

... mange proprement !

... ne mets pas les coudes sur la table !

...tiens-toi normalement !

... regarde moi, en face !

... ne regarde pas tes pieds !

... arrête ce vacarme !

... pourquoi es-tu si tranquille ?

... dis ; il te plaît" !

... dis "Merci" !

... mieux que ça !

... ne pleure pas !

...ne souris pas bêtement !

... le soir, moi, ...le bel âge ... j'en ai ras le bol !

E. Scan the cartoon and find the French for: See answers below.
   1. Don't cry!
   2. Stop that noise!
   3. Sit up straight!
   4. Don't drag your feet!

F. Have a partner cover up the captions in the first row of pictures on pages 72 and 73. Then, ask your partner to point out the pictures that match these commands as you read them.
   1. Tiens-toi droit!
   2. Mange proprement!
   3. Finis ta soupe!
   4. Réponds-moi!

   How did your partner do? Now switch roles. You cover up the captions in the second row on both pages. Try to find the pictures as your partner reads these commands.
   1. Regarde où tu marches!
   2. Ne regarde pas tes pieds!
   3. Parle intelligiblement!
   4. Regarde-moi en face!

G. Go back to part B where you wrote what adults always told you not to do. Draw a stick figure for each command and write a caption in French.

H. Can you think of five commands or orders you would like to give adults? Be sure to use the **vous** form. Compare your ideas with a partner's and illustrate the five best.

I. Why is there a question mark after **le bel âge** in the boy's speech bubble? How does he feel about **le bel âge**? How did you? What would you consider **le bel âge**? See answers below.

soixante-treize 73

Answers

E 1. Ne pleure pas!
 2. Arrête ce vacarme!
 3. Tiens-toi normalement!
 4. Ne traîne pas les pieds!

I He's questioning whether his age is a good age; He's tired of it; Answers will vary.

READING
Activities D–F

Language Note

You might want to review the use of the imperative. Remind students how to form affirmative and negative commands, noting that **me** and **te** in negative commands become **moi** and **toi** in affirmative commands, attached to the verb with a hyphen. (**Réponds-moi! Ne me réponds pas!**) You may also need to remind students that with regular -**er** verbs, the **s** of the **tu** form is dropped in commands. (**Lève-toi! Ne te lève pas!**)

TPR Have students work in pairs. One student reads a caption and the other acts it out.

Thinking Critically

Comparing and Contrasting
Ask students which captions resemble what adults tell children in English.

POSTREADING
Activities G–I

For Individual Needs

H. Slower Pace Write some of the captions from the reading on the board or on a transparency and write the same captions next to them using the **vous** form.

Group Work

H. Form groups of three and have each group choose five commands. Then, have them present the commands to the class, with one student reading them and the other two acting them out.

The **Mise en Pratique** reviews and integrates all four skills and culture in preparation for the Chapter Test.

 For Individual Needs

Challenge Ask students to write a recipe in French for their favorite sandwich or some other easily-prepared dish.

(TPR) Read the recipes, modeling each step with gestures. Have students mimic your gestures as they repeat the instructions. Choose several students to perform the gestures as you call out various steps.

Teaching Suggestion

Have individuals randomly choose some steps of a recipe to mime, while others guess what they are doing. **(Tu mélanges. Tu mets le plat au four.)** Finally, call for volunteers to try to recall a recipe from memory, miming each step as they call them out.

Language Notes

- You may wish to point out the use of the infinitive in written instructions, such as recipes, directions on product packages, and assembly instructions.
- Students might want to know the following vocabulary from the recipes: **en rondelle** *(in round slices);* **haché fin** *(finely chopped);* **des gousses d'ail écrasées** *(crushed cloves of garlic);* **râpé** *(grated);* **remuer** *(to stir);* **saupoudrer** *(sprinkle);* **dorer** *(to brown);* **de la cannelle** *(cinnamon);* **des bleuets** (the Canadian word for *blueberries);* **des grains de poivre concassés** *(ground pepper);* **aplatir** *(to flatten);* **saler** *(to salt);* **de la crème fraîche** *(heavy cream).*

MISE EN PRATIQUE

GRATIN DE BANANES JAUNES *Martinique*

INGRÉDIENTS
- 1 banane jaune [par personne] coupée en rondelles
- 1 oignon haché fin
- 2 gousses d'ail écrasées
- 50 grammes de beurre
- 3 cuillerées à soupe de farine
- 3/4 de litre de lait
- 110 grammes de fromage râpé
- sel et poivre

PRÉPARATION
1. Faire revenir l'oignon et l'ail dans le beurre, jusqu'à la couleur blonde. Ajouter un peu de sel et poivre.
2. En remuant constamment, rajouter la farine.
3. Hors du feu, ajouter le lait petit à petit.
4. Remettre sur le feu et amener à ébullition.
5. Retirer du feu et mettre la moitié du fromage.
6. Beurrer un plat qui va au four.
7. Alterner des couches de sauce et bananes, terminant avec la sauce.
8. Saupoudrer avec le reste du fromage.
9. Mettre au four à 425 degrés Fahrenheit et laisser dorer.

Servir chaud avec toutes viandes.

Pouding au pain et aux bleuets
Canada

INGRÉDIENTS
- 4 tasses de cubes de pain
- 1 cuillerée à thé de cannelle
- 1/4 tasse de sucre granulé
- 3/4 tasse de beurre fondu
- 2 tasses de bleuets frais
- 1/2 tasse de sucre brun

PRÉPARATION
1. Chauffer le four à 350 degrés Fahrenheit.
2. Placer les cubes dans un grand bol.
3. Ajouter la cannelle et le sucre granulé.
4. Verser le beurre fondu et bien mêler.
5. Mélanger les bleuets et le sucre brun.
6. Dans un plat qui va au four, alterner des rangs de bleuets et pain.
7. Faire cuire au four pendant 30 minutes.

Servir chaud.

STEAK AU POIVRE — France

Ingrédients — par personne
- 1 steak
- 1/2 cuillerée à soupe de grains de poivre concassés
- 1/2 cuillerée à soupe de beurre
- 1/2 cuillerée à soupe d'huile
- 2 cuillerées à soupe de bouillon de bœuf
- 1/4 tasse de crème fraîche

Préparation
1. Répartir le poivre sur le steak.
2. Aplatir avec la main.
3. Saler le steak.
4. Faire cuire dans l'huile et le beurre.
5. Sortir le steak et réserver au chaud.
6. Dans la poêle outer le bouillon de bœuf et la crème fraîche.
7. Mélanger la sauce et ajouter un peu de sel.

Servir chaud, la sauce sur le steak.

74 *soixante-quatorze*   CHAPITRE 3   Un repas à la française

Math Link

Have students convert the metric measurements in the Martinique recipe to American equivalents, using the following approximations:

- 1 tablespoon = 15 milliliters
- 1 ounce = 30 grams
- 1 quart = 1 liter
- 1 pound = 450 grams

Have students convert the measurements in the recipes from Canada and France to their metric equivalents, using these approximations:

- 1 teaspoon = 5 milliliters
- 1 tablespoon = 15 milliliters
- 1 cup = 250 milliliters

1 Read the recipes and answer these questions.

1. In what order is the following information given?
   a. serving instructions 3
   b. ingredients 1
   c. cooking instructions 2

2. Which recipe(s) would you choose to make if . . .
   See answers below.
   a. you loved fruit?
   b. you were tired of the usual rice and potatoes?
   c. you had a lot of leftover bread?
   d. you were going to a potluck dinner and had to bring a vegetable dish?
   e. you liked spicy food?

2 Listen to the following conversations and decide which recipe on page 74 each person is going to make. Answers on p. 51D.

3 The French Club is planning a **soirée francophone.** In groups of four, choose a recipe that you'd like to make. Decide what ingredients you'll need and make a shopping list. If you were shopping in France, which specialty stores would you have to visit? One person can buy the ingredients, while the others play the roles of salespeople at the various stores.

4 At the **soirée,** you want to present your club sponsor with a gift. With a partner, make suggestions about what you might give. Decide on an appropriate gift.

5 Make a program for your francophone banquet. Be sure to include a menu with the courses of the banquet and a list of the entertainment you'll provide. You might even do some research on the dishes you'll be serving and put the information in your program.

6

JEU DE ROLE

Create a humorous skit for entertainment at the **soirée francophone.** Choose one of these scenarios or invent your own.
—A guest at a home in France does not act appropriately!
—Someone who knows little about French dining customs eats a meal in an elegant French restaurant.
—Two people meet for the first time, and one asks questions that shock the other.

MISE EN PRATIQUE   *soixante-quinze* **75**

Answers

1 2. a. gratin de bananes jaunes, pouding au pain et aux bleuets
   b. gratin de bananes jaunes
   c. pouding au pain et aux bleuets
   d. gratin de bananes jaunes
   e. steak au poivre

📁 **Portfolio**

6 Written/Oral Have students include the script of this skit in their written portfolios, or have them make an audio recording of their performance to be included in their oral portfolios. For portfolio information, see *Assessment Guide,* pages 2–13.

Teaching Suggestion

1 You might have students work in groups to answer these questions. Have reporters from each group present their findings and compare them.

Group Work

3 Have the groups demonstrate making their recipe. Have them bring ingredients and explain the process as they demonstrate. Have them bring enough of the food prepared in advance so that each student can taste the final product. If a group makes something that requires cooking or baking, have them demonstrate up to that point, but they should also bring the prepared food ready to share.

 **Video Wrap-Up**

• *VIDEO PROGRAM*
• *EXPANDED VIDEO PROGRAM,* Videocassette 1, 35:32–48:45
• *VIDEODISC PROGRAM,* Videodisc 2A

At this time, you might want to use the video resources for additional review and enrichment. See *Video Guide* or *Videodisc Guide* for suggestions regarding the following:
• **Un repas à la française** (Dramatic episode)
• **Panorama Culturel** (Interviews)
• **Vidéoclips** (Authentic footage)

This page is intended to help students prepare for the test. It is a brief checklist of the major points covered in the chapter. The students should be reminded that this is only a checklist and does not necessarily include everything that will appear on the test.

Teaching Suggestion

Type all of the answers to the questions in **Que sais-je?** in random order and number them according to their new order. Before distributing the copies, have students work in groups of three, reading the questions and deciding how to answer them. Next, distribute copies of the answers you've typed and have the groups match them to the questions. Finally, choose one student to come to the front of the class. Provide him or her with the answer key. Have the student call on individuals for answers and praise correct answers by saying **Oui, très bien! Excellent! Superbe! Magnifique! Tu as raison! C'est ça!**

QUE SAIS-JE?

Can you use what you've learned in this chapter?

Can you make purchases? p. 58

1 In France, how would you . . .

1. ask how much the shrimp costs? Combien coûtent les crevettes?
2. ask for two kilograms (of them)? Je vais en prendre deux kilos.
3. ask how much all your purchases cost? Ça fait combien?

2 Where would you go to buy . . . See answers below.

1. a pastry? 3. snails? 5. chicken?
2. eggs? 4. ham? 6. a croissant?

Can you ask for, offer, accept, and refuse food? p. 64

3 What would you expect to have for a typical French breakfast, lunch, and dinner? See answers below.

4 How would you . . . See answers below.

1. ask for more of your favorite dessert?
2. ask someone to pass your favorite main dish?
3. offer someone something to drink?

5 How would you respond if you were offered a second helping?

1. You'd like some more. 2. You just couldn't eat any more.
   Oui, je veux bien. Merci, je n'ai plus faim.

Can you pay and respond to compliments? p. 64

6 What would you say to compliment the meal you've just eaten? How would you respond to a compliment? See answers below.

Can you ask for and give advice? p. 68

7 How would you ask for advice about what to give someone for his or her birthday? Qu'est-ce que je pourrais offrir à... pour son anniversaire?

8 How would you advise your friend to give his or her grandmother these gifts? See answers below.

1. 2. 3.

9 At what stores would you buy the gifts in number 8?
1. à la boutique de cadeaux 2. à la maroquinerie 3. à la maroquinerie

10 How would you respond to a gift idea if . . . Possible answers:

1. you didn't like the idea? C'est banal. Ce n'est pas son style. Il/Elle en a déjà un(e).
2. you did like the idea? Bonne idée! C'est original. Tu as raison... ; D'accord.

Can you extend good wishes? p. 71

11 What would you say to someone who is . . . See answers below.

1. leaving by car on vacation?
2. having a birthday party?
3. not feeling well?

76 *soixante-seize*

CHAPITRE 3 Un repas à la française

Answers
2 1. à la pâtisserie
 2. à la crémerie
 3. à la poissonnerie
 4. à la charcuterie
 5. à la boucherie
 6. à la boulangerie
3 *Possible answers*
 Breakfast: croissants, tartines, café
 Lunch: entrée, plat principal, fromage, dessert
 Dinner: same as lunch

4 *Possible answers*
 1. Je pourrais avoir encore de la glace?
 2. Tu pourrais me passer le poulet?
 3. Tu veux de l'eau?
6 *Possible answers*
 C'était délicieux; C'est gentil.
8 1. Offre-lui un cadre.
 2. Tu pourrais lui offrir un sac.
 3. Tu peux lui offrir un foulard.
11 1. Bonne route!
 2. Joyeux (Bon) anniversaire!
 3. Bon rétablissement!

PREMIERE ETAPE

Making purchases

C'est combien, s'il vous plaît?
How much is it, please?
Combien coûte(nt)... ?   *How much is (are) . . . ?*
Combien en voulez-vous?   *How many/much do you want?*
Je voudrais une livre (un kilo) de...
I'd like a pound (kilo) of . . .
Je vais (en) prendre...   *I'll take . . . (of them).*
Ça fait combien?   *How much does that make?*

Stores and products

la boucherie   *butcher shop*
la boulangerie   *bakery*
la charcuterie   *delicatessen*
la crémerie   *dairy*
la pâtisserie   *pastry shop*
la poissonnerie   *fish shop*
la baguette   *long loaf of bread*
le beurre   *butter*
le bifteck   *steak*
les crevettes (f.)   *shrimp*
les croissants (m.)   *croissants*
les escargots (m.)   *snails*
le fromage   *cheese*
les fruits de mer (m.)   *seafood*
les huîtres (f.)   *oysters*

le lait   *milk*
le jambon   *ham*
le mille-feuille   *layered pastry*
les œufs (m.)   *eggs*
le pain au chocolat   *croissant with a chocolate filling*
le pâté   *paté*
le poisson   *fish*
le poulet   *chicken*
la religieuse   *cream puff pastry*
le rôti de bœuf   *roast beef*
le saucisson   *salami*
la tarte aux pommes   *apple tart*
la viande   *meat*
la volaille   *poultry*

DEUXIEME ETAPE

Asking for, offering, accepting, and refusing food

Je pourrais avoir... s'il vous plaît?
May I have some . . . please?
Vous pourriez (Tu pourrais) me passer...   *Would you pass . . . ?*
Vous voulez (Tu veux)... ?   *Do you want . . . please?*
Encore... ?   *Some more . . . ?*
Voilà.   *Here it is.*
Tenez (Tiens).   *Here you are.*

Oui, je veux bien.   *Yes, I would.*
Merci, ça va.   *No thank you, I've had enough.*
Je n'ai plus faim/soif.   *I'm not hungry/thirsty any more.*

Paying and responding to compliments

C'est vraiment bon!   *This is really good!*
C'était délicieux!   *That was delicious!*

Ce n'est pas grand-chose.   *It's nothing special.*
C'est gentil!   *That's nice of you!*

Meal vocabulary

une tartine   *bread, butter, jam*
le café au lait   *coffee with milk*
des céréales (f.)   *cereal*
le chocolat chaud   *hot chocolate*
l'entrée (f.)   *first course*
le plat principal   *main course*
le dessert   *dessert*

TROISIEME ETAPE

Asking for and giving advice

Tu as une idée de cadeau pour... ?
Have you got a gift idea for . . . ?
Qu'est-ce que je pourrais offrir à... ?   *What could I give to . . . ?*
Offre-lui (-leur)...   *Give him/her (them) . . .*
Tu pourrais lui (leur) offrir...   *You could give him/her (them) . . .*
..., peut-être   *. . . , maybe*
Bonne idée!   *Good idea!*
C'est original.   *That's unique.*
Tu as raison...   *You're right . . .*
D'accord.   *OK.*
C'est trop cher.   *It's too expensive.*
C'est banal.   *That's ordinary.*

Ce n'est pas son style.   *That's not his/her style.*
Il/Elle en a déjà un(e).   *He/She already has one (of them).*

Gifts and shops

les bonbons (m.)   *candies*
la boîte de chocolats   *box of chocolates*
le cadre   *photo frame*
les fleurs (f.)   *flowers*
le foulard   *scarf*
le portefeuille   *wallet*
le sac à main   *purse*
le vase   *vase*
la boutique de cadeaux   *gift shop*
la confiserie   *candy shop*
le fleuriste   *florist's shop*

la maroquinerie   *leather shop*

Extending good wishes

Bonne fête!   *Happy holiday! (Happy saint's day!)*
Joyeux (Bon) anniversaire!   *Happy birthday!*
Bonne fête de Hanoukka!   *Happy Hanukkah!*
Joyeux Noël!   *Merry Christmas!*
Bonne année!   *Happy New Year!*
Meilleurs vœux!   *Best wishes!*
Félicitations!   *Congratulations!*
Bon voyage!   *Have a good trip! (by plane, ship)*
Bonne route!   *Have a good trip! (by car)*
Bon rétablissement!   *Get well soon!*

Game

DEVINE!   Form teams of three or four. Each team must compose a list of clues for words and expressions in the **Vocabulaire**. (C'est là qu'on achète des escargots (à la poissonnerie). On le dit le premier janvier (Bonne année!). On y met une photo (un cadre).) Have teams take turns reading their clues. Each team should appoint a spokesperson to call out the answer. Points are given for guessing a word or expression correctly. You may decide to award the other teams one point each if a clue is incorrect or inappropriate.

Game

SOUVIENS-TOI!   Gather objects to represent as many of the vocabulary items as possible. Place twenty of them on a tray and cover the tray with a towel. Form teams of five. Uncover and show the tray to one team for one minute and then cover the tray again. Have the students in the team write down as many of the objects as they can remember. Repeat the process for each team. Next, project a list of the items on the tray on the overhead projector. The team whose list most closely matches yours wins.

CHAPTER 3 ASSESSMENT

CHAPTER TEST

- *Chapter Teaching Resources, Book 1*, pp. 141–146
- *Assessment Guide*, Speaking Test, p. 29
- *Assessment Items, Audiocassette 7A Audio CD 3*

TEST GENERATOR, CHAPTER 3

ALTERNATIVE ASSESSMENT

Performance Assessment

You might want to use Activity 3 (p. 75) as a cumulative performance assessment activity.

Portfolio Assessment

- **Written:** Activity 25, *Pupil's Edition*, p. 65
  Assessment Guide, p. 16
- **Oral:** Activity 26, *Pupil's Edition*, p. 65
  Assessment Guide, p. 16

EXPANDED VIDEO
PROGRAM,
Videocassette 2
01:23–04:06

OR *VIDEODISC PROGRAM,*
Videodisc 2B

Search 1, Play To 4865

Motivating Activity

Have students look at the photos on pages 78–81 and tell what these photos suggest to them about the climate, natural resources, food, occupations, and leisure activities in Martinique. Ask students if they've ever visited a country or part of the United States that has a tropical climate. If so, ask them to describe the climate, the vegetation, and the animals that live there.

Background Information

Madinina, the Carib Indian name of **la Martinique,** means *island of flowers.* The colorful flowers and plants contribute to the charm of the island. A tropical island of steep hills, volcanoes, palm trees, and beautiful beaches, Martinique has an average temperature of 77°F. People of a variety of racial and ethnic backgrounds live in Martinique: the **Créoles,** the largest ethnic group on the island, who are of mixed African and European descent; the **Békés,** or **Blancs-Pays,** who are white inhabitants born in Martinique; and the **Blancs-France,** or white residents from France. There are also a number of Asian and Indian immigrants.

CHAPITRE 4

Allez, viens à la Martinique!

La plage des Salines et le Rocher du Diamant

Culture Notes

• **La plage des Salines,** located at the southernmost tip of Martinique, is lined with coconut palms and is considered Martinique's best beach. It is located near a large salt pond and a petrified forest. The beach consists of approximately one and a half miles of white sand and calm waters.

• **Le Rocher du Diamant,** located off the southwest shore of the island opposite the fishing village of **le Diamant,** was commandeered in 1804 by the British navy, who fortified it with cannons as they fought for possession of Martinique. After nearly 17 months of British occupation, the French commander Villeneuve finally recaptured the 575-foot rock in June of 1805.

La Martinique

Population : 345.000

Points d'intérêt : la Pagerie, le Rocher du Diamant, la plage des Salines, le musée Gauguin du Carbet, la bibliothèque Schœlcher

Parcs et jardins : le jardin de Balata, la Savane, les Ombrages

Martiniquais célèbres : Aimé Césaire, Joséphine de Beauharnais, Euzhan Palcy

Ressources et industries : bananes, ananas, canne à sucre

Spécialités : boudin créole, acras de morue, crabes farcis, colombo de mouton

Festivals : la semaine internationale de la voile, le Festival de Sainte-Marie, Mai de Saint-Pierre

soixante dix-neuf 79

Using the Almanac and Map

Terms in the Almanac

- **La Pagerie** was the family estate of Napoléon Bonaparte's first wife Joséphine, who was born there in 1763.
- The **musée Gauguin du Carbet** contains some of painter Paul Gauguin's original works and memorabilia related to his stay in Martinique in 1887. Christopher Columbus landed in **le Carbet** in 1502, and d'Esnambuc arrived there in 1635 with the first French settlers.
- **La bibliothèque Schœlcher** is a library named after Victor Schœlcher, who worked in the nineteenth century to abolish slavery in Martinique.
- **La Savane,** a beautiful park in Fort-de-France, was once a battlefield where the French fought the English and the Dutch in the seventeenth century for possession of Martinique.
- **Aimé Césaire** is a poet and playwright who co-founded the literary movement called **Négritude,** which sought to restore the cultural identity of black Africans. His works include the poem *Cahier d'un retour au pays natal* (1939) and the play *La tragédie du roi Christophe* (1963).
- **Joséphine de Beauharnais** (1763–1814) was born in **la Pagerie.** She married Napoléon Bonaparte in 1796. When she was unable to provide him with the heir he so desperately wanted, Napoléon divorced her in 1809.

Some culinary specialties of Martinique include:
- **boudin créole:** a spicy sausage
- **acras de morue:** cod fritters
- **crabes farcis:** stuffed crab
- **colombo de mouton:** curried lamb stew with rice.

Art Link

Paul Gauguin (1848-1903) was a painter, sculptor, and printmaker, who has greatly influenced twentieth-century art. During his voyage to Martinique in 1887, he was influenced by the brilliant colors of the tropics. His paintings are generally simple with many bright colors that he uses for expressive and symbolic purposes.

Geography Link

Ask students to name some agricultural products of Martinique. Then, ask them if they know where in the United States these same products are grown. (They might mention sugar cane in Louisiana and pineapples in Hawaii.) Ask students to name other foods native to the Americas (corn and popcorn, cranberries, blueberries, turkeys, and various types of squash).

LOCATION OPENER
CHAPTER
4

Using the Photo Essay

① Sugar cane (**canne à sucre**) was introduced to the West Indies during the 1400s. Slaves were later brought to Martinique from Africa to work on the sugar plantations. Pineapples were one of the first products from the New World presented at court by Spanish explorers in the sixteenth century. The word **ananas** is derived from the Carib word for fruit. Bananas (**bananes**) are plentiful on the islands. A larger variety of banana, the plantain, is starchy, not sweet. It must be cooked before it is eaten and is usually served as a side dish. The most common type of plantain is the "Martinique."

Teaching Suggestion

② Ask students to name common spices and where they think the following spices are grown. They might know that one of the reasons Columbus set out to discover a new route to the Orient was to search for spices. Have students research the origin and history of the spices listed below:

black pepper	**le poivre noir**
cinnamon	**la cannelle**
cloves	**les clous de girofle**
coriander	**la coriandre**
cumin	**le cumin**
curry	**le curry**
ginger	**le gingembre**
nutmeg	**la muscade**

Thinking Critically

③ **Observing** Have students look at the photos on pages 80–81 and try to determine what products people might buy or sample when visiting a market in Martinique. (They might mention local fruits and vegetables, seafood, flowers, baskets, cloth, dolls, and art work.)

La Martinique

La Martinique est une petite île de la mer des Caraïbes que l'on appelle aussi «la perle des Antilles françaises». On y vit au rythme créole : on danse la biguine et le zouk, on mange piquant, mais il ne faut pas oublier que la Martinique est un département de la France. Ses habitants sont français. Ils votent comme s'ils habitaient en France métropolitaine. Le français est la langue officielle et on paie ses achats en francs.

① La Martinique produit surtout de la canne à sucre, des ananas et des bananes qu'on appelle «l'or vert» de l'île.

② La Martinique produit beaucoup d'épices.

③ Ce Martiniquais cueille des feuilles de cocotier pour en faire des objets qu'il vendra au marché.

80 *quatre-vingts*

Language Note

① Bananas are referred to as **l'or vert** and sugar cane as **l'or blanc.** Ask students if they can imagine why. (**L'or** *(gold)* is a symbol of money or wealth. Bananas are harvested when green, and sugar is harvested when white. Since the island's economic prosperity is dependent upon bananas and sugar, their importance is implied by the expressions.) Ask students if they can imagine how the French sometimes refer to oil (**l'or noir**).

Agriculture Link

① Much of the terminology for the processing of sugar cane comes from French. In order to extract sugar from the canes, they are crushed and sprayed with hot water to extract the juice. The juice that results (**bagasse**) is purified, leaving a mixture of syrup and crystals called **massecuite.** A centrifuge then separates the syrup or molasses from the sugar crystals.

④ Des milliers d'espèces de fleurs poussent dans **le jardin de Balata.**

⑤ Ces bateaux multicolores que l'on appelle des gommiers sont utilisés pour la pêche.

quatre-vingt-un **81**

④ Landscaper and horticulturalist Jean-Philippe Thoze spent approximately 20 years developing **le jardin de Balata.** In the gardens are thousands of varieties of tropical flowers and plants. The term **balata** is the Carib name for a rare native tree. The town of Balata boasts a replica of the Sacré-Cœur basilica in Paris.

④ Martinique is known as **l'île aux fleurs,** and there is a rich array of flowers almost everywhere you turn. The orchids, frangipani, oleanders, hibiscus, jade vines, flamingo flowers, bougainvillea, and anthuriums paint the countryside with swatches of color. Trees such as the flame and tulip trees are magnificent when they are in bloom. Fruit trees abound, and tropical fruits such as mangoes, papayas, bright red West Indian cherries, lemons, limes, and bananas are grown throughout the island.

⑤ Fishing is an important livelihood for many **Martiniquais.** Among the many varieties of fish that live in the sea are the **oursins blancs** *(white sea urchins),* **étoiles de mer** *(starfish),* **dorades** *(sea bream),* and **poissons volants** *(flying fish).* The front part of the **gommiers** (fishing boats) are made of the trunk of the gum tree **(gommier),** with boards added to complete the structure of the boat.

Teacher Note

④ The tree in the center photo is called a "traveler's palm." Originating in Madagascar, the tree has two vertical rows of leaves whose stalks contain large quantities of clear watery sap from which comes a refreshing drink. Travelers who are short on water can always count on obtaining refreshment from this tree.

Culture Note

⑤ **Gommier** or **yole** races, which usually take place on saints' days throughout the year, are a village tradition.

Chapitre 4 : Sous les tropiques
Chapter Overview

Mise en train pp. 84–86	Un concours photographique		Practice and Activity Book, p. 37		Video Guide OR Videodisc Guide

	FUNCTIONS	GRAMMAR	CULTURE	RE-ENTRY
Première étape pp. 87–91	Asking for information and describing a place, p. 90	The use of **de** before a plural adjective and noun, p. 89	• **Note Culturelle, La ville de St. Pierre,** p. 87 • **Panorama Culturel,** Places to visit in different regions, p. 91	• Descriptive adjectives • Weather expressions
Deuxième étape pp. 92–97	• Asking for and making suggestions, p. 94 • Emphasizing likes and dislikes, p. 96	• Recognizing reflexive verbs, p. 93 • The reflexive verbs **se coucher** and **se lever,** p. 96	• **Note Culturelle, Yoles rondes** (fishing boats), p. 92 • **Note Culturelle,** The **créole** language, p. 94 • Realia: Calendar of events in Martinique, p. 95 • **Rencontre Culturel, Carnaval** in Martinique, p. 97	• Sports • Making and responding to suggestions
Troisième étape pp. 98–101	Relating a series of events, p. 99	The present tense of reflexive verbs, p. 100	**Note Culturelle,** Music and dance in Martinique, p. 98	• Pronunciation: **e muet** • Adverbs of frequency

Lisons! pp. 102–103	**An sèl Zouk** (A **zouk** song by Kassav')		**Reading Strategy:** Looking for the main idea and decoding

Review pp. 104–107	**Mise en pratique,** pp. 104–105	**Que sais-je?** p. 106	**Vocabulaire,** p. 107

Assessment Options

Etape Quizzes
• *Chapter Teaching Resources, Book 1*
  Première étape, Quiz 4-1, pp. 191–192
  Deuxième étape, Quiz 4-2, pp. 193–194
  Troisième étape, Quiz 4-3, pp. 195–196
• *Assessment Items, Audiocassette 7B/Audio CD 4*

Chapter Test
• *Chapter Teaching Resources, Book 1,* pp. 197–202
• *Assessment Guide,* Speaking Test, p. 29
• *Assessment Items, Audiocassette 7B/Audio CD 4*

Test Generator, Chapter 4

RESOURCES: Print	RESOURCES: Audiovisual

Video Program OR *Expanded Video Program, Videocassette 2*
OR *Videodisc Program, Videodisc 2B*   *Textbook Audiocassette 2B/Audio CD 4*

Textbook Audiocassette 2B/Audio CD 4

Practice and Activity Book, pp. 38–40
Chapter Teaching Resources, Book 1
• Teaching Transparency Master 4-1, pp. 175, 178 . . . . *Teaching Transparency 4-1*
• Additional Listening Activities 4-1, 4-2, p. 179 . . . . *Additional Listening Activities, Audiocassette 9B/Audio CD 4*
• Realia 4-1, pp. 183, 185
• Situation Cards 4-1, pp. 186–187
• Student Response Forms, pp. 188–190
• Quiz 4-1, pp. 191–192 . . . . *Assessment Items, Audiocassette 7B/Audio CD 4*
Video Guide . . . . *Video Program* OR *Expanded Video Program, Videocassette 2*
Videodisc Guide . . . . *Videodisc Program, Videodisc 2B*

Textbook Audiocassette 2B/Audio CD 4

Practice and Activity Book, pp. 41–43
Chapter Teaching Resources, Book 1
• Communicative Activity 4-1, pp. 171–172
• Teaching Transparency Master 4-2, pp. 176, 178 . . . . *Teaching Transparency 4-2*
• Additional Listening Activities 4-3, 4-4, p. 180 . . . . *Additional Listening Activities, Audiocassette 9B/Audio CD 4*
• Realia 4-2, pp. 184, 185
• Situation Cards 4-2, pp. 186–187
• Student Response Forms, pp. 188–190
• Quiz 4-2, pp. 193–194 . . . . *Assessment Items, Audiocassette 7B/Audio CD 4*
Videodisc Guide . . . . *Videodisc Program, Videodisc 2B*

Textbook Audiocassette 2B/Audio CD 4

Practice and Activity Book, pp. 44–46
Chapter Teaching Resources, Book 1
• Communicative Activity 4-2, pp. 173–174
• Teaching Transparency Master 4-3, pp. 177, 178 . . . . *Teaching Transparency 4-3*
• Additional Listening Activities 4-5, 4-6, p. 181 . . . . *Additional Listening Activities, Audiocassette 9B/Audio CD 4*
• Realia 4-2, pp. 184, 185
• Situation Cards 4-3, pp. 186–187
• Student Response Forms, pp. 188–190
• Quiz 4-3, pp. 195–196 . . . . *Assessment Items, Audiocassette 7B/Audio CD 4*
Videodisc Guide . . . . *Videodisc Program, Videodisc 2B*

Practice and Activity Book, p. 47

Video Guide . . . . *Video Program* OR *Expanded Video Program, Videocassette 2*
Videodisc Guide . . . . *Videodisc Program, Videodisc 2B*

Alternative Assessment
• Performance Assessment   • Portfolio Assessment
  Première étape, p. 90   Written: **Mise en pratique,** Activity 4, *Pupil's Edition,* p. 105
  Deuxième étape, p. 96   *Assessment Guide,* p. 17
  Troisième étape, p. 101   Oral: Activity 15, *Pupil's Edition,* p. 90
                                        Assessment Guide, p. 17

For Student Response Forms, see *Chapter Teaching Resources, Book 1,* pp. 188–190.

Première étape

8 Ecoute! p. 89

Venez à la Martinique! A vous la mer, le soleil, le ciel bleu, les plages et les cocotiers... A vous le poisson grillé, les fleurs, les épices! Visitez la forêt tropicale, escaladez les pentes de la Montagne Pelée, regardez les magnifiques champs de canne à sucre. Venez à la Martinique, une histoire d'amour entre ciel et mer.

Answers to Activity 8
les cocotiers, la forêt tropicale, la Montagne Pelée, les champs de canne à sucre

Deuxième étape

17 Ecoute! p. 94

MAGALI   Alors, qu'est-ce que tu veux faire aujourd'hui?

CÉSAR   Je ne sais pas... Ça te dit d'aller à la pêche?

MAGALI   Non, c'est barbant. On attend pendant des heures, c'est tout!

CÉSAR   Eh bien, tu as une autre idée?

MAGALI   On pourrait faire du deltaplane. Ça, c'est original!

CÉSAR   Pas question. Je n'ai pas envie de me casser une jambe! Pourquoi pas faire de la plongée?

MAGALI   C'est une bonne idée... mais je n'ai pas de masque, moi.

CÉSAR   On pourrait se promener sur la plage, alors.

MAGALI   D'accord. On y va!

Possible answers to Activity 17
fishing, hang gliding, scuba diving, walking on the beach; walking on the beach

22 Ecoute! p. 96

1. — Qu'est-ce que tu aimes faire pendant les vacances?
   — Ce que je préfère, c'est me lever tard parce que je dois me lever à six heures quand je vais à l'école. Et ça, je déteste!

2. — Et toi, qu'est-ce que tu aimes faire?
   — Ce que j'aime bien, c'est faire de l'équitation le long de la plage.

3. — Qu'est-ce que tu aimes faire le week-end?
   — Ben, ce qui me plaît, c'est me baigner toute la journée.

4. — Et toi, qu'est-ce que tu aimes faire?
   — J'aime rester à la maison. Tous mes copains aiment sortir, mais moi, ça ne me plaît pas.

Answers to Activity 22
1. getting up late; like
   getting up at 6:00 A.M.; dislike
2. horseback riding; like
3. swimming; like
4. staying at home; like
   going out; dislike

*T*roisième étape

26 Ecoute! p. 99

Le matin? Ben, c'est assez banal. Je me lève à sept heures et demie. Puis, je me lave le visage pour me réveiller un peu. Ensuite, je vais à la cuisine pour prendre le petit déjeuner : des tartines et peut-être du chocolat, si j'ai le temps. Je m'habille, d'habitude en jean et en tee-shirt. Euh, enfin, je me brosse les dents super vite, et je cours au lycée.

Answers to Activity 26
e, b, c, d, a

*M*ise en pratique

2 p. 105

Il y a beaucoup de circuits pittoresques à faire. Je crois que celui-ci vous intéressera. On commence le matin par une visite de la Soufrière. Vous verrez un volcan actif de près. Ensuite, vous prendrez l'autocar pour aller déguster la cuisine locale dans un petit restaurant typique. Vers deux heures, visite de la forêt tropicale pour voir nos fameuses chutes d'eau, les chutes du Carbet. Enfin, vous pourrez visiter une plantation de café. Personnellement, c'est le circuit que je vous recommande.

Answers to Mise en pratique Activity 2
visit "La Soufrière" and see an active volcano, lunch at the local restaurant, visit the tropical forest and the waterfalls of Carbet, visit a coffee plantation

Une publicité française
(Cooperative Learning Project)

ASSIGNMENT

Students will create and perform a television commercial for the **Office de tourisme de la Martinique** to encourage visitors to come to Martinique.

MATERIALS

✂ **Students may need**
For making props:
- Posterboard
- Construction paper
- Glue
- Markers
- Scissors

SUGGESTED SEQUENCE

1. In order to motivate students and give them ideas about the elements of a successful commercial, try to obtain videos from travel agencies that promote vacation packages.

2. Each group chooses a theme that determines which features of Martinique they will emphasize. The theme should be clearly stated in the commercial.

3. The script must include a physical description of the island and name at least five things to do there. Each group member should have a speaking part.

4. After the script is written, each group member should proofread it to check for variety of vocabulary and language accuracy.

5. When the script has been edited and recopied, students should gather and/or make props, and rehearse. Have students perform their commercials for the class. You might also videotape their commercials, if possible.

GRADING THE PROJECT

Each group member should receive a collective grade based on completion of the requirements, language use, and creativity and overall presentation. Each group member should receive an individual grade based on pronunciation, and effort and participation.

Suggested Point Distribution (total = 100 points)

Completion of requirements	20 points
Language use.	20 points
Creativity/presentation	20 points
Pronunciation	20 points
Effort/participation	20 points

TEACHER NOTE

You might prefer to give students the option of promoting any francophone country, province, or department in their commercials.

Chapitre 4 : Sous les tropiques
♜ *Games*

MOT DE PASSE

In this game, students will practice the vocabulary of the chapter.

Procedure Form two or three teams. Have one player from each team stand at the front of the classroom, facing his or her teammates. Choose a word from the chapter vocabulary to be the password and show it only to the players in front of the class. The first player may choose to pass or play. To play, he or she gives a one-word clue to try to get his or her teammates to say the password within ten seconds. If the player's teammates do not guess the word, the next player gives his or her teammates an additional clue and play continues. Give five points for guessing a word after the first clue, four points for guessing correctly after the second clue, and so on.

LA QUEUE

In this game, students will practice the vocabulary words and expressions from this chapter.

Procedure To start, one student calls out a word or expression from the chapter. The next student must call out a word, expression, or a sentence that incorporates the vocabulary and begins with the last letter of whatever the first student called out. Hence, the name **La queue.** For example, if the first student says **un moustique**, the second student's offering must begin with an **e.** If the second student says **est,** then the third student must say something that begins with a **t (Tu vas à la pêche?)**, and so on. Articles do not count as the first letter of a word. For example, if one student says **un ananas,** then another student can appropriately follow with **le sable.** A student who cannot respond within ten seconds is out, but may get back in the game by responding correctly when another student cannot.

Chapitre 4
Sous les tropiques
pp. 82–107

*U*sing the Chapter Opener

Motivating Activity

Have students locate Martinique on the map of the francophone world on pupil page xxiii or on *Map Transparency 4.* Ask them what they think it would be like living on a tropical island. Ask them what they remember about Martinique from Level 1. Remind them that Martinique and Guadeloupe are overseas departments (**départements d'outre-mer**) of France, and therefore are guaranteed the services of the French government and the educational system.

Teaching Suggestion

Have students look at the photographs and then ask the following questions:
- **Quel est le sujet de ce chapitre?**
- **Qu'est-ce qu'on fait à la Martinique?**
- **C'est beau, la Martinique? Pourquoi?**

Photo Flash!

① After the French settled in Martinique in 1635 under Louis XIII, **fort Saint-Louis** was constructed in 1640 in order to protect ships that were being repaired and cleaned. By 1681, a town began to emerge around the fort, known at this time as Fort Royal. Starting in 1759, the fort went from British to French occupation in a series of struggles lasting for more than thirty years. In 1802, the French gained final control of the fort and renamed it **fort Saint-Louis.** In 1973, the fort became a historical monument.

CHAPITRE

4
Sous les tropiques

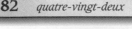
① Qu'est-ce qu'on peut faire à la Martinique?
On peut visiter le fort Saint-Louis.

82 *quatre-vingt-deux*

Culture Note

All of Martinique's beaches are open to the public, but hotels charge a fee for nonguests to use their changing rooms or facilities. The soft, white-sand beaches begin south of Fort-de-France. To the north, the beaches are made up of hard-packed gray or even black volcanic sand. **Pointe-du-Bout** is a man-made soft white beach lined with luxury resorts. South of **Pointe-du-Bout** is **Anse-Mitan,** a natural white-sand beach surrounded by perfect snorkeling waters. Some beaches offer the convenience of picnic tables and nearby **bistros** and **cafés,** while others are more secluded and offer nothing but sea and sand.

Traveling to a tropical island . . . what images come to your mind? Palm trees, beaches, bright flowers, and turquoise seas? Martinique has all those things, plus a fascinating history, world-renowned music, and, above all, warm, friendly people!

In this chapter you will learn

- to ask for information and describe a place
- to ask for and make suggestions; to emphasize likes and dislikes
- to relate a series of events

And you will

- listen to a radio ad for Martinique and to people making plans
- read the lyrics of a zouk song
- write a description of your daily activities
- find out about Carnival in Martinique and what French speakers like to do in their countries

② Ce qui me plaît, c'est déguster de la cuisine antillaise.

③ D'abord, je veux me baigner.

Focusing on Outcomes

Point out that the three photo captions are examples of the three functional chapter outcomes. Ask students if they can pick out the words in the captions that perform these functions. After they've read the photo captions, ask students their preference: **Qu'est-ce qui te plaît : visiter le fort Saint-Louis, déguster de la cuisine antillaise, ou te baigner à la plage?** Prompt **Ce qui me plaît, c'est...**
NOTE: You may want to use the video to support the objectives. The self-check activities in **Que sais-je?** on page 106 help students assess their achievement of the objectives.

Photo Flash!

② Antillean cuisine, which is known for its essential spiciness, often uses hot peppers for seasoning, and seafood dishes are common throughout the islands. However, the similarities end there. For example, the cuisine in Barbados is known for its West African influence, with an abundance of rice, peas, beans, and okra, which are added to meat and fish dishes. Martinique and Guadeloupe are known for their classic French and Creole dishes. Puerto Rican cuisine includes a wide variety of rice, beans, yams, and the ever-present **tostones** *(fried green plantains)* and **amarillos** *(baked ripe plantains)*.

③ There are many beautiful beaches on both the Atlantic and Caribbean coasts of Martinique, but probably the most popular is **Les Salines** near the small town of Sainte-Anne at the southern tip of the island. There is even a black sand beach near Saint-Pierre, formed from the eruption of nearby Mount Pelée.

Culture Note

Call attention to the fabric pictured under the bowl of peppers in Photo 2. This material is called **madras,** a brightly-colored, woven, cotton plaid of various designs. This fabric is used to make the traditional costume of Martinique, as well as everyday clothing. You might challenge students to find all the appearances of this unique cloth in the chapter (pages 97, 98, 101, 102, and 104).

History Link

The bright magenta flowers pictured next to Photo 3 are called **Bougainvillea.** The flower was named after Louis-Antoine de Bougainville, a French navigator who explored areas of the South Pacific and sailed around the world from 1766–1769 as leader of the French naval force. He wrote a widely-read account of his journey in 1771 called *Voyage autour du monde.*

VIDEO PROGRAM OR EXPANDED VIDEO PROGRAM,
Videocassette 2
04:07–09:26

OR VIDEODISC PROGRAM,
Videodisc 2B

Search 4865, Play To 14460

Video Synopsis

In this segment of the video, Agnès and Jean-Philippe see an announcement of a photography contest at their school. They decide to enter it together and plan to photograph the beauty of Martinique. Lisette and Stéphane hear them and discuss how they could do a more interesting project. They decide to show how people live in Martinique. Agnès and Jean-Phillipe photograph and describe the scenery. Stéphane and Lisette interview and photograph people at work. Stéphane talks about the work and what he likes to do. The four friends meet the next day at school and wonder who is going to win the contest!

Motivating Activity

Tell students that **un concours** is *a contest.* Based on that information, ask them what they think is happening in the story. Ask students if they like to take photos and if any of them has ever entered a photo contest. Ask them what they think makes a good photograph. Ask students to imagine they are the judges of the contest as they view the video and read the **Mise en train.**

Teaching Suggestion

Have students scan the flyer and ask them the following questions: Who is sponsoring the contest? What is its theme? Whom do you contact for information?

Mise en train

Agnès Stéphane

Jean-Philippe Lisette

Un concours photographique

Look at the two photo projects. Can you guess the theme of each one?

CONCOURS

Reportage Photographique

Le Club Photo vous invite à participer à son concours annuel

Thème:
Découvrir la Martinique

Nombreux prix!

Alors, à vos appareils-photos et vive l'imagination!

Pour tous renseignements, contactez M. Lucas, salle 310

C'est une bonne idée, ce concours photographique. Ça te tente de le faire avec moi? J'ai mon nouvel appareil-photo!

Pourquoi pas? Il y a beaucoup de choses à voir.

LA MARTINIQUE...
autrefois appelée Madinina, l'île aux fleurs. Une île parmi tant d'autres, mais si belle, colorée, chaleureuse...

On se promène, on se baigne, on se bronze. La mer, le sable, le soleil, les cocotiers, l'eau couleur turquoise, les sports nautiques... la Martinique — c'est magnifique!

Chez nous, il fait beau, chaud même parfois, mais il y a toujours un peu de pluie. C'est pour ça que notre île est si verte toute l'année. Il y a des fleurs de toutes les couleurs : rouges, jaunes, mauves, bleues, et blanches!

Plus vers le nord, c'est la jungle tropicale, les arbres immenses, le paradis des plantes et des moustiques.

C'est l'éternel printemps. Quand on voit le soleil se coucher dans la mer ou bien se lever au petit matin, déjà on est amoureux.

84 *quatre-vingt-quatre*

CHAPITRE 4 Sous les tropiques

RESOURCES FOR MISE EN TRAIN
Textbook Audiocassette 2B/Audio CD 4
Practice and Activity Book, p. 37
Video Guide
  Video Program
  Expanded Video Program, Videocassette 2
Videodisc Guide
  Videodisc Program, Videodisc 2B

Multicultural Link

Ask students if they have ever traveled to another town, state, or country and found it to be different from what they had expected, and if so, how. Ask them what opinions they have of other countries and why they hold these opinions. Ask how the media (TV programs, commercials, advertisements, newspapers, magazines) influence what they think about other places.

MISE EN TRAIN
CHAPITRE 4

Presentation

Before they view the video, tell students that the teenagers they're going to see are entering a contest. Ask students to try to answer these questions as they watch the episode: 1. Are all the students going to do the same thing? 2. What are they going to do differently? Then, have students look at the photos and read the text in the **Mise en train.** Ask them to determine which participants in the photo contest took which group of photos and for what reason.

Thinking Critically
Comparing and Contrasting Have students compare the two sets of photos in the **Mise en train.** Ask them what has been emphasized in each set and which one they prefer.

For Individual Needs

Challenge In groups of three, have students write one sentence captions for the photos, using their own words. Write their captions on the board or on a transparency and have the class choose the best ones.

Slower Pace Have students cover the text of the **Mise en train** with pieces of paper. Write paraphrased captions of the photos on a transparency in random order and have students match the captions with the photos.

Auditory Learners Describe each photo aloud in random order. Have students identify the photo you're describing.

Visual Learners Distribute a written version of your descriptions (see Auditory Learners). Have students match the descriptions with the photos.

Video Integration

- **EXPANDED VIDEO PROGRAM,** Videocassette 2, 09:27–17:11
- **VIDEODISC PROGRAM,** Videodisc 2B

Search 14460, Play To 28410

You may choose to continue with **Un concours photographique (suite)** or wait until later in the chapter. When the story continues, Lisette and Stéphane interview a bank employee. Agnès and Jean-Philippe take pictures of a rain forest and Mount Pelée in the north. Later, at school, the winning projects are displayed. The two pairs of friends both win prizes: Agnès and Jean-Philippe for their technical expertise, and Lisette and Stéphane for their originality.

For videodisc application, see *Videodisc Guide.*

For Individual Needs

2 Challenge Have students work in pairs to make up additional sentence starters based on the **Mise en train** for their classmates to complete. Have them write their work on a transparency and present it to the class.

2 Tactile/Visual Learners Have students write the sentence starters in the left column on strips of paper of one color, and the sentence completions in the right column on strips of paper of a second color. Have students add their own sentence starters and completions (see Challenge above) on the appropriate colored strips. Afterwards, have students shuffle the strips and pass them to a partner who will arrange the matching strips.

Teaching Suggestions

2 Once students have completed this activity, have them read aloud the sentence endings and have others supply appropriate beginnings, without looking at their books.

3 Have students write captions for each photo.

3 Describe the photos one at a time in random order and have students write the number of the photo that matches your description.

Thinking Critically

3 Synthesizing Have students explain why they believe certain photos belong to one or the other photo essay theme. Then, ask them which photos they prefer and why.

---

1 Tu as compris?

1. Why are the students taking pictures? for a photo essay contest
2. What do Agnès and Jean-Philippe take pictures of? nature
3. What do they emphasize in their presentation of Martinique? the beauty of the island
4. What do Stéphane and Lisette take pictures of? people
5. What are they trying to show in their photo-essay? everyday life

2 Pourquoi?

Complète les phrases suivantes.

1. L'île est verte toute l'année... d
2. C'est un paradis pour les pêcheurs... c
3. Beaucoup de gens se lèvent à 4h... e
4. C'est une île très colorée... a
5. On aime se balader ensemble le samedi après-midi ou le dimanche... b

a. parce qu'il y a des fleurs de toutes les couleurs.
b. parce que c'est quand la famille peut être réunie.
c. parce que le climat est doux et la mer est toujours bleue.
d. parce qu'il y a toujours un peu de pluie.
e. parce que le travail commence très tôt.

3 A qui, les photos?

Here are some more photos Agnès, Jean-Philippe, Stéphane, and Lisette took. Based on what you know about the themes of their photo essays, who do you think took them?

Stéphane, Lisette: 1, 3, 5; Agnès, Jean-Philippe: 2, 4

4 Cherche les expressions

In **Un concours photographique** what do the students say to . . . See answers below.

1. suggest that they participate in the photo contest?
2. accept a suggestion?
3. describe what's on the island?
4. describe the weather?
5. tell when and how often they do something?

5 Et maintenant, à toi

If you entered a photo contest about your state or hometown, what would you take pictures of?

Culture Note

3 Refer students to Photo 3. Head wraps in Martinique are more than a fashion. They also convey information about the women who wear them. Traditionally, a wrap with one peak indicates a woman is single. Two peaks indicate she is engaged, and three mean she is married.

Answers

4 1. Ça te tente de le faire avec moi?
2. Pourquoi pas?
3. *Possible answers:* Il y a beaucoup de choses à voir! La mer, le sable, le soleil, parfois, les cocotiers, l'eau couleur tourquoise, les sports nautiques...
4. Il fait beau, chaud même parfois, mais il y a toujours un peu de pluie.
5. *Possible answers:* le soir, le samedi après-midi, le dimanche, à quatre heures, très tôt, d'habitude, toute l'année.

PREMIERE ETAPE

Asking for information and describing a place

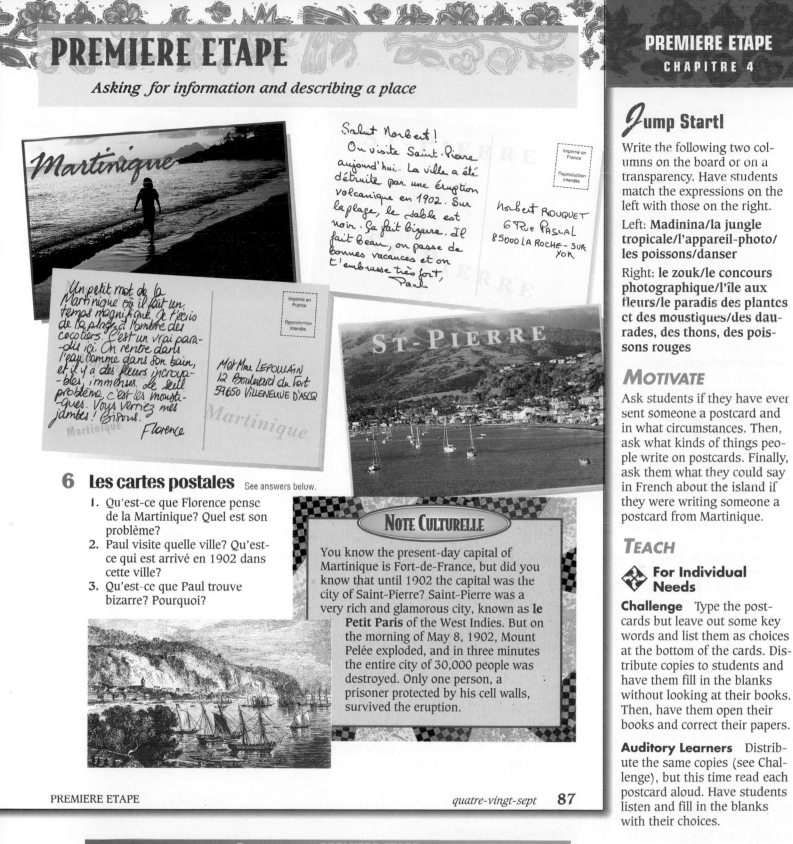

Salut Norbert!
On visite Saint-Pierre aujourd'hui. La ville a été détruite par une éruption volcanique en 1902. Sur la plage, le sable est noir. Ça fait bizarre. Il fait beau, on passe de bonnes vacances et on t'embrasse très fort,
Paul

Imprimé en France
Reproduction interdite

Norbert ROUQUET
6 Rue PASCAL
85000 LA ROCHE-SUR-YON

Un petit mot de la Martinique où il fait un temps magnifique. Je t'écris de la plage, à l'ombre des cocotiers. C'est un vrai paradis ici. On rentre dans l'eau comme dans son bain, et il y a des fleurs incroyables, immenses. Le seul problème c'est les moustiques. Vous verriez mes jambes! Bisous.
Florence

Imprimé en France
Reproduction interdite

Mr et Mme LEPOULLAIN
12 Boulevard du Fort
59650 VILLENEUVE D'ASCQ

Martinique

ST-PIERRE

6 Les cartes postales *See answers below.*

1. Qu'est-ce que Florence pense de la Martinique? Quel est son problème?
2. Paul visite quelle ville? Qu'est-ce qui est arrivé en 1902 dans cette ville?
3. Qu'est-ce que Paul trouve bizarre? Pourquoi?

NOTE CULTURELLE

You know the present-day capital of Martinique is Fort-de-France, but did you know that until 1902 the capital was the city of Saint-Pierre? Saint-Pierre was a very rich and glamorous city, known as **le Petit Paris** of the West Indies. But on the morning of May 8, 1902, Mount Pelée exploded, and in three minutes the entire city of 30,000 people was destroyed. Only one person, a prisoner protected by his cell walls, survived the eruption.

Jump Start!

Write the following two columns on the board or on a transparency. Have students match the expressions on the left with those on the right.

Left: **Madinina/la jungle tropicale/l'appareil-photo/ les poissons/danser**

Right: **le zouk/le concours photographique/l'île aux fleurs/le paradis des plantes et des moustiques/des daurades, des thons, des poissons rouges**

MOTIVATE

Ask students if they have ever sent someone a postcard and in what circumstances. Then, ask what kinds of things people write on postcards. Finally, ask them what they could say in French about the island if they were writing someone a postcard from Martinique.

TEACH

For Individual Needs

Challenge Type the post-cards but leave out some key words and list them as choices at the bottom of the cards. Distribute copies to students and have them fill in the blanks without looking at their books. Then, have them open their books and correct their papers.

Auditory Learners Distribute the same copies (see Challenge), but this time read each postcard aloud. Have students listen and fill in the blanks with their choices.

Answers
6 1. C'est un paradis; Il y a des moustiques.
2. Saint-Pierre; une éruption volcanique
3. le sable; parce qu'il est noir

Presentation

Vocabulaire Sketch a map of the United States on the board. Add several major cities and a compass labeled **nord, sud, ouest,** and **est.** Have students repeat the compass directions after you. Then, ask either-or questions (**Los Angeles est dans l'est ou dans l'ouest des Etats-Unis?**) and questions to elicit information. (**C'est où, New York?**) Have students open their books and repeat the vocabulary after you. Then, ask questions about the map of Martinique similar to those you asked about the United States. (**C'est où, le jardin de Balata? Quelle est la ville principale de l'île? Où est-ce qu'il y a un village de pêcheurs?**)

⬥ For Individual Needs

Tactile/Visual/Auditory Learners Trace an outline of Martinique on a transparency and label several cities. Draw several vocabulary items on small, separate pieces of transparency (tropical forest, mosquitos, sugar cane field). Have students draw the same map on a sheet of paper and the vocabulary items on small, separate pieces of paper. Describe Martinique, using the vocabulary, and ask students to place the vocabulary item on the map according to what you say in French. (**Au Morne Rouge, il y a le jardin de Balata. Au nord du jardin, il y a une forêt tropicale. Dans la forêt tropicale, il y a beaucoup de moustiques!**) Turn on the overhead projector after every two or three sentences and place the vocabulary items on your map so that students can check theirs.

VOCABULAIRE

7 Vrai ou faux?

1. La Martinique est dans la mer des Caraïbes. vrai
2. La capitale de la Martinique est la Montagne Pelée. faux
3. Dans le sud, il y a de belles plages. vrai
4. Dans le nord de la Martinique, il y a une forêt tropicale. vrai
5. Il y a des villages de pêcheurs dans l'ouest de la Martinique. faux

Note de Grammaire

When you want to say *some,* simply use **de** if there's an adjective before a plural noun:

des conseils → **de bons** conseils

des plages → **de belles** plages

CHAPITRE 4   Sous les tropiques

Teaching Suggestions

7 Have students write additional true-false statements about the map and read them to a partner. The partner should answer **vrai** or **faux** and correct any false statements.

Note de grammaire Show pictures and ask questions about them. (**Ce sont de grosses voitures, ou ce sont de petites voitures?**)

(**TPR**) On a large sheet of butcher paper, sketch an outline of Martinique, label the towns, and tape it to the board. On small, separate pieces of butcher paper, draw the vocabulary items (a waterfall, a pineapple, a fishing village). Tell students to tape the pictures of the vocabulary items to the map where you indicate. (**Max, mets le sable à Sainte-Anne.**)

8 Ecoute!

While in France, you hear the following ad for Martinique on the radio. Which features of the island are mentioned?
Answers on p. 81C.

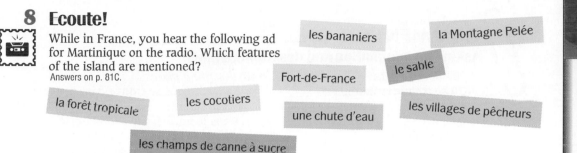

les bananiers   la Montagne Pelée

Fort-de-France   le sable

la forêt tropicale   les cocotiers   une chute d'eau   les villages de pêcheurs

les champs de canne à sucre

9 A la Martinique

Complete the following sentences, using the features of Martinique presented in Activity 8. Create your own sentences with the features you don't use.

1. Le volcan qui a détruit l'ancienne capitale s'appelle _____.   la Montagne Pelée
2. Si vous adorez le poisson, visitez _____.   les villages de pêcheurs
3. Il pleut beaucoup dans _____.   la forêt tropicale
4. Attention à ta tête quand tu marches sous _____.   les cocotiers
5. À la Martinique il y a des plages où _____ est noir.   le sable
6. La capitale de la Martinique s'appelle _____.   Fort-de-France

10 Vingt questions

Write down a feature of Martinique. Your classmates will ask you questions to try to guess the feature. You can only answer yes or no. When someone guesses correctly, the turn passes to that person.

—C'est un fruit?   —Non.   —C'est une ville?   —Oui.
—C'est un arbre?   —Non.   —C'est dans le nord?   —Non.
—C'est un lieu *(a place)*?   —Oui.   —C'est Fort-de-France?   —Oui.

11 Une visite guidée

Your guided tour of Martinique included the following sights. Your friend, who would like to take the same tour, asks about each place. With a partner, take turns asking about and describing each place.

—C'est comment, la plage des Salines?
—C'est magnifique! Le sable est blanc et il y a des palmiers.

la ville de Saint-Pierre   le jardin de Balata   le marché   la forêt tropicale

---

Teaching Suggestion

8 On the board or on a transparency, list all of the features in random order and number each one. Then, play the recording and have students reorder the features as they are mentioned.

For Individual Needs

9 Challenge Have students design a crossword puzzle that uses these sentence starters as clues. Have them create additional clues and supply the answers.

11 Challenge Encourage students to say as much as they can in French about each photo. Help them recall facts they've learned so far about the places pictured. For example, have them reread Paul's postcard and the **Note Culturelle** on page 87 and answer the following: **La ville de Saint-Pierre s'appelait comment avant? (le Petit Paris) Qu'est-ce qui est arrivé dans cette ville? (une éruption volcanique) En quelle année? (1902) Il y avait combien d'habitants? (30,000).**

Building on Previous Skills

11 To re-enter the pronoun **en**, have partners secretly choose one of the four places in the photos. One student asks questions to try to guess the place his or her partner chose. **(Il y a du sable?)** The other must answer, using the pronoun **en. (Oui, il y en a. Non, il n'y en a pas.)**

 For videodisc application, see *Videodisc Guide.*

Science Link

The climate of the mountainous northern region of Martinique is typical of the subtropical rain forest. Between 160 to 200 inches of annual rainfall and high humidity produce lush vegetation consisting of palm, rosewood, logwood, breadfruit, and mahogany trees, oleander, ferns, and orchids. Volcanoes tend to produce rich soil. However, the permanently moist rain forest soil is not very fertile since the hot and humid weather causes organic matter to decompose rapidly and to be quickly absorbed by tree roots and fungi. The plant development in rain forests exhibit vertical stratification in which the highest plant layer extends beyond 100 feet. Most trees have a very shallow root system because rain falls in the forest, drips down the leaves, and trickles down the tree trunk to the ground, moistening, but not drenching it.

Presentation

Comment dit-on... ? Sketch a map of the United States on the board and add several cities and attractions such as Disney World or the Grand Canyon. Ask questions about various states, such as **Où se trouve la Floride? Qu'est-ce qu'il y a à voir là-bas? Il y fait chaud? La Floride est plus grande ou plus petite que le Texas?** Then, as students look at the map of Martinique on page 88, ask similar questions about the island.

Mon journal

14 Written For an additional journal entry suggestion for Chapter 4, see *Practice and Activity Book,* page 148.

Portfolio

15 Oral This activity is appropriate for students' oral portfolios. For portfolio suggestions, see *Assessment Guide,* page 17.

Language Note

Point out that some names of countries or departments are masculine and other names are feminine, so the adjectives used to describe them will vary in form according to this difference in gender. (**La Martinique est charmante. Le Japon est charmant.**)

CLOSE

Group Work

To close this **étape**, form groups of three and have students write and perform skits that incorporate as many of the functions, grammatical structures, and vocabulary from this **étape** as possible.

COMMENT DIT-ON... ?

Asking for information and describing a place

To ask about a place:

Où se trouve la Martinique?
Where is . . . located?
Qu'est-ce qu'il y a à voir?
What is there . . . ?

Il fait chaud?

C'est comment? *What's it like?*

To describe a place:

La Martinique **se trouve** dans la mer des Caraïbes.
Dans le nord, il y a la forêt tropicale et **dans le sud,** il y a de belles plages. La capitale se trouve **dans l'ouest** et il y a des villages de pêcheurs **dans l'est.**
Il fait toujours très chaud et il pleut souvent.
C'est **plus grand que** New York.
. . . bigger than . . .
C'est **moins grand qu'**Oahu.
. . . smaller than . . .
La Martinique est une île **charmante, colorée** et **vivante!**
. . . charming, colorful, lively

12 Ma ville

Complète les phrases pour faire une description de ta ville.

_____ se trouve dans l'état de/d' _____. Dans le nord, il y a _____ et dans le sud, il y a _____. Il fait _____ chez nous. Ma ville est plus grande que _____ et moins grande que _____. C'est une ville _____ et _____.

13 Jeu d'identification

Pense à une ville importante aux Etats-Unis ou ailleurs *(elsewhere).* Tes camarades de classe vont te poser des questions pour deviner le nom de cette ville.

Où se trouve cette ville?   C'est petit?   Qu'est-ce qu'il y a à voir?   C'est comment?

C'est plus grand que... ?   Il fait froid en hiver?

14 Mon journal

Would you like to travel? Where would you like to go? Write a description of your destination, including what there is to do and see there. You might want to illustrate your entry.

15 Et toi, tu voudrais aller où?

Now, interview a partner about his or her destination. Ask at least five questions about the geography, the weather, and the attractions. Then, reverse roles.

ASSESS

Quiz 4-1, *Chapter Teaching Resources, Book 1,* pp. 191–192

Assessment Items, Audiocassette 7B Audio CD 4

Performance Assessment

Have students imagine they are in Martinique and are sending a postcard to a friend or family member. The postcard should have a picture on one side and a short message on the other. The message should include three things the students have done or seen. Grades should be based on appropriateness of the picture, accuracy of the language, and variety of vocabulary used.

PANORAMA CULTUREL

VIDEO PROGRAM
OR EXPANDED VIDEO PROGRAM,
Videocassette 2
17:12–22:05

OR VIDEODISC PROGRAM,
Videodisc 2B

Search 28410, Play To 32315

Célestine • Côte d'Ivoire

Thomas • France

Marie • France

We asked some francophone people what there is to see in their area. Here's what they had to say.

Qu'est-ce qu'il y a à visiter dans cette région?

«En Côte d'Ivoire, ce qu'il y a à voir en touriste je dirais... Je pense souvent au niveau de Man, c'est-à-dire, la ville de Man. Il y a les montagnes et puis, il y a des cascades et ensuite, il y a la ville de Korhogo qui recouvre beaucoup de culture, c'est à dire les danses. Et il y a beaucoup de choses à apprendre, surtout pour les étrangers. Il y a les masques à découvrir. Il y en a plein. Il y a trop de choses. Je ne peux pas les citer.»

—Célestine

«[Paris,] c'est une ville de touristes quand même. C'est une grande ville parce que c'est la capitale de la France quand même. C'est une des plus belles villes du monde et il y a beaucoup de lieux touristiques. Il y a beaucoup de musées. Il y a des sculptures. Il y a des cinémas, beaucoup de cinémas pour les sorties entre copains. Et il y a la tour Eiffel, la tour Montparnasse, les grands sites.»

—Thomas

«En Provence, il y a surtout la mer. Moi, j'aime bien. C'est pas très loin. C'est à une demi-heure d'ici. Il y a la mer. On peut se baigner. Aussi, il y a toutes les villes de Côte d'Azur qui sont très jolies, où on peut aller se promener. Voilà.»

—Marie

Qu'en penses-tu?

1. Which of the places mentioned would you most like to visit? What makes it attractive to you?
2. What is there to see and do where you live?
3. Plan a sight-seeing trip for a tourist who is coming to spend one day in your area. Be sure to include the most interesting and enjoyable things to see and do.

Questions

1. D'après Célestine, qu'est-ce qu'il y a à voir à Man? (les montagnes et les cascades) Et à Korhogo? (la culture et la danse)
2. Qu'est-ce que Thomas pense de Paris? (C'est une ville de touristes, et c'est une des plus belles villes du monde.)
3. Qu'est-ce qu'il y a à Paris pour les touristes? (des musées, des sculptures, des cinémas, la tour Eiffel, la Tour Montparnasse, les grands sites)
4. D'après Marie, quelle est l'attraction touristique principale de la Provence? (la mer)
5. Qu'est-ce qu'on peut faire dans toutes les villes de Côte d'Azur? (On peut se promener.)

DEUXIEME ETAPE

Asking for and making suggestions; emphasizing likes and dislikes

Qu'est-ce qu'on peut faire à la Martinique?

Il y a beaucoup de choses à faire!

On peut faire de la plongée, faire de la voile, ou tout simplement se promener sur la plage.

Ceux qui ne sont pas très sportifs peuvent faire les boutiques à Fort-de-France. Ça vous tente?

16 Tu veux visiter la Martinique?

Would this travel brochure attract you to Martinique? Why or why not?

NOTE CULTURELLE

Among the most beautiful sights in Martinique are the **yoles rondes,** the traditional fishing boats that are also used for racing. People come from all over the world to watch the "nautical ballet" of these brightly painted boats that are unique to Martinique.

Jump Start!

Have students identify the following: **un arbre tropical/ un fruit tropical/un volcan/ l'ancien nom de la Martinique/le contraire de nord/ on fait du sucre avec** (*Answers:* **un cocotier, un palmier, un bananier/un ananas, une banane/la Montagne Pelée/Madinina/ sud/la canne à sucre**)

MOTIVATE

Have students name some activities they would associate with Martinique. Ask them which of these activities they would highlight if they were making a travel brochure about Martinique.

TEACH

Teaching Suggestion

16 Read the travel brochure with students and ask the following questions: **Qui aime faire de la plongée? Où est-ce que tu en fais? Qui aime faire de la voile? Tu as un bateau? Qui aime faire les boutiques? Qu'est-ce que tu aimes acheter?** Then, have students make substitutions in the captions of the travel brochure to adapt them to their own city, state, or region.

 Culture Note
Shoppers can find good buys in Fort-de-France on designer scarves, French fragrances, fine china, crystal, and leather goods. The area around the cathedral has many small boutiques that carry luxury items. The **Centre des métiers d'art** and the **marché artisanal sur la Savane** in Fort-de-France carry local crafts, including dolls, straw goods, tapestries, pottery, jewelry, and beads. A **collier chou** is a traditional style necklace, and a **chaîne forçat** is a traditional bracelet.

RESOURCES FOR DEUXIEME ETAPE

Textbook Audiocassette 2B/Audio CD 4
Practice and Activity Book, pp. 41–43
Videodisc Guide
   Videodisc Program, Videodisc 2B

Chapter Teaching Resources, Book 1
• Communicative Activity 4-1, pp. 171–172
• Teaching Transparency Master 4-2, pp. 176, 178
   Teaching Transparency 4-2
• Additional Listening Activities 4-3, 4-4, p. 180
   Audiocassette 9B/Audio CD 4
• Realia 4-2, pp. 184, 185
• Situation Cards 4-2, pp. 186–187
• Student Response Forms, pp. 188–190
• Quiz 4-2, pp. 193–194
   Audiocassette 7B/Audio CD 4

VOCABULAIRE

A la Martinique, on aime bien...

faire de la planche à voile.

faire du deltaplane.

faire de la plongée sous-marine.

aller à la pêche.

faire de la plongée avec un tuba.

danser le zouk.

déguster des fruits tropicaux.

se promener.

se baigner.

s'amuser.

Note de Grammaire

Did you notice the word **se** before some of the verbs in the **Vocabulaire?** The pronoun **se** tells you that the subject of the sentence receives the action of the verb. Verbs with this pronoun before them are called *reflexive verbs.* You'll learn how to make the forms of the reflexive verbs later in this chapter.

DEUXIEME ETAPE

quatre-vingt-treize 93

Presentation

Vocabulaire Show pictures of the vocabulary items and have students repeat after you. Then, ask questions about the activities, such as **Qui a déjà fait du deltaplane? Qui voudrait essayer? Qui aime aller à la pêche?** Next, draw a grid on the board, listing several activities vertically and several questions horizontally, such as **Qui a déjà fait... ? Qui aime beaucoup... ? Qui n'aime pas du tout... ?** Ask a student to poll the class and tally the results on the board.

For videodisc application, see *Videodisc Guide.*

(TPR) Tell students to do these activities (**Jean, danse le zouk!**) and have them respond to demonstrate their comprehension.

Thinking Critically

Comparing and Contrasting Ask students which of these activities they can do in or near their own town and which ones are limited to a particular environment. Ask them what they do in their area that they couldn't do on a tropical island.

Presentation

Note de grammaire Demonstrate the difference between **promener** and **se promener** by drawing stick figures on the board or on a transparency. Point to an appropriate drawing, saying **Le garçon se promène. Ici, il promène son chien.** Do the same with the verbs **amuser** and **s'amuser.** (**La fille s'amuse. Ici, elle amuse le bébé.**)

Language Notes

• Call attention to the word **tropicaux** and ask students to try to guess the singular form (**tropical**). Discuss the formation of this adjective and its plural form. Have students suggest other nouns that might be used with **tropical.** (**une île/des îles, un arbre/des arbres, une forêt/des forêts, un menu/des menus**)

• **Déguster** means much more than **manger.** It means to *savor* whatever you eat or drink and to truly appreciate it. **Une dégustation** implies a *sampling* of something. Sometimes, a grocery store will offer **une dégustation gratuite** to offer samples of a new product. **Un dégustateur/une dégustatrice** is a person who tests the quality of wine.

Answers on p. 81C.

Teaching Suggestion

17 Draw pictures of the activities or items mentioned in random order on the board or on a transparency (a fishing pole, a hang glider, scuba gear, a mask, and a beach), and number them. As students listen to the recording, have them write the numbers of the pictures in the order they hear them mentioned.

Building on Previous Skills

18 Have students draw on a sheet of paper a desktop that would reflect their interests. Have them show the drawing to a partner who will guess what they like to do. (**Tu aimes lire? Tu aimes jouer au basket?**) The artist should confirm a correct guess (**Oui, c'est ça.**) or encourage a different response. (**Non, pas exactement.**)

Presentation

Comment dit-on... ? Type and distribute copies of the listening script for Activity 17. Draw three columns on the board or on a transparency and label them as follows: *Asking for suggestions, Making suggestions,* and *Accepting and Refusing suggestions.* Have students pick out the sentences from the listening script that accomplish these functions and write them under the appropriate columns. Finally, introduce the expressions in **Comment dit-on... ?** and ask students which ones they recall from Chapter 1. (**Qu'est-ce qu'on fait? Si tu veux, on peut... ; Tu as envie de... ? On pourrait... ; Ça te dit de (d')... ?**)

17 Ecoute!

Listen as Magali and César decide what to do today. List two things they suggest. What do they finally decide to do? Answers on p. 81C.

18 Qu'est-ce qu'ils aiment? See answers below.

Regarde les bureaux de José et de Jocelyne. A ton avis, qu'est-ce qu'ils aiment faire?

Le bureau de José

Le bureau de Jocelyne

COMMENT DIT-ON... ?

Asking for and making suggestions

To ask for suggestions about what to do:

Qu'est-ce qu'on peut faire?

To make suggestions:

On peut se promener sur la plage.
We can . . .

Ça te dit d'aller manger une glace?
What do you think of going . . . ?

Si on allait se baigner?
How about going . . . ?

NOTE CULTURELLE

In Martinique, people speak French and **créole**, a mixture of French and African languages with some Spanish, English, and Portuguese words. Here's how to respond in Creole to someone's suggestions:

Oui / Non *Ouai / Han-Han*
Chouette! *I bon!*
D'accord. *D'accó.*
C'est une bonne idée. *Ce'an bon bagaï.*

Je ne peux pas. *Mwen pé pa.*
Ça ne me dit rien. *Sa pa ka di mwen ayen.*
Pas question! *Awa!*

---

94 *quatre-vingt-quatorze*

CHAPITRE 4 Sous les tropiques

Teaching Suggestion

Note Culturelle Before reading the **Note Culturelle** with students, write these expressions on the board or on a transparency. Put the French expressions in one column and the Creole expressions in random order in a second column. Have students try to match the French expressions to their Creole equivalents.

Teacher Note

For more information on the Creole language, see **Lisons!** on page 103.

Answers

18 José: la musique, la natation, le deltaplane, la pêche, la plongée

Jocelyn: se promener sur la plage, les fruits, les copains, la natation ou la plongée, faire de la voile

19 Une journée touristique

Fais des projets pour une journée touristique à la Martinique avec un(e) camarade. Décidez de ce que vous allez faire le matin, l'après-midi et le soir.

déguster des spécialités antillaises

visiter Saint-Pierre

faire des photos des chutes d'eau

écouter de la musique antillaise et danser

aller voir la forêt tropicale

visiter un village de pêcheurs

– ? –

se promener à Fort-de-France

s'amuser sur la plage

20 Qu'est-ce qu'il y a à faire?

Scan the calendar of events to find the answers to these questions.

1. How many countries participate in the **Championnat de tennis de la Caraïbe et des Amériques?**
2. What are three types of plays presented at the **Rencontres caribéennes de théâtre?**
3. Where do the artists come from for the **Festival de Fort-de-France?**
4. Who dreams of being at the **Tour des yoles rondes de la Martinique?**
5. What event replaces **Jazz à la Martinique** every other year?
   See answers below.

21 Si on allait... ?

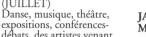

You're going to Martinique with the French Club, but you must decide in which month to go. With a group of classmates, decide on the best time to go, suggesting what you might do then. Consult the calendar of events so you'll know what to suggest.

—Si on y va en décembre, on peut écouter de la musique.
—Non, c'est barbant. En juillet, au Festival de Fort-de-France, on peut danser...

CALENDRIER DES ÉVÉNEMENTS

CHAMPIONNAT DE TENNIS DE LA CARAÏBE ET DES AMÉRIQUES

(MAI)
Se déroule chaque année sur la commune du Lamentin (Petit Manoir). Ce championnat réunit pas moins de 40 pays de la Caraïbe et des Amériques ; un carrefour d'échanges sportifs mais également culturels.

RENCONTRES CARIBÉENNES DE THÉÂTRE

(MAI)
Des troupes théâtrales martiniquaises, de la Caraïbe et d'Europe présentent chaque année des pièces classiques, drôles et parfois nouvelles.

FESTIVAL DE FORT-DE-FRANCE

(JUILLET)
Danse, musique, théâtre, expositions, conférences-débats, des artistes venant de tous les pays du monde, ce festival des vacances est l'un des plus grands temps forts de la vie culturelle martiniquaise, avec un accent particulier sur la culture noire.

TOUR DES YOLES RONDES DE LA MARTINIQUE

(AOUT)
Un sujet rêvé pour les photographes professionnels ou amateurs présents au mois d'août. Ce spectacle populaire et unique au monde laisse admirer la technique des équipes qui ont fait, à partir de splendides embarcations traditionnelles de pêche, un outil de course.

SEMI-MARATHON

(NOVEMBRE)
Au mois de novembre a lieu, depuis 1985, le semi-marathon international de Fort-de-France. Il suscite tellement d'intérêt que pas moins de 350 coureurs viennent de l'étranger pour y participer. Plus de 3 000 coureurs y participent chaque année.

JAZZ A LA MARTINIQUE

(DECEMBRE)
En alternance chaque année avec le Carrefour International de la guitare, ces deux grands moments culturels et musicaux présentent en concert début décembre des musiciens du monde entier : Dee Dee Bridewater, Eddy Louis, Baden Powell, Victoria de Los Angeles, Ichiro Suzuki, Manuel Brueco, beaucoup d'artistes de la Caraïbe et des styles très différents.

Answers
20 1. 40
   2. classical, funny, new
   3. from everywhere
   4. professional photographers
   5. Carrefour International de la guitare

Cooperative Learning

21 Have small groups create a **Calendrier des événements** for their town or school. Have students mention two or three events. They might use the newspaper to find out about town happenings or write about school events. Assign a leader to gather information, a writer to record it, and an artist to find or create illustrations for the calendar.

Teaching Suggestions

19 Encourage students to respond to their partner's suggestions in Creole (see **Note Culturelle** on page 94). Students might present their conversations to the class.

19 After students have finished their pair work, have individuals ask their classmates questions to find out whose plans are similar to theirs. (**Qui va visiter Saint-Pierre le matin? Qui va danser le soir?**)

20 Ask additional comprehension questions, such as the following:
1. When does the marathon take place? (in November) How many people participate? (3,000)
2. Where does the tennis championship take place? (in Le Lamentin) Can you find it on the map on page 88?
3. What happens at the Fort-de-France festival? (dance, music, theater, exhibitions, lectures, debates) What culture is emphasized? (the black culture)
4. Where do the theatrical groups come from that present the plays in May? (from all over the world)

Additional Practice

20 For additional listening and speaking practice, ask questions in French, such as the following: **En quel mois est-ce qu'on peut voir des troupes théâtrales? (en mai) Qu'est-ce qu'il y a au mois de juillet? (le festival de Fort-de-France) Combien de coureurs viennent de l'étranger pour participer au semi-marathon? (trois cent cinquante)**

21 Have each group report to the class the particular month they chose to go to Martinique and why.

96 **DEUXIEME ETAPE**   **CHAPITRE 4**

Presentation

Comment dit-on... ? Write the following question and answers on the board or on a transparency: *What do you like to do on the weekend?*
1. *I like to go shopping.*
2. *What I really like to do is go shopping.*
Ask students to explain the difference between the two responses. Model each statement in **Comment dit-on... ?**, telling what you really like or dislike. Have students repeat each expression after you, substituting their own likes or dislikes. Then, write times on the board such as **le week-end** or **le samedi soir**. Have students tell what they really like or dislike doing at these times. (**Ce que j'aime le week-end, c'est me lever très tard.**) Finally, have partners ask each other questions using the expressions and the times on the board.

◆ For Individual Needs

Auditory Learners Have students complete each expression in **Comment dit-on... ?**, according to their own likes and dislikes. Have them read their sentences to the class and have others respond **Moi aussi!** or **Moi non plus!**

Language Note

In the expressions from **Comment dit-on... ?** that use the verbs **se plaire** and **s'ennuyer** (**Ce qui me plaît...** , **Ce qui ne me plaît pas...** , **Ce qui m'ennuie...**), it is acceptable to use **de** before the infinitive. (**Ce qui me plaît, c'est de dormir tard. Ce qui m'ennuie, c'est de rester à la maison.**)

COMMENT DIT-ON... ?
Emphasizing likes and dislikes

> *Ce qui me plaît, c'est jouer au frisbee®!*

To emphasize what you like:

    Ce que j'aime bien le week-end, **c'est** me coucher très tard.
      What I like is . . .
    Ce que je préfère, c'est me promener sur la plage.
      What I prefer is . . .
    Ce qui me plaît à la Martinique, **c'est** la mer!
      What I like is . . .

To emphasize what you don't like:

    Ce que je n'aime pas, c'est les maths!
      What I don't like is . . .
    Ce qui ne me plaît pas, c'est me lever à 6h du matin.
      What I don't care for is . . .
    Ce qui m'ennuie, c'est rester à la maison le week-end.
      What bothers me is . . .

22 Ecoute!

What activities are these people talking about? Do they like or dislike the activities?
Answers on p. 81C.

23 Qu'est-ce que tu aimes faire?

Qu'est-ce que tu aimes faire dans les situations suivantes? Pose les questions à un(e) camarade et puis, changez de rôles.

   —Qu'est-ce que tu aimes faire quand il pleut?
   —Ce qui me plaît, c'est lire un roman.

> le samedi matin
> quand il fait très chaud
> quand il pleut
> après l'école
> quand il neige

24 Une publicité

Write a commercial to attract tourists to one of your favorite places. Describe the place and tell what you can do there and what you like most about it. Use props, photos or art, and music to entice people to visit.

Note de Grammaire

When you're using a reflexive verb to talk about yourself, use **me** before the verb instead of **se**. Can you figure out what **me lever** and **me coucher** mean in **Comment dit-on...?** **Se lever** *(to get up)* and **se coucher** *(to go to bed)* are among the most frequently used reflexive verbs.

De bons conseils

If you look up specific words or phrases in an English-French dictionary, here are a few hints:

• Some words can have several different meanings in English or in French. If you look up the word *pool* for example, do you mean a *swimming pool* or a *billiard game*? Be sure to choose the correct French equivalent.
  • Pay attention to the part of speech of the word you're looking for. Are you looking for the noun *snack*, as in *a quick snack*, or the verb *snack*, as in *I snack between meals*?
  • To be sure you have the appropriate definition, look up the French word you want to use in the French-English part of the dictionary. Is the English equivalent what you had in mind?

CLOSE

To close this **étape,** have one student begin by making a suggestion. (**Ça te dit d'aller au cinéma?**) The next student should refuse (**Non, ce qui ne me plaît pas, c'est aller au cinéma**) and then make a suggestion to the next student (**Si on allait au parc?**) and so on.

ASSESS

Quiz 4-2, *Chapter Teaching Resources, Book 1,* pp. 193–194

Assessment Items, Audiocassette 7B Audio CD 4

Performance Assessment

Use Activity 24 to assess students' performance of this **étape.**

RENCONTRE CULTURELLE

Qu'en penses-tu?

1. What celebration is pictured above?   Carnival
2. What festivals and celebrations do you have in your area?

Savais-tu que... ?

Carnival (**Carnaval**) is a well-known tradition in French-speaking countries. It takes place the week before Lent (**le Carême**), ending on Shrove Tuesday (**Mardi gras**), at the stroke of midnight. In Martinique, however, Carnival lasts until midnight of Ash Wednesday (**Mercredi des cendres**), and is celebrated with parades, music, dancing, feasting, and colorful costumes. Queens are elected to reign over the festivals, and on the Sunday before Ash Wednesday, they parade through the streets of the city to the beat of Creole songs. On Monday, mock weddings are held in which the participants dress in burlesque costumes. On Tuesday, Carnival performers dance wildly in red costumes decorated with mirrors. Finally, on Ash Wednesday, people dress in black and white costumes to mourn the death of the cardboard king, **Roi Vaval**, who symbolizes the spirit of Carnival. At the stroke of midnight, the dancing and music stop, and Lent begins. Other cities famous for their Carnival celebrations are Nice in France, Quebec City in Canada, and New Orleans in Louisiana.

Teacher Note

Lent (**le Carême**) is a Christian religious season meant as a time of spiritual discipline and renewal; it lasts approximately 40 days. Ash Wednesday marks the first day of penitence that begins the season of Lent. On this day in many churches, the priest or pastor blesses ashes from burned palms and uses them to mark a cross on the worshiper's forehead, symbolizing purification and penitence. Shrove Tuesday, the day before Ash Wednesday, originated with the custom of seeking forgiveness for sin (being *shriven*) on that day.

Multicultural Link

Have students do research to find out about **Carnaval** or **Mardi gras** in other parts of the world, such as Rio de Janeiro, Nice, and Quebec, where the greatest celebrations occur. Have them compare these celebrations and their traditions to those in Martinique.

Motivating Activity

Have students tell what they know about Mardi Gras. Ask them if it is celebrated where they live, and if so, how. Then, ask if they know of other festivals that involve music, dancing, and costumes.

Presentation

Read **Savais-tu que... ?** with students. Have them match each photo with the day on which it was taken, according to the descriptions in **Savais-tu que... ?** (top left photo: Ash Wednesday; bottom left photo: Sunday before Ash Wednesday; photo on right: Shrove Tuesday)

History Link

French colonists introduced Mardi Gras to North America in the early 1700s. It especially became popular in the south and is a legal holiday in Alabama, Florida, and parts of Louisiana. It dates back to the ancient Roman custom of celebrating before a period of fast. In French, **Mardi gras** means *Fat Tuesday,* originating from the custom of parading a fat ox through the streets of Paris on Shrove Tuesday.

Culture Note

In New Orleans during the two weeks before Mardi Gras, elaborate parades and masked balls are held every night. They are sponsored by civic clubs called Krewes, who each choose a king, usually a senior member, and a queen, usually the daughter of a member, to reign over the festivities. This is considered such an honor that some of the members put their daughters' names on a list the day they are born, so that they might be queen 18 years later.

Jump Start!

Write the following scrambled conversation on the board and have students rewrite it in the correct order.

— Bonne idée. L'aventure, j'adore!

— Non, il fait trop chaud. Si on allait faire du delta-plane?

— On pourrait regarder une vidéo.

— Qu'est-ce qu'on peut faire cet aprèm?

— Non, c'est barbant. Ça te dit d'aller à la plage?

MOTIVATE

Ask students to describe a typical day from the time they get up until the time they go to bed.

TEACH

Teaching Suggestions

• Using props, act out some of the sentences by describing your daily routine. Have students repeat the sentences and mimic your gestures. Then, have them cover the caption below each illustration. Call out one sentence from each caption at random and have students point to the appropriate illustration.

25 Students might write down all of the sentences that describe their own day as well.

 Culture Note

At one time, the only relief for the slaves was to join a rebel group called the Maroons, which was dedicated to the preservation of African culture in the Caribbean. Finally, Victor Schœlcher prepared the decree that abolished slavery in the colonies in 1848.

Teacher Note

For more information on Antillean music and dance, see **Lisons!** on page 102.

TROISIEME ETAPE
Relating a series of events

SALUT, JE M'APPELLE AGATHE ET JE T'INVITE À PASSER UNE JOURNÉE TYPIQUE CHEZ MOI, ALLEZ, VIENS!

D'abord, je me lève à 7h du matin.

Puis, je me lave.

Je me brosse les dents.

Vers 7h30, je m'habille.

Ensuite je prends mon petit déjeuner et je vais au lycée.

Après l'école, je rentre chez moi. Le mercredi et le vendredi, je vais à un cours de percussions. Après, on mange en famille.

Enfin, en semaine, je me couche assez tôt, vers 9h. Mais le weekend, je me couche beaucoup plus tard.

25 Et toi?

How is your weekday schedule similar to Agathe's? How is it different?

NOTE CULTURELLE

Music and dance are an integral part of life in Martinique. A popular saying is that in Martinique **tout finit par une chanson.** Much of the music arises from the time the first Africans were brought as slaves to work in the sugarcane fields. The rhythms of the songs and the steps of the dances they created are still in existence today in the **biguine, mazurka,** and the internationally popular **zouk.**

RESOURCES FOR **TROISIEME ETAPE**

Textbook Audiocassette 2B/Audio CD 4
Practice and Activity Book, pp. 44–46
Videodisc Guide
   Videodisc Program, Videodisc 2B

Chapter Teaching Resources, Book 1
• Communicative Activity 4-2, pp. 173–174
• Teaching Transparency Master 4-3, pp. 177, 178
   Teaching Transparency 4-3
• Additional Listening Activities 4-5, 4-6, p. 181
   Audiocassette 9B/Audio CD 4
• Realia 4-2, pp. 184, 185
• Situation Cards 4-3, pp. 186–187
• Student Response Forms, pp. 188–190
• Quiz 4-3, pp. 195–196
   Audiocassette 7B/Audio CD 4

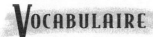

VOCABULAIRE

se lever	to get up	Je me lève.	I get up.
se laver	to wash (oneself)	Je me lave.	I wash (myself).
se brosser les dents	to brush one's teeth	Je me brosse les dents.	I brush my teeth.
s'habiller	to get dressed	Je m'habille.	I get dressed.
se coucher	to go to bed	Je me couche.	I go to bed.
		tôt	early
		tard	late

COMMENT DIT-ON... ?
Relating a series of events

To start:
   D'abord, je me lève.

To continue:
   Ensuite, je me lave.
   Et puis, je m'habille.
   Vers 8h, je mange.
      At about . . .
   Après ça, j'attends le bus.
      After that, . . .

To end:
   Finalement, je vais au lycée.
      Finally, . . .

26 Ecoute!

André décrit ses préparatifs du matin. Mets les images en ordre. e, b, c, d, a

a.

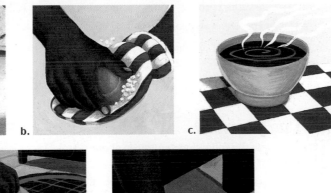
b.

c.

d.

e.

Presentation

Vocabulaire/Comment dit-on... ? Model and act out the sentences in the **Vocabulaire.** You might use props to illustrate your actions (an alarm clock, a washcloth). Have students repeat after you and imitate your gestures. Repeat the process, this time including sequencing words and times of day in your sentences. Then, have a student come to the front of the classroom to model your sentences. (**D'abord, je me lève à sept heures. Ensuite, je me lave. A sept heures et demie, je prends mon petit déjeuner...**) He or she may look at the book for support.

For videodisc application, see *Videodisc Guide.*

TPR Give commands using the **Vocabulaire** (**Brossez-vous les dents! Levez-vous!**) and have students act out the commands at their desks.

For Individual Needs

26 Slower Pace Before you play the recording, have students suggest a sentence from the **Vocabulaire** to describe each illustration.

Culture Note

Call attention to the **gant de toilette** in illustration **b.** The French use a wash cloth that is sewn together to fit over the hand and worn like a "glove." Students might also notice the bowl pictured in the third illustration. Usually, the French will drink their hot chocolate (**chocolat chaud**), coffee, or **café au lait** in a large bowl.

27 Tactile/Visual Learners Have students write the activities on separate, small strips of paper. On other small pieces of paper, have students sketch representations of each activity. Finally, have them match the sketches to the strips and arrange them in the order in which they do the activities.

Presentation

Grammaire After reading through the **Grammaire** with students, act out your daily routine, asking **Qu'est-ce que je fais?** Prompt students to reply **Vous vous levez.** Confirm each reply: **Oui, je me lève.** Then, ask a volunteer to act out his or her daily routine. Ask students **Qu'est-ce qu'il/elle fait?** to elicit **Il/Elle se lève.** Next, have two students go through the routine, and ask **Qu'est-ce qu'ils/elles font?** Have the two students confirm **Oui, nous nous levons** after each reply. Finally, have students work in pairs acting out their daily routine and telling each other what they are doing. (**Tu te lèves.**)

Building On Previous Skills

Re-enter the names of rooms in the house and places in town by asking **Où est-ce qu'on se lave? Où est-ce qu'on s'habille? Où est-ce qu'on déjeune?** and so on.

Teaching Suggestion

28 Have students take notes as they complete this activity. Then, have them write sentences, comparing themselves to their partners. (**Moi, en semaine, je me lève à 7h, mais Thomas se lève à 6h.**)

---

27 Un matin typique

Which of these activities do you do in the morning? Put them in the order in which you do them, adding any other activities that are part of your morning routine.

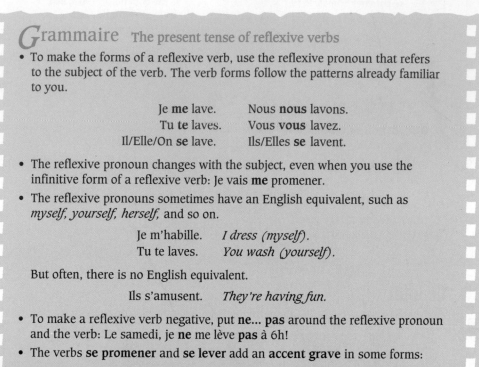

Je me brosse les dents. — ? — Je me lève.
Je vais au lycée. Je me lave. Je me lève.
Je prends mon petit déjeuner. Je m'habille.

> ### 𝒢rammaire   The present tense of reflexive verbs
>
> - To make the forms of a reflexive verb, use the reflexive pronoun that refers to the subject of the verb. The verb forms follow the patterns already familiar to you.
>
> | | |
> |---|---|
> | Je **me** lave. | Nous **nous** lavons. |
> | Tu **te** laves. | Vous **vous** lavez. |
> | Il/Elle/On **se** lave. | Ils/Elles **se** lavent. |
>
> - The reflexive pronoun changes with the subject, even when you use the infinitive form of a reflexive verb: Je vais **me** promener.
> - The reflexive pronouns sometimes have an English equivalent, such as *myself, yourself, herself,* and so on.
>
> | | |
> |---|---|
> | Je m'habille. | *I dress (myself).* |
> | Tu te laves. | *You wash (yourself).* |
>
> But often, there is no English equivalent.
>
> | | |
> |---|---|
> | Ils s'amusent. | *They're having fun.* |
>
> - To make a reflexive verb negative, put **ne... pas** around the reflexive pronoun and the verb: Le samedi, je **ne** me lève **pas** à 6h!
> - The verbs **se promener** and **se lever** add an **accent grave** in some forms:
>
> | | |
> |---|---|
> | Je me promène/lève. | Nous nous promenons/levons. |
> | Tu te promènes/lèves. | Vous vous promenez/levez. |
> | Il/Elle/On se promène/lève. | Ils/Elles se promènent/lèvent. |

28 Une interview

Complete the following sentences about yourself and then find out about your partner.

1. En semaine, je me lève vers _____ h. Et toi?
2. Le samedi, je me lève vers _____ h. Et toi?
3. Je m'habille _____ (cool, chic, relax) pour aller à l'école. Et toi?
4. Pour aller à une boum, je m'habille _____ (cool, chic, relax). Et toi?
5. Le week-end, je me couche vers _____ h. Et toi?
6. D'habitude, j'arrive à l'école _____ (tôt, à l'heure, en retard). Et toi?

Tu te rappelles ❓

When you're listening to people or reading books and magazines, keep in mind that the unaccented **e** is often dropped:

Je me lave.	Je m'lave.
On se promène.	On s'promène.
Tu te couches?	Tu t'couches?

100   *cent*   CHAPITRE 4   Sous les tropiques

♖ Game

A TOI! To practice reflexive verbs, have students form a circle (or two). Call out a sentence containing a reflexive verb. (**Nous nous levons à six heures.**) Then, toss a soft ball to a student as you call out a different subject (**mon père**). The student catches the ball, replaces the subject of the original sentence with the new one, and says the new sentence. (**Mon père se lève à six heures.**) Then, he or she tosses the ball to another student, calling out a new subject. A student who does not respond within five seconds is out of the game, but may get back in by correcting another's error. After several tosses, start a new sentence. You might also substitute different verbs in addition to subjects, saying **Je me lave** and calling out **s'habiller** as you throw the ball.

29 A la Martinique...

Complète les phrases pour décrire chaque photo.

1. Les enfants _____ en costumes traditionnels pendant les fêtes.
   s'habillent

2. Ils _____ bien ensemble.
   s'amusent

3. Le soleil _____ sur la mer.
   se couche

30 Nos emplois du temps

a. Qu'est-ce que tu fais en général...

1. à 10h le samedi matin?
2. à 8h le vendredi soir?
3. à midi le dimanche?
4. à 7h le mercredi matin?
5. à 11h le jeudi soir?
6. à 9h le lundi matin?

b. Maintenant, demande à tes camarades de classe ce qu'ils font à ces heures-là. Qui fait les mêmes choses que toi?

31 Chère Marie-Line, ...

Read this letter from Marie-Line, a student in Martinique. Then, write a reply, telling what you normally do after school and mentioning differences you've noticed between life in Martinique and life in the United States.

Tu te rappelles ?

To tell how often you do something, you need adverbs. Do you remember these?

d'habitude	usually
souvent	often
quelquefois	sometimes
ne... jamais	never

To tell what you usually do on a certain day, use **le** with the name of the day.
Le samedi, je me lève très tard!

Après l'école, je rentre chez moi. D'abord, je prends mon goûter : souvent des tartines ou un fruit et quelquefois, de la canne à sucre. Puis, je fais mes devoirs. Comme je ne suis pas très forte en maths, je dois passer beaucoup de temps à faire mes devoirs de maths et je n'aime pas beaucoup ça. Vers 8 h, mon père rentre à la maison et toute la famille dîne ensemble. Après, si j'ai le temps, je regarde la télé. J'aime surtout les films américains et les clips vidéo de Zouk Machine, mon groupe préféré. Enfin, vers 10h, je vais me coucher car je dois me lever à 6 h les jours de classe. C'est dur!
Et toi, qu'est-ce que tu fais après l'école? Tu as beaucoup de devoirs? C'est comment, ta vie aux États-Unis? Raconte-moi. J'attends ta lettre.

Je t'embrasse,
Marie-Line

Teaching Suggestions

30 Students might write a diary entry for each time and day mentioned, telling not only what they're doing at the moment, but also how they feel about it. Refer students to the Supplementary Vocabulary in the back of the book for additional daily activities.

31 You might first use the letter as the basis of a reading activity. Have students read the letter and then respond to your questions, true-false statements, or other means of assessing their comprehension.

Cooperative Learning

31 Form groups of four and have students peer-edit their letters. Have one student check for accents and spelling, one for subject-verb agreement, one for correct use of possessive adjectives, and one for correct use of connectors and adverbs of frequency. All students should check for comprehensibility and make suggestions for improvement.

CLOSE

Have students write a paragraph describing their daily routine. Have them peer-edit their paragraphs as they did in Activity 31 and then rewrite each sentence on a strip of paper. Have them shuffle the strips of paper and pass them to a partner. The partner rearranges the strips in the original or a logical order. The writer of the paragraph then checks for accuracy and offers corrections, if necessary. (**Non, d'abord, ma mère rentre du travail, et après mon père prépare le dîner.**)

ASSESS

Quiz 4-3, *Chapter Teaching Resources, Book 1,* pp. 195–196

*Assessment Items, Audiocassette 7B
Audio CD 4*

Performance Assessment

Form groups of four and have students tell each other what they normally do from the time they wake up until the time they fall asleep. They should act out the activities, using sequencing words, adverbs of frequency, and times of day.

Music allows people to express the feelings and ideas closest to their hearts and minds. That's the basis of **zouk**, a music unique to the French West Indies.

DE BONS CONSEILS

Reading in a foreign language can be intimidating. After previewing, skimming, and scanning, look for the main idea of what you're reading. Then, it's easier to figure out the details.

A. What would you write a song about? Your feelings? Global politics? Injustice? Your home? The things you love, or things that bother you? List three things you might write about in a song.

B. What are you going to read here? Can you tell what two languages are represented? Do you think Kassav' sings *An sèl zouk* in French or in Creole? What's the title of the CD? Do you know what it means? (hint: it's from English) See answers below.

C. Skim the French lyrics. Which of the following do you think is the focus of the song?

   a. the songwriter's feelings about France

   b. <u>Martinique, Guadeloupe, the Caribbean</u>

   c. life as a sailor

D. Where is the songwriter from? How does he feel about his homeland? What words and phrases tell you? See answers below.

AN SÈL ZOUK
UN SEUL ZOUK

Fout' sa jéyan / lè mwen Gwadloup' / Mwen a kaze an mwen / Mwen byen kontan / Ké ni bon tan / Tchè mwen souri pou Matinik / Sé kon si sé la mwen wè jou / Bondyé / Sa ou pé di di sa zanmi / Yo tou piti /Sé la nou grandi / Epi mizik an tout' kwen kaÿ la / **An sèl Gwadloup ki ni** / **Sé an sèl Matinik / Pou an zèl Zouk nou ni / Madikéra** / Pa lé kwè dé bèl péyi kon sa / Fo nou pa viv' kon nou yé a / Rété tou sa / Sa ou ka di ya / Mwen ja réfléchi asou tou sa / Mé pa ka konpwann / éti nou kaÿ épi sa / Yo pa byen gran / Mé yo ni balan / E yo ka ba dousè chalè lov' / **Ki nou la Gwadloup / Ki nou Matinik / Ki nou Guyann / Nou sé karáyib /** **An nou mété nou / O dyapazon /** Lésé tchè nou palé / Pou nou pé sanblé / **An sèl Gwadloup ki ni /** **Sé an sèl Matinik / Pou an zèl Zouk nou ni /** **Madikéra** / An gran makè té di / Yo kon pousyè lò épi lajan / Ki tonbé dépi zétwal / E pozé an lan mè / Lè an ka sonjé sé la nou vwè jou / Bondyé mèsi / An mété an jounou /I ka fè révé / I ka fè chanté / Bondyé mèsi sé la nou vwè jou /**Woyoyoÿ /** **An nou alé / woyoyoÿ / Bagaÿ la fè zip zip /** **Biten la fè zip zip zip /**

Paroles & Musique César DURCIN

READING STRATEGY

Looking for the main idea

Teacher Note

For an additional reading, see *Practice and Activity Book*, page 47.

PREREADING
Activities A–C

Motivating Activity

A. Ask students what types of things their favorite musical groups and artists write about in their songs. Ask them if they are ever affected by the message in a song and why.

Multicultural Link

B. Ask students if they are familiar with any music from a different culture. Ask them if any of their favorite songs in English are sung by British, Canadian, or Australian artists, or English-speaking artists of other nationalities, and if they can detect different accents or meanings of words in these songs.

Culture Note

The basic sound of **zouk** comes from the traditional **gwo ka** drums, which are made from barrels that once held salted meat, the former food of slaves. The rhythm of **zouk** comes from the French West Indies, and the guitar and vocal arrangements have their roots in West Africa. **Zouk** is also related to two dance forms and their music: **biguine,** *a rhythmic native dance of Martinique,* and **mazurka,** *a lively Polish folk dance.*

Culture Note

Zouk is an integral part and a unique expression of French Antillean culture. Emigrants from Martinique and Guadeloupe brought their island music with them to Paris, where they encountered the rhythms of French-speaking Africa. Catalyzed by the high-energy tunes of Parisian discos, the hybrid sound was christened *zouk,* the Creole term for *party.* Dynamic groups like Kassav' and Zouk Machine have brought this music world-wide attention.

Answers

B a song; French and Creole; Creole; Tékitizi; take it easy

D Guadeloupe; *Possible answers:* love, warmth, beauty, sweetness; "Elles ont de l'allure, elles nous donnent de la douceur, de la chaleur, de l'amour."

For Activities E and H, see answers below.

E. Which lines of the song are the chorus? How do you know? **Madikera** is a word made from **Madinina**, a name for Martinique, and **Karukéra**, a name for Guadeloupe. What is the message of the chorus?

F. Try to pronounce each Creole word below and find its French equivalent. If you can't figure out the word's meaning by its sound, compare the Creole text with the French text. Which Creole word comes from English? lov'

1. Gwadloup   d   a. les étoiles
2. Matinik   f   b. content
3. kontan   b   c. la mer
4. piti   g   d. Guadcloupe
5. mizik   e   e. musique
6. zétwal   a   f. Martinique
7. lan mè   c   g. petites
8. lov'   h   h. l'amour

Try to match these phrases.   **1.** a **2.** c **3.** b

1. Mwen byen kontan.   a. Je suis bien content.
2. Pou an zèl Zouk.   b. C'est là que nous avons grandi.
3. Sé la nou grandi.   c. Pour un seul zouk.

G. Write a list of other Creole words you can figure out and pass it to a classmate, who will try to write the French words next to the Creole ones.

H. Looking at all the words and phrases you have decoded, what are the songwriter's feelings about **zouk**? How does the title of the song relate to his ideas?

I. Write a brief song in French about one of the topics you listed in Activity A and set it to a favorite piece of music. Use some of the expressions you've learned in this chapter to express what you like and dislike about your topic.

⑮

C'est super / Lorsque je suis à la Guadeloupe / Je suis chez moi / Content / Je prends du bon temps / J'ai le cœur qui sourit pour la Martinique / C'est comme si j'y étais né / Qu'en dis-tu / Elles sont petites / C'est là que nous avons grandi / Avec de la musique dans toute la maison / **Il n'y a qu'une seule Guadeloupe / Une seule Martinique / Pour un seul zouk / Madikera** / Mais je ne peux admettre / Que nous vivons comme nous le faisons / Il faut que ça change / J'ai déjà pensé à tout ce dont tu parles / Et je ne vois pas / Où cela nous mène / Elles ne sont pas très grandes / Mais elles ont de l'allure / Et elles nous donnent de la douceur, de la chaleur, et de l'amour / **Que nous soyons à la Guadeloupe / à la Martinique / En Guyane / Dans la Caraïbe / Accordons nos violons** / Laissons parler nos cœurs / Pour nous rassembler / **Il n'y a qu'une seule Guadeloupe / Une seule Martinique / Pour un seul zouk / Madikera** / Un grand écrivain a dit / Qu'elles sont comme des pièces d'or et d'argent / Tombées de la bourse aux étoiles / Et posées sur la mer / Lorsque je pense que c'est là que nous avons vu le jour / Je me mets à genoux / Pour remercier Dieu /

cent trois **103**

Answers

E "Il n'y a qu'une seule Guadeloupe... Madikera."; it repeats itself, and it's in bold type; to present a strong, unified Guadeloupe and Martinique.

H *Possible answers:* He wants to unify all of the French speaking areas of the Carribean; He uses the word "un seul," only one (all together).

Language Note

Write the following Kassav' song titles on the board or on a transparency, have students pronounce them the way they are written, and then ask students if they recognize any French words in the Creole: **Palé mwen dous'** (*Tell Me Sweet Things*); **Zôt Vini Pou** (*Others Come For . . .*); **Lévé Tèt' Ou** (*Lift Your Head Up*); **Mwen Alé** (*I'm Going/Leaving*); **Ou Chanjé** (*You've Changed*).

READING
Activities D–G

Teaching Suggestion

E. Ask how the chorus relates to the main idea and title of the song.

For Individual Needs

F., G. Slower Pace Have students do these activities in pairs rather than individually.

POSTREADING
Activities H–I

For Individual Needs

Challenge Type the lyrics of the Creole song and number the lines. Type the lines of the French song in a different order and precede each one with a letter of the alphabet. Have students match the Creole lyrics with their French equivalents.

Teaching Suggestion

I. If some students choose to set their song to rap music, you might play the song *S'appeler rap* from *Allez, viens!,* Level 1, recorded on *Textbook Audiocassette 1* and *Audio CD 1.*

Language Note

The Creole that is spoken in Martinique, Guadeloupe, and Haiti is of French and African origin. Words written in Creole are usually spelled phonetically. These words often resemble (in spelling and pronunciation) words in one of the languages of origin. Examples in Creole/French include: **jou/jour, mèsi/merci, lajan/l'argent,** and **konpwann/comprendre.** Creole languages often originate when the speakers of two different languages attempt to communicate, resulting in a simplified form of one of the languages.

The **Mise en pratique** reviews and integrates all four skills and culture in preparation for the Chapter Test.

For Individual Needs

Visual/Tactile Learners
Read the brochure with students and ask them to find and touch the areas on the map that the brochure refers to. Students might work with partners to verify that they've found the correct area.

Geography Link

Guadeloupe consists of two main islands, Grande-Terre and Basse-Terre, in addition to five smaller islands: Marie-Galante, L'île des Saintes, La Désirade, Saint-Barthélemy, and the northern half of Saint-Martin. Basse-Terre, twenty-seven miles long and fifteen miles wide, is thickly forested and mountainous. The dormant volcanic summit, La Soufrière, which is 4,868 feet above sea level, is located on this island. Cattle, sheep, goats, and pigs are raised 3,000 feet above sea level in the savanna (tropical grassland) region. Coffee, cacao, vanilla bean, and banana plantations are plentiful throughout Basse-Terre, while sugar cane is cultivated on the island of Grande-Terre. The fauna of Guadeloupe include lizards, raccoons, agouti (a type of rodent), mongooses, wild ducks, and hummingbirds.

History Link

The Carib Indians originally occupied the islands of Guadeloupe. In 1626, the Spanish established a colony there, but were driven away by the French, who colonized the island in 1635. It remained essentially French, except for temporary British occupations between 1759 and 1813.

MISE EN PRATIQUE

Où se trouve la Guadeloupe?

Dans la mer des Caraïbes, dans les Antilles françaises, près de la Martinique.

Qu'est-ce qu'il y a à voir à la Guadeloupe? Il y a deux îles, Basse-Terre et Grande-Terre. Les deux îles sont liées par la Rivière Salée. À l'ouest, en Basse-Terre, il y a le volcan de la Soufrière, près de la ville de Basse-Terre, qui est la capitale de la Guadeloupe. À l'est, en Grande-Terre, il y a des champs de canne à sucre. Comme à la Martinique, il fait toujours chaud, entre 16 et 27 degrés Celsius. La Guadeloupe est plus grande que la Martinique, mais moins grande que Porto Rico. C'est une île accueillante, vivante, et tout à fait charmante!

Guadeloupe

L'île de Basse Terre

104   *cent quatre*   CHAPITRE 4   Sous les tropiques

Math Link

Have students convert the Celsius temperatures in the brochure to Fahrenheit to find out how warm it is in Guadeloupe and Martinique. To convert Celsius into degrees Fahrenheit, multiply Celsius by 1.8 and add 32. Then, have students convert the average seasonal temperatures where they live into Celsius. To convert degrees Fahrenheit into Celsius, subtract 32 from Fahrenheit and divide by 1.8.

Government Link

Guadeloupe, like Martinique, is a French overseas **département,** or *administrative district,* which is represented in the French National Assembly by three deputies, and in the French senate by two senators. The citizens of Guadeloupe are entitled to the same social welfare programs as in France, including old-age and disability pensions, family allowances, unemployment relief, and health insurance.

1 Like Martinique, Guadeloupe is an island in the French West Indies. What is the island of Guadeloupe like? Read the brochure on page 104 and match these areas with the numbered labels on the map.   welcoming, lively, charming

    a. les champs de canne à sucre   3   **d.** la Rivière Salée   2
    b. la mer des Caraïbes   5   **e.** l'île de Grande-Terre   4
    c. la Soufrière   6   **f.** la ville de Basse-Terre   1

 2 A travel agent in Guadeloupe is describing a tour you're interested in taking. As she speaks, write down, in order, what you will do on the tour.   Answers on p. 81D.

 3 With a partner, plan a day of sightseeing in Guadeloupe. Using the brochure, the map, and the information from the tour guide in Activity 2, choose three things that you'd like to do and see. Then, ask your partner what he or she would like to do, give your suggestions, and make a plan for your day together.

4 Create a brochure about a city, state, or country. Describe the place and its inhabitants. Make suggestions about things to do and sites to visit. Illustrate your brochure with drawings or magazine cutouts.

un musée   un cinéma   un théâtre   de belles plages   un zoo   un parc

une fête   des concerts   des montagnes   des monuments historiques   de bons restaurants

5 If you had to give a ten-minute presentation on the people, places, and culture of Martinique, what would you talk about? Write an outline for your presentation.

6

JEU DE ROLE

If you were rich and famous, would you change your daily routine? Imagine that you and your partner have suddenly become rich and famous. Take turns interviewing each other about your new lifestyles. Be sure to ask your partner . . .

- when he or she gets up and goes to bed.
- what he or she eats for breakfast, lunch, and dinner.
- what he or she wears.
- how he or she spends the rest of the day.

MISE EN PRATIQUE   *cent cinq*   **105**

Family Link

5 You might have students give a ten-minute presentation on the people, places, and culture of Martinique to a family member.

Community Link

Arrange to have your students visit an elementary school classroom and share what they have learned about Martinique with younger students.

For Individual Needs

4 Challenge Have students use their brochures to perform an extemporaneous skit in which they discuss plans as they did in Activity 3. Have pairs of students bring their brochures to the front of the class. Have them first choose one of the two places to visit, and then three things to do, according to the brochure of the place they've chosen. They should ask for and make suggestions, emphasize likes and dislikes, and relate a series of events.

Portfolio

4 Written This activity is appropriate for students' written portfolios. For portfolio suggestions, see *Assessment Guide,* page 17.

Teaching Suggestion

5 You might have students make their presentations to the class and have the class choose the best ones. These students might enjoy "taking their show on the road" (see Community Link below).

Video Wrap-Up

- *Video Program*
- *Expanded Video Program,* Videocassette 2, 04:07–25:55
- *Videodisc Program,* Videodisc 2B

At this time, you might want to use the video resources for additional review and enrichment. See *Video Guide* or *Videodisc Guide* for suggestions regarding the following:
- **Un concours photographique** (Dramatic episode)
- **Panorama Culturel** (Interviews)
- **Vidéoclips** (Authentic footage)

QUE SAIS-JE?

This page is intended to help students prepare for the test. It is a brief checklist of the major points covered in the chapter. The students should be reminded that this is only a checklist and does not necessarily include everything that will appear on the test.

♜ Game

SERPENT! Prepare a board game on a sheet of paper on which squares "snake" across the page. Number each square and label the first one **Départ**, and the last one, **Arrivée**. In each square, write an answer to one of the questions in **Que sais-je?** On a separate sheet of paper, type the numbers and letters of the questions in **Que sais-je?** that correspond to the squares on the board game. Form groups of three. Give each group one board for two players and an answer sheet for the judge. The players will need one die and two game pieces (coins will work nicely). Have them take turns rolling the die and moving from square to square. They must read what's on the square, look at the **Que sais-je?** and determine which question is answered by that square. The judge must verify the players' responses. If students are wrong, they must return to the square where they began their turn. The first person to reach **Arrivée** wins!

Can you ask for information? p. 90

Can you describe a place? p. 90

Can you ask for and make suggestions? p. 94

Can you emphasize likes and dislikes? p. 96

Can you relate a series of events? p. 99

Can you use what you've learned in the chapter?

1 How would you ask . . .   See answers below.
  1. the location of a place?
  3. what attractions there are?
  2. what it's like?
  4. what the weather is like?

2 How would you describe your state? Tell . . .
  1. where it's located.
  3. how big it is.
  2. what's in the north, south, east, and west.
  4. what there is to do there.
  5. what there is to see there.

3 How would you ask what there is to do in Martinique?
Qu'est-ce qu'on peut faire à la Martinique?

4 How would you suggest these activities to your friend?   See answers below.

1.
2.
3.
4.

5 How would you tell someone what you really like to do . . .
  1. on Saturday mornings?
  2. on weekends?   See answers below.

6 How would you tell someone what you really don't like to do . . .
  1. on Sundays?
  2. when it's cold?
  3. at school?
  See answers below.

7 How would you tell someone . . .
  1. what you do first thing in the morning?   D'abord,...
  2. what you do after that?   Ensuite,... ; Et puis,... ; Après ça,...
  3. what you finally do before leaving for school?   Finalement,...

8 Explain what you usually do after school.

106   *cent six*   CHAPITRE 4   Sous les tropiques

Possible answers
1 1. Où se trouve... ?
    2. C'est comment?
    3. Qu'est-ce-qu'il y a à voir?
    4. Quel temps fait-il?
4 1. Ça te dit d'aller à la plage?
    2. Si on allait faire du deltaplane?
    3. On peut aller se promener?
    4. Si on allait faire de la plongée?

5 1. Ce que j'aime bien le samedi matin, c'est...
    2. Ce qui me plaît le weekend, c'est...
6 1. Ce que je n'aime pas le dimanche, c'est...
    2. Ce qui ne me plaît pas quand il fait froid, c'est...
    3. Ce qui m'ennuie à l'ecole, c'est...

PREMIERE ETAPE

Asking for information and describing a place

Où se trouve... ?   *Where is . . . ?*
Qu'est-ce qu'il y a... ?   *What is there . . . ?*
Il fait...?   *Is it . . . ? (weather)*
C'est comment?   *What's it like?*
...se trouve...   *. . . is located . . .*
dans le nord   *in the north*
dans le sud   *in the south*
dans l'est   *in the east*
dans l'ouest   *in the west*
plus grand(e) que...   *bigger than . . .*

moins grand(e) que...   *smaller than . . .*
charmant(e)   *charming*
coloré(e)   *colorful*
vivant(e)   *lively*

Places, flora, and fauna

un ananas   *pineapple*
un bananier   *banana tree*
la capitale   *capital*
des champs (m.) de canne à sucre   *sugarcane fields*
une chute d'eau   *waterfall*

un cocotier   *coconut tree*
la forêt tropicale   *tropical rain forest*
l'île   *island*
la mer   *sea*
un moustique   *mosquito*
un palmier   *palm tree*
les plages (f.)   *beaches*
le sable   *sand*
un village de pêcheurs   *fishing village*
le volcan   *volcano*

DEUXIEME ETAPE

Asking for and making suggestions

Qu'est-ce qu'on peut faire?   *What can we do?*
On peut...   *We can . . .*
Ça te dit d'aller... ?   *What do you think of going . . . ?*
Si on allait... ?   *How about going . . . ?*

Emphasizing likes and dislikes

Ce que j'aime bien, c'est...   *What I like is . . .*

Ce que je préfère, c'est...   *What I prefer is . . .*
Ce qui me plaît, c'est...   *What I like is . . .*
Ce que je n'aime pas, c'est...   *What I don't like is . . .*
Ce qui ne me plaît pas, c'est...   *What I don't care for is . . .*
Ce qui m'ennuie, c'est...   *What bothers me is . . .*

Activities

aller à la pêche   *to go fishing*

danser le zouk   *to dance the zouk*
faire du deltaplane   *to hang glide*
faire de la planche à voile   *to windsurf*
faire de la plongée sous-marine   *to scuba dive*
faire de la plongée avec un tuba   *to snorkel*
déguster   *to taste, enjoy*
s'amuser   *to have fun*
se baigner   *to go swimming*
se promener   *to go for a walk*

TROISIEME ETAPE

Relating a series of events

D'abord,...   *First, . . .*
Ensuite,...   *Next, . . .*
Et puis,...   *And then, . . .*
Vers...   *About (a certain time) . . .*
Après ça,...   *After that, . . .*
Finalement,...   *Finally, . . .*

Daily activities

se brosser les dents   *to brush one's teeth*
se coucher   *to go to bed*
s'habiller   *to get dressed*

se lever   *to get up*
se laver   *to wash (oneself)*
tôt   *early*
tard   *late*

VOCABULAIRE   *cent sept* **107**

For Individual Needs

Challenge   To review vocabulary, have students group words and expressions from the vocabulary list that are related. For example, **la mer** and **se baigner**, or **les plages** and **le sable**. Then, have them write sentences showing the relationship between the two words they have chosen to group together. (**On se baigne dans la mer. C'est une plage de sable blanc.**)

CHAPTER 4 ASSESSMENT

CHAPTER TEST

• *Chapter Teaching Resources, Book 1,* pp. 197–202
• *Assessment Guide,* Speaking Test, p. 29
• *Assessment Items, Audiocassette 7B Audio CD 4*

TEST GENERATOR, CHAPTER 4

ALTERNATIVE ASSESSMENT

Performance Assessment
You might want to use the **Jeu de rôle** (p. 105) as a cumulative performance assessment activity.

Portfolio Assessment
• **Written: Mise en pratique,** Activity 4, *Pupil's Edition,* p. 105
  Assessment Guide, p. 17
• **Oral:** Activity 15, *Pupil's Edition,* p. 90
  Assessment Guide, p. 17

♟ Game

AUTOUR DU MONDE   Prepare several one-word clues for each vocabulary word or expression. For example, **l'eau, le sel, les poissons,** or **le sable** could elicit **la mer.** Have the first student of the first row stand next to the student seated behind him or her. Call out a clue. The first student who calls out the vocabulary item you have in mind moves on to the next student. A student may continue moving "around the world," or he or she must take the seat of the one who guesses before him or her. If neither student guesses within five seconds, give the next clue. The first student to move "around the world" and return to his or her seat wins.

EXPANDED VIDEO
PROGRAM,
Videocassette 2
26:22–29:14

OR *VIDEODISC PROGRAM,*
Videodisc 3A

Search 1, Play To 5130

Motivating Activity

Have students look at pages 108–109 and ask them what they think the region of **la Touraine** is famous for (châteaux). Ask if this is a scene in the south of France (No; no tiled roofs). Ask students if they know the names of any rivers in this region. (The Vienne River is pictured on pages 108–109.) Finally, have them look at the map on page 109 and identify the capital of **Touraine** (Tours).

Background Information

Touraine was recaptured from the English by Joan of Arc in 1429 during the Hundred Years' War (1337–1453). The region was long a favorite getaway of French kings because of its mild climate, beautiful countryside, numerous rivers, and fine forests for hunting. From the fifteenth to the seventeenth centuries, medieval and Renaissance rulers from Charles VII to Henri III built their châteaux in this region. In fact, within a 60-kilometer radius of the city of Tours, there are over 200 châteaux. Also known for its flowers, fruits, vegetables, and vineyards, Touraine is called **le jardin de la France.**

CHAPITRES 5, 6, 7

Allez, viens en Touraine!

Le château de Chinon

History Link

The **château de Chinon,** a medieval fortress prized by both the French and the English, was built on a rocky promontory overlooking the Vienne River and surrounding countryside. From the reign of Henri d'Anjou (later Henry II of England) to that of his son, Richard the Lionhearted, the castle remained in English hands, but was finally captured by the French king Philippe II Auguste. It was here that Charles VII first received Joan of Arc. In the seventeenth century, the château came into the possession of Cardinal Richelieu, prime minister of Louis XIII, and remained in his family until after the Revolution. It is now in ruins.

𝒰sing the Almanac and Map

Terms in the Almanac

- **La cathédrale Saint-Gatien,** built between the thirteenth and sixteenth centuries, displays the evolution of Gothic architecture.
- **L'hôtel Goüin,** a typical Renaissance building, houses a Gallo-Roman museum containing medieval and Renaissance works of art.
- **Le musée des Beaux-Arts,** built during the seventeenth and eighteenth centuries, displays paintings by artists such as Rubens, Rembrandt, Delacroix, Monet, and Degas.
- **L'Historial de Touraine** is a museum that details the history of the province.
- **La Loire,** the longest river in France, is more than 1,020 kilometers long.
- **Le Cher,** a tributary of the Loire River, joins it at Tours. The château of Chenonceau is built over the Cher River.
- **Saint Grégoire de Tours** (538-594) wrote *Historia Francorum* in Latin. It remains today the primary source for historical research about this period.
- **Saint Martin de Tours** was a former Roman soldier who became bishop of Tours.
- **François Rabelais** (c. 1495–1553), priest, doctor, and author, wrote *Gargantua* and *Pantagruel,* which satirized the society of his time and presented his views on education, religion, and philosophy.
- **René Descartes** (1590–1650) was a philosopher and mathematician known for his famous phrase "Cogito ergo sum" («**Je pense, donc je suis**»).

La Touraine

Population : plus de 500.000

Points d'intérêt : la place Plumereau, la cathédrale Saint-Gatien, l'hôtel Goüin, le musée des Beaux-Arts, l'Historial de Touraine

Châteaux : Amboise, Azay-le-Rideau, Chenonceau, Chinon, Loches, Ussé, Villandry

Fleuves et rivières : la Loire, le Cher, l'Indre, la Vienne, la Creuse

Tourangeaux célèbres : saint Grégoire, Honoré de Balzac, saint Martin, François Rabelais, René Descartes

Spécialités : tarte Tatin, saumon au beurre blanc, crottins de Chavignol, ragoût d'escargots aux cèpes

Map labels: ANGLETERRE, BELGIQUE, ALLEMAGNE, LUXEMBOURG, Lille, Paris, Strasbourg, Chartres, SUISSE, Tours, Poitiers, FRANCE, Lyon, ITALIE, Océan Atlantique, Bordeaux, Nice, Arles, Aix-en-Provence, CORSE, ESPAGNE, Mer Méditerranée, N

cent neuf **109**

Teacher Note

The following are some of the regional food specialties of Touraine:

- **tarte Tatin:** a caramelized, upside-down apple tart, originally made at the hôtel Tatin in the Loire Valley by two sisters (**les demoiselles Tatin**), who accidentally cooked an apple tart upside down and created a culinary sensation.

- **saumon au beurre blanc:** salmon cooked in a sauce of butter, wine, and shallots.
- **crottins de Chavignol:** a popular goat cheese (**chèvre**).
- **ragoût d'escargots aux cèpes:** a stew made with snails (**escargots**) known as **petits gris,** and wild mushrooms (**cèpes**) peculiar to Touraine.

Using the Photo Essay

① **Amboise,** a royal château, was the preferred residence of Louis XI, Charles VIII, and François I. After the **Conjuration d'Amboise,** a massacre of French Protestants in 1560, it was abandoned by the monarchy. The tower on the left side has a huge spiral ramp that allowed men on horseback to ride up to meet with the king.

② Located on the Indrois River, **Montrésor** is a medieval fortress that once belonged to the counts of Anjou. The village at the foot of the château is known today for its collection of medieval furniture.

③ **Azay-le-Rideau** was built partly in the Indre River during the Renaissance. In fact, the **donjon** *(castle tower)* is in the middle of the river. The château is known for its main staircase, which is straight rather than spiral. There is an excellent **son et lumière** show during which spectators stroll around the château, following the performers who re-enact its history.

④ **Villandry** is famous for its sixteenth-century Renaissance gardens, built in three terraces with a large lake at the top that provides water pressure for irrigation and the fountains. Ask students if they can tell which part of the château dates from a period earlier than the Renaissance (the heavily fortified tower that was built for defense).

⑤ **Chenonceau,** constructed around 1520, is built over the Cher River. The approach to Chenonceau is a magnificent shaded **allée,** and its **son et lumière** show is highlighted by the reflection of the bridge's illuminated arches in the water.

La Touraine

La Touraine, célèbre pour ses abondantes cultures de fruits et de légumes et pour ses vignes, est souvent appelée «le jardin de la France». C'est aussi une importante région historique. Les rois aimaient y séjourner en raison de son climat doux et de ses forêts abondantes en gibier. Ils y ont construit de merveilleux châteaux que l'on connaît aujourd'hui sous le nom de «châteaux de la Loire».

① **Amboise**

② **Montrésor**

③ **Azay-le-Rideau**

④ **Villandry**

⑤ **Chenonceau**

Teaching Suggestion

You might have students work in groups to look up additional information on the châteaux shown on these pages, or any of the other châteaux located in Touraine and the Loire Valley. These include Langeais, Blois, Chambord, Chaumont, and others. Encourage students to find interesting stories connected with the châteaux. To expand this activity, see the project on page 135E.

Culture Note

There were both royal châteaux and private châteaux built in Touraine. In general, the king had only one set of furnishings, which was transported from château to château as he traveled. That is why many of the royal châteaux are today quite sparsely furnished. In most private châteaux, a guest room was always set aside for the king.

⑥ On dit que c'est **le château d'Ussé** qui a inspiré à Charles Perrault l'histoire de *La belle au bois dormant*.

Tours est une ville historique, mais c'est aussi une ville très vivante. Il y a des festivals de musique, de théâtre et de cinéma. Viens avec nous faire la connaissance de quatre lycéens qui y habitent. Dans les chapitres 5, 6 et 7, ils vont te faire découvrir cette belle région.

⑥ The **château d'Ussé** has beautiful terraces facing the Indre River. The château was used as a model for the castle in *Sleeping Beauty (La belle au bois dormant)*. Several rooms in the château display various scenes of the story. The château, built at the beginning of the Renaissance, has a variety of steeples, turrets, towers, chimneys, and dormer windows set upright in a sloping roof.

⑦ Léonard de Vinci a habité au manoir du **Clos-Lucé.** C'est aujourd'hui un musée où l'on peut voir ses inventions reconstituées d'après ses plans.

⑦ **Le manoir du Clos-Lucé** is a fifteenth-century house made of brick and stone. François I convinced Leonardo da Vinci, whom he named "the great master in all forms of art and science," to live and work there. The lower level contains scale models made by IBM® from some of da Vinci's drawings: the first airplane, the first self-propelled vehicle, the helicopter, the parachute, the tank, the machine gun, and the swing bridge.

⑧ **La place Plumereau,** située au cœur de la ville de Tours, est un des endroits préférés des étudiants et des élèves.

⑨ Le grand écrivain **Honoré de Balzac** a écrit certains de ses romans au château de Saché, à 20 kilomètres au sud-ouest de Tours.

⑧ **La place Plumereau,** located in the center of Tours, is known for its fifteenth-century houses. The wooden beams supporting the structures are covered with slate tiles to protect them from the weather. Numerous cafés, boutiques, galleries, concerts, and other types of entertainment make the square a popular gathering place.

⑨ **Honoré de Balzac** (1799–1850) was a French novelist known for the detailed, accurate descriptions of his more than 2,000 characters, who were portrayed as the product of their heredity and environment. His most famous work is the 90-volume *La comédie humaine.* Other works by Balzac include *Le curé de Tours* (1829), *Le père Goriot* (1834), and *Les illusions perdues* (1839).

cent onze **111**

Thinking Critically

Observing   Point out to students that most of the châteaux were built along rivers. Have them suggest reasons why this was done (transportation, water supply, fishing, defense, scenery).

Drawing Inferences   Have students imagine what it would be like to live in an ancient building. How would it be different from a modern home? (Even when ancient structures are modernized with electricity and conveniences, there are certain characteristics of these old buildings that cannot be changed. The thick stone walls are very humid and cold, especially if the building is built in water or has a moat. There is a musty smell that is hard to eradicate. Floors and walls are often uneven or cracked. Stone staircases become worn and uneven.)

Chapitre 5 : Quelle journée!
Chapter Overview

Mise en train pp. 114–116	**C'est pas mon jour!**		*Practice and Activity Book*, p. 49	*Video Guide* OR *Videodisc Guide*
	FUNCTIONS	**GRAMMAR**	**CULTURE**	**RE-ENTRY**
Première étape pp. 117–121	Expressing concern for someone, p. 119	The **passé composé** with **avoir**, p. 120	• **Note Culturelle, Carnet de correspondance,** p. 117 • French tardy slip, p. 117	• Connector words • Sports and leisure activities
Deuxième étape pp. 122–125	• Inquiring; expressing satisfaction and frustration, p. 123 • Sympathizing with and consoling someone, p. 125	Introduction to verbs that use **être** in the **passé composé**, p. 124	**Note Culturelle,** Meals at school, p. 122	• Pronunciation: the nasal sound [ɛ̃] • Reflexive verbs
Troisième étape pp. 126–129	• Giving reasons and making excuses, p. 127 • Congratulating and reprimanding someone, p. 127		• Realia: **Bulletin Trimestriel,** p. 126 • **Note Culturelle,** French grades and report cards, p. 126 • **Panorama Culturel,** School life in francophone countries, p. 129	Question words

Lisons! pp. 130–131	**Le cancre** and **Page d'écriture** Two poems by Jacques Prévert	**Reading Strategy:** Deducing the main idea

Review pp. 132–135	**Mise en pratique,** pp. 132–133	**Que sais-je?** p. 134	**Vocabulaire,** p. 135

Assessment Options	**Etape Quizzes**
	 • *Chapter Teaching Resources, Book 2*
	   Première étape, Quiz 5-1, pp. 23–24
	   Deuxième étape, Quiz 5-2, pp. 25–26
	   Troisième étape, Quiz 5-3, pp. 27–28
	 • *Assessment Items, Audiocassette 7B/Audio CD 5*
		Chapter Test
		 • *Chapter Teaching Resources, Book 2,* pp. 29–34
		 • *Assessment Guide,* Speaking Test, p. 30
		 • *Assessment Items, Audiocassette 7B/Audio CD 5*
		
		 Test Generator, Chapter 5

Video Program OR Expanded Video Program, Videocassette 2
OR Videodisc Program, Videodisc 3A   Textbook Audiocassette 3A/Audio CD 5

RESOURCES: Print	RESOURCES: Audiovisual
	Textbook Audiocassette 3A/Audio CD 5
Practice and Activity Book, pp. 50–52	
Chapter Teaching Resources, Book 2	
• Teaching Transparency Master 5-1, pp. 7, 10 . . . . Teaching Transparency 5-1	
• Additional Listening Activities 5-1, 5-2, p. 11 . . . . Additional Listening Activities, Audiocassette 9B/Audio CD 5	
• Realia 5-1, pp. 15, 17	
• Situation Cards 5-1, pp. 18–19	
• Student Response Forms, pp. 20–22	
• Quiz 5-1, pp. 23–24 . . . . Assessment Items, Audiocassette 7B/Audio CD 5	
Videodisc Guide . . . . Videodisc Program, Videodisc 3A	
	Textbook Audiocassette 3A/Audio CD 5
Practice and Activity Book, pp. 53–55	
Chapter Teaching Resources, Book 2	
• Communicative Activity 5-1, pp. 3–4	
• Teaching Transparency Master 5-2, pp. 8, 10 . . . . Teaching Transparency 5-2	
• Additional Listening Activities 5-3, 5-4, p. 12 . . . . Additional Listening Activities, Audiocassette 9B/Audio CD 5	
• Realia 5-2, pp. 16, 17	
• Situation Cards 5-2, pp. 18–19	
• Student Response Forms, pp. 20–22	
• Quiz 5-2, pp. 25–26 . . . . Assessment Items, Audiocassette 7B/Audio CD 5	
Videodisc Guide . . . . Videodisc Program, Videodisc 3A	
	Textbook Audiocassette 3A/Audio CD 5
Practice and Activity Book, pp. 56–58	
Chapter Teaching Resources, Book 2	
• Communicative Activity 5-2, pp. 5–6	
• Teaching Transparency Master 5-3, pp. 9, 10 . . . . Teaching Transparency 5-3	
• Additional Listening Activities 5-5, 5-6, p. 13 . . . . Additional Listening Activities, Audiocassette 9B/Audio CD 5	
• Realia 5-2, pp. 16, 17	
• Situation Cards 5-3, pp. 18–19	
• Student Response Forms, pp. 20–22	
• Quiz 5-3, pp. 27–28 . . . . Assessment Items, Audiocassette 7B/Audio CD 5	
Video Guide . . . . Video Program OR Expanded Video Program, Videocassette 2	
Videodisc Guide . . . . Videodisc Program, Videodisc 3A	
Practice and Activity Book, p. 59	
Video Guide . . . . Video Program OR Expanded Video Program, Videocassette 2	
Videodisc Guide . . . . Videodisc Program, Videodisc 3A	

Alternative Assessment
- Performance Assessment
  Première étape, p. 121
  Deuxième étape, p. 125
  Troisième étape, p. 128
- Portfolio Assessment
  Written: Activity 22, *Pupil's Edition*, p. 124
    Assessment Guide, p. 18
  Oral: **Mise en pratique,** Activity 5, *Pupil's Edition*, p. 133
    Assessment Guide, p. 18

Chapitre 5 : Quelle journée!
Textbook Listening Activities Scripts

For Student Response Forms, see *Chapter Teaching Resources, Book 2,* pp. 20–22.

Première étape

7 Ecoute! p. 119

1. — Tu n'as pas tes devoirs aujourd'hui, Sara?
   — Excusez-moi, monsieur, mais j'ai perdu mon livre d'anglais.

2. — Pourquoi tu n'es pas venue avec nous hier après-midi? On a fait les magasins!
   — Désolée, mais c'était impossible. J'ai été collée.

3. — Tu en fais une tête. Qu'est-ce qui se passe?
   — Ben, j'ai eu une mauvaise note en maths après tout le temps que j'ai passé à étudier!

4. — Pourquoi tu es arrivé en classe avec quinze minutes de retard?
   — J'ai raté le bus.

Answers to Activity 7
1. c   2. d   3. a   4. b

9 Ecoute! p. 119

FRANCINE   Salut, Luc. Te voilà enfin. Dis donc, ça n'a pas l'air d'aller. Qu'est-ce qui t'arrive?

LUC   Désolé d'être en retard. Tout a été de travers ce matin!

FRANCINE   Qu'est-ce qui s'est passé?

LUC   J'avais oublié mon livre d'histoire, donc à midi, je suis rentré chez moi pour aller le chercher.

FRANCINE   Et après?

LUC   Ben, je ne l'ai pas trouvé et en plus, en descendant l'escalier, j'ai raté une marche, je suis tombé et j'ai déchiré mon pantalon.

FRANCINE   Pauvre vieux!

LUC   Attends! J'ai vite mis un autre pantalon, et j'ai couru pour attraper le bus. Mais je l'ai raté, donc, j'ai décidé de venir à pied.

FRANCINE   Tu es venu à pied? Mais ça fait presque deux kilomètres! Tu aurais dû me téléphoner.

Answers to Activity 9
1, 3

12 Ecoute! p. 121

1. — Tiens, Marie, qu'est-ce qui t'arrive?
   — J'ai eu une interro de français, et j'ai eu sept!

2. — J'ai attendu le bus pendant vingt minutes aujourd'hui. Et toi?
   — Moi, je l'ai attendu un quart d'heure!

3. — Salut, Marc! Tu attends le bus?
   — Non, j'attends ma mère. Elle vient me chercher.

4. — Eh ben, qu'est-ce qui s'est passé?
   — D'abord, je n'ai pas entendu mon réveil. Ensuite, j'ai eu une interro de français, et après l'école, on a perdu le match de basket.

5. — Tu as été collé aujourd'hui?
   — Oui, malheureusement.

Answers to Activity 12
1. past   3. now   5. past
2. past   4. past

Deuxième étape

18 Ecoute! p. 123

1. — Salut, Georges. Comment ça s'est passé, ton week-end au lac?
   — Oh, tout a été de travers!

2. — Salut, Eliane. Comment s'est passé ton week-end?
   — Ça s'est très bien passé, merci.
   — Et toi, comment s'est passé ton week-end?

3. — Moi? J'ai travaillé tout le week-end. C'était horrible!

4. — Martine, comment s'est passé ton week-end?
   — J'ai fait de la natation, et je suis allée à la boum de Denise. C'était super!

5. — Et toi, Bruno?
   — J'ai vu un bon film comique au cinéma, et j'ai regardé un match de foot à télé. Mon équipe a gagné! Quel week-end formidable!

Answers to Activity 18

1. bad   3. bad   5. good
2. good   4. good

Troisième étape

30 Ecoute! p. 128

1. — Combien tu as eu à ta rédaction de français?
   — A ma rédaction? Ben, j'ai eu seize.
   — Seize? Bravo!

2. — Eh, salut! Combien tu as eu à ton interro d'histoire?
   — J'ai eu quinze.
   — Félicitations! Moi, j'ai eu onze.

3. — Et à l'interro de sciences-éco? Combien tu as eu?
   — Euh, ce n'est pas mon fort. J'ai eu dix.
   — C'est pas terrible, ça. Tu dois mieux travailler.

4. — Combien tu as eu en biologie?
   — J'ai eu huit. Je ne suis pas doué pour les sciences.
   — Mais, c'est inadmissible! Tu ne dois pas faire le clown en classe!

Answers to Activity 30

1. congratulating
2. congratulating
3. reprimanding
4. reprimanding

Mise en pratique

2 p. 133

LE PERE Je vous ai demandé un rendez-vous parce que je ne suis pas content des notes de Ginette. Elle a eu huit à la dernière interro. Qu'est-ce qui se passe?

LE PROF Le huit, c'est qu'elle n'a pas assez étudié. Et, la semaine passée, elle est arrivée en retard tous les jours!

LE PERE Eh bien, elle dit que l'histoire, ce n'est pas son fort. Elle dit aussi que vous ne l'aimez pas!

LE PROF N'importe quoi! Ce n'est pas du tout vrai! Elle est très intelligente, mais elle doit mieux travailler. Elle doit être plus sérieuse, et surtout, elle ne doit pas faire le clown en classe!

LE PERE Bon, je vais lui parler. C'est inadmissible, un huit en histoire-géo!

Answers to Mise en pratique Activity 2

1. faux   3. faux   5. faux
2. faux   4. vrai   6. vrai

Chapitre 5 : Quelle journée!
Projects

Une bande dessinée
(Cooperative Learning Project)

ASSIGNMENT

In groups of four, students will create, write, and illustrate a comic strip of ten frames entitled **Une journée horrible.** Students should use at least six of the nine functions in this chapter and the **passé composé** of verbs conjugated with both **être** and **avoir.** Assign the roles of leader/creator, writer, proofreader, and artist. All group members will participate in all aspects of the project, but these roles will define the principal tasks of the group members.

MATERIALS

✂ **Students may need**

- Notebook paper
- Posterboard or butcher paper
- Scissors
- Glue
- Pencils
- Markers or colored pencils

SUGGESTED SEQUENCE

1. Each group creates the characters for its comic strip.

2. Students create the story and outline what will happen in each frame of the comic strip.

3. Two members begin to write the script while the others sketch possible illustrations or find pictures from magazines or catalogues. Each member proofreads the finished script for accuracy and makes suggestions for improvement. Students then submit the rewritten copy and drawings of each character.

4. Correct the rough draft, using correction symbols so that the group is held accountable for correcting its grammatical errors. For example, use **sp** to indicate a spelling error, or **ag** to signal incorrect subject-verb or noun-adjective agreement.

5. Group members then rewrite the rough draft and complete the comic strip. The frames can be drawn on separate sheets of paper and glued to a posterboard. Each frame should be large enough to accommodate the speech bubbles and/or captions. The title and the names of the creators, writers, and illustrators of the comic strip should be clearly written on the posterboard.

GRADING THE PROJECT

Each group should receive a collective grade for the inclusion of all required elements, accuracy of language, variety of vocabulary, and creativity and overall appearance. Each member should receive an individual grade for his or her effort and participation in the project.

Suggested Point Distribution (total = 100 points)

Inclusion of requirements . . . . 20 points
Language use . . . . 20 points
Vocabulary . . . . 20 points
Creativity/overall appearance . . . . 20 points
Effort/participation . . . . 20 points

Chapitre 5 : Quelle journée!
♜ Games

LE JEU DU PENDU

In this game, students will practice the French alphabet and the vocabulary and expressions from this chapter.

Procedure

1. Prepare a list of vocabulary words or expressions from this chapter to use in a game of "Hangman" in which you play against the class. Write the name of each student on a slip of paper and place all of the names in a box.

2. To play the game, draw on the board or on a transparency a scaffold from which the man will hang. Next to the scaffold, draw lines to represent the number of letters in the word or expression you have chosen. The man will have only six parts: a head, a torso, two arms, and two legs.

3. Have volunteers call out a letter in French that they think might appear somewhere in the word or expression. If the student guesses correctly, write that letter on all the lines where it appears in the word or expression.

4. If the letter that the student calls out does not appear, write it on the board and draw the head of the man.

Continue in this manner until you've drawn all six parts of the man, in which case you receive a point, or until the students have guessed all the letters of your word or expression.

5. If students have guessed all the letters, have them tell you where accents, if any, are needed. (**Le premier e a un accent grave.**)

6. If students place the accents correctly, the class may receive a point only after two students create and perform a short dialogue using the word or expression. To decide who will create the dialogue, pick two names from the box. For example, if the expression the class guessed is **Ça n'a pas l'air d'aller,** one student begins a dialogue with that expression, and the other must reply logically. (**J'ai eu 5 à mon devoir d'anglais.**) If the word is **Courage!,** one student starts a dialogue that would require this word as a response. (**J'ai été collé(e).**) If the word is **perdre,** one student begins a dialogue with a sentence containing this verb and the other student replies logically. If the two students create an appropriate dialogue, the class scores a point. If not, you score a point. Continue to play for a specified length of time.

Chapitre 5
Quelle journée!
pp. 112–135

𝒰sing the Chapter Opener

Motivating Activity

Ask students what kinds of things cause them to have a good or a bad day. Ask them what a friend might say to make them feel better.

Teaching Suggestion

Have students guess the meaning of the expression **Quelle journée!** as you say the expression with appropriate intonation and gestures. Have students look at the photos and read the opening paragraph on page 113. Ask them to describe in French what they see in each photo. Elicit suggestions about what the people might be feeling and why. Students might also pair off and create two-line dialogues based on Photo 1.

◆ For Individual Needs

Slower Pace Have students work in pairs to create several one- or two-word captions for each photo. For example, for Photo 1, students could write **Les copains, Au café,** or **Après l'école.**

Challenge Have students compete to create the best or most humorous caption for each photo.

Additional Practice

Ask students to name the objects pictured on this page (**une trousse, des crayons, une gomme, une calculatrice, un tableau**).

CHAPITRE

5 Quelle journée!

① Raconte!

Language Note

Point out that the word **journée** is a **faux ami;** it is not the equivalent of the English word *journey.* Have students guess the root word (**jour**). **Journée** is used to talk about the duration of a day (**J'ai lu toute la journée.**), whereas **jour** refers to the day as a whole. (**Quel jour on est?**)

H
ave you ever had a day when everything goes wrong—or something wonderful happens? At times like that, it's always nice to have a friend who will listen to you and understand how you feel.

In this chapter you will learn

- to express concern for someone
- to inquire; to express satisfaction and frustration; to sympathize with and console someone
- to give reasons and make excuses; to congratulate and reprimand someone

And you will

- listen to students telling what happened earlier and making excuses
- read poems about school
- write a letter about your last vacation
- find out what French-speaking teenagers like and dislike about high school

② C'est pas de chance, ça!

③ Félicitations!

cent treize 113

Focusing on Outcomes

As you read each of the outcomes for the chapter, ask students in what situations they would use these functions. Then, have students look at the photos and match them with the outcomes listed. NOTE: You may want to use the video to support the objectives. The self-check activities in **Que sais-je?** on page 134 help students assess their achievement of the objectives.

Photo Flash!

② Point out the notebooks in Photo 2 and the paper in the lower right-hand corner of this page. French notebooks contain graph paper rather than lined paper. Generally, students can choose the notebook they want to use, but some teachers may require a specific type.

③ Ask students what game the boys are playing in Photo 3 (soccer). French **lycéens** are required to take two hours of physical education a week. There is usually a choice between track and field (**athlétisme**), gymnastics, soccer, volleyball, and basketball. However, schools do not have teams that compete against other school teams. Therefore, there are no cheerleaders, marching bands, or student athletes, even at the university level. Students who wish to compete in team sports must join city leagues or clubs outside of school.

 Culture Note

From elementary to junior high, French schools provide students with books, which must be covered and returned at the end of the school year. High school students, however, must buy their own books. They commonly buy used books from classmates, who post notices in the hallways announcing the books they have for sale.

 Culture Note

Les écoles maternelles accept children ages three to five. Children then attend **l'enseignement élémentaire** for five years. **L'enseignement secondaire** in the **collège** lasts for four years and is for students ages eleven to fifteen. In the first two years, **sixième** and **cinquième**, students share a common curriculum. In grades **quatrième** and **troisième**, students begin to choose **options** to orient themselves towards a particular course of study. After **collège**, students may choose a vocational **lycée** that prepares them for a professional certificate. Students may also opt for a three-year academic cycle that prepares them for the **baccalauréat**, a rigorous exam that guarantees students the right to enter any French university. During the last year of high school (**terminale**), students must orient their coursework towards the **bac** they choose. For example, they might choose **L (littéraire)**.

VIDEO PROGRAM OR EXPANDED VIDEO PROGRAM, Videocassette 2 29:15–32:52

OR **VIDEODISC PROGRAM,** Videodisc 3A

Search 5130, Play To 11695

Video Synopsis

In this segment of the video, Céline is at a café with Hector. She tells him that nothing has gone right for her today. First, her alarm didn't go off, and she woke up late. She missed her bus and arrived late to school. Then, she realized she didn't have her homework. Finally, she got a 10 on a math quiz. Hector is sympathetic and consoles her. She says she's going home to go to bed so nothing else can happen to her.

Motivating Activity

Ask students what kind of day they're having so far today, and ask them what has made it good or bad. Ask them to look at the photos in the **Mise en train** and tell what kind of day they think Céline is having and why.

Teaching Suggestion

Have students look at the photos in **C'est pas mon jour!** and try to determine all the things that happened to Céline during the day.

Mise en train

C'est pas mon jour!

What are some unpleasant things that can happen to you on a school day? See if you can relate to what happened to Céline.

Céline   Hector

RESOURCES FOR MISE EN TRAIN

Textbook Audiocassette 3A/Audio CD 5
Practice and Activity Book, p. 49
Video Guide
   Video Program
   Expanded Video Program, Videocassette 2
Videodisc Guide
   Videodisc Program, Videodisc 3A

Mais, ce n'est pas tout! J'avais oublié mes devoirs!

Ce n'est pas dramatique. Moi aussi, j'oublie mes devoirs quelquefois.

Oui, mais ça m'énerve! Je les avais faits, ces devoirs.

Et après, ta matinée s'est bien passée?

Pas du tout! Ça a été de pire en pire! Devine combien j'ai eu à mon interro de maths... 10!

C'est pas mal!

Tu sais, il y a des jours comme ça. Ça va aller mieux!

Pas mal? D'habitude, j'ai 15.

Pas moi. Les maths, ce n'est pas mon fort.

Je ne sais pas. Cet après-midi, je vais me coucher. Comme ça, je ne risque rien.

MISE EN TRAIN

cent quinze 115

Presentation

Write the sentences that explain what happened to Céline on the board in random order. Convey the meaning through gestures or mime. Then, show the video and have students reorder the actions as they occur in the video. Finally, have students pair off to read the **Mise en train** aloud. Circulate around the room to help with pronunciation and intonation.

Teacher Note

Remind students that the French grading system is based on 20, so Céline's grade of 10 is considered average. You might point out that it is extremely rare for a student to receive a perfect score of 20, and that a score of 18 or 19 is also very rare and considered exceptional.

Group Work

Students might work in groups of three to act out the dialogue in **C'est pas mon jour!** Have two students read the dialogue between Hector and Céline and the third student act out Céline's flashbacks.

Culture Note

Students might notice that Céline's classroom seems bare and undecorated. French junior high/middle school (**collège**) or high school (**lycée**) classrooms are not reserved for a particular teacher or class. Instead, students and teachers move about from room to room. Classes are usually one or two hours long, and students have about five minutes between classes, which is called **l'interclasse**. Usually, the same students change classes together, since they are grouped according to the course of study they have chosen.

Video Integration

- **EXPANDED VIDEO PROGRAM,** Videocassette 2, 32:53–37:59
- **VIDEODISC PROGRAM,** Videodisc 3A

Search 11695, Play To 20870

You may choose to continue with **C'est pas mon jour! (suite)** or wait until later in the chapter. When the story continues, everything starts to go wrong for Hector. First, the bookstore doesn't have the books he needs, so he buys a different book. While at a café, Hector notices his sack is missing and sees a man leaving with what he thinks is his sack. He follows and stops the man. The waiter thinks Hector, who can't find his money, is leaving without paying! At that moment, Céline arrives. She pays Hector's bill, and the waiter finds Hector's sack with his money inside. All's well that ends well!

For Individual Needs

2 Tactile/Visual Learners
Have students write the sequencing expressions as well as the sentence fragments on separate, small strips of paper. Then, have them put the sentences in order according to Céline's day and attach the appropriate sequencing expressions.

3 Slower Pace Have students write the text in the speech bubbles on separate, small strips of paper. Have them place each strip next to the appropriate situation in the activity.

Teaching Suggestion

3 Have students pair off to do this activity. Assign each pair numbers 1 and 2, 3 and 4, or 5 and 6. When partners have identified the functional expressions, have them practice the two-line dialogue. They might make substitutions to vary the exchange.

For Individual Needs

4 Auditory Learners
Create other unfortunate situations to read to the class in addition to the ones written in Activity 4. (J'ai perdu mon livre d'histoire. Je n'ai pas fait mes devoirs. Je n'ai pas entendu mon réveil. Je n'ai pas eu le temps de prendre mon petit déjeuner. J'ai mangé de la pizza pour le petit déjeuner. Je n'ai pas fini mes devoirs. J'ai raté le bus.) Have individuals respond after each sentence, using one of the responses presented in the activity. (Ça m'arrive aussi. Ça ne risque pas de m'arriver.)

For videodisc application, see *Videodisc Guide.*

---

1 Tu as compris? See answers below.

1. What kind of mood is Céline in? Why?
2. Name three unfortunate things that happened to Céline.
3. How does Hector react to Céline's story?
4. What are Céline's plans for the afternoon?

2 Mets en ordre

Mets les phrases en ordre d'après la journée de Céline dans **C'est pas mon jour!** See answers below.

1. D'abord,...
2. Ensuite,...
3. Et puis,...
4. Après ça,...
5. Et puis,...
6. Enfin,...

elle n'avait pas ses devoirs.

son réveil n'a pas sonné.

Hector a renversé son verre sur sa jupe.

elle est arrivée à l'école en retard.

elle a raté son bus.

elle a eu dix à son interro de maths.

3 Cherche les expressions

What do Céline and Hector say in each of these situations?

1. Hector apologizes.
2. Céline makes light of an accident.
3. Hector wants to know what happened to Céline.
4. Céline complains about her bad day.
5. Céline is upset with herself.
6. Hector consoles Céline.

> 2 C'est pas grave.

> 4 Tout a été de travers!

> 6 Ça va aller mieux!

> 5 Ça m'énerve!

> 3 Raconte!

> 1 Désolé.

4 Ça t'arrive aussi?

If Céline or Hector said the following to you, would you say **Ça m'arrive aussi** *(That happens to me, too)* or **Ça ne risque pas de m'arriver** *(That will never happen to me)*?

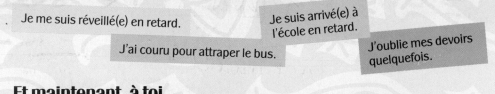

Je me suis réveillé(e) en retard.

Je suis arrivé(e) à l'école en retard.

J'ai couru pour attraper le bus.

J'oublie mes devoirs quelquefois.

5 Et maintenant, à toi

Have you ever had a day like Céline's? What happened? How did you react?

116 *cent seize*   CHAPITRE 5   Quelle journée!

Answers

1 1. bad mood; Everything went wrong.
  2. *Possible answers:* Her alarm didn't go off, she woke up late, she didn't have time for breakfast, she missed her bus, she got to school late, she forgot her homework, she got a 10 on her math quiz, Hector spilled his drink on her.
  3. He sympathizes with and consoles her.
  4. to go to bed so nothing else can happen to her

2 1. D'abord, son reveil n'a pas sonné.
  2. Ensuite, elle a raté son bus.
  3. Et puis, elle est arrivée à l'école en retard.
  4. Après ça, elle n'avait pas ses devoirs.
  5. Et puis, elle a eu dix à son interro de maths.
  6. Enfin, Hector a renversé son verre sur sa jupe.

PREMIERE ETAPE

Expressing concern for someone

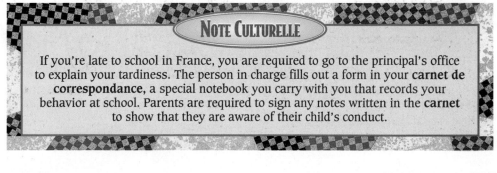

LYCEE ALFRED KASTLER
Ministère de l'Education Nationale
ETABLISSEMENT PUBLIC D'ENSEIGNEMENT GENERAL ET TECHNOLOGIQUE
29 Boulevard QUITTON · Tél: 51.36.24.46

carnet de correspondance

BULLETIN D'ABSENCE

L'élève
fréquentant la classe de
a été absent le
ou du
MOTIF
au
Le Surveillant
Le Conseiller d'Éducation ou
Le Directeur Adjoint.
Signature des Parents.

BILLET DE RETARD

Elève: Céline Déroulède

Classe: 2de

Motif: m'a pas entendu son réveil et a raté son bus

Signature du proviseur: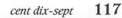
Lycée Alfred Kastler
Le Surveillant Général

6 Qu'est-ce que c'est?

What do you suppose a **billet de retard** is? What information does it give? What happened to Céline this morning?

> ### NOTE CULTURELLE
>
> If you're late to school in France, you are required to go to the principal's office to explain your tardiness. The person in charge fills out a form in your **carnet de correspondance**, a special notebook you carry with you that records your behavior at school. Parents are required to sign any notes written in the **carnet** to show that they are aware of their child's conduct.

PREMIERE ETAPE   *cent dix-sept* **117**

Jump Start!

Write the following scrambled monologue on the board or on a transparency. Have students rearrange the sentences to form a logical sequence of events. 1. **Donc, je suis arrivée au lycée en retard.** 2. **Je n'ai pas pris mon petit déjeuner.** 3. **Mon réveil n'a pas sonné.** 4. **En cours, j'ai vu que j'avais oublié mes devoirs.** 5. **J'ai couru pour attraper le bus.** 6. **Je me suis réveillée en retard.** 7. **Mais bien sûr, je l'ai raté.** (*Answers:* 3, 6, 2, 5, 7, 1, 4)

MOTIVATE

To arouse students' curiosity, arrive late to class. Apologize in French and give several excuses for being late. Then, ask students what excuses they give when they are late.

TEACH

Teaching Suggestion

After students do Activity 6 and read the **Note Culturelle**, ask the following questions: **Céline est en quelle classe? Quel est son nom de famille? Elle va à quel lycée? Qu'est-ce qu'on lui a donné? Qui a signé le billet? Où est-ce qu'on met le billet de retard? Pourquoi est-ce que Céline est arrivée en retard? Qui va signer ce billet de retard?**

Culture Note

Le **proviseur** (**Madame le proviseur**) is the actual director of the **lycée**. Most students might never see the **proviseur**. In **école primaire**, the head of the school is called **le directeur** (**la directrice**).

Answers

6 a tardy slip; name of student, grade level, reason for being late, signature of principal; She did not hear her alarm clock and missed her bus.

RESOURCES FOR PREMIERE ETAPE

Textbook Audiocassette 3A/Audio CD 5
Practice and Activity Book, pp. 50–52
Videodisc Guide
  Videodisc Program, Videodisc 3A

Chapter Teaching Resources, Book 2
• Teaching Transparency Master 5-1, pp. 7, 10
  Teaching Transparency 5-1
• Additional Listening Activities 5-1, 5-2, p. 11
  Audiocassette 9B/Audio CD 5
• Realia 5-1, pp. 15, 17
• Situation Cards 5-1, pp. 18–19
• Student Response Forms, pp. 20–22
• Quiz 5-1, pp. 23–24
  Audiocassette 7B/Audio CD 5

Presentation

Vocabulaire Gather props to present the sentences (an alarm clock, a torn shirt, a math book, and a report card). Act out each sentence and have students repeat after you, mimicking your gestures. Then, call out sentences in random order and have students mime the appropriate gestures for each sentence. Next, ask nine volunteers to come to the front of the class. Have each one repeat a sentence after you and mime the gestures. Other students should continue to participate by repeating and miming as well. Finally, as the nine individuals act out their sentences, have the class give the sentence associated with the mime. (**J'ai raté une marche. J'ai été collée.**)

Additional Practice

Ask students to tell which of these things has ever (**déjà**) happened to them and which has never (**ne... jamais**) happened. (**Tu as déjà été collé(e)? Oui, j'ai déjà été collé(e). Non, je n'ai jamais été collé(e).**)

Teaching Suggestion

Trace each illustration and enlarge it on a photocopier. Tape the pictures to the board and number them one through nine. Call out sentences (**J'ai eu une colle.**) and have students give the number of the corresponding picture. (**C'est le numéro huit.**) According to the level of your students, you might then call out a number (**numéro trois**) and have students supply the sentence. (**J'ai raté une marche.**)

Vocabulaire

J'ai passé une journée épouvantable!

D'abord, je n'ai pas entendu mon réveil.

Ensuite, j'ai raté une marche. Je suis tombé...

... et j'ai déchiré ma chemise.

Après ça, j'ai raté le bus...

... et j'ai perdu mon livre de maths.

Ensuite, **le prof a rendu les interros et j'ai eu une mauvaise note**...

... donc, **j'ai été collé.**

Finalement, **j'ai reçu mon bulletin trimestriel.** Quelle journée!

118 *cent dix-huit*

CHAPITRE 5   Quelle journée!

♜ Game

QU'EST-CE QUI SE PASSE? Trace the illustrations from the **Vocabulaire** without the captions, number each square, photocopy, and distribute one to each student. Form groups of four or five. Give each group a pair of dice and an answer sheet to the judge. To play the game, students take turns throwing the dice and telling what happened in the illustration that corresponds to the number they threw. For example, if a student throws a six, he or she would say **J'ai perdu mon livre de maths,** and six points would be awarded for the correct answer. A student who throws a ten, eleven, or twelve, loses a turn.

7 Ecoute! 1. c 2. d 3. a 4. b

Listen to these dialogues and decide which of the excuses illustrated below is given in each one.

a.

b.

c.

d.

8 La suite

Choose the appropriate completions for these sentences.

1. J'ai déchiré mon jean... c
2. J'ai reçu mon bulletin trimestriel... d
3. J'ai perdu mes devoirs d'histoire... a
4. Je n'ai pas entendu mon réveil... e
5. Mon prof n'était pas content... b

a. donc, mon prof était furieux, et j'ai eu zéro.
b. parce que j'ai perdu mon livre de français.
c. quand je suis tombé(e).
d. et j'ai eu de très bonnes notes!
e. donc, j'ai raté le bus.

COMMENT DIT-ON... ?

Expressing concern for someone

Ça n'a pas l'air d'aller. *You look like something's wrong.*
Qu'est-ce qui t'arrive? *What's wrong?*
Qu'est-ce qui se passe? *What's going on?*
Raconte! *Tell me!*

---

9 Ecoute!

Luc is late for his lunch meeting with Francine at a café. Listen to his excuses and decide which of the following happened to make him late.

1. Luc est rentré chez lui à midi.
2. Il a trouvé son livre d'histoire.
3. Il a raté une marche et il est tombé.
4. Il a pris le bus pour aller au café.

Culture Note

Call attention to illustration **a** in Activity 7. In labeling their school papers, French students usually write their last names first in capital letters, followed by their first names in lowercase letters. They usually don't write their teachers' names or class periods since the school day isn't divided into class periods as it is in the United States. The **term A1** written below this student's name refers to **terminale A1,** which means that the student

is in **terminale** (the last year of the **lycée**) and has chosen section **A1** of the **baccalauréat.** However, in 1993, the French government simplified the nomenclature of **bac** choices, which had ranged from **A** to **E**, and from **1** to **3** for each letter. Currently, there are only three sections for the general **bac: ES** (**économique et social**), **L** (**littéraire**), and **S** (**scientifique**). There are also four technological sections.

Teaching Suggestion

7 Call students attention to illustration **a**. Ask them how they know this is a French student's paper, other than the language (graph paper, number seven is crossed, the grade is based on twenty points).

For Individual Needs

7 Slower Pace Before you play the recording, ask students to imagine what excuse each illustration might suggest. Then, ask questions about the illustrations. (**Sept sur vingt, c'est une bonne ou une mauvaise note? Le bus arrive ou il part? Le bureau est bien rangé, ou il est en désordre? La fille est heureuse ou triste?**)

8 Challenge Have partners create additional sentence starters and completions and present them to the class on a transparency for other students to match.

Presentation

Comment dit-on... ? Ask students to imagine that something unfortunate just happened to them, and to be prepared to talk about it. Then, go around the room asking students what's wrong. (**Ça n'a pas l'air d'aller, Paul. Qu'est-ce qui t'arrive? Qu'est-ce qui se passe, Anne?**)

For videodisc application, see *Videodisc Guide.*

Teaching Suggestion

9 Have students listen to the recording a second time and identify the expressions of concern that Francine uses. Then, have them correct the false statements.

Presentation

Grammaire Have students look at the sentences in the **Vocabulaire** on page 118. Ask them what the teenager is talking about. Point out that since he's talking about what *happened,* he's using the **passé composé.** Ask students how the **passé composé** is formed. List the past participles in the **Vocabulaire** and have students try to deduce their infinitive forms. Then, remind students how the negative is formed in the **passé composé** and call on individuals to make the sentences in the **Vocabulaire** on page 118 negative. Finally, read the **Grammaire** with students.

Teaching Suggestion

Show magazine pictures and ask questions to elicit students' use of the **passé composé.** (Qu'est-ce qu'elle a bu hier soir? Qu'est-ce qu'il a pris pour le petit déjeuner? Qu'est-ce qu'ils ont fait cet après-midi?)

Game

TIC-TAC-TOE Make three or four tic-tac-toe grids and one answer sheet. In each square write an infinitive in parentheses followed by a sentence without the verb. (voir— J' ____ Marc.) Distribute copies to groups of two players and one judge. Players take turns reading aloud a sentence and supplying the verb in the **passé composé.** The judge verifies the answers. When the answer is correct, a student puts a marker in that square. (A coin works well.) A student wins when three squares in a row are marked horizontally, vertically, or diagonally.

10 Qu'est-ce que tu dis?

If you saw Jean, Colette, and Gérard at the end of the day, how would you ask about their day? How do you think they would respond? See answers below.

Jean   Colette   Gérard

11 Encore en retard!

You're the principal! When your partner arrives at school late, question him or her and write out a **billet de retard.** Don't forget to sign it! Then, reverse roles.

> Vous vous appelez comment?   en terminale
>
> Qu'est-ce qui vous est arrivé?   en seconde
>
> Vous êtes en quelle classe?   en première

*G*rammaire   The passé composé

You already know how to say that something happened in the past: for most verbs, you use a form of **avoir** and the past participle of the main verb.

j' **ai mangé**	nous **avons mangé**
tu **as mangé**	vous **avez mangé**
il/elle/on **a mangé**	ils/elles **ont mangé**

- To form past participles of **-er** verbs, drop **-er** from the infinitive and add **-é**:
  J'ai **raté** le bus.
  To form past participles of **-re** verbs, drop **-re** from the infinitive and add **-u**:
  Zut! On a **perdu** le match!
  To form past participles of **-ir** verbs, drop **-ir** from the infinitive and add **-i**:
  Enfin! On a **fini**!

- Many verbs have an irregular past participle, just as they do in English.

  Il a **été** collé aujourd'hui. (**être**)   Elle a **pris** un sandwich. (**prendre**)
  Vous avez **fait** vos devoirs? (**faire**)   Il a **bu** de l'eau. (**boire**)
  On a **eu** une interro. (**avoir**)   Tu as **lu** ce roman? (**lire**)
  J'ai **reçu** mon bulletin. (**recevoir**)   On a **vu** un film hier. (**voir**)

- To say that something didn't happen, put **ne... pas** around the form of **avoir**:
  Je **n'ai pas** entendu mon réveil.

120 *cent vingt*   CHAPITRE 5   Quelle journée!

Additional Practice

To give students practice forming the **passé composé,** prepare several flashcards. On one side, write sentences in the present tense. (**Sophie prend une tartine.**) Have students read the card and say the sentence in the **passé composé.** (**Sophie a pris une tartine.**) To help visual learners, show the sentence in the **passé composé** that you've written on the other side of the card.

Possible answers

10 1. Qu'est-ce-qui s'est passé? Je suis arrivé en retard au lycée.
2. Comment a été ta journée? J'ai oublié mes devoirs.
3. Qu'est-ce-qui s'est passé à l'école? J'ai eu huit à mon interro.

12 Ecoute!

Listen to these students. Are they talking about something that is happening now or something that happened in the past? Answers on p. 111C.

13 Bonne ou mauvaise journée?

Est-ce que ces personnes ont passé une bonne ou une mauvaise journée? Ecris trois phrases pour décrire ce qui est arrivé à chaque personne.

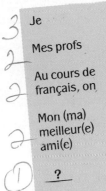

Je	perdre	une bonne note en...
Mes profs	rater	le devoir de...
Au cours de français, on	prendre	un déjeuner de...
	avoir	l'interro de...
	faire	du deltaplane
Mon (ma) meilleur(e) ami(e)	ne pas entendre	le réveil
	rencontrer	collé
	trouver	20 dollars
	regarder	un match entre... et...
?	recevoir	le bus pour aller...
	voir	une vedette de cinéma
	être	un film
	?	?

14 L'heure de la sortie

Write down four activities you think your classmates do after school. Then, ask a partner if he or she did them yesterday.

—Tu as joué au foot?
—Non, j'ai joué au tennis.

jouer au foot
regarder la télé
écouter de la musique
faire les devoirs

15 Qu'est-ce qu'on a tous fait?

In groups of four, try to find three things that everyone did last weekend and three things that no one did. Report your findings to the class, using **On a tous...** and **On n'a pas...** As the groups report, note the activities that most people did or didn't do.

16 Jeux de rôle

With a partner, choose two of these situations and take turns expressing concern for each other and explaining what happened.

1. Tu arrives au cours de maths avec vingt minutes de retard. Le prof n'est pas content!
2. Tu n'étais pas à la boum de ton ami(e) samedi soir. Il/Elle veut savoir ce qui s'est passé.
3. Tu arrives chez toi à une heure du matin. Ton père (ta mère) est furieux (furieuse).
4. Tu n'es pas allé(e) faire les magasins avec tes copains hier après l'école. Ton ami(e) te téléphone pour savoir pourquoi.

PREMIERE ETAPE
cent vingt et un **121**

Additional Practice

12 On separate slips of paper, write an infinitive, either **le présent** or **le passé composé**, and a subject in parentheses. Have pairs of students draw a slip of paper and work together to write a sentence, using the subject and the verb in the specified tense. Then, have one student read the sentence aloud. The class will decide if the students are talking about something that is happening now or something that happened in the past.

For Individual Needs

12 Challenge Have students listen to the recording a second time and tell what happened or what is happening in each situation.

Teaching Suggestion

14 For additional sports and weekend activities, refer students to the **Si tu as oublié...** section and the Supplementary Vocabulary in the back of the book.

Building on Previous Skills

15 To re-enter leisure activities and numbers, write several activities on the board. Have volunteers poll the class to see how many people did the activities last weekend. **(Qui a écouté de la musique?)** Have the polltakers count their classmates' raised hands aloud in French before writing the totals on the board.

CLOSE

Use Activity 16 to close this étape. Form small groups and assign one of the four situations to each one. Group members should work together to create the conversation and present it to the class.

ASSESS

Quiz 5-1, *Chapter Teaching Resources, Book 2,* pp. 23–24

*Assessment Items, Audiocassette 7B
Audio CD 5*

Performance Assessment

Have students write a composition about a bad day a fictitious character has had recently. They could use a cartoon character or a character in a TV program. They should describe the events of the day from start to finish, using the **passé composé.** Grades should be based on accuracy, comprehensibility, and variety of vocabulary.

DEUXIEME ETAPE

Inquiring; expressing satisfaction and frustration; sympathizing with and consoling someone

*J*ump Start!

Have students write down three things that happened to them during the week or on the weekend.

MOTIVATE

Ask students what people usually ask one another first when they meet at the end of the day. *(How was your day?)* Have students scan the conversation to see if they can find out how to ask this question in French. **(Alors, comment s'est passée ta journée?)** Then, ask them to name some of the good things that can happen in a school day.

TEACH

Teaching Suggestion

Play the role of Benoît and tell the class about your bad day, using gestures, props, and mime. Then, smile and play the role of Yves, telling the class about your good day. Interject the expressions from **Comment dit-on... ?** on page 123 as you tell about all the things that happened to you. Once meaning has been established in this manner, distribute typed copies of randomly ordered sentences in the conversation that tell what happened and the functional expressions that demonstrate satisfaction or frustration. Have students label two columns on a sheet of paper: **Une bonne journée** and **Une mauvaise journée.** Have them rewrite the sentences of the conversation under the appropriate column. Visual learners might put a smiling face and a frowning face at the top of the appropriate columns.

YVES	Oh là là, ça a pas l'air d'aller, toi! Qu'est-ce qui s'est passé?
BENOIT	Ben, j'ai reçu un ballon dans la figure en gym et j'ai dû aller à l'infirmerie! Décidément, c'est pas mon jour, aujourd'hui!
YVES	Ah, bon? Qu'est-ce qui t'est arrivé d'autre?
BENOIT	Tout a été de travers! D'abord, je suis arrivé en retard à l'école. Ensuite, je suis tombé dans l'escalier. Et puis, à la cantine, quelqu'un a renversé une assiette de spaghettis sur mon pantalon.
YVES	Pauvre vieux!
BENOIT	Enfin... Et toi, au fait? J'espère que ta journée s'est mieux passée que la mienne.
YVES	Oui, elle s'est même très bien passée. En géo, j'ai eu 18. Ensuite, en français, j'ai eu 16. Le prof a même lu ma rédaction à la classe! Après, à la récré, Julien m'a invité à son anniversaire. Et finalement, en anglais, on a vu un bon film.

17 C'est Yves ou Benoît?

1. Il a eu une bonne note en géo. Yves
2. Il est allé à l'infirmerie. Benoît
3. Il a vu un bon film. Yves
4. Quelqu'un a renversé une assiette de spaghettis sur son pantalon. Benoît
5. Il est arrivé en retard à l'école. Benoît
6. Il a eu 16 en français. Yves
7. Il va aller à une fête. Yves
8. Il est tombé dans l'escalier. Benoît

NOTE CULTURELLE

Many students who do not live close enough to go home for lunch eat in the school cafeteria **(la cantine).** The meals served follow the French sequence: a first course, a main dish with vegetables, then cheese, fruit, or yogurt. Students might stand in line for their meals, or they might be served at their table. Since the lunch period lasts for about two hours, students usually have time to study, play a game, or go to a café after they eat.

RESOURCES FOR DEUXIEME ETAPE

Textbook Audiocassette 3A/Audio CD 5
Practice and Activity Book, pp. 53–55
Videodisc Guide
  Videodisc Program, Videodisc 3A

Chapter Teaching Resources, Book 2
• Communicative Activity 5-1, pp. 3–4
• Teaching Transparency Master 5-2, pp. 8, 10
  Teaching Transparency 5-2
• Additional Listening Activities 5-3, 5-4, p. 12
  Audiocassette 9B/Audio CD 5
• Realia 5-2, pp. 16, 17
• Situation Cards 5-2, pp. 18–19
• Student Response Forms, pp. 20–22
• Quiz 5-2, pp. 25–26
  Audiocassette 7B/Audio CD 5

COMMENT DIT-ON... ?
Inquiring; expressing satisfaction and frustration

To inquire:

Comment ça s'est passé? *How did it go?*

Comment s'est passée ta journée (hier)? *How was your day (yesterday)?*

Comment s'est passé ton week-end? *How was your weekend?*

Comment se sont passées tes vacances? *How was your vacation?*

To express satisfaction:

C'était... *It was . . .*
  incroyable! *amazing!*
  super!
  génial!
Ça s'est très bien passé!
  It went really well!
Quelle journée formidable!
  What a great day!
Quel week end formidable!
  What a great weekend!

To express frustration:

C'était incroyable!
  It was unbelievably bad!
J'ai passé une journée
  horrible!
  I had a terrible day!
C'est pas mon jour!
  It's just not my day!
Tout a été de travers!
  Everything went wrong!
Quelle journée!/Quel week-end!
  What a (bad) day!/ . . . weekend!

18 Ecoute!

Listen as some friends discuss their weekends.
Did they have a good weekend or a bad one?
Answers on p. 111D.

19 Sondage

Poll five classmates to find out how their weekends were.
Did more people have good weekends or bad weekends?

20 Et toi, qu'est-ce que tu as fait?

Ask a partner how his or her day went yesterday. Your partner should mention three things
that made the day good or bad. Then, reverse roles.

Tu te rappelles ?

Do you remember how to pronounce the
nasal sound (ɛ̃) in **incroyable**? When you
see the letters **in, im, ain, aim,** or **(i)en,**
don't pronounce the *n* sound as in the
English word *fine,* but make a pure nasal
sound where part of the air goes through
the back of your mouth and nose, as in
the French **fin.** Try pronouncing these
words with the nasal (ɛ̃): **bulletin,
bien, faim, soudain.** Remember
that if another vowel follows the **n** or **m,**
(**inadmissible**), there is no nasal sound.

À la française

There are many expressions you can use to show
interest and get someone to continue a story in
English. You can do the same in French. Say **Ah
bon?** or **Ah oui?** *(Really?),* **Et après?** *(And then
what?),* and **Et ensuite?** *(And what next?).*

Teaching Suggestions

20 After the pairs have finished their conversation, ask volunteers to come to the front
of the class and tell about their partner's day
(**Hier, Claire a passé une bonne journée.
Elle...**). Have the class take notes during the
presentations. Then, question students about
what happened to their classmates based on
the presentations. (**Qui a été collé? Qui a eu
cent à son interro d'algèbre?**)

20 Before doing this activity, have students
read **A la française.** Encourage them to use
these expressions in their dialogues.

Tu te rappelles? Have students look at the
Supplementary Vocabulary at the back of the
book to find as many words as possible that
use the nasal [ɛ̃] sound. Then, have them
write and act out short skits, using as many
of the words as possible.

Comment dit-on... ? Have
students ask you how your
day was, using the informal
questions in the dialogue on
page 122 as a model. After
each question, smile or look
sad as you respond with one
of the expressions in **Comment
dit-on... ?** After several examples, ask students how their
day was, allowing them to
look at the expressions in the
function box as they respond.

For videodisc
application, see
Videodisc Guide.

For Individual
Needs

**Visual Learners/Slower
Pace** Write each expression
from **Comment dit-on... ?** on
separate strips of transparency
and label the following columns on a transparency: *To
inquire, To express satisfaction,* and *To express frustration.* Place the transparency on
the overhead projector and the
strips one at a time in random
order. Have students tell you
under which column to place
each strip. You might say each
expression aloud with the
appropriate intonation to help
auditory learners.

18 Challenge Play the
recording again and have students tell what the speakers
did over the weekend.

Additional Practice

18 Have students write
down the expressions in
Comment dit-on... ? Then, as
they listen to the recording,
have them place a check next
to the expressions they hear
that demonstrate either satisfaction or frustration.

Presentation

Note de grammaire Have students do Activity 21, and then ask them what tense they think the sentences are written in and how they know. Then, have students point out all of the helping verbs and indicate which sentences contain the verb **avoir** and which contain **être**. Ask if they can find a reflexive verb among the sentences and tell which helping verb it uses.

Teaching Suggestions

• Write various verb infinitives on index cards. Hold them up one at a time, asking **avoir ou être?** You might also call out a singular subject (**il**) as you hold up a card (**aller**), and have students form the **passé composé.** (**Il est allé.**) Finally, ask questions about pictures to elicit the **passé composé.** (**Qu'est-ce qu'elle a fait ce matin?**)

21 For more practice with the **passé composé,** have students rewrite the account of the incident in the third person, telling what happened to Emilie and her friends.

📁 Portfolio

22 Written This activity is appropriate for students' written portfolios. For portfolio suggestions, see *Assessment Guide,* page 18.

◈ For Individual Needs

22 Challenge Have students arrange "photographs" of an actual or imaginary vacation on posterboard. They could use real or drawn photographs or magazine cut-outs. Have them write a caption and a short description for each photograph, telling about the vacation in the **passé composé.**

---

21 Qu'est-ce qu'ils ont fait?

Emilie et ses amis sont allés à la plage hier. Choisis les dessins qui correspondent à leurs activités.

1. Ce week-end, on est allés à la plage. Moi, je suis arrivée à l'heure. Les autres sont arrivés en retard. c
2. On a joué au volley, on a lu des romans et on a écouté de la musique. a
3. Plus tard, on s'est promenés et on a vu un château de sable magnifique. d
4. Malheureusement, je suis tombée sur le château. Quelle maladroite! b

a.

b.

c.

d.

Note de *Grammaire*

You use **être** instead of **avoir** as the helping verb to make the **passé composé** of some verbs. Many of these are verbs of motion, such as **aller, tomber,** and **arriver.**

> Je suis allé(e)
> Tu es allé(e)
> Il est allé   ⎱
> Elle est allée   ⎰ au lycée.
> On est allé(e)(s)

You have to use **être** to make the **passé composé** of all reflexive verbs as well.

> Je me suis levé(e).
> Tu t'es levé(e).
> Il s'est levé.
> Elle s'est levée.
> On s'est levé(e)(s).

Notice that when you write these forms, the past participle has to agree with the subject or the reflexive pronoun. You'll learn more about this in Chapter 6.

22 ✒ Comment se sont passées tes vacances?

Ton correspondant Marc raconte ses vacances dans une lettre. Réponds à sa lettre. Raconte tes vacances, réelles ou imaginaires.

> Salut!
> Comment ça s'est passé tes vacances? Nous, on est partis faire du ski dans les Alpes. C'était super! J'ai fait du ski pour la première fois. Je suis souvent tombé! Les montagnes sont magnifiques. Attends de voir mes photos. Et toi? Tu as passé de bonnes vacances? Qu'est-ce que tu as fait? Raconte-moi!
> Marc

124 *cent vingt-quatre*   CHAPITRE 5   Quelle journée!

Additional Practice

Type and distribute copies of the following paragraph and have students supply the **passé composé** of the verbs in parentheses. Ce matin, le réveil de Sylvie ____ (ne pas sonner). Donc, elle ____ (se réveiller) en retard. Puis, elle ____ (se laver) et ____ (s'habiller) très vite. Elle ____ (ne pas avoir) le temps de prendre son petit déjeuner, alors elle ____ (manger) juste une pomme, et elle ____ (boire) du jus d'orange.

Elle ____ (aller) à l'arrêt de bus, mais elle ____ (rater) le bus. Pauvre Sylvie! A cause de tout ça, elle ____ (arriver) en retard à l'école, et en plus, en entrant dans la salle de classe, elle ____ (ne pas voir) la marche, et elle ____ (tomber). Quel désastre! (*Answers:* n'a pas sonné, s'est réveillée, s'est lavée, s'est habillée, n'a pas eu, a mangé, a bu, est allée, a raté, est arrivée, n'a pas vu, est tombée)

23 Devine!

Put the letters you wrote for Activity 22 together face down. Each person selects a letter and reads it silently. The rest of the group asks yes-no questions to determine where the writer went and what he or she did on vacation.

—Cette personne est allée en France?   —Oui.
—Elle est allée à la plage?   —Non.
—Elle a fait du ski?   —Non.
—   ?

COMMENT DIT-ON... ?
Sympathizing with and consoling someone

To sympathize with someone:
Oh là là! *Oh no!*
C'est pas de chance, ça! *Tough luck!*
Pauvre vieux/vieille!
You poor thing!

To console someone:
Courage! *Hang in there!*
Ça va aller mieux. *It'll get better.*
T'en fais pas. *Don't worry.*
C'est pas grave. *It's not serious.*

---

24 Les pauvres!

What would you say to sympathize with and console the following people?   See answers below.

1.

2.

3.

25 Une mauvaise journée

Make a list of five things that can make your day go wrong.

Ma journée se passe mal si je ne prends pas mon petit déjeuner.
je rate le bus.
    ?

26 La plus mauvaise journée de ma vie

Imagine that all the things you listed in Activity 25 happened to you yesterday. Describe your day to a friend, who urges you to continue telling about your day, reacts sympathetically, and tries to console you. Then, reverse roles.

Presentation

Comment dit-on... ? Have students find the expressions in the **Mise en train** on pages 114 and 115 that Hector uses to sympathize with and console Céline. (**T'inquiète pas. C'est pas grave. Ce n'est pas dramatique. Ça va aller mieux.**) Write them on the board and add others from **Comment dit-on... ?** Have students say the expressions. Then, have them console you as you tell stories to elicit their sympathy.

For Individual Needs

Visual Learners Have students bring to class a magazine picture that shows someone who is sad, hurt, or upset. Have them mount it on construction paper and attach to it a caption telling what happened. Form groups of five and have everyone show his or her picture and read the caption to the group. Students then pass the pictures to the group members, who each write a different expression of sympathy or consolation under the caption. Students should vary the expressions they use.

CLOSE

Group Work

Form groups of six. In each group, distribute six different paragraph-starters. (**Hier, quand je suis arrivé(e) chez moi,...**) To start, each member completes the sentence and continues writing for one minute. When you call time, students pass their papers to the next student, who adds to the paragraph. With each pass, extend the time. When everyone has written on every paper, have students choose the best paragraph within their group and read it to the class.

ASSESS

Quiz 5-2, *Chapter Teaching Resources, Book 2,* pp. 25–26

Assessment Items, Audiocassette 7B Audio CD 5

Performance Assessment

Form small groups and have a "sob story" contest. Each group is to create and write the saddest story they can imagine. Have each group read its story to the class. Students will sympathize with the person and vote on who gets the "teardrop" award.

Possible answers

24 1. Oh là là! C'est pas grave.   2. C'est pas de chance ça!   3. Courage, t'en fais pas!

*J*ump Start!

Have students list in French four good and two unfortunate things that happened to them during the past week.

MOTIVATE

Ask students to suggest as many excuses as they can that students traditionally use to explain low grades to parents.

TEACH

Teaching Suggestions

- For listening and speaking practice, ask the following questions about the **bulletins: Quel est le nom de famille de Caroline? Comment s'appelle son lycée? Elle habite où? Elle est en quelle classe? Elle a combien de cours? Combien elle a eu en latin? Que dit son prof de latin?**
- After students have read the **Note Culturelle,** ask them the following questions: **En quels cours avez-vous des exposés? Préférez-vous les interros orales ou écrites? Pourquoi? Vous avez combien d'interros par semaine? Pour quels cours avez-vous beaucoup de devoirs?**

Thinking Critically

Comparing and Contrasting
Ask students how the **bulletins** are similar to or different from their own report cards.

Culture Notes

- French high school students usually have at least two hours of homework every day.
- French high school teachers generally teach fewer hours per week and are provided with more preparation time at school than their American counterparts.

TROISIEME ETAPE

Giving reasons and making excuses; congratulating and reprimanding someone

Lycée Balzac
Académie de Tours

BULLETIN TRIMESTRIEL

NOM et prénom : PUECH Jean Classe de 2de 7

MATIERES D'ENSEIGNEMENT	MOYENNE DE L'ELEVE	APPRECIATIONS
Français	15	Travail sérieux
Mathématiques	12	A fait beaucoup de progrès
Sc. Physiques	15	Bon élève
Sc. Naturelles	9	Travail moyen.
Histoire-Géographie	16	Bon travail
Anglais	13	Résultats encourageants
Latin	11	A fait beaucoup de progrès
Arts plastiques	10	Peut mieux faire
Education physique	10	Doit s'appliquer davantage

Lycée Balzac
Académie de Tours

BULLETIN TRIMESTRIEL

NOM et prénom : GUY Caroline Classe de 2de 7

MATIERES D'ENSEIGNEMENT	MOYENNE DE L'ELEVE	APPRECIATIONS
Français	12	Satisfaisant
Mathématiques	14	A fait beaucoup de progrès
Sc. Physiques	15	Bon travail
Sc. Naturelles	9	Peut mieux faire
Histoire-Géographie	18	Très bonne élève!
Allemand	15	Travail sérieux
Anglais	11	Assez bien
Education musicale	17	Elève très sérieuse
Education physique	12	A fait beaucoup de progrès

27 Tu comprends?

1. Qui a eu la meilleure note en français? En maths?
2. En quelle matière est-ce que Jean est le plus fort? Et Caroline?
3. En quelle matière est-ce qu'il est le moins bon? Et Caroline?
4. Tu es plutôt comme Jean ou comme Caroline?

1. Jean; Caroline
2. histoire-géographie; histoire-géographie
3. sciences naturelles; sciences naturelles

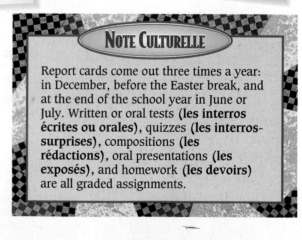

NOTE CULTURELLE

Report cards come out three times a year: in December, before the Easter break, and at the end of the school year in June or July. Written or oral tests (**les interros écrites ou orales**), quizzes (**les interros-surprises**), compositions (**les rédactions**), oral presentations (**les exposés**), and homework (**les devoirs**) are all graded assignments.

RESOURCES FOR **TROISIEME ETAPE**

Textbook Audiocassette 3A/Audio CD 5
Practice and Activity Book, pp. 56–58
Video Guide
  Video Program
  Expanded Video Program, Videocassette 2
Videodisc Guide
  Videodisc Program, Videodisc 3A

Chapter Teaching Resources, Book 2
- Communicative Activity 5-2, pp. 5–6
- Teaching Transparency Master 5-3, pp. 9, 10
  Teaching Transparency 5-3
- Additional Listening Activities 5-5, 5-6, p. 13
  Audiocassette 9B/Audio CD 5
- Realia 5-2, pp. 16, 17
- Situation Cards 5-3, pp. 18–19
- Student Response Forms, pp. 20–22
- Quiz 5-3, pp. 27–28
  Audiocassette 7B/Audio CD 5

COMMENT DIT-ON... ?
Giving reasons and making excuses

To give reasons:

Je suis assez bon (bonne) en français. *I'm pretty good at . . .*
C'est en maths **que je suis le/la meilleur(e).** *I'm best in . . .*
L'anglais, c'est mon fort! *. . . is my strong point.*

To make excuses:

L'histoire, c'est pas mon fort. *. . . isn't my best subject.*
J'ai du mal à comprendre. *I have a hard time understanding.*
Je suis pas doué(e) pour les sciences. *I don't have a talent for . . .*

28 Comment tu trouves tes cours?

Make a list of the classes you have this year and write down your comments about each one. Share them with a friend. Do you have the same opinions?

> Je suis fort(e) en...   J'adore...
>
> difficile   chouette   C'est intéressant!
>
> Le prof est super.   facile   amusant

29 Le jour des bulletins trimestriels

a. You're the teacher! Make a list of six subjects and give a partner a grade for each one. Don't forget to write your comments (**appréciations**).

b. You and your partner exchange the report cards you made. Ask each other about your grades, giving reasons or excuses for each one.

> —Combien tu as eu en maths?
> —J'ai eu 15. Je suis assez bon (bonne) en maths. Et toi?
> —Moi, j'ai eu 8. C'est pas mon fort!

COMMENT DIT-ON... ?
Congratulating and reprimanding someone

To congratulate someone:

Félicitations! *Congratulations!*
Bravo! *Terrific!*
Chapeau! *Well done!*

To reprimand someone:

C'est inadmissible. *That's unacceptable.*
Tu dois mieux travailler en classe. *You have to work harder in class.*
Tu ne dois pas faire le clown en classe! *You can't be goofing off in class!*
Ne recommence pas. *Don't do it again.*

Presentation

Comment dit-on... ? Write the expressions on the board in two columns: *To give reasons* and *To make excuses*. Then, ask who has a particular class (**Qui a algèbre?**) and how they do in it. (**Tu es assez bon (bonne) en algèbre, ou tu as du mal à comprendre?**) Students might accompany their answer with a thumbs-up or thumbs-down gesture. Finally, have students write down the classes they have and tell a partner what they think of each class, using the expressions in **Comment dit-on... ?**

Teaching Suggestion

28 You might take a class poll of the most and least popular classes.

Presentation

Comment dit-on... ? Circulate among the students handing them papers with French grades written on them, some good, some bad. As you hand a paper to a student, show the grade to the class and congratulate or reprimand the student based on the grade. Then, write the expressions from **Comment dit-on... ?** on the board. Have each student write a school subject in French on a slip of paper and next to that, a grade based on 20 points. Have students exchange their slips and then circulate around the room talking about their grades and congratulating or reprimanding each other.

For videodisc application, see *Videodisc Guide.*

Language Notes

- Ask students what English expression corresponds to the French expression **Chapeau!** *(Hats off!)*
- In the expression **faire le clown**, the word **clown** is pronounced *cloon*.

Portfolio

29 Written Have students write their own ideal **bulletin** to include in their portfolios. Have them write their courses in French, give themselves French grades, and write in French some **appréciations** their teachers might give them for those classes. For portfolio information, see *Assessment Guide,* pages 2–13.

For Individual Needs

30 Challenge Play the recording a second time and have students write each school subject and grade they hear mentioned.

Teaching Suggestion

33 Have students take notes as they interview their partner and then write a paragraph describing their partner's week at school.

📖 **Mon journal**

34 For an additional journal entry suggestion for Chapter 5, see *Practice and Activity Book,* page 149.

CLOSE

To close this **étape,** have students write letters to a French pen pal in which they tell about a fictitious report card. They should give excuses for any bad grades and give reasons for good ones.

ASSESS

Quiz 5-3, *Chapter Teaching Resources, Book 2,* pp. 27–28

Assessment Items, Audiocassette 7B/Audio CD 5

Performance Assessment

Have students act out the roles of student and parent on report card day. On separate slips of paper, write several classes and grades in French and place them in a box. On index cards, write either **parent** or **élève.** Students will choose a card to establish their role. Then, the **élève** chooses a slip of paper from the report-card box. The **parent** asks about the grade and congratulates or reprimands the **élève,** and the **élève** comments or makes an excuse for the grade. Continue until everyone has participated.

30 Ecoute!

Listen as Gilbert's father and friends ask him about his schoolwork. Are they reprimanding or congratulating him?   Answers on p. 111D.

31 Vraiment, Gilbert...

Regarde les notes que Gilbert a eues à ses autres devoirs. Qu'est-ce que tu peux lui dire à propos de ses notes?

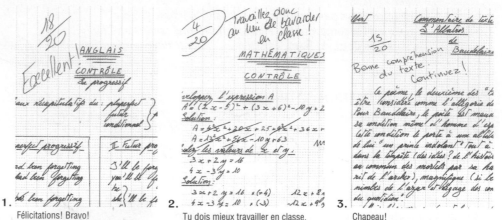

Possible answers:

1. Félicitations! Bravo!   2. Tu dois mieux travailler en classe.   3. Chapeau!

32 Le meilleur et le pire

Write down a good test grade, a bad test grade, and subjects for each. Your partner will play the role of your parent and ask you about your grades. Give reasons or excuses for each one.

—Combien tu as eu à l'interro de géométrie?
—J'ai eu 100! La géo, c'est mon fort!
—Chapeau! Et à ton interro d'anglais?
—Euh...

33 Ta semaine à l'école

How was your week at school? Interview a partner. Be sympathetic, or scold your partner if necessary!

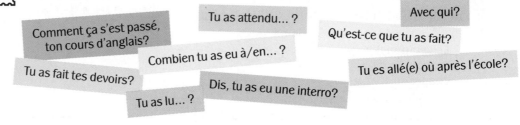

Comment ça s'est passé, ton cours d'anglais?

Tu as attendu... ?

Avec qui?

Qu'est-ce que tu as fait?

Combien tu as eu à/en... ?

Tu as fait tes devoirs?

Tu es allé(e) où après l'école?

Tu as lu... ?

Dis, tu as eu une interro?

34 Mon journal

In Chapter 1 you wrote your resolutions for the school year in your journal. Reread them now. How are you doing? Report on your progress.

🌐 **Culture Note**

Call attention to the grades on the papers in Activity 31. The grade is written over 20 on each paper. However, many teachers will actually write only 18, 4, or 15 since it's known that all grades are based on 20. The average grades students receive vary depending on the subject matter. For example, it is considered easier to get a higher grade in math because the answers are either right or wrong, as opposed to philosophy or literature, which require critical thinking and the writing of analytical essays. A grade of 12 in math would be considered just above average, whereas it would be a very good grade in philosophy or literature.

Panorama Culturel

Franck • Martinique

Virginie • France

Emmanuel • France

VIDEO PROGRAM
OR EXPANDED VIDEO
PROGRAM,
Videocassette 2
38:00–42:23

OR VIDEODISC PROGRAM,
Videodisc 3A

Search 20870, Play To 24670

What do you like and dislike about school? We asked several francophone students for their opinions. Here's what they had to say.

Qu'est-ce que tu aimes à l'école?

«Les mathématiques. J'aime bien. On travaille. Ça permet de réfléchir. J'aime bien.»

Et tes professeurs, ils sont comment?

«En général, assez sympathiques; ils sont très proches de nous. Ils nous comprennent le plus souvent. Ils nous aident si on a de petits problèmes. S'ils voient que ça ne va pas trop, ils nous conseillent. Ils sont très sympathiques.»

—Franck

«Ce que j'aime à l'école? Les récréations... parce qu'on peut se voir entre copains. Ça fait une pause entre chaque heure de cours. Et puis, on peut discuter, se désaltérer... Mon cours préféré, c'est l'anglais, parce que j'aime la langue anglaise.»

Qu'est-ce que tu n'aimes pas à l'école?

«Ce que je n'aime pas à l'école? Les sciences physiques. J'aime pas du tout.»

—Virginie

«Ben, à l'école, ce que j'aime en particulier, c'est les copains. C'est tout, hein. Parce que, bon, il y a certains profs qui sont sympa... Autrement le lycée... [ce que j'aime] c'est les copains, et se retrouver entre nous, j'aime bien.»

Qu'est-ce que tu n'aimes pas à l'école?

«Les surveillants. Je n'aime pas les surveillants à l'école, parce que... bon il y en a qui sont sympa, mais il y en a d'autres qui sont trop stricts, et puis c'est même pénible, quoi.»

—Emmanuel

Qu'en penses-tu? See answers below.

1. What do these students say they like most about school?
2. What complaints do they have?
3. Are your likes and dislikes similar to those these students mentioned? In what way?

Teacher Notes

- See *Video Guide, Videodisc Guide,* and *Practice and Activity Book* for activities related to the **Panorama Culturel**.
- Remind students that cultural material may be included in the Chapter Quizzes and Test.
- The interviewees' language represents informal, unrehearsed speech. Occasionally, edits have been made for clarification.

Motivating Activity

Ask students what they like and dislike about school, their classes, and their teachers.

Presentation

Have students view the video and listen for one or two things that each interviewee likes or dislikes. Ask the **Questions** below to check for comprehension, and then have students discuss **Qu'en penses-tu?** in small groups. Finally, ask them which of the three students they identify with the most and why.

Multicultural Link

Have students interview people from other countries or do research about their educational systems. Have them report their findings to the class.

Questions

1. **Pourquoi est-ce que Franck aime les maths? (Ça permet de réfléchir.)**
2. **Pourquoi est-ce que Franck trouve que les profs sont sympa? (Ils aident et conseillent les élèves.)**
3. **Quel est le cours préféré de Virginie? (l'anglais)**
4. **Qu'est-ce qu'Emmanuel préfère à l'école? (les copains) Qu'est-ce qu'il n'aime pas? (les surveillants)**

Teaching Suggestion

Have students conduct an interview with a partner in which they ask the following interview questions: **Qu'est-ce qui te plaît à l'école? Qu'est-ce que tu n'aimes pas à l'école? Et tes profs, ils sont comment?**

Answers
1. nice teachers, breaks, friends
2. The supervisors are too strict.

READING STRATEGY

Deducing the main idea

Teacher Note

For an additional reading, see *Practice and Activity Book*, page 59.

PREREADING
Activities A–C

Motivating Activity

Ask students to recall any humorous experiences they had in elementary school.

Teaching Suggestion

After students do Activities A–C, read *Le cancre* aloud to the class. Pass out typed copies of the poem and have students underline every word they <u>do</u> know (including the words translated in Activity C). Then, have them read the poem to themselves, trying to determine meaning from the underlined words before looking up new words in the dictionary.

READING
Activities D–K

 Cooperative Learning

Have groups of five dramatize *Le cancre* by acting out the meaning of each line of the poem. Assign a leader, readers, and actors for each group. Then, have each group decide on the actions, props, and sound effects they will use to present the poem to the class. One or two group members might read the poem aloud while the others act.

Thinking Critically

Analyzing Ask students if they think it's a good idea to single out young students as a dunce (**un cancre**) and why or why not?

LISONS!

$\mathcal{D}$o you have days when you would rather be anywhere else but in school? If you have, you can relate to these poems.

DE BONS CONSEILS

Sometimes, in order to figure out what a reading means, you have to understand the separate parts of it first. In a poem, it's helpful to examine the words, images, and symbols used before you decide what the main idea or message is.

A. What do you think will happen in the poems based on the illustrations? See answers below.

B. What drives you crazy about school? Make a list. What words can you find in the two poems that relate to what you don't like about school?

C. Here's some vocabulary you might need to understand these poems. How many sentences can you write with these words?

le rire	laugh
le visage	face
les chiffres	numbers
le pupitre	desk
la craie	chalk
effacer	to erase
le maître	grade school teacher
faire le pitre	to goof off
ils s'en vont	they leave

Le cancre See answers below.

D. Un cancre is *a dunce*. What is a dunce? French schoolchildren who got into trouble used to have to wear donkey ears. What donkey-like quality is the boy in

---

Le Cancre

Il dit non avec la tête
mais il dit oui avec le cœur
il dit oui à ce qu'il aime
il dit non au professeur
il est debout
on le questionne
et tous les problèmes sont posés
soudain le fou rire le prend
et il efface tout
les chiffres et les mots
les dates et les noms
les phrases et les pièges
et malgré les menaces du maître
sous les huées des enfants prodiges
avec des craies de toutes les couleurs
sur le tableau noir du malheur
il dessine le visage du bonheur

Page d'écriture

Deux et deux quatre
quatre et quatre huit
huit et huit font seize...
Répétez ! dit le maître
Deux et deux quatre
quatre et quatre huit
huit et huit font seize.
Mais voilà l'oiseau-lyre
qui passe dans le ciel
l'enfant le voit
l'enfant l'entend
l'enfant l'appelle :
Sauve-moi
joue avec moi
oiseau !
Alors l'oiseau descend
et joue avec l'enfant
Deux et deux quatre...
Répétez ! dit le maître
et l'enfant joue
l'oiseau joue avec lui...
Quatre et quatre huit
huit et huit font seize
et seize et seize qu'est-ce qu'ils font ?
Ils ne font rien seize et seize

Teacher Notes

- You and your students may be interested in a book called *La foire aux cancres* (by Jean-Charles, published in Paris by Calmann-Lévy). It is a humorous compilation of the mistakes made by **cancres** in French classrooms.
- Call students' attention to the donkey ears that the boy is wearing in the illustration. As punishment, French children wore them instead of the dunce cap that used to be worn in the United States.

Answers

A *Possible answers:* A boy will erase something on the chalkboard. A bird will enter the classroom.

D a bad student; stubbornness; "Il dit non avec la tête... ," "Il dit non au professeur... "

et surtout pas trente-deux
de toute façon
et ils s'en vont.
Et l'enfant a caché l'oiseau
dans son pupitre
et tous les enfants
entendent sa chanson
et tous les enfants
entendent la musique
et huit et huit à leur tour s'en vont
et quatre et quatre et deux et deux
à leur tour fichent le camp
et un et un ne font ni une ni deux
un à un s'en vont également.
Et l'oiseau-lyre joue
et l'enfant chante
et le professeur crie :
Quand vous aurez fini de faire le pitre!
Mais tous les autres enfants
écoutent la musique
et les murs de la classe
s'écroulent tranquillement.
Et les vitres redeviennent sable
l'encre redevient eau
les pupitres redeviennent arbres
la craie redevient falaise
le porte-plume redevient oiseau.

the poem displaying? What lines in the poem show this?

E. What else does the boy do to express his negative attitude toward school?　See answers below.

F. There are some expressions that show the poet has the same attitude. Can you match them to their English equivalents?

1. **les phrases et les pièges**　c
2. **les menaces du professeur**　a
3. **les huées des enfants prodiges**　d
4. **le tableau noir du malheur**　b

   a. *the teacher's threats*
   b. *the blackboard of unhappiness*
   c. *the sentences and the traps*
   d. *the boos of the gifted students*
       G. See answers below.

G. Despite his negative attitude about school, the boy has an essentially positive attitude about life. How do you know? Is he really **un cancre**?

H. Draw **le visage du bonheur** as you imagine it.

Page d'écriture　See answers below.

I. How does the poem begin? Do you do these kinds of drills in class? What happens to these numbers as the poem goes on?

J. Other classroom objects are transformed at the end of the poem. What quietly falls down? What turns into sand? What does the ink turn into? The desks? The chalk? The pen?

K. What does the student invite into the classroom that causes these transformations? In your opinion, what does this guest in the classroom symbolize?

L. What is the common theme that links these two poems? How does the student in each poem escape from the oppression of the classroom?

cent trente et un　**131**

POSTREADING
Activity L

Group Work

Have groups of five divide the text of *Page d'écriture* evenly among themselves and illustrate each line of the poem. Give students the option of using magazine cut-outs. You may help them decide what constitutes a line. Have students use one piece of paper for each illustration, drawing anything they think represents the meaning of the line. Have them write the line on the back of and below the illustration. Then, have groups sit in front of the class and show their illustrations as they read their lines of the poem. Students may choose the best illustrations from different groups to represent the entire poem and display them in the classroom.

Literature Link

Jacques Prévert (1900–1977) was a popular French poet who published a highly successful volume of poetry: *Les Paroles (Words).* Some of these poems were put to music. Young people related to Prévert because he wrote about happiness and love, lashed out at hypocrisy and stupidity, and playfully mocked respected human institutions. He wrote in free verse, irregular verse, occasional rhymes, and puns.

Language Note

Un vers is a line of poetry (**au troisième vers:** *in the third line;* **vers blancs/libres:** *blank/free verse*). **Une strophe** is a *stanza*.

Teaching Suggestion

You might show *Les Quatre Cents Coups (400 Blows),* a 1959 film by director François Truffaut, which depicts a 1950s classroom setting.

Answers

E He's rebellious. He erases "knowledge" off the board.
G He draws "the face of happiness" on the chalkboard; No.
I with addition problems; *Answers will vary;* They leave the classroom.
J the classroom walls; the windows; water; trees; stone; bird
K bird; *Possible answers:* Freedom, the power of the pen to transport you to another place through the imagination.
L children seeking liberation from the oppressive classroom; by using the imagination

Culture Note

Long ago, French schoolchildren used to write with a quill **(une plume),** a feather made into a pen that was dipped in ink. The quill was attached to a wooden holder called a **porte-plume.** Good handwriting was emphasized. Even today, French children learn cursive writing before they learn to print. This was also the case with American children until about 1940.

MISE EN PRATIQUE

The **Mise en pratique** reviews and integrates all four skills and culture in preparation for the Chapter Test.

Teaching Suggestion

Prepare and distribute similar versions of the three documents for students to fill out and include in their portfolios.

For Individual Needs

Slower Pace For listening and reading practice, assign a number to each document. Make random statements about the three documents and have students write the number(s) of the document(s) to which each of your statements refers. (**L'élève est en seconde. Le professeur s'appelle Monsieur Mabille. C'est le 12 novembre. Elle n'a pas sport aujourd'hui. Madame Garin a signé. L'élève s'appelle Ginette. L'infirmier ou l'infirmière a signé. L'élève est arrivée avec trente minutes de retard. Le surveillant général a signé. L'élève s'est fait mal à la main. L'élève n'a pas entendu son réveil.**)

Culture Note

The **surveillant général** stamp seen on the **billet de retard** probably contains the signature of the **surveillant** rather than the **surveillant général**. Surveillants, familiarly called **les pions** by students, are usually university students who take on part-time jobs to help the **lycée** administration with tasks, such as monitoring halls and signing various student forms. Above the **surveillants** are the **surveillant général** and the **conseiller d'éducation** who are on campus at all times and are responsible for scheduling classes, among other things.

DEMANDE

Je sollicite un rendez-vous avec

M _Mabille_

Professeur de _Histoire-géographie_

Date et Signature des Parents,

12 novembre

H. Garin

DEMANDE DE DISPENSE EXCEPTIONNELLE D'EDUCATION PHYSIQUE
(à remplir par les parents et à remettre au Conseiller d'Education avant le cours)

Nom de l'élève _GARIN_ Prénom _Ginette_ Classe _2nde_

Date du cours _12/11_

Motif de la demande _s'est fait mal à la main — dispense d'EPS_

Ci-joint certificat médical: (1) Oui - Non

Date _12/11_ Signature, _Mme Garin_

Lycée Balzac Tours — *INFIRMERIE*

BILLET DE RETARD

Lycée Balzac Tours — *Le Surveillant Général*

Nom _GARIN_ Le _12/11_

Prénom _Ginette_ élève de _seconde_

arrivé(e) à _8h30_ heures avec _30 min._ de retard

POUR LE MOTIF SUIVANT _n'a pas entendu son réveil et a raté le bus_

_____ Peut être admis(e) en classe.

Teacher Note

You might remind students that **seconde** is the first year of the **lycée, première** is the second year, and **terminale** is the last.

Language Note

Tell students that the -**c** in **seconde** is pronounced as a hard -**g** sound.

1 1. Look at the first document. What information is given? Who filled this out? Why?

2. What information is filled out in the second document? What happened to Ginette? What does this note excuse her from?

3. At what time did Ginette arrive at school? Why?

4. How was Ginette's day?
See answers below.

2 Ecoute la conversation entre le père de Ginette et son professeur d'histoire-géo. Décide si les phrases suivantes sont vraies ou fausses. Answers on p. 111D.

1. Ginette a eu 9 à l'interro d'histoire-géo.

2. La semaine passée, elle est arrivée en classe à l'heure.

3. D'après Ginette, l'histoire est son fort.

4. D'après Ginette, le prof ne l'aime pas.

5. Le prof de Ginette ne l'aime pas.

6. D'après le prof, Ginette ne doit pas faire le clown en classe.

3 Write Ginette's diary entry for November 12.

4 How much do you know about French schools?

1. What's in a **carnet de correspondance**? a record of a student's behavior at school

2. What happens in **la cantine**? Students eat lunch.

3. How often do report cards come out in France? three times a year

4. Match the following assignments to their English equivalents:

   1. **les rédactions** d   a. *oral presentations*

   2. **les interros orales** c   b. *homework*

   3. **les exposés** a   c. *oral tests*

   4. **les devoirs** b   d. *compositions*

5. Would you like to attend a French high school? List three reasons why you would and three reasons why you wouldn't.

5 You just got back to school from a weekend out of town. Ask a friend how the weekend was, being sure to ask where he or she went and what happened. Don't forget to sympathize if things went badly! Then, reverse roles.

6

JEU DE ROLE

You've been having problems in one of your classes and decide to meet with your teacher after school today. Act out the situation with a partner.

- Be sure to bring up your latest grades, good and bad.
- Give reasons for tardiness, bad grades, or lost homework.
- The teacher may be sympathetic, reprimanding, or both.

Answers

1 1. teacher's name, subject, date and signature of parent; parent; to make an appointment

2. student's name and grade, date, excuse and signature of parent; She hurt her hand; to skip a P.E. class

3. 8h30; She didn't hear her alarm and missed her bus.

4. a disaster

Teaching Suggestions

2 After students listen to the recording, have them correct the false statements.

2 After students have done this activity, you might distribute typed copies of the script and have students rewrite the conversation as if Ginette were an excellent student.

For Individual Needs

3 Challenge After students fill out similarly prepared documents (see Teaching Suggestion on page 132), have them write their own diary entry for November 12. They might include these in their written portfolios.

4 Challenge Have students write a letter to a French pen pal explaining American school procedures in terms the French correspondent will understand.

Portfolio

5 Oral This activity is appropriate for students' oral portfolios. For portfolio suggestions, see *Assessment Guide*, page 18.

Video Wrap-Up

- *VIDEO PROGRAM*
- *EXPANDED VIDEO PROGRAM, Videocassette 2, 29:15–44:00*
- *VIDEODISC PROGRAM, Videodisc 3A*

At this time, you might want to use the video resources for additional review and enrichment. See *Video Guide* or *Videodisc Guide* for suggestions regarding the following:

- **C'est pas mon jour!** (Dramatic episode)
- **Panorama Culturel** (Interviews)
- **Vidéoclips** (Authentic footage)

This page is intended to help students prepare for the test. It is a brief checklist of the major points covered in the chapter. The students should be reminded that this is only a checklist and does not necessarily include everything that will appear on the test.

Teaching Suggestion

Have students work in pairs to find as many responses as possible to each of the questions in **Que sais-je?**

♜ **Game**

▌ **TIC-TAC-TOE** Create three to five transparencies of tic-tac-toe grids. Number the squares and write one of the questions from **Que sais-je?** in each square. You might write the same question in two squares and require different responses for each one. You might also change the questions to instructions: *Show concern for someone and ask what happened.* Then, project a grid on the overhead. Form two teams and have them take turns trying to answer a square correctly in order to place their team's X or O in that square. Individuals should choose a square (**J'aimerais le numéro sept, s'il vous plaît**), and you mark an X or an O in that square if they respond appropriately. The first team to mark three squares in a row wins!

QUE SAIS-JE?

Can you use what you've learned in the chapter?

1 How would you show concern for someone by asking what happened? *Possible answers:* Ça n'a pas l'air d'aller. Qu'est-ce qui se passe? Qu'est-ce qui t'arrive?

2 How would your friend answer you if the following happened to him?

1. J'ai déchiré ma chemise.   2. J'ai raté le bus.   3. J'ai reçu mon bulletin trimestriel.

3 How would you inquire about your friend's . . .   See answers below.

1. day yesterday?   2. weekend?   3. vacation?

4 How would you respond to someone's question about your weekend if it went really well? *Possible answers:* C'était incroyable/super/génial! Ça s'est très bien passé! Quel week-end formidable!

5 How would you respond to someone's question about your vacation if everything went wrong?   Tout a été de travers!

6 What would you say to sympathize with and console these people?

1. Céline a raté le bus.   See answers below.   3. Henri est arrivé en retard au
2. Véronique a été collée.   cours de français.

7 How would you explain the following grades on your report card?

See answers below.

MATIERES	MOYENNE	APPRECIATIONS
Informatique	11	Peu d'effort!
Anglais	16	Bon travail
Français	10	Travail moyen

8 What would you say to a friend who . . .   *Possible answers:*

1. got a good grade in French?   Bravo!   3. received a scholarship to
2. won an athletic competition?   college?   Chapeau!
   Félicitations!

9 How would you reprimand a friend who . . .
Tu dois mieux travailler en classe!   Tu ne dois pas faire le clown en classe!
1. got a low grade in English?   2. is always joking in class?

Can you express concern for someone? p. 119

Can you inquire? p. 123

Can you express satisfaction and frustration? p. 123

Can you sympathize with and console someone? p. 125

Can you give reasons and make excuses? p. 127

Can you congratulate and reprimand someone? p. 127

Possible answers

3 1. Comment ça s'est passé hier?
2. Comment s'est passé ton week-end?
3. Comment se sont passées tes vacances?

6 1. Oh, là là! Courage!
2. C'est pas de chance, ça! Ça va aller mieux.
3. Pauvre vieux! T'en fais pas. C'est pas grave.

7 1. L'informatique, c'est pas mon fort!
2. L'anglais, c'est mon fort!
3. Je suis pas doué(e) pour le français.

PREMIERE ETAPE

Expressing concern for someone

Ça n'a pas l'air d'aller. *You look like something's wrong.*
Qu'est-ce qui se passe? *What's going on?*
Qu'est-ce qui t'arrive? *What's wrong?*
Raconte! *Tell me!*

School day vocabulary

passer une journée épouvantable *to have a horrible day*
entendre le réveil *to hear the alarm clock*
rater le bus *to miss the bus*
rater une marche *to miss a step*
tomber *to fall*
déchirer *to rip*

rendre les interros *to return tests*
avoir une mauvaise note *to get a bad grade*
être collé(e) *to have detention*
perdre *to lose*
recevoir le bulletin trimestriel *to receive one's report card*

DEUXIEME ETAPE

Inquiring; expressing satisfaction and frustration

Comment ça s'est passé? *How did it go?*
Comment s'est passée ta journée (hier)? *How was your day (yesterday)?*
Comment s'est passé ton week-end? *How was your weekend?*
Comment se sont passées tes vacances? *How was your vacation?*
C'était incroyable! *It was amazing/unbelievably bad!*

Ça s'est très bien passé! *It went really well!*
Quelle journée formidable! *What a great day!*
Quel week-end formidable! *What a great weekend!*
J'ai passé une journée horrible! *I had a terrible day!*
C'est pas mon jour! *It's just not my day!*
Tout a été de travers! *Everything went wrong!*
Quelle journée! *What a (bad) day!*
Quel week-end! *What a (bad) weekend!*

Sympathizing with and consoling someone

Oh là là! *Oh no!*
C'est pas de chance, ça! *Tough luck!*
Pauvre vieux/vieille! *You poor thing!*
Courage! *Hang in there!*
Ça va aller mieux. *It'll get better.*
T'en fais pas. *Don't worry.*
C'est pas grave. *It's not serious.*

Other expressions

arriver *to arrive*

TROISIEME ETAPE

Giving reasons and making excuses

Je suis assez bon (bonne) en... *I'm pretty good at . . .*
C'est en... que je suis le/la meilleur(e). *I'm best in . . .*
..., c'est mon fort. *. . . is my strong point.*
..., c'est pas mon fort. *. . . isn't my best subject.*
J'ai du mal à comprendre. *I have a hard time understanding.*
Je suis pas doué(e) pour... *I don't have a talent for . . .*

Congratulating someone

Félicitations! *Congratulations!*
Bravo! *Terrific!*
Chapeau! *Well done!*

Reprimanding someone

C'est inadmissible. *That's unacceptable.*
Tu dois mieux travailler en classe. *You have to work harder in class.*
Tu ne dois pas faire le clown en classe! *You can't be goofing off in class!*
Ne recommence pas. *Don't do it again.*

VOCABULAIRE

cent trente-cinq **135**

Chapitre 6 : A nous les châteaux!
Chapter Overview

Mise en train pp. 138–140	Le disparu		Practice and Activity Book, p. 61		Video Guide OR Videodisc Guide
	FUNCTIONS	**GRAMMAR**	**CULTURE**	**RE-ENTRY**	
Première étape pp. 141–145	Asking for opinions; expressing enthusiasm, indifference, and dissatisfaction, p. 144	The phrase **c'était**, p. 144	• **Note Culturelle,** Types of **châteaux** in France, p. 141 • Realia: *Les exclus du loisir* (chart), p. 145	• Pronunciation: **[y]** versus **[u]** • Expressing satisfaction and frustration	
Deuxième étape pp. 146–150	Expressing disbelief and doubt, p. 148	The **passé composé** with **être**, p. 147	• Realia: *Les personages de Chenonceau,* p. 149 • **Panorama Culturel,** Studying historical figures in school, p. 150	The **passé composé** with **avoir**	
Troisième étape pp. 151–153	Asking for and giving information, p. 152	• Formal and informal phrasing of questions, p. 152 • The verb **ouvrir**, p. 153	• Realia: Brochure of bus tours in Touraine, p. 151 • **Note Culturelle,** Buses and trains in France, p. 151 • *Renseignements pratiques* for Fontaine-bleau, p. 153 • Realia: Train schedule, p. 153	• Question words • Telling time • Phone vocabulary	

Lisons! pp. 154–155	Posters from an **Office de tourisme** in Touraine	**Reading Strategy:** Taking notes

Review pp. 156–159	**Mise en pratique,** pp. 156–157	**Que sais-je?** p. 158	**Vocabulaire,** p. 159

Assessment Options	**Etape Quizzes** • *Chapter Teaching Resources, Book 2* **Première étape,** Quiz 6-1, pp. 79–80 **Deuxième étape,** Quiz 6-2, pp. 81–82 **Troisième étape,** Quiz 6-3, pp. 83–84 • *Assessment Items, Audiocassette 7B/Audio CD 6*	**Chapter Test** • *Chapter Teaching Resources, Book 2,* pp. 85–90 • *Assessment Guide,* Speaking Test, p. 30 • *Assessment Items, Audiocassette 7B/Audio CD 6* **Test Generator, Chapter 6**

Video Program OR Expanded Video Program, Videocassette 2
OR Videodisc Program, Videodisc 3B

Textbook Audiocassette 3B/Audio CD 6

RESOURCES: Print	RESOURCES: Audiovisual

Textbook Audiocassette 3B/Audio CD 6

Practice and Activity Book, pp. 62–64
Chapter Teaching Resources, Book 2
• Teaching Transparency Master 6-1, pp. 63, 66. . . . . Teaching Transparency 6-1
• Additional Listening Activities 6-1, 6-2, p. 67 . . . . Additional Listening Activities, Audiocassette 9B/Audio CD 6
• Realia 6-1, pp. 71, 73
• Situation Cards 6-1, pp. 74–75
• Student Response Forms, pp. 76–78
• Quiz 6-1, pp. 79–80 . . . . Assessment Items, Audiocassette 7B/Audio CD 6
Videodisc Guide. . . . . Videodisc Program, Videodisc 3B

Textbook Audiocassette 3B/Audio CD 6

Practice and Activity Book, pp. 65–67
Chapter Teaching Resources, Book 2
• Communicative Activity 6-1, pp. 59–60
• Teaching Transparency Master 6-2, pp. 64, 66. . . . . Teaching Transparency 6-2
• Additional Listening Activities 6-3, 6-4, p. 68 . . . . Additional Listening Activities, Audiocassette 9B/Audio CD 6
• Realia 6-2, pp. 72, 73
• Situation Cards 6-2, pp. 74–75
• Student Response Forms, pp. 76–78
• Quiz 6-2, pp. 81–82 . . . . Assessment Items, Audiocassette 7B/Audio CD 6
Video Guide. . . . . Video Program OR Expanded Video Program, Videocassette 2
Videodisc Guide. . . . . Videodisc Program, Videodisc 3B

Textbook Audiocassette 3B/Audio CD 6

Practice and Activity Book, pp. 68–70
Chapter Teaching Resources, Book 2
• Communicative Activity 6-2, pp. 61–62
• Teaching Transparency Master 6-3, pp. 65, 66. . . . . Teaching Transparency 6-3
• Additional Listening Activities 6-5, 6-6, p. 69 . . . . Additional Listening Activities, Audiocassette 9B/Audio CD 6
• Realia 6-2, pp. 72, 73
• Situation Cards 6-3, pp. 74–75
• Student Response Forms, pp. 76–78
• Quiz 6-3, pp. 83–84 . . . . Assessment Items, Audiocassette 7B/Audio CD 6
Videodisc Guide. . . . . Videodisc Program, Videodisc 3B

Practice and Activity Book, p. 71

Video Guide. . . . . Video Program OR Expanded Video Program, Videocassette 2
Videodisc Guide. . . . . Videodisc Program, Videodisc 3B

Alternative Assessment
• Performance Assessment
  Première étape, p. 145
  Deuxième étape, p. 149
  Troisième étape, p. 153

• Portfolio Assessment
  Written: Activity 23, Pupil's Edition, p. 149
    Assessment Guide, p. 19
  Oral: Activity 28, Pupil's Edition, p. 152
    Assessment Guide, p. 19

Midterm Exam
Assessment Guide, pp. 35–42
Assessment Items,
  Audiocassette 7B
  Audio CD 6

Chapitre 6 : A nous les châteaux!
Textbook Listening Activities Scripts

For Student Response Forms, see *Chapter Teaching Resources, Book 2,* pp. 76–78.

Première étape

7 Ecoute! p. 143

1. Elle a donné à manger aux animaux.
2. Elle a fait un tour sur la grande roue.
3. Elle a assisté à un spectacle son et lumière.
4. Elle est montée dans des tours.
5. Elle est allée dans un parc d'attractions.
6. Elle a fait une visite guidée.

Answers to Activity 7

1. Han   4. Mariyam
2. Perrine   5. Perrine
3. Mariyam   6. Han

10 Ecoute! p. 144

1. — Eh, Dien, tu as passé un bon week-end?
   — Ben, oui.
   — Qu'est-ce que tu as fait?
   — Ben, je suis allée au château de Fontainebleau.
   — Vraiment? Ça t'a plu?
   — Oui, beaucoup. C'était magnifique.
2. — Salut, Bertrand. C'était comment, ton week-end?
   — Oh, pas mal. Je suis allé au zoo.
   — Tu t'es bien amusé?
   — Oh, plus ou moins.
3. — C'était comment, la boum hier soir?
   — La fête de Béatrice? C'était sensas! Je me suis beaucoup amusée.
4. — Salut, Amina. Qu'est-ce que tu as fait hier?
   — Je suis allé dans un parc d'attractions.
   — Tu t'es bien amusée?
   — Pas vraiment. Je me suis plutôt ennuyée. C'était nul.

Answers to Activity 10

1. enthusiastic   3. enthusiastic
2. indifferent   4. dissatisfied

Deuxième étape

16 Ecoute! p. 147

1. — Dis, tu as vu Paul?
   — Paul? Je crois qu'il est retourné dans l'autocar.
2. — Bon. Et Laurence? Où est-elle?
   — Je crois qu'elle est restée au café.
   — Va la chercher, s'il te plaît.

3. — Où est Ali?
   — Il est descendu au bord de la rivière.
   — Oh là là! Va le chercher tout de suite!
4. — Et Guillaume?
   — Euh, je ne sais pas. Peut-être qu'il est monté au premier étage?
   — Bon... va le chercher.
5. — Et Mireille? Tu l'as vue?
   — Oui... elle est allée dans le jardin de Diane de Poitiers. Je vais la chercher.
6. — Enfin, il n'y a plus que Marcel qui manque.
   — Je crois qu'il est parti avec les Américains!

Answers to Activity 16

1. in the bus   4. on the second floor
2. at a café   5. in the castle garden
3. at the riverbank   6. with some Americans

20 Ecoute! p. 149

1. MAI   Salut, Daniel. Comment s'est passé ton week-end?
    DANIEL Très bien, merci.
    MAI   Qu'est-ce que tu as fait?
    DANIEL D'abord, je suis allé au supermarché. Et tu ne vas pas croire qui j'ai vu! J'ai fait la connaissance de Vanessa Paradis!
    MAI   Ça m'étonnerait!
2. MAI   Eh bien, Agnès, qu'est-ce qui s'est passé?
    AGNES   Oh, je suis tombée, et j'ai déchiré ma robe.
    MAI   Oh là là! Pauvre vieille!
3. MAI   Salut, Richard. Tu as passé un bon week-end?
    RICHARD Oui, c'était super! Je suis allé visiter le château de Versailles, et j'ai vu le fantôme de Louis Quatorze.
    MAI   Mon œil!
4. MAI   Et toi, Valérie, comment ça s'est passé, ton week-end?
    VALERIE Bof. J'ai lu un roman, et j'ai fait du vélo, c'est tout.
    MAI   Oh, c'est pas si mal.
5. MAI   Mohammed, qu'est ce que tu as fait ce week-end?
    MOHAMMED J'ai fait un vidéo-clip avec Kassav'.
    MAI   N'importe quoi!
    MOHAMMED Mais si, c'est vrai! Tu vas voir!

Answers to Activity 20

1. no   2. yes   3. no   4. yes   5. no

Troisième étape

26 Ecoute! p. 152

L'EMPLOYÉ Bonjour, mademoiselle.

NATHALIE Bonjour, monsieur. A quelle heure est-ce que le train pour Paris part?

L'EMPLOYÉ Dans une demi-heure, à quatorze heures vingt-cinq.

NATHALIE Combien coûte un aller simple?

L'EMPLOYÉ Soixante francs.

NATHALIE Bon, alors un aller simple, s'il vous plaît. Le train part de quel quai?

L'EMPLOYÉ Du quai dix, par là.

NATHALIE Bien. Merci beaucoup!

Answers to Activity 26

1. Paris
2. quatorze heures vingt-cinq
3. aller simple
4. soixante francs
5. dix

Mise en pratique

2 p. 156

Horaires pour samedi et dimanche. Ligne douze, destination Blois avec arrêts à Amboise et Monteaux. Départ de la gare routière de Tours à neuf heures. Arrivée Amboise à neuf heures trente, Monteaux à neuf heures cinquante-cinq, Blois à dix heures quarante-cinq. Pour le retour, départ Blois à quinze heures trente, Monteaux à seize heures vingt, Amboise à seize heures quarante-cinq, arrivée Tours à dix-sept heures quinze. Prix aller simple : adulte quarante francs, enfants de huit à treize ans vingt-cinq francs, gratuit pour les enfants de moins de huit ans. Prix aller-retour : adulte, soixante-cinq francs, enfants de huit à treize ans quarante francs, gratuit pour les enfants de moins de huit ans.

Answers to Mise en pratique Activity 2

To Amboise: 9:00
From Amboise: 4:45
Price for 13 years old or younger: 40 francs
Price for 14 years old or above: 65 francs

Des châteaux vivants
(Cooperative Learning Project)

ASSIGNMENT

Students will give an oral presentation in English on the château of their choice. Groups of four will use visual and/or auditory aids to present a colorful history of the château. Their presentations might include original songs, raps, skits, puppet shows, computer assistance, or any other imaginative ideas. Students should also prepare five test questions about the château for their classmates to answer after the presentation. Assign the roles of organizer, writer, editor, and artist in each group. Although group members will participate in all aspects of the project, they will each serve as a leader in a particular area.

MATERIALS

✄ Students may need
(depending upon the chosen format)
- Posters
- Slides
- Videocassette
- Props
- Computer-generated graphics
- Costumes
- Puppets and stage

SUGGESTED SEQUENCE

1. Each group chooses and researches a château. You might give students the following guidelines:
   - Tell when the château was built, by whom, and for what reason.
   - Name three unique features of the architecture of this château.
   - Tell about two important events that occurred there.
   - Talk about two important people who lived there.
   - Tell why you like the château and if you would like to have lived there. Give reasons.
2. Group members decide on the format for their presentation.
3. Students write and edit the script and five test questions.
4. Students write a final version of the script and test questions.
5. Members prepare the visual aids and rehearse their presentation.
6. The group hands in a final copy of the script and test questions before performing.
7. As part of the project, or as a challenge for some groups, students might present a commercial in French about their château.

GRADING THE PROJECT

Each group should receive a collective grade based on the content of their presentation and creativity and overall presentation. Group members should receive individual grades based on effort and participation in their own presentation, and the written tests administered by the other groups.

Suggested Point Distribution (total = 100 points)

Content	40 points
Creativity/overall presentation	20 points
Effort/participation	20 points
Written test grades	20 points

TEACHER NOTE

There are many travel guides that provide information about châteaux, such as *Let's Go France* (Saint Martin's Press) and *Frommer's Comprehensive Travel Guide* (Prentice Hall Travel). You might write or call the tourist office in Tours at Office de Tourisme, Hôtel de Ville, Place Jean Jaurès, 37000 Tours (Tel. 47.05.58.08.). You might also refer students to the Location Opener on pages 108–111 for the names and photos of several châteaux.

Chapitre 6 : A nous les châteaux!
♜ Games

VINGT QUESTIONS

In this game, students will practice asking questions.

Procedure Form four teams. Each team secretly chooses a famous historical figure and the other teams try to guess the identity of the person by asking only yes-no questions in French. Before beginning, students might brainstorm a list of questions and question starters they can use to play the game. **(C'est un homme/une femme? Il/Elle est mort(e)? Il/Elle est né(e) à(au/en)... ? C'était un(e) Américain(e)... ? Il/Elle a fait... ? Il/Elle a découvert... ? Il/Elle a inventé... ? Il/Elle était chanteur (chanteuse), acteur (actrice), homme (femme) d'affaires** *(business-man/businesswoman),* **homme (femme) politique** *(politician),* **joueur (joueuse) de... ? Il/Elle est allé(e)... ? Il/Elle a habité à (au/en)... ?)**

The teams take turns asking questions, but all the teams combined may ask only twenty questions. The first team that guesses the identity of the historical figure wins.

LE BASE-BALL

In this game, students will practice the **passé composé.**

Procedure Draw a baseball diamond on the board. Write sentences in the present tense on some flashcards and infinitives on others. Form two teams and explain the requirements for reaching each base. To hit a single, students must give the past participle of an infinitive. To hit a double, students must read the present tense of the sentence on the card and restate it in the **passé composé.** For a triple, students must listen to a sentence that you read in the present tense and restate it in the **passé composé.** All responses are oral. Each team gets one out, and there are no home runs. To begin the game, a player from one team chooses the hit he or she would like to try for. If the player chooses a double, for example, he or she must read the sentence on the flashcard in the present tense **(Mon frère étudie le français)** and change it to the **passé composé. (Mon frère a étudié le français.)** If the player is correct, write his or her initials on the appropriate base. Then, the next player chooses a hit and tries to answer. If a player gets a hit, all teammates on base may or may not advance an equal number of bases, depending on their position on base at the time of the hit. For example, if the batter hits a single and a teammate is on first base, then the teammate on first base moves to second base. However, if the batter hits a single and a teammate is on second base, the teammate stays on second base. Runs are scored when a teammate crosses home plate. A team continues at bat until a player makes an out by answering incorrectly. In this case, erase the initials from the board, and the opposing team comes to bat. Continue to play for a specified number of innings or amount of time.

Chapitre 6
A nous les châteaux!

pp. 136–159

𝒰sing the Chapter Opener

Motivating Activity

Ask students what comes to mind when they think of castles. They might suggest knights, kings and queens, or dragons and dungeons. Point out that while Americans see the medieval world as remote, Europeans live with evidence of that world in their everyday lives. Ask students if they have ever visited or would like to visit a castle and why.

Photo Flash!

① The Chenonceau château was constructed in the sixteenth century. It is referred to as the **château des six femmes** because of six influential women who lived there at one time or another until the nineteenth century. Its two gardens are named after two of the women: Catherine de Médicis and Diane de Poitiers. Catherine de Médicis' contribution to the château was a gallery she had built on the bridge that crosses the Cher River. Its floor is made of black and white diamond-shaped stones. (See Photo 7 on page 139 and Photo 5 on page 110.)

CHAPITRE

6
A nous les châteaux!

① C'était magnifique, Chenonceau!

136 *cent trente-six*

Teacher Notes

The town of Chenonceaux is spelled with an –x, whereas the château of Chenonceau does not have a final –x.

After a hard week at school, it's nice to spend the day having fun with your family or friends. Around Tours, people visit the many châteaux of the region to explore the castles and find out about their history.

In this chapter you will learn

- to ask for opinions; to express enthusiasm, indifference, and dissatisfaction
- to express disbelief and doubt
- to ask for and give information

And you will

- listen to friends telling about their weekends
- read about attractions in the Tours area
- write about a trip you've taken
- find out about some of the châteaux and the historical figures francophone students learn about in school

② C'est combien, un aller-retour pour Chenonceaux?

③ C'est pas vrai! Tu plaisantes!

Focusing on Outcomes

Ask students to say as much as they can in French about the photos. Read the list of outcomes with students and have them try to match the photos with the outcomes. NOTE: You may want to use the video to support the objectives. The self-check activities in **Que sais-je?** on page 158 help students assess their achievement of the objectives.

Photo Flash!

② Virginie, Hector, and Céline are buying their bus tickets in a **gare routière** in the town of Tours to go visit the Chenonceau château. Tours is located within 60 kilometers (37 miles) of some of the loveliest châteaux in France. Because of its location, Tours is an excellent central point from which to visit the châteaux of the Loire Valley.

③ Céline, Hector, and Virginie are standing above the Cher River. The Chenonceau château is built across the Cher, which is a tributary of the Loire. During World War II, the Cher formed part of the boundary between northern, occupied France and the southern, unoccupied zone. The château was sometimes used by members of the French resistance to smuggle Jews, prisoners, and downed Allied aviators out of the occupied zone. They would cross the river through the gallery that Catherine de Médicis had built, and exit safely through the door on the other side of the river.

Thinking Critically

Comparing and Contrasting Have students look at the photos and read the introductory paragraph at the top of this page. Ask them what they think the students in the photographs did over the weekend and whether it is something they would do. Point out that while French teenagers also go out with friends, go shopping, go to the movies and to parties as American teens do, it is not unusual for them to visit a historical site or a museum.

VIDEO PROGRAM
OR EXPANDED VIDEO
PROGRAM,
Videocassette 2
44:13–49:34

OR VIDEODISC PROGRAM,
Videodisc 3B

Search 1, Play To 9635

Video Synopsis

In this segment of the video, Céline is telling Bruno about her weekend excursion to the château de Chenonceau with Hector and Virginie. She tells him that they took the bus to the town of Chenonceaux, rented bicycles, and then rode the rest of the way. Céline read aloud from her guidebook, and they toured the château. At the end of the visit, Céline and Virginie noticed that Hector was missing!

Motivating Activity

Ask several students what they did over the weekend. **(Qu'est-ce que tu as fait le week-end dernier?)** Ask if they might visit a historical site with a group of friends. Have students look at the photos and tell what they think Céline and her friends did. Tell them that something unusual happened and have them try to guess what it was.

Math Link

Call attention to the road signs in Photo 4. The numbers on the signs indicate the distance in kilometers to the destination. Have students calculate the distance in miles by multiplying the number of kilometers by 0.62 (Loches, 16.74 miles; Chisseaux, 1.24 miles; Montrichard, 6.2 miles).

Mise en train

Le disparu

Have you ever visited a castle or other historical site? What did you find interesting about it?

Céline   Hector   Virginie

138 cent trente-huit

CHAPITRE 6   A nous les châteaux!

RESOURCES FOR MISE EN TRAIN

Textbook Audiocassette 3B/Audio CD 6
Practice and Activity Book, p. 61
Video Guide
  Video Program
  Expanded Video Program, Videocassette 2
Videodisc Guide
  Videodisc Program, Videodisc 3B

«Le château a été construit entre 1513 et 1521 par Thomas Bohier. On l'appelle «le château des six femmes». Eh, Hector, tu m'écoutes?

On a visité le château...

Oui, oui... Vous savez, on dit qu'il y a des gens qui disparaissent dans ces châteaux.

Sans blague? Tu plaisantes!

Je ne te crois pas.

Et puis, on a remarqué qu'Hector n'était plus là!

Tiens. Où est Hector?

Je ne sais pas.

On a cherché partout, mais on ne l'a pas trouvé.

On l'a perdu?

Il a disparu!

MISE EN TRAIN

cent trente-neuf 139

Video Integration

- **EXPANDED VIDEO PROGRAM,**
  Videocassette 2, 49:35–54:23
- **VIDEODISC PROGRAM,**
  Videodisc 3B

Search 9635, Play To 18255

You may choose to continue with **Le disparu (suite)** at this time or wait until later in the chapter. When the story continues, Céline and Virginie find a note from Hector near the bicycles. It's a riddle telling them to go to the garden of Diane de Poitiers. There, they find another riddle directing them to go to the garden of Catherine de Médicis. They can't find Hector, but they hear a voice calling for help. On the bank below, they see Hector, who needs help getting back up to the bridge. The trick Hector played on them didn't work out exactly as he had planned! Hector apologizes as Céline and Virginie go for help.

MISE EN TRAIN
CHAPITRE 6

Presentation

Show the video and ask the questions in Activity 1 on page 140. Then, play the recording and have students read along. Next, form groups of two or three and assign each group a speech bubble or photo caption. Have students cover the text in their books with pieces of paper. Then, call on groups at random to uncover and read aloud their speech bubble or photo caption. Have students try to identify the photo that accompanies what they hear. (**C'est la première photo.**)

Thinking Critically

Drawing Inferences Ask students how often they use buses and trains to get around town. Point out that most Americans depend more on cars than on public transportation—unless they live in one of a few very large cities—and that French teenagers rely more on public transportation than on cars. Ask students to imagine why. (French teenagers can't get a driver's license until they're eighteen. Cars and gasoline are expensive. The public transportation system is more convenient and much more developed. French students usually don't work after school, so they don't need a car to get to work.)

Culture Note

Students may notice the tourists at the château in Photos 8 and 9. The Chenonceau château is one of the most frequently visited châteaux in France. It receives visitors, not only from France, but frequently from the United States, Japan, and all the western European countries.

Teaching Suggestion

2 Have pairs of students create additional questions about the **Mise en train** for their classmates to answer.

For Individual Needs

3 Challenge Have students cover the word box before completing Céline's journal. Afterwards, compile a list on the board or on a transparency of the words students used to correctly complete the journal so that they can compare the possibilities.

3 Slower Pace Read the letter aloud and have students listen with their books closed. As you read the letter, fill in the blanks, so students hear the letter as it should be. Convey the meaning with gestures, actions, and intonation as you read. Then, have students open their books and do the activity. You might have them work with a partner.

For videodisc application, see *Videodisc Guide.*

Teaching Suggestion

5 Form small groups and ask each one to imagine how this episode might end. Have them write down the endings. Then, either now or later, share with them the synopsis of **Le disparu (suite)** on page 139 and have them compare their endings to what really happens. Have the class select the ending they prefer.

---

1 Tu as compris?

1. Where did Céline and her friends go for the day? *to visit Chenonceau*
2. How did they get there? *by bus and by bicycle*
3. How did they find out about the history of the château? *from a guide book*
4. What did they do at the château? *They explored it.*
5. What happens at the end of the story? *Hector disappears.*

2 Qui....

1. n'est pas allé au château? *Bruno*
2. a visité le château? *Céline, Hector, Virginie*
3. a trouvé Chenonceau magnifique? *Céline*
4. a lu le guide du château? *Céline*
5. a dit qu'il y a des gens qui disparaissent? *Hector*
6. a disparu? *Hector*
7. a cherché Hector partout? *Céline, Virginie*

Virginie   **Bruno**   **Céline**   **Hector**

3 Le journal de Céline

Complète le journal de Céline.

est parti	visiter
des vélos	est arrivés
magnifique	a remarqué
a cherché	a acheté

See answers below.

Ce week-end, je suis allée ____ le château de Chenonceau. C'était ____! On ____ les billets à la gare et le car ____ à 8h10. On y ____ à 8h55. On est allés directement louer ____. J'ai lu mon guide du château à haute voix, mais Hector ne s'y intéressait pas. Il nous a dit que des gens disparaissent dans les châteaux, mais je ne l'ai pas cru. Enfin, après la visite guidée du château, on ____ qu' Hector n'était plus là! On l'____ partout mais il avait disparu sans laisser de traces! La suite au prochain numéro...

4 Cherche les expressions

What do the teenagers in **Le disparu** say to . . .   See answers below.

1. ask for an opinion?
2. express enthusiasm?
3. inquire about the cost of a round-trip ticket?
4. express disbelief?

5 Et maintenant, à toi

What do you think happened to Hector? What would you do if you were in Céline and Virginie's situation?

CHAPITRE 6   A nous les châteaux!

Language Note

Point out the use of the word **le car** for the intercity bus that Céline and her friends took to Chenonceaux. **Le bus** refers only to city buses.

Answers

3 visiter, magnifique, a acheté, est parti, est arrivés, des vélos, a remarqué, a cherché

4 1. C'était comment?
2. C'était magnifique!
3. C'est combien un aller-retour?
4. Sans blague? Tu plaisantes! Je ne te crois pas.

PREMIERE ETAPE

Asking for opinions; expressing enthusiasm, indifference, and dissatisfaction

Es-tu déjà allé à Loches? On a vu des cachots et je suis montée dans la vieille tour en ruine. C'est très intéressant... on se sent vraiment transporté au Moyen Age. Au fait, je t'ai acheté un souvenir... mais c'est une surprise! Je t'embrasse. Adèle

Jean Brami
Bâtiment Le Fanal n°8
Esplanade de l'Europe
34000 MONTPELLIER

LOCHES

Le château d'Azay-le-Rideau

Si tu voyais Azay-le-Rideau! C'est incroyable comme château. On s'est promenés dans le parc, puis on a fait un pique-nique. Le spectacle son et lumière sur la vie dans un château de la Renaissance était superbe. C'est vraiment à voir!
Frédéric

Véronique Fabre
8, rue de Liège
75 009 PARIS

NOTE CULTURELLE

Most castles in France are of two types. **Châteaux forts,** such as Loches, were built for protection in the Middle Ages. They are massive buildings with thick walls, often surrounded by a moat and built in a strategic location. **Châteaux de la Renaissance,** such as Chenonceau or Azay-le-Rideau, date from the sixteenth century when more thought was given to comfort than to defense. **Châteaux de la Renaissance** feature large windows, ornate sculptures or stonework, and often highly decorated interiors.

See answers below.

6 C'est Loches ou Azay-le-Rideau?

1. a. On peut monter dans une vieille tour.
   b. C'est un château du Moyen Age.
   c. On peut se promener dans le parc ou pique-niquer.
   d. On peut descendre voir les cachots *(dungeons).*
   e. On l'a construit à l'époque de la Renaissance.
2. Quel château est-ce que tu préfères? Pourquoi?

Jump Start!

Draw two columns on the board or on a transparency.

In the left column, write: **C'est combien un aller-retour pour Chenonceaux? Ça t'a plu? Qu'est-ce que tu as fait pendant le week-end? On dit qu'il y a des gens qui disparaissent dans ces châteaux. Où est Hector?**

In the right column, write: **Je suis allée visiter le château de Chenonceau. Tu plaisantes! Il a disparu! Vingt-cinq francs. Oui, je me suis beaucoup amusée!**

Have students match the questions and statements with the appropriate responses.

MOTIVATE

Ask students how their lives would be different if they lived in a castle.

TEACH

For Individual Needs

Auditory Learners If possible, display large photos of Azay-le-Rideau and Loches, either from travel posters or books. Read the two postcards aloud, omitting the names of the châteaux. Have students listen with their books closed and try to identify the château each postcard describes.

RESOURCES FOR PREMIERE ETAPE

Textbook Audiocassette 3B/Audio CD 6
Practice and Activity Book, pp. 62–64
Videodisc Guide
   Videodisc Program, Videodisc 3B

Chapter Teaching Resources, Book 2
• Teaching Transparency Master 6-1, pp. 63, 66
   Teaching Transparency 6-1
• Additional Listening Activities 6-1, 6-2, p. 67
   Audiocassette 9B/Audio CD 6
• Realia 6-1, pp. 71, 73
• Situation Cards 6-1, pp. 74–75
• Student Response Forms, pp. 76–78
• Quiz 6-1, pp. 79–80
   Audiocassette 7B/Audio CD 6

Answers
6 1. a. Loches
   b. Loches
   c. Azay-le-Rideau
   d. Loches
   e. Azay-le-Rideau

Presentation

Vocabulaire First, relate each of these experiences in the **Vocabulaire** as if it were yours. Sketch on the board as you speak or use pictures you've gathered. Then, write **au parc d'attractions, au zoo,** and **aux châteaux** on the board. Tell students again what you did (**J'ai donné à mangé aux animaux.**) and have them tell you where you went. (**Vous êtes allé(e) au zoo.**) Finally, have students open their books and cover the text in the **Vocabulaire** with pieces of paper. Read aloud the captions of the photos in random order and have students try to match them with the appropriate photos.

Building on Previous Skills

Have students look at the **Vocabulaire** and find the verbs in the **passé composé** that are conjugated with the helping verb **être.** Ask if they can guess why some of the past participles have an extra **-e.**

Language Notes

- **Un cachot** is the French word for *dungeon.* **Un donjon** is a **faux ami.** Le donjon is *the castle keep,* a high, fortified tower.
- The word **zoo** in French is pronounced **[zo]** as in **zoologique [zo o lo jik].**
- Call students' attention to the false cognate **assister.** It means *to attend,* not *to help,* which is **aider.**

Vocabulaire

Qu'est-ce que tu as fait pendant le week-end?

Perrine

Je suis allée dans un parc d'attractions.

J'ai fait un tour sur les montagnes russes…

et sur la grande roue.

Han

Ce week-end, moi, je suis allée au zoo!

J'ai fait une visite guidée,…

on a fait un pique-nique…

et on a donné à manger aux animaux. Ça m'a beaucoup plu!

Mariyam

Moi, je suis allée faire un circuit des châteaux!

Je suis montée dans des tours…

et après, on a assisté à un spectacle son et lumière. C'était magnifique!

142 *cent quarante-deux*

CHAPITRE 6   A nous les châteaux!

🌐 **Culture Note**

There are three major theme parks in France. **Euro Disney,** located in Marne-la-Vallée, is 32 kilometers (20 miles) east of Paris. The park covers 99 acres of the 1,500 acre resort. It has five themes: Frontierland, Adventureland, Main Street USA, Fantasyland, and Discoveryland. The resort has numerous restaurants, hotels, and sports and camping facilities. **Parc Astérix,** located a short distance north of the Charles-de-Gaulle airport in Paris, was inspired by the popular heroes from the comic strip. Fairground attractions range from high-speed water rides to merry-go-rounds. The **Rue de Paris** leads visitors on a historical reconstruction of Paris through the centuries. **Futuroscope,** near Poitiers, is an extraordinary theme park that features modern visual technology in a futuristic setting. Visitors can sit on a "magic carpet" in a cinematic theater and "ride" to witness panoramic views presented on the screen.

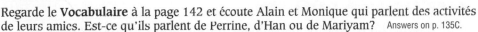
7 Ecoute!

Regarde le **Vocabulaire** à la page 142 et écoute Alain et Monique qui parlent des activités de leurs amics. Est-ce qu'ils parlent de Perrine, d'Han ou de Mariyam?   Answers on p. 135C.

8 Alors, tu as fait le circuit....

Imagine you've taken one of the colorful trips advertised on these fliers. Your partner will ask you questions until he or she guesses which trip you took. Then, reverse roles.

—Tu es allé(e) dans un parc d'attractions?   — Oui.
—Tu as fait une visite guidée des châteaux?   — Non.
—   ?   —   ?
—Alors, tu as fait le circuit vert!   —   ?

Faites le circuit jaune! On va... faire une visite guidée des châteaux, monter dans une tour, aller au zoo et donner à manger aux animaux!

ESSAYEZ LE CIRCUIT BLEU! VOUS POUVEZ... aller au zoo, donner à manger aux animaux, faire un pique-nique et aller dans un parc d'attractions!

Choisissez le circuit rose où vous pouvez... faire un pique-nique, aller au zoo, donner à manger aux animaux et assister à un spectacle son et lumière!

Amusez-vous en faisant le circuit vert! Vous pouvez... aller dans un parc d'attractions, faire un tour sur les montagnes russes, faire un pique-nique et assister à un spectacle son et lumière!

ON VA FAIRE LA FÊTE SUR LE CIRCUIT ORANGE! ALLONS... FAIRE UN PIQUE-NIQUE, ASSISTER À UN SPECTACLE SON ET LUMIÈRE, FAIRE UNE VISITE GUIDÉE DES CHÂTEAUX ET MONTER DANS UNE TOUR!

9 Jeu

Draw a grid of nine boxes: three across and three down. Write a weekend activity in each box. Find someone in your class who's done one of the activities in your grid. That person signs the appropriate box and writes where he or she did the activity. The first person to get five different signatures that form an **x** or a **+** wins.

—Tu as déjà donné à manger à un éléphant?
—Non, jamais! *or* Oui, au zoo à New York.

Culture Note

Sound and light shows (**des spectacles son et lumière**), are a popular form of summer entertainment in France. They take on many forms, often using actors and props in addition to film, audio recordings, and light displays. The lights and film are often projected onto historic buildings: cathedrals, monuments, castles, and châteaux. The shows usually have historic themes, so they are educational, as well as entertaining.

Teaching Suggestions

8 Remind students to use the helping verb **être** with the verbs **aller** and **monter**. (**Tu es allé(e) au zoo? Tu es monté(e) dans une tour?**) After students have done this activity in pairs, ask individuals to tell which excursion they chose and why.

• Hold up a piece of yellow, blue, pink, green, or orange construction paper. Have students tell one thing they did on the tour that corresponds to that color. (**Je suis allé(e) au zoo.**)

For Individual Needs

8 Visual Learners Have students sketch an illustration of all the things they could do on one of the excursions. Then, have them show the sketch to a partner, who will try to guess which trip is represented. (**Tu as choisi le circuit rouge.**)

Teaching Suggestion

9 Have the winner tell which student did each activity. (**Heidi est montée dans une tour.**) Then, ask that student if it's true and have them reassure you. (**Oui, c'est vrai, je suis montée dans une tour à Paris.**)

Language Note

9 Point out the adverb **déjà** that comes after the helping verb in the **passé composé**. (**Tu as déjà donné à manger à un éléphant?**) Students might try to answer using this construction. (**Oui, j'ai déjà donné à manger à un éléphant. Non, je n'ai jamais donné à manger à un éléphant.**)

Presentation

Comment dit-on... ? On a transparency, write the new expressions for *expressing enthusiasm, indifference, and dissatisfaction* in three columns. Above the appropriate columns, draw a smiling face, an indifferent face with a straight line for a mouth, and a frowning face. Then, list places that are commonly visited in your area. Ask students **Tu es allé(e) au ciné ce week-end? C'était comment?** Point to the sentences that express enthusiasm, gesture thumbs-up, and ask **C'était superbe? C'était sensas?** Have students repeat your response (**Oui, c'était sensas!**), making the appropriate gesture. Proceed in a similar manner for the other groups of expressions, using other places to visit.

For videodisc application, see *Videodisc Guide.*

For Individual Needs

Visual Learners Write the four functions on the board and have students copy them. Scatter transparency strips with the expressions from **Comment dit-on... ?** written on them on the overhead projector. Have students copy the expressions under the appropriate function.

Additional Practice

10 Have students listen to the recording a second time and tell where the friends went over the weekend.

COMMENT DIT-ON... ?

Asking for opinions; expressing enthusiasm, indifference, and dissatisfaction

To ask for an opinion:
C'était comment? *How was it?*
Ça t'a plu? *Did you like it?*
Tu t'es bien amusé(e)?
Did you have fun?

To express enthusiasm:
C'était... *It was . . .*
  magnifique! *beautiful!*
  incroyable! *incredible!*
  superbe! *great!*
  sensas! *sensational!*
Ça m'a beaucoup plu.
  I really liked it.
Je me suis beaucoup amusé(e).
  I had a lot of fun.

To express indifference:
C'était... *It was . . .*
  assez bien. *OK.*
  comme ci, comme ça. *so-so.*
  pas mal. *all right.*
Mouais. *Yeah.*
Plus ou moins. *More or less.*

To express dissatisfaction:
C'était... *It was . . .*
  ennuyeux. *boring.*
  mortel. *deadly dull.*
  nul. *lame.*
  sinistre. *awful.*
Sûrement pas! *Definitely not!*
Je me suis ennuyé(e). *I was bored.*

Note de Grammaire

You've probably noticed that **c'était** *(it was)* uses a form of the verb **être** you haven't studied yet. To describe what things were like in the past, you use this verb tense called the **imparfait** *(imperfect).* You'll learn more about it in Chapter 8.

Tu te rappelles ?

• Two of the most difficult vowels for English speakers to produce in French are the sound (y) in **tu** and the sound (u) in **tout.**

• To produce the (y) sound, start by saying *me* in English, then round your lips, keeping your tongue pressed behind your lower teeth. Practice by saying **Ça t'a plu?** and **Sûrement pas!** There's no equivalent to this sound in English, so it takes some practice to get it right.

• The (u) sound is like the vowel sound in the English word *fool.* Practice this sound by saying **beaucoup** and **un tour.**

• Learning to distinguish between these sounds is important. There's a big difference between a **pull** and a **poule** *(a hen)* in French!

10 Ecoute!

Listen to several friends discuss what they did over the weekend. Are they enthusiastic, indifferent, or dissatisfied? Listen again and write down each response.
Answers on p. 135C.

11 C'était comment?

Ton ami(e) te pose la question **C'était comment?** Comment est-ce que tu réponds si...

1. tu es allé(e) à une boum chez ton/ta meilleur(e) ami(e) hier soir?
2. tu as fait une visite guidée d'une maison historique?
3. tu as vu un film français avec Gérard Depardieu?
4. tu es allé(e) à un concert de jazz?
5. tu es allé(e) dans un musée d'art moderne?
6. tu as fait un pique-nique à la plage avec ta famille?
7. tu as passé un examen de français?

144 *cent quarante-quatre*

CHAPITRE 6   A nous les châteaux!

Teaching Suggestion

11 This activity lends itself to pair work. Have one student tell that he or she did one of these activities. (**Je suis allé(e) à une boum chez... hier soir.**) The partner asks how it was. (**C'était comment?**) Have students take turns. Then, for additional practice, have students describe what they did over the weekend (**Je suis allé(e) au match de basket.**), and have the partner ask **C'était comment?**

Language Note

Point out that the word **mouais** is slang and should only be used in informal situations and not in written language. It is a combination of the hesitative sound **Hmmm** and the word **ouais**, which is slang for **oui**.

12 En famille

Ces familles sont parties en week-end. Où est-ce qu'elles sont allées? Qu'est-ce qu'elles ont fait? C'était comment pour chaque personne dans la famille? *See answers below.*

1.

2.

3.

4.

13 Qu'est-ce qu'on fait en France?

D'après les pourcentages à droite,...

1. quelle est l'activité la plus populaire chez les Français?
2. quel spectacle de musique est le plus populaire? le moins populaire?
3. quel pourcentage de Français a visité au moins *(at least)* un musée? un monument historique? un parc d'attractions?
4. est-ce que les Américains aiment faire les mêmes choses que les Français? Et toi? Qu'est-ce que tu aimes faire?

See answers below.

Les exclus du loisir

Au cours de leur vie, 82 % des Français (15 ans et plus) ne sont jamais allés à l'opéra. 82 % n'ont jamais assisté à un concert de jazz.

- 77 % ne sont jamais allés voir une opérette.
- 76 % n'ont jamais assisté à un spectacle de danse.
- 75 % n'ont jamais assisté à un concert de rock.
- 71 % n'ont jamais assisté à un concert de musique classique.
- 62 % n'ont jamais visité une galerie d'art.
- 57 % ne sont jamais allés dans un parc d'attractions.
- 55 % ne sont jamais allés au théâtre.
- 46 % n'ont jamais assisté à un match sportif payant.
- 45 % ne sont jamais allés dans une discothèque.
- 28 % n'ont jamais visité un monument historique.
- 26 % n'ont jamais visité un musée.
- 12 % ne sont jamais allés au cinéma.
- 7 % ne sont jamais allés au restaurant.

14 Nos distractions

Make a list of six attractions in your region and ask your classmates if they've been there. Then, ask them how they liked each place. According to your poll, which place is the most popular? The least?

—Tu es déjà allé(e) à Mount Rushmore?
—Oui.
—Ça t'a plu?
—Beaucoup. C'était superbe!

15 Le week-end

Prépare un dialogue avec un(e) camarade de classe. Qu'est-ce que tu as fait ce week-end? Où es-tu allé(e)? Qu'est-ce que tu as fait là-bas? C'était comment?

Answers

12 *Possible answers*

1. au zoo; Pour le garçon, c'était nul! Pour sa sœur, c'était magnifique!
2. faire un pique-nique; C'était comme ci, comme ça/superbe!
3. sur les montagnes russes; C'était incroyable/sinistre!
4. visiter les châteaux; C'était mortel/pas mal.

13 1. aller au restaurant
2. la musique classique; une opérette
3. 74%; 72%, 43%

Performance Assessment

On a transparency, draw and project three illustrations: an amusement park, a château, and a zoo. For each picture, have students imagine they went there, mention at least two things they did, and tell what they thought of it. (**Je suis allé(e) dans un château. J'ai fait une visite guidée, et j'ai fait un pique-nique. C'était bien.**)

Math Link

13 Convert the realia into a questionnaire and distribute copies to students. For example, write **Es-tu déjà allé(e) voir une opérette?** After students have completed the questionnaires, collect them and compile the totals. Then, have groups of students calculate the percentage of their classmates who haven't done these activities. For example, if there are eight in a class of 30 who have never been to a concert, divide 8 by 30 (.267) and multiply by 100 to get 26.7%.

Group Work

14 Have groups of four create a radio commercial for a tour company. They should describe one or more of the attractions in their region, invent a day tour by bus or train, and include the prices. Students may wish to record the commercial on an audiocassette for their oral portfolios. You might also use this activity as a chapter project.

CLOSE

On index cards, write the names of several places to visit during a weekend. Distribute one to each student. Have each student tell what he or she did at the place on the card, using *y* to replace it. (**J'y ai vu des sculptures.**) The student should also tell what he or she thought of it. (**C'était ennuyeux.**) The others try to guess where the students went. (**Il/Elle est allé(e) dans un musée.**)

ASSESS

Quiz 6-1, *Chapter Teaching Resources, Book 2,* pp. 79–80

Assessment Items, Audiocassette 7B/Audio CD 6

146   DEUXIEME ETAPE

Jump Start!

Write the following sentences on the board or on a transparency. Have students deduce from each one where the person went.

1. **Han a donné à mangé aux animaux.**
2. **Anne a fait un tour sur les montagnes russes.**
3. **Marc a visité des cachots.**
4. **Marie a vu un film français.**
5. **Jean a fait un pique-nique.**

MOTIVATE

Ask students if they have ever been on a school field trip and if so, where they went. You might also ask them where they would go if they lived in Touraine.

TEACH

 For Individual Needs

Tactile/Auditory Learners
Have students copy the captions of the illustrations on separate slips of paper and cover the captions in their book with paper. Students should then shuffle the slips, select one, and read aloud the caption to a partner, who will point to the illustration that fits the caption.

Kinesthetic Learners Ask for volunteers to come to the front of the room and act out one of the captions. Classmates try to guess the caption that corresponds to the gestures.

Teaching Suggestion

Ask students what they notice about all of the verbs in the **passé composé** (**être** is the helping verb). Then, call their attention to the spelling of the past participles and ask them why they think there are letters added to some of them.

DEUXIEME ETAPE

Expressing disbelief and doubt

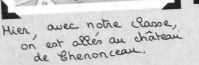

Le 21 avril à Chenonceau...

Hier, avec notre classe, on est allés au château de Chenonceau.

On est arrivés au château de bonne heure. Jean-Claude n'est pas venu avec nous.

Than et Mathieu sont entrés pour la visite guidée. Ali est directement monté au premier étage.

Anaïs est descendue au bord du Cher.

Charlotte est tombée dans le jardin de Diane de Poitiers.

Catherine et Suriya sont restées longtemps au café.

Des touristes américains sont partis à vélo.

On est rentrés tout contents!

RESOURCES FOR DEUXIEME ETAPE

Textbook Audiocassette 3B/Audio CD 6
Practice and Activity Book, pp. 65–67
Video Guide
    Video Program
    Expanded Video Program, Videocassette 2
Videodisc Guide
    Videodisc Program, Videodisc 3B

Chapter Teaching Resources, Book 2
• Communicative Activity 6-1, pp. 59–60
• Teaching Transparency Master 6-2, pp. 64, 66
    Teaching Transparency 6-2
• Additional Listening Activities 6-3, 6-4, p. 68
    Audiocassette 9B/Audio CD 6
• Realia 6-2, pp. 72, 73
• Situation Cards 6-2, pp. 74–75
• Student Response Forms, pp. 76–78
• Quiz 6-2, pp. 81–82
    Audiocassette 7B/Audio CD 6

16 Ecoute!

Listen as the teacher tries to locate all the students to head back to the bus. Where are these students? Answers on p. 135C.

1. Paul
2. Laurence
3. Ali
4. Guillaume
5. Mireille
6. Marcel

VOCABULAIRE

entrer (entré)	to enter	mourir (mort)	to die
venir (venu)	to come	sortir (sorti)	to go out
rester (resté)	to stay	partir (parti)	to leave
monter (monté)	to go up	rentrer (rentré)	to go back (home)
descendre (descendu)	to go down	revenir (revenu)	to come back
naître (né)	to be born	retourner (retourné)	to return
devenir (devenu)	to become		

Grammaire   The passé composé with être

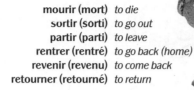

- To form the **passé composé** of some verbs, you use **être** instead of **avoir** as the helping verb. The verbs you've just learned follow this pattern, as do the verbs **aller, tomber,** and **arriver** from Chapter 5.

Je **suis rentré(e).**	Nous **sommes rentré(e)s.**
Tu **es rentré(e).**	Vous **êtes rentré(e)(s).**
Il/Elle/On **est rentré(e)(s).**	Ils/Elles **sont rentré(e)s.**

- When you form the **passé composé** with **être,** the past participle agrees in gender and number with the subject, just as an adjective agrees with the noun it describes. If the subject of the verb is feminine, add an **-e** to the past participle. If the subject is feminine plural, add **-es.** If it's masculine plural, add an **-s.** Don't forget that a compound subject with one masculine element is considered masculine.

17 Une journée au château

Tes copains et toi, vous êtes allés au château samedi dernier. Décris ce que chacun de vous a fait.

Je	arriver	au château de ___?___
On	aller	à pied/à vélo/en train
Les filles	monter	dans une tour
Les garçons	descendre	dans le jardin
___?___	rester	dans la chambre du roi
___?___ et ___?___	tomber	dans la boutique de souvenirs
	retourner	dans l'escalier
	___?___	___?___

DEUXIEME ETAPE

cent quarante-sept   **147**

Presentation

Vocabulaire Make a house out of a cardboard box with an opening for a door. Use a stuffed animal to demonstrate a story in the **passé composé,** using all the verbs that have **être** as their helping verb. (M. Ours est né à Chartres. Un jour, il est sorti de sa maison. Il est descendu en ville, et il est allé à la gare. Son train est parti pour Paris à six heures. Il est revenu à Chartres vers midi, et il est retourné chez lui. A deux heures, il est reparti pour Paris. Il est monté au troisième étage de la tour Eiffel. Il est tombé! Aïe! Il est mort. Il n'est jamais rentré chez lui.) On the board, draw the Eiffel Tower and whatever else you may need to tell the story. Retell the story, having students repeat. Then, ask for volunteers to reconstruct the story.

Group Work

Have groups create a story, using verbs that are conjugated with **être** in the **passé composé.** They might present the stories to the class, using props and illustrations.

Presentation

Grammaire On strips of transparency, write several sentences in large letters, using verbs in the **passé composé** conjugated with both **être** and **avoir.** Cut the strips into subject pronouns, helping verbs, past participles, and past participle endings, and shuffle the pieces. After reading **Grammaire,** have two students come up to the overhead projector and try to rearrange the pieces into sentences. You might prepare index cards in the same manner for small groups to use.

Teaching Suggestion

18 After students tell what Annick did, ask questions such as **Qu'est-ce qu'elle a fait avant de monter dans l'arbre? Qu'est-ce qu'Annick a fait après avoir joué avec le chien?**

Teacher Note

18 Many local newspapers carry the comic *Family Circus*®. It occasionally has a similar drawing in which the child engages in several activities while running an errand. This cartoon can be used to reteach or review the **passé composé** and vocabulary.

For Individual Needs

18 Slower Pace In random order, list the things Annick did on the board or on a transparency and have students rewrite them in the correct order, according to the illustration. Then, have students take turns telling the story to a partner, using adverbs of sequence, such as **d'abord, après, puis, ensuite,** and so on.

Presentation

Comment dit-on... ? Have partners think of two unbelievable things that have happened to them. Then, as students tell you these things, respond with the expressions of disbelief and doubt in **Comment dit-on... ?** Finally, tell outrageous tales to students and prompt them to respond with the new expressions in the function box.

For videodisc application, see *Videodisc Guide.*

18 La petite Annick

Qu'est-ce qu'Annick a fait cet après-midi? See answers below.

19 Qu'est-ce qu'il/elle a fait?

Choose a famous person and write down three things the person did. Without giving the person's name, read your list to your group. The first one to guess the person's name takes the next turn.

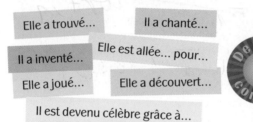

Elle a trouvé...   Il a chanté...

Il a inventé...   Elle est allée... pour...

Elle a joué...   Elle a découvert...

Il est devenu célèbre grâce à...

How can you remember when to use **avoir** to form the past tense and when to use **être**? A general rule of thumb is that you often associate **être** with verbs of motion. Think of a house. You use **être** with any verb that will get you *into* the house, *upstairs* and *downstairs* (even by falling!), and *out* of the house. Also, if you *stay* in the house, and are *born* or *die* in the house, you will use **être** with these verbs. Draw a picture to illustrate this and keep it as a study guide.

De bons conseils

COMMENT DIT-ON... ?
Expressing disbelief and doubt

To express disbelief and doubt:

Tu plaisantes!	**C'est pas vrai.**	**N'importe quoi!**
You're joking!	*You're kidding.*	*That's ridiculous!*
Pas possible!	**Ça m'étonnerait.**	**Mon œil!**
No way!	*I doubt it.*	*Yeah, right!*

Culture Note

To express disbelief, French people will often place their index finger just below their eye, pull down the bottom lid slightly, and say **Mon œil!** Sometimes they will make this gesture and frown without speaking to convey their meaning. The French also will protrude their jaw and lips and say **Peuh!** to express disbelief. This gesture is often accompanied by the expression **N'importe quoi!** *(That's ridiculous!)*

Possible answers

18 Elle est rentrée chez elle, et elle est montée dans sa chambre. Après, elle est descendue, et elle est sortie dans son jardin. Elle est montée sur un arbre, et elle est tombée. Ensuite, elle est allée chez les voisins, elle est entrée chez eux et elle a mangé du pain et du chocolat. Finalement, elle est retournée dans son jardin, et elle a joué avec son chien. Elle a parlé avec son copain, et elle est retournée chez elle pour regarder la télé.

20 Ecoute!

Listen to Mai as she asks her friends about their weekends. Does she believe what they tell her or not? *Answers on p. 135C.*

21 C'est vrai?

What would you say if a friend made one of the following statements? *Possible answers:*

1. «J'ai fait du jogging à 4h ce matin.»
2. «J'ai vu Elvis Presley hier.»
3. «La France est en Afrique.»
4. «On doit aller à l'école dimanche.»
5. «Hier, j'ai gagné un million de dollars.»
6. «En Espagne, on parle allemand.»

1. Tu plaisantes!	**4.** Ça m'étonnerait!
2. Mon œil!	**5.** Pas possible!
3. C'est pas vrai!	**6.** N'importe quoi!

22 Un jour...

Imagine three extraordinary things that happened to you and tell your partner about them. Your partner will express disbelief and ask for more details. Then, reverse roles.

—Un jour, je suis arrivé(e) à l'école avec le président de la République française.
—Tu plaisantes! Pourquoi est-ce qu'il est venu avec toi?
—...

23 Mon œil!

a. In your group, take turns telling tall tales about yourselves. The entire group will respond with expressions of doubt and disbelief. When you have told your stories, choose the best one from your group.

b. Put together your own newspaper of sensational stories. Each group will write up its best story, adding some details to make the story even more interesting and unbelievable.

24 Dans le guide du château

Lis cette page du guide de Chenonceau et réponds aux questions. *See answers below.*

Qui...

1. était la femme du roi?
2. était la favorite du roi?
3. est mort pendant un tournoi de joute?
4. est devenue régente de France?
5. a donné des fêtes extravagantes?
6. a d'abord possédé Chenonceau?
7. a reçu Chenonceau en cadeau?
8. a accepté le château de Chaumont en échange de Chenonceau?
9. est finalement devenue propriétaire de Chenonceau?

Les personnages de Chenonceau

Henri II, le roi
Il est né en 1519. Roi de France de 1547 à 1559, il était marié à Catherine de Médicis, qui a longtemps pleuré sa mort accidentelle pendant un tournoi de joute.

Diane de Poitiers, la toujours belle
La jeune femme est devenue la favorite du roi Henri II. En 1547, quand Henri II est monté sur le trône, il lui a donné Chenonceau. A la mort du roi, la reine Catherine de Médicis a contraint Diane à accepter le château de Chaumont en échange de Chenonceau.

Catherine de Médicis, la fastueuse
Née en 1519, elle était la femme et la reine d'Henri II. Quand le roi est mort, elle est devenue régente de la France. Elle a réclamé le château de Chenonceau à Diane de Poitiers. Elle y a ensuite donné des fêtes extravagantes.

Additional Practice

20 Have students listen to the recording a second time and tell what each person did or where he or she went.

Teacher Note

22, 23 A source of true, extraordinary accomplishments that students might use is the *Guinness Book of World Records.*

📁 **Portfolio**

23 Written Part b of this activity is appropriate for students' written portfolios. For portfolio suggestions, see *Assessment Guide,* page 19.

Close

On index cards, write several unusual activities that your students did on an imaginary field trip (**revenir tout(e) seul(e), rester dans le car**). Write each expression on two cards, so that two students will have a card with the same expression. Distribute one card to each student. Have students circulate around the room, trying to find the person who did the same thing they did. If a student's card reads **arriver en retard,** he or she asks **Tu es arrivé(e) en retard?** Students should answer according to their own card. (**Oui, moi aussi, je suis arrivé(e) en retard. Non, je suis venu(e) à pied.**) If the cards don't match, students should react with disbelief. (**Mon œil!**) When students find their match, they should report to you.

Answers
24 1. Catherine de Médicis
   2. Diane de Poitiers
   3. Henri II
   4. Catherine de Médicis
   5. Catherine de Médicis
   6. Henri II
   7. Diane de Poitiers
   8. Diane de Poitiers
   9. Catherine de Médicis

Assess

Quiz 6-2, *Chapter Teaching Resources, Book 2,* pp. 81–82

Assessment Items, Audiocassette 7B Audio CD 6

Performance Assessment

Write several subjects and infinitives on separate slips of paper and place them in two boxes. Have a pair of students draw a slip of paper from each box. Using the subject and verb they drew, both students should make a sentence that relates an unbelievable incident. For example, for **ma mère** and **aller,** a student might say **Ma mère est allée sur la lune.** The other student should react appropriately. (**Mon œil!**)

VIDEO PROGRAM
OR EXPANDED VIDEO
PROGRAM,
Videocassette 2
54:24–59:14

OR VIDEODISC PROGRAM,
Videodisc 3B

Search 18255, Play To 21985

Teacher Notes

- See *Video Guide, Videodisc Guide,* and *Practice and Activity Book* for activities related to the **Panorama Culturel.**
- Remind students that cultural material may be included in the Chapter Quizzes and Test.
- The interviewees' language represents informal, unrehearsed speech. Occasionally, edits have been made for clarification.

Motivating Activity

Ask students to name their favorite historical or literary figures and tell why they like them.

Presentation

Before you show the video, have students list all the French historical figures they know. Then, show the video. Have students list all the names they hear mentioned and compare the two lists.

Thinking Critically

Comparing and Contrasting

Ask students how the history they learn differs from the history the interviewees learn.

Multicultural Link

Have students research historical figures from other cultures and present their findings to the class.

PANORAMA CULTUREL

Hervé • Martinique   Pauline • France   Evelyne • France

We asked students what famous people they have studied in school. Here are their responses.

Qui sont les personnages historiques que tu as étudiés?

«Je connais tous les personnages historiques français et je vais en citer quelques-uns. Bien, on peut parler des rois de France, par exemple de Louis XIV, de Louis XV, d'Henri IV en Angleterre et en Martinique, notre impératrice Joséphine qui s'est mariée avec Napoléon.»

Il y a quelqu'un que tu admires en particulier?
«J'apprécie beaucoup Joséphine, l'impératrice, tout d'abord parce que c'est une compatriote et voilà.»

—Hervé

«On a étudié surtout des auteurs, comme Victor Hugo ou Maupassant, mais aussi des personnages historiques de l'histoire de France, comme Napoléon.»

Il y a quelqu'un que tu admires en particulier?
«Que j'admire... Je vois pas spécialement. J'aime bien Victor Hugo. J'aime bien les poètes.»

—Pauline

«Les personnages qu'on a étudiés en histoire sont Hitler, Mussolini, Vercingétorix et Jules César... Louis XVI et tous les rois de France, les rois d'Angleterre aussi.»

—Evelyne

Qu'en penses-tu?

1. Which of the famous people mentioned have you studied? What did they do?
2. Which of these people do you find most interesting? Why?
3. What other French-speaking historical figures do you know about? What did they do?
4. Choose a well-known francophone person you have not studied and find out why he or she is famous.

Questions

1. Avec qui est-ce que l'impératrice Joséphine s'est mariée? (avec Napoléon)
2. Quel auteur est-ce que Pauline admire le plus? (Victor Hugo)
3. Qui a étudié Jules César? (Evelyne)
4. Qui est Maupassant? (C'est un auteur.)
5. Pourquoi est-ce qu'Hervé, qui est Martiniquais, connaît les personnages français? (La Martinique est un département français.)

History Link

Point out that America and France have been linked many times throughout history. Ask students if they can think of any examples. (Benjamin Franklin was ambassador to France. He and others gleaned many of our democratic principles from the writings of Diderot, Rousseau, and Montesquieu. The French helped us fight our revolution, and then staged their own thirteen years later.)

TROISIEME ETAPE

Asking for and giving information

CIRCUITS D'UNE JOURNEE

Départ à 9 h 00, place de la Gare, quai n° 6

10 - TOURS, Cormery, vallée de l'Indre, **LOCHES** (visite, déjeuner libre), **CHENONCEAU** (visite), **AMBOISE** (visite), Montlouis, TOURS (vers 18 h 45).

> *Les samedis, du 10 avril au 25 septembre.*
> *Les mardis, du 6 juillet au 28 septembre.*
> Car : **145 F**
> Droits d'entrée : **65 F**

11 - TOURS, Amboise (vue sur le château), Chaumont, **BLOIS** (visite, déjeuner libre), Ménars, **CHAMBORD** (visite), **CHEVERNY** (visite), vallée du Cher, TOURS (vers 18 h 45).

> *Les lundis et vendredis, du 12 avril au 27 septembre.*
> Car : **145 F**
> Droits d'entrée : **65 F**

Les circuits de jour sont accompagnés et commentés par des guides-interprètes de Touraine (français-anglais).

CIRCUITS D'UNE DEMI-JOURNEE

Départ à 13 h 15, place de la Gare, quai n° 6

12 - TOURS, Vouvray, **CHAUMONT** (visite), **LE CLOS-LUCE** à Amboise, demeure de Léonard de Vinci (visite), TOURS (vers 18 h 45).

> *Les samedis, du 3 juillet au 11 septembre.*
> Car : **93 F**
> Droits d'entrée : **42 F**

13 - TOURS, Savonnières, Villandry, **USSE** (visite), **LANGEAIS** (visite), TOURS (vers 18 heures).

> *Les mardis, du 6 juillet au 31 août.*
> Car : **93 F**
> Droits d'entrée : **35 F**

SPECTACLES *SON ET LUMIERE*

Départ place de la Gare, quai n° 6

14 - **LE LUDE** : "Les glorieuses et fastueuses soirées au bord du Loir". Départ à 21 heures jusqu'au 31 juillet, à 20 h 30 au mois d'août.

> *Les samedis, du 26 juin au 21 août.*
> *Les vendredis, du 25 juin au 20 août.*
> Car et droits d'entrée : **140 F**

15 - **AMBOISE** : "A la Cour du Roy François". Départ à 21 h 30 jusqu'au 31 juillet, à 21 heures à partir du 1er août.

> *Les mercredis, du 7 juillet au 25 août.*
> Car et droits d'entrée : **120 F**

25 A lire avec attention

Ces gens choisissent quel(s) tour(s) ?

1. Julien voudrait visiter Chaumont et Clos-Lucé. **12**
2. Francine veut voir un spectacle son et lumière mercredi. **15**   **3. 13, 15**
3. Hélène a 128 F pour le car et l'entrée.
4. Cam voudrait assister à un spectacle son et lumière jeudi ou vendredi. **14**
5. Luc veut voir Amboise et visiter Chambord. **11**
6. En avril, Marion voudrait visiter des châteaux. **10, 11**
7. Robert veut faire une visite guidée en anglais. **10, 11**

NOTE CULTURELLE

The intercity bus **(le car)** and the train **(le train)** are two excellent ways to see France. Trains run frequently between larger towns and cities. They are known for running on time. Nearly all train lines are electrified and computerized. The **train à grande vitesse (TGV)**, a high-speed train that covers long distances with only a few stops, is the most popular. At the **gare routière,** usually located at the train station, you can take the bus to the smaller towns in the region you are visiting. Some of the bus stations also offer tours, like the ones you see here in the brochure.

TROISIEME ETAPE   *cent cinquante et un*   **151**

Jump Start!

Write the mnemonic device *Dr. & Mrs. Vandertramp* on the board or on a transparency. Using this device as an aid, have students list the infinitives and the past participles of all the verbs that are conjugated with **être** in the **passé composé.**

MOTIVATE

Ask students what they would need to ask transportation employees if they wanted to take a tour by bus or train. Ask them if they would ask formal questions in French and why.

TEACH

Teaching Suggestion

Ask questions about the tour schedules, such as the following: **Il y a combien de spectacles son et lumière? Le car pour Cormery part à quelle heure? C'est combien le car pour Vouvray? Qu'est-ce qu'on peut faire au mois de juin? C'est combien les circuits d'une journée?**

Additional Practice

For listening practice, describe a tour you took, without naming the place. Have students tell you where you went.

Culture Note

The national railroad in France is operated by a government agency called the **Société Nationale des Chemins de Fer,** or **SNCF.** The TGV travels at speeds up to 185 miles per hour. **TGV nord** from Paris' **Gare du nord** travels due north through Normandy. **TGV atlantique** from Paris' **Gare Montparnasse** branches out through Brittany **(Bretagne)** and southwestern France from Bordeaux to the Spanish border. **TGV sud-est** from Paris' **Gare de Lyon** travels southeast through Lyon to the Côte d'Azur.

Presentation

Comment dit-on... ? Draw a train schedule on the board and label clearly the towns the trains go to, the departure and arrival times, the **quais** the trains leave from, and the prices of one-way and round-trip tickets. On another section of the board, draw a ticket window for the entrance to a château and mark clearly the visiting hours and the entrance fee (**l'entrée**). Then, have students play the roles of the two ticket agents at the station and at the château. Play the role of a tourist and ask all of the questions in **Comment dit-on... ?**, pointing to the information on the board to prompt students. Repeat with other students.

For videodisc application, see *Videodisc Guide.*

Presentation

Note de grammaire Read formal questions **De quel quai est-ce que le train part?** and have students form an informal question. (**Le train part de quel quai?**)

For Individual Needs

27 Challenge Have students rewrite the conversation, using the same sentences, but changing the information to represent one of the tours described on page 151.

Portfolio

28 Oral This activity is appropriate for students' oral portfolios. For portfolio suggestions, see *Assessment Guide,* page 19.

COMMENT DIT-ON... ?
Asking for and giving information

To ask for information:	*To respond:*
A quelle heure est-ce que le train (le car) pour Blois **part?**	**A 14h40.**
What time does the train (the bus) for . . . leave?	
De quel quai?	**Du quai 5.**
From which platform?	
A quelle heure est-ce que vous ouvrez (fermez)?	**A 10h (à 18h).**
What time do you open (close)?	

To ask for prices:	*To ask for what you want:*
Combien coûte un aller-retour?	**Je voudrais un aller-retour.**
How much is a round-trip ticket?	*I'd like a round-trip ticket.*
Combien coûte un aller simple?	**Un aller simple, s'il vous plaît.**
How much is a one-way ticket?	*A one-way ticket, please.*
C'est combien, l'entrée?	**Trois tickets, s'il vous plaît.**
How much is the entrance fee?	*Three (entrance) tickets, please.*

26 Ecoute!

Nathalie achète un billet à la gare. Ecoute sa conversation avec l'employé de la gare. Ensuite, complète les phrases suivantes.
Answers on page 135D.

1. Nathalie veut aller à...
2. Le train part à...
3. Elle voudrait un...
4. Ça coûte...
5. Le train part du quai...

> **Note de Grammaire**
>
> • To ask a question formally, use the question word(s) followed by **est-ce que: A quelle heure est-ce que le train arrive?**
> • To make an informal question, you may put the question word(s) at the end of the question: **Le train arrive à quelle heure?**

27 Méli-mélo!

Mets en ordre cette conversation entre l'employée de la gare routière et un touriste.

28 Une excursion

Look at the brochure on page 151. Choose a trip you would like to take and buy your ticket from the agent. Be sure to ask for all the information you need. Act out the scene with a partner and then reverse roles.

Culture Note

Although trains and buses are commonly used by tourists, some take advantage of the extensive road system in France and rent cars. On the national highways (**les autoroutes**), the speed limit (**la limite de vitesse**) is 130 kilometers per hour, on divided highways, it's 115 kilometers per hour; on rural roads, it's 80 kilometers per hour; and in all towns, the speed limit is 50 kilometers per hour.

Teacher Note

Note de Grammaire You might tell students that a third, more formal way to form questions in French is by using *inversion,* reversing the order of the subject pronoun and the verb. Tell them that a -t- is inserted after a third person singular verb that ends with a vowel. (**Je prends le train pour Paris. A quelle heure arrive-t-il?**)

29 Au château de Fontainebleau

Lis les renseignements pratiques pour Fontainebleau et réponds aux questions suivantes. See answers below.

1. Les jardins ouvrent à quelle heure?
2. A quelle heure est-ce qu'ils ferment? Pourquoi est-ce que l'heure de fermeture change?
3. Le château ouvre à quelle heure? Il ferme à quelle heure pour le déjeuner?
4. A quelle heure est-ce que le château rouvre? Il ferme à quelle heure le soir?

RENSEIGNEMENTS PRATIQUES:

Les cours et jardins sont ouverts tous les jours dès 8 h du matin et ferment entre 17 et 20 h 30 suivant la saison.

Le château est ouvert tous les jours (sauf mardi) de 9 h 30 à 12 h 30 et de 14 h à 17 h. Fermeture des caisses à 11 h 30 et 16 h.

L'entrée générale pour les grands et petits appartements, le Musée Napoléon et le Musée Chinois se fait au milieu du bâtiment de droite de la cour du cheval blanc.

Renseignements : tél. (1) 64 22 27 40.

30 A la boutique de cadeaux

You've decided to open a gift shop near Fontainebleau. Decide what your business hours will be, remembering that it is normal for stores to close for a long lunch. Then take turns with your partner, answering the phone as a tourist calls to ask for your hours.

Note de Grammaire

Ouvrir *(to open)* ends in **-ir**, but it's conjugated like a regular **-er** verb. Drop the **-ir** and add the endings **-e, -es, -e, -ons, -ez,** or **-ent.**

31 Jeu de rôle

This Saturday you're leaving Tours to see the château at Azay-le-Rideau. Choose the train you'll take. Answer your parent's questions about what you're doing and when you're leaving. Act out the scene with a partner and then reverse roles.

32 Mon journal

Write about a real or imaginary trip you've taken. Tell when you left, how you got there, what you did, and whether or not you had a good time.

Notes à consulter		7141 1	241 2	4087 3	4001 4	7143 5	4325 6	7145 7	245 8
TOURS	A		08.27	08.37			09.22		
TOURS	D	05.53		08.51					11.47
JOUE-les-TOURS	A	06.06				08.51		09.30	
BALLAN	A	06.07				08.58		09.37	
DRUYE	A					09.06		09.45	
VALLERES	A							09.52	
AZAY-le-RIDEAU	A	06.19						09.56	
AZAY-le-RIDEAU	D	06.20				09.19		10.01	
LA CHAPPELLE/ ST BLAISE	A					09.20		10.02	
CHEILLE	A								
QUINCAY	A								
RIVARENNES	A	06.27							
RIGNY-USSE	A							10.10	
HUISMES	A								
CHINON	A	06.43							
CHINON	D		06.50			09.40		10.25	
LOUDUN	A		07.15					10.30 11.03	

1 - Circule les lundis et le 15 juillet - AUTORAIL

2 - Circule les lundis - Autocar

3 - Circule tous les jours sauf samedis, dimanches et fêtes. Corail.

4 - Circule tous les jours sauf dimanches et fêtes. Corail.

5 - Circule tous les jours sauf dimanches et fêtes. Autorail.

6 - Circule tous les jours. Corail.

7 - Circule les dimanches et fêtes. Autorail.

8 - Circule les dimanches et fêtes. Autocar.

📖 Mon journal

32 For an additional journal entry suggestion for Chapter 6, see *Practice and Activity Book,* page 150.

CLOSE

To close this **étape,** hand out the following sentences, and then have students rearrange them to form a dialogue. Afterwards, project the dialogue on the overhead and have students check their papers. **Du quai six./Voilà, mademoiselle./C'est 25 francs./De quel quai est-ce que le train part?/Alors, une place pour le train de 8h20, s'il vous plaît./Pardon, monsieur. Combien coûte un aller-retour pour Blois?**

ASSESS

Quiz 6 3, *Chapter Teaching Resources, Book 2,* pp. 83–84

Assessment Items, Audiocassette 7B/Audio CD 6

Performance Assessment

Use Activity 28 to assess students' performance for this **étape.** On separate index cards, write **l'agent, le/la touriste,** and the numbers 10–15. Then, have two students choose a card to establish their roles. Have the **agent** use the brochure on page 151, and have the **touriste** choose a number to determine the tour he or she is to inquire about. In their dialogue, the **touriste** should inquire about the days and times of the tour, from which **quai** and at what time the bus leaves, and the cost of the tour. Finally, he or she should buy a bus ticket.

Answers

29 1. à 8h
   2. entre 17h et 20h30 suivant la saison
   3. 9h30; 12h30
   4. 14h; 17h

Language Notes

29 Point out that **rouvre** is a form of the verb **ouvrir** with the prefix **re-,** meaning *again,* attached to it; the **-e** is dropped because **ouvre** begins with a vowel sound. Other words formed in this manner are **récrire, rhabiller, rasseoir,** and **rassurer.**

If the prefix is **ré-,** the **-é** is not always dropped before a vowel, as in **réinventer** and **réarmer.**

Note de grammaire The English word *overture,* meaning the music played at the beginning or *opening* of a performance, comes from the French word **l'ouverture.**

READING STRATEGY
Taking notes

Teacher Note

For an additional reading, see *Practice and Activity Book,* page 71.

PREREADING

Motivating Activity

Have students imagine they are phoning a travel agency to ask for information about an excursion. Ask them how taking notes might be helpful in this situation. Point out that it might save them a second call, and that it might even prevent them from missing the tour! Similarly, taking notes while reading increases understanding of a text, condenses the information, and makes a second reading easier.

READING
Activities A–C

Teaching Suggestion

A. Have students read the likes and dislikes of their imaginary friends before they attempt to read the posters. Students should then scan for specific information to try to match their friends' interests to the available activities.

For Individual Needs

B. Slower Pace Have students compare the notes they took for the remaining posters with a partner's. Have them discuss why they found certain details important.

Teaching Suggestion

Rappel Have students write the categories *Who? What? When? Where? Why?* and write something for each category as they take notes.

LISONS!

TOURISME FLUVIAL
DANS LES PAYS DE LA LOIRE
LOUEZ VOTRE BATEAU HABITABLE SANS PERMIS

Découvrir le plaisir sauvage d'une nature tranquille!

Des châteaux de la Loire à l'Océan Atlantique, partez à la découverte des rivières de la région (Maine, Mayenne, Oudon, Sarthe, Erdre et canal de Nantes à Brest) : plus de 350 kms de paysages sans cesse renouvelés entre Angers et Redon.

En famille ou entre amis, louez l'un des 180 bateaux SANS PERMIS (de 2 à 12 personnes). Vous découvrirez le plaisir de la navigation, les châteaux, manoirs, abbayes et de nombreux villages typiques. Les écluses au nombre restreint sont ouvertes tous les jours. Vous vous amarrez où et quand vous voulez pour inventer vos loisirs : équitation, pêche, vélo, baignade, promenade...

A QUI VOUS ADRESSER?

Notre brochure est à votre disposition auprès de nos 2 centrales de réservation.

RIVIERES D'ANJOU & DU MAINE 13 bases - 150 bateaux **MAINE RESERVATION** B.P. 2224 - 49022 ANGERS CEDEX 02 Tél. 41 23 51 30 - Fax. 41 23 51 35 Télex. 723 070	**RIVIERE DE L'ERDRE** **& CANAL DE NANTES A BREST** 3 bases - 30 bateaux **LOISIRS ACCUEIL** Place du Commerce - 44000 NANTES Tél. 40 89 50 77 - Fax. 40 20 44 54 Télex. 711 505

ℐn most towns in France, you can visit the **Office de tourisme** to find out what activities are available in that area.

 DE BONS CONSEILS
How do you remember what you read? You take notes, of course! But you certainly can't write down everything you read. You have to choose the information you think is important to remember.

A. You have four friends who would be happy to join you on one of these excursions or at one of these events. Match one of these activities to each friend's likes and dislikes.

1. Latif is artistic, and he's always looking for something unusual to do.
2. Denise likes to be active outdoors, and she loves to travel.
3. Nicole loves romantic novels and films.
4. Paul plays chess and collects books on castles and knights. See answers below.

RAPPEL Remember to look for the answers to the questions *Who? What? When? Where?* and *Why?* when you are choosing information you think is important to remember.

B. Read the poster for **A la recherche de la lumière,** taking notes as you read.

154 *cent cinquante-quatre*

Culture Note

You might point out the addresses in the brochure for **Tourisme fluvial.** The **B.P.** in the first address stands for **boîte postale** *(post office box).* The five-digit number next to the post office box number is the postal code (**le code postal**). The first two digits of the postal code represent the **département.** (France has 96 departments.) If the first two digits are followed by three zeroes, this indicates the main town in the department. For example, the postal code for Bordeaux is 33000. Paris, Lyons, and Marseilles are divided into **arrondissements,** which are shown in the last two digits of the postal code. The **cedex** number is a routing code indicating a zone within a postal code area, and is used by businesses to expedite the mailing service.

Answers
A 1. Saran   3. Valençay
2. Tourisme fluvial   4. Taillebourg

VALENÇAY

La "belle", dans le parc aux daims

Dans un lieu qui n'est autre que ce vague pays des contes de fées, un riche marchand, ruiné par une tempête, habite avec ses trois filles et son

fils... C'est ainsi que commence, "La belle et la bête", conte qui inspira le poète et cinéaste Jean Cocteau, pour la réalisation de son célèbre film. Aujourd'hui, le texte original du film sert de support à la mise en scène d'un nouveau spectacle son et lumière, dans le cadre prestigieux du château de Valençay. Jean-Claude Baudoin, son réalisateur, fait évoluer dans le parc aux daims, 200 figurants jouant avec l'eau, la pyrotechnie et les costumes du XVIe siècle. Le nouveau cadre de ce parc, inutilisé jusqu'à présent, avec ses arbres séculaires et son étang, permet d'obtenir le miracle de la double image, puisque la plupart des scènes se reflètent dans l'eau.

"La belle et la bête" - Château - Jusqu'au 28 août ☎ *54 00 04 42 A71, sortie Salbris puis D724 et D956.*

SARAN

A la recherche de la lumière

Peintre, graveur, sculpteur, illustrateur, lauréat du prix international de New York, Gilbert Sabatier, artiste contemporain, expose 40 nouvelles toiles dans le magnifique cadre du château de l'Etang, à Saran. Il s'agit de peintures acryliques de grand format (1,70 x 1,30 m), auxquelles s'ajoutent plusieurs sculptures. Les toiles traitent de la lumière et de ses déclinaisons, elles sont en relief avec apport de matériaux divers (tissus, sable, plexiglas...). Elles ressemblent à des kaléidoscopes, ou bien encore à des vitraux surréalistes. Une démarche logique, lorsque l'on sait que la recherche de la lumière est devenue une véritable obsession chez l'artiste.

"Déclinaison de lumière" - Château de l'Etang - 4 au 29 août - ☎ *38 53 14 25 A10, sortie Orléans Nord.*

TAILLEBOURG

"Le génie du château" Spectacle son et lumière

Venez voyager avec nous au cœur du moyen âge ; par-delà le spectacle, c'est toute la mémoire d'une cité qui est retrouvée...

4 au 8 et 10 au 15 août à 22h (Ouverture des guichets à 21 h)
Prix des places : Adultes 65 F, Enfants 35 F
Groupes : Adultes 55 F, Enfants 30 F
Réservations : Mairie de TAILLEBOURG :
☎ 46 91 80 42
Office de tourisme de SAINTES :
☎ 46 74 23 82

L'hébergement de notre spectacle est entièrement assuré par l'hôtel 2 étoiles "Les chênes verts" à St-Savinien, où 25 chambres tout confort vous attendent dans une forêt de chênes verts. La restauration est également assurée sur place.

Then, compare your notes with a partner's. What did you each think were important items to note? You probably noted four or five key words or phrases to explain further what is happening in Saran. Try this method of taking notes as you read the remaining posters.

C. Now, check your note-taking. Can you answer these questions about the remaining posters, using only your notes?

Where can you . . . See answers below.
- travel back to the Middle Ages?
- experience a sound and light show?
- see châteaux from a boat?
- look at a contemporary artist's work?

D. Using your notes, write three brief postcards about three of the activities you'd

most like to try. Address them to friends you think would enjoy the activities. Use sentence starters like **Si tu veux, on pourrait...**, or **Ici, on peut...**

E. Make a travel poster to publicize an interesting event that you enjoyed. Be sure to include (a) a heading that tells where the event takes place, (b) a subheading that catches the reader's attention and gives the main theme of the event, and (c) a short text that offers four or five pieces of information that would make the reader want to attend. Draw a picture or find one in a magazine to illustrate the poster.

cent cinquante-cinq 155

Thinking Critically

D. Drawing Inferences/ Synthesizing Ask students for whom the information in the posters is intended. Then, have them reread the likes and dislikes of their imaginary friends in Activity A on page 154. Ask them to keep these preferences in mind as they think about their own friends' likes and dislikes and begin to tailor the information in their postcards for their intended readers.

Cooperative Learning

E. You might have groups of four make travel posters. Assign leaders to help the groups decide what to advertise and what to include in the advertisement. Have tactile learners collect and outline the information, visual learners arrange the layout of the information, and creative individuals illustrate or collect pictures for the poster.

Culture Note

The château of Valençay is a beautiful Renaissance château in the Loire region. It was built in 1550 on the site of an old feudal castle. The dungeon, a tower, and the main body of the building date from this period. In the seventeenth and eighteenth centuries, additional wings were added. Talleyrand, the foreign minister of Napoleon in 1803, received foreign dignitaries there as ambassador to France. The interior of the château is lavishly furnished in the Empire and Louis XIV styles. Ten private apartments are open to the public.

Radio-Television-Film Link

If possible, you might show Jean Cocteau's *La Belle et la bête,* a fantasy based on the children's tale. Jean Cocteau (1889–1963) was a French poet, novelist, actor, film director, and painter. In the 1940s, he returned to and concentrated on filmmaking, first as a screenwriter, and then as a director. It was during these years that he directed the classic *Beauty and the Beast.* The more recent Walt Disney

animated version is available in French through several foreign language educational video distributors.

Answers

C • Taillebourg
- Taillebourg, Valençay
- on a boat rented from Tourisme fluvial
- Saran

The **Mise en pratique** reviews and integrates all four skills and culture in preparation for the Chapter Test.

Teaching Suggestion

1 As an extension of this activity, have pairs of students create a telephone conversation between a travel agent and a tourist inquiring about the château. Ask for volunteers to present their conversation to the class.

Language Note

1 You might write the following words on the board for students to refer to as they read the brochure and take notes: **patrimoine** (*heritage*); **dès** (*from*); **achevé** (*accomplished*); **grandir** (*to grow up*); **relié** (*linked*); **souterrain** (*underground*).

Additional Practice

2 For additional listening practice, list in random order on the board the times and destinations, and the prices and ages mentioned in the recording. Have students listen to the recording again and match the times with the destinations and the prices with the ages.

✦ For Individual Needs

3 Slower Pace You might have students work in pairs to do this activity. In addition, you might translate the following expressions if students find they inhibit their comprehension of the text: **Depuis toujours, les châtelaines recevaient...** (*The ladies of the château had always . . .*); **ainsi que la façon dont elles étaient traitées...** (*as well as the way they were treated . . .*); **et attendait de tous les hommes... qu'ils en fassent autant...** (*and expected all the men . . . to do the same . . .*).

MISE EN PRATIQUE

You and a friend are going to visit Amboise. You want to see the castle where Francis I was raised and spent the early years of his reign.

See answers below.

1 You see this poster about Amboise and take down some notes about visiting hours, entrance fees, the sound and light show, and some facts about Amboise and Clos-Lucé.

A LA COUR DU ROY FRANÇOIS - AMBOISE

Le château d'Amboise est un des trésors du patrimoine français. Sa construction, commencée dès le XIème siècle, a finalement été achevée par Charles VIII au XVème siècle. Mais c'est le roi François I qui a rendu Amboise célèbre. A l'âge de six ans, il y a établi sa résidence et c'est là qu'il a grandi. Passionné par les arts, il a même invité Léonard de Vinci à venir travailler à Clos-Lucé, un manoir du XVème siècle relié à Amboise par des passages souterrains. De Vinci est resté à Clos-Lucé jusqu'à sa mort et on peut aujourd'hui y admirer certaines de ses inventions.

Le château est ouvert tous les jours de 9h à 12h et de 14h à 18h30, et sans interruption de 9h à 18h30 aux mois de juillet et d'août. Fermeture en hiver à 17h30. Spectacle son et lumière, du 7 juillet au 25 août, "A la cour du Roy François", à 22h30 le mercredi et le samedi. Droit d'entrée : 27F Tarif enfant : 10F

2 You call the bus station in Tours, but you get a recorded message. Listen carefully and note the times you'll need to catch the bus to and from Amboise and how much your ticket will be. Answers on p. 135D.

3 When you arrive at the château, you buy a pamphlet about Amboise. Read the information in the pamphlet on page 157 and answer the questions as best you can.

1. How were women treated before Francis I? without much respect
2. How did he treat the women in his court? with respect
3. What became of them when Francis I became king? They became a more visible part of court life.
4. What did he spend a lot of money on? Why? clothes; to show the beauty of the women in his court
5. How did the French court change under his reign? It became a place where the arts and sciences flourished.
6. What did he organize? festivals

CHAPITRE 6   A nous les châteaux!

🌐 Culture Note

Leonardo da Vinci (1452–1519) was an Italian painter, sculptor, architect, and engineer whose genius was centuries ahead of its time (see page 20). In 1516, King Francis I invited him to live at Clos Lucé. The king would often visit Da Vinci by way of the underground tunnel from the château to Clos Lucé. Da Vinci died after spending three years at Clos Lucé.

Answers

1 Visiting hours: every day 9 A.M. to 12 P.M. and 2 to 6:30 P.M.; 9 A.M. to 6 P.M. in July and August; closes at 5:30 P.M. in winter.

Entrance fees: 27 F for adults and 10 F for children.

Sound and light show: from the 7th of July until the 25th of August, at 10:30 P.M., Wednesdays and Saturdays.

Amboise: built by Charles VIII in fifteenth century; Francis I was raised there;

Clos Lucé: Leonardo de Vinci lived and died there.

Un homme de goût

Depuis toujours, les châtelaines recevaient peu de respect et d'attention de la part des hommes de la cour. Mais, sous François I, leur rôle dans la société ainsi que la façon dont elles étaient traitées ont commencé à changer. Le roi François aimait les femmes, les respectait et attendait de tous les hommes de sa cour qu'ils en fassent autant. Si un homme disait du mal d'une femme, il était pendu. François I dépensait beaucoup pour les vêtements de ses courtisanes. Il voulait qu'elles montrent leur beauté. Sous son règne, la Cour de France est devenue une école d'élégance, de goût et de culture où les arts, les sciences et la poésie étaient célébrés lors des nombreux festivals organisés par le roi lui-même.

 **4** When you get back from your trip to Amboise, one of your friends asks you what it was like, how you got there, what you saw, and what you learned. Tell your friend all about your trip. Act this out with a partner.

5 Who's a famous person from your region? Write a summary of that person's life and accomplishments to give to French tourists who visit your area of the country.

6 How much cultural information do you remember? Match the following people, places, and things from this chapter.

1. Azay-le-Rideau   c
2. Joséphine   e
3. TGV   f
4. Victor Hugo   a
5. Moyen âge   d
6. le car   b

a. poète
b. gare routière
c. château de la Renaissance
d. château fort
e. Martinique
f. train à grande vitesse

7

JEU DE ROLE

While you're at Amboise, one of your friends disappears! Act out the scene with two classmates.

- Make suggestions about what might have happened to your friend.
- React with doubt to the suggestions.
- Resolve the problem.

Culture Note

Amboise was the first French castle to reflect the style of the Italian Renaissance. The structure of the château is a mixture of both the Gothic and Renaissance styles. Two squat towers were built with ramps to accommodate horses and carriages. The château was built in the fifteenth century by Charles VIII, who died in 1498 after banging his head on a very low door in the château.

The château enjoyed its heyday under King Francis I, who was known as the Chevalier King. He sponsored many outlandish festivals, the most memorable of which was in honor of the arrival of the Holy Roman Emperor Charles V in 1539. Torchbearers led the way as the emperor made a grand entrance up one of the tower's ramps. A torch ignited one of the fabric-draped towers and nearly burned Charles V alive.

Teaching Suggestions

4 After students talk about their trip to Amboise, have them conduct a similar conversation in which they talk about a real or imaginary excursion they took with friends, family, or classmates. Have them begin by telling where they went. (**L'année dernière, je suis allé(e) visiter une maison historique en ville.**)

5 Ask students to find a picture of the person and mount it on construction paper with their description. They might display these at school as a local "Hall of Fame."

 **Video Wrap-Up**

- *VIDEO PROGRAM*
- *EXPANDED VIDEO PROGRAM,* **Videocassette 2, 44:13–60:34**
- *VIDEODISC PROGRAM,* **Videodisc 3B**

At this time, you might want to use the video resources for additional review and enrichment. See *Video Guide* or *Videodisc Guide* for suggestions regarding the following:
- **Le disparu** (Dramatic episode)
- **Panorama Culturel** (Interviews)
- **Vidéoclips** (Authentic footage)

QUE SAIS-JE?

This page is intended to help students prepare for the test. It is a brief checklist of the major points covered in the chapter. The students should be reminded that this is only a checklist and does not necessarily include everything that will appear on the test.

Teaching Suggestion

Have partners answer all the questions in **Que sais-je?** Then, have them write humorous skits in which all of the elements in **Que sais-je?** appear. For example, John asks Mary about her weekend (#1), and then Mary asks John about a recent trip he took (#2). Then, Mary talks about her last trip (#3). She talks about the unusual things that happened during her vacation, and John responds with disbelief (#4). Finally, John and Mary discuss the next trip they're going to take and ask and answer each other's questions about tourist information (#5 and #6). Have the pairs present the skits to the class.

◆ For Individual Needs

6 Slower Pace Have students organize the information in chart format to help them as they do this activity.

Can you ask for opinions? p. 144

Can you express enthusiasm, indifference, and dissatisfaction? p. 144

Can you express disbelief and doubt? p. 148

Can you ask for and give information? p. 152

Can you use what you've learned in the chapter?

1 How would you ask . . . *Possible answers:*
  1. how your friend's weekend was? C'était comment, ton week-end?
  2. how your friend liked what he or she did? Ça t'a plu?
  3. if your friend had fun? Tu t'es bien amusé(e)?

2 You're just back from a trip, and your friend asks you how it was. How would you respond if you had visited these places? See answers below.

1. 2. 3.

3 How would you tell what you did on your last vacation and how you liked it?

4 How would you respond if your friend told you . . . See answers below.
  1. she got lost in the dungeon while visiting a castle?
  2. he saw the ghost of Francis I arguing with Leonardo da Vinci?
  3. she found 100 gold coins in the gardens at Chenonceau?
  4. he just inherited the château of Azay-le-Rideau?

5 How would you find out . . . See answers below.
  1. the cost of a round-trip ticket to your destination?
  2. which platform the train leaves from?
  3. at what time the train leaves?
  4. when a place opens and closes?
  5. how much it costs to get into a place?

6 Can you tell someone . . . See answers below.
  1. at what times this museum opens?
  2. what time it closes in the spring?
  3. what the regular entrance fee is?
  4. what the fee for teenagers is?

7 Can you ask for the information above?
See answers below.

> (Musée Archéologique de l'Hôtel Goüin) 25 rue de Commerce - Tél. 47.66.22.32
> Du 1er février au 14 mars et du 1er octobre au 30 novembre de 10h à 12h30 et de 14h à 17h30, fermé le vendredi. Tous les jours du 15 mars au 14 mai de 10h à 12h30 et de 14h à 18h30. Du 15 mai au 30 septembre de 10h à 19h. Entrée : Plein tarif : 18 F - Groupes + 15 pers. et 3e âge : 15 F - Enfants de 7 à 18 ans : 12 F - Scolaires : 5 F.

158 *cent cinquante-huit*   CHAPITRE 6   A nous les châteaux!

Possible answers

2 1. C'était sensas!
  2. Je me suis beaucoup amusé(e)!
  3. C'était pas mal.
4 1. Pas possible!
  2. Mon œil!
  3. C'est pas vrai!
  4. Tu plaisantes!

5 1. Combien coûte un aller-retour pour Paris?
  2. De quel quai est-ce que le train part?
  3. A quelle heure est-ce que le train part?
  4. A quelle heure est-ce que vous ouvrez et fermez?
  5. Combien coûte l'entrée?
6 1. Le musée ouvre à dix heures.
  2. Le musée ferme à douze heures trente et à dix-huit heures trente.
  3. 18 francs
  4. 12 francs

7 1. A quelle heure est-ce que le musée ouvre?
  2. A quelle heure est-ce que le musée ferme au printemps?
  3. Combien coûte l'entrée?
  4. Combien coûte l'entrée pour les enfants de treize à dix-huit ans?

PREMIERE ETAPE

Asking for opinions; expressing enthusiasm, indifference, and dissatisfaction

C'était comment? *How was it?*
C'était... *It was . . .*
  magnifique *beautiful*
  incroyable *incredible*
  superbe *great*
  sensas *sensational*
  assez bien *OK*
  comme ci, comme ça *so-so*
  pas mal *all right*
  ennuyeux *boring*
  mortel *deadly dull*
  nul *lame*
  sinistre *awful*
Ça t'a plu? *Did you like it?*

Ça m'a beaucoup plu. *I really liked it.*
Mouais. *Yeah.*
Sûrement pas! *Definitely not!*
Tu t'es amusé(e)? *Did you have fun?*
Je me suis beaucoup amusé(e). *I had a lot of fun.*
Plus ou moins. *More or less.*
Je me suis ennuyé(e). *I was bored.*

Activities

assister à un spectacle son et lumière *to attend a sound and light show*
faire un pique-nique *to have a picnic*

visiter un parc d'attractions *to visit an amusement park*
faire un tour sur la grande roue *to ride on the ferris wheel*
faire un tour sur les montagnes russes *to ride on the roller coaster*
faire un circuit des châteaux *to tour some châteaux*
faire une visite guidée *to take a guided tour*
monter dans une tour *to go up in a tower*
visiter un zoo *to visit a zoo*
donner à manger aux animaux *to feed the animals*

For Individual Needs

Challenge Have students create a crossword puzzle that uses the verbs in the **Vocabulaire**. Students might give clues for the meaning of a verb found in the puzzle. (**C'est le contraire de «monter».**) They might also create incomplete sentences as clues to indicate that either the helping verb, the past participle, or the subject pronoun is found in the puzzle. (**Les filles sont ____ (aller). Christian ____ venu avec moi. ____ suis sorti avec mes amis.**)

DEUXIEME ETAPE

Expressing disbelief and doubt

Tu plaisantes! *You're joking!*
Pas possible! *No way!*
Ça m'étonnerait. *I doubt it.*
C'est pas vrai! *You're kidding!*
N'importe quoi! *That's ridiculous!*
Mon œil! *Yeah, right!*

Verbs

entrer *to enter*
venir *to come*
rester *to stay*
monter *to go up*
descendre *to go down*
partir *to leave*
sortir *to go out*
rentrer *to go back (home)*
revenir *to come back*

retourner *to return*
naître *to be born*
devenir *to become*
mourir *to die*

CHAPTER 6 ASSESSMENT

CHAPTER TEST
• *Chapter Teaching Resources, Book 2,* pp. 85–90
• *Assessment Guide,* Speaking Test, p. 30
• *Assessment Items, Audiocassette 7B Audio CD 6*

TEST GENERATOR, CHAPTER 6

ALTERNATIVE ASSESSMENT

Performance Assessment
You might want to use the **Jeu de rôle** (p. 157) as a cumulative performance assessment activity.

Portfolio Assessment
• **Written:** Activity 23, *Pupil's Edition,* p. 149
  Assessment Guide, p. 19
• **Oral:** Activity 28, *Pupil's Edition,* p. 152
  Assessment Guide, p. 19

MIDTERM EXAM
• *Assessment Guide,* pp. 35–42
• *Assessment Items, Audiocassette 7B Audio CD 6*

TROISIEME ETAPE

Asking for and giving information

A quelle heure est-ce que le train (le car) pour... part? *What time does the train (the bus) for . . . leave?*
De quel quai? *From which platform?*
Du quai... *From platform . . .*

A quelle heure est-ce que vous ouvrez (fermez)? *What time do you open (close)?*
Combien coûte... ? *How much is . . . ?*
un aller-retour *a round-trip ticket*

un aller simple *a one-way ticket*
C'est combien, l'entrée? *How much is the entrance fee?*
Je voudrais... *I'd like . . .*
Un..., s'il vous plaît. *A . . . , please.*
...tickets, s'il vous plaît. *. . . (entrance) tickets, please.*

Game

LE JEU DU PENDU Have partners play *Hangman.* One student draws on a piece of paper a scaffold from which a man will hang and lines to represent the number of letters in any word or expression from the **Vocabulaire**. The other student calls out letters in French that he or she thinks might appear in the word or expression. If correct, the opponent fills in that letter wherever it occurs in the word or expression. If the letter doesn't occur in the word or expression, the opponent draws a part of the man (a head, torso, two arms, and two legs). If the drawing is completed first, no point is scored. If the word or expression is completed first, the student who guessed the letters gets a point.

Chapitre 7 : En pleine forme
Chapter Overview

Mise en train pp. 162–164	Trop de conseils		Practice and Activity Book, p. 73		*Video Guide* OR *Videodisc Guide*

	FUNCTIONS	GRAMMAR	CULTURE	RE-ENTRY
Première étape pp. 165–169	Expressing concern for someone; complaining, p. 165	Reflexive verbs in the **passé composé,** p. 168	• **Note Culturelle,** Pharmacies in France, p. 167 • **Rencontre Culturelle,** Figures of speech, p. 169	Expressing doubt
Deuxième étape pp. 170–175	• Giving advice; accepting and rejecting advice, p. 173 • Expressing discouragement; offering encouragement, p. 174	The pronoun **en** with activities, p. 172	• Realia: Schedule of activities offered at **Gymnase Club,** p. 170 • **Note Culturelle,** Teens' exercise habits, p. 171 • Realia: *Le sport et les jeunes* (brochure excerpt), p. 171 • **Panorama Culturel,** Staying healthy, p. 175	• Telling how often you do something • Sports activities • Pronunciation: the [r] sound
Troisième étape pp. 176–179	Justifying your recommendations; advising against something, p. 178	The verb **se nourrir,** p. 177	• Realia: *Des astuces pour bien se nourrir* (brochure), p. 176 • **Note Culturelle,** Mineral water, p. 176 • Realia: **Test Super-forme!** (health quiz), p. 177 • Realia: Government health poster, p. 179	Food vocabulary

Lisons! pp. 180–181	Sports à la carte		Reading Strategy: Paraphrasing

Review pp. 182–185	Mise en pratique, pp. 182–183	Que sais-je? p. 184	Vocabulaire, p. 185

Assessment Options	**Etape Quizzes**
	• *Chapter Teaching Resources, Book 2*
	  Première étape, Quiz 7-1, pp. 135–136
	  Deuxième étape, Quiz 7-2, pp. 137–138
	  Troisième étape, Quiz 7-3, pp. 139–140
	• *Assessment Items, Audiocassette 8A/Audio CD 7*
		Chapter Test
		• *Chapter Teaching Resources, Book 2,* pp. 141–146
		• *Assessment Guide,* Speaking Test, p. 31
		• *Assessment Items, Audiocassette 8A/Audio CD 7*
		
		Test Generator, Chapter 7

Video Program OR *Expanded Video Program, Videocassette 3*
OR *Videodisc Program, Videodisc 4A*

Textbook Audiocassette 4A/Audio CD 7

RESOURCES: Print	**RESOURCES: Audiovisual**

Textbook Audiocassette 4A/Audio CD 7

Practice and Activity Book, pp. 74–76
Chapter Teaching Resources, Book 2
• Teaching Transparency Master 7-1, pp. 119, 122 . . . . *Teaching Transparency 7-1*
• Additional Listening Activities 7-1, 7-2, p. 123 . . . . *Additional Listening Activities, Audiocassette 10A/Audio CD 7*
• Realia 7-1, pp. 127, 129
• Situation Cards 7-1, pp. 130–131
• Student Response Forms, pp. 132–134
• Quiz 7-1, pp. 135–136 . . . . *Assessment Items, Audiocassette 8A/Audio CD 7*
Videodisc Guide . . . . *Videodisc Program, Videodisc 4A*

Textbook Audiocassette 4A/Audio CD 7

Practice and Activity Book, pp. 77–79
Chapter Teaching Resources, Book 2
• Communicative Activity 7-1, pp. 115–116
• Teaching Transparency Master 7-2, pp. 120, 122 . . . . *Teaching Transparency 7-2*
• Additional Listening Activities 7-3, 7-4, p. 124 . . . . *Additional Listening Activities, Audiocassette 10A/Audio CD 7*
• Realia 7-2, pp. 128, 129
• Situation Cards 7-2, pp. 130–131
• Student Response Forms, pp. 132–134
• Quiz 7-2, pp. 137–138 . . . . *Assessment Items, Audiocassette 8A/Audio CD 7*
Video Guide . . . . *Video Program* OR *Expanded Video Program, Videocassette 3*
Videodisc Guide . . . . *Videodisc Program, Videodisc 4A*

Textbook Audiocassette 4A/Audio CD 7

Practice and Activity Book, pp. 80–82
Chapter Teaching Resources, Book 2
• Communicative Activity 7-2, pp. 117–118
• Teaching Transparency Master 7-3, pp. 121, 122 . . . . *Teaching Transparency 7-3*
• Additional Listening Activities 7-5, 7-6, p. 125 . . . . *Additional Listening Activities, Audiocassette 10A/Audio CD 7*
• Realia 7-2, pp. 128, 129
• Situation Cards 7-3, pp. 130–131
• Student Response Forms, pp. 132–134
• Quiz 7-3, pp. 139–140 . . . . *Assessment Items, Audiocassette 8A/Audio CD 7*
Videodisc Guide . . . . *Videodisc Program, Videodisc 4A*

Practice and Activity Book, p. 83

Video Guide . . . . *Video Program* OR *Expanded Video Program, Videocassette 3*
Videodisc Guide . . . . *Videodisc Program, Videodisc 4A*

Alternative Assessment
• Performance Assessment
  Première étape, p. 168
  Deuxième étape, p. 174
  Troisième étape, p. 179
• Portfolio Assessment
  Written: Activity 37, *Pupil's Edition,* p. 179
    Assessment Guide, p. 20
  Oral: Activity 38, *Pupil's Edition,* p. 179
    Assessment Guide, p. 20

For Student Response Forms, see *Chapter Teaching Resources, Book 2,* pp. 132–134.

Première étape

6 Ecoute! p. 165

1. — Salut, Edouard. Ça ne va pas?
   — Oh, j'ai mal à la tête.
   — Tu devrais boire de l'eau et prendre de l'aspirine.

2. — Et bien, Jérôme, qu'est-ce que tu as?
   — J'ai un rhume. Je n'arrête pas d'éternuer, et j'ai le nez qui coule.
   — Pauvre vieux!

3. — Jean-Claude. Jean-Claude! Psst! Tu n'as pas l'air en forme, toi. Quelque chose ne va pas?
   — Oh, j'ai mal dormi hier soir. J'ai passé une nuit blanche.
   — Tu devrais te reposer!

Answers to Activity 6
1. b   3. c
2. a   d. J'ai mal à la gorge.

9 Ecoute! p. 166

1. — Et vous, qu'est-ce que vous avez?
   — Aïe, j'ai mal aux dents!

2. — Qu'est-ce que vous avez?
   — J'ai mal au bras et à la main. Je jouais au foot pendant le cours de sport et je suis tombé.

3. — Qu'est-ce qu'il y a?
   — J'ai fait de la natation hier, et maintenant, j'ai vraiment mal à l'oreille.

4. — Qu'est-ce que vous avez?
   — J'ai joué au volley pendant le cours de sport, et maintenant, j'ai mal à la main.

Answers to Activity 9
1. d 2. c, b 3. a 4. b

13 Ecoute! p. 168

1. On a pas mal de clients ce matin! D'abord, quelqu'un s'est foulé la cheville en faisant une randonnée.

2. Et il y a quelqu'un qui s'est fait mal au coude, mais ça va maintenant.

3. Il y a aussi quelqu'un qui s'est coupé le doigt, mais ce n'est pas grave.

Answers to Activity 13
1. Véronique 2. Fatima 3. Tranh

Deuxième étape

19 Ecoute! p. 172

1. — Salut, Josée. Dis, qu'est-ce que tu fais comme sport?
   — Ben, moi, j'aime surtout faire du jogging. J'en fais deux ou trois fois par semaine. Quelquefois, je fais aussi de l'aérobic.

2. — Et toi, Christelle?
   — Le mardi et le jeudi, je fais de la gymnastique, et je fais de la musculation trois fois par semaine.

3. — Khalid, qu'est-ce que tu fais comme sport?
   — J'aime faire de la natation de temps en temps. En ce moment, je m'entraîne tous les jours au football américain.

Answers to Activity 19
Josée: jogging two or three times a week, aerobics sometimes
Christelle: gymnastics twice a week, weight lifting three times a week
Khalid: swimming from time to time, football every day

23 Ecoute! p. 173

1. — Ben, Bertrand, tu dois vraiment te mettre en condition. Pourquoi tu ne joues pas au tennis avec moi?
   — Oh, je n'ai pas le temps! En plus, je déteste le sport.

2. — Hélène? Ça n'a pas l'air d'aller.
   — Je suis toute raplapla.
   — Mais tu n'es pas en forme! Tu pourrais faire de l'exercice, faire de la gymnastique. C'est génial!
   — C'est une bonne idée. Peut-être que j'irai à la MJC demain.

3. — Ça va, Michel?
   — Non, je n'ai pas bien dormi hier soir.
   — Tu devrais peut-être te coucher plus tôt.
   — Tu as raison. Ce soir, je me couche à neuf heures!

4. — Tu sais, Cécile, tu devrais faire du sport. Pourquoi tu ne fais pas de la musculation ou au moins de l'exercice? On peut en faire ensemble!
   — C'est gentil, mais ce n'est pas mon truc, la musculation.

Answers to Activity 23
1. refuse   3. accepte
2. accepte 4. refuse

26 Ecoute! p. 174

SABRINA Salut, Emile.

EMILE Salut, Sabrina. On commence?

SABRINA Oui, alors, tu vois, je commence par des pompes. Voilà, je te montre comment on fait. J'en fais... cinq. Alors... une, deux, trois, quatre... Et cinq! Ouf!

EMILE Bon. A mon tour. J'en fais cinq aussi! Une, deux, trois,... Oh, je n'en peux plus!

SABRINA Tu y es presque!

EMILE quatre...

SABRINA Encore un effort!

EMILE cinq!

Answers to Activity 26
Sabrina encourage Emile.

Troisième étape

32 Ecoute! p. 177

1. — Et toi, Marie-Ange, tu te nourris bien?
   — Bof. Je ne sais pas. Je suis toujours pressée, donc, je saute souvent le petit déjeuner.
   — Est-ce que tu grignotes entre les repas?
   — Oui, des frites ou des chips. Mais au moins je ne mange jamais de confiseries; je n'aime pas ça.

2. — Tu crois que tu te nourris bien, Ali?
   — Oui, je mange toujours des crudités, et je bois deux litres d'eau par jour. Je fais aussi beaucoup de sport.
   — Tu grignotes entre les repas?
   — Oui, mais c'est toujours des fruits.

3. — Et toi, Philippe, tu te nourris bien?
   — Ben, je ne sais pas. Je mange souvent du riz et des pâtes pour avoir de l'énergie. J'évite de manger des produits riches en matières grasses.
   — Tu grignotes entre les repas?
   — Oui, malheureusement, j'adore les pâtisseries!

Answers to Activity 32
Good habits: Ali, Philippe
Bad habits: Marie-Ange, Philippe
Ali is the healthiest.

35 Ecoute! p. 178

JULIE Mais qu'est-ce que tu as, David? Tu n'as pas l'air en forme!

DAVID Je me sens tout raplapla.

JULIE Alors, ça te fera du bien de m'accompagner au gymnase.

DAVID Quoi, faire de l'exercice? Non, c'est pas mon truc, ça.

JULIE On peut jouer au tennis, alors. Le tennis, c'est une bonne façon de se mettre en condition.

DAVID D'accord, d'accord. Un match, c'est tout.

JULIE Et après, tu devrais venir manger végétarien chez moi. Manger beaucoup de légumes, c'est bon pour la santé!

DAVID Bonne idée. J'aime bien les légumes... mais pas de petits pois, d'accord?

JULIE D'accord. Et tu devrais boire beaucoup d'eau... tiens, bois de l'eau minérale. C'est meilleur que le coca! Tu devrais éviter les boissons sucrées!

DAVID Merci. Alors, on va le faire, ce match?

Answers to Activity 35
De l'accompagner au gymnase, de manger beaucoup de légumes, de boire beaucoup d'eau, d'éviter les boissons sucrées

Mise en pratique

4 p. 183

Venez au Centre Equilibre Santé! Vous voulez vous mettre en forme et vous reposer en même temps? Chez nous, on offre des activitiés pour tous. On vous proposera un programme individuel en fonction de vos possibilités physiques : musculation, gymnastique, natation et des exercices de relaxation. Après, le sauna et les massages sont à votre disposition. Si vous téléphonez maintenant, on vous propose des excursions spéciales : choisissez l'excursion rafting, l'équitation ou le vélo tout terrain. Téléphonez maintenant pour profiter de ces excursions à prix spécial! Combattez le stress! Vous deviendrez une nouvelle personne!

Answers to Mise en practique Activity 4
1. weightlifting, gymnastics, swimming, relaxation exercises
2. sauna and massage
3. rafting, horseback riding, mountain biking
4. call now

Chapitre 7 : En pleine forme
Projects

A votre santé!
(Cooperative Learning Project)

ASSIGNMENT

In groups of four, students will create a "slide" presentation to promote a ficticious health resort. Each group will choose a leader, a writer, a proofreader, and an artist. Although all group members will participate in all aspects of the project, they will each serve as a leader in a particular area and delegate tasks to other group members. Students are to imagine they work for a spa or health resort in the United States. As employees, their job is to recruit clients by highlighting in a slide presentation all the features and activities the resort offers. They are to send slides and an audiocassette to health resorts in France in order to attract potential visitors to the United States. The slides will actually be transparencies that students draw and project on the overhead projector.

MATERIALS

✄ **Students may need**
- Transparencies
- Colored transparency pens
- An audiocassette
- An audiocassette recorder

SUGGESTED SEQUENCE

1. The groups name their resort, choose its location, and invent an address and phone number.

2. The group members decide what features to highlight in their presentation. They should describe the meals served and the activities offered, and tell how each is beneficial to the participants.

3. Students write the script for the presentation, keeping in mind which sections they would like to illustrate with slides. If some groups need more guidelines in writing their scripts, have them refer to the **Comment dit-on... ?** and **Grammaire** boxes on pages 165, 166, 168, 171, 173, 174, 177, and 178 for expressions and structures. All group members proofread and edit the script. Each member might be responsible for proofreading one section of the text or the entire text. Students write a final draft and hand it in.

4. Correct the scripts using correction symbols (see Projects page, Chapter 5). While you correct their papers, students should prepare the transparencies and the audiocassette. Students might use background music or sound effects in their recording as long as it doesn't render their speech inaudible. Students might complete the recording outside of class. If students don't have access to an audiocassette recorder, they should arrange a time to use one before or after school.

5. Students hand in a final copy before the presentation.

6. One or more of the members may change the slides during the presentation as the recording is playing. Students may wish to include an auditory signal in the recording that indicates when it's necessary to change slides.

GRADING THE PROJECT

Each group should receive a collective grade based on content, accuracy of written work, and creativity and overall presentation. Group members should receive individual grades based on comprehensibility, and effort and participation in the project. You might have the class suggest grades for the content and overall quality of the presentations. Each group might also suggest grades for its members on individual effort and participation.

Suggested Point Distribution (total = 100 points)

Content	20 points
Accuracy of written work	20 points
Creativity/presentation	20 points
Comprehensibility	20 points
Effort/participation	20 points

CHARADES

In the two games on this page, students will practice the vocabulary and expressions from this chapter.

Procedure   On separate slips of paper, write all the expressions from the **Vocabulaire** on page 185. Form teams of five. A player from one team goes to the front of the room and draws a slip of paper. The player mimes the word or expression written on the paper for his or her team members, who call out their guesses. (**Qu'est-ce que tu as?** or **J'ai mal au dos.**) The object of the game is to use the least amount of time to get your team members to say the word or expression. Time students, using a watch or a stopwatch. Keep score by recording the number of seconds it takes a team to guess the correct word or expression. If a team cannot guess the word or expression in one minute, record a score of sixty seconds. In this case, you might give other teams a chance to erase five seconds from their total by trying to guess the word or expression. As the ultimate bonus, you might give the team that guesses correctly the opportunity to subtract ten seconds from their score by writing the word or expression correctly on the board. The team with the least amount of recorded time after a set number of rounds is the winner.

MEMOIRE

Procedure   Choose several expressions from the **Vocabulaire** for the **Première étape** on page 185. Write each expression on two separate index cards. Distribute one card to every student, except for two to six students that you ask to serve as the players in front of the class. These players take turns asking the others **Quelque chose ne va pas?** or **Qu'est-ce que tu as?** The object of the game is for players to find two students who respond in the same way (**J'ai un rhume**), according to the expression written on their card. When a player finds two students in the class who answer in the same way, he or she collects their cards. When all of the cards have been collected, the player who holds the most cards wins.

Chapitre 7
En pleine forme
pp. 160–185

Using the Chapter Opener

Motivating Activity

Ask students why it is important to be concerned with good eating habits and exercising. Ask if they admire the physical condition of an athlete and to imagine how rigorous his or her exercise routine or diet must be.

Photo Flash!

① Ask students what game the girls are playing in Photo 1 (soccer). Soccer was introduced to France in 1890 and has since become the most popular sport there. Each year, the French Federation of Soccer organizes championships and the **Coupe de France.** Its final match is attended by the president of France. There are two million soccer players in France, of whom 650 are professionals. French soccer enthusiasts can choose from among 20,000 soccer clubs.

Teaching Suggestion

Gather magazine pictures of healthful food, tired-looking people, and energetic people playing sports. Have students look at the three photos in the Chapter Opener and help them understand the captions by using gestures and synonyms. Then, hold up the pictures one at a time and have students suggest the caption that best relates to each one.

CHAPITRE

7
En pleine forme

① Tu devrais faire du sport!

160   cent soixante

Staying in good health and physical condition is important. Although you can't avoid getting sick from time to time, you can stay healthy and energetic by eating right and exercising while still having fun with your friends!

In this chapter you will learn

- to express concern for someone; to complain
- to give, accept, and reject advice; to express discouragement; to offer encouragement
- to justify your recommendations; to advise against something

And you will

- listen to friends giving advice about health and sports
- read about different sports
- write a health brochure
- find out what people in francophone countries do to stay in shape

② C'est bon pour toi!

③ Je suis tout raplapla.

161

Focusing on Outcomes

Have students look at the photos and say as much as they can about them in French. Then, have them match the photos with the outcomes listed. NOTE: You may want to use the video to support the objectives. The self-check activities in **Que sais-je?** on page 184 help students assess their achievement of the objectives.

Photo Flash!

② The French generally eat fruits and vegetables at both lunch and dinner. Even busy working families tend to buy and prepare fresh produce rather than frozen or canned goods. Children are generally accustomed to eating salads, vegetables, and fruit or yogurt at lunchtime, since many return home for a long lunch.

③ Point out to students the caption for this photo that reads **Je suis tout raplapla.** The word **raplapla** comes from the word **raplati,** meaning *flattened.* Other related French words are **plat** *(flat)*; **l'eau minérale plate** *(flat, non-carbonated mineral water);* **à plat-ventre** *(lying flat);* and **un plateau** *(a flat tray, raised flat surface, plateau).*

Culture Note

The French pride themselves not only on the freshness and high quality of the ingredients they use in their cooking, but also on the presentation of their dishes, which they consider just as important. For a large majority of French people, cuisine is an art form as well as a ritual, with its own rules and methods that must be followed. The French culinary tradition dates to the Renaissance, and the first restaurants to the French Revolution. Since the beginning of the nineteenth century, literary figures have written about French food. Berchoux wrote a poem entitled *La gastronomie,* and Brillat-Savarin wrote the celebrated work on gastronomy, *La physiologie du goût.* Because of these works and others, French cuisine gained world-wide recognition.

VIDEO PROGRAM
OR EXPANDED VIDEO
PROGRAM,
Videocassette 3
01:25–05:07

OR VIDEODISC PROGRAM,
Videodisc 4A

Search 1, Play To 6670

Video Synopsis

In this segment of the video, Céline, Bruno, and Hector are at a café. Bruno complains that he is not feeling well. Céline and Hector show their concern by asking him about his diet, if he's exercising, and whether he's getting enough sleep. Hector suggests that Bruno join him in working out at the gym. At the gym, Hector helps Bruno warm up and do some weight training. While they are practicing some aerobic exercises, Bruno twists his ankle. Hector tries to help, but Bruno is fed up with all of his friends' suggestions.

Motivating Activity

Draw two columns on the board or on a transparency and label them **De bonnes habitudes** and **De mauvaises habitudes.** Ask students to name all the good and bad health habits they can think of. Write their suggestions in the appropriate column. You may wish to provide the French equivalents for the expressions they give.

Mise en train

Trop de conseils

What do you do when you're feeling out of sorts? Look at the photos and read the story to see what kind of advice Bruno gets from his friends.

Bruno   Céline   Hector

162   *cent soixante-deux*   CHAPITRE 7   En pleine forme

RESOURCES FOR MISE EN TRAIN
Textbook Audiocassette 4A/Audio CD 7
Practice and Activity Book, p. 73
Video Guide
  Video Program
  Expanded Video Program, Videocassette 3
Videodisc Guide
  Videodisc Program, Videodisc 4A

Culture Note

Most of the gymnasiums and sports complexes in France **(les salles et les centres de sport)** that offer aerobics, body-building, water aerobics, and weightlifting have been created only in recent years.

Au gymnase...

Tiens, pourquoi tu ne viens pas avec moi au gymnase?

Au début, il faut s'échauffer. Doucement, il ne faut pas forcer. Va à ton propre rythme.

6

7

Ensuite, il faut tonifier les muscles... Un peu plus haut!

Je n'en peux plus!

Encore un effort. Tu y es presque.

On fait de l'aérobic pour élever le rythme cardiaque.

Ouf! Je suis déjà crevé.

Courage!

9

8

Aïe!

Tu peux marcher? Tu devrais mettre une compresse froide dessus.

Ecoute! J'en ai marre de tes conseils!

Ça va, Bruno?

Non, pas terrible. J'ai mal à la cheville.

Mais, ça te fera du bien.

10

11

MISE EN TRAIN

cent soixante-trois **163**

You may choose to continue with **Trop de conseils (suite)** or wait until later in the chapter. When the story continues, Bruno is at home with his ankle bandaged. Céline and Hector bring him a cake and fruit juice. They are trying to help, but Hector bumps Bruno's foot and Céline spills cake on Bruno's new pants. Bruno tries to be gracious, but he's glad when Céline and Hector finally leave!

Video Integration

- *EXPANDED VIDEO PROGRAM,* Videocassette 3, 05:08–09:17
- *VIDEODISC PROGRAM,* Videodisc 4A

Search 6670, Play To 14125

Presentation

To begin, have students view the video with their books closed. Then, play the recording and have students read along. Next, have them read the text aloud in pairs. Ask the questions in Activity 1 on page 164. Finally, ask questions such as **Qui n'est pas en pleine forme? Est-ce qu'il mange bien? Est-ce qu'il fait de l'exercice? Qui lui donne des conseils? Est-ce qu'ils lui donnent trop de conseils?**

For Individual Needs

Challenge/Auditory Learners Type the text of the **Mise en train,** changing some of the words and numbering the lines. For example, for the first line, instead of **Eh bien, qu'est-ce que tu as, Bruno?,** type **Alors, qu'est-ce que tu vois, Annick?** As a listening exercise, play the recording and have students cross out each word on the typed copy of the text that is different from what they hear. Play the recording again and have them write the words they hear in place of the words they crossed out. Pause the recording frequently to allow time for corrections.

Additional Practice

For additional speaking practice after completing the Challenge activity above, project a transparency of your revised version of the **Mise en train** on the overhead projector, and have students tell you what changes they made. (A la première ligne, ce n'est pas Alors, c'est Eh, bien; ce n'est pas vois, c'est as; ce n'est pas Annick, c'est Bruno. A la ligne deux,...) Make the changes on the transparency as students suggest them so that all can check their papers.

For Individual Needs

2 Auditory Learners
Read this activity aloud and have volunteers answer. For non-auditory learners, you might give students the option of looking at their books as you read aloud.

For videodisc application, see *Videodisc Guide.*

Teaching Suggestion

4 Have students select additional quotations and take turns with a partner reading them aloud to one another and trying to guess who the speaker is.

Thinking Critically

5 Synthesizing Ask students if they might have a conversation with their friends similar to the one Céline and Hector had with Bruno. Why or why not? Ask them what they think of offering unsolicited advice to a friend. Is it acceptable or wise to do so? Why or why not?

Drawing Inferences Ask students if they think Americans are concerned with their diet because of health or for other reasons. Ask them to imagine why these French teenagers are so concerned about their friend's health.

Language Note

To help students understand and remember the verb **sauter** *(to skip, to jump),* point out that we use this word in English *(to sauté vegetables).* (When vegetables are sautéed, the hot butter or oil makes them jump around in the pan.) Call students' attention to the difference in pronunciation between the French **sauté** and the English *sauté.*

1 Tu as compris? See answers below.

1. How does Bruno feel at the beginning of the story?
2. What three things do Céline and Hector ask him about?
3. What do they suggest to help him feel better?
4. Where do Hector and Bruno go? What do they do there?
5. How does Bruno feel at the end of the story?

2 Fais ton choix

Complète ces phrases d'après **Trop de conseils.**

1. Bruno s'est couché vers...
   a. dix heures.
   b. onze heures et demie.
   c. minuit.

2. Au petit déjeuner, Bruno...
   a. a mangé une pomme.
   b. a mangé des céréales.
   c. n'a rien mangé.

3. D'après Céline, il est important de...
   a. se coucher tard.
   b. bien se nourrir.
   c. sauter des repas.

4. Bruno fait du sport...
   a. rarement.
   b. souvent.
   c. de temps en temps.

5. D'après Hector, pour élever le rythme cardiaque, il faut...
   a. s'échauffer.
   b. tonifier les muscles.
   c. faire de l'aérobic.

6. Bruno s'est fait mal...
   a. à la main.
   b. à la cheville.
   c. à la tête.

3 Cherche les expressions See answers below.

What does Céline or Hector say to . . .
1. find out what is wrong with Bruno?
2. give him advice?
3. justify their advice?
4. offer encouragement?

What does Bruno say to . . .
5. tell how he's feeling?
6. express his discouragement?
7. complain about an injury?
8. express his annoyance with his friend?

4 Qu'est-ce qu'ils disent? 1. b 2. c 3. a 4. d

1.   2.   3.   4.

a. «Il est important de bien se nourrir.»
b. «Je me sens tout raplapla.»
c. «J'ai sauté le petit déjeuner ce matin.»
d. «On doit tonifier ses muscles.»

5 Et maintenant, à toi

What do you think of the advice Bruno's friends gave him? What would you advise Bruno to do? How do you react when your friends give you advice about your health?

Answers

1 1. tired
2. what's wrong, what time he went to bed, whether he ate breakfast that morning
3. Don't skip meals. Eat a balanced diet with lots of fruits and vegetables.
4. to a gym; ride stationary bicycles, lift weights, do aerobics
5. He is fed up with his friend's advice.

3 1. Qu'est-ce que tu as?
2. Tu ne dois pas sauter les repas. Mange des fruits et des légumes. Tu ferais bien de t'entraîner. Tu devrais faire de l'exercice. Pourquoi tu ne viens pas avec moi au gymnase? Ça te fera du bien.
3. C'est bon pour toi.
4. Encore un effort. Tu y es presque! Courage!
5. Je me sens tout raplapla. Je suis fatigué. J'ai mal dormi.
6. Je n'en peux plus. Ouf! Je suis déjà crevé!
7. J'ai mal à la cheville.
8. J'en ai marre de tes conseils.

PREMIERE ETAPE

Expressing concern for someone; complaining

COMMENT DIT-ON... ?

Expressing concern for someone; complaining

To express concern for someone:

Quelque chose ne va pas? *Is something wrong?*

Qu'est-ce que tu as? *What's wrong?*

Tu n'as pas l'air en forme. *You don't look well.*

To complain:

Je ne me sens pas bien. *I don't feel well.*

Je suis tout(e) raplapla. *I'm wiped out.*

J'ai mal dormi. *I didn't sleep well.*

J'ai mal partout! *I hurt all over!*

VOCABULAIRE

Je suis malade.	*I'm sick.*
J'ai mal au cœur.	*I'm sick to my stomach.*
J'ai...	*I have . . .*
un rhume.	*a cold.*
la grippe.	*the flu.*
des allergies.	*allergies.*
mal à la tête.	*a headache.*
mal à la gorge.	*a sore throat.*
le nez qui coule.	*a runny nose.*

6 Ecoute!

Listen to Lucien's friends complain about how they feel. Match the person's name with his picture. What would the person in the remaining picture say?

1. Edouard   2. Jérôme   3. Jean-Claude

a. 2   b. 1

c. 3   d. J'ai mal à la gorge.

RESOURCES FOR PREMIERE ETAPE

Textbook Audiocassette 4A/Audio CD 7
Practice and Activity Book, pp. 74–76
Videodisc Guide
  Videodisc Program, Videodisc 4A

Chapter Teaching Resources, Book 2
• Teaching Transparency Master 7-1, pp. 119, 122
  Teaching Transparency 7-1
• Additional Listening Activities 7-1, 7-2, p. 123
  Audiocassette 10A/Audio CD 7
• Realia 7-1, pp. 127, 129
• Situation Cards 7-1, pp. 130–131
• Student Response Forms, pp. 132–134
• Quiz 7-1, pp. 135–136
  Audiocassette 8A/Audio CD 7

Jump Start!

Have students list the communicative objectives from page 161 and find an expression in the **Mise en train** to illustrate each one.

MOTIVATE

Ask students what they say in English to show their concern for a friend who is not feeling well. Ask them how they can tell when someone is not feeling well.

TEACH

Presentation

Comment dit-on... ? Prepare three students in advance to express concern for you, using the expressions from **Comment dit-on... ?** Use facial expressions and gestures as you answer them with complaints. Have the class repeat after you and mimic your gestures. Then, express concern for students, and have them complain as you did.

Vocabulaire Act out these illnesses, using gestures and props to convey their meaning. Have students repeat after you and mimic your gestures. Assign individuals certain illnesses. (**Joël, tu as un rhume.**) As they act out their illness, ask the others **Qu'est-ce qu'il/elle a? Il/Elle a mal à la gorge ou un rhume?**

For videodisc application, see *Videodisc Guide.*

For Individual Needs

Kinesthetic Learners Say an expression of complaint or illness. (**Tu as un rhume.**) Have students respond by making an appropriate gesture or facial expression.

PREMIERE ETAPE

Teaching Suggestions

• Do Activities 7 and 8 first, and then present the **Vocabulaire.** Finally, do Activity 9.

8 Circulate among the students and eavesdrop on their conversations. Ask individuals **Pauvre vieux/vieille, qu'est-ce que tu as?** When they answer, offer some advice. **(Bois du jus d'orange.)**

Presentation

Vocabulaire Teach the French word **le bras** by pointing to your arm and having students repeat as they touch their arm. Continue in this manner for other parts of the body. Then, use a doll to teach various ailments by making several cause-and-effect statements. **(Elle a fait du jogging, et maintenant, elle a mal aux pieds.)** Point to where the doll hurts. Then, have the doll run into things or fall and have students tell where the doll hurts. Finally, describe a situation **(Elle est allée chez le dentiste.)** and have students describe the doll's ailment suggested by the situation. **(Elle a mal aux dents.)**

❖ For Individual Needs

Visual/Tactile/Auditory Learners Have groups of students draw people with various ailments on index cards. Have them write a description of the ailment on the back of the card. **(Il/Elle a mal au dos.)** Have group members take turns showing the pictures to the group. The others in the group must tell what's wrong with the person shown on the card. Have students show the reverse side of the ____ help visual learners.

---

7 **Tu n'as pas l'air en forme!**

Tu n'as pas l'air en forme aujourd'hui et ton ami(e) te demande ce que tu as. Qu'est-ce que tu réponds si... See answers below.

1. tu t'es couché(e) à deux heures du matin?
2. tu es allergique aux chats?
3. tu es fatigué(e)?
4. tu as besoin d'aspirine?
5. tu éternues *(sneeze)* et tu as le nez qui coule?
6. tu es allé(e) au championnat de foot hier soir et tu as beaucoup crié?
7. tu as la grippe?

8 **C'est pas de chance, ça!**

You came to school sick today. Your friend responds sympathetically to your complaints and tells you what to do. Act out the scene, and then reverse roles.

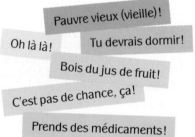

Pauvre vieux (vieille)!

Oh là là!   Tu devrais dormir!

Bois du jus de fruit!

C'est pas de chance, ça!

Prends des médicaments!

9 **Ecoute!**

Listen as several students talk to the pharmacist. Where are their aches and pains?
1. d   2. c, b   3. a   4. b

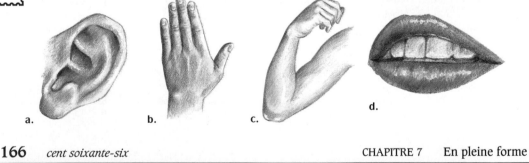

a.   b.   c.   d.

166 *cent soixante-six*   CHAPITRE 7   En pleine forme

VOCABULAIRE

J'ai mal partout!
J'ai mal...

à l'oreille (f.)

au cou

au bras

aux dents (f.)

au dos

au ventre

à la main

au pied

à la jambe

Building on Previous Skills

Review the preposition **à** and its contractions **au** and **aux.** Then, name a part of the body using a definite article **(le dos).** Have students say that they have an ache or pain there, using the correct form of **à. (J'ai mal au dos.)**

TPR Give students commands to follow, such as **Touchez votre pied droit avec la main gauche.** Then, have students write commands to give their classmates.

Possible answers

7 1. Je suis tout(e) raplapla.   5. J'ai un rhume.
  2. J'ai des allergies.   6. J'ai mal à la gorge.
  3. J'ai mal dormi.   7. J'ai mal partout.
  4. J'ai mal à la tête.

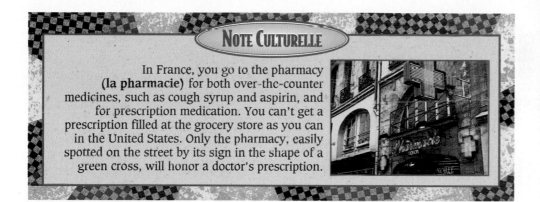

NOTE CULTURELLE

In France, you go to the pharmacy **(la pharmacie)** for both over-the-counter medicines, such as cough syrup and aspirin, and for prescription medication. You can't get a prescription filled at the grocery store as you can in the United States. Only the pharmacy, easily spotted on the street by its sign in the shape of a green cross, will honor a doctor's prescription.

For Individual Needs

10 Visual Learners/ Slower Pace Write the questions on a transparency and project them on the overhead. Have a student come up to the projector and call on volunteers to answer the questions. The student-teacher should then write the answers beside or underneath each question.

10 Challenge Have students work in groups and write each cause and its effect on separate index cards. **(J'ai mangé trop de pizza. J'ai mal au ventre.)** Challenge them to invent additional causes for pains or aches and their effects. Then, have them pass the shuffled cards to another group, who will match the causes to the effects.

10 J'ai mal à...

Qu'est-ce qui te fait mal si... See answers below.

1. tu as mangé trop de pizza?
2. tu as joué au volley-ball toute la journée?
3. tu as fait cent abdominaux *(sit-ups)*?
4. tu as passé deux heures à faire du jogging?
5. tu as dansé jusqu'à minuit?
6. tu as passé la nuit à étudier?
7. tu es allé(e) chez le dentiste?
8. tu es assis(e) tout près des enceintes *(speakers)* à un concert de rock?

11 Jacques a dit

Your group leader tells you where you ache: **Vous avez mal au dos.** The group acts it out, but only if the leader begins by saying **Jacques a dit.** You're out if you act out a pain when the leader doesn't say **Jacques a dit.** The winner becomes the next leader.

12 Aïe! J'ai mal partout!

You worked out last night and now you're sore all over. When your friend asks how you are, complain about all that hurts. Your friend should react sympathetically. Then, reverse roles.

À la française

When you're not feeling well or when you hurt yourself accidentally, say **Aïe!** *(Ow!)* or **Ouille!** *(Ouch!)*. When you've finished doing something physically difficult, say **Ouf!** *(Whew!)*.

VOCABULAIRE

Qu'est-ce qui t'est arrivé?

Presentation

Vocabulaire Using small strips of an old bedsheet, bandage your elbow, leg, ankle, and finger. Pointing to the bandages, act out the expressions and have students repeat after you. You may wish to use a crutch and bandage to help illustrate the different verbs or add context, such as **Ce weekend, j'ai fait du ski, et je me suis cassé la jambe.** Then, ask students to substitute other parts of the body in each expression. **(Je me suis cassé le bras.)** Finally, hand out the bandages, ask students to create their own injuries, and circulate around the room, asking individuals **Qu'est-ce qui t'est arrivé?** Allow them to look at their books as they respond.

Possible answers

10 1. le ventre
2. les mains, les bras
3. le ventre
4. les jambes, les pieds
5. les jambes, les pieds
6. la tête, les yeux, le dos
7. les dents
8. les oreilles

Language Note

Point out that you use the definite article, not the possessive adjective, with parts of the body after the verbs **se couper, se casser,** and **se fouler. (Je me suis cassé la jambe.)**

Additional Practice

13 Have students listen to the recording again and ask them the following questions: **Qu'est-ce que Véronique faisait quand elle s'est foulé la cheville? Fatima va mieux? L'accident de Tranh est grave ou pas?**

Presentation

Note de grammaire On strips of transparency, write the sentences in the **Note de grammaire** in large letters and cut them apart into words. Guide volunteers through the process of putting the sentences together. Explain the difference between **Elle s'est coupée** and **Elle s'est coupé le doigt.** Afterwards, you might have small groups complete a similar exercise, using photocopied sentence strips cut apart into words.

CLOSE

Group Work

Form groups of five and have each group write on separate index cards 25 expressions from the **Comment dit-on... ?** and **Vocabulaire** sections of this **étape** that relate to an injury or illness. Have each student in the group make five line drawings of a human figure on a sheet of paper. One student chooses five cards and reads them to the group. **(Il a mal au dos. Il a un rhume.)** The other group members draw the injuries or illnesses described on their human figures. Afterwards, students should take turns explaining the injuries and illnesses of each person in their drawings. The student who reads the cards should compare what the members say with what is written on the card. Each group member chooses and reads five cards.

---

13 **Ecoute!**   Answers on p. 159C.

You're helping out the nurse at a **colonie de vacances** this summer. Listen as she tells you about the patients who have come in this morning. Which of the people in the **Vocabulaire** on page 167 is she talking about? Fatima? Guy? Véronique? Tranh?

14 **Comme la vie est dure!**

Accidents will happen! Complete these sentences in as many ways as you can.

1. Quand mes amis et moi sommes allés faire du ski, je n'ai pas eu de chance! Je me suis cassé __?__ .   la jambe, le bras...

2. Mon amie faisait la cuisine et elle s'est coupé __?__ .   le doigt

3. A la fin de la soirée, mon meilleur ami s'est foulé __?__ .   la cheville

4. En rentrant chez moi, je me suis fait mal __?__ .   au dos, au pied...

15 **Le maladroit**

Ton ami Pascal a passé un mauvais week-end. Qu'est-ce qui lui est arrivé? Complète ce paragraphe.

J'ai passé un week-end épouvantable! D'abord, vendredi,
je _(... me suis foulé la cheville)_ , donc je n'ai pas pu aller faire du ski avec mes copains. Ensuite, samedi
après-midi, je faisais un sandwich quand je _(... me suis coupé le doigt)_ . Et c'est
pas tout! Samedi soir, en entrant dans ma chambre,
je _(... me suis fais mal à la jambe)_ . Dimanche, j'allais répondre au téléphone quand je suis
tombé dans l'escalier et je _(... me suis cassé le bras)_ . Je craque, moi!

16 **Qu'est-ce qui s'est passé?**

You phone a friend to find out why he or she didn't meet you after school. Your friend says he or she is hurt and tells you what's wrong. React with sympathy, or react with doubt if you think your friend is making excuses. Make your conversation humorous or serious. Then, reverse roles.

Si tu as oublié how to express doubt va à la page 148.

168   *cent soixante-huit*   CHAPITRE 7   En pleine forme

Note de Grammaire

- Many of the verbs you use to tell about injuries are reflexive. They follow the same pattern in the past tense as other reflexive verbs you've learned:

  Je **me suis cassé** la jambe.
  Nous **nous sommes cassé** la jambe.
  Tu **t'es cassé** le doigt.
  Vous **vous êtes cassé** le bras.
  Elle **s'est cassé** la cheville.
  Ils **se sont cassé** les doigts.

- When a direct object follows a reflexive verb, the past participle does not change:

  Elle s'est **coupée.**
  but
  Elle s'est **coupé** le doigt.

ASSESS

Quiz 7-1, *Chapter Teaching Resources, Book 2,* pp. 135–136

Assessment Items, Audiocassette 8A Audio CD 7

Performance Assessment

Use Activity 16 as an assessment activity for this **étape.** Have each pair present their phone conversation to the class. You might grade the students on accuracy, comprehensibility, originality, and effort.

RENCONTRE CULTURELLE

1. Elle a un chat dans la gorge.
2. Il a pris ses jambes à son cou!
3. Ça coûte les yeux de la tête!
4. Tu me casses les pieds!

Qu'en penses-tu?

1. How would you translate these expressions literally? Can you figure out what the expressions mean figuratively? What would the English equivalents be?
2. Think of expressions like these in English. Then, find out what they are in French.

Savais-tu que... ?

Different cultures sometimes use very different images to convey the same idea. Did you figure out the English equivalents of the French expressions above?

1. Literal meaning:
She's got a cat in her throat.
English equivalent:
She's got a frog in her throat.
2. Literal meaning:
He took his legs to his neck.
English equivalent:
He ran like the wind.
3. Literal meaning:
It costs the eyes from the head.
English equivalent:
It costs an arm and a leg.
4. Literal meaning:
You're breaking my feet!
English equivalent:
You're a pain in the neck!

Teaching Suggestion

Have students try to match the following figures of speech and their equivalents: **Il n'a pas mis le nez dehors de la journée.** (Il n'est pas sorti pendant toute la journée.) **Ils se sont bouffé le nez.** (Ils se sont fâchés.) **Il a la langue bien pendue.** (Il parle beaucoup.) **Je donne ma langue au chat.** (Dis-moi la réponse. Je ne peux plus deviner.) **Il conduit comme un pied.** (Il conduit très mal.) **Ils sont comme dos et chemise.** (Ils sont très bons amis.) **Il a fait ça les deux doigts dans le nez.** (Il a fait ça facilement.) **Il a le cœur sur la main.** (Il est très généreux.) **Il a réussi haut la main.** (Il a réussi facilement.) **La moutarde me monte au nez.** (Je suis très fâché(e).)

RENCONTRE CULTURELLE
CHAPITRE 7

Motivating Activity

Have students recall expressions in English that use parts of the body. *(My eye! My foot! You're pulling my leg! My eyes are bigger than my stomach. I put my foot in my mouth. I made it by the skin of my teeth. Could you give me a hand? He cut off his nose to spite his face. You're shooting yourself in the foot.)* Ask students how such expressions add to a language. (They make it more expressive and colorful.) Ask why students should learn these kinds of expressions in a foreign language. (It makes their informal speech more authentic.)

Presentation

For each illustration, ask **Qu'est-ce que ça veut dire?** and prompt students to give an explanation of the expression in French. (**Elle ne peut pas parler. Il va très vite. C'est très cher. Elle l'embête.**) Then, ask the questions in **Qu'en penses-tu?**

For Individual Needs

Visual Learners Have students draw or find descriptive or humorous pictures to illustrate the idioms on the pupil's page as well as those listed in the Teaching Suggestion at the bottom of this page. Have them write the idiom below their illustration. You might display the pictures in the classroom.

Language Arts Link

Point out that the figures of speech on this page are called *idiomatic expressions* and cannot be translated literally.

DEUXIEME ETAPE

Giving, accepting, and rejecting advice; expressing discouragement; offering encouragement

Place d'Italie Centre Italie II, 14, rue Vandrezanne 13ᵉ / 45.80.34.16

Heures d'ouverture : du lundi au vendredi de 8 H à 22 H. Samedi de 8 H à 19 H. Dimanche de 9 H à 17 H.

[Brochure: Circuit Gymnase Club — Entraînement individuel - Plan d'entraînement personnalisé établi par votre professeur. Cardio-training, circuit training, exercices d'abdominaux et d'assouplissement. Musculation — Plan d'entraînement personnalisé établi par votre professeur. Culture physique, Relaxation, Danse, Arts martiaux, Sports de combat, Sports aquatiques, Détente schedules. Piscine - Bains à remous - Sauna - Hammam - UVA* - Bar* - Restaurant*.]

Ces horaires sont indicatifs et susceptibles de modifications. Renseignez-vous à l'accueil.

17 A lire avec attention   See answers below.

1. What's the purpose of this brochure?
2. How many major categories are there? What are they?
3. In the courses listed under each category, find at least four words that come from English. Can you guess what the other courses are?
4. What do you think **Détente** means, judging from the activities listed next to it?

18 Qu'est-ce qu'on choisit?   1. **a.** en bleu **b.** en rouge **c.** en vert

1. Au Gymnase Club, est-ce qu'on choisit les cours en vert, en bleu, ou en rouge...
   a. pour se tonifier les muscles?   **b.** si on est déjà en forme?   **c.** si on est stressé(e)?
2. Tu choisis quelles activités? A quel niveau? Quels jours? Pourquoi?

NOTE CULTURELLE

There has been a growing interest among French teenagers in both individual and team sports. Although there are no athletic teams that represent the **lycées**, students can join informal teams in their town or city. Many students have some sort of regular athletic activity, and some belong to private sports clubs like **Gymnase Club**. People can also take a variety of dance, martial arts, and weight-training classes at the **Maison des jeunes et de la culture (MJC).**

LE SPORT ET LES JEUNES

60% des jeunes français font du sport : 37% en font régulièrement, 16% pratiquent de temps en temps, 5% rarement, 2% pendant les vacances seulement. Trois jeunes sur dix font partie d'une association sportive. Les jeunes ont tendance à faire plus de sport depuis quelques années: un jeune sur deux fait régulièrement de la gymnastique ou du jogging. 28% pratiquent régulièrement un sport individuel (athlétisme, judo, natation, tennis, ski) et 33% un sport d'équipe. Les sports les plus populaires sont le football (45%) et la natation (31%) puis le jogging et la gymnastique (27%).

VOCABULAIRE

Qu'est-ce que tu fais pour te mettre en condition?

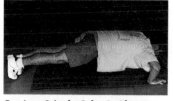

Quelquefois, **je fais de l'exercice. J'aime faire des pompes.**

Moi, **je fais de la musculation.**

Moi, **je fais des abdominaux** tous les jours!

Moi, **je fais** souvent **de la gymnastique.**

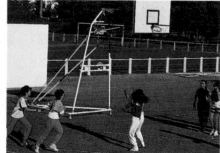

Moi, **je m'entraîne au** basket.

Je fais de l'aérobic deux fois par semaine.

Health Link

Obtain from the health or physical education teacher a chart that gives the number of calories burned per hour doing various physical activities. Have students calculate how many calories the people in the photos would burn in an hour doing the activities pictured. Some students may want to calculate how many calories they burn in a week according to their own physical activity.

Math Link

Once students have finished their calculations (see Health Link), have them draw a graph demonstrating the relationship between physical activity and calories burned and have them write an explanation in French. Students might also use the sports statistics in the **Note Culturelle** on this page to create a graph showing the percentages of young French people who engage in various sports.

Teaching Suggestions

21 Have students include in their sentences how often these athletes must do certain activities to stay in condition. (**Il doit faire de la musculation trois fois par semaine.**)

22 Ask for volunteers to comment on the most physically active person they talked to. (**Paul est très sportif. Il fait du jogging quatre fois par semaine. Il s'entraîne au basket trois fois par semaine, et il fait des pompes tous les jours.**)

Presentation

Note de grammaire Write the questions and answers from the **Note de grammaire** in large letters on strips of posterboard and cut them into words. Have students in front of the class form a question with the words. (**Tu fais de la natation?**) Ask an individual that question. When the person answers, have the students rearrange themselves to form the response, starting with **Je**, taking out **de la natation**, and adding **en** and perhaps **n'... pas** in the appropriate places. (**Je n'en fais pas.**) Repeat the process with other questions and answers.

Additional Practice

Have students conduct a chain activity in which they ask each other whether they participate in certain sports activities and answer, using the pronoun **en** or an expression of frequency. One student begins by asking **Tu fais de la musculation, Sophie?** Sophie answers **Non, je n'en fais pas** or **Oui, j'en fais _souvent_**. Sophie then asks a student another question, and so on. You might list sports or activities on the board to prompt students.

19 Ecoute! Answers on p. 159C.

a. Simone asked her friends Josée, Christelle, and Khalid what they do to keep in shape. What does each person do?
b. Listen again to Josée, Christelle, and Khalid and write down how often they do each activity.

Tu te rappelles ?

Here are some expressions you've already learned to tell how often you do something:
Je m'entraîne à la natation **tous les jours.**
Je fais de l'exercice **trois fois par semaine.**
Je joue au tennis **deux fois par mois.**
Je **ne** fais **jamais** d'aérobic.
Je fais de la gymnastique **le lundi** et **le jeudi.**

20 Sportif ou pas?

Décris ce que ta famille, tes amis et toi, vous faites comme sports. Choisis un mot ou une expression dans chaque boîte et fais des phrases.

Je	faire de la musculation	tous les jours
Ma mère/mon père	faire de l'aérobic	deux fois par semaine
Ma meilleure amie	faire du jogging	ne... jamais
Mon meilleur ami	faire des abdominaux	le week-end
Ma sœur/mon frère	faire de la gymnastique	le matin
Avec l'équipe de..., on...	faire de l'exercice	l'après-midi
___?___	s'entraîner au/à la...	le soir
	___?___	___?___

21 Les sportifs See answers below.

Qu'est-ce qu'ils doivent faire pour se mettre en condition?

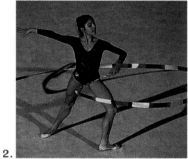

1.   2.   3.

22 Tu en fais souvent?

Est-ce que tes camarades de classe sont en forme? Fais une liste de cinq sports et activités. Ensuite, demande à trois de tes camarades s'ils en font et s'ils en font souvent. Qui est le plus sportif?

— Tu fais de la gymnastique?
— Oui.
— Tu en fais souvent?
— Ben... deux fois par semaine.

Note de *G*rammaire

You can use **en** to replace a phrase beginning with **de la, du, de l'**, or **des** that refers to an activity:

—Tu fais **de la natation?**
—Non, je n'**en** fais pas. Et toi?
—Moi, j'**en** fais souvent.

Possible answers
21 1. Il doit s'entraîner au football américain tous les jours. Il doit faire de la musculation, des abdominaux et des pompes.
2. Elle doit faire de la musculation, de la danse et de l'aérobic.
3. Ils doivent faire de la danse et de la musculation. Ils doivent s'entraîner au patin.

COMMENT DIT-ON... ?
Giving, accepting, and rejecting advice

To give advice:

Tu dois te mettre en condition.
You've got to . . .

Tu devrais faire du sport.
You should . . .

Tu ferais bien de t'entraîner au basket.
You would do well to . . .

Tu n'as qu'à te coucher plus tôt.
All you have to do is . . .

Pourquoi tu ne fais **pas** de la gymnastique?
Why don't you . . . ?

To accept advice:

Tu as raison.
Bonne idée!
D'accord.

To reject advice:

Je ne peux pas.
Non, je n'ai pas très envie.
Non, je préfère faire de la musculation!
Pas question!
Je n'ai pas le temps.
I don't have time.
Ce n'est pas mon truc.
It's not my thing.

23 Écoute!

Olivier donne des conseils à ses amis. Est-ce qu'ils acceptent ou refusent ses conseils? Answers on p. 159C.

24 Tu ferais bien de... See answers below.

Donne des conseils à tes amis.

1. Jean-Paul s'est endormi pendant le cours de maths.
2. Cam ne peut pas porter ses gros livres.
3. Arnaud a grossi pendant l'hiver.
4. Mireille est crevée à la fin de la journée.
5. Raoul a des difficultés à monter l'escalier.
6. André ne peut pas toucher ses pieds.

Tu te rappelles ?

When you're pronouncing the French **r**, keep the tip of your tongue pressed against your lower front teeth. Arch the back of your tongue upward, almost totally blocking the passage of air in the back of your throat. Practice by saying **tu ferais** and **tu devrais.** Then try **tu as raison, très envie,** and **mon truc.**

25 Tu devrais t'entraîner!

Ton ami(e) ne se sent pas bien. Demande-lui comment il ou elle va. Ensuite, va à la page 170 et conseille-lui de faire deux activités au **Gymnase Club.** Faites un emploi du temps sportif pour une semaine.

DEUXIEME ETAPE

cent soixante-treize **173**

Presentation

Comment dit-on... ? On separate strips of transparency, write several sentences that state a health problem, give advice, and either accept or reject advice. Color-code the sentences according to the function they serve. For example, write **Je suis tout raplapla** (stating a health problem) in black, **Tu n'as qu'à te coucher plus tôt** (giving advice) in green, **Tu as raison** (accepting advice) in blue, and **Je ne peux pas** (rejecting advice) in red. Arrange the strips to form conversations, read them, and have students repeat after you. Then, ask students which sentences state a health problem (black), which ones give advice, and so on. Finally, place the strips randomly on the overhead projector and have students rearrange them to form other conversations.

Teaching Suggestion

Have each student write a complaint from the **Première étape** on a sheet of paper and pass it to a classmate. The classmate writes a reply, giving some advice from **Comment dit-on... ?** and passes it back. The first student then writes back, accepting or rejecting the advice. Allow students to continue their correspondence as long as they can. Circulate around the classroom, checking the notes. You might read humorous ones to the class.

Possible answers

24 1. Tu devrais te coucher plus tôt.
2. Tu ferais bien de faire de la musculation.
3. Pourquoi tu ne fais pas de l'exercice?
4. Tu n'as qu'à te coucher plus tôt.
5. Tu dois te mettre en condition.
6. Pourquoi tu ne fais pas de la gymnastique?

Additional Practice

24 For additional listening practice to help auditory learners, you might first read the sentences aloud with students' books closed.

Presentation

Comment dit-on... ?

Prepare four students ahead of time to offer you encouragement, using the expressions in **Comment dit-on... ?** Do three aerobic activities for fifteen seconds each. As you give up on each one, express your discouragement. After each activity, the four students will encourage you. Then, show magazine pictures of people who are exhausted, discouraged, or frustrated. (Students could gather these in advance for extra credit points.) For each picture, ask **Qu'est-ce qu'il/elle dit?** When a student responds **J'abandonne,** for example, ask another student **Tu peux l'encourager?**

For videodisc application, see *Videodisc Guide.*

CLOSE

To close this **étape,** draw or gather several pictures of people engaged in physical activity, some who are out of shape or tired, and some who are discouraged. Show the pictures and ask a variety of questions about them in order to elicit the functional expressions from this **étape.** For example, for a picture of someone doing push-ups, ask **Qu'est-ce qu'il fait? Combien de fois par semaine est-ce qu'il en fait?** For a picture of a tired person, say **Il ne dort pas assez. Quels conseils est-ce que tu lui donnes?** For a picture of someone studying very hard, ask **Qu'est-ce qu'il se dit?** and **Qu'est-ce que tu peux lui dire pour l'encourager?** and so on.

COMMENT DIT-ON... ?
Expressing discouragement; offering encouragement

To express discouragement:	To offer encouragement:
Je n'en peux plus!	**Allez!** *Come on!*
I just can't do any more!	**Courage!** *Hang in there!*
J'abandonne. *I give up.*	**Encore un effort!** *One more try!*
Je craque! *I'm losing it!*	**Tu y es presque!** *You're almost there!*

26 Ecoute!

Sabrina et Emile sont au gymnase. Qui encourage qui? Answers on p. 159D.

27 Qu'est-ce qu'ils disent? *Possible answers:*

1. Encore un effort!/Je n'en peux plus!

2. J'abandonne./Courage!

3. Allez! Tu y es presque!

28 Allez-y, allez-y!

Write a cheer for your favorite team.

29 Les copains d'abord

Chaque personne dans ton groupe est découragée pour une des raisons suivantes. Les autres l'encouragent et lui donnent des conseils. Joue la scène avec trois de tes camarades.

Vocabulaire à la carte

Allez, les bleus!	*Go, blue team!*
A bas les verts!	*Down with the green team!*
Vivent les rouges!	*Hurray for the red team!*
Ecrasez-les!	*Crush them!*
gagner	*to win*
l'équipe	*the team*
marquer un (des) point(s)	*to score*
marquer un but	*to make a goal*

Je me sens tout(e) raplapla et je n'arrive pas à dormir.

Je voudrais être en forme mais je n'aime pas le sport.

Mon équipe de football ne gagne jamais.

Je suis toujours en retard pour l'école le matin et mes notes ne sont pas très bonnes.

ASSESS

Quiz 7-2, *Chapter Teaching Resources, Book 2,* pp. 137–138

Assessment Items, Audiocassette 8A Audio CD 7

Performance Assessment

To assess students' performance for this **étape,** have them create a dialogue that incorporates as many of the functions and as much of the vocabulary of this **étape** as possible. For example, have them imagine a doctor's visit. One partner is the patient who complains of some injury or ailment; the other partner is the doctor who gives advice and recommends treatment. You may wish to have students submit a written copy as well.

PANORAMA CULTUREL

Mélanie • Québec

Patricia • Québec

Sébastien • France

We asked some francophone people what to do to stay in shape. Here's what they had to say.

Qu'est-ce qu'il faut faire pour être en forme?

«Pour être en forme, il faut faire beaucoup d'exercice. Il faut bien manger. C'est important. Et après ça, il faut... Moi, j'ai un régime alimentaire... Il faut faire très attention à ce qu'on mange et puis il faut se coucher de bonne heure. Il faut dormir.»

—Mélanie

«Alors, il faut pratiquer au moins un sport ou une activité physique trois fois par semaine, à raison d'une heure à la fois et de façon assez intensive.»

Qu'est-ce qu'il faut éviter de manger?

«Eh bien, des chips, du chocolat, des liqueurs, des choses comme ça. Il faut surtout s'alimenter avec des fruits, des légumes, manger de la viande en portion réduite, etc.»

—Patricia

«Pour être en forme, je fais beaucoup de sport. Surtout du basket, du foot et du tennis. Sinon, je mange bien, le petit déjeuner surtout, et voilà.»

—Sébastien

Qu'en penses-tu?

1. What do these people do to stay healthy?
2. What else might someone do to stay in shape?
3. In your opinion, what is a healthy lifestyle?
   1. exercise, participate in sports, play basketball, soccer, and tennis, eat fruits and vegetables, eat breakfast and eat less meat, avoid unhealthy food, go to bed early

Questions

1. Qui dit qu'il faut beaucoup dormir pour être en forme? (Mélanie)
2. D'après Patricia, qu'est-ce qu'il faut éviter de manger ou de boire? (des chips, du chocolat, des liqueurs)
3. Selon Patricia, qu'est-ce qu'il faut manger? (des fruits, des légumes, de la viande en portion réduite)
4. Quels sports est-ce que Sébastien fait pour être en forme? (du basket, du foot et du tennis)

Community Link

If there is a gym, fitness club, or community center that offers sports activities in your town, have a group of students visit one and interview people who attend. Have them find out why people exercise and what else they do to stay healthy. Other groups could interview student athletes. Have the groups report the information to the class and compare their answers with those of Mélanie, Patricia, and Sébastien.

PANORAMA CULTUREL
CHAPITRE 7

VIDEO PROGRAM OR EXPANDED VIDEO PROGRAM, Videocassette 3 09:18–13:30

OR VIDEODISC PROGRAM, Videodisc 4A

Search 14125, Play To 17395

Teacher Notes

- See *Video Guide, Videodisc Guide,* and *Practice and Activity Book* for activities related to the **Panorama Culturel.**
- Remind students that cultural material may be included in the Chapter Quizzes and Test.
- The interviewees' language represents informal, unrehearsed speech. Occasionally, edits have been made for clarification.

Motivating Activity

Ask students the same questions that the interviewees answer. Write their responses on the board or on a transparency.

Presentation

Show the video and ask students what they can tell about each interviewee. Then, have them compare the interviewees' responses with those that were compiled in the Motivating Activity.

Thinking Critically

Analyzing Ask students which they think is more important, looking good or feeling good, and why. Ask how the media can influence our attitudes about feeling or looking good.

Jump Start!

Ask students to imagine they have a friend who has very unhealthy habits. Have them write five sentences, offering the person advice on what to do to get in shape.

MOTIVATE

Bring a grocery store advertisement from the newspaper to class and have students name the foods that are healthful and those that aren't.

TEACH

Language Notes

• Have students deduce the meaning of the word **astuces** *(ways, tricks, tips)*. Point out that the word **trucs** *(things)* may be used to mean the same thing in informal conversation.

• Tell students that if they want tap water, they should ask for **une carafe d'eau** *(a pitcher of water)* or **de l'eau du robinet** *(tap water)*. In either case, the server will bring tap water served in a pitcher. If they just ask for **de l'eau,** the server may bring bottled water, which they will have to pay for.

For Individual Needs

30 Kinesthetic/Auditory Learners After students have read the realia and answered the questions, call out the foods mentioned in the realia and have students gesture thumbs-up if they should consume the food, or thumbs-down if they should avoid the food.

Possible answers

30 1. how to eat well
2. Foods You Should Eat Every Day
3. Foods You Should Avoid

TROISIEME ETAPE

Justifying your recommendations; advising against something

DES ASTUCES POUR BIEN SE NOURRIR

Chaque jour tu devrais consommer :	Tu devrais aussi éviter de :

Chaque jour tu devrais consommer :

• de la viande, du poisson ou des œufs.
• des pommes de terre, des pâtes, du riz.
• de l'eau (au moins 1,5 litre par jour).
• des fruits et des légumes.
• du lait.
• du pain.

Tu devrais aussi éviter de :

• grignoter entre les repas des produits riches en matières grasses (chips) ou en sucre (confiseries, gâteaux, pâtisseries).
• sauter des repas.
• rajouter du sel à tous les plats.

30 ## A lire avec attention

See answers below.

1. Look at the pictures in *Des astuces pour bien se nourrir.* What is the pamphlet about?
2. Now look at the list under **Chaque jour tu devrais consommer.** What English title would you give to this list?
3. Look at the pictures in the second category. What English title would you give to this list?

VIVE L'EAU

• boire 1,5 l d'eau par jour.
• c'est la seule vraie boisson zéro calorie.
• elle facilite l'élimination des toxines.
• elle contribue au fonctionnement du transit intestinal.
• certaines eaux minérales apportent des éléments indispensables au bon fonctionnement de l'organisme : magnésium, calcium,... ce qui limite les risques de carence en cas de régime.

NOTE CULTURELLE

Drinking mineral water has long been part of the French way of life. If you ask for mineral water in a restaurant, you have a choice of either carbonated (**gazeuse**) or non-carbonated (**plate**). You will also find that beverages are usually served without ice. If you want ice, ask for **des glaçons.**

RESOURCES FOR TROISIEME ETAPE

Textbook Audiocassette 4A/Audio CD 7
***Practice and Activity Book,** pp. 80–82*
Videodisc Guide
    Videodisc Program, Videodisc 4A

Chapter Teaching Resources, Book 2
• Communicative Activity 7-2, pp. 117–118
• Teaching Transparency Master 7-3, pp. 121, 122
    Teaching Transparency 7-3
• Additional Listening Activities 7-5, 7-6, p. 125
    Audiocassette 10A/Audio CD 7
• Realia 7-2, pp. 128, 129
• Situation Cards 7-3, pp. 130–131
• Student Response Forms, pp. 132–134
• Quiz 7-3, pp. 139–140
    Audiocassette 8A/Audio CD 7

VOCABULAIRE

On doit...	Everyone should . . .		Evitez de...	Avoid . . .
bien se nourrir.	eat well.		grignoter entre les repas.	snacking between meals.
manger des légumes.	eat vegetables.		sauter des repas.	skipping meals.
manger des pâtes.	eat pasta.		consommer trop de sucre,	eating too much sugar,
manger du riz.	eat rice.		de sel,	salt,
boire de l'eau.	drink water.		de matières grasses.	fat.
			suivre un régime trop strict.	following a diet that's too strict.

31 Le test super-forme

Est-ce que tu te nourris bien? Essaie ce petit test.

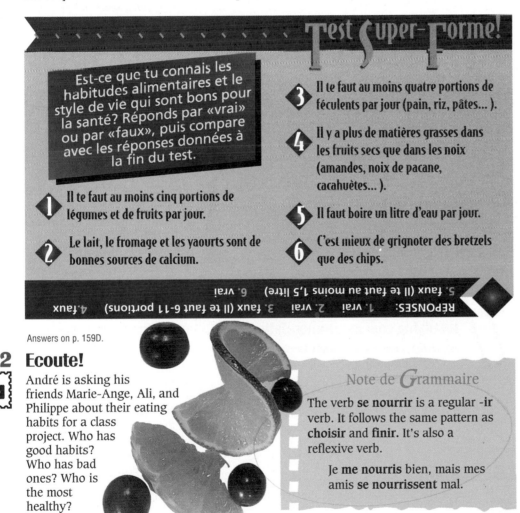

Test Super-Forme!

Est-ce que tu connais les habitudes alimentaires et le style de vie qui sont bons pour la santé? Réponds par «vrai» ou par «faux», puis compare avec les réponses données à la fin du test.

1. Il te faut au moins cinq portions de légumes et de fruits par jour.

2. Le lait, le fromage et les yaourts sont de bonnes sources de calcium.

3. Il te faut au moins quatre portions de féculents par jour (pain, riz, pâtes...).

4. Il y a plus de matières grasses dans les fruits secs que dans les noix (amandes, noix de pacane, cacahuètes...).

5. Il faut boire un litre d'eau par jour.

6. C'est mieux de grignoter des bretzels que des chips.

RÉPONSES: 1. vrai 2. vrai 3. faux (Il te faut 6-11 portions) 4. faux 5. faux (Il te faut au moins 1,5 litre) 6. vrai

Answers on p. 159D.

32 Ecoute!

André is asking his friends Marie-Ange, Ali, and Philippe about their eating habits for a class project. Who has good habits? Who has bad ones? Who is the most healthy?

Note de Grammaire

The verb **se nourrir** is a regular -ir verb. It follows the same pattern as **choisir** and **finir**. It's also a reflexive verb.

Je **me nourris** bien, mais mes amis **se nourrissent** mal.

TROISIEME ETAPE
cent soixante-dix-sept 177

Building on Previous Skills

- Tell students that **éviter, sauter,** and **consommer** are regular -er verbs. You might have students conjugate and use them in sentences for practice.
- Have students guess from the context what **la santé** (health) and **les féculents** (starchy food) mean. Then, tell students the meaning of **les noix** (nuts) and have them try to guess what **les amandes** (almonds) and **les noix de pacane** (pecans) are.

Teaching Suggestion

Note de grammaire Write the conjugations of **choisir** and **finir** on the board, and then write the infinitive **se nourrir** and the subject pronouns. Have one student write the reflexive pronouns next to the subject pronouns. Have another write the stem of the verb next to each reflexive pronoun. Have a third student write the ending of each verb form on the stem of the verb. All students should follow the same procedure on a sheet of paper.

Presentation

Vocabulaire Bring as many of the vocabulary items as possible to class. You might show and talk about sugar and butter, incorporating the new expressions. (**C'est du sucre. Où est-ce qu'on trouve du sucre? Dans les pâtisseries? Qu'est-ce qu'il y a d'autre dans les pâtisseries? Beaucoup de matières grasses? Pour bien se nourrir, il faut consommer beaucoup de sucre? Il faut consommer beaucoup de matières grasses?** and so on.) Then, have students draw two columns on a sheet of paper and label them **On doit...** and **Evitez de...** Make some recommendations preceded by a number. (**1. Manger beaucoup de sucre.**) Have students write the number of your statement in the appropriate column. Then, repeat your remarks and have volunteers say them, beginning with **On doit...** or **Evitez de...** (**Evitez de manger beaucoup de sucre.**)

For Individual Needs

32 Auditory Learners/ Challenge Have students draw a chart with three columns. In the first column, they write the names of the three friends, and they label the other two columns **De bonnes habitudes** and **De mauvaises habitudes.** Play the recording and have students write the good and bad habits mentioned in the appropriate columns. Then, project the same chart on a transparency and ask students how to fill it in.

— **Quelles sont les bonnes habitudes de Marie-Ange?**

— **Elle ne mange pas de confiseries.**

For Individual Needs

33 Slower Pace Before students look at this activity, read the letter as it should be, filling in the blanks with the words. Use pictures, gestures, and intonation to get the meaning across. Then, have students open their books and complete the paragraph.

34 Slower Pace Before students begin the activity, have them list their habits in one column and the changes they would like to make in another. Circulate to check their notes and offer help. Then, have them use their notes to write a paragraph.

Mon journal

34 For an additional journal entry suggestion for Chapter 7, see *Practice and Activity Book*, page 151.

Presentation

Comment dit-on... ? Hold up a vegetable or a picture of one and say **C'est bon pour toi!** with appropriate inflection and gesture. With the other hand hold up a picture of a cigarette and say **Ce n'est pas bon pour toi! Evite de fumer des cigarettes!** Present the remaining expressions in this manner, using additional pictures or objects.

For videodisc application, see *Videodisc Guide*.

Additional Practice

35 After students do this activity, have them write down all the expressions in **Comment dit-on... ?** Play the recording a second time and have students number the expressions in the order they occur in Julie and David's conversation.

---

33 Mes habitudes

Charlotte's dance instructor had her write a paragraph about her eating and exercise habits. Read the paragraph first. Then, fill in the blanks. See answers below.

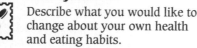

Je ne __1__ pas toujours très bien. Je n'aime pas __2__, donc, je ne mange pas trop souvent de bifteck; je préfère __3__: les spaghettis, par exemple. Je mange rarement des fruits et des __4__; je préfère les chips. Je suis souvent pressée, donc, je __5__ parfois le petit déjeuner ou le dîner. Mais au déjeuner, je prends toujours du poulet ou du poisson et je ne rajoute jamais de __6__ aux plats. Je n'aime pas trop les produits __7__ en __8__: les confiseries, les gâteaux. Mon faible, c'est les chips et les frites. Je suis assez sportive. Je fais de la natation deux __9__ par semaine et je joue quelquefois au foot avec des copains. Je n'ai jamais fait de danse, mais j'ai très envie de commencer un nouveau __10__ sportif!

34 Mon journal

Describe what you would like to change about your own health and eating habits.

Maintenant je saute le petit déjeuner mais je voudrais prendre des céréales et du lait. Je fais de la natation deux ou trois fois par mois. Je voudrais en faire plus souvent.

COMMENT DIT-ON... ?

Justifying your recommendations; advising against something

To justify your recommendations:
C'est bon pour toi. *It's good for you.*
Ça te fera du bien. *It'll do you good.*
C'est meilleur que de manger dans un fast-food. *It's better than . . .*

To advise against something:
Evite de fumer des cigarettes. *Avoid . . .*
Ne saute pas de repas. *Don't skip . . .*
Tu ne devrais pas te faire bronzer. *You shouldn't . . .*

35 Ecoute!

Julie et David sont au café. Ecoute leur conversation. Qu'est-ce que Julie conseille à David?
Answers on p. 159D.

Teaching Suggestion

Write the following examples on the board or on a transparency: <u>Manger des fruits</u>, c'est meilleur que de <u>manger des chips</u>. <u>Le poisson</u>, c'est meilleur que <u>la pizza</u>. Have students write five sentences substituting other verb phrases and nouns for what you've underlined. Ask volunteers to read some of their sentences aloud and have the class agree (**Je suis d'accord.**) or disagree. (**Je ne suis pas d'accord.**)

Language Note

Point out the difference between **C'est meilleur que de** + infinitive and **C'est meilleur que** + noun.

Answers

33 1. me nourris 6. sel
2. la viande 7. riches
3. les pâtes 8. sucre
4. légumes 9. fois
5. saute 10. programme

36 A toi de donner des conseils

Donne des conseils à ces gens. Qu'est-ce qu'ils devraient éviter de faire? Qu'est-ce qu'ils devraient faire? See answers below.

1.

2.

3.

37 En pleine forme!

Make your own health brochure! Draw pictures or use cutouts from magazines to show what people should do and what they should avoid.

Vocabulaire à la carte

se ronger les ongles	to bite one's nails
mâcher du chewing-gum	to chew gum
boire de l'alcool	to drink alcohol
fumer	to smoke
se faire bronzer	to get a tan

Sans tabac ça va!

Il n'y a pas de tabac sans dégats !

Alcool, ras-le-bol.

Jeu de vin, jeu de vilains

Céréales, on se régale
Légumes et fruits, c'est oui!

Je mange, donc je suis!

38 Jeu de rôle

Write down three habits that could harm an athlete's performance. Then, with a partner, act out a scene between an athlete who has those habits and his or her coach. The coach should advise the athlete against the three bad habits, suggest how the athlete can change, and justify the recommendations he or she makes.

Possible answers

36 1. Evite de fumer des cigarettes. Tu dois mâcher du chewing-gum.
2. Evite de te faire bronzer. Tu devrais mettre un tee-shirt.
3. Tu ne devrais pas manger des matières grasses. Mange de la salade. Ça te fera du bien.

Community Link

37 Have students display their posters in elementary or other schools. They might make their posters bilingual if French isn't offered at these schools.

Group Work

36 Form small groups and assign one photo to each group. Have the groups create a conversation between the person(s) shown in their photo and a friend. Have groups present their conversations to the class. The class should select the best conversation for each photo.

📁 **Portfolio**

37 Written This activity is appropriate for students' written portfolios.

38 Oral This activity is appropriate for students' oral portfolios. For portfolio suggestions, see *Assessment Guide*, page 20.

CLOSE

To close this **étape**, ask an artistic student to draw a picture of a person doing all the things listed in the **Vocabulaire à la carte.** Ask another to draw a picture of a person eating a variety of unhealthy foods. Make transparencies of both pictures and have the class give these people advice about what they should and should not do and then justify their advice.

ASSESS

Quiz 7-3, *Chapter Teaching Resources, Book 2,* pp. 139–140

Assessment Items, Audiocassette 8A/Audio CD 7

Performance Assessment

Use Activity 38 to assess students' performance for this **étape**. To get started, students might reread Charlotte's paragraph on page 178 and their journal entries from Activity 34. You might base students' oral grades on content, accuracy, variety of vocabulary, comprehensibility, creativity, and effort.

READING STRATEGY
Paraphrasing

Teacher Note

For an additional reading, see *Practice and Activity Book,* page 83.

PREREADING
Activity A

Motivating Activity

Ask students if they have ever been to the Olympic Games **(Les Jeux olympiques)** or if they have ever watched them on television. Ask them which of the sports shown here they have seen in the Olympic Games and which they prefer watching. Ask also if students participate or are interested in any of these sports.

READING
Activities B-G

Teaching Suggestion

B.–D. You may want to have students do these activities with a partner.

Culture Note

The Winter Olympic Games debuted in 1924 in Chamonix, France. In the winter of 1992, they were held in Albertville, France. Lausanne, Switzerland, is the home of the International Olympic Committee. Baron Pierre de Coubertin (1863–1937) was a French educator who was responsible for the reinstatement of the Olympic Games in 1896 after a 1,500 year hiatus. He had traveled to Greece where excavators were uncovering an ancient Olympic site and decided that the revival of the Olympic Games would ease world tensions. Therefore, he proposed the modern Olympic Games and became president of the International Olympic Committee.

---

*W*hich of these sports do you practice? Which would you like to try?

DE BONS CONSEILS
There is often more than one way to express an idea. Have you ever tried to explain something to a friend, only to be met with a confused look? You probably tried to explain again using different words. This technique, *paraphrasing,* can also help you when you read. If you can restate what you've just read in your own words, you can understand and remember what you've just read much better.

For Activities A, B, C, and D, see answers below.

A. How many sports are represented in these posters and what are they?

B. Each poster presents at least four categories of information. What are the categories? Which posters offer five categories? What is the fifth one?

C. Scan the posters to find the following information.
1. Which sport is the most popular in France? How do you know?
2. Which sports offer several different types of events?
3. Which sports do not have their headquarters in Paris?

D. Who is speaking in each poster? Scan the posters to find . . .
1. a gold medalist.
2. a silver medalist in Barcelona.
3. a bronze medalist.
4. a doctor.
5. a World Cup co-president.

180   *cent quatre-vingts*

Sports À La Carte

BASKET

- Particularités : C'est un sport qui compte de plus en plus d'adeptes, notamment grâce au succès du basket américain.
- Nombre de licenciés (adhérents à la Fédération française) : Près de 400 000.
- Adresse : Fédération française de basket-ball, 14, rue Froment, 75011 Paris.
- À lire : *Basket-ball,* de J.Chazalon et A. Gilles, éditions Amphora.
- «En basket, il faut beaucoup d'adresse, bien sûr, mais aussi de la rapidité et de la tonicité. Pour progresser, il faut aimer les sports techniques, car il y a beaucoup de règles à connaître.» (Frédéric Hufnagel, joueur professionnel.)

CYCLISME

- Particularités : Convient bien aux amoureux de la nature. Grand avantage : il peut être pratiqué partout ! Vélo de randonnée, VTT, cyclisme de compétition...
- Nombre de licenciés : 90 000.
- Adresse : Fédération française de cyclisme, 5, rue de Rome, 93561 Rosny-sous-Bois Cedex.
- À lire : *Vélo et cycles passion,* de R. Ballantine et R. Grant, éditions Hachette.
- «Le cyclisme, c'est une bonne école pour l'équilibre, pour la confiance en soi. C'est aussi un sport d'équipe.» (Patrick Nédélec, médecin fédéral du Tour de France.)

ATHLÉTISME

- Particularités : 3 disciplines : la course, le saut et le lancer, avec de multiples épreuves, en stade, et aussi parfois, en forêt. Age de début : 8-9 ans. On peut choisir sa spécialisation à partir de 13-15 ans.
- Nombre de licenciés : Plus de 130 000.
- Adresse : Fédération française d'athlétisme, 10, rue du Faubourg-Poissonnière, 75010 Paris.
- «La coureuse de 400 mètres doit être à la fois rapide et résistante. Moi, au collège, je courais plus vite que les autres. Alors j'ai travaillé, je me suis entraînée. J'adore la compétition.» (Marie-José Pérec, médaille d'or aux jeux Olympiques de Barcelone, en 1992.)

NATATION

- Particularités : la natation favorise un développement musculaire à la fois solide et harmonieux. Elle permet d'apprendre à mieux maîtriser sa respiration. Compétitions à partir de 10 ans.
- Nombre de licenciés : 150 000.
- Adresse : Fédération française de natation, 148, avenue Gambetta, 75020 Paris.
- «En natation, il faut être sérieux à l'entraînement, travailleur, généreux. Il faut essayer de bien nager techniquement, mais surtout, il faut aimer l'eau. A chaque entraînement, on a des sensations différentes. On sent son corps vivre.» (Catherine Plewinski, médaille de bronze à Barcelone.)

Answers

A eight; basketball, cycling, track and field, swimming, tennis, skiing, soccer, skating

B specifics of the sport, number of sports organization members, address, quotes; basketball, cycling, tennis; what to read

C 1. soccer; There are nearly 2 million organization members, and the article claims it's **le roi.**
2. track and field, skating, skiing
3. cycling, skiing

D 1. Marie-José Pérec
2. Isabelle Duchesnay
3. Catherine Plewinski
4. Patrick Nédélec
5. Michel Platini

Et si vous essayiez un nouveau sport ?
Voici 8 fiches pour vous aider à choisir.

TENNIS

- Particularités : C'est le «sport-phare». Pour éviter des problèmes de dos, complétez le tennis par un autre sport.
- Nombre de licenciés : Près de 1 400 000.
- Adresse : Fédération française de tennis, stade Roland-Garros, 2, avenue Gordon-Bennett, 75016 Paris.
- A lire : *Vous et le tennis*, éditions Larousse.
- «A chaque fois que je joue, je retrouve la joie de voir partir une balle avec une trajectoire bien nette. J'ai toujours du plaisir à faire un beau coup, surtout quand j'ai frappé d'instinct.» (Pascale Paradis, ancienne championne du monde junior.)

SKI

- Particularités : Trois disciplines : ski alpin, ski de fond, saut à ski. Pour le ski alpin, mieux vaut commencer le plus tôt possible !
- Nombre d'adhérents : 635 000.
- Adresse : Fédération française de ski, 50, rue des Marquisats, Boîte postale 2451, 74011 Annecy Cedex.
- «Le ski est un sport très complet, qui demande à la fois de la puissance et de l'agilité. Il faut prendre des risques. Il y a aussi la vitesse et, par-dessus tout, la glisse, cette sensation exceptionnelle.» (Franck Piccard, médaille d'argent aux jeux Olympiques d'Albertville, en 1992.)

FOOTBALL

- Particularités : C'est le sport-roi, évidemment. Le plus pratiqué, le plus télévisé, le plus commenté. Les filles sont encore peu nombreuses dans les clubs.
- Nombre de licenciés : Près de 2 millions.
- Adresse : Fédération française de football, 60 bis, avenue d'Iéna, 75016 Paris.
- «Je n'aurais jamais pu faire un sport individuel. J'aime trop vivre et partager avec les autres. Mon grand plaisir, c'était de m'entraîner avec mon équipe, de gagner avec elle, et, s'il le fallait, d'accepter ensemble nos défaites.» (Michel Platini, co-président de l'organisation de la Coupe du Monde 1998.)

PATINAGE

- Particularités : Patinage artistique, danse sur glace, hockey, patinage de vitesse... On choisit sa discipline en s'inscrivant en club. Certains clubs ne proposent qu'une seule discipline.
- Nombre de licenciés : Près de 30 000.
- Adresse : Fédération française des sports de glace, 42, rue du Louvre, 75001 Paris.
- «Quand on patine, il faut penser aux pieds, aux jambes, aux bras, au port de tête, mais aussi aux expressions... On peut être très bon techniquement, si on n'a aucun sentiment, ça ne sert à rien.» (Isabelle Duchesnay, médaille d'argent en danse sur glace, à Barcelone.)

For Activities E and F, see answers below.

E. Complete the following sentences with information from the poster on each sport.

Le basket: C'est un sport qui __1__ de plus en plus d'adeptes.

L'athlétisme: On peut choisir __2__ à partir de 13–15 ans.

La natation: La natation permet d'apprendre à mieux __3__ sa respiration.

Le tennis: Je retrouve la joie de voir partir une balle avec une trajectoire bien __4__ .

Le football: Mon grand plaisir, c'était... de __5__ avec elle.

Le patinage: Certains clubs ne __6__ qu'une seule discipline.

Le cyclisme: Le cyclisme, c'est __7__ pour l'équilibre.

Le ski: Il y a aussi... la glisse, cette sensation __8__ .

F. To paraphrase, it helps to use synonyms. Match these synonyms to the words you used in 1–8 above.

a	sa discipline particulière
un bon exercice	formidable
remporter la victoire	
offrent	contrôler	régulière

G. Choose one of the sports, and read carefully the **Particularités** section and the section where a person is talking about the sport. Then, write the information about the sport in your own words. Share your paraphrased version with a partner.

H. Make a poster to promote your favorite sport. Include reasons why your sport is the best and the most enjoyable. You can also interview and quote classmates who like that sport and use art or magazine cutouts to make your poster convincing and eye-catching.

cent quatre-vingt-un **181**

LISONS!
CHAPITRE 7

For Individual Needs

G. Auditory Learners/Slower Pace You might have students work in pairs and read the **Particularités** together to ensure their comprehension.

POSTREADING
Activity H

Cooperative Learning

H. Some students may prefer to work in groups so that the task of making the poster is broken down into smaller steps. Create a cooperative learning assignment in which one student is the writer, one is the interviewer, and another gathers artwork and arranges the layout of the poster.

Thinking Critically

H. Synthesizing Have students interview their classmates in French. The interviewers should practice paraphrasing and write key words and phrases of the interviewees' responses in French. Then, have students change roles.

Physical Education Link

H. Display the posters in a prominent place in the school to draw attention to the sports, to bring recognition to the creators of the posters, and to increase awareness of foreign language as an enjoyable and relevant school subject. Students might also volunteer to present their posters in English to a physical education or health class.

Answers

E 1. compte
2. sa spécialisation
3. maîtriser
4. nette
5. gagner
6. proposent
7. une bonne école
8. exceptionnelle

F 1. a
2. sa discipline particulière
3. contrôler
4. régulière
5. remporter de la victoire
6. offrent
7. un bon exercice
8. formidable

Teacher Note

Point out the French method of writing numbers in the brochures next to the categories **Nombres de licenciés** and **Nombres d'adhérents.** Tell students that while we write 300,000 with a comma, the French write 300 000 without one or with a period (300.000).

The **Mise en pratique** reviews and integrates all four skills and culture in preparation for the Chapter Test.

Thinking Critically

1 **Comparing and Contrasting** Have students compare Claudia Schiffer's habits with their own. How are their habits different or similar?

For Individual Needs

1 **Challenge** Students might create their own column to explain how they stay healthy.

Language Notes

1 Students might want to know the following vocabulary from the article: **une rubrique** *(a column);* **livrer** *(to reveal);* **repérer** *(to spot);* **une boîte de nuit** *(a night club);* **dès** *(from);* **un defilé** *(a fashion show);* **peser** *(to weigh);* **faire une razzia** *(to indulge in);* **fantaisiste** *(whimsical);* **les laitages** *(dairy products);* **allongée** *(stretched out);* **rattraper son retard** *(to catch up on).*

2 Point out the play on words in the names in Activity 2: **Jean Fairien (Fait rien).** Students might have fun inventing similar names.

Teaching Suggestion

2 Before students write their name on their cartoon, pass the cartoons around the class. Students might choose the one they prefer and write a comic book episode involving the character.

Answers

1 1. des fruits, du poisson, des laitages
2. deux
3. la gymnastique—une heure par jour, le jogging ou le vélo—une heure une à deux fois par semaine
4. le plus tôt possible; huit heures

MISE EN PRATIQUE

1 Lis cet article sur les habitudes de Claudia Schiffer et réponds aux questions suivantes. *See answers below.*

  1. Qu'est-ce qu'elle mange?
  2. Elle boit combien de litres d'eau par jour?
  3. Elle fait quels sports? Est-ce qu'elle en fait souvent?
  4. Elle se couche à quelle heure en général? Elle a besoin de combien d'heures de sommeil?

SECRET DE BEAUTE

Dans cette rubrique les plus belles stars vous livrent leur secret de beauté. Leurs coiffures, leurs maquillages, leur régime n'auront plus de secret pour vous !

CLAUDIA SCHIFFER

Repérée dans une boîte de nuit de Düsseldorf par des agents de l'agence de mannequin Metropolitan, Claudia est devenue une star dès son premier défilé pour Chanel en 1990.

★ MON REGIME

« Avant, je pesais 60 kilos (maintenant 57) pour 1,79 m. J'ai supprimé les sucreries pour faire une razzia de fruits et de poissons. Je fais de temps en temps des régimes un peu fantaisistes : un jour "tout fruits", le lendemain "tout laitages"… Je bois deux litres d'eau par jour.

★ DU SPORT

Je m'oblige à une heure de gymnastique par jour, des exercices simples à faire chez soi. Allongée sur le dos, des ciseaux avec mes jambes pour faire travailler mes abdominaux. J'essaie de faire, une à deux fois par semaine, une heure de jogging ou de vélo.

★ BEAUCOUP DE SOMMEIL

J'essaie de me coucher le plus tôt possible. J'ai besoin d'un minimum de 8 heures de sommeil. Comme ce n'est pas toujours possible, je rattrape mon retard dans les avions et les taxis.

2 Invent a cartoon character who has really bad health habits. Write a physical description of your character and describe his or her daily activities and what he or she eats. Give your character a name from the boxes below or make up your own name. Make a drawing of your character, or assemble a picture from magazine cutouts.

Nicole Estérol
Gaston Gourmand
Monsieur Bouchasucre
Jean Fairien
Julien Bougepas
Annie Cotine
Madame Mangetout
Laurent Lafumée

182 *cent quatre-vingt-deux*   CHAPITRE 7   En pleine forme

Math Links

• Have students calculate Claudia's weight in pounds, and her height from meters to feet and inches. One kilogram equals 2.2 pounds. To convert kilograms into pounds, multiply the number of kilograms (57) by 2.2 (125.4 pounds). One meter equals 3.28 feet. To convert meters to feet and inches, multiply the meters (1.79) by 3.28 (5.87). Then, multiply .87 by 12 to find the number of inches (10.45). Claudia is five feet ten inches tall.

• Have students calculate their own height and weight into kilograms and meters. To convert inches to meters, multiply by .0254. A student who is five feet four inches tall multiplies the height in inches (64) by .0254 (1.6 meters). Imagine the student weighs 115 pounds. To convert the weight into kilograms, divide 115 by 2.2 (52 kilos).

3 Have a partner read your cartoon character's description. Then, play the role of your character. Your partner should give you advice on what you should do to improve your health and encourage you to change your habits. You should respond to the advice as you think your character would. Then, your partner should play the role of his or her character and you should give advice and encouragement.

4 Listen to a radio commercial for the health spa **Centre Equilibre Santé** and answer the following questions.   Answers on p. 159D.

1. What exercise activities are offered?
2. What is available after you work out?
3. What special excursions are offered?
4. What do you have to do to get the excursions in the package?

5 If you were in France, . . .   See answers below.

1. where would you go to have a prescription filled?
2. what symbol would you look for to find that place?
3. where could you go to take an aerobics class?
4. what two kinds of mineral water could you order in a restaurant?
5. when would you tell someone **J'ai un chat dans la gorge!**?
6. when would you say **Aïe!** and **Ouf!**?

CENTRE
Équilibre Santé

LES QUATRE-TEMPS

LAC BEAUPORT

6

JEU DE ROLE

Play the role of a whining (or accident-prone!) patient who comes to a doctor with several ailments or injuries, thinking that everything is extremely serious. The doctor asks what happened and what is wrong, then gives advice on what the patient should and shouldn't do.

MISE EN PRATIQUE   *cent quatre-vingt-trois* **183**

Answers
5 1. to a pharmacy
2. a green cross
3. gym club
4. carbonated or non-carbonated
5. when you cannot talk
6. **Aïe!** when you are hurt, and **Ouf!** after doing something physically difficult to express relief

Teaching Suggestion

3 You might have students present their dialogue to the class as a skit.

For Individual Needs

4 Challenge Type the listening script, substituting blanks for ten to twelve words, and distribute copies to students. Play the recording two or three times and have students write the words they hear or can guess from context in the blank spaces.

4 Slower Pace Use the listening script as suggested for the Challenge activity above and supply the missing words at the bottom of the script for students to use in completing the sentences.

5 Challenge Have students incorporate all of the answers to these questions in a letter to a friend or relative back home describing their home-stay in France.

Video Wrap-Up

• *VIDEO PROGRAM*
• *EXPANDED VIDEO PROGRAM,*
  Videocassette 3, 01:25–15:13
• *VIDEODISC PROGRAM,*
  Videodisc 4A

At this time, you might want to use the video resources for additional review and enrichment. See *Video Guide* or *Videodisc Guide* for suggestions regarding the following:

• **Trop de conseils**
  (Dramatic episode)
• **Panorama Culturel**
  (Interviews)
• **Vidéoclips**
  (Authentic footage)

This page is intended to help students prepare for the test. It is a brief checklist of the major points covered in the chapter. The students should be reminded that this is only a checklist and does not necessarily include everything that will appear on the test.

Teaching Suggestion

Have students work in pairs to answer the questions in **Que sais-je?**

♜ Game

QUE SAIS-JE? Form two teams and have the members of each team count off. Have the first student from each team go to the board. Call out a question at random from **Que sais-je?** The first student to write a complete, correct answer wins a point for his or her team. Continue with the second player from each team, and so on. The team with the most points at the end of the game wins.

QUE SAIS-JE?

Can you use what you've learned in this chapter?

Can you express concern for someone and complain? p. 165

1 What would you say to a friend if . . .   *Possible answers:*
1. he didn't look well?   Tu n'as pas l'air en forme.
2. something seemed to be wrong?   Quelque chose ne va pas?
3. she were on crutches?   Qu'est-ce que tu as?

2 How would you respond to a friend's concern if . . .   *Possible answers:*
1. you were very tired?   J'ai mal dormi. Je suis tout(e) raplapla.
2. you weren't feeling well?   Je ne me sens pas bien.
3. your arm were in a sling?   Je me suis cassé le bras.
4. you had a cold?   J'ai un rhume.
5. you'd cut your finger?   Je me suis coupé le doigt.
6. you'd lifted weights for the first time?   J'ai mal partout!

Can you give advice? p. 173

3 How would you suggest that your friend do the following?   See answers below.

 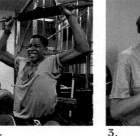 

1.   2.   3.

Can you accept and reject advice? p. 173

4 How would you respond to the suggestions you made in number 3? See answers below.

Can you express discouragement and offer encouragement? p. 174

5 How would you express discouragement if you were . . .   *Possible answers:*
1. on the last mile of a marathon?   Je n'en peux plus!
2. studying for final exams?   Je craque!
3. in the final minutes of your aerobics class?   J'abandonne!

6 How would you encourage someone who . . .   *Possible answers:*
1. can't go on?   Encore un effort!
2. is almost finished?   Tu y es presque!
3. is discouraged about grades?   Courage!

Can you justify your recommendations and advise against something? p. 178

7 How would you tell someone what he or she should do on a regular basis and explain why?   See answers below.

8 If a friend were trying to lead a healthy lifestyle, what are three things you would advise him or her to avoid?   *Possible answers:* Evite de fumer des cigarettes! Ne saute pas de repas! Tu ne devrais pas te faire bronzer!

184   *cent quatre-vingt-quatre*   CHAPITRE 7   En pleine forme

Possible answers
3 1. Tu dois faire des pompes.
  2. Tu ferais bien de faire de la musculation.
  3. Pourquoi tu ne manges pas de fruits?
4 *Accept:* Tu as raison. Bonne idée! D'accord.
  Reject: Je ne peux pas. Non, je n'ai pas très envie.
  Non, je préfère... ; Pas question! Je n'ai pas le temps. Ce n'est pas mon truc.

7 Tu devrais faire du sport parce que c'est bon pour toi. Tu ferais bien de te coucher plus tôt. Ça te fera du bien. Pourquoi tu ne manges pas de fruits et de légumes? C'est meilleur que de manger des hamburgers et des fruits.

PREMIERE ETAPE

Expressing concern for someone; complaining

Quelque chose ne va pas? *Is something wrong?*
Qu'est-ce que tu as? *What's wrong?*
Tu n'as pas l'air en forme. *You don't look well.*
Je ne me sens pas bien. *I don't feel well.*
Je suis tout(e) raplapla. *I'm wiped out.*
J'ai mal dormi. *I didn't sleep well.*
J'ai mal partout! *I hurt all over!*

Illnesses, aches, pains, and injuries

Je suis malade. *I'm sick.*
J'ai mal au cœur. *I'm sick to my stomach.*
J'ai le nez qui coule. *I've got a runny nose.*
J'ai un rhume. *I've got a cold.*
J'ai la grippe. *I've got the flu.*
J'ai des allergies. *I have allergies.*
J'ai mal... *My . . . hurts.*
  à la gorge *throat*
  à la tête *head*
  au dos *back*
au pied *foot*
au bras *arm*
à la main *hand*
au ventre *stomach*
à l'oreille (f.) *ear*
aux dents (f.) *teeth*
au cou *neck*
à la jambe *leg*
se faire mal à... *to hurt one's . . .*
se casser... *to break one's . . .*
se fouler la cheville *to sprain one's ankle*
se couper le doigt *to cut one's finger*

DEUXIEME ETAPE

Giving, accepting, and rejecting advice

Tu dois... *You've got to . . .*
Tu devrais... *You should . . .*
Tu ferais bien de... *You would do well to . . .*
Tu n'as qu'à... *All you have to do is . . .*
Pourquoi tu ne... pas... ? *Why don't you . . . ?*
Tu as raison. *You're right.*
Bonne idée! *Good idea!*
D'accord. *OK.*
Je ne peux pas. *I can't.*
Non, je n'ai pas très envie. *No, I don't feel like it.*
Non, je préfère... *No, I prefer . . .*
Pas question! *No way!*
Je n'ai pas le temps. *I don't have time.*
Ce n'est pas mon truc. *It's not my thing.*

Expressing discouragement; offering encouragement

Je n'en peux plus! *I just can't do any more!*
J'abandonne. *I give up.*
Je craque! *I'm losing it!*
Allez! *Come on!*
Courage! *Hang in there!*
Encore un effort! *One more try!*
Tu y es presque! *You're almost there!*

At the gym

se mettre en condition *to get into shape*
faire des abdominaux *to do sit-ups*
faire de l'aérobic *to do aerobics*
faire de l'exercice *to exercise*
faire de la gymnastique *to do gymnastics*
faire de la musculation *to lift weights*
faire des pompes *to do push-ups*
s'entraîner à... *to train for*

TROISIEME ETAPE

Justifying your recommendations; advising against something

C'est bon pour toi. *It's good for you.*
Ça te fera du bien. *It'll do you good.*
C'est meilleur que de... *It's better than . . .*
Evite de... *Avoid . . .*
Ne saute pas... *Don't skip . . .*
Tu ne devrais pas... *You shouldn't . . .*

Eating right

On doit... *Everyone should . . .*
  bien se nourrir *eat well*
  manger des légumes/des pâtes/du riz *eat vegetables/pasta/rice*
Evitez de... *Avoid . . .*
  suivre un régime trop strict *following a diet that's too strict*
consommer trop de sucre *eating too much sugar*
  de sel *salt*
  de matières grasses *fat*
grignoter entre les repas *snacking between meals*
sauter des repas *skipping meals*

Game

Loto! So that students can practice writing, reading, and hearing the expressions and vocabulary from this chapter, have them draw a large 5 × 5 grid on a sheet of paper and write in each square one of the expressions from the **Vocabulaire.** While students are making their grid, write the expressions from the **Vocabulaire** on separate slips of paper and place them in a box. When students have completed their grid, begin the game of "Bingo." The first student to mark five squares in a row (with small bits of paper), calls out **Loto!** and should then say and mime the French expressions he or she marked while showing you their grid.

CHAPTER 7 ASSESSMENT

CHAPTER TEST

- *Chapter Teaching Resources, Book 2,* pp. 141–146
- *Assessment Guide,* Speaking Test, p. 31
- *Assessment Items,* Audiocassette 8A Audio CD 7

TEST GENERATOR, CHAPTER 7

ALTERNATIVE ASSESSMENT

Performance Assessment
You might want to use the **Jeu de rôle** (p. 183) as a cumulative performance assessment activity.

Portfolio Assessment

- **Written:** Activity 37, *Pupil's Edition,* p. 179
  Assessment Guide, p. 20
- **Oral:** Activity 38, *Pupil's Edition,* p. 179
  Assessment Guide, p. 20

Game

DIS-MOI! Write 20 words or expressions from the vocabulary on a grid of 20 squares. Photocopy one for every two students and distribute to partners. Have them cut apart the squares and take ten each. Each student alternately tries to get his or her partner to say the words or expressions on the ten squares by giving clues in French and gesturing. If he or she fails to convey the item, the square is set aside. If the player giving the clues doesn't know the word or expression, he or she sets that square aside as well. When they have finished, each may have a set of words or expressions that have not been guessed. He or she looks these up in the book and writes a complete sentence or short dialogue containing the word or expression. The partners then trade sets of squares and repeat the last step.

EXPANDED VIDEO PROGRAM, Videocassette 3
15:36–18:14

OR VIDEODISC PROGRAM, Videodisc 4B

Search 1, Play To 4710

Motivating Activity

Have students share what they know about Côte d'Ivoire, or any impressions they may have of Africa in general. Have them imagine differences between living in an Ivorian village and living in a city like Abidjan. Then, have students point out the differences that they observe in the photos on pages 186–189.

Background Information

Côte d'Ivoire got its name from the ivory trade, which once flourished, but has since been banned in many countries around the world. The size of the country belies the diversity of its land and peoples. Consisting mostly of rain forest, the southern half of the country has a tropical climate with oppressive humidity and abundant rainfall. The northern half, which is savanna, tends to be hotter and drier. Until drought and falling market prices caused economic setbacks, the country had enjoyed a fairly high standard of living. In addition to French, which is the national language, more than 60 ethnic languages are spoken in Côte d'Ivoire. Djoula, the market language, is spoken at least minimally by most Ivorians.

CHAPITRE 8

Allez, viens en Côte d'Ivoire!

Un village Sénoufo

Culture Note

Have students look at the Sénoufo village on pages 186–187. The structure of the buildings is economical, practical, and comfortable at the same time. Villagers use straw from the surrounding fields for the roofs and beaten or stabilized earth bricks for the walls. With this kind of structure, air-conditioning is not needed despite the hot temperatures, since the straw roof ensures that the temperature is spread out evenly, and the gap between the top of the walls and the roof provides for a cooling flow of air. The narrower structures in the photo are granaries used to store sorghum, millet, and other grains. They are elevated on clay supports **(pieds de terre)** in order to protect the grains from the humidity and the rodents **(rongeurs)**.

La République de Côte d' Ivoire

Population : plus de 13.000.000

Villes principales : Abidjan, Yamoussoukro, Bouaké, Korhogo

Peuples ethniques : Baoulé, Agni, Bété, Yacouba, Sénoufo, Malinké

Points d'intérêt : le parc national de Taï, la basilique de Notre-Dame-de-la-Paix, le parc national de la Comoë

Ivoiriens célèbres : la reine Abla Pokou, Félix Houphouët-Boigny, Alpha Blondy, Désiré Ecaré, Bamba Adama

Ressources et industries : café, cacao, bois, bananes

Festivals : la Fête des ignames, la Fête des générations, la Fête des masques

cent quatre-vingt-sept 187

Using the Almanac and Map

Terms in the Almanac

- **Yamoussoukro,** the administrative capital of Côte d'Ivoire since 1983, is the hometown of former president **Félix Houphouët-Boigny.** In fact, the name **Yamoussoukro** means "city of Yamoussou" (Houphouët Boigny's mother). The city is known for its wide, brightly-lit highways, the five-star Hôtel Président, Notre Dame Basilica, and the Presidential Palace, famous for its **caïmans sacrés** *(sacred crocodiles)*.

- The **Baoulé,** the largest ethnic group in Côte d'Ivoire, migrated from Ghana over two hundred years ago. They are known as excellent goldsmiths and weavers.

- The **Agni** also originated in Ghana and settled primarily in eastern Côte d'Ivoire.

- The **Bété,** who settled in the southwestern forest region of Côte d'Ivoire more than 1,000 years ago, are known for their masks.

- The **Sénoufo** settled in the northern part of the country in the sixteenth century. They are known for their elaborate statues and masks.

- The **Malinké,** originally from what is now Guinea and Mali, live in northern Côte d'Ivoire and are famous for their rich musical heritage and pottery.

- **Le parc national de Taï,** a rain forest located near the Liberian border, is home to many wild animals.

- **Le parc national de la Comoë** is the largest game park in West Africa.

- **Alpha Blondy,** an advocate of Africa and the poor, is a popular reggae musician. One of his most popular hits is *Cocody Rock.*

Using the Map

Have students look at the map of Côte d'Ivoire on this page. Ask them why they think it is hotter and drier the farther north you go, and wetter and more humid as you travel south. (As you travel north, you move towards the desert, so you encounter fewer trees and less rain. As you travel south, you see more and more tropical rain forest. Also, Côte d'Ivoire is located approximately seven degrees north of the equator.) Ask students if they know the capitals of the countries surrounding Côte d'Ivoire (Monrovia, Liberia; Conakry, Guinea; Bamako, Mali; Ouagadougou, Burkina Faso; Accra, Ghana).

Culture Note

La reine Abla Pokou, the famous queen of the **Baoulé** people, led the migration of the Baoulé from Ghana to Côte d'Ivoire in the eighteenth century.

Using the Photo Essay

① Korhogo, located in northern Côte d'Ivoire, is the main city of the Sénoufo. The Korhogo region is surrounded by artisan villages, known for their weavers, blacksmiths, potters, woodcarvers, and painters of tapestry and cloth. **Batiks** (*tapestry or painted cloth pictures*), or **toiles** (*painted canvas or cloth*), similar to the one shown in this photo, are made in the villages of Fakaha and Katia. These tapestries or cloth pictures are generally pieces of canvas, burlap, or gunnysack with images of black and brown animals and other patterns painted on them.

Art Link

① The paint used for the **batiks** is made with various dyes taken from millet. The different colors are made by mixing the dyes together to produce blacks, browns, and whites.

② The **Yacouba** people live primarily in western Côte d'Ivoire in and around the city of Man, and are admired for their acrobatic dancing. You might point out to students the numerous, decorative cowry shells that adorn the costumes of the dancers in this photo. Their ceremonial masks, often featuring plumes, shells, and even tin cans, can be seen in museums all over the world.

③ One of Côte d'Ivoire's most interesting fishing villages is Sassandra, located on the Atlantic coast five to six hours west of Abidjan. Apparently, Sassandra is a contraction of San Andrea, a name given by the Portuguese, who were visitors to the area in the fifteenth and sixteenth centuries. The town is inhabited by the Néyo people, who are well-known as fishermen (**pêcheurs**).

La République de Côte d'Ivoire

Au XVe siècle, les navigateurs français sont arrivés sur la côte ouest de l'Afrique, une région riche en ivoire, et l'ont baptisée Côte d'Ivoire. Elle est devenue colonie française en 1893 et en 1960, pays indépendant sous le nom de République de Côte d'Ivoire. Le cacao, le café et les bananes sont en tête de la production ivoirienne. Grâce à sa grande forêt tropicale, la Côte d'Ivoire est aussi un grand exportateur de bois précieux comme l'ébène et l'acajou.

① Les artisans en Côte d'Ivoire font beaucoup de produits originaux commes **les batiks.**

② **Les danseurs yacoubas** sont connus pour leurs talents d'acrobatie.

③ La pêche est une activité traditionnelle et les pêcheurs tiennent à leur indépendance.

Culture Note

② Various tribal dance performances and numerous festivals are held throughout Côte d'Ivoire during the year.

La Fête des ignames is a harvest ritual observed by the Agni and the Abron, who belong to the Akan ethnic group. As the Akan migrated from Ghana to Côte d'Ivoire in the eighteenth century, they survived on yams, which they introduced to Côte d'Ivoire.

La Fête des générations is a celebration of various generations throughout the country. The Adioukrou hold this festival just before the children return to school.

During **la Fête des masques,** held in Man every November, one can see more than 100 masks from nearby villages. Throughout West Africa, it is believed that masks appease the ancestors and minor deities who are intermediaries between man and God. They are also thought to ward off evil.

④ **Abidjan** est un des grands centres commerciaux de l'Afrique occidentale.

⑤ **La cascade de mont Tonkoui** est une des merveilles de la Côte d'Ivoire.

⑥ **Ce pont de lianes** se trouve près de la ville de Man.

⑦ **La plage d'Assinie** est un des endroits préférés non seulement des touristes étrangers mais aussi des Ivoiriens.

⑧ **La basilique de Notre-Dame-de-la-Paix** à Yamoussoukro est la plus grande église du monde.

cent quatre-vingt-neuf 189

④ **Abidjan,** no longer the capital of Côte d'Ivoire, remains the diplomatic and economic center of the country. The city grew rapidly after the Vridi Canal was built in 1951. The canal connected the city to the lagoon and created a protected deep water port.

Thinking Critically

④ **Observing** Ask students if the skyline of Abidjan resembles that of an American or a European city. Have them look for clues in the photo to justify their answers. Ask if they notice anything in the photo that suggests Abidjan is an African city.

⑤ **La cascade de mont Tonkoui,** the most famous attraction in the Man region, is a waterfall located in a bamboo forest five kilometers outside of the city. Approximately 20 kilometers from Man is **mont Tonkoui,** which, at 1,218 meters, is the highest point in Côte d'Ivoire. From this vantage point, one can see neighboring Guinea and its dense forests and rolling hills.

⑥ In western Côte d'Ivoire, travelers encounter various **ponts de lianes,** which enable them to cross the streams and rivers. These swinging bridges are made of tough, slender vines called **lianes,** rope, and several thin branches. They are considered sacred and must not be touched by the soles of shoes; the bridges must be crossed barefoot. Although they are destroyed every year by torrential rains, they are patiently rebuilt by the local villagers, sometimes overnight!

⑦ **La plage d'Assinie,** located two hours east of Abidjan, is reputed to be one of the best beaches in Côte d'Ivoire.

 Culture Note

⑥ Another attraction in the Man region, especially for hikers, is the **Dent de Man,** a steep, jagged, tooth-shaped mountain located 14 kilometers northeast of town. To climb this 75-foot summit, known as the "guardian angel of Man," visitors will need a guide to avoid losing the jungle path.

Architecture Link

⑧ **La basilique de Notre-Dame-de-la-Paix,** a replica of St. Peter's Basilica in Rome, is larger than St. Peter's and is the world's largest church. It was built in only three years compared to 100 years for St. Peter's. Designed to hold 7,000 people, the basilica contains 30 acres of marble and four times the amount of stained glass found in the Notre-Dame Cathedral in Chartres, France. It is also the world's largest air-conditioned space.

Chapitre 8 : C'était comme ça
Chapter Overview

Mise en train pp. 192–194	La nostalgie		Practice and Activity Book, p. 85	Video Guide OR Videodisc Guide

	FUNCTIONS	GRAMMAR	CULTURE	RE-ENTRY
Première étape pp. 195–199	• Telling what or whom you miss; reassuring someone, p. 197 • Asking and telling what things were like, p. 198	Introduction to the **imparfait**, p. 199	• **Rencontre Culturelle,** Village life in Côte d'Ivoire, p. 195 • **Note Culturelle,** Ethnic groups in West Africa, p. 196	• Sympathizing with and consoling someone • The phrase **c'était**
Deuxième étape pp. 200–205	Reminiscing, p. 201	Formation of the **imparfait**, p. 202	• **Note Culturelle,** High school in Côte d'Ivoire, p. 201 • **Note Culturelle,** Félix Houphouët-Boigny and his birthplace, Yamoussoukro, p. 203 • **Panorama Culturel,** City living versus country living, p. 205 • Realia: *Un jeune Ivoirien s'en souvient,* p. 203	• Pronunciation: The [ɛ] sound • Adjectives of physical traits and personality
Troisième étape pp. 206–209	Making and responding to suggestions, p. 209	**si on** + the **imparfait**, p. 209	• Markets in Abidjan, pp. 206–207 • **Note Culturelle,** Abidjan, p. 207	Responding to suggestions

Lisons! pp. 210–211	An excerpt from **La belle histoire de Leuk-le-Lièvre**	**Reading Strategy:** Linking words and pronouns

Review pp. 212–215	**Mise en pratique,** pp. 212–213	**Que sais-je?** p. 214	**Vocabulaire,** p. 215

Assessment Options

Etape Quizzes
• *Chapter Teaching Resources, Book 2*
  Première étape, Quiz 8-1, pp. 191–192
  Deuxième étape, Quiz 8-2, pp. 193–194
  Troisième étape, Quiz 8-3, pp. 195–196
• *Assessment Items, Audiocassette 8A/Audio CD 8*

Chapter Test
• *Chapter Teaching Resources, Book 2,* pp. 197–202
• *Assessment Guide,* Speaking Test, p. 31
• *Assessment Items, Audiocassette 8A/Audio CD 8*

Test Generator, Chapter 8

*Video Program OR Expanded Video Program, Videocassette 3
OR Videodisc Program, Videodisc 4B*   *Textbook Audiocassette 4B/Audio CD 8*

RESOURCES: Print	**RESOURCES: Audiovisual**
	Textbook Audiocassette 4B/Audio CD 8
Practice and Activity Book, pp. 86–88 *Chapter Teaching Resources, Book 2* • Teaching Transparency Master 8-1, pp. 175, 178 . . . . • Additional Listening Activities 8-1, 8-2, p. 179 . . . . • Realia 8-1, pp. 183, 185 • Situation Cards 8-1, pp. 186–187 • Student Response Forms, pp. 188–190 • Quiz 8-1, pp. 191–192 . . . . *Videodisc Guide*	 *Teaching Transparency 8-1* *Additional Listening Activities, Audiocassette 10A/Audio CD 8* *Assessment Items, Audiocassette 8A/Audio CD 8* *Videodisc Program, Videodisc 4B*
	Textbook Audiocassette 4B/Audio CD 8
Practice and Activity Book, pp. 89–91 *Chapter Teaching Resources, Book 2* • Communicative Activity 8-1, pp. 171–172 • Teaching Transparency Master 8-2, pp. 176, 178 . . . . • Additional Listening Activities 8-3, 8-4, p. 180 . . . . • Realia 8-2, pp. 184, 185 • Situation Cards 8-2, pp. 186–187 • Student Response Forms, pp. 188–190 • Quiz 8-2, pp. 193–194 . . . . *Video Guide* . . . . *Videodisc Guide*	 *Teaching Transparency 8-2* *Additional Listening Activities, Audiocassette 10A/Audio CD 8* *Assessment Items, Audiocassette 8A/Audio CD 8* *Video Program OR Expanded Video Program, Videocassette 3* *Videodisc Program, Videodisc 4B*
	Textbook Audiocassette 4B/Audio CD 8
Practice and Activity Book, pp. 92–94 *Chapter Teaching Resources, Book 2* • Communicative Activity 8-2, pp. 173–174 • Teaching Transparency Master 8-3, pp. 177, 178 . . . . • Additional Listening Activities 8-5, 8-6, p. 181 . . . . • Realia 8-2, pp. 184, 185 • Situation Cards 8-3, pp. 186–187 • Student Response Forms, pp. 188–190 • Quiz 8-3, pp. 195–196 . . . . *Videodisc Guide*	 *Teaching Transparency 8-3* *Additional Listening Activities, Audiocassette 10A/Audio CD 8* *Assessment Items, Audiocassette 8A/Audio CD 8* *Videodisc Program, Videodisc 4B*
Practice and Activity Book, p. 95	
Video Guide . . . . *Videodisc Guide*	*Video Program OR Expanded Video Program, Videocassette 3* *Videodisc Program, Videodisc 4B*

Alternative Assessment
- Performance Assessment
  Première étape, p. 199
  Deuxième étape, p. 204
  Troisième étape, p. 209
- Portfolio Assessment
  Written: **Mise en pratique,** Activity 4, *Pupil's Edition,* p. 213
      Assessment Guide, p. 21
  Oral: **Mise en pratique,** Activity 6, *Pupil's Edition,* p. 213
      Assessment Guide, p. 21

For Student Response Forms, see *Chapter Teaching Resources, Book 2,* pp. 188–190

Première étape

7 Ecoute! p. 197

1. — Qu'est-ce qu'il y a, Sylvie?
   — Oh, mon village me manque. C'était tellement calme là-bas.
   — T'en fais pas! Tu vas t'y faire. Tu vas voir, il y a beaucoup de choses à voir et à faire ici.

2. — Ça va, Emile?
   — Tu vois, mes copains me manquent. On jouait toujours ensemble dans le village.
   — Mais tu vas te plaire ici aussi! Tout le monde est très sympa.

3. — Pourquoi tu fais la tête, Francine?
   — Ce qui me manque, c'est faire du ski. Mais c'est impossible ici! Il ne neige jamais!
   — Allez! Fais-toi une raison. Pourquoi pas faire du ski nautique? Tu vas voir, c'est super cool!

4. — Ça va, Bertrand?
   — Oh, je regrette les repas en famille. Toute la famille se réunissait pour le dîner. Ici, je mange seul.
   — Tu vas voir, tu vas te faire des amis.

Answers to Activity 7
1. a   2. c   3. b   4. d

11 Ecoute! p. 199

JUSTIN   Alors Mamadou, comment tu trouves notre grande ville? Géniale, hein?

MAMADOU   Euh... C'est très différent de mon village, ça c'est sûr! C'est beaucoup plus animé.

JUSTIN   Tu vois, je t'avais dit qu'Abidjan te plairait.

MAMADOU   Oui, c'est vrai, mais qu'est-ce que je suis fatigué! Avec toutes ces voitures, c'est impossible de bien dormir. C'est beaucoup trop bruyant!

JUSTIN   Ben moi, je préfère ça à un petit village isolé et mortel. Tu verras, d'ici peu, tu t'habitueras au bruit.

MAMADOU   Et puis, mon village était quand même plus propre et moins dangereux, et ça, ça me manque vraiment.

JUSTIN   Ecoute, on ne peut pas tout avoir! En tout cas, moi, j'adore Abidjan. C'est peut-être un peu moins tranquille et un peu plus sale que chez toi, mais au moins, c'est très vivant.

MAMADOU   Oui, tu as raison. Après tout, j'ai beaucoup de chance de pouvoir habiter avec toi et de pouvoir continuer mes études. Bon, j'arrête de me plaindre! Et si on allait se promener?

JUSTIN   Oui, bonne idée! Je vais te montrer des endroits que tu n'as encore jamais vus. Ça va être super!

MAMADOU   D'accord, allons-y!

Answers to Activity 11
His village was quieter, cleaner, and safer; go for a walk in the city

Deuxième étape

17 Ecoute! p. 201

YAPO   Alors, Mme Koré, vous étiez comment quand vous étiez enfant?

MME KORÉ   Oh, j'étais parfois pénible. Je posais constamment des questions à ma mère. Oui, je l'ennuyais beaucoup.

YAPO   Et est-ce que vous l'aidiez aussi?

MME KORÉ   Oui, j'avais des responsabilités à la maison. Je devais sortir la poubelle, balayer la terrasse et aider ma mère à faire la cuisine. J'aimais faire tout ça. C'était amusant de faire la cuisine avec ma mère.

YAPO   Vous aviez des frères et sœurs?

MME KORÉ   Oui, j'avais deux frères. On s'entendait très bien. Je ne les taquinais jamais. Ils étaient gentils.

YAPO   Vous faisiez des bêtises?

MME KORÉ   Bien sûr, comme tous les enfants! J'étais parfois embêtante, mais pas trop. Mais je n'avais pas de soucis! Ah, que c'était bien, quand j'étais petite.

Answers to Activity 17
Elle ne taquinait pas ses frères. Elle faisait des bêtises.

19 Ecoute! p. 202

Oh, pour vous, les jeunes d'aujourd'hui, la vie est plus facile qu'avant. Quand j'étais enfant, la vie était dure. Les filles n'avaient pas le droit d'aller à l'école; ça, c'était pour les garçons. Nous, les filles, on restait à la maison, on faisait le ménage et on s'occupait de nos frères et sœurs. C'était beaucoup plus difficile que maintenant. Je devais travailler tous les jours! Oh, la vie était dure! Je ne la regrette pas.

Answers to Activity 19
1. faux   2. faux   3. vrai   4. faux

*T*roisième étape

27 Ecoute! p. 208

1. JUSTIN Tu sais, l'architecture à Abidjan n'est pas toujours moderne. Là, par exemple, ce style est très différent de celui de la cathédrale que tu as vue tout à l'heure.

   MAMADOU Oui, c'est beaucoup plus traditionnel. Je préfère ça.

2. MAMADOU Où est-ce qu'on va maintenant?

   JUSTIN C'est une surprise, mais je suis sûr que tu vas aimer.

   MAMADOU Allez, dis-moi.

   JUSTIN Sois patient. Tu verras, c'est un endroit super où on peut trouver des tas de choses géniales, surtout des tissus. Voilà. On y est.

3. MAMADOU Dis donc, qu'est-ce qu'il fait chaud!

   JUSTIN Oui, tu as raison. Et puis, on a aussi beaucoup marché. Je suis un peu fatigué, moi. Pas toi?

   MAMADOU Si. On s'arrête quelques minutes pour se reposer? Et si on allait boire un verre?

   JUSTIN D'accord.

4. MAMADOU Oh là là! Avec tout ça, j'ai complètement oublié d'acheter des cadeaux pour mes frères.

   JUSTIN Ce n'est pas trop tard. On peut s'arrêter ici, si tu veux.

   MAMADOU Bonne idée. Comme ça, je pourrai acheter un masque pour Henri et un tam-tam pour Félix. Ça lui fera plaisir, il adore la musique.

Answers to Activity 27

1. b   2. e   3. a   4. c

*M*ise en pratique

3 p. 213

KOFFI Dis, Sandrine, il y a plein de choses à faire en ville en ce moment.

SANDRINE Oh, vraiment, tu sais, je n'ai pas envie de faire grand-chose. Mon village me manque tellement.

KOFFI Ecoute, fais-toi une raison! Tu sais, Abidjan, c'est pas mal comme ville. Tiens, si on faisait une promenade dans la lagune? Tu pourrais voir ta nouvelle ville!

SANDRINE Non, je n'ai pas très envie. Je suis malade en bâteau.

KOFFI Tu as envie de manger de la daurade fraîche? Si on pêchait cet aprèm, on pourrait manger du poisson ce soir!

SANDRINE Mmm... c'est une bonne idée. Mais je n'ai pas d'argent pour le matériel, moi.

KOFFI Moi non plus.

SANDRINE Bon, si on rendait visite à des amis, alors?

KOFFI Non, je préfère faire quelque chose en ville.

SANDRINE Tiens, j'ai une idée! Si on visitait le musée? C'est gratuit, c'est en ville, et moi, je n'y suis jamais allée!

KOFFI D'accord. Allons-y!

Answers to Mise en pratique Activity 3

go for a boat ride, go fishing, visit some friends, visit the museum in Abidjan; They decide to visit the museum.

des tissus (m.)   un masque   de la poterie   des tam-tams

Chapitre 8 : C'était comme ça
Projects

Livres pour enfants
(Individual Project)

ASSIGNMENT

Students will write and illustrate a children's book in French, using the **imparfait** and the present tense. The story should be about a character whose situation has recently changed. It should describe the way things were as opposed to how they are now, and the character should express nostalgia for the way things used to be. Other characters then console him or her and suggest ways to improve the present situation. The story should be about ten pages long with an average of three sentences per page. The text may be handwritten or typed. Each page should be illustrated with original drawings, cutouts from magazines or catalogues, or computer-generated graphics.

TEACHER NOTE

If students have access to a computer and software such as Hypercard®, Hyperstudio® (Macintosh), or Linkway® (IBM & compatibles), they might write and illustrate their stories on the computer and animate them as well.

MATERIALS

✄ **Students may need**
- Posterboard or construction paper
- Unlined paper
- Markers, colored pencils, or crayons
- Magazine or catalogue pictures
- Scissors
- Glue or tape
- Hole punch
- Yarn or ribbon
- Typewriter or word processor
- Computer and software mentioned in Teacher Note

SUGGESTED SEQUENCE

1. As a prewriting activity, ask students about their favorite childhood stories. Ask them who their favorite characters were and what made the stories interesting.

2. Each student creates characters (people, animals, or animated objects) and a story line that meets the specifications given in the Assignment. The students should turn in a plan in French or English, in which they briefly describe the story line, the characters, and their relationship to one another.

3. Students begin writing the story. They might complete the project outside of class, or you might allow them class time.

4. Students might hand in a rough draft of each page of the story as it is completed. Set deadlines for completion of the pages. Students should either describe or sketch the illustration that will appear on each page.

5. Correct the text as it is handed in, using correction symbols so that students are responsible for correcting their mistakes. For example, if a student has an incorrect ending on the **imparfait,** you might write "ending" above the mistake. If the student uses the present tense where the **imparfait** is needed, you might write "tense" to indicate the error.

6. When students have corrected and rewritten the entire text, they should complete the illustrations, create a title page, and assemble the book.

7. When the books are completed, students might circulate them in class for others to read. You might even leave the books in a designated area in the room so that students can read them at their leisure. Have students write positive feedback on index cards and place them in the books. You might display some books in a showcase in the library or have a student write an article for the school newspaper telling about the project.

GRADING THE PROJECT

Each student should be graded on the content of the story, the accuracy of the language, the variety of vocabulary used, his or her creativity and effort, and the overall appearance of the project.

Suggested Point Distribution (total = 100 points)

Content	20
Language use	20
Variety of vocabulary	20
Creativity/effort	20
Overall appearance	20

COMMUNITY LINK

As a community-service project, you might send the book to an elementary school with a cassette tape of students reading the story, complete with music and sound effects.

AWALE

Awalé *is a traditional game similar to backgammon that was originally played in Egypt thousands of years ago. Awalé is uniquely representative of African culture and is also an intellectually challenging source of entertainment. Played by Africans of all ages, it is known by different names, depending on the country. In Côte d'Ivoire, the game is called* **awalé.** *In Senegal, it is known as* **ouri;** *in Togo and Benin, it is* **aju;** *the Masai in Kenya call it* **dodoi;** *in Zaire, it is called* **mankala.**

Materials
✂ **To make the game board, each pair of students will need**
- An egg carton (with two rows of six cups each)
- Two paper cups, one for each end of the carton
- 48 beans, pebbles, or seeds

Object
The object of the game is to "capture" beans, and the player with the most beans at the end of the game wins.

Procedure
1. To begin, players place four beans in each cup of the egg carton. Players will sit on opposite sides of the game board, and a move can be made starting from any cup containing beans on their side.
2. Either player may start the game. Moves are made counterclockwise around the board.
3. Player A starts by picking up all the beans from one of the cups on his or her side of the board and dropping them one at a time in each consecutive cup to the right.

4. The two cups at either end of the board are for captured beans. Beans are captured when the last bean (or beans) falls into a cup (or cups) containing one or two beans. Potentially, a player may capture the beans of several cups at a time if each of those cups contains one or two beans prior to the move. For example, if the player's last three beans fall into three consecutive cups, each containing one or two beans, he or she would capture the beans in those three cups, including the bean that completed the move.

However, if the player's last three beans fall into three cups containing two, four, and two beans respectively, he or she would only capture the two beans in the last cup, since the four beans in the next-to-last cup break the sequence. To prevent the capture of beans, players should either try to fill as many cups as possible with more than two beans or try to leave several cups empty.

5. Players take turns until one player has no beans on his or her side, and the other player cannot reach the other side of the board with two consecutive moves.

6. At the end of the game, players count their captured beans, plus any beans left on their opponent's side of the board. One point is given for each captured bean.

7. A match can consist of a particular number of games (4), or points (50, 100, 200, . . .), or a certain amount of time (30 minutes).

Chapitre 8
C'était comme ça
pp. 190–215

*U*sing the Chapter Opener

Motivating Activity

Ask students if they have ever moved to a new town or neighborhood. If so, ask them how they felt when they first arrived in their new home and what they liked or disliked about moving. Ask them what they would say to a new student in their school to make him or her feel more at home. Be sensitive to students for whom such moves may have been the results of unfortunate circumstances.

Photo Flash!

① Koffi and Sandrine, two students in Abidjan, are talking about Sandrine's recent move to Abidjan. She is telling Koffi about the village she is from. Although more than two million people live in Côte d'Ivoire's largest city, Abidjan, more than half of the country's population lives in rural areas (**en brousse,** *in the bush*).

Teaching Suggestions

• Have students read the captions and say as much as they can in French about each photo.
• Write the expression from Louisiana, **Laissez les bons temps rouler** *(Let the good times roll),* on the board or on a transparency and ask students if they know what it means. Once students understand this expression, have them deduce the meaning of **le bon vieux temps** in the caption of Photo 1.

CHAPITRE 8
C'était comme ça

① Si on parlait du bon vieux temps?

190 *cent quatre-vingt-dix*

Group Work

Have students work in groups to list all the problems or difficulties they imagine a young Ivorian from a small town or village might encounter when coming to live in the city for the first time.

Culture Note

Call attention to the cowry shells that decorate the jewelry on pages 190–191. During the eighteenth century, Djoula traders brought the cowry shell, originally from the Indian Ocean, to Côte d'Ivoire. These shells were used as currency in parts of the country until World War II. Because of their history, today they are a symbol of success. They are used not only to make jewelry, but also to decorate elaborate costumes worn in tribal rituals.

In Côte d'Ivoire, students have to leave their home villages to go to a large town to attend high school. Life is suddenly different for them. What about you? What was life like when you were younger? Did you have different friends, go to a different school, or live in another city, state, or country?

In this chapter you will

- tell what or whom you miss; reassure someone; ask and tell what things were like
- reminisce
- make and respond to suggestions

And you will

- listen to a grandmother reminisce about her childhood
- read a folktale from West Africa
- write about what you were like as a child and what you miss about your childhood
- learn about villages in Côte d'Ivoire and how francophone people feel about living in the city and the country

② La vie était plus tranquille au village.

③ On était contents!

Culture Note

In Ivorian villages (au village), houses might be made of cement, cinder blocks, mud bricks, and even bamboo. Animals such as goats, dogs, and chickens can be seen everywhere, and may even travel with their owners on buses and in taxis!

Language Note

Ask students if they recognize any verbs in the photo captions. Remind them that the phrase C'était was introduced in Chapter 6. Ask them to recall in what context it was used. (It was used to tell how an event was.) Ask them how its use is similar here. (It's used to tell how life was and what people were like.)

Focusing on Outcomes

Ask students to read the chapter outcomes, and taking into account the meaning of **du bon vieux temps**, tell what they think the two people in the photo on page 190 are talking about. (Sandrine is probably telling Koffi about what she and her friends and family used to do in the *good old days.*) Then, have them tell how they think the photos on both pages relate to the outcomes listed. NOTE: You may want to use the video to support the objectives. The self-check activities in **Que sais-je?** on page 214 help students assess their achievement of the objectives.

Photo Flash!

② This photo shows the inhabitants of a village in Côte d'Ivoire. Since African villages are generally small, it is common for everyone to know everyone else's business. There are very few secrets in the village. The village residents (**les villageois**) are usually very welcoming and generous, and they are especially appreciative if you know enough of the local language to properly greet the elders. Life moves at a slower pace in the village, and traditions are much stronger than in the city.

③ This photo shows junior high (**collège**) students at their school in Côte d'Ivoire.

Culture Note

 All students in Côte d'Ivoire wear uniforms. In high school, boys wear khaki shirts and pants, and girls generally wear blue skirts and white blouses. Many **lycées** include grades **sixième** through **terminale**. In elementary school, girls wear blue or brown gingham dresses.

**VIDEO PROGRAM
OR EXPANDED VIDEO
PROGRAM,**
Videocassette 3
18:15–22:00

OR *VIDEODISC PROGRAM,*
Videodisc 4B

Search 4710, Play To 11515

Video Synopsis

In this segment of the video, Sandrine and Koffi are talking in a park in Abidjan. Sandrine has just moved to the city from her village, and she's home-sick. She describes her village and its people to Koffi, and compares village and city life. Koffi reassures her that she will grow to like Abidjan and offers to show her around.

Motivating Activity

Compile a list of the problems and difficulties that a person from a small town might en-counter when coming to the city for the first time. Then, have students look at the pho-tos in the **Mise en train** and tell whether they suggest any of the problems on their list.

Presentation

Have students view the first segment of the video. Stop the video after Photo 7 in the book. Ask students what Sandrine misses about her vil-lage. Then, play the rest of the video and have students give Sandrine's impression of the city of Abidjan. Next, play the recording and have students read along as they listen. Finally, have students answer the questions in Activity 1 on page 194.

Mise en train

Sandrine   Koffi

La Nostalgie

Look at the title, photos, and captions of this story. What do you think Sandrine is talking to Koffi about? Does she seem happy or sad?

Koffi et Sandrine sont camarades de classe. Sandrine est née dans un village en Côte d'Ivoire. Ça fait trois semaines qu'elle habite à Abidjan.

C'était comment, là-bas dans ton village?

Oh, c'était tellement mieux. J'avais beaucoup d'amis. Ils me manquent beaucoup.

1

J'allais au collège de Sakassou. C'était un petit collège. Nous étions une cinquantaine d'élèves.

2

Après l'école, j'avais des responsabilités. On travaillait…

3

mais on s'amusait aussi. On ne faisait pas grand-chose, mais c'était bien. On se promenait ensemble. On écoutait de la musique…

4

192   *cent quatre-vingt-douze*   CHAPITRE 8   C'était comme ça

---

RESOURCES FOR MISE EN TRAIN

Textbook Audiocassette 4B/Audio CD 8
Practice and Activity Book, p. 85
Video Guide
  Video Program
  Expanded Video Program, Videocassette 3
Videodisc Guide
  Videodisc Program, Videodisc 4B

Culture Note
③ The women in this photo are mak-ing **foutou,** the national dish of Côte d'Ivoire. Here, they are pounding the ingredients (boiled plantains, manioc, or yams) into a paste that will be eaten with one of several spicy sauces.

Il y avait des animaux : des vaches, des chèvres, des poules…

De temps en temps, on organisait des fêtes. Ça me plaisait beaucoup. On chantait et on dansait. On discutait. C'était super.

5

6

On se réunissait souvent : les cousins, les oncles et les tantes, les grands-parents. C'était merveilleux.

7

Ici à Abidjan, j'ai l'impression que les gens sont plus seuls qu'en brousse. On vit dans des appartements. On ne se connaît pas autant.

8

Ici, c'est tellement plus grand! Si on veut aller voir quelqu'un, il faut prendre le bus. Là-bas, tout le monde se connaît dans le village.

Ici à Abidjan, c'est pas si mal. Tu vas voir… Eh! Si on visitait la ville ensemble? Si tu veux, je vais te faire voir tout. Je suis sûr que dans quelques semaines tu en tomberas amoureuse!

9

10

MISE EN TRAIN

cent quatre-vingt-treize **193**

 Video Integration

- *EXPANDED VIDEO PROGRAM,* Videocassette 3, 22:01–29:47
- *VIDEODISC PROGRAM,* Videodisc 4B

Search 11515, Play To 25495

You may choose to continue with **La Nostalgie (suite)** or wait until later in the chapter. When the story continues, it is several weeks later and Sandrine's sister, Albertine, has just arrived from the village to visit. Albertine is excited but completely unaccustomed to being in a big city. Sandrine, however, has changed. She is confident and very much at home in Abidjan. Sandrine gives her sister a tour, and Albertine is amazed at how she has become a city-dweller.

Teaching Suggestion

Write one sentence from each photo caption on the board. Have students copy the sentences on separate slips of paper and shuffle them. Then, play the recording and have students arrange the sentences in the order in which they hear them mentioned in the recording.

For Individual Needs

Slower Pace Draw two columns on the board or on a transparency and label them **En brousse** and **En ville**. For visual learners, put a symbol next to each label, such as a palm tree next to **En brousse** and a skyscraper next to **En ville**. Have students do the same on a sheet of paper. Then, have partners find the sentences in the **Mise en train** that refer to Sandrine's village and those that refer to Abidjan and write them in the appropriate column. Afterwards, have them tell you what to write in the columns on the board or transparency.

Culture Note

Point out the wooden elephant pictured on this page. It is made of ebony, the heartwood of many tropical trees common in western Africa. The bark of these trees is jet-black, yet the wood just under the bark is white. It is the interior heartwood of the tree, the dark brown ebony streaked with black, that is commonly used for many Ivorian crafts. This hard, close-grained wood typically polishes to a high gloss and is ideal for cabinet-making, piano keys, and knife handles, as well as statues and masks.

1 Tu as compris? See answers below.

1. Where did Sandrine move from? Where does she live now?
2. Where does Koffi live? Does he like it there?
3. What was it like where Sandrine used to live? What did she do there?
4. According to Sandrine, what is Abidjan like?
5. What does Koffi offer to do?

2 Ville ou village?

Est-ce que Sandrine parle de son village ou d'Abidjan?

1. «Il y avait des chèvres.»   de son village
2. «On organisait des fêtes.»   de son village
3. «C'est tellement grand!»   d'Abidjan
4. «Nous étions une cinquantaine d'élèves.»   de son village
5. «On vit dans des appartements.»   d'Abidjan
6. «Les gens sont plus seuls.»   d'Abidjan

3 C'était le bon vieux temps

Sandrine parle de quelle image?

1. «On se promenait ensemble.»   a
2. «On chantait et on dansait.»   c
3. «On se réunissait souvent.»   b

a.

b.

c.

4 Cherche les expressions See answers below.

1. What does Sandrine say to . . .
   a. tell what she thinks of her life in the village?
   b. recall what she used to do?
   c. give her impressions of Abidjan?

2. What does Koffi say to . . .
   a. ask how life was in Sandrine's village?
   b. reassure Sandrine?

5 Et maintenant, à toi

Have you ever moved from one place to another? What do you miss about where you used to live? How would you feel if you had to move now?

RENCONTRE CULTURELLE

What can you tell about everyday life in an African village from these photos?

Qu'en penses-tu?

1. What are these people from different villages in Côte d'Ivoire doing?
2. How does this differ from the way things are done in the United States?

> **1.** spinning yarn, carving wood, making foutou, carrying fruit
>
> **2.** In the United States, people buy what they need from stores, whereas in a small village in Côte d'Ivoire, people make many of the things they need from raw materials.

Savais-tu que... ?

Small villages in Côte d'Ivoire are plentiful and rich in local culture. Certain regions of Côte d'Ivoire, as well as individual towns, villages, and ethnic groups, are known for their particular customs, crafts, and costumes. The town of Korhogo is famous for its painted woven fabrics; the Sénoufo are known for their weaving; the people in Katiola are noted for their pottery. In areas where electricity and machinery are not available, everyday life requires many physical tasks. Life is simpler; people cook over open fires, carry water, use large communal bowls in place of table settings and silverware, and walk instead of riding in cars.

Culture Note

In Côte d'Ivoire, living in the city has its advantages, especially in Abidjan. There are better health-care facilities, a greater selection of food, more social activities, and better educational opportunities. Unfortunately, as in the United States, city life is also more stressful and expensive. Village life, on the other hand, can be quite simple. Villages can range in size from less than 100 inhabitants to more than 25,000. Larger villages are likely to have water and electricity, whereas people living in smaller villages may have to depend on a well or stream for water, and campfires and lanterns for cooking and lighting.

(Refer to the Photo Flash! on page 190.)

Motivating Activity

Ask students to imagine living in a small rural village like those pictured. Ask them what they think they would like or dislike about the lifestyle. Ask them to compare city life and country life in the United States. Ask them which they prefer in the United States, city or country life, and why.

Presentation

Have students look at the pictures and tell what the people are doing. Ask them to recall the expression that tells where these people live (**en brousse**). (Refer to the Photo Flash! on page 190.) Discuss the questions in **Qu'en penses-tu?** and the information in **Savais-tu que... ?** with students. Afterwards, ask them to imagine what a typical day might be like for a teenager living **en brousse.** You might have them discuss this in groups.

Thinking Critically

Synthesizing Ask students to name some of the ways in which life would be less complicated in a small village. Ask them if they think it would be easier for them to adjust to the village or for the villagers to adjust to the city and why. Then, ask students if they think it's possible to live a less complicated life in this country. How? Is it desirable? Why or why not?

Multicultural Link

Have students research villages or peoples in other parts of Africa or the world to find out what particular craft(s), if any, they are known for. Students might then report their findings to the class.

196   PREMIERE ETAPE

Jump Start!

Write the following sentences on the board or on a transparency. For each sentence, students decide whether it describes life **en brousse, en ville,** or **les deux.**

1. **Il n'y a pas de voitures.**
2. **On y écoute de la musique.**
3. **On vit dans des appartements.**
4. **Tout le monde se connaît.**
5. **Il faut prendre le bus pour aller voir quelqu'un.**
6. **On organise des fêtes.**
7. **Il y a une cinquantaine d'élèves dans le collège.**
8. **On discute avec des amis.**

(*Answers:* 1. **en brousse** 2. **les deux** 3. **en ville** 4. **en brousse** 5. **en ville** 6. **les deux** 7. **en brousse** 8. **les deux**)

MOTIVATE

Ask students if they have ever been homesick. Ask volunteers to share their experiences and tell what they missed about their homes, friends, families, and school.

TEACH

Teaching Suggestion

Ask two volunteers to read the dialogue aloud. Then, have pairs of students write each character's lines on separate slips of paper, shuffle them, and pass them to another pair of students to rearrange in the original order. Then, write a few key words from each line on the board and have partners try to create a similar conversation, using the words as cues.

Thinking Critically

Synthesizing Ask students if they know someone who has gone away to school after high school. Have them discuss the advantages and the disadvantages of living at home and living on campus while attending college.

PREMIERE ETAPE

Telling what or whom you miss; reassuring someone; asking and telling what things were like

ADJOUA Alors, ça va, Adama? Tu te débrouilles dans notre grande ville?

ADAMA Oui, mais je regrette mon village. Il me manque beaucoup.

ADJOUA Je comprends. Dis-moi, il se trouve où, ton village?

ADAMA Koni est au nord, près de Korhogo.

ADJOUA C'était tellement différent là-bas?

ADAMA Bien sûr! La vie était plus tranquille, on était moins pressés. Il y avait des coutumes, des cérémonies avec des danses traditionnelles.

ADJOUA Mais il y a des danses ici aussi! Et il y a tant d'autres choses à voir... et beaucoup de monde!

ADAMA Là-bas, j'avais un tas d'amis. On jouait au foot... on jouait aux cartes... et à l'awalé, j'étais le champion!

ADJOUA T'en fais pas. Tu trouveras des amis ici aussi. Et c'est bien de vivre en ville. Tu vas voir que c'est plus animé ici.

6 Tu as compris?

1. Adama est d'où?
2. Qu'est-ce qu'Adama regrette *(miss)*?
3. Comment était la vie là-bas?
4. Qu'est-ce qu'on faisait là-bas?
5. D'après Adjoua, comment est la vie à Abidjan?

1. Koni
2. son village
3. différente, plus tranquille, on était moins pressés
4. on jouait au foot, aux cartes et à l'awalé
5. très animée

NOTE CULTURELLE

Most high schools in West Africa are in large cities or towns, so students have to leave their home village if they want to continue their studies beyond the junior high level. Students who go to a big city to study usually live with a relative or friend from the same village who will take them in as a family member. People from the same ethnic group often live in the same neighborhood. You can usually tell a person's ethnic group from his or her name: **Adjoua** and **Koffi** are Baoulé names, and **Adama** is a Sénoufo name. French West Africans usually have both an African and French first name. They always give their family name first, followed by their African first name and then their French first name: **TRAORE Adama Eric** or **KOUASSI Adjoua Désirée.**

RESOURCES FOR PREMIERE ETAPE

Textbook Audiocassette 4B/Audio CD 8
Practice and Activity Book, pp. 86–88
Videodisc Guide
    Videodisc Program, Videodisc 4B

Chapter Teaching Resources, Book 2
- Teaching Transparency Master 8-1, pp. 175, 178
    Teaching Transparency 8-1
- Additional Listening Activities 8-1, 8-2, p. 179
    Audiocassette 10A/Audio CD 8
- Realia 8-1, pp. 183, 185
- Situation Cards 8-1, pp. 186–187
- Student Response Forms, pp. 188–190
- Quiz 8-1, pp. 191–192
    Audiocassette 8A/Audio CD 8

COMMENT DIT-ON... ?
Telling what or whom you miss; reassuring someone

To tell what or whom you miss:

Je regrette la campagne. *I miss . . .*
Mon école **me manque.** *I miss . . .*
Mes copains **me manquent.**
Ce qui me manque, c'est mon ancienne maison.
What I really miss is . . .

To reassure someone:

Tu vas t'y faire. *You'll get used to it.*
Fais-toi une raison.
Make the best of it.
Tu vas te plaire ici.
You're going to like it here.
Tu vas voir que tout le monde est sympa ici. *You'll see that . . .*

7 Ecoute!

Ecoute ces élèves. Qu'est-ce qui leur manque?

1. Sylvie   a
2. Emile   c
3. Francine   b
4. Bertrand   d

8 Qu'est-ce que tu as?   *Possible answers:*

a. Your friends want to know what's wrong. What would you tell them if . . .

1. your best friend had just moved away?   Mon meilleur ami (Ma meilleure amie) me manque.
2. your bike were stolen?   Ce qui me manque, c'est mon vélo.
3. the snow had melted and you loved to ski?   Je regrette le ski et la neige.
4. your mom were away on a long trip?   Ma mère me manque.
5. your favorite teacher had moved to a different school?   Mon prof me manque.

b. What would you like your friends to say to make you feel better?
Tu vas t'y faire. Fais-toi une raison. Tu vas voir que ça va aller mieux.

9 Ils ont le mal du pays   *They're homesick*

Il y a de nouveaux élèves à ton école cette année. A ton avis, qu'est-ce qui leur manque? Fais une liste de trois choses pour chaque élève.   See answers below.

Lisa est de Tours.

Philippe vient de Québec.

Karine est de Paris.

José vient de la Martinique.

Presentation

Comment dit-on... ?   Give each of four students an index card on which you've written one expression for reassuring someone. Tell them that you've just moved here from Paris. Bring photos, postcards, or souvenirs from Paris and show them as you tell students what you miss about the city. Write the expressions in **Comment dit-on... ?** as you say them. Have the four students take turns reassuring you by saying what's on their card. Finally, trade places with students who, by using your pictures, will tell what they miss about the city.

Additional Practice

7 Have students tell what each person in the recording misses. Ask **Qu'est-ce que Sylvie regrette? Qu'est-ce qu'Emile regrette?** and so on. Then, ask students to imagine they are the individuals in the recording. Ask them what they miss (**Qu'est-ce que tu regrettes, Sylvie?**) and have them tell what they miss. (**Ce qui me manque, c'est mon village.**)

Teaching Suggestions

8 Ask students to write answers to the questions. For listening practice, have volunteers read any one of their answers aloud. Their classmates write the number of the question in the activity that corresponds to the answer they hear. For example, if a student reads **Mon prof me manque,** the others would write **5.**

9 Have students role-play this activity, with one partner playing the new student and the other reassuring him or her.

Language Notes

• To explain how the verb **manquer** is used, ask students to compare the verb forms in **Mon école me manque** and **Mes copains me manquent.** Ask them to compare how **manquer** is used in French as opposed to the way *to miss* is used in English. (Literally, **me manque(nt)** means *is (are) lacking to me.*) Finally, ask students how they would say *I miss you* in French. (**Tu me manques. Vous me manquez.**)

• Tell students that **ce qui** is used only for objects and places, not people.

Possible answers

9 *José:* la plage, la mer, la planche à voile
Lisa: ses copains, sa maison, ses profs, les châteaux
Karine: la tour Eiffel, le métro, les musées
Philippe: le ski, la neige, le hockey

Teaching Suggestion

10 Ask volunteers to present their dialogue as a skit. Have the class take notes and tell at least one thing the American student in each pair misses (**... lui manque(nt)**).

Presentation

Comment dit-on... ?
Describe an imaginary town where you supposedly used to live, using magazine pictures or drawings. Then, ask if anyone has ever lived in another home or city. Ask students several either-or questions to elicit the expressions in **Comment dit-on... ?** (**C'était comment la ville? La vie, c'était simple ou compliqué? Il y avait beaucoup d'habitants ou peu d'habitants?**)

For videodisc application, see *Videodisc Guide.*

Presentation

Vocabulaire To illustrate the adjectives, gather magazine pictures and describe them. (**Ce paysage est tranquille, mais cette ville est bruyante.**) Then, ask either-or questions. (**Cette ville est tranquille ou bruyante?**) Next, have students repeat the vocabulary after you. Finally, have volunteers describe the city and the country, using your pictures and the adjectives. (**La ville, c'est animé. La campagne, c'est calme.**)

Teaching Suggestion

Ask volunteers to use gestures, sounds, props, or drawings on the board to try and get their classmates to say one of the adjectives in the Vocabulaire.

10 Fais-toi une raison

You've just moved to Abidjan. Tell your new Ivorian friend three things you miss about your home, and he or she will reassure you. Act out the scene with a partner and then change roles.

—Qu'est-ce que tu as?
—Ma ville me manque.
—Ah, bon? Pourquoi?
— ...

la cuisine américaine   ma meilleure amie   ___?___   mon chat   la neige   mon lycée   les fêtes   mon chien   mon meilleur ami

COMMENT DIT-ON... ?
Asking and telling what things were like

To ask what things were like:
C'était comment? *What was it like?*
C'était tellement différent? *Was it really so different?*

To tell what things were like:
C'était beau. *It was . . .*
Il y avait de jolies maisons. *There were . . .*
La vie était plus simple, **moins** compliquée! *Life was more . . . , less . . .*

VOCABULAIRE

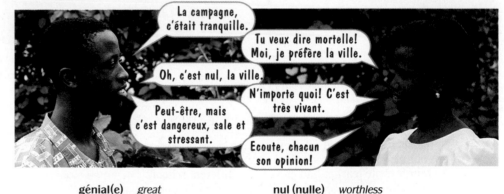

La campagne, c'était tranquille.
Tu veux dire mortelle! Moi, je préfère la ville.
Oh, c'est nul, la ville.
N'importe quoi! C'est très vivant.
Peut-être, mais c'est dangereux, sale et stressant.
Ecoute, chacun son opinion!

génial(e)	*great*	**nul (nulle)**	*worthless*
calme	*calm*	**très vivant(e)**	*very lively*
tranquille	*peaceful*	**bruyant(e)**	*noisy*
propre	*clean*	**sale**	*dirty*
relaxant(e)	*relaxing*	**stressant(e)**	*stressful*
mortel (mortelle)	*dull*	**animé(e)**	*lively*
		dangereux (dangereuse)	*dangerous*

Language Note

Remind students that an adjective is invariable when it directly follows **c'est** and **c'était**. (**La ville, c'est amusant.**) However, the adjective must reflect the gender and number when a noun or **il(s)/elle(s)** are used: **Les villes sont bruyantes. Elles sont animées.**

Additional Practice

Have students ask those who have lived in another state or town what their former hometowns were like. Help them by asking either-or questions. As an extension of this activity, students might invent an imaginary town and describe it.

11 Ecoute!

Listen to the conversation between Justin and his cousin Mamadou, who has just moved to Abidjan to go to school. List three things Mamadou misses about his village. What do he and Justin decide to do? Answers on p. 189C.

12 La vie en ville

Adjoua is comparing her life in the city to life in the country. Agree or disagree with her statements, adding your own opinion.

La ville, c'est super.

La vie à la campagne, c'est tranquille.

La ville, c'est toujours bruyant.

La campagne, c'est relaxant.

—La vie en ville, c'est super.
—Oui, c'est génial. *ou* Mais non, c'est nul.

13 C'était plus relax...

Choose a place you have lived or where you would like to have lived. Make a list of the advantages and disadvantages of life there. Then, make a similar list for the place you live now. Which place do you prefer? Why?

A Paris	Ici
C'était très animé	C'est tranquille.
Il y avait beaucoup à faire.	J'ai beaucoup d'amis.
J'avais un chat.	J'ai trois chats!

Note de Grammaire

- When you describe what things were like, you use the *imperfect* tense (**l'imparfait**). You've already seen two forms, **c'était** and **il y avait**.
- To form the imperfect, add the appropriate ending to the stem. For the verb **avoir**, the stem is **av-**. The imperfect endings are:

  j'av**ais**
  tu av**ais**
  il/elle/on av**ait**
  nous av**ions**
  vous av**iez**
  ils/elles av**aient**

- For the verb **être**, the stem is **ét-**.

14 Interview

Maintenant, interviewe un(e) camarade. Demande-lui comment c'était là où il/elle habitait avant et comment c'est maintenant. Demande-lui quel endroit il/elle préfère.

—Où est-ce que tu habitais avant?
—A...
—C'était comment?
—C'était super! La vie là-bas, c'était plus...
—Qu'est-ce qu'il y avait là-bas?
—...

15 Tu vas t'y faire

Your pen pal from Abidjan, who will be spending a year at your school, is worried about moving to your town and going to your school. Write a letter reassuring your friend. Tell him or her the advantages of your town and school.

ASSESS

Quiz 8-1, *Chapter Teaching Resources, Book 2,* pp. 191–192

Assessment Items, Audiocassette 8A Audio CD 8

Performance Assessment

Have groups of three role-play a situation in which one student is homesick and the other two comfort him or her. Challenge them to include as many functions and as much vocabulary from this **étape** as possible.

Presentation

Note de grammaire Tell students to reread **La Nostalgie** on pages 192–193 and find all the verbs that describe how things used to be for Sandrine. Based on all the imperfect verbs they see, have them try to deduce how to conjugate the verbs **être** and **avoir** in the **imparfait**.

Geography Link

13 Hang a world map on the wall and place a large pin in the location of your city or town. Teach students the phrase **Avant, j'habitais...** Then, have students who have lived in another city or country mark their previous hometown with a pin and tell where they used to live and what it was like. To involve the entire class, have students pretend they lived in another town and mark their imaginary hometowns on the map with a pin.

CLOSE

Game

CATÉGORIES Write the four functions from this **étape** plus *adjectives for describing places* on the board. Form two teams. Name a category *(reassuring someone)* and have the two teams take turns reassuring someone about something. (**Tu vas voir, c'est sympa ici.**) Continue until a team cannot add another appropriate sentence. The last team to say something appropriate to the category scores a point. When students have exhausted a category, choose another one and start a new round.

DEUXIEME ETAPE
Reminiscing

Jump Start!

Ask students to imagine they have just moved and write five sentences describing the town they left and telling what and whom they miss.

MOTIVATE

Recall the expression used in the Chapter Opener: **le bon vieux temps**. Ask students when their **bon vieux temps** was and what it was like. Was it when they were five years old? Ten? At a summer camp? Do they ever reminisce about these times? Why?

TEACH

Presentation

Vocabulaire Use puppets to tell Yapo's story. Tell students that Yapo is reminiscing about his childhood. Introduce his mother and brother and proceed to tell the story, using the puppets and other props to get the meaning across. Then, have students open their books and read along as you read the sentences aloud. Finally, ask the following questions: **Qu'est-ce que Yapo faisait tous les jours?** (la sieste) Il avait des responsabilités? (Il n'avait pas de responsabilités.) Il avait des problèmes ou des soucis? (Il n'avait pas de problèmes/soucis.) Qui est-ce qu'il taquinait? (son frère) Qu'est-ce qu'il conduisait? (une voiture super) Qui est-ce qu'il ennuyait? (sa mère) Que faisait-il toujours? (des bêtises)

Culture Note

In West African countries, it is very common for children to share a bed or a mat since there are often not enough for each child to have his or her own.

VOCABULAIRE

Yapo

 je faisais la sieste tous les jours.

 **Je faisais** toujours **des bêtises.**

 **Je taquinais** mon frère…

 et **je conduisais une voiture** super.

 **J'ennuyais** ma mère.

 Je n'avais pas de responsabilités, pas de soucis.

Qu'est-ce qui s'est passé??!!

200 *deux cents*

CHAPITRE 8   C'était comme ça

RESOURCES FOR DEUXIEME ETAPE

Textbook Audiocassette 4B/Audio CD 8
Practice and Activity Book, pp. 89–91
Video Guide
   Video Program
   Expanded Video Program, Videocassette 3
Videodisc Guide
   Videodisc Program, Videodisc 4B

Chapter Teaching Resources, Book 2
• Communicative Activity 8-1, pp. 171–172
• Teaching Transparency Master 8-2, pp. 176, 178
   Teaching Transparency 8-2
• Additional Listening Activities 8-3, 8-4, p. 180
   Audiocassette 10A/Audio CD 8
• Realia 8-2, pp. 184, 185
• Situation Cards 8-2, pp. 186–187
• Student Response Forms, pp. 188–190
• Quiz 8-2, pp. 193–194
   Audiocassette 8A/Audio CD 8

16 Moi aussi!

Est-ce que tu étais comme Yapo quand tu étais enfant? Avec un(e) camarade, lis ce qu'il a dit dans le **Vocabulaire** et réponds **Moi aussi! Moi, non! Moi non plus!** ou **Moi, si!** à chaque phrase. Est-ce que toi et ton/ta camarade, vous aviez le même caractère quand vous étiez jeunes?

17 Ecoute! *Answers on p. 189C.*

Yapo interviewe son professeur sur son enfance. Ecoute l'interview. Ensuite, lis ses notes. Sont-elles correctes? Corrige les erreurs s'il y en a.

> *Elle était pénible; elle ennuyait sa mère.*
> *Elle aidait sa mère; elle faisait la cuisine avec elle.*
> *Elle taquinait ses deux frères.*
> *Elle ne faisait jamais de bêtises.*

NOTE CULTURELLE

Some families in Côte d'Ivoire may only be able to send one child to high school, so being a student like Yapo is a respected privilege. High school is very competitive, and students devote most of their time to their studies. When they do have free time, they often visit relatives and friends, play soccer, or get together to listen to music and discuss the latest family events, such as marriages, initiations, and baptisms.

COMMENT DIT-ON...?

Reminiscing

Quand j'étais petit(e), j'étais très pénible! *When I was little, ...*
Quand ma meilleure amie **était petite,** elle était gentille. *When ... was little, ...*
Quand j'avais deux **ans,** je n'étais pas facile! *When I was ... years old, ...*

18 La vie à cinq ans

A reporter for your school paper is interviewing you about your childhood. Answer the questions.

1. Quand tu avais cinq ans, tu étais comment?
2. Tu avais un ou une meilleur(e) ami(e)?
3. Il ou elle était comment?
4. Comment était ta vie quand tu avais cinq ans?

Vocabulaire *à la carte*

rigolo	*funny*
polisson (polissonne)	*naughty*
mal luné(e)	*moody*
capricieux (capricieuse)	*temperamental*
coquin(e)	*mischievous*
sage	*well-behaved*
timide	*shy*
calme	*calm*
un petit diable	*a little devil*
un petit ange	*a little angel*

DEUXIEME ETAPE

deux cent un 201

Culture Notes

• Other pastimes of Ivorian teenagers include dancing, singing, discussing current events, playing a variety of sports, and card or board games. Girls enjoy braiding each other's hair, which can be a very elaborate, time-consuming procedure.

• In Côte d'Ivoire, students often write their school work on small chalkboards. They are issued books and study a variety of subjects, including three languages in high school (French, English, and Spanish or German). Course work is usually quite rigorous, and all lessons are given in French. This can be difficult for children who grow up speaking their ethnic language and little or no French.

Teaching Suggestion

17 As a variation, have students listen to the recording before they open their books. Tell them to take notes (not complete sentences) as the teacher describes her childhood. Then, have students open their books and compare their notes with Yapo's.

Presentation

Comment dit-on... ?/ Vocabulaire à la carte
Label two columns on the board **Un petit diable** and **Un petit ange** and sketch a picture to illustrate each label. Write the other vocabulary words on separate flashcards. Then, describe how you were and how your imaginary brother or sister was when you were little. (**Moi, quand j'étais petit(e), j'étais un petit ange, bien sûr! Mon frère/ma sœur, par contre, était un petit diable!**) Tape the vocabulary words under the appropriate columns as you use them. (**Moi, j'étais sage. Mais mon frère/ma sœur était polisson(ne)!**) Use facial expressions, gestures, and intonation to help convey the meaning of the words.

For videodisc application, see *Videodisc Guide.*

For Individual Needs

18 Slower Pace Ask either-or questions to help students answer the questions. (**Quand tu étais petit(e), tu étais rigolo ou timide?**)

18 Challenge Ask students to imagine what their favorite celebrities were like when they were little and to describe them (**Quand Tom Cruise était petit, il était...**).

Grammaire The imperfect

You've already learned how to use the imperfect of **être** and **avoir** to tell *what things were like* in the past. You also use the imperfect when you're talking about *what used to happen* in the past.

- You've seen the imperfect endings -**ais**, -**ais**, -**ait**, -**ions**, -**iez**, and -**aient**.
- All verbs use the same endings, which are added to a stem. The stem of most verbs is the **nous** form of the verb in the present tense without -**ons**.

nous **avons** ⟶	av- ⟶	j'**av**ais *(I had, used to have)*
nous **faisons** ⟶	fais- ⟶	elle **fais**ait *(She did/made, used to do/make)*
nous **allons** ⟶	all- ⟶	ils **all**aient *(They went, used to go)*

- The stem of **être**, as you know, is **ét-**.

19 Ecoute! Answers on p. 189C.

Ecoute la grand-mère de Sandrine qui parle de son enfance. Est-ce que ces phrases sont vraies ou fausses?

1. D'après la grand-mère, quand elle était jeune la vie était plus facile.
2. Les filles allaient à l'école.
3. Les filles travaillaient plus dur.
4. Son enfance lui manque.

20 Tu avais une vie facile?

L'année dernière, qu'est-ce que tu faisais chez toi? Pose des questions à un(e) camarade pour savoir quelles responsabilités il/elle avait. Il/Elle va répondre avec **jamais, quelquefois, d'habitude,** ou **toujours.** Qui avait la vie la plus facile?

1. Tu faisais la vaisselle?
2. Tu gardais ton frère ou ta sœur?
3. Tu lavais la voiture?
4. Tu promenais le chien?
5. Tu sortais la poubelle?
6. Tu faisais la lessive *(washed clothes)*?
7. Tu rangeais ta chambre?
8. Tu passais l'aspirateur?
9. Tu faisais la cuisine?
10. Tu tondais le gazon?

Tu te rappelles ?

Do you remember how to pronounce the (ɛ) sound represented by the letters **ais, ait, ê** and **è**? It sounds like the *e* in *pet*. Don't let the sound glide; keep it tense and short. Practice saying this sentence: **Il faisait des bêtises et ennuyait sa mère, mais il n'était pas très embêtant.**

When you're learning the forms of a new verb or verb tense, it often helps to look for patterns to help you remember how to spell the verbs. For example, to remember the endings of the imperfect tense, notice that the **nous** and **vous** stems have the familiar present tense endings with just one difference: an added **i** for **i**mperfect. How could you remember the other endings? Taking a minute to analyze verb forms makes it easy to recall them when you want to write in French.

21 Que faisait Yapo?

Qu'est-ce que Yapo faisait quand il était plus jeune?

1. Il étudiait avec un copain. **2.** Il jouait à l'awalé. **3.** Il se baignait. **4.** Il allait à l'école.

22 Papa Houphouët, tu nous manqueras!

Complete this young Ivorian's story about shaking hands with the former president of Côte d'Ivoire by using the **imparfait** form of the verbs in parentheses.

UN JEUNE IVOIRIEN S'EN SOUVIENT...

J'ai rencontré Félix Houphouët-Boigny un après-midi de l'an 1977. C' _1_ (être) à l'occasion d'une finale de Coupe nationale de football. Ce jour-là, j' _2_ (être) ramasseur de balle. Je _3_ (devoir) avoir 12 ou 13 ans.

Nous, les ramasseurs de balle, _4_ (être) placés après les joueurs. Le président a salué tous les joueurs. Le chef du protocole _5_ (vouloir) lui indiquer le chemin des tribunes mais Houphouët a dit : «Laissemoi saluer mes enfants. Ils font aussi partie du match.» Je croyais rêver lorsque j'ai vu la main de

Notre Père prendre la mienne... Quelle émotion! Je _6_ (serrer) la main à Félix Houphouët-Boigny! Pendant une semaine, j'ai mangé avec la main gauche.

Plus tard, quand je _7_ (raconter) l'histoire à mes amis, ils _8_ (être) très impressionnés.

D'ABIDJAN N°001   3

1. était   2. étais   3. devais   4. étions   5. voulait   6. serrais   7. racontais   8. étaient

NOTE CULTURELLE

Félix Houphouët-Boigny, affectionately called **Papa Houphouët** or **Le Vieux**, was elected as Côte d'Ivoire's first president in 1960 when the country gained independence from France. His presidency was marked by economic prosperity, owing to his support of agriculture and his willingness to foster a close relationship with France. Houphouët-Boigny served as president of Côte d'Ivoire until his death in December 1993. His funeral was held two months later in Yamoussoukro. Because of its distinction as the native village of the president, Yamoussoukro has been built up more than any other town in Côte d'Ivoire, with the exception of Abidjan. Some impressive sights in town are the Presidential Palace, the Basilica of Our Lady of Peace (the largest basilica in the world), and large four-lane highways lined with towering street lights and trees for miles in both directions.

DEUXIEME ETAPE   *deux cent trois* **203**

Culture Notes

• Before Côte d'Ivoire's independence in 1960, Félix Houphouët-Boigny became the first African to hold a cabinet post in the French government. While his West African counterparts were stressing nationalism in the early post-independence years (1960s), the Ivorian president continued to use France's resources to aid in the growth and modernization of his country and the betterment of his people.

• When foreign dignitaries would visit Côte d'Ivoire, the President would take them to Yamoussoukro. These days were declared holidays, and school children would line the streets waving and greeting the President and his guests. To commemorate this special occasion, women would wear skirts **(pagnes)** with pictures of the President and his guest printed on them.

Teaching Suggestion

21 Ask students to bring in a photo of themselves at a younger age that shows what they used to do, and tell their classmates about it. Give students the option of bringing in magazine or catalogue pictures instead of a photo so they can "invent" their childhood, if they prefer.

For Individual Needs

22 Slower Pace Write all the verbs needed to complete the article in their correct form and in random order. Then, photocopy and distribute them to students. Have them number the verbs in the order they should appear in the article. You may wish to have students rewrite the text, completing it with the verbs from your list. Then, read the article aloud with the correct verb forms and have students check their papers.

Teaching Suggestion

22 When the activity has been completed, ask the following comprehension questions: **Qui est-ce que ce jeune homme a rencontré?** (Félix Houphouët-Boigny) **En quelle année?** (1977) **Où était-il?** (à une finale de Coupe nationale de football) **Quel âge avait-il?** (douze ou treize ans) **Qui est-ce que le président a salué?** (tous les joueurs) **Pourquoi est-ce que le jeune Ivoirien a mangé avec la main gauche pendant une semaine?** (parce qu'il avait serré la main à Félix Houphouët-Boigny) **Quelle a été la réaction de ses amis?** (Ils étaient très impressionés.)

For Individual Needs

22 Challenge Ask students if they've ever met anyone famous, and if so, to recount the event in French.

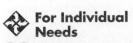

Teaching Suggestion

24 Have students write the answers to this quiz in complete sentences without writing their names. Form groups of five and have the group members take someone else's paper and read it aloud. The others in the group try to guess whose paper is being read, based on what they know of their classmates.

Presentation

Vocabulaire à la carte
Draw or gather pictures or objects to represent the vocabulary. Show the pictures or objects, say the French name, and have students repeat after you. Then, while holding up the picture or object, ask questions, such as **Tu jouais aux billes quand tu étais petit(e)? Qui avait une poupée? Comment s'appelait-elle? Tu avais un nounours? Il était comment?**

 Mon journal

25 For an additional journal entry suggestion for Chapter 8, see *Practice and Activity Book,* page 152.

Building on Previous Skills

25 Help students transfer the expressions for emphasizing they learned in the present tense to the **imparfait.** (Ce que j'aimais surtout, c'était... , Ce qui me plaisait, c'était...)

CLOSE

 Game

CHARADES Form groups of five. Have students take turns acting out what they did when they were little. The others should try to guess, using the **imparfait. (Tu faisais la sieste.)** The student who guesses correctly scores a point.

---

23 Devine!

Find the following words in the quiz below. What do you think they mean in English?

la nourriture	agité	un jouet	imaginaire	un surnom	dessins animés
food	restless	a toy	imaginary	a nickname	cartoons

24 Une enquête

a. Take the quiz in Activity 23.
b. Poll four of your classmates. Make a list of the most popular answers for each question.

25 Mon journal

Comment étais-tu quand tu étais enfant? Qu'est-ce que tu faisais? Comment était ta vie? Qu'est-ce que tu regrettes de ton enfance?

On m'appelait…
Je mangeais…
Je n'aimais pas…
Je faisais…   ?   J'aimais surtout…

Vocabulaire à la carte

un tricycle	a tricycle
un nounours	a stuffed animal
une couverture	a blanket
un bac à sable	a sandbox
une poupée	a doll
un train électrique	a train
un ballon	a ball
des cubes (m.)	blocks
des billes (f.)	marbles

204 *deux cent quatre*   CHAPITRE 8 C'était comme ça

Performance Assessment

Have groups of three write a story about someone's childhood (a celebrity, an imaginary character, or a cartoon character). Have them tell what the character was like when he or she was little and what he or she used to do. Then, students should contrast the way things were with how they are now for the character. Have a narrator read the story while two students act it out.

PANORAMA CULTUREL

Jacques • Québec

Onélia • France

Céline • Viêt-nam

VIDEO PROGRAM
OR EXPANDED VIDEO
PROGRAM,
Videocassette 3
29:48–34:48

OR VIDEODISC PROGRAM,
Videodisc 4B

Search 25495, Play To 28070

We asked some French-speaking people whether they would prefer to live in the city or the country and why. Here's what they had to say.

 Est-ce que tu préfères la vie en ville ou à la campagne? Pourquoi?

«J'aime les deux. J'aime bien vivre à la ville à cause de toutes les commodités qu'on y retrouve, mais j'aime bien partir les fins de semaines, ou pendant les vacances, pour me rendre à la campagne.»
—Jacques

«[En ville,] on peut sortir quand on veut. On n'a pas besoin des parents qui nous emmènent et ramènent en voiture. C'est plus pratique. On peut inviter des amis et sortir ensemble. Je trouve que c'est un avantage.»
—Onélia

«[A la campagne,] il n'y a pas de pollution. C'est plus... C'est mieux pour respirer. C'est plus agréable et, par exemple, il n'y a pas de bruit comme tout à l'heure là. Et on est plus au calme et il y a moins de voleurs, aussi.»
—Céline

Qu'en penses-tu?

1. According to these people, what are the advantages and disadvantages of living in the city? In the country? See answers below.
2. Do you agree or disagree with the interviewees?
3. Which of these advantages or disadvantages apply to where you live? Which don't?
4. Can you think of other reasons why you might prefer living in the country or in the city?
5. How might your life be different if you lived in a small town, a big city, or an African village?

Teacher Notes

• See *Video Guide, Videodisc Guide,* and *Practice and Activity Book* for activities related to the **Panorama Culturel.**
• Remind students that cultural material may be included in the Chapter Quizzes and Test.
• The interviewees' language represents informal, unrehearsed speech. Occasionally, edits have been made for clarification.

Motivating Activity

Ask students which they prefer, city or country life, and why.

Presentation

Have students view the video and say as much as they can about the interviews. Ask them the **Questions** below to check comprehension. Finally, have students work in small groups to discuss the questions in **Qu'en penses-tu?**

For Individual Needs

Challenge Ask a few students who feel strongly about either city or country life to try to convince their classmates that theirs is the better lifestyle. You might form two teams and debate the topic. (Vivre en ville ou à la campagne. Que choisir?)

Answers

1. *In the city:* more convenient; teenagers don't need rides from their parents; it's easy to go out with friends.
   In the country: no pollution; not as noisy; people are calmer; less crime.

Questions

1. Qui préfère la campagne? La ville? Qui aime les deux? (Céline; Onélia; Jacques)
2. Quand est-ce que Jacques aime aller à la campagne? (en fins de semaines ou pendant les vacances)
3. Pourquoi est-ce qu'Onélia préfère la ville? (On peut sortir quand on veut.)
4. Pourquoi est-ce que Céline préfère la campagne? (Il n'y a pas de pollution, c'est moins bruyant et c'est plus calme.)

*J*ump Start!

Have students copy and complete the following sentence starters, using different verbs in the **imparfait**.
1. **Quand j'avais six ans...**
2. **Quand ma grand-mère était jeune...**
3. **Quand nous étions jeunes, mon meilleur ami (ma meilleure amie) et moi...**

MOTIVATE

Ask students to recall Sandrine's problem in the **Mise en train**. How did Koffi try to help her? Ask students what kinds of places Koffi and Sandrine might have visited and if they think Sandrine's opinion of Abidjan might have improved after her tour of the city.

TEACH

Teaching Suggestion

Read the letter and the photo captions aloud as students listen with their books closed. Then, ask them if Sandrine still feels the way she did in the **Mise en train**. Have them describe her mood and tell what she is doing in Abidjan. Then, project a transparency of sentences that paraphrase those in the letter. For example, instead of **J'espère que vous allez bien**, write **J'espère que tout va bien.** Write the sentences in random order. Have students write each sentence on a separate strip of paper. Finally, have students arrange the strips to match the order of the letter. When they have finished, have them compare the letter in the book with the new version.

Geography Link

Cocody, Treichville, and Plateau (where **le stade** and **la cathédrale Saint-Paul** are located) are three major neighborhoods in Abidjan.

TROISIEME ETAPE

Making and responding to suggestions

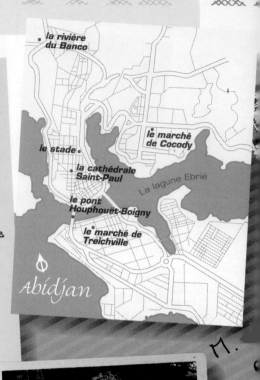

Chers Papa et Maman
J'espère que vous allez bien. Ici, tout va bien. Abidjan, c'est pas mal comme ville et je commence à m'y faire. J'ai pensé que ça vous ferait plaisir si je vous envoyais quelques photos pour vous donner une idée de ce que je fais. Ici, c'est très animé comme vous pouvez le remarquer et il y a des tas de choses à voir. Je n'ai vraiment pas le temps de m'ennuyer mais je pense quand même beaucoup à vous, et je dois dire que notre petit village me manque un peu. Bon, je dois vous quitter. Tante Adèla m'appelle pour le dîner. Donnez mon bonjour à tout le monde.
A bientôt. Grosses bises.
Sandrine

A Abidjan, il y a des mosquées dont l'architecture est très traditionnelle.

On voit aussi des bâtiments super modernes comme cette cathédrale, par exemple.

Ça, c'est le marché de Treichville, on peut y acheter toutes sortes de choses.

206 *deux cent six*   CHAPITRE 8   C'était comme ça

A Cocody, on vend surtout des tissus. Il y en a de toutes les couleurs.

D'ailleurs, j'y ai acheté un pagne. Comment le trouvez-vous?

Ça, c'est un maquis. Quand il fait chaud, c'est agréable d'y boire une boisson rafraîchissante.

C'est un marché d'artisans. J'adore la poterie, les paniers et les masques.

NOTE CULTURELLE

Abidjan is Côte d'Ivoire's main city, although in 1983 the political capital was officially transferred to Yamoussoukro, the birthplace of former president Félix Houphouët-Boigny. As Abidjan's population has grown from just a few hundred thousand in 1960 to over 2 million today, so has its diversity. Now you can see modern skyscrapers and European-style office buildings in the Plateau and Cocody regions as well as the traditional African-style marketplaces in Treichville. Known as the "Paris" and the "melting pot" of Africa, Abidjan is home to many people from Côte d'Ivoire's 60 different ethnic groups.

26 Qu'est-ce qu'il y a? See answers below.

Qu'est-ce qu'il y a sur les photos de Sandrine? Qu'est-ce que tu voudrais voir à Abidjan?

TROISIEME ETAPE

deux cent sept 207

Answers
26 une mosquée, une cathédrale, le marché de Treichville, des tissus au marché de Cocody, un pagne, un maquis, un marché d'artisans

Culture Note

In the **marché d'artisans,** prices are rarely marked since merchants expect customers to bargain for what they buy. **Pagnes** and **tissu** *(fabric/cloth)* can be made of cotton, rayon, blends, or wax, which is the most expensive. Authentic masks can be quite expensive, especially if made of ebony **(ébène)** (see Culture Note on page 193). Bracelets, necklaces, and earrings can be made of wood, silver, gold, bronze, bone, plastic, or glass beads.

Teaching Suggestion

Read the captions for the photos as students read along in their book. Then, ask questions about the photos. (**Où est-ce qu'on peut boire quelque chose? Où est-ce qu'il y a des poteries? Où est-ce qu'on vend des tissus? Où voyez-vous un pagne?**) Have students point to the photo in their book that answers each question. Next, have students work in pairs. Have one partner cover the captions of the photos in his or her book with pieces of paper and the other read the captions aloud in random order one at a time. The other partner will point to the photo that matches the caption being read.

Culture Notes
• Abidjan, located on the inland Ebrié Lagoon, was a small town until 1950, when a canal was completed to link the lagoon with the ocean, making Abidjan a major port.
• Towns, villages, and ethnic groups are known for their particular crafts. The town of Man (in western Côte d'Ivoire) is known for its masks and panther dance dolls. In and around Yamoussoukro and Bouaké (north of Yamoussoukro), the Baoulé are known for their gold jewelry and beautiful woven blankets.

Thinking Critically

Synthesizing Have students suggest American cities that would be considered a "Paris" or a "melting pot."

Presentation

Vocabulaire Talk about each picture, using synonyms, gestures, and drawings, and then ask questions about them. (Avez-vous déjà visité une mosquée? Quel tissu préférez-vous? Que porte la femme dans son pagne? Combien de masques voyez-vous? Que font les gens au maquis? Comment s'appelle le maquis? Avez-vous déjà fait de la poterie? A quoi ça sert, un tam-tam? Savez-vous jouer du tam-tam? Qu'est-ce qu'on met dans un panier?)

Teaching Suggestion

27 Play the recording again and pause it after each dialogue to ask a question.
1. De quoi est-ce qu'ils parlent?
2. Qu'est-ce qu'on peut trouver à cet endroit?
3. Qu'est-ce qu'ils vont faire ici?
4. Qu'est-ce que Mamadou veut faire?

Additional Practice

27 Have students create descriptive comments that might be overheard at certain places in their town or area. Classmates will try to guess what place it is.

✦ For Individual Needs

28 Challenge Have students imagine they are Thomas and write home to their mother to tell her about where they have gone, what they've done, and the souvenirs they've bought for people.

Teaching Suggestion

28 Ask students to suggest what an Ivorian student visiting their town might buy as a souvenir to take back home.

VOCABULAIRE

une mosquée   des tissus (m.)   un pagne *   un masque

un maquis   de la poterie   des tam-tams (m.)   des paniers (m.)

27 Ecoute!

Justin is giving Mamadou a tour of Abidjan. Listen to the following conversations. Where is each one taking place? **1.** b **2.** e **3.** a **4.** c
  a. devant un maquis
  b. devant une mosquée
  c. près d'un marché d'artisans
  d. à la cathédrale
  e. près du marché de Cocody

* a 2½-meter piece of Ivorian cloth used to make skirts, shirts, head wraps, or baby slings

208   *deux cent huit*

28 Des souvenirs   See answers below.

Thomas, un Parisien, visite Abidjan et il cherche des souvenirs pour sa famille. Où est-ce qu'il va pour trouver ces cadeaux?

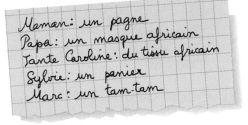

Maman: un pagne
Papa: un masque africain
Tante Caroline: du tissu africain
Sylvie: un panier
Marc: un tam-tam

CHAPITRE 8   C'était comme ça

🌐 Culture Note

A **maquis** is an outdoor restaurant where people socialize. At a typical **maquis,** there are usually several wooden tables covered with plastic tablecloths and surrounded by wooden chairs. A menu lists what is served, but what is actually available depends on the season of the year, the time of day, the day of the week, and when the owner last went to the market. There is loud music and good food: chicken and rice with various sauces; fried plantains (**aloco**); spaghetti with a sauce of palm oil and tomato paste; rice made with tomato paste, palm oil, and hot pepper (**riz gras**); and omelettes served with bread.

Answers
28 un pagne — au marché de Cocody
un masque africain — à un marché d'artisans
du tissu africain — au marché de Cocody
un panier — à un marché d'artisans
un tam-tam — à un marché d'artisans

COMMENT DIT-ON... ?

Making and responding to suggestions

To make suggestions:

Si on allait au stade pour voir un match de foot?
Si on achetait un pagne au marché?
Si on visitait la mosquée?
Si on jouait du tam-tam?

To respond to suggestions:

D'accord.
C'est une bonne idée.
Bof.
Comme tu veux. *It's up to you.*
Non, je préfère...
Non, je ne veux pas.

Note de *G*rammaire

Notice that you can use the imperfect tense to make suggestions. To say *How about . . .* , use the phrase **si on** + the verb in the imperfect tense.

29 Si on...?

Propose ces activités à ton ami(e). Il/Elle va accepter ou refuser. Ensuite, changez de rôle. *Possible answers:*

1. Si on jouait du tam-tam?
2. Si on jouait au foot?
3. Si on achetait de la poterie?
4. Si on mangeait dans un maquis?

30 Que faire en ville?

Aujourd'hui, tu vas visiter Abidjan avec ton correspondant ivoirien (ta correspondante ivoirienne). Décidez de ce que vous allez faire le matin, l'après-midi et le soir.

31 Jeu de rôle

Upon your return to France after living in Abidjan for several months, you find that you really miss Africa. Role-play the situation with two friends, who ask you what Abidjan was like, what you did there, and reassure you.

TROISIEME ETAPE

deux cent neuf **209**

ASSESS

Quiz 8-3, *Chapter Teaching Resources, Book 2,* pp. 195–196

Assessment Items, Audiocassette 8A
Audio CD 8

Performance Assessment

Use Activity 31 to assess students' performance in this **étape.** You might base students' oral grades on content, accuracy, comprehensibility, creativity, and effort.

Presentation

Comment dit-on... ? On a transparency, draw several places to visit in Abidjan. On a transparency, draw and cut out some smiling faces, frowning faces, and indifferent faces. Then, propose things to do (**Si on allait au musée?**) and respond in a different voice. (**Bof.**) Put a face that represents your answer in the appropriate place on the transparency. Then, repeat the suggestions and have students answer, using the faces as cues. Next, read **Comment dit-on... ?** with students. Suggest going somewhere and have individuals respond. Finally, have partners take turns making and responding to suggestions.

For videodisc application, see *Videodisc Guide.*

CLOSE

Have students draw a map of Abidjan like the one on page 206. Then, have them draw and cut out small pictures of things to buy at the places labeled on the map. Next, have them suggest doing something with their partner. (**Si on allait au marché pour acheter un panier?**), placing the object (**le panier**) on the map in the appropriate place (**le marché**). The partner accepts (**D'accord**), and the cutout is left in place, or he or she refuses (**Non, je préfère acheter un masque** or **Non, je ne veux pas**), and the cutout is changed or removed. Students take turns. When they have agreed upon three things, they write sentences telling about what they have decided to do. (**On va acheter un panier au marché.**)

READING STRATEGY

Linking words and pronouns

Teacher Note

For an additional reading, see *Practice and Activity Book*, page 95.

PREREADING
Activity A

Motivating Activity

Ask students if they can re-count any folktales they may have read. Have them identify the moral to each story, if any.

Culture Notes

• The stories in this book are based on African folktales, retold in French for elementary school children who are learning French. The main character in this tale is Leuk, a clever rabbit who sets out on a journey and meets all kinds of animals and people who teach him lessons about life.

• The feisty nature of Bugs Bunny comes from Br'er Rabbit of Joel Chandler Harris' Uncle Remus stories, which are also based on African folktales. Both Bugs Bunny and Br'er Rabbit owe much of their characterization to Leuk-le-Lièvre—their distant cousin!

A. Leopold Sédar Senghor, born in Senegal in 1906 to a wealthy merchant family, was educated by Europeans, first at the seminary of Ngasobil, then in Dakar and finally, in France. He received a degree in litera-ture and taught in a French **lycée**. Although he was influ-enced by his exposure to Euro-pean philosophy, he became the leader of a group of Africans who wanted to return to the source of their culture. Senghor served as the first president of Senegal from 1960 until his resignation in 1981.

$\mathcal{W}$hat folktales do you know?

DE BONS CONSEILS

If you drive a car, you know that signs are important. Signs tell you when and where to go, what streets you're looking for, and how fast you may drive. When you're reading, look for *linking words* and *pronouns*. These signs help you understand a story. Linking words indicate when events occur, and pronouns help you keep track of who's doing what.

A. Preview the pictures, titles, and organization of the reading.

1. What kind of book is this?
   a. a textbook about rabbits
   b. <u>a reading book for elementary students</u>
   c. an African history book

2. What is the hare's name?
   a. Senghor   c. <u>Leuk</u>
   b. Sadji

3. What's the purpose of the activities at the end of the story? <small>See answers below.</small>

B. Paraphrase the definitions in the **Que signifie?** activity by choosing synonyms for the words or phrases in italics in the following sentences. Based on these words, can you guess what the story will be about?

1. **Un philtre** est *un breuvage* qui possède un pouvoir extraordinaire.
   a. <u>une boisson</u>   b. un homme

2. **Un prétendant** est celui qui veut *épouser* une jeune fille.
   a. rencontrer
   b. <u>se marier avec</u>

L. SENGHOR & A. SADJI

LA BELLE HISTOIRE DE LEUK-LE-LIÈVRE

Cours Elémentaire des écoles d'Afrique Noire

HACHETTE · EDICEF

78. – Les questions difficiles (suite)

« Trois jeunes hommes aimaient une même jeune fille et chacun d'eux voulait l'épouser. Tous trois possédaient un savoir très étendu.

« Le premier pouvait voir ce qui se passait à des milliers de kilomètres. Son regard traversait les forêts les plus épaisses, passait par-dessus la montagne la plus haute et rien ne pouvait l'arrêter.

« Le deuxième possédait une peau de mouton qui, rapide comme l'éclair, vous transportait d'un lieu à un autre, instantanément. Sur cette peau, pouvait prendre place un nombre considérable de personnes.

« Le troisième avait un philtre• qui redonnait la vie aux morts. Il suffisait d'en verser quelques gouttes dans leurs narines.

« Les trois jeunes hommes partirent ensemble pour rendre visite à la belle jeune fille. Chacun d'eux cachait aux autres le pouvoir qu'il détenait. Chacun croyait qu'à leur arrivée il triompherait de ses camarades. En chemin, ils causaient comme de bons amis, lorsque, tout à coup, le prétendant• qui avait la vue longue et perçante déclara :

« — Tiens, tiens, la jeune fille vers qui nous allons est décédée. Je vois qu'on l'a emmenée au cimetière. La fosse est déjà creusée, le cortège• est debout et les fossoyeurs• s'apprêtent à l'enterrer. Quel malheur, les amis! Je vois cela, mais nous n'avons aucun moyen, ni vous ni moi, d'arracher cette jeune et belle personne à la mort.

« — J'ai, dit le second, le moyen de vous

Language Arts Links

B. Review the definition of *paraphrasing* before beginning this activity. Make sure students know what a *synonym* is.

• Point out the narrative structure of the tale. The quotation marks indicate that it is a story told within a story. At the end of the tale, students discover the name of the narrator (Leuk-le-Lièvre).

Language Note

Point out the use of the **passé simple** in the fifth paragraph (**partirent, déclara**). Tell stu-dents that this is a written, not a spoken, verb form used instead of the **passé composé** in literary and historical texts.

Answers

A 3. to explain new vocabulary, to check for under-standing, to discuss the story, to practice grammar functions

transporter immédiatement à ce cimetière. Mais à quoi bon puisque nous ne pourrons que regarder enterrer la jeune fille? Aucun de nous, en effet, n'est capable de la ressusciter.

« — Emmène-nous toujours, si tu le peux, jusqu'au cimetière, dit le troisième. Nous verrons bien.»

« L'homme tire, de son vêtement, la peau de mouton sur laquelle les trois compagnons prennent place. En un clin d'œil, les voilà arrivés au cimetière, près de la fosse ouverte où la jeune fille doit être ensevelie.

« Alors le troisième prétendant prend le philtre magique, le philtre qui ressuscite les morts. Il en verse quelques gouttes dans les narines de la morte. Aussitôt celle-ci se redresse, éternue trois fois, et regarde tout le monde, l'air étonné. Elle est sauvée.

« On demande, dit encore Leuk, quel est, de ces trois prétendants, celui qui méritait d'épouser la jeune fille. »

Que signifie? philtre : breuvage qui possède un pouvoir extraordinaire — **prétendant :** celui qui veut épouser une jeune fille — **cortège :** ensemble des personnes qui accompagnent un vivant ou un mort — **fossoyeur :** homme chargé de creuser la tombe d'un mort.

Pourquoi et comment?
1. Dites quel pouvoir possédait chacun des trois prétendants.
2. Pourquoi chacun cachait-il son secret?
3. Quel est celui des trois que la jeune fille va épouser et

pourquoi?

Ecrivez. — Grammaire : Accord du sujet avec le verbe. Les pronoms personnels du singulier sont : je, tu, il ou elle, moi, toi, lui ou elle.
Exercice : Accorder, à l'indicatif présent, les verbes avec les pronoms sujets. — Je (partir) pour un long voyage — Tu (vouloir) épouser la belle fille — Elle (habiter) très loin — Il (posséder) un philtre magique — Tu (avoir) une vue perçante — C'est moi qui (voir) la jeune fille morte — C'est toi qui (offrir) la peau.

3. **Un cortège** est *l'ensemble* des personnes qui accompagnent un vivant ou un mort.
   a. plusieurs   b. le groupe
4. **Un fossoyeur** est un homme chargé de *creuser* la tombe d'un mort.
   a. faire   b. acheter

C. In **Les questions difficiles,** three suitors vie for the hand of a beautiful girl. Read the story and make a chart of the powers and actions of each suitor. See answers below.

D. Look for the following linking words in the text and figure out what's happening at the point they appear. See answers below.

en chemin   *on the way*
lorsque   *when*
en effet   *in fact*
en un clin d'œil   *in the wink of an eye*
aussitôt   *right away*

E. Find the following sentences in the story. Then, identify what the italicized pronouns refer to.

1. Trois jeunes hommes aimaient une même jeune fille et chacun d'eux voulait *l'*épouser.
   a. chacun des hommes
   b. la jeune fille
2. Emmène-*nous* toujours...
   a. le troisième jeune homme et la jeune fille
   b. les trois jeunes hommes
3. Aussitôt *celle-ci* se redresse...
   a. la peau   b. la morte
4. ... quel est, de ces trois prétendants, *celui* qui méritait d'épouser la jeune fille.
   a. le prétendant   b. la fille

F. Answer the questions in the **Pourquoi et comment?** activity. Take a poll to find out who the class thinks will marry the girl. See answers below.

deux cent onze **211**

READING
Activities B–E

Thinking Critically
B. Drawing Inferences
Before they begin this activity, have students read *Que signifie?* at the end of the story. Ask them what they think these four words mean. Ask if they can make any predictions about the plot of the story based on their understanding of these words.

Language Note
E. Stress the importance of pronouns in order to avoid repetition. Ask students to imagine how it would sound if a story always referred to its characters by name.

POSTREADING
Activity F

Teaching Suggestion
F. Students might answer these questions with a partner or in small groups.

Thinking Critically
Synthesizing Point out that the story is about three young men and that the number three is also a common element in our fairytales and folklore. Ask students to name other folktales where there is a cluster of three characters or elements. (Examples include *Goldilocks and the Three Bears, The Three Little Pigs,* and three wishes from a genie.)

Terms in Lisons!
Students might want to know the following vocabulary: **epaisse** *(thick);* **une peau de mouton** *(lambskin);* **l'éclair** *(lightning);* **cacher** *(to hide);* **détenir** *(to hold);* **décédée** *(deceased);* **emmener** *(to take away);* **enterrer, ensevelir** *(to bury);* **arracher** *(to rescue from).*

Answers
C **Le premier:** He had extraordinary vision; He saw the girl being buried in the cemetery.
Le deuxième: He had a magic sheepskin that could transport people anywhere; He transported the other two men and himself to the cemetery.
Le troisième: He had a drink that brought the dead back to life. He brought the girl back to life.
D **en chemin** — They're going to visit the girl.
lorsque — The man with extraordinary vision notices that the girl is dead.

en effet — The second man is saying that the men are not able to bring the girl back to life.
en un clin d'œil — They arrive at the cemetery.
aussitôt — The girl is saved.
F 1. **Le premier:** He had extraordinary vision.
Le deuxième: He had a magic sheepskin that could transport people anywhere.
Le troisième: He had a drink that brought the dead back to life.
2. They wanted to impress the girl.
3. Answers will vary.

The **Mise en pratique** reviews and integrates all four skills and culture in preparation for the Chapter Test.

Teaching Suggestions

• Have students first try to guess the story line by looking at the pictures. Have them write down what they think it's about. Later, they can compare their guesses with what really happens in the story.

• Read the story aloud to students as they listen with their books closed. Tell them to listen for the gist of the story and not try to grasp the meaning of every word.

Thinking Critically

Analyzing If students were to write their own African folktale, in which country would it take place and why? Ask students where the story of Mamy Wata takes place and if they usually think of water when they think of Africa. Ask them why this might be a popular folktale in Africa. (Since water is scarce in many parts of Africa, folktales dealing with an abundance of water are prevalent.) In this tale, the queen of water provided the animals with plenty of water and allowed the men to fish where they pleased.

1 Comparing and Contrasting Ask students if they can think of any other stories that involve a human in the form of an animal who is eventually restored to his original form (*Beauty and the Beast* and *The Frog Prince*). How are they similar to or different from the story of *Mamy Wata?*

Family Link

Students might recount this story in English to a family member.

MISE EN PRATIQUE

L'HISTOIRE DE MAMY WATA

Mamy Wata, reine des eaux, était très généreuse. Elle laissait les animaux boire dans tous les points d'eau et les hommes avaient en plus le droit de pêcher partout où ils le désiraient.

Un jour, quand Mamy Wata nageait paisiblement dans une rivière avec quelques gros poissons, on est venu l'avertir qu'à plusieurs kilomètres de là, un horrible monstre terrorisait les habitants des villages riverains.

Mamy Wata a décidé d'aller voir ce qui se passait. On lui a indiqué la grotte dans laquelle le monstre se retirait la nuit pour dormir. Elle s'est cachée dans un coin. Lorsque le monstre est rentré se coucher, elle s'est mise à l'observer. Le monstre ne pouvait pas dormir. Il pleurait et grondait beaucoup, et faisait beaucoup de bruit en respirant.

Mamy Wata a compris que le monstre était malheureux. Elle a inventé des jeux. Elle lui a appris à jouer du tam-tam. Elle lui a appris à chanter et à danser. Le monstre était tellement content d'avoir une amie qu'il s'est mis à rire.

Soudain, alors qu'il riait encore, il s'est aperçu qu'il avait complètement changé. Il était redevenu le jeune homme d'avant! Il était en réalité un jeune homme qu'une méchante sorcière avait un jour changé en monstre!

212 *deux cent douze*   CHAPITRE 8   C'était comme ça

Language Note

Students may want to know the following vocabulary words from *L'histoire de Mamy Wata:* **une reine** *(a queen)*; **le droit** *(the right/privilege)*; **paisiblement** *(peacefully)*; **avertir** *(to warn)*; **une grotte** *(a cave)*; **se mettre à** *(to begin)*; **gronder** *(to groan)*; **s'apercevoir** *(to notice)*.

Multicultural Link

Have students find out about folktales from different cultures. Students might do research to find folktales or ask people they know from other cultures. Students might then recount these tales to the class.

1 Read *L'histoire de Mamy Wata* and answer the questions.　See answers below.

1. Who was Mamy Wata? What was she like?
2. What did she do for animals? And for people?
3. When Mamy Wata first sees the monster, what is he like? What is he doing in his cave?
4. What does Mamy Wata do for the monster?
5. What had happened to the monster?

2 Does *L'histoire de Mamy Wata* remind you of any stories? Think of a character from your favorite fairy tale. Describe him or her to a partner, telling what the character was like and what he or she would do. Your partner will try to guess who the character is. Then, change roles.

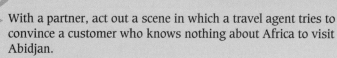

> Elle était...
> Il avait...
> Elle habitait...
> Il aimait...
> Elle avait le pouvoir de...

3 Read the tourist brochure *Cette semaine à Abidjan.* Then, listen to Koffi and Sandrine talking about what they'd like to do in Abidjan. What suggestions do they make? What do they finally decide on?　Answers on p. 189D.

4 Write a postcard to your former host family in Abidjan, telling them what you miss about being there. Describe how your life at home is different from life in Abidjan.

5 From what you know about the culture of Côte d'Ivoire, answer the following questions.　See answers below.

1. How can you tell to which ethnic group someone belongs?
2. If you were a high school student, how would you spend your free time?
3. Describe what Ivorian villages are like.

CETTE SEMAINE A ABIDJAN

La pêche, sport très populaire, est pratiquée le long des côtes ou de la lagune. Parmi les nombreux types de poissons, on compte des thons, des requins, des espadons voiliers, des raies, des barracudas, des coryphères, des liches, des daurades, des bourtes... Matériel et bateaux à louer.

Promenade en Lagune pour voir la ville moderne en bateau le jour et la nuit. Voir la pyramide, les gratte-ciels, et le pont Houphouët-Boigny. Départ à 10h, 12h, 14h, 17h, 22h, 23h. Durée 35 min.

Le Musée National d'Abidjan renferme plus de 19.000 pièces d'art et d'artisanat ivoiriens : sculptures sur bois, poteries, tissages, bijoux, instruments de musique, accessoires de danse, de chasse, de pêche, d'agriculture et de transport. Situé au croisement des boulevards Cadre et Nangui Abrogoua. Ouvert de 9h à 12h et de 15h à 18h, tous les jours sauf le lundi. Entrée gratuite.

6

J E U　D E　R O L E

With a partner, act out a scene in which a travel agent tries to convince a customer who knows nothing about Africa to visit Abidjan.

- The travel agent suggests the city and describes its advantages.
- The customer asks what there is to see, do, and buy there.
- The customer has false, preconceived notions about the city and Côte d'Ivoire. The agent corrects the customer's false impressions.

MISE EN PRATIQUE　　　　*deux cent treize* **213**

Answers

1 1. the queen of the waters, very generous
2. She let animals drink from all the bodies of water and let men fish wherever they wanted.
3. He was unhappy; He was crying and groaning.
4. She played with him, taught him how to play the drums, sing, and dance.
5. He was a young man who had been turned into a monster by an evil sorceress.

5 *Possible answers*
1. from their names
2. studying, visiting relatives and friends, playing soccer, listening to music and discussing the latest family events with friends
3. quiet, clean, everyone knows one another; usually the same ethnic group; people make many of the things they need; chickens and goats are common; people cook over open fires; they walk rather than drive; bowls are used without silverware; there are usually no high schools.

Teaching Suggestion

2 Students might work together to describe a character from a cartoon, a television show, or a movie character from their childhood. Have students read their description to their classmates, who will try to guess the character's identity. Refer students to the Supplementary Vocabulary in the back of the book for additional adjectives.

For Individual Needs

3 Slower Pace Have students read the brochure with a partner before they listen to the recording. Ask them which of the three activities they would choose and why. Then, play the recording, asking students to listen for the activity Koffi and Sandrine finally decide on.

Portfolio

4 Written This activity is appropriate for students' written portfolios.

6 Oral This activity is appropriate for students' oral portfolios. For portfolio suggestions, see *Assessment Guide,* page 21.

Video Wrap-Up

- *VIDEO PROGRAM*
- *EXPANDED VIDEO PROGRAM,* Videocassette 3, 18:15–38:00
- *VIDEODISC PROGRAM,* Videodisc 4B

At this time, you might want to use the video resources for additional review and enrichment. See *Video Guide* or *Videodisc Guide* for suggestions regarding the following:
- **La Nostalgie** (Dramatic episode)
- **Panorama Culturel** (Interviews)
- **Vidéoclips** (Authentic footage)

This page is intended to help students prepare for the test. It is a brief checklist of the major points covered in the chapter. The students should be reminded that this is only a checklist and does not necessarily include everything that will appear on the test.

Teaching Suggestion

You might have pairs of students work together to answer the questions in **Que sais-je?** or divide the class into two teams and have them compete to see who can be the first to answer the questions correctly.

Cooperative Learning

Have students work in groups to answer the questions in **Que sais-je?** Assign one student to read aloud each question to the group. Have one student turn to the page where the answer is found and suggest two answers for each question. Designate one student to decide on and choose the best answer. Finally, one student should write down the answer chosen as the best response for each question.

QUE SAIS-JE?

Can you tell what or whom you miss?
p. 197

Can you reassure someone? p. 197

Can you ask and tell what things were like?
p. 198

Can you reminisce?
p. 201

Can you make and respond to suggestions? p. 209

Can you use what you've learned in this chapter?

1 If you moved to a new city, how would you say you missed . . . *Possible answers:*

1. Ce qui me manque, c'est ma maison.
2. Mon chat me manque.
3. Mes copains me manquent.

2 How would you reassure someone who had just moved to your town and was homesick? *Possible answers:* Tu vas t'y faire. Fais-toi une raison. Tu vas te plaire ici. Tu vas voir que tout le monde est sympa ici.

3 How would you ask your homesick friend what his or her former town was like? C'était comment?

4 How would you describe how things were . . .
1. in medieval times?   2. in the 60s?   3. when you were five?

5 How would you tell what these people used to do when they were young? See answers below.

1. Yapo   2. Tes amis et toi   3. Anne et Agathe

6 How would you tell what you usually did after school when you were ten years old? Quand j'avais dix ans, après l'école, je (j')...

7 How would you suggest . . .
1. visiting a place in Abidjan? Si on visitait... ?
2. buying something from the market? Si on achetait... ?
3. playing your favorite game or sport? Si on jouait... ?

8 How would you respond if a friend invited you to . . . *Possible answers:*
1. play tennis?   2. eat barbecue?   3. visit a museum?
D'accord. Comme tu veux. C'est une bonne idée. Non, je préfère... Bof. Non, je ne veux pas.

Game

QUE SAIS-JE? Write the questions from **Que sais-je?** on separate index cards and shuffle them. Form five or six teams and number them one through six. Have a member of the first team choose a card and read the question aloud. If he or she answers the question correctly, his or her team receives two points, and play passes to the next team. If he or she cannot answer the question correctly, the next team may try to answer for one point. If they do not succeed, the question is placed back in the stack of questions. The game is over when all of the questions have been answered.

Answers

5 1. Yapo taquinait son frère.
2. Nous jouions du tam-tam.
3. Anne et Agathe faisaient des tours sur les montagnes russes.

PREMIERE ETAPE

Telling what or whom you miss

Je regrette... *I miss . . .*
... me manque. *I miss . . . (singular subject)*
... me manquent. *I miss . . . (plural subject)*
Ce qui me manque, c'est... *What I really miss is . . .*

Reassuring someone

Tu vas t'y faire. *You'll get used to it.*
Fais-toi une raison. *Make the best of it.*

Tu vas te plaire ici. *You're going to like it here.*
Tu vas voir que... *You'll see that . . .*

Asking and telling what things were like

C'était comment? *What was it like?*
C'était tellement différent? *Was it really so different?*
C'était... *It was . . .*
Il y avait... *There were . . .*
La vie était plus..., moins... *Life was more . . . , less . . .*

Describing places

animé(e) *exciting*
bruyant(e) *noisy*
calme *calm*
dangereux (dangereuse) *dangerous*
génial(e) *great*
mortel (mortelle) *dull*
nul (nulle) *worthless*
propre *clean*
relaxant(e) *relaxing*
sale *dirty*
stressant(e) *stressful*
tranquille *peaceful*
très vivant(e) *very lively*

DEUXIEME ETAPE

Reminiscing

Quand j'étais petit(e),... *When I was little, . . .*
Quand il/elle était petit(e),... *When he/she was little, . . .*
Quand j'avais... ans,... *When I was . . . years old, . . .*

Activities

avoir des responsabilités *to have responsibilities*
avoir des soucis *to have worries*
conduire une voiture *to drive a car*

faire des bêtises *to do silly things*
faire la sieste *to take a nap*
ennuyer *to bother*
taquiner *to tease*

TROISIEME ETAPE

Making and responding to suggestions

Si on allait... ? *How about going . . . ?*
Si on achetait... ? *How about buying . . . ?*
Si on visitait... ? *How about visiting . . . ?*
Si on jouait... ? *How about playing . . . ?*
D'accord. *OK.*
C'est une bonne idée. *That's a good idea.*
Bof. *(expression of indifference)*

Comme tu veux. *It's up to you.*
Non, je préfère... *No, I prefer . . .*
Non, je ne veux pas. *No, I don't want to.*

Things to see and buy in Abidjan

un maquis *popular Ivorian outdoor restaurant*
un masque *mask*
une mosquée *mosque*

un pagne *piece of Ivorian cloth*
des paniers (m.) *baskets*
de la poterie *pottery*
un tam-tam *African drum*
le tissu *fabric, cloth*

VOCABULAIRE

deux cent quinze **215**

Allez, viens en Provence!

pp. 216–293

EXPANDED VIDEO PROGRAM,
Videocassette 3
38:20–41:07

OR *VIDEODISC PROGRAM,*
Videodisc 5A

Search 1, Play To 4995

Motivating Activity

Have students share what they know about southern France, and then have them look at the photos on pages 216–219. Ask them how **la Provence** is different from the French regions they have previously studied (**Paris et ses environs**, pages xxiv–3; **la Touraine**, pages 108–111). You might also ask students to compare the different regions of the United States. Have them tell what each region of the country is known for.

Background Information

Equally influenced by the Greeks and the Romans, **Provence** (formerly **Gallia Transalpina**, the first Roman **provincia** in the second century B.C.) is known for the beauty and variety of its countryside, the Mediterranean nature of the weather and crops, and the vestiges of past civilizations found at every turn. Even in modern cities, the ancient monuments make it seem as if time has stood still. The rugged areas of the region are dotted with tiny villages, many of which are built on cliffs, and most of the houses are built of limestone and have roofs made of terracotta tiles.

CHAPITRES 9, 10, 11

Allez, viens en Provence!

Un paysage provençal typique

Culture Note

The photo spread on pages 216–217 shows a lavender field, a common sight in the Provence region. Because of an abundance of flowers, such as lavender, jasmine, tuberoses, violets, and orange blossom, Provence, and particularly the town of Grasse, has become known for its perfume. In the sixteenth century, distillation of the essences of the flowers in Grasse began. Then, in the nineteenth century, Paris became the center for perfume production, while Grasse continued to provide the raw materials. Three perfumeries in Provence that still offer tours are **Galimard, Molinard,** and **Fragonard.**

La Provence

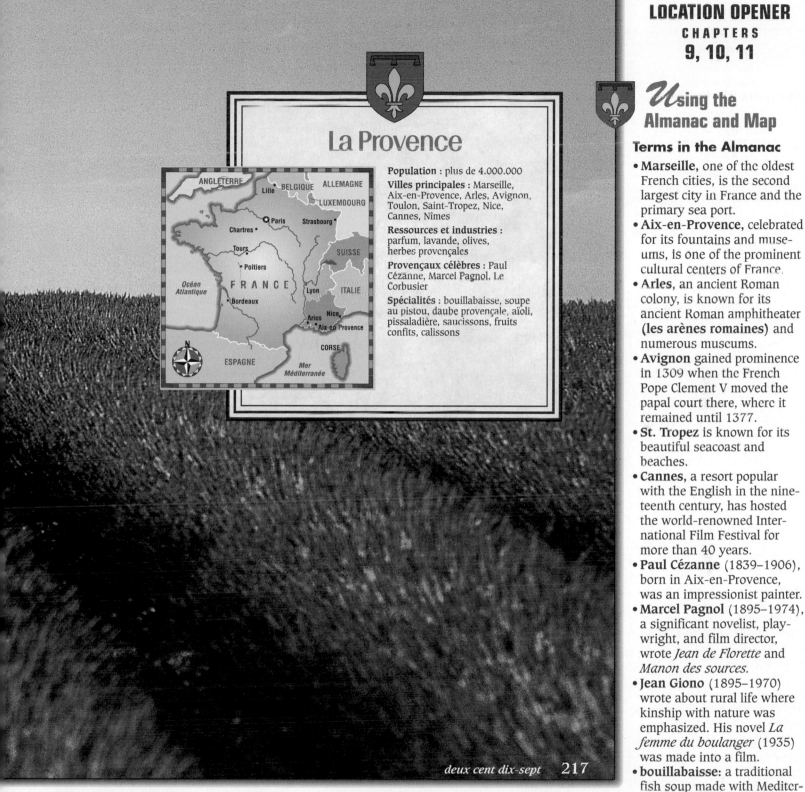

Population : plus de 4.000.000

Villes principales : Marseille, Aix-en-Provence, Arles, Avignon, Toulon, Saint-Tropez, Nice, Cannes, Nîmes

Ressources et industries : parfum, lavande, olives, herbes provençales

Provençaux célèbres : Paul Cézanne, Marcel Pagnol, Le Corbusier

Spécialités : bouillabaisse, soupe au pistou, daube provençale, aïoli, pissaladière, saucissons, fruits confits, calissons

deux cent dix-sept 217

Using the Almanac and Map

Terms in the Almanac

- **Marseille,** one of the oldest French cities, is the second largest city in France and the primary sea port.
- **Aix-en-Provence,** celebrated for its fountains and museums, is one of the prominent cultural centers of France.
- **Arles,** an ancient Roman colony, is known for its ancient Roman amphitheater (**les arènes romaines**) and numerous museums.
- **Avignon** gained prominence in 1309 when the French Pope Clement V moved the papal court there, where it remained until 1377.
- **St. Tropez** is known for its beautiful seacoast and beaches.
- **Cannes,** a resort popular with the English in the nineteenth century, has hosted the world-renowned International Film Festival for more than 40 years.
- **Paul Cézanne** (1839–1906), born in Aix-en-Provence, was an impressionist painter.
- **Marcel Pagnol** (1895–1974), a significant novelist, playwright, and film director, wrote *Jean de Florette* and *Manon des sources.*
- **Jean Giono** (1895–1970) wrote about rural life where kinship with nature was emphasized. His novel *La femme du boulanger* (1935) was made into a film.
- **bouillabaisse:** a traditional fish soup made with Mediterranean fish and shellfish.
- **soupe au pistou:** a vegetable and bean soup flavored with **pistou,** a sauce of basil, garlic, and olive oil.
- **daube provençale:** a stew traditionally made with **herbes provençales,** tomatoes, and lamb.
- **aïoli:** a strong garlic mayonnaise made with olive oil.

Culture Notes

- *La Marseillaise,* the French national anthem, was adopted and sung by a regiment from **Marseille,** which is how the song got its name. It was composed in Strasbourg by Rouget de Lisle.
- Most French cities have tourist offices (**Syndicats d'Initiative**) that sell posters (**affiches**) of the region. One poster for Aix-en-Provence bears a reproduction of Cézanne's painting, *la montagne Sainte-Victoire.*

Language Notes

- **Aix** is a derivation of the Latin word for water (**aquae**), which is **eaux** in modern French. Many towns that include the name **Aix** or **Ax** are famous for their mineral springs: Aix-la-Chapelle (Aachen in German), Aix-les-Bains, and Ax-les-Thermes.
- The city of **Marseille** is written with a final -*s* in English (Marseilles).

Using the Photo Essay

① **La Promenade des Anglais,** a famous boulevard that extends from one end of Nice's waterfront to the other, is lined with luxury hotels. This eight-lane, five-kilometer highway was built in 1830, and its name reflects the influx of the English, who established Nice as a major resort. It is also the central parade route of Nice and the site of the Carnaval celebration for Mardi Gras and the **bataille des fleurs** in the summer.

① **Nice,** located on the **baie des Anges,** is the capital of the Côte d'Azur. The city was founded in 350 B.C. by the Greeks, and later colonized by the Romans. In 1814, France lost possession of Nice to the Italians until 1861, when it was reclaimed by the French after the people voted in favor of its return. As a result, there is a distinctive Italian influence in the city.

② **Gordes,** a Provençal village built high on a cliff, boasts the Renaissance **Château de Gordes,** which is really a fortress. The château was built in the eleventh century and later rebuilt in the sixteenth century. Inside the château is the **Musée Vasarély,** named after the artist Victor Vasarély, one of the founders of kinetic art. The museum houses many tapestries and works of art.

③ A tributary of the Durance River, the Verdon River has carved out a canyon, **les Gorges du Verdon,** or the **Grand Canyon de Verdon,** which varies in depth from 250 to 700 meters. It is known as the deepest canyon in Europe, and the view from Point Sublime is breathtaking. A walking path was built in 1928, and a corniche road was built in 1947 to accommodate automobile traffic.

La Provence

La Provence offre une grande variété de paysages : la Côte d'Azur a de belles plages, la Haute-Provence a les Alpes et la Camargue a des chevaux sauvages et des flamants roses. En Provence, on peut aussi voir des forêts de pins et des champs de lavande. Depuis les années 1900, les touristes viennent en grand nombre y passer leurs vacances. Chaque été, des centaines de festivals de toutes sortes attirent aussi un grand nombre de personnes.

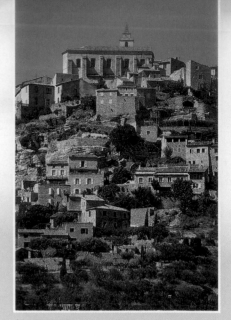

① La Côte d'Azur est célèbre pour ses plages, ses hôtels et ses boutiques de grand luxe. **La Promenade des Anglais** à Nice est un lieu touristique très connu.

② La plupart des villages perchés comme Gordes ont été construits il y a 500 ans à cause de fréquentes attaques de maraudeurs.

③ **Les gorges du Verdon** sont le *Grand Canyon* français. A 700 mètres plus bas se trouve la rivière où l'on fait du canoë.

Culture Note

The **Camargue** consists of over 300,000 acres of wetlands, pastures, dunes, and salt flats. It is home to an incredible collection of flora, such as tamarisk and narcissi, and fauna, including the egret (similar to a heron) and the ibis (a large wading bird).

Geography Link

③ A **corniche** is a roadway that winds along a cliff or steep slope.

Language Link

During the Dark Ages (the fifth through the tenth century A.D.), one of the Romance languages that evolved was the **langue d'oc,** or **Occitan.** The numerous variations of **Provençal,** which are spoken today throughout Provence, are dialects of this language.

④ **le pont du Gard** est un aqueduc de 49 mètres de haut construit par les Romains il y a 2.000 ans.

④ **Le pont du Gard,** a remnant of the aqueduct that once brought fresh water from a spring at Uzès to the city of Nîmes, was built in 19 B.C. by the Romans, a testimony to their desire for large quantities of fresh water and to their engineering skills. The entire aqueduct was 17 kilometers (10.5 miles) long, and therefore vulnerable during times of war. By the fourth century, the bridge was no longer maintained, and local people carried off stones for building. Napoléon III had the bridge restored in the nineteenth century. The aqueduct is made of enormous dry blocks set together with no mortar, and the arches vary in size.

Depuis l'époque des Romains, Aix-en-Provence est la capitale de la Provence. Aujourd'hui, c'est surtout une ville d'art, peuplée d'étudiants en raison de sa célèbre université. Dans les chapitres 9, 10 et 11, quelques élèves d'Aix-en-Provence vont te montrer leur belle ville.

⑤ **Aix-en-Provence** was founded by the Romans in 103 B.C. and became the capital of Provence in the twelfth century. The town's university was built in 1409, and the area became a part of France in 1486.

⑤ A Aix-en-Provence, les jeunes aiment bien se retrouver dans les cafés du Cours Mirabeau. Haute de 1.000 mètres et située à l'est de la ville, **la montagne Sainte-Victoire** attire beaucoup de monde le week-end.

⑥ **Cassis** is a fishing port east of Marseille. The **calanques,** which are deep, narrow arms of the sea enclosed by rugged white limestone cliffs, are sometimes used as natural yacht harbors. They also provide a real challenge for rock climbers. The calanques are celebrated in the poem *Calendal,* by Frédéric Mistral, the famous Provençal poet.

⑥ A trente minutes de Marseille, **les calanques de Cassis** offrent un total dépaysement : falaises blanches plongeant dans l'eau turquoise.

deux cent dix-neuf **219**

Thinking Critically

Observing Ask students to determine from the photos the kinds of activities that are available to residents and tourists in Provence.

Comparing and Contrasting Ask students to think of popular tourist resorts in the United States and compare them to Provence. Have them compare the kinds of activities available in both places and who goes there.

Geography Link

Have students compare the geography of Provence and Touraine and consider how it influenced the development of the two regions. (Both the Rhône River and the Loire River have been major transportation and trade arteries throughout history. Both provinces have moderate climates. Provence was influenced by the early Greeks and Romans (Marseilles was a Greek settlement founded in the seventh century B.C.), whereas Touraine was influential in the development and the government of central France, especially during the late Middle Ages and the Renaissance years.)

Language Note

⑥ The name of the town **Cassis** is pronounced without the final **-s**, while the final **-s** is pronounced in the name of the fruit, **cassis** *(black currants).*

Chapitre 9 : Tu connais la nouvelle?
Chapter Overview

Mise en train pp. 222–224	Il ne faut pas se fier aux apparences		Practice and Activity Book, p. 97		Video Guide OR Videodisc Guide
	FUNCTIONS	**GRAMMAR**	**CULTURE**	**RE-ENTRY**	
Première étape pp. 225–229	Wondering what happened; offering possible explanations; accepting and rejecting explanations, p. 228	**avoir l'air** + adjective, p. 227	• **Note Culturelle**, The **Cours Mirabeau**, Aix-en-Provence, p. 225 • **Panorama Culturel**, Friendship, p. 229		
Deuxième étape pp. 230–234	Breaking some news; showing interest, p. 231	The **passé composé** vs. the **imparfait**, p. 233	• **Note Culturelle, Histoires marseillaises**, p. 233	The **passé composé** of reflexive verbs	
Troisième étape pp. 235–237	Beginning, continuing, and ending a story, p. 235	• The **passé composé** and the **imparfait** with interrupted actions, p. 237 • **être en train de**, p. 237			

Lisons! pp. 238–239	La cantatrice chauve: scène IV		**Reading Strategy:** Reading with a purpose

Review pp. 240–243	**Mise en pratique**, pp. 240–241	**Que sais-je?** p. 242	**Vocabulaire**, p. 243

Assessment Options	**Etape Quizzes**
	• *Chapter Teaching Resources, Book 3*
	  Première étape, Quiz 9-1, pp. 23–24
	  Deuxième étape, Quiz 9-2, pp. 25–26
	  Troisième étape, Quiz 9-3, pp. 27–28
	• *Assessment Items, Audiocassette 8A/Audio CD 9*
		Chapter Test
		• *Chapter Teaching Resources, Book 3*, pp. 29–34
		• *Assessment Guide*, Speaking Test, p. 32
		• *Assessment Items, Audiocassette 8A/Audio CD 9*
		
		Test Generator, Chapter 9

Video Program OR *Expanded Video Program, Videocassette 3* OR *Videodisc Program, Videodisc 5A*	*Textbook Audiocassette 5A/Audio CD 9*

RESOURCES: Print	RESOURCES: Audiovisual

Textbook Audiocassette 5A/Audio CD 9

Practice and Activity Book, pp. 98–100
Chapter Teaching Resources, Book 3
• Teaching Transparency Master 9-1, pp. 7, 10 . . . . *Teaching Transparency 9-1*
• Additional Listening Activities 9-1, 9-2, p. 11 . . . . *Additional Listening Activities, Audiocassette 10A/Audio CD 9*
• Realia 9-1, pp. 15, 17
• Situation Cards 9-1, pp. 18–19
• Student Response Forms, pp. 20–22
• Quiz 9-1, pp. 23–24 . . . . *Assessment Items, Audiocassette 8A/Audio CD 9*
Video Guide . . . . *Video Program* OR *Expanded Video Program, Videocassette 3*
Videodisc Guide . . . . *Videodisc Program, Videodisc 5A*

Textbook Audiocassette 5A/Audio CD 9

Practice and Activity Book, pp. 101–103
Chapter Teaching Resources, Book 3
• Communicative Activity 9-1, pp. 3–4
• Teaching Transparency Master 9-2, pp. 8, 10 . . . . *Teaching Transparency 9-2*
• Additional Listening Activities 9-3, 9-4, p. 12 . . . . *Additional Listening Activities, Audiocassette 10A/Audio CD 9*
• Realia 9-2, pp. 16, 17
• Situation Cards 9-2, pp. 18–19
• Student Response Forms, pp. 20–22
• Quiz 9-2, pp. 25–26 . . . . *Assessment Items, Audiocassette 8A/Audio CD 9*
Videodisc Guide . . . . *Videodisc Program, Videodisc 5A*

Textbook Audiocassette 5A/Audio CD 9

Practice and Activity Book, pp. 104–106
Chapter Teaching Resources, Book 3
• Communicative Activity 9-2, pp. 5–6
• Teaching Transparency Master 9-3, pp. 9, 10 . . . . *Teaching Transparency 9-3*
• Additional Listening Activities 9-5, 9-6, p. 13 . . . . *Additional Listening Activities, Audiocassette 10A/Audio CD 9*
• Realia 9-2, pp. 16, 17
• Situation Cards 9-3, pp. 18–19
• Student Response Forms, pp. 20–22
• Quiz 9-3, pp. 27–28 . . . . *Assessment Items, Audiocassette 8A/Audio CD 9*
Videodisc Guide . . . . *Videodisc Program, Videodisc 5A*

Practice and Activity Book, p. 107

Video Guide . . . . *Video Program* OR *Expanded Video Program, Videocassette 3*
Videodisc Guide . . . . *Videodisc Program, Videodisc 5A*

Alternative Assessment
• Performance Assessment   • Portfolio Assessment
  Première étape, p. 228   Written: Activity 28, *Pupil's Edition,* p. 237
  Deuxième étape, p. 234   *Assessment Guide,* p. 22
  Troisième étape, p. 237   Oral: Activity 29, *Pupil's Edition,* p. 237
                                     Assessment Guide, p. 22

Chapitre 9 : Tu connais la nouvelle?
Textbook Listening Activities Scripts

For Student Response Forms, see *Chapter Teaching Resources, Book 3*, pp. 20–22

Première étape

7 Ecoute! p. 227

— Tu as vu Kim hier soir? Elle avait l'air déprimée. Qu'est-ce qu'elle a, à ton avis?

— Rien du tout. Je crois qu'elle était juste fatiguée. Mais Serge avait l'air mal à l'aise, par contre.

— Oui, je crois qu'il n'est pas très sociable. Maria était de bonne humeur, en tout cas. Elle est vraiment sympa, cette fille!

— Oui, c'est une bonne copine. Dis donc, tu as vu Maud casser le vase?

— Non, c'est pas vrai!

— Mais si! Elle était vraiment gênée!

— Ah ouais? J'ai raté ça.

— En tout cas, Paul et Victor se sont fait remarquer par tout le monde.

— Ah oui, alors! Ces deux-là, ils ne peuvent pas jouer aux cartes sans se disputer. Victor était furieux!

— Eh, tu as remarqué que Guillaume avait l'air inquiet? Je me demande pourquoi...

— Ben... Je crois qu'il attendait sa petite amie et qu'elle n'est jamais arrivée. Elle était malade, et elle n'a pas pu lui téléphoner.

Answers to Activity 7
1. f   2. b   3. e   4. d   5. g   6. c

11 Ecoute! p. 228

1. — Salut, Patricia. J'ai un petit problème... Pascale ne me parle plus, et je ne sais pas pourquoi.
   — T'en fais pas. Peut-être qu'elle a passé une mauvaise journée.
   — Oui, tu as peut-être raison.

2. — Eh, toi, Jérôme, qu'est-ce que t'en penses?
   — Peut-être qu'elle est de mauvaise humeur parce qu'elle a eu une mauvaise note.
   — Ça m'étonnerait. Elle étudie tout le temps!

3. — Marc, qu'est-ce que tu en dis?
   — Ecoute, elle est sans doute déprimée parce qu'elle n'a pas pu sortir ce week-end.
   — C'est possible.

4. — Thuy, tu as une idée?
   — Je parie que tu as oublié de lui téléphoner.
   — Là, tu te trompes. Je lui ai téléphoné hier soir, mais elle a refusé de me parler.

Answers to Activity 11
1. accept   2. reject   3. accept   4. reject

Deuxième étape

15 Ecoute! p. 231

1. — Tu as entendu la nouvelle? Sa voiture est tombée en panne quand elle allait chez ses grand-parents.

2. — Figure-toi qu'il a rencontré une fille au parc, et il est tombé amoureux d'elle!

3. — Tu sais qu'il s'est disputé avec sa copine? D'ailleurs, ils ont cassé.

4. — Tu connais la nouvelle? Oui, un accident de vélo, c'est pas marrant, ça. Mais quand on trouve cent francs, c'est pas si mal!

5. — Oh, il a été privé de sortie, c'est tout.

Answers to Activity 15
1. Amina   3. Romain   5. Thibaut
2. Didier   4. Marie

17 Ecoute! p. 232

1. — Eh, Jérémy, devine ce que j'ai vu hier!
   — Aucune idée. Dis vite!
   — J'ai vu Philippe et Julie sortir ensemble du cinéma!

2. — Salut, Carole. Tu connais la nouvelle?
   — Non, quoi?
   — Diane et Frédéric se sont disputés. Ils ont cassé!
   — C'est pas vrai!

3. — Tu ne devineras jamais ce qui s'est passé!
   — Je ne sais pas. Raconte!
   — Thierry faisait du ski ce week-end, et il s'est cassé la jambe!
   — Pas possible! Pauvre Thierry!

4. — Tu sais ce que j'ai entendu dire?
   — Aucune idée. Quoi?
   — Charlotte a trouvé un billet de cent francs dans la rue!

Answers to Activity 17
1. b   2. d   3. c   4. a

*T*roisième étape

24 Ecoute! p. 236

— A propos, tu sais ce qui m'est arrivé?

— Aucune idée. Raconte!

— Quelle journée, je te dis pas! J'avais rendez-vous avec Annick à deux heures. J'attendais le bus pour aller chez elle quand j'ai vu ma copine Sylvie qui marchait dans la rue. On a parlé. Je lui ai raconté la boum de samedi dernier, l'interro de français, Patrick — il est tellement beau, celui-là! —, mes parents...

— Et après?

— Bref, il était deux heures et quart quand je me suis rendu compte que j'étais en retard pour mon rendez-vous. J'avais aussi un autre problème : je n'avais plus mon sac! Je savais bien qu'Annick m'attendait chez elle, mais je devais d'abord retrouver mon sac, quoi!

— Alors qu'est-ce que tu as fait?

— Tu ne devineras jamais ce qui s'est passé. Je commençais à me désespérer quand j'ai vu Patrick qui courait vers moi. Il avait mon sac à la main! Une sacrée coïncidence, non? Il m'a donné mon sac, et je l'ai remercié.

— Et Annick?

— Je lui ai téléphoné. Heureusement, elle n'était pas fâchée. Patrick et moi sommes allés au café, et Annick nous a rejoints plus tard. Finalement, ça a été un après-midi super!

Answers to Activity 24

b, a, d, c

*M*ise en pratique

2 p. 241

1. Cher Je-sais-tout,
   Je me demande depuis longtemps pourquoi le ciel est bleu. Vous pouvez me l'expliquer?

2. Cher Je-sais-tout,
   Je perds toujours des chaussettes quand je fais la lessive, et je ne les retrouve jamais. Ma question : où vont toutes ces chaussettes?

3. Cher Je-sais-tout,
   Hier je mangeais du fromage quand j'ai remarqué que le Gruyère avait des trous. D'où viennent donc les trous dans le Gruyère?

Answers to Mise en pratique Activity 2

1. c   2. b   3. a

Chapitre 9 : Tu connais la nouvelle?
Projects

Les informations
(Class Project)

ASSIGNMENT
The class will create and videotape a French television newscast, using news and sports stories they have written.

MATERIALS
✂ **Students may need**
- Posterboard or butcher paper
- Colored markers
- Video camera
- Videocassette
- Computer-generated graphics

PREPARATION
First, the class decides on the content of the newscast. The news stories may focus on current events, human interest, or sports, and should be a mixture of serious and humorous incidents.

SUGGESTED SEQUENCE
1. Partners write news stories to submit for the newscast. They should keep their identities secret by using pen names. Students will use both the **passé composé** and the **imparfait** in the stories and should try to include as many of the functions and vocabulary from this chapter as possible.

2. Post the articles around the classroom and have students vote for their five favorite stories, ranking each from one to five.

3. Tally the points for each story and select the seven to nine most popular ones. Of these, choose two or three lead stories, three or four on-the-spot stories, and two or three sports stories. Then, form groups and distribute one story to each group for editing. Have students recopy and submit the edited stories for final corrections. Use symbols to indicate corrections to be made (see Projects, Chapter 8).

4. Ask for volunteers to read the stories "on the air." There may be as many as two anchorpeople, three or four on-the-spot reporters, and two sportscasters. Next, ask for three volunteers to write scripts to open the newscast, to introduce the on-the-spot stories and sports, and to end the newscast. Assign a student to select and play background music at the beginning and end of the show, and another student who has experience with video to tape the broadcast. The remaining students will create the set.

5. To create the set for the newscast, students might make a banner displaying the name of the station. Have students use posterboard for illustrations to accompany the lead stories. For the on-the-spot or sports stories, have students draw the background scene on butcher paper.

6. Allow students time in class to rehearse the show. Assign pronunciation coaches to listen to the anchorpeople and make suggestions on how to improve their delivery. Then, videotape the broadcast and show the final product to the class and to other French classes.

GRADING THE PROJECT
Because of the diversity of students' tasks, this project lends itself to holistic grading of the overall quality of the newscast. You might base students' grades on content, use of language, overall presentation, and effort and participation.

Suggested Point Distribution (total = 100 points)

Content	25 points
Language use	25 points
Overall presentation	25 points
Effort/participation	25 points

LE FOOTBALL AMERICAIN

In this game, students will practice the functions and vocabulary from this chapter.

Preparation

1. Make fourteen cards with the following words written on them: eight with *rush*, three with *pass*, one with *fumble,* and one with *penalty.*
2. Draw a football field on the board, marking off every five yards.
3. Form two teams that will take turns playing offense.

Procedure

1. A member of the offense draws a card from the stack. If the card says *rush* or *pass,* that player must answer a question. If the player answers correctly, he or she rolls one die.
   * For a *rush,* the player doubles the number rolled, and the team advances that number of yards on the board.
   * For a *pass,* the number rolled on the die is multiplied by ten, and the team advances that number of yards on the board.
2. If a player draws the card marked *penalty,* ask a member of the defensive team a question. If the person answers correctly, he or she rolls the die and the number is doubled to determine the number of yards the offense will be penalized.
3. If a player for the offense draws a card marked *interception* or *fumble,* the defensive team takes the next turn if a team member can correctly answer a question.
4. Whenever the ball changes hands, play always starts on the offensive team's twenty-yard line.
5. A team that crosses the goal line receives six points and a bonus question to try for an extra point.

Questions should require the players to do the following:

1. Form sentences with adjectives that describe emotional states.
   * Show a picture of a person showing a particular emotion and have the student tell why the person feels that way. (**Elle est fâchée parce qu'elle est privée de sortie.**)
   * Show a picture and have the student tell why the person seemed to feel that way last night. (**Il avait l'air déprimé parce qu'il était fatigué.**)
2. Offer possible explanations.
   * Show a picture and ponder **Je me demande pourquoi...** Have the student offer a possible explanation (**A mon avis,...**).
3. Accept and reject possible explanations.
   * Show a picture and offer an explanation for the way someone feels. (**Je crois qu'elle est inquiète parce que... Qu'est-ce que tu en penses?**) Have the student accept or reject your explanation. (**Ça se voit.**)
4. Show interest.
   * Break some news (**Tu sais qui j'ai vu?**) and have the student show interest. (**Raconte!**)
5. Use both the **passé composé** and the **imparfait** correctly.
   * Prepare flashcards of sentences that involve both the **passé composé** and the **imparfait** with one of the verbs in the infinitive form: **1. Quand j'avais douze ans, je (jouer) ___ du piano. 2. Ma mère (travailler) ___ quand je suis entré(e) hier soir. 3. Je faisais mes devoirs quand tu me (m') (téléphoner) ___ .** Have the student read the sentence, supplying the verb in the correct tense.

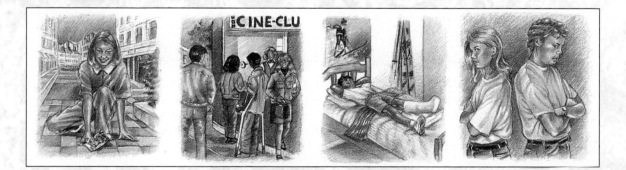

Chapitre 9
Tu connais la nouvelle?
pp. 220–243

𝒰sing the Chapter Opener

Motivating Activity

Poll the class to find out how many students have talked about the following topics in the past 24 hours:

1. your boyfriend or girlfriend
2. someone else's boyfriend or girlfriend
3. what you or someone else is wearing
4. a quarrel with someone or someone else's quarrel
5. a test
6. homework
7. music
8. the latest episode of (name a TV program)
9. the new movie (name a movie)
10. the latest sports match or game

Photo Flash!

① Cédric, Odile, and Pascale are talking together in a café called the **Café du Cours** on the famous **Cours Mirabeau** in Aix-en-Provence. Cédric is drinking a **menthe à l'eau,** a popular drink made with mint syrup and water.

Teaching Suggestion

Ask students to look at Photo 1 and to suggest reasons why Cédric, Odile, and Pascale might be sitting in a café. (In France, the café is an important meeting place for friends to get together.)

CHAPITRE **9** Tu connais la nouvelle?

① A propos, tu sais qui j'ai vu hier?

220 *deux cent vingt*

History Link

Aix-en-Provence is known as the historical and cultural capital of Provence. Its history dates to 123 B.C., when a Roman consul named Caius Sextius Calvinus founded the thermal baths of **Aquae Sexitae** in Aix.

Language Note

Explain that **nouvelle** means *news.* Then, ask students to guess the meaning of **Tu connais la nouvelle?** *(Did you hear the latest?)*

When you get together with friends, what do you talk about? Yourselves, of course! What you've been doing, whom you've talked to . . . and what your friends who aren't there are doing, too.

In this chapter you will learn

- to wonder what happened; to offer possible explanations; to accept or reject explanations
- to break some news; to show interest
- to begin, continue, and end a story

And you will

- listen to friends discuss what happened at a party
- read a scene from a play
- write about your personality
- find out about friendship in the francophone world

② Je me demande pourquoi elle a l'air fâchée!

③ Tu ne devineras jamais ce qui s'est passé!

8
9 FRANÇAIS   14 MATHS
10
11   HIST-GÉO
                                VENDR
                                (04) Av
            ÉPHANE
        Rendre disse
        e La fontain

        INTERRO !!!

      - Exposé s
        Guerre de

    19H RENDEZ-vous

- Call attention to the clay figurine pictured to the left of Photo 3. This is a representation of a typical farmhouse in Provence called **un mas provençal.** The distinctive features of the **mas** are their low, sloping profiles, natural stone-colored walls, and windows that are larger on the ground floor than on the second floor. The term **mas,** used for this typical rural dwelling, originated in the eleventh century when it meant

a house or *a barn,* and was even used to refer to a group of buildings. The basic design has remained constant throughout the centuries and allows for its expansion to mirror the occupants' financial growth.
- Point out the red-tiled roof of the structure, typical of the south of France. The distinctive roofs are made from red-canal, curved, clay tiles. The roofs are gently sloped to keep the tiles from sliding off.

Video Synopsis

In this segment of the video, Odile is walking in the park when she sees Cédric and Arlette together on a bench. They appear to be talking tenderly, and then, Cédric kisses Arlette's hand. Odile assumes they are having a romantic tête-à-tête. Odile breaks the news to Charlotte, who knows that Odile likes to imagine romances and warns her not to jump to conclusions. Just then, Pascale, Cédric's girlfriend, joins Charlotte and Odile. Because they are acting secretive, Pascale guesses that something is going on between Cédric and Arlette. Next, Cédric arrives, but Pascale leaves before he can talk to her. He doesn't understand what's going on.

Motivating Activity

Ask students if they have ever jumped to conclusions about something they witnessed. Ask them to recall a television program, movie, or book in which a character erroneously assumed something from the way a situation appeared. Ask them what the consequences of their own assumptions or those of the character were.

Mise en train

Il ne faut pas se fier aux apparences

Have you ever made assumptions about people or situations and then discovered they were all wrong? How many different ways can you interpret the photo on the right?

Cédric   Arlette

Odile   Charlotte

Pascale

ODILE	Devine qui j'ai vu ici dans le parc.
CHARLOTTE	Aucune idée... Dis un peu!
ODILE	Cédric et Arlette.
CHARLOTTE	Et alors?
ODILE	A mon avis, ça cache quelque chose.
CHARLOTTE	J'ai du mal à le croire. Toi, tu vois des histoires d'amour partout.
ODILE	Ils avaient l'air de bien s'entendre.
CHARLOTTE	Je n'y crois pas. Tu sais bien que Cédric est le petit copain de Pascale.
ODILE	Mais, je t'assure que c'est vrai.
CHARLOTTE	En tout cas, ça ne nous regarde pas...
ODILE	Mais, je les ai vus. Ils se parlaient tendrement et puis, Cédric lui a embrassé la main.

1

2

Ecoute, il ne faut pas se fier aux apparences.

Bon, comme tu veux... Pauvre Pascale!

Chut! La voilà!

3

Bonjour! Comment vas-tu?

Super. Qu'est-ce que vous avez à me regarder comme ça? Qu'est-ce que j'ai?

Rien du tout.

222 *deux cent vingt-deux*

CHAPITRE 9   Tu connais la nouvelle?

Language Note

Call attention to the way Charlotte warns Odile to be quiet when Pascale approaches in Photo 2. Point out that while we say *Shhh!* in English, the French say **Chut!**, pronouncing the –t.

PASCALE   Allez, quoi!
              Dites-le-moi!
ODILE   On a vu Cédric
              et Arlette dans
              le parc...
CHARLOTTE ...en train de se
              parler.
PASCALE   Et alors?
CHARLOTTE Alors, rien.

4

Mais quoi?
Je ne comprends rien.
Qu'est-ce que vous racontez?
Ah, je commence à comprendre.
Vous voulez dire que Cédric
et Arlette...

Mais non,
pas du tout!

5

Tiens,
le voilà, Cédric!

Eh bien,
au revoir! J'ai du travail à
faire. A lundi. Salut.

6

Salut. Où est-ce que
Pascale est partie? Elle va revenir?

Non, elle
est rentrée chez
elle.

Pourquoi? Elle
est fâchée? Elle ne m'a même
pas dit bonjour.

Elle avait
du travail à
faire.

7

Pascale!!

Moi,
j'adore quand ça
se complique!

8

MISE EN TRAIN   *deux cent vingt-trois* **223**

Presentation

Before students read the **Mise en train,** have them look at the photos. Ask if they can guess who is making assumptions about whom, what those assumptions might be, and what consequences this might have for the people involved. Ask students to suggest some possible explanations for Cédric's and Arlette's behavior. Then, show the video and ask the questions in Activity 1 on page 224. Have students compare the story with the assumptions they made before reading. Finally, ask them if they can guess what the title **Il ne faut pas se fier aux apparences** means, judging from the story in the **Mise en train.** You might have students suggest additional titles for the story.

Group Work

Have groups of five read the **Mise en train,** with each group member assuming the role of one of the characters. Ask them to imitate the characters in the video and act out the roles with appropriate emotion and gestures. After the groups have practiced the scene several times, ask volunteers to act it out in front of the class.

Thinking Critically

Analyzing Ask students to analyze the factors that contributed to the misunderstanding in the **Mise en train.** Have them suggest ways that certain characters could have behaved in order to prevent a misunderstanding. (Odile might have asked Cédric and Arlette what they were doing. Pascale might have asked Odile to explain her implication. Charlotte and Odile might have told Cédric why Pascale left.)

📺 Video Integration

- **EXPANDED VIDEO PROGRAM,**
  Videocassette 3, 44:40–49:11
- **VIDEODISC PROGRAM,**
  Videodisc 5A

Search 11355, Play To 19500

You may choose to continue with **Il ne faut pas se fier aux apparences (suite)** at this time or wait until later in the chapter. When the story continues, Cédric and Arlette are talking in front of school. Pascale walks by, and Cédric asks her what's wrong. She doesn't want to talk to him and continues walking. Cédric can't understand what's wrong. Then, Odile overhears Cédric and Arlette making plans to meet the next day. She tells Pascale, and the next day, they discover that Cédric and Arlette are in a play! They are rehearsing the same scene Odile witnessed in the park.

1 Tu as compris? See answers below.

1. What did Odile see in the park?
2. What does Odile think is going on?
3. What does Charlotte think is going on?
4. Why does Pascale leave so quickly?
5. How does Odile feel about what happened?

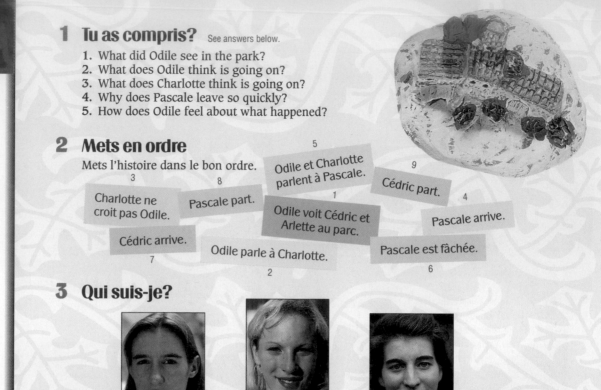

2 Mets en ordre

Mets l'histoire dans le bon ordre.

3 · Charlotte ne croit pas Odile.
8 · Pascale part.
5 · Odile et Charlotte parlent à Pascale.
1 · Odile voit Cédric et Arlette au parc.
9 · Cédric part.
4 · Pascale arrive.
· Cédric arrive. 7
· Odile parle à Charlotte. 2
· Pascale est fâchée. 6

3 Qui suis-je?

Arlette

Odile

Charlotte

1. «Moi, j'adore quand ça se complique!» Odile
2. «Je vois des histoires d'amour partout.» Odile
3. «Nous avions l'air de bien nous entendre.»
4. «J'ai embrassé la main d'Arlette.» Cédric
5. «Je suis fâchée.» Pascale
6. «Je suis le petit copain de Pascale.» Cédric
7. «Je ne crois pas que Cédric et Arlette flirtaient.» Charlotte
8. «J'ai dit que j'avais du travail à faire.» Pascale

3. Cédric et Arlette

Cédric

Pascale

4 Cherche les expressions

What do the people in **Il ne faut pas se fier aux apparences** say to . . .

1. break some news? Devine qui j'ai vu...
2. show interest in hearing some news? Aucune idée... Dis un peu!
3. reject explanations about what might have happened? J'ai du mal à le croire. Je n'y crois pas.
4. ask what's going on? Allez, quoi! Dites-le-moi!

5 Et maintenant, à toi

If you were Pascale, what would you have done?

Answers

1 1. She saw Cédric kissing Arlette's hand.
2. Cédric has found a new girlfriend.
3. Nothing.
4. She is angry at Cédric.
5. She is enjoying the situation.

PREMIERE ETAPE

Wondering what happened; offering possible explanations; accepting or rejecting explanations

> A mon avis, il est amoureux d'elle.

> Je crois que ça cache quelque chose. Pascale va être furieuse!

> Mais non! Je parie qu'elle s'est coupé le doigt et que Cédric l'aide à mettre un sparadrap.

> Peut-être que Pascale et Cédric se sont disputés... alors, Cédric s'est trouvé une nouvelle copine!

6 A ton avis...

What explanations do their friends give for Cédric and Arlette's behavior? How would you explain the situation? Cédric is in love with Arlette. Arlette cut her finger, and Cédric is applying a bandage. Pascale and Cédric had an argument, and Cédric has found a new girlfriend; Answers will vary.

NOTE CULTURELLE

Where do you go to see and talk about what's happening in your town? In Aix-en-Provence, the **Cours Mirabeau** provides entertainment and refreshment to tourists and inhabitants alike. Often called one of the most beautiful streets in Europe, the **Cours Mirabeau** is the main street in Aix. Plane trees and fountains run the length of the broad boulevard, making it a cool place even in the summer when the **provençal** sun is strong. The shadier side of the street has banks and mansions (**hôtels particuliers**) from the seventeenth and eighteenth centuries, while the sunnier side of the street is famous for its shops and sidewalk cafés. One of these, the **Deux Garçons**, is the place in Aix to see and be seen.

RESOURCES FOR PREMIERE ETAPE

Textbook Audiocassette 5A/Audio CD 9
Practice and Activity Book, pp. 98–100
Video Guide
  Video Program
  Expanded Video Program, Videocassette 3
Videodisc Guide
  Videodisc Program, Videodisc 5A

Chapter Teaching Resources, Book 3
• Teaching Transparency Master 9-1, pp. 7, 10
  Teaching Transparency 9-1
• Additional Listening Activities 9-1, 9-2, p. 11
  Audiocassette 10A/Audio CD 9
• Realia 9-1, pp. 15, 17
• Situation Cards 9-1, pp. 18–19
• Student Response Forms, pp. 20–22
• Quiz 9-1, pp. 23–24
  Audiocassette 8A/Audio CD 9

𝒥ump Start!

Write the following sentences on the board or on a transparency. Students decide which character from the **Mise en train** would most likely say each sentence, and write the name of that character next to the appropriate number.

1. Je crois qu'Odile voit des histoires d'amour partout.
2. Pascale est furieuse contre moi, mais je ne sais pas pourquoi.
3. Je suis la petite amie de Cédric.
4. Cédric m'a embrassé la main.
5. J'ai vu Arlette et Cédric ensemble dans le parc.

(*Answers:* 1. Charlotte   2. Cédric   3. Pascale   4. Arlette   5. Odile)

MOTIVATE

Gather magazine pictures of people showing different emotions. Ask students to imagine how the people feel and why they feel that way.

TEACH

Teaching Suggestion

Have students look at the photo of Arlette and Cédric in the park. Ask them for all possible explanations concerning their behavior and compile a list in French on the board. Then, read aloud the four explanations on this page. Ask students which of the four explanations they find the most believable. Then, compare these explanations with those on the board. Next, ask students to look at the text and find the expressions that introduce a supposition (A mon avis... ; Je crois que... ; Je parie que... ; Peut-être que...).

Language Note

You might point out that the words **copain** and **copine** are also used for *boyfriend* and *girlfriend.*

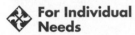
Vocabulaire

Comment sont les clients des Deux Garçons aujourd'hui?

226 *deux cent vingt-six*   CHAPITRE 9   Tu connais la nouvelle?

7 Ecoute!

Ecoute Raoul et Philippe qui sont au café Les Deux Garçons en train de parler de la fête d'hier soir. D'après leur conversation, comment étaient leurs amis?

1. Kim   f
2. Serge   b
3. Maria   e
4. Maud   d
5. Victor g
6. Guillaume c

a. énervé(e)
b. mal à l'aise
c. inquiet (inquiète)
d. gêné(e)
e. de bonne humeur
f. déprimé(e)
g. furieux (furieuse)
h. de mauvaise humeur

Note de Grammaire

- Remember that you use the **imparfait** to tell what people were like in the past:

    Il **était** triste.

- You can also use the expression **avoir l'air** + an adjective to tell how people *seemed* to be:

    Elle **avait l'air fâchée.**

    The adjective agrees with the person you're describing.

8 Qu'est-ce qui s'est passé?

Décris les réactions de tes amis dans ces situations. Complète chaque phrase avec un adjectif qui convient.   *Possible answers:*

1. Pierre est tombé devant son prof d'histoire. Il était _____.   gêné
2. Marion est allée à une boum où elle ne connaissait personne. Elle était _____.   mal à l'aise
3. Jean a eu 20 à l'interro d'anglais. Il était _____.   de bonne humeur
4. Le chat d'Ali est mort soudainement. Ali avait l'air _____.   déprimé
5. Li est sortie avec un beau garçon. Elle avait l'air _____.   amoureuse
6. Jean-Michel n'a pas pu trouver son portefeuille ce matin. Il était _____.   de mauvaise humeur
7. On a fait une surprise-partie pour Eric. Il était vachement _____!   étonné

9 Alors, raconte!

Avec qui as-tu parlé hier? Fais une liste et décris l'humeur de ces personnes.

Melissa était de bonne humeur mais Manuel avait l'air plutôt déprimé. Sheryl était vachement inquiète parce qu'elle ·it en ret~

A la française

To better describe people and things, you can use words like **assez** (*sort of*) and **plutôt** (*rather*) to modify adjectives. When you're talking to people your own age, you can use the informal expressions **vachement** (*really*) and **super** (*really, ultra-*) before adjectives for emphasis: Elle était **vachement énervée.** Il est **super sympa.**

10 Mon journal

Complète les phrases suivantes pour décrire ta personnalité.

Je suis énervé(e) quand...
Je suis fâché(e) quand...
Je suis déprimé(e) quand...

Je suis de bonne humeur quand...
Je suis mal à l'aise quand...
Je suis étonné(e) quand...

Language Notes

- Another colloquial way to say *very* or *really* is **hyper.** (Il/Elle était **hyper** fâché(e).)
- Tell students that **une vache** is *a cow* in English. The term developed from the fact that the French use **vache** as an adjective,

meaning **méchant.** (Il/Elle est **vache.**) The word **méchant** is also used to mean *great.* (Il a une **méchante** moto.) **Vachement** came to be used as **méchamment** (*really*) as in **Ce gâteau est vachement bon,** similar to *You make a mean cake.*

Presentation

Note de grammaire   Use the pictures of various people showing emotion that students gathered (see For Individual Needs on page 226). Show each picture, asking **Il/Elle a l'air comment?** Have students tell you how the person seems to be feeling. **(Il a l'air déprimé. Elle a l'air étonnée.)**

For Individual Needs

7 Slower Pace   Have students copy the names and choices on a sheet of paper. Then, have them draw lines from the names to the appropriate emotions as they listen to the recording.

7 Tactile Learners   Have students list the emotions on a sheet of paper and the names on small pieces of paper. As they listen to the recording, have them place the names next to the appropriate emotion.

7 Challenge   Have students listen to the recording a second time and tell why each of the people felt or appeared to feel the way they did, according to Raoul or Philippe.

Group Work

8   Have groups of students create other sentences about imaginary people and call on another group to guess how the person might have felt.

 **Mon journal**

10   For an additional journal entry suggestion for Chapter 9, see *Practice and Activity Book,* page 153.

Additional Practice

10   Have students talk about other people in their journals (**Mes parents sont de bonne humeur quand...**).

For videodisc application, see *Videodisc Guide.*

Presentation

Comment dit-on... ?
Obtain a picture of the *Mona Lisa* from the library, show it, and muse **Je me demande pourquoi elle sourit.** Offer an explanation. (**A mon avis, elle était amoureuse.**) Encourage students to accept or reject the explanation by asking either-or questions. (**Ça se voit, Jean, ou ce n'est pas possible? J'ai peut-être raison, ou je me trompe?**) With each choice, offer the *acceptance* with a nod of the head *(yes),* and the *rejection,* while shaking the head *(no).*

For Individual Needs

Challenge Make statements in which you wonder why the people feel the way they do in the **Vocabulaire** on page 226. (**Je me demande pourquoi le serveur est de mauvaise humeur.**) Encourage students to respond, using the expressions in **Comment dit-on... ?** (**Je parie qu'il est de mauvaise humeur parce qu'un client a oublié de payer.**)

CLOSE

To close this **étape,** choose five pictures of people who are showing different emotions and tape them to the board. Have students choose three of the pictures and write a short paragraph for each one, telling how the person feels and offering possible explanations for those feelings. Then, ask volunteers to read one of their paragraphs aloud and have the other students guess which picture it describes.

COMMENT DIT-ON... ?

Wondering what happened; offering possible explanations; accepting or rejecting explanations

To wonder what happened:
Je me demande pourquoi elle sourit comme ça. *I wonder. . .*

To offer possible explanations:
A mon avis, elle était amoureuse. *In my opinion, . . .*
Peut-être qu'elle a passé une bonne journée. *Maybe . . .*
Je crois qu'elle a gagné à la loterie. *I think that . . .*
Je parie qu'elle a mangé trop vite. *I bet that . . .*

To accept an explanation:
Tu as peut-être raison. *Maybe you're right.*
C'est possible. *That's possible.*
Ça se voit. *That's obvious.*
Evidemment. *Obviously.*

To reject an explanation:
A mon avis, tu te trompes. *In my opinion, you're mistaken.*
Ce n'est pas possible. *That's not possible.*
Je ne crois pas. *I don't think so.*

11 Ecoute!

Listen as Cédric asks his friends why Pascale doesn't talk to him. Does he accept or reject the explanations they offer? Answers on p. 221C.

12 Je me demande pourquoi!

Qu'est-ce qui est arrivé à Nora, à Thierry et à Didier? Imagine trois événements qui peuvent expliquer leur humeur. Parles-en avec un(e) camarade qui va te dire s'il/elle est d'accord avec toi ou pas.

—Je me demande pourquoi Nora a l'air fatiguée aujourd'hui.
—Peut-être qu'elle a mal à la tête.
—Non, je ne crois pas. Je parie qu'elle...

Nora

Thierry

Didier

13 Charades

a. Pick an emotion from the **Vocabulaire** and write down a reason you might feel that way. Act out the emotion and then the reason. Your group will offer possible explanations. The first person to guess the reason acts out his or her charade.

b. After playing charades in your group, decide which one was the best and act it out as a group for the class.

ASSESS

Quiz 9-1, *Chapter Teaching Resources, Book 3,* pp. 23–24

Assessment Items, Audiocassette 8A Audio CD 9

Performance Assessment

Have students write a paragraph in which they speculate about the feelings of a real or imaginary person. Students should explain the circumstances, tell how the person appeared to be feeling, imagine why he or she was feeling that way, and offer two possible explanations for the person's emotional state. They should accept one explanation as possible and reject the other one as improbable.

PANORAMA CULTUREL

Marius • Côte d'Ivoire

Yannick • Martinique

Jennifer • France

**VIDEO PROGRAM
OR EXPANDED VIDEO
PROGRAM,**
Videocassette 3
49:12–53:43

OR **VIDEODISC PROGRAM,**
Videodisc 5A

Search 19500, Play To 23490

We talked to some French-speaking teenagers about friendships. Here's what they had to say.

Comment est l'ami idéal?

«Pour moi, un ami idéal, c'est l'ami qui sait t'écouter, qui sait te comprendre et puis qui a beaucoup d'attentions pour toi. Et aussi, cet ami-là cherche toujours à t'aider quand tu as des problèmes... et qui ne trahit pas tes secrets-et puis aussi c'est un ami qui te soutient toujours. Voilà.»

—Marius

«L'amie parfaite, eh bien, c'est celle qui ne sera pas fayot, c'est-à-dire, enfin, fayotte, du moins c'est celle qui n'ira pas répéter à tout bout de champ «Mais oui, tiens, elle a tel et tel problème.» C'est l'idéal à la fin.

Moi, je crois que, l'idéal comme amie, c'est, enfin, qu'elle me ressemble un peu.»

—Yannick

Quelle est la différence entre un copain et un ami?

«Je pense qu'un copain, c'est quelqu'un qu'on voit un peu tous les jours, à qui on dit bonjour, mais sans vraiment se confier. Alors qu'une amie on lui confie beaucoup de choses, on reste souvent avec elle, on est très proches.»

—Jennifer

«Eh bien, une copine, c'est par exemple... elle est dans la même classe. On discute avec elle des cours... je sais pas, moi... des bobards qu'on raconte à tout le monde. Et l'amie, on lui confie plus ce qui se passe dans l'intimité, ce qu'on ne doit pas dire à sa mère ou à quelqu'un d'autre, de se confier vraiment, on irait plutôt vers l'amie que vers la copine.»

—Yannick

Qu'en penses-tu? See answers below.

1. What are the qualities of a good friend according to these people?
2. What characteristics do you look for in a friend?
3. According to these people, what is the difference between **un copain** and **un ami**?

Answers

1. Someone who listens to you, understands you, helps when you have problems, doesn't betray your confidence, and supports you.
3. **Un ami** is a closer friend than **un copain. Un copain** might be a classmate or an acquaintance, but **un ami** is someone you confide in and trust.

Questions

1. Qui pense que l'amie idéale doit lui ressembler un peu? (Yannick)
2. D'après Yannick, une camarade de classe est une amie ou plutôt une copine? (une copine)
3. Selon Jennifer, à qui est-ce qu'on se confie? (à un ami ou une amie)

Teacher Notes

• See *Video Guide, Videodisc Guide,* and *Practice and Activity Book* for activities related to the **Panorama Culturel.**
• Remind students that cultural material may be included in the Chapter Quizzes and Test.
• The interviewees' language represents informal, unrehearsed speech. Occasionally, edits have been made for clarification.

Motivating Activity

Ask students what the difference is between an acquaintance and a friend. Ask what the difference is between a friend and a best friend.

Presentation

Have students view the video. Ask them if the definitions of a friend offered by the interviewees were similar to those suggested for the Motivating Activity above. Ask them if they can discern from the interviews whether **un(e) ami(e)** is the equivalent of *a friend* or *an acquaintance.*

Language Note

Point out that **un fayot (une fayotte)** is slang for a student who is *a tattletale* or *a teacher's pet.* **Un bobard** is slang for *a fib* or *a tall tale.*

*J*ump Start!

Write some suppositions on the board or on a transparency. **(Je parie que le prof est étonné parce que tout le monde a fait ses devoirs.)** Have students either accept or reject them in writing.

*M*OTIVATE

Ask students to imagine that something wonderful just happened to them. Ask them how they would break the news to their best friend. Ask what they would say to their best friend who just said *You'll never guess what happened!*

*T*EACH

Teaching Suggestion

Trace the pictures on a transparency without the speech bubbles and write in the names of the characters. Write the speech bubbles on separate, small pieces of transparency. Project the transparency on the overhead and ask questions to prompt students to talk about the pictures. Have them guess the relationships of the people to each other and where they are. Then, ask questions in the **passé composé** to emphasize that the illustrations represent what happened. **(Qui est tombé? Qui est resté dans sa chambre? Qui est tombé amoureux? Qui est fâché contre sa mère? Qui n'a plus de copine? Qui est allé chez ses grand-parents? Qui a trouvé cent francs? Qui a rencontré une fille au parc? Qui a eu un problème avec sa voiture?)** Then, place the speech bubbles randomly on the overhead and read them one at a time. Have students tell you on which picture to place each speech bubble.

Language Note

For an explanation of **un coup de foudre**, see page 240.

DEUXIEME ETAPE

Breaking some news; showing interest

Marie

Romain

Thibaut

Amina

Didier

14 Tu as compris?

Qui a passé un bon week-end? Un mauvais week-end?

Bon week-end : Marie, Didier
Mauvais week-end : Romain, Thibaut, Amina

RESOURCES FOR **DEUXIEME ETAPE**	
Textbook Audiocassette 5A/Audio CD 9	***Chapter Teaching Resources, Book 3***
Practice and Activity Book, pp. 101–103	• Communicative Activity 9-1, pp. 3–4
Videodisc Guide	• Teaching Transparency Master 9-2, pp. 8, 10
Videodisc Program, Videodisc 5A	*Teaching Transparency 9-2*
	• Additional Listening Activities 9-3, 9-4, p. 12
	Audiocassette 10A/Audio CD 9
	• Realia 9-2, pp. 16, 17
	• Situation Cards 9-2, pp. 18–19
	• Student Response Forms, pp. 20–22
	• Quiz 9-2, pp. 25–26
	Audiocassette 8A/Audio CD 9

VOCABULAIRE

avoir un accident	to have an accident
avoir (prendre) rendez-vous (avec quelqu'un)	to have (make) a date (with someone)
se disputer (avec quelqu'un)	to have an argument (with someone)
casser (avec quelqu'un)	to break up (with someone)
être privé(e) de sortie	to be "grounded"
faire la tête	to sulk
tomber en panne	to break down (in a vehicle)
se perdre	to get lost
rencontrer	to meet
tomber amoureux(-euse) (de quelqu'un)	to fall in love (with someone)

15 Ecoute!

Regarde les images à la page 230. Ecoute Catherine qui décrit ses amis. De qui parle-t-elle?
Answers on p. 219C.

16 Et toi?

Réponds à ces questions. Ensuite, pose les mêmes questions à un(e) camarade.

1. Est-ce que tu as déjà eu un accident? Où? Qu'est-ce qui t'est arrivé?
2. Est-ce que tu as déjà été privé(e) de sortie? Pourquoi?
3. Est-ce que tu t'es déjà perdu(e)? Où? Comment est-ce que tu as retrouvé ton chemin?
4. Est-ce que tu es déjà tombé(e) amoureux (amoureuse) de quelqu'un?

Si tu as oublié the passé composé of reflexive verbs va à la page 168.

COMMENT DIT-ON... ?
Breaking some news; showing interest

To break some news:

Tu connais la nouvelle? *Did you hear the latest?*
Tu ne devineras jamais ce qui s'est passé.
   You'll never guess what happened.
Tu sais qui j'ai vu? *Do you know who . . . ?*
Tu sais ce que Robert a fait? *Do you know what . . . ?*
Devine qui Marion a vu! *Guess who . . .*
Devine ce que j'ai fait! *Guess what . . .*

To show interest:

Raconte!
Aucune idée. *No idea.*
Dis vite! *Let's hear it!*

Presentation

Vocabulaire Write the French expressions and their English equivalents on index cards. Give one card to each pair of students or to groups of three. The partners or groups must devise a way to teach that expression to their classmates, without using English. In large classes, you might write the same expression on two or three cards.

Teaching Suggestion

16 Tell students that they can invent answers if they prefer. Have them take notes as they conduct this interview. Afterwards, ask them to talk about the person they interviewed, without naming him or her. (**Cette personne a eu un accident de vélo quand elle avait cinq ans, mais ce n'était pas grave...**)

Presentation

Comment dit-on... ? Write the expressions for showing interest on the board and prompt three students to say them after each of three "news-breaking" statements you make. (**Tu connais la nouvelle?**) After the first student responds (**Raconte!**), tell a far-fetched story. Repeat the process with the remaining two students. Then, ask the class to guess the meanings of the expressions that you used and the responses that students gave.

For videodisc application, see *Videodisc Guide.*

Language Note

Students might be interested in the following expressions related to **tomber en panne**: **tomber en panne d'essence** *(to run out of gas)*; **une panne d'électricité** *(a power failure)*; **Je suis en panne de radio** *(My radio is broken)*; **être en panne** *(to be out of words, or to be stumped)*; **dépanner** *(to repair)*; **un dépanneur** *(a repairman)*.

Additional Practice

To re-enter the **passé composé** of verbs that have **avoir** or **être** as their helping verbs and the **passé composé** of reflexive verbs, prepare several flashcards. On one side, write sentences in the present tense. (**Eric cherche son livre. Les filles sortent. Je me perds.**) Have students give the **passé composé** of each sentence. After students respond, show the other side of the card on which you've written the sentence in the **passé composé.**

For Individual Needs

17 Slower Pace Have students look at the illustrations and predict what each conversation might be about.

17 Challenge Before students listen to the recording, have partners write a short dialogue to accompany each illustration. Tell students that the illustrations represent the news they are to break to someone in the dialogue. Then, play the recording and have students complete the activity. Play the recording again and have students compare their dialogues with those in the recording.

18 Challenge Ask students to find an account of an unusual incident in the newspaper and write about it in French.

Additional Practice

18 Ask the following questions about the news item:

1. **Dans quelle ville se trouve la centrale nucléaire? (à Fouilly-des-Oies)**
2. **A quelle heure est-ce que le président s'est fait mal à la main? (à sept heures ce matin)**
3. **Qu'est-ce que le président a dit quand il s'est fait mal au petit doigt? («Ouille! Ouille! Ouille!»)**
4. **Que faisait Elvis quand l'habitant d'Aix l'a vu? (Il sortait d'une boulangerie.)**
5. **Quand est-ce que les habitants de la région provençale ont vu un OVNI? (vers dix-sept heures hier après-midi)**
6. **Dans quelle ville se trouve le restaurant de Monsieur Rintintin? (en Arles)**
7. **Ce restaurant a combien d'étoiles? (quatre)**
8. **Quand est-ce que le propriétaire a ouvert son restaurant? (la semaine dernière)**

---

17 Ecoute! 1. b 2. d 3. c 4. a

Ecoute ces conversations et choisis l'image qui correspond à chaque conversation.

a.   b.   c.   d.

18 Tu connais la nouvelle? See answers below.

a. Lis **Sur le vif** et réponds aux questions suivantes.

1. Qu'est-ce qui est arrivé au président?
2. Est-ce qu'il a visité la centrale nucléaire?
3. Qu'est-ce que l'habitante d'Aix faisait quand elle a vu Elvis?
4. Qu'est-ce qu'Elvis a acheté?
5. Qu'est-ce que c'est qu'un OVNI?
6. Comment était l'OVNI que le témoin *(eyewitness)* a vu?
7. Qui sont les clients de M. Rintintin?

b. With a partner, take turns breaking and responding to the news in **Sur le vif**!

SUR LE VIF

LE PRESIDENT A BOBO
Le président de la République a dû annuler sa visite à la centrale nucléaire de Fouilly-les-Oies. Le porte-parole du gouvernement a annoncé hier : « Le Président a eu un petit accident. Il s'est fait mal au petit doigt à sept heures ce matin. » Son épouse précise qu'au moment de l'incident, le président a dit : « Ouille! Ouille! Ouille! »

LE «KING» PARMI NOUS
Une habitante d'Aix-en-Provence a eu la surprise de sa vie ce matin. Elle promenait son chien au centre-ville quand elle a aperçu Elvis Presley en personne qui sortait d'une boulangerie. Elle a dit que le roi du rock avait un sac plein de pains au chocolat.

UNE VRAIE HISTOIRE MARSEILLAISE
Plusieurs habitants de la région provençale déclarent avoir vu un OVNI vers 17 heures hier après-midi. Un témoin a dit : « J'ai vu un énorme objet dans le ciel. Je savais que ce n'était pas un avion parce qu'il y avait des lumières vertes, jaunes, et violettes qui clignotaient. C'était comme un ballon de football! C'était un spectacle incroyable! »

UNE AUBERGE POUR TOUTOU
Les habitants d'Arles peuvent maintenant amener leurs chiens et chats dans un restaurant quatre étoiles fait exclusivement pour eux. Le propriétaire du restaurant, M. Médor Rintintin, a ouvert son établissement la semaine dernière. Des centaines de maîtres ont déjà invité leurs petites bêtes préférées à un repas grand luxe.

Language Notes

- While American children call a small wound *a boo-boo*, French children refer to it as **un bo-bo.**
- **OVNI** stands for **objet volant non-identifié.**

18 Explain the origin of the name **Monsieur Médor Rintintin.** (**Médor** is a common name for a dog in France. Rin-Tin-Tin was the canine star of a 1950s American television drama of the same name.)

Answers

18 1. Il s'est fait mal au petit doigt.
2. Non.
3. Elle promenait son chien au centre-ville.
4. un sac de pains au chocolat
5. a UFO, an unidentified flying object
6. C'est comme un ballon de football, un spectacle incroyable.
7. les chiens et les chats

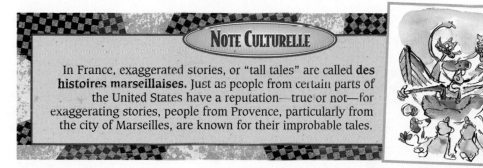

Note Culturelle

In France, exaggerated stories, or "tall tales" are called **des histoires marseillaises.** Just as people from certain parts of the United States have a reputation— true or not—for exaggerating stories, people from Provence, particularly from the city of Marseilles, are known for their improbable tales.

---

*G*rammaire The passé composé vs. the imparfait

- You already know you use the **passé composé** to *tell what happened.*

    Elle **a eu** un accident.   Nous **avons joué** au tennis.

- You use the **imparfait** . . .

    —to *describe how people or things were* in the past.
    Quand elle **avait** cinq ans, elle **était** pénible.

    —to talk about repeated actions in the past, to *tell what used to happen.*
    Quand j'**avais** huit ans, je **faisais** toujours des bêtises. Je **jouais** du piano, mais maintenant je n'en joue plus.

    —to describe general conditions in the past, to *set the scene.*
    Il **était** deux heures de l'après-midi; il **faisait** beau.

- You often need to use both the **passé composé** and the **imparfait** to tell what took place in the past.

    Il **faisait** gris et il **pleuvait.** J'**étais** de mauvaise humeur; ma mère **travaillait** et mon frère, qui **était** privé de sortie, **faisait** la tête. Soudain, j'**ai pris** une décision : pourquoi ne pas aller au cinéma? Je **suis allée** au Ciné 4 voir le nouveau film de Gérard Depardieu. Après, j'**ai rencontré** des copains et on **est allés** au café. Bref, j'**ai passé** une bonne journée!

19 Passé composé ou imparfait?

Reread the short story in the **Grammaire.** Tell why each verb in bold type is in the **passé composé** or the **imparfait.** See answers below.

De bons conseils

Here are a few hints to help you decide when to use the **passé composé** and when to use the **imparfait.**

- Words like **d'abord, puis,** and **ensuite** that tell in what order events happened often signal the **passé composé.**

    - Words that indicate a specific moment in the past, like **soudain** *(suddenly),* **tout à coup** *(suddenly),* and **au moment où** *(just when),* also signal the **passé composé.**

- Words that indicate a repeated action, like **toujours, d'habitude, tous les jours, souvent,** and **de temps en temps,** usually signal the **imparfait.**

Answers

19 Il **faisait** gris et il **pleuvait:** *sets the scene*
J'**étais:** *describes how people were in the past*
ma mère **travaillait:** *sets the scene*
mon frère, qui **était:** *describes how people were in the past*
faisait la tête: *sets the scene*
j'**ai pris** une décision; Je **suis allée** au Ciné 4; j'**ai rencontré** des copains; on **est allés;** j'**ai passé:** *tells what happened*

Language Notes

- Point out that **Je jouais du piano** means *I played piano, I would play piano,* or *I used to play piano.* All imply that *playing piano* took place often and over an indefinite period of time.
- You may wish to tell students that the imperfect of **être** means *was* and *were* and the imperfect of other verbs <u>sometimes</u> means *was/were* + verb + *ing.* (**Ma mère travaillait.** *My mother was working.)*

Grammaire Read the **Grammaire** with students. Then, draw a timeline on the board, mark events, and label them. **(Je me suis levé(e) à 6h30. J'ai mangé le petit déjeuner à 7h30. Je suis parti(e) à 8h.)** Then, write sentences randomly around the timeline. **(Il faisait beau. Mon frère m'embêtait. J'étais content(e).)** Explain that these sentences can't be marked on the timeline at a specific point, because they express background circumstances, feelings, or occurrences over an extended period of time.

Teacher Note

Point out to students that when someone asks what they did over the weekend, they usually talk about completed activities, thereby using the past tense. In French, they would answer similarly, using the **passé composé. (J'ai fait des magasins, je suis allé(e) à une boum, et j'ai eu un accident de voiture.)** However, when someone asks for further information about the event, they are asking for *background information* or a *description* of the event. *(What was the party like? Who was there? Who was driving when you had the accident? Was it raining?)* In French, these questions and their responses would be in the **imparfait. (Comment était la boum? Qui était là? Qui conduisait quand l'accident a eu lieu? Il pleuvait?)**

Additional Practice

Have students look at **Sur le vif** on page 232 and examine each verb. Have them try to explain why these verbs are in the **imparfait** or the **passé composé.**

Teaching Suggestion

20 Have students work in pairs to complete this activity. Then, write the activity on a transparency and project it. Have a volunteer call on students to tell him or her which form of the verb to write in the blanks. Discuss why the **imparfait** or the **passé composé** is used in each case.

 Portfolio

22 Written You might have students include their **histoires marseillaises** in their written portfolios. For portfolio information, see *Assessment Guide,* pages 2–13.

CLOSE

To close this **étape,** have students present to the class one of the **histoires marseillaises** they created in Activity 21.

ASSESS

Quiz 9-2, *Chapter Teaching Resources, Book 3,* pp. 25–26

Assessment Items, Audiocassette 8A/Audio CD 9

Performance Assessment

Have students write an account of something that happened to them this weekend, on a vacation, or on another real or imaginary occasion. Have them write it in dialogue form, using Activity 21 as a model.

20 Sur le vif

Finish the following reporter's story for **Sur le vif** by putting the verbs in the **passé composé** or the **imparfait.** See answers below.

Patrick Bruel continue sa tournée de concerts dans le sud de la France. Hier, le chanteur __1__ (être) à Montpellier où des centaines de jeunes __2__ (aller) l'applaudir. A leur grande joie, quelques-uns __3__ (avoir) la chance de le rencontrer en personne. Il __4__ (être) environ minuit au restaurant La Côte à l'Os quand tout à coup, Patrick lui-même __5__ (entrer). Il __6__ (être) accompagné de quelques-uns de ses musiciens. Il __7__ (demander) le menu au serveur qui n'en __8__ (croire) pas ses yeux. Bruel __9__ (sembler) très content et il __10__ (rire) beaucoup. Il a dit au serveur que les concerts le __11__ (mettre) toujours de bonne humeur mais lui __12__ (donner) aussi très faim. Il __13__ (regarder) la carte que le serveur lui avait apportée, puis il __14__ (commander) des escargots et un steak au poivre. Après le repas, il __15__ (boire) un café. Ensuite, Bruel __16__ (payer) l'addition et il __17__ (partir) après avoir donné son autographe au serveur qui __18__ (ne pas regretter) d'avoir travaillé ce soir-là.

21 Tu plaisantes!

Take turns telling some **histoires marseillaises** to a partner. Try the following suggestions.

rencontrer le président
à Washington
visiter la Maison Blanche
dîner avec lui

—Tu sais qui j'ai rencontré?
—Non, raconte!
—J'ai rencontré le président des Etats-Unis!
—Mon œil! Tu étais où?
—J'étais à Washington, évidemment!
—Mais qu'est-ce que tu faisais?
—Je visitais la Maison Blanche.
—Alors, qu'est-ce que tu as fait?
—J'ai dîné avec lui.

1. voir un extra-terrestre
chez moi
regarder la télé
visiter sa planète

2. rencontrer le loup du Gévaudan *(the Bigfoot of France)*
dans la forêt
faire du camping
prendre une photo

3. trouver 500 F
dans le parc
promener le chien
faire du shopping

4. avoir rendez-vous avec (ta star préférée)
sur le Cours Mirabeau
écouter de la musique
demander son autographe

22 Mon œil!

Write down three activities, a place, and an emotion. Then, exchange papers with a partner and write **une histoire marseillaise,** using the information your partner gave you.

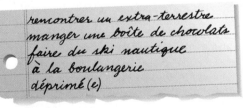

Answers

20 1. était
2. sont allés
3. ont eu
4. était
5. est entré
6. était
7. a demandé
8. croyait
9. semblait

10. riait
11. mettaient
12. donnaient
13. a regardé
14. a commandé
15. a bu
16. a payé
17. est parti
18. ne regrettait pas

Additional Practice

For additional reading, listening, and speaking practice, ask the following questions about the article for **Sur le vif:**

1. **Où était le chanteur quand il a donné son concert? (à Montpelier)**
2. **Combien de jeunes sont allés l'applaudir? (des centaines)**
3. **Il était quelle heure quand Patrick est entré dans un restaurant? (minuit)**
4. **Comment s'appelait le restaurant? (La Côte à l'Os)**
5. **Qu'est-ce que Patrick a demandé au serveur? (le menu)**
6. **Est-ce qu'il était de bonne humeur? (oui)**
7. **Comment le sais-tu? (Il riait beaucoup.)**
8. **Qu'est-ce qu'il a commandé? (des escargots et un steak au poivre)**
9. **Qu'est-ce qu'il a bu après? (un café)**
10. **Est-ce que le serveur regrettait d'avoir travaillé ce soir-là? (non)**

TROISIEME ETAPE

Beginning, continuing, and ending a story

Antoine

TROISIEME ETAPE

*J*ump Start!

Have students complete the following paragraph with the appropriate form of the **imparfait** or the **passé composé.**

> **Tu sais qui j'ai vu? Je (J')** ___ (rencontrer) Michael Jordan! Bref, j' ___ (être) au fastfood, quand il ___ (entrer). Il m'a dit qu'il ___ (s'ennuyer) chez lui, et il m'___ (inviter) à venir jouer au basket. C' ___ (être) vachement chouette! (*Answers:* **ai rencontré, étais, est entré, s'ennuyait, a invité, était**)

*M*OTIVATE

Poll the class to find out who likes to talk on the phone with friends. Ask them how they begin, continue, and end their conversations.

*T*EACH

Presentation

Comment dit-on... ? Tell students that you are going to recount a story, using expressions to begin, continue, and end it. Then, tell the story, raising your hand each time you use one of the functions. Then, write the three categories *begin, continue,* and *end* on the board, and have students cover **Comment dit-on... ?** with a sheet of paper. Have volunteers read the phone conversation and tell which words belong in each category.

Pascale téléphone à Antoine . . .

— A propos, Antoine, qu'est-ce que tu as fait hier soir?

— Je m'ennuyais chez moi, alors, j'ai décidé d'aller au cinéma. A ce moment-là, le téléphone a sonné. C'était Arlette. Elle s'ennuyait aussi et voulait faire quelque chose avec moi

— Donc, vous êtes allés au cinéma!

— Eh bien... c'est-à-dire que... je suis timide.

— Tu veux dire que tu ne l'as pas invitée?!

— Je n'ai pas eu le courage!

— Mais tu es dingue!

— Attends! Elle m'a proposé d'aller voir *Germinal* au Cinéma Cézanne.

— Heureusement!

— Oui, mais tu vois, ce cinéma est à l'autre bout d'Aix.

— Et alors?

— Ben, on a décidé de s'y retrouver une demi-heure plus tard. Alors, j'ai pris le bus, mais à cette heure-là, il y avait beaucoup de circulation et je suis arrivé très en retard. Arlette était déjà partie.

— Pauvre vieux! Maintenant, c'est à toi de l'inviter quelque part.

— Tu crois?

Pascale

23 Tu as compris?

Qu'est-ce qui est arrivé à Antoine hier soir? Pourquoi n'a-t-il pas invité Arlette? A ton avis, qu'est-ce qu'il va faire maintenant? See answers below.

COMMENT DIT-ON... ?
Beginning, continuing, and ending a story

To begin a story:
A propos,...
   By the way, . . .

To continue a story:
Donc,... *Therefore, . . .*
Alors,... *So . . .*
A ce moment-là,...
   At that point, . . .
Bref,... *Anyway, . . .*
C'est-à-dire que...
   That is, . . .
... quoi. *. . . you know.*
... tu vois. *. . . you see.*

To end a story:
Heureusement,...
   Fortunately, . . .
Malheureusement,...
   Unfortunately, . . .
Finalement,...

RESOURCES FOR **TROISIEME ETAPE**

Textbook Audiocassette 5A/Audio CD 9
Practice and Activity Book, pp. 104–106
Videodisc Guide
   Videodisc Program, Videodisc 5A

Chapter Teaching Resources, Book 3
- Communicative Activity 9-2, pp. 5–6
- Teaching Transparency Master 9-3, pp. 9, 10
   Teaching Transparency 9-3
- Additional Listening Activities 9-5, 9-6, p. 13
   Audiocassette 10A/Audio CD 9
- Realia 9-2, pp. 16, 17
- Situation Cards 9-3, pp. 18–19
- Student Response Forms, pp. 20–22
- Quiz 9-3, pp. 27–28
   Audiocassette 8A/Audio CD 9

Answers

23 Arlette called Antoine and asked him to go to a movie. Because of traffic, Antoine arrived very late, and Arlette had already left; He is shy; Answers will vary.

Teaching Suggestions

24 Before playing the recording, have students look at the pictures and imagine a logical order in which they might be placed. Then, play the recording, and have students verify or correct their guesses.

25 After students complete this activity, ask them the following comprehension questions:
1. Qui a téléphoné à Odile? (Pascale)
2. Pour faire quoi? (Pour aller faire du roller en ligne.)
3. Comment Odile est-elle allée au parc? (en bus)
4. Est-ce que Pascale était au parc? (non)
5. Combien de temps est-ce qu'Odile a attendu au parc? (vingt minutes)
6. Odile était de bonne humeur après avoir attendu? (non, fâchée)
7. Qu'est-ce qu'elle a fait ensuite? (Elle a essayé de téléphoner à Pascale, et elle est rentrée chez elle.)
8. Qui a téléphoné à Odile la deuxième fois? (Pascale)
9. Qu'est-ce qu'elle a dit? (Elle était au Jardin Rambot et Odile s'est trompée.)

For Individual Needs

25 Challenge Have students work in pairs to complete the exercise. Have one partner cover the word box on this page, and have the other partner turn to the **Comment dit-on... ?** on pages 231 and 235. Have students decide together which words to use to complete the sentences. Afterwards, compile a list on the board or on a transparency of the words students chose. Have the class decide which are logical choices.

---

24 Ecoute! b, a, d, c

Ecoute l'histoire de Caroline. Remets les images suivantes en ordre d'après son histoire.

a.   b.   c.   d.

25 Qu'est-ce qu'ils disent?

Complète la conversation entre Odile et Arlette.

> heureusement   à ce moment-là
> à propos   aucune idée
> dis vite!   bref
> devineras   malheureusement

— Salut, Odile.
— Salut, Arlette. Tu sais ce qui m'est arrivé hier?
— __1__. Raconte!   Aucune idée
— Je faisais mes devoirs chez moi quand Pascale m'a téléphoné. Elle s'ennuyait chez elle et elle voulait aller faire du roller en ligne. Moi, j'étais d'accord. Simple, tu vois? Mais non! J'ai pris le bus pour aller au parc, mais Pascale n'était pas là.
— Vraiment? Mais elle est toujours à l'heure!
— Exactement! Donc, j'ai attendu vingt minutes...
— Vingt minutes!
— __2__, elle n'est jamais arrivée et j'étais fâchée. J'ai essayé de lui téléphoner, mais elle n'était pas là.   Malheureusement/Bref
— Et alors?
— __3__, j'ai décidé de rentrer chez moi. Après ça, tu ne __4__ jamais ce qui s'est passé!   3. A ce moment-là   4. devineras
— __5__!   Dis vite
— Le téléphone a sonné. C'était Pascale!
— Qu'est-ce qu'elle t'a dit?
— Euh... tu vois, c'était de ma faute. Elle était au Jardin Rambot, et moi, je suis allée au Parc Joseph Jourdan! __6__, elle n'était pas trop fâchée contre moi. __7__, on s'est donné rendez-vous pour demain au Jardin Rambot.   6. Heureusement   7. Bref
— Tout est bien qui finit bien!

26 Le jeu du cadavre exquis

In your group, choose a main character for a story. One person begins by writing the first sentence or two of the story, folds the paper to cover all but the last few words, and passes it to the next person who writes another sentence, folds the paper again, and passes it on. Remember, anything can happen! When you've finished, read the story to the class.

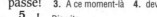

Caroline a un mom...
Donc, elle a cassé avec Martin.

Literature Link

26 Point out the title of the activity: **Le jeu du cadavre exquis.** André Breton (1896–1966), Louis Aragon (1897–1982), and Philippe Soupault (1897–1990) were cofounders of the Surrealist movement, which sought to eliminate the distinction between dream and reality, objectivity and subjectivity, and reason and madness. Together, they experimented with the revolutionary technique of *automatic writing* and were known to sit in cafés and practice this process in the form of **Le jeu du cadavre exquis.** Breton and Soupault explored this concept in a jointly authored work, *The Magnetic Fields (Les champs magnétiques;* 1920). In 1924, Breton's *Manifeste du surréalisme* defined Surrealism as "pure psychic automatism, by which it is intended to express . . . the real process of thought. It is the dictation of thought free from any control by the reason and of any aesthetic or moral occupation."

27 Qu'est-ce qu'on faisait quand... ?

How many sentences can you make using the **passé composé** and the **imparfait** in each one?

—Je faisais mes devoirs quand un extra-terrestre est entré dans ma chambre.
—Mon ami visitait Paris quand il est tombé amoureux.

faire mes devoirs danser le zouk manger de la pizza se disputer avec... visiter... faire la tête conduire la voiture faire la sieste faire des pompes être collé(e) être à... se promener ?	**quand**

rencontrer... avoir un accident décider de... voir... recevoir... tomber amoureux (amoureuse) de... perdre... casser (avec...) se casser... déguster... ?

28 Quelle surprise!

Imagine an unexpected guest paid you a surprise visit at home last night. Write about what everyone was doing when the surprise took place. Then, describe the guest and tell why he or she came to your home.

29 Jeu de rôle

Choose a well-known fairy tale. Each person plays the role of a character in the tale and tells the story from his or her point of view. Present your versions to the class, and see if they can guess what tale you are telling.

La belle et la bête (Beauty and the Beast)

Les trois petits cochons (The Three Little Pigs)

La belle au bois dormant (Sleeping Beauty)

Cendrillon (Cinderella)

Le petit chaperon rouge (Little Red Riding Hood)

Blanche-Neige (Snow White)

Note de Grammaire

- Sometimes you have to use both the **imparfait** and the **passé composé** in the same sentence. For example, you might want to say that one action *was going on* (imparfait) when another action *happened* (passé composé):

  Je **faisais** mes devoirs quand le téléphone **a sonné.**

- To emphasize that you were *in the middle of* or *busy doing* something, you can use the imperfect of the expression **être en train de** with an infinitive:

  J'**étais en train de** faire mes devoirs quand le téléphone **a sonné.**

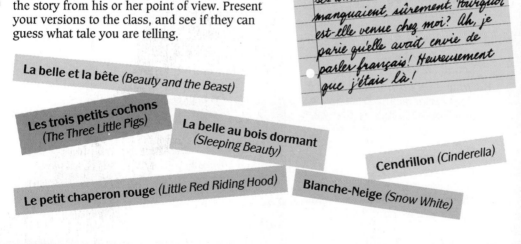

> Tu ne devineras jamais ce qui s'est passé hier soir! Mon père regardait la télé et moi, j'écoutais mon CD préféré de Céline Dion quand elle est entrée dans le salon! Elle était sympa, mais elle avait l'air un peu déprimée. Ses amis à Montréal lui manquaient, sûrement. Pourquoi est-elle venue chez moi? Ah, je parie qu'elle avait envie de parler français! Heureusement que j'étais là!

TROISIEME ETAPE

deux cent trente-sept **237**

Presentation

Note de grammaire Write the following activities on the board: **faire les devoirs, écrire au tableau, regarder par la fenêtre, lire une bande dessinée, dormir, parler à un(e) camarade.** As you leave the classroom, tell six volunteers to do these activities. Then, after leaving for a few moments, make a grand entrance, and ask each volunteer what he or she was doing when you came in. (**Qu'est-ce que tu faisais quand je suis entré(e) dans la salle de classe?**) Then, ask the other students what the volunteers were doing. (**Qu'est-ce que... faisait?**) Involve the other students by asking them what they were doing when you came in. You might repeat this, using **être en train de.**

 For videodisc application, see *Videodisc Guide.*

Portfolio

28 Written This activity is appropriate for students' written portfolios.

29 Oral This activity is appropriate for students' oral portfolios. For portfolio suggestions, see *Assessment Guide,* page 22.

Teaching Suggestion

29 Try to obtain one of these stories in French from the public library or from a foreign language bookstore. You might read it aloud to the class in one sitting or over several days. Students might follow along, reading photocopies you've distributed. Often, the French and English story lines will differ. Students might try to tell how the two versions differ, if they are familiar with the story in English.

CLOSE

Have students reread the conversation between Pascale and Antoine on page 235. Then, have partners create and act out the phone conversation in which Antoine explains to Arlette what happened and invites her to go out.

ASSESS

Quiz 9-3, *Chapter Teaching Resources, Book 3,* pp. 27–28

Assessment Items, Audiocassette 8A
Audio CD 9

Performance Assessment

Use Activity 29 to assess students' performance for this **étape.** You might base students' oral grades on content and comprehensibility.

READING STRATEGY

Reading with a purpose

Teacher Note

For an additional reading, see *Practice and Activity Book,* page 107.

Motivating Activity

Ask students if they have ever read a play or have seen one in a theater, whether they liked it, and why or why not. If students have ever acted in a play, ask them to describe their experience.

PREREADING
Activities A–B

Teacher Note

Eugène Ionesco, the author of *La cantatrice chauve,* began to learn English in 1948, according to a method that required him to memorize dialogues. The dialogues were supposed to reflect daily life, but in fact, had little to do with real life or authentic conversation. Ionesco noticed that people say many things every day that make little sense when taken out of context. It was this experience that inspired the writing of *La cantatrice chauve.*

For Individual Needs

B. Challenge Have students use a French-French dictionary to find synonyms for **absurde** (futile, inconscient, dérangé, désarticulé, sot, sans sens) and **banal** (commun, quotidien, ordinaire, rebattu, usé). Have students write sentences using these words.

Multicultural Link

Have students research playwrights from other cultures to see if any have made significant contributions to the theater of the absurd.

LISONS!

For Activities B-I, see answers below.

*M*isunderstandings can occur between friends. What do you think of the misunderstanding in this scene from the play *La cantatrice chauve?*

DE BONS CONSEILS

Before you read, make some theories about what the reading will be about or what's going to happen. Then, read to see if your ideas are correct or incorrect. You'll understand and remember much more if you read with a purpose.

A. Have you ever had the experience of saying something over and over and suddenly realizing that what you were saying seemed completely meaningless? The playwright Eugène Ionesco had just such an experience in the late 1940s and wrote *La cantatrice chauve* about it. When you read this scene from the play, keep in mind that this is an example of the theater of the absurd. Then, reread the scene to see if you think Ionesco has made his point: the endless repetition of common, polite words and phrases makes them sound absurd.

B. What does *absurd* mean? What does *banal* mean? What are some of the banalities that we say all the time (things we've said so often we don't even think about their meaning anymore)? Can polite phrases seem absurd sometimes? List five words or phrases you think people use without thinking.

Culture Note

Ionesco was born in 1912 in Romania. From the age of six, he lived in France and witnessed the first World War. Ionesco was disturbed by the rise of Nazism in Romania and France and revolted against it in his writing. He became one of Europe's foremost playwrights and wrote *Rhinocéros,* one of the definitive plays of the theater of the absurd. When he died in Paris in 1994, his plays were still in production.

SCENE IV

Mme et M. Martin, s'assoient l'un en face de l'autre, sans se parler. Ils se sourient, avec timidité.

M. MARTIN *(le dialogue qui suit doit être dit d'une voix traînante, monotone, un peu chantante, nullement nuancée).*
– Mes excuses, Madame, mais il me semble, si je ne me trompe, que je vous ai déjà rencontrée quelque part.

Mme MARTIN. – A moi aussi, Monsieur, il me semble que je vous ai déjà rencontré quelque part.

M. MARTIN. – Ne vous aurais-je pas déjà aperçue, Madame, à Manchester, par hasard?

Mme MARTIN. – C'est très possible. Moi, je suis originaire de la ville de Manchester! Mais je ne me souviens pas très bien, Monsieur, je ne pourrais pas dire si je vous y ai aperçu, ou non!

M. MARTIN. – Mon Dieu, comme c'est curieux! moi aussi je suis originaire de la ville de Manchester, Madame!

Mme MARTIN. – Comme c'est curieux!

. . .

M. MARTIN. – Depuis que je suis arrivé à Londres, j'habite rue Bromfield, chère Madame.

Mme MARTIN. – Comme c'est curieux, comme c'est bizarre! moi aussi, depuis mon arrivée à Londres j'habite rue Bromfield, cher Monsieur.

M. MARTIN. – Comme c'est curieux, mais alors, mais alors, nous nous sommes peut-être rencontrés rue Bromfield, chère Madame.

Mme MARTIN. – Comme c'est curieux; comme c'est bizarre! c'est bien possible, après tout! Mais je ne m'en souviens pas, cher Monsieur.

M. MARTIN. – Je demeure au n° 19, chère Madame.

Mme MARTIN. – Comme c'est curieux, moi aussi j'habite au n° 19, cher Monsieur.

M. MARTIN. – Mais alors, mais alors, mais alors, mais alors, mais alors, nous nous sommes peut-être vus dans cette maison, chère Madame?

Mme MARTIN. – C'est bien possible, mais je ne m'en souviens pas, cher Monsieur.

M. MARTIN. – Mon appartement est au cinquième étage, c'est le n° 8, chère Madame.

Mme MARTIN. – Comme c'est curieux, mon Dieu, comme c'est bizarre! et quelle coïncidence! moi aussi j'habite au cinquième étage, dans l'appartement n° 8, cher Monsieur!

Answers

B *Absurd:* ridiculous, nonsensical; *Banal:* unoriginal, dull, trite; Answers will vary; Yes; *Possible answers:* How are you? Fine. You know? Okay. Have a nice day; *Possible answers:* Ça va? Ça va bien. Ah, bon? Bon. Ben. Et la famille? Il fait beau. Vous allez bien?

M. MARTIN, *songeur.* – Comme c'est curieux, comme c'est curieux, comme c'est curieux et quelle coïncidence! vous savez, dans ma chambre à coucher j'ai un lit. Mon lit est couvert d'un édredon vert. Cette chambre, avec ce lit et son édredon vert, se trouve au fond du corridor, entre les water et la bibliothèque, chère Madame!

Mme MARTIN. – Quelle coïncidence, ah mon Dieu, quelle coïncidence! Ma chambre à coucher a, elle aussi, un lit avec un édredon vert et se trouve au fond du corridor, entre les water, cher Monsieur, et la bibliothèque!

M. MARTIN. – Comme c'est bizarre, curieux, étrange! alors, Madame, nous habitons dans la même chambre et nous dormons dans le même lit, chère Madame. C'est peut-être là que nous nous sommes rencontrés!

Mme MARTIN. – Comme c'est curieux et quelle coïncidence! C'est bien possible que nous nous y soyons rencontrés, et peut-être même la nuit dernière. Mais je ne m'en souviens pas, cher Monsieur!

M. MARTIN. – J'ai une petite fille, ma petite fille, elle habite avec moi, chère Madame. Elle a deux ans, elle est blonde, elle a un œil blanc et un œil rouge, elle est très jolie, elle s'appelle Alice, chère Madame.

Mme MARTIN. – Quelle bizarre coïncidence! moi aussi j'ai une petite fille, elle a deux ans, un œil blanc et un œil rouge, elle est très jolie et s'appelle aussi Alice, cher Monsieur!

M. MARTIN, *même voix traînante, monotone.* – Comme c'est curieux et quelle coïncidence! et bizarre! c'est peut-être la même, chère Madame!

Mme MARTIN. – Comme c'est curieux! c'est bien possible cher Monsieur.

Un assez long moment de silence... La pendule sonne vingt-neuf fois.

M. MARTIN, *après avoir longuement réfléchi, se lève lentement et, sans se presser, se dirige vers Mme Martin qui, surprise par l'air solennel de M. Martin, s'est levée, elle aussi, tout doucement; M. Martin a la même voix rare, monotone, vaguement chantante.* – Alors, chère Madame, je crois qu'il n'y a pas de doute, nous nous sommes déjà vus et vous êtes ma propre épouse… Elisabeth, je t'ai retrouvée!

Mme MARTIN *s'approche de M. Martin sans se presser. Ils s'embrassent sans expression. La pendule sonne une fois, très fort. Le coup de la pendule doit être si fort qu'il doit faire sursauter les spectateurs. Les époux Martin ne l'entendent pas.*

Mme MARTIN. – Donald, c'est toi, darling!

What are five polite phrases you might say in French?

C. What phrases do you find in the first few lines that indicate the Martins are strangers when the scene begins, in spite of the fact they are married?

D. In the first 20 lines, find two things that Mr. and Mrs. Martin have in common. Based on what you've just read, what do you think will happen in the scene?

E. Find examples of phrases that are repeated throughout this scene. What is the effect of the repetition of these phrases?

F. Why are the remarks **Comme c'est curieux** and **Quelle coïncidence** ridiculous as used here by the Martins? What is curious and bizarre about their conversation?

G. Reread the last lines of Mr. Martin and Mrs. Martin. What is the significant change in their attitude toward each other? How is this change signaled in their language? Give two examples.

H. Reread the stage directions. Why does Ionesco want the characters to present their lines in this way? Find the lines punctuated with an exclamation point. Practice reading them aloud with a monotonous, singsong, expressionless voice. How easy is this to do?

I. What is the main point that Ionesco is trying to make? Can you find enough evidence to prove that the play is about the absurdity of daily life? Do you think that Ionesco has successfully created a scene that convinces you of this absurdity?

J. Using some of the small talk and polite phrases you noted in part B, write a brief, absurd dialogue with a partner. Then, perform your scene for the class.

READING
Activities C–I

Drama Link

C. Ask students to read the opening directions of this scene in lines one through four. Ask them what information they would get from reading the play as opposed to seeing it produced. (They would know what the playwright intended as opposed to a director's or actor's interpretation.) Ask students why it is important to read stage directions and other directions interspersed in the text that are printed in italics. If there are students in your class who have acted in some of the school plays or are in a drama or theater class, ask them to give advice on following stage directions.

Group Work

C.–I. You may want to have students work in small groups to find and discuss the answers.

POSTREADING
Activity J

Teaching Suggestion

J. Since plays are meant to be read aloud and performed, give students ample opportunity to practice reading this scene aloud with appropriate intonation and facial expressions. You might have partners volunteer to present half or all of the scene to the class. You might consider staging it for other French classes.

Answers

C *Possible answers:* Mes excuses, Madame, mais il me semble... que je vous ai déjà rencontrée quelque part; A moi aussi, Monsieur; Ne vous aurais-je pas déjà aperçue, Madame, à Manchester... ?

D *Possible answers:* Both are originally from Manchester. Both live on Bromfield Street; Answers will vary.

E *Possible answers:* Comme c'est curieux! Comme c'est bizarre! Mais alors... ! Quelle coïncidence; The repetition of the phrases increases the absurdity of the situation and satirizes polite conversation.

F The Martins are married, so there is nothing curious or coincidental about the things they have in common. They do not recognize each other immediately.

G The Martins act like husband and wife; They talk more familiarly with each other; They use **tu** instead of **vous**. Mme Martin calls M. Martin "darling."

H The lines are presented in a monotone voice to exaggerate the banality of polite conversation.

I *Possible answer:* Daily life is full of absurdities. Our lives become mundane and empty when we speak to each other in platitudes and meaningless phrases.

MISE EN PRATIQUE

The **Mise en pratique** reviews and integrates all four skills and culture in preparation for the Chapter Test.

Teaching Suggestion

Have students scan the table of contents to find answers to the following questions:

1. Il y a combien de catégories d'articles dans *Paris Match?* (sept)
2. Comment s'appelle la femme sur la photo? (Veronica Berlusconi)
3. Il y a combien d'articles dans la catégorie "Match de Paris?" (cinq)
4. L'article *Cinéma, arts et théâtre* se trouve à quelle page? (à la page 20)
5. Quel article se trouve à la page 25? (*Rabin-Arafat : Les secrets de la grande réconciliation*)
6. Qui a écrit *La vie parisienne* dans la catégorie "Match de la vie?" (Agathe Godard)
7. Il y a combien de jeux dans cet exemplaire de *Paris Match?* (trois)
8. Qui est l'auteur des anacroisés? (Michel Duget)

 Culture Note

Call students' attention to the black and white photograph in the upper right-hand corner of this page. Robert Doisneau (1912–1994), a free-lance photographer, was a master at capturing humorous and tender moments in every-day life. Throughout his life-time, he exhibited his works in major museums in France and in the United States. Permanent collections of his work reside in the **Bibliothèque Nationale** and the **Musée d'Art Moderne** in Paris and in the Museum of Modern Art in New York.

Veronica Berlusconi.

MATCH DE PARIS

LES GENS

L'ACTUALITE

«Les frères », 1934, par Robert Doisneau.
«J'écrivais. Il illustrait. Ses photos de rêve nous faisaient oublier nos misères ».
Par Edmonde Charles-Roux de l'académie Goncourt 90

MATCH DE LA SEMAINE

MATCH DE LA VIE

JEUX

240   *deux cent quarante*   CHAPITRE 9   Tu connais la nouvelle?

 **Culture Note**

Paris Match is a popular weekly magazine somewhat comparable to *People* magazine in the United States, with articles that often focus on the lives of famous people. *Paris Match* is known for its sensationalism and full-page photographs.

Language Notes

- **Mon beauf,** under the last entry for *Match de Paris,* is slang for **mon beau-frère** *(my brother-in-law).* The adjective **beau/belle** is used to refer to *in-laws.* (**Ma belle-mère** means *my mother-in-law.*)
- In the category *Les gens,* **le coup de foudre** (literally *a bolt of lightning*) is an idiomatic expression meaning *love at first sight.* (**J'ai eu le coup de foudre pour...** *I fell head over heels in love with . . .*)

1 1. Skim the titles of the different categories in *Paris Match* magazine and the articles listed under each. Can you figure out what each category is about?

2. Who is featured in **Les Gens**? Which of these articles would you want to read?

3. Look at the **L'Actualité** section. Are these statements true?

  a. Veronica Berlusconi fait de la politique. c. La «chasse» aux œufs est une surprise.

  b. Les Zoulous sont ennemis de l'A.n.c. d. Doisneau était photographe.
  See answers below.

2 a. Listen to some readers call in on the hotline of the know-it-all column, **Je-sais-tout**, to ask questions they've been wondering about. Match their questions with the pictures that the editor chose to illustrate them. 1. c 2. b 3. a

a.

b.

c.

b. Now, act as Monsieur or Madame Je-sais-tout and write a brief answer to each caller in part a, giving a possible explanation. Make your answers humorous or serious.

3 Compare your explanations in number 2b with those of a classmate. Try to arrive at the most logical—or most interesting—explanation for each question.

4 You've decided to start your own magazine, like *Paris Match*, to keep your classmates informed of what's going on at your school. Make a table of contents for your magazine. First choose categories that you think your classmates would be interested in. You might want to create new categories like **la cantine**, **après l'école**, or **les sports**. Then, create some article titles and summaries and include photos or art about your feature articles. You might even design a cover for your newsmagazine.

5

JEU DE ROLE

With your classmates, create an informal television news broadcast about the happenings in your school. Using the table of contents of your magazine as a guide, break the top news stories for your class. You can even assign a "correspondent" who reports from the scene. Be sure to:
• break the news to the class.
• begin, continue, and end the stories.
• offer possible explanations for anything strange that happened.

MISE EN PRATIQUE *deux cent quarante et un* **241**

Answers
1 1. **Match de Paris:** articles related to culture and the arts
   Documents: articles about current political and social issues
   Les Gens: articles about famous people
   L'Actualité: articles about world and national news
   Match de la Semaine: weekly news
   Match de la Vie: articles concerning daily living
   Jeux: games

2. Kim Basinger, Jean-Claude Van Damme
3. a. true
   b. true
   c. false
   d. true

For Individual Needs

2 Slower Pace Before playing the recording, have students imagine what the people in the illustrations are going to ask about. Encourage them to say as much as possible about the pictures in French.

3 Challenge Have students invent and write their own **je-sais-tout** letter to pass to a partner, who will answer it.

Portfolio

4 Written You may want students to include this table of contents in their written portfolios. For portfolio information, see *Assessment Guide*, pages 2–13.

Teaching Suggestion

5 This activity is expanded in the project on page 219E.

Video Wrap-Up

• **VIDEO PROGRAM**
• **EXPANDED VIDEO PROGRAM,** Videocassette 3, 41:08–57:50
• **VIDEODISC PROGRAM,** Videodisc 5A

At this time, you might want to use the video resources for additional review and enrichment. See *Video Guide* or *Videodisc Guide* for suggestions regarding the following:
• **Il ne faut pas se fier aux apparences** (Dramatic episode)
• **Panorama Culturel** (Interviews)
• **Vidéoclips** (Authentic footage)

QUE SAIS-JE?

This page is intended to help students prepare for the test. It is a brief checklist of the major points covered in the chapter. The students should be reminded that this is only a checklist and does not necessarily include everything that will appear on the test.

Teaching Suggestions

• Have students work in pairs to find the answers to **Que sais-je?** Then, give each pair eighteen index cards or have them cut sheets of paper into eighteen pieces about the size of index cards. Have students number the cards in the corner from one to eighteen and shuffle them. Then, have students write each answer to **Que sais-je?** on the cards. They should lay out the answers in sequential order to match the order of the questions in **Que sais-je?** Once students have done this, have them copy down the numbers they wrote on the cards in the order they appear. This will serve as an answer key. Finally, the partners shuffle their cards and pass them to another pair of students, who will arrange the answers to match the order of the questions in **Que sais-je?** Afterwards, have students check their work, using the answer key.

2, 3 You might have small groups work together to complete these activities. Have students create additional situations for Activity 2, and the other group members will try to offer possible explanations for them. For Activity 3, have students invent additional quotes for group members to respond to.

Can you wonder what happened and offer possible explanations? p. 228

Can you accept and reject explanations? p. 228

Can you break some news? p. 231

Can you show interest? p. 231

Can you begin, continue, and end a story? p. 235

Can you use what you've learned in this chapter?

1 If you didn't know why your friend was late for your meeting after school, how would you say that you wonder what happened? Je me demande...

2 What possible explanations could you give for each of these situations? *Possible answers:*
1. Ton ami(e) était déprimé(e). A mon avis,...
2. Tes parents avaient l'air fâchés aujourd'hui. Peut-être que...
3. Ton prof était de bonne humeur. Je crois que...
4. Tes amis étaient étonnés. Je parie que...

3 How would you respond if your friends made these remarks? *Possible answers:*
1. «A mon avis, il va faire beau aujourd'hui.» Tu as peut-être raison.
2. «Je crois que Paris est la plus grande ville de France.» Evidemment.
3. «Je parie que j'ai raté mon interro d'anglais.» Je ne crois pas.
4. «Peut-être que notre prof est en retard.» C'est possible.
5. «J'ai vu un extra-terrestre dans le jardin.» Ce n'est pas possible. A mon avis, tu te trompes.

4 How would you break the following news to a friend? *Possible answers:*

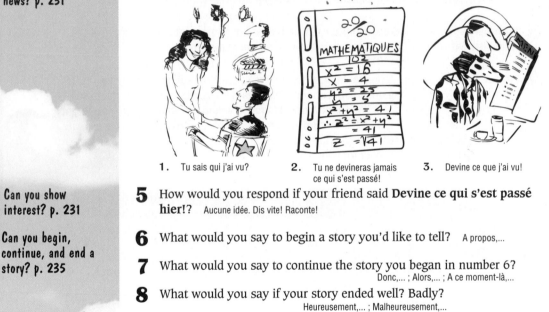

1. Tu sais qui j'ai vu?   2. Tu ne devineras jamais ce qui s'est passé!   3. Devine ce que j'ai vu!

5 How would you respond if your friend said **Devine ce qui s'est passé hier!**? Aucune idée. Dis vite! Raconte!

6 What would you say to begin a story you'd like to tell? A propos,...

7 What would you say to continue the story you began in number 6? Donc,... ; Alors,... ; A ce moment-là,...

8 What would you say if your story ended well? Badly? Heureusement,... ; Malheureusement,...

242   *deux cent quarante-deux*   CHAPITRE 9   Tu connais la nouvelle?

♜ Game

JE L'AI TROUVÉE Write the answers to the questions in the **Que sais-je?** on separate index cards and scatter them face up on the floor. Form two teams. Call out a question at random. Have one student from each team race to try to find the card that contains the answer to that question. The first student to find the correct answer calls out **Je l'ai trouvée** and scores a point for his or her team.

PREMIERE ETAPE

Wondering what happened; offering possible explanations

Je me demande... *I wonder . . .*
A mon avis,... *In my opinion, . . .*
Peut-être que... *Maybe . . .*
Je crois que... *I think that . . .*
Je parie que... *I bet that . . .*

Accepting or rejecting explanations

Tu as peut-être raison. *Maybe you're right.*
C'est possible. *That's possible.*

Ça se voit. *That's obvious.*
Evidemment. *Obviously.*
A mon avis, tu te trompes. *In my opinion, you're mistaken.*
Ce n'est pas possible. *That's not possible.*
Je ne crois pas. *I don't think so.*

Feelings

amoureux (amoureuse) *in love*
de bonne humeur *in a good mood*
de mauvaise humeur *in a bad mood*
déprimé(e) *depressed*

énervé(e) *annoyed*
étonné(e) *surprised*
fâché(e) *angry*
furieux (furieuse) *furious*
gêné(e) *embarrassed*
inquiet (inquiète) *worried*
mal à l'aise *uncomfortable*
avoir l'air *to seem*

Other useful expressions

assez *sort of*
plutôt *rather*
vachement *really*
super *really, ultra-*

Cooperative Learning

Have groups of students write and stage a play in which they use as many of the words and expressions in the **Vocabulaire** as possible. Have each group choose a playwright to invent the story line, a writer to script the play in French, a director to create the stage directions, and have students choose the actors and actresses.

DEUXIEME ETAPE

Breaking some news; showing interest

Tu connais la nouvelle? *Did you hear the latest?*
Tu ne devineras jamais ce qui s'est passé. *You'll never guess what happened.*
Tu sais qui... ? *Do you know who . . . ?*
Tu sais ce que... ? *Do you know what . . . ?*
Devine qui... *Guess who . . .*
Devine ce que... *Guess what . . .*

Raconte! *Tell me!*
Aucune idée. *No idea.*
Dis vite! *Let's hear it!*

Personal happenings

avoir un accident *to have an accident*
avoir (prendre) rendez-vous (avec quelqu'un) *to have (make) a date (with someone)*
être privé(e) de sortie *to be "grounded"*
faire la tête *to sulk*

casser (avec quelqu'un) *to break up (with someone)*
rencontrer *to meet*
se disputer (avec quelqu'un) *to have an argument (with someone)*
se perdre *to get lost*
tomber amoureux (amoureuse) (de quelqu'un) *to fall in love (with someone)*
tomber en panne *to break down (vehicle)*

TROISIEME ETAPE

Beginning, continuing, and ending a story

A propos,... *By the way, . . .*
Donc,... *Therefore, . . .*
Alors,... *So, . . .*
A ce moment-là,... *At that point, . . .*

Bref,... *Anyway,. . .*
C'est-à-dire que... *That is, . . .*
... quoi. *. . . you know.*
... tu vois. *. . . you see.*
Heureusement,... *Fortunately, . . .*
Malheureusement,... *Unfortunately, . . .*

Finalement,... *Finally,. . .*
être en train de *to be in the process of (doing something)*

CHAPTER 9 ASSESSMENT

CHAPTER TEST

• *Chapter Teaching Resources,* Book 3 pp. 29–34
• *Assessment Guide,* Speaking Test, p. 32
• *Assessment Items,* Audiocassette 8A Audio CD 9

TEST GENERATOR, CHAPTER 9

ALTERNATIVE ASSESSMENT

Performance Assessment

You might want to use the Jeu de rôle (p. 241) as a cumulative performance assessment activity.

Portfolio Assessment

• **Written:** Activity 28, *Pupil's Edition,* p. 237
  Assessment Guide, p. 22
• **Oral:** Activity 29, *Pupil's Edition,* p. 237
  Assessment Guide, p. 22

Game

CATÉGORIES Form rows of five or six students. Write the categories from the **Vocabulaire** on the board. The first person in each row has a sheet of paper, and everyone has a pen or pencil. First, name a category and secretly write five words or expressions from it on a transparency. Then, call out **Commencez!** The first student in the row writes one expression from the category and quickly passes the paper to the next student who writes a different one, and so on. The last student in the row returns the paper to the first. The teams continue in this manner for one minute. Call time and project the transparency. The student who has the paper at the end of one minute tells you how many of the expressions on the transparency appear on the paper and are written correctly. The row that most closely matches your five words or expressions wins that round.

Chapitre 10 : Je peux te parler?
Chapter Overview

Mise en train pp. 246–248	Qu'est-ce que je dois faire?		Practice and Activity Book, p. 109	Video Guide OR Videodisc Guide
	FUNCTIONS	**GRAMMAR**	**CULTURE**	**RE-ENTRY**
Première étape pp. 249–253	• Sharing a confidence, p. 250 • Asking for and giving advice, p. 250	Placement of object pronouns, p. 252		Accepting and refusing advice
Deuxième étape pp. 254–257	Asking for and granting a favor; making excuses, p. 255	Direct object pronouns with the **passé composé**, p. 257	• **Note Culturelle, Le parc des Thermes**, p. 254 • **Note Culturelle**, Provençale cuisine, p. 257 • Realia: Recipe for **pissaladière**, p. 257	Pronunciation: the nasal sound [ã]
Troisième étape pp. 258–261	Apologizing and accepting an apology; reproaching someone, p. 258	Object pronouns before an infinitive, p. 259	**Panorama Culturel**, Talking about personal problems, p. 261	Making excuses in the past tense

Lisons! pp. 262–263	Etes-vous un bon copain?		**Reading Strategy:** Reading inductively

Review pp. 264–267	Mise en pratique, pp. 264–265	**Que sais-je?** p. 266	**Vocabulaire**, p. 267

Assessment Options	**Etape Quizzes** • *Chapter Teaching Resources, Book 3* 　**Première étape,** Quiz 10-1, pp. 79–80 　**Deuxième étape,** Quiz 10-2, pp. 81–82 　**Troisième étape,** Quiz 10-3, pp. 83–84 • *Assessment Items, Audiocassette 8B/Audio CD 10*	**Chapter Test** • *Chapter Teaching Resources, Book 3*, pp. 85–90 • *Assessment Guide*, Speaking Test, p. 32 • *Assessment Items, Audiocassette 8B/Audio CD 10* **Test Generator, Chapter 10**

Video Program OR *Expanded Video Program, Videocassette 4*
OR *Videodisc Program, Videodisc 5B*

Textbook Audiocassette 5B/Audio CD 10

RESOURCES: Print	**RESOURCES: Audiovisual**

Textbook Audiocassette 5B/Audio CD 10

Practice and Activity Book, pp. 110–112
Chapter Teaching Resources, Book 3
• Teaching Transparency Master 10-1, pp. 63, 66 . . . . *Teaching Transparency 10-1*
• Additional Listening Activities 10-1, 10-2, p. 67 . . . . *Additional Listening Activities, Audiocassette 10B/Audio CD 10*
• Realia 10-1, pp. 71, 73
• Situation Cards 10-1, pp. 74–75
• Student Response Forms, pp. 76–78
• Quiz 10-1, pp. 79–80 . . . . *Assessment Items, Audiocassette 8B/Audio CD 10*
Videodisc Guide . . . . *Videodisc Program, Videodisc 5B*

Textbook Audiocassette 5B/Audio CD 10

Practice and Activity Book, pp. 113–115
Chapter Teaching Resources, Book 3
• Communicative Activity 10-1, pp. 59–60
• Teaching Transparency Master 10-2, pp. 64, 66 . . . . *Teaching Transparency 10-2*
• Additional Listening Activities 10-3, 10-4, p. 68 . . . . *Additional Listening Activities, Audiocassette 10B/Audio CD 10*
• Realia 10-2, pp. 72, 73
• Situation Cards 10-2, pp. 74–75
• Student Response Forms, pp. 76–78
• Quiz 10-2, pp. 81–82 . . . . *Assessment Items, Audiocassette 8B/Audio CD 10*
Videodisc Guide . . . . *Videodisc Program, Videodisc 5B*

Textbook Audiocassette 5B/Audio CD 10

Practice and Activity Book, pp. 116–118
Chapter Teaching Resources, Book 3
• Communicative Activity 10-2, pp. 61–62
• Teaching Transparency Master 10-3, pp. 65, 66 . . . . *Teaching Transparency 10-3*
• Additional Listening Activities 10-5, 10-6, p. 69 . . . . *Additional Listening Activities, Audiocassette 10B/Audio CD 10*
• Realia 10-2, pp. 72, 73
• Situation Cards 10-3, pp. 74–75
• Student Response Forms, pp. 76–78
• Quiz 10-3, pp. 83–84 . . . . *Assessment Items, Audiocassette 8B/Audio CD 10*
Video Guide . . . . *Video Program* OR *Expanded Video Program, Videocassette 4*
Videodisc Guide . . . . *Videodisc Program, Videodisc 5B*

Practice and Activity Book, p. 119

Video Guide . . . . *Video Program* OR *Expanded Video Program, Videocassette 4*
Videodisc Guide . . . . *Videodisc Program, Videodisc 5B*

Alternative Assessment
• Performance Assessment
  Première étape, p. 253
  Deuxième étape, p. 257
  Troisième étape, p. 260
• Portfolio Assessment
  Written: Activity 31, *Pupil's Edition,* p. 260
    Assessment Guide, p. 23
  Oral: Activity 29, *Pupil's Edition,* p. 260
    Assessment Guide, p. 23

Chapitre 10 : Je peux te parler?
Textbook Listening Activities Scripts

For Student Response Forms, see *Chapter Teaching Resources, Book 3,* pp. 76–78.

Première étape

7 Ecoute! p. 250

1. — Mohamed, je peux te parler?
 — Oui, qu'est-ce qu'il y a?
 — Tu vois, Li m'a prêté son livre d'histoire.
 — C'est gentil.
 — Le problème, c'est que je l'ai perdu!

2. — Tu as une minute?
 — Oui, je t'écoute.
 — Je suis embêtée. Hier soir, je devais retrouver Emile au café, mais j'ai été privée de sortie, et j'ai pas pu y aller. Il ne me parle plus, mais ce n'était pas de ma faute!

3. — J'ai un problème.
 — Je peux peut-être faire quelque chose?
 — Ben... c'est que j'ai eu dix en histoire-géo.
 — Tu avais étudié?
 — Ben... pas beaucoup. Je n'ai pas eu le temps!

Answers to Activity 7
1. b   2. c   3. a

10 Ecoute! p. 252

1. — Salut, Hubert. Je peux te parler?
 — Oui, je t'écoute.
 — Je me suis disputée avec Luc. C'était un petit malentendu, mais il ne me parle plus.
 — C'est ridicule! Tu devrais lui téléphoner pour te réconcilier avec lui.

2. — Salut, Florence. Tu sais que je me suis disputée avec Luc?
 — Non! Qu'est-ce qui s'est passé?
 — Ben, tu vois, il était en retard à notre rendez-vous au ciné.
 — Mais c'est pas grave ça! Tu devrais lui pardonner.

3. — Salut, Jacques. Tu as une minute? Je me suis disputée avec Luc, et j'ai besoin de conseils.
 — Qu'est-ce qu'il a fait?
 — Il était en retard pour notre rendez-vous au ciné.
 — Alors ça, c'est impardonnable! Il ne te respecte pas. A mon avis, tu devrais casser.

4. — Eh, Marie, tu as une minute? Je ne sais pas quoi faire.
 — Mais qu'est-ce qu'il y a?
 — Luc était en retard à notre rendez-vous hier soir et on s'est disputés.

 — Tu t'es fâchée contre lui?
 — Oui, mais c'était tellement bête.
 — Ecoute. Tu devrais t'excuser et lui dire que tu l'aimes. C'est vrai, non?

Answers to Activity 10
1. Call Luc and make up with him.
2. Forgive him.
3. Break up with him.
4. Apologize and tell him you love him.

Deuxième étape

16 Ecoute! p. 255

1. — Gisèle, tu peux me prêter ta jupe bleue pour la fête ce soir?
 — Bien sûr! Je peux te la prêter sans problème.

2. — Stéphane, ça t'ennuie de sortir la poubelle?
 — Désolé, je n'ai pas le temps. Je dois retrouver des amis dans dix minutes!

3. — Chantal, tu pourrais faire la vaisselle pour moi?
 — Je voudrais bien, sœurette, mais je dois faire mes devoirs.

4. — Papa, tu as une minute pour m'aider à ranger le salon?
 — Désolé, mais j'ai quelque chose d'important à faire. Demande à ta mère.

5. — Maman, ça t'embête de m'aider à ranger le salon?
 — Pas du tout.

Answers to Activity 16
1. helps
2. makes excuse
3. makes excuse
4. makes excuse
5. helps

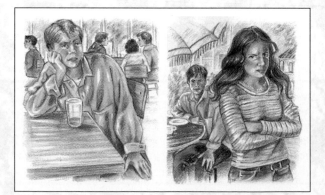

18 Ecoute! p. 256

PASCALE Vraiment, je ne sais pas par où commencer!

JEAN-CLAUDE Calme-toi, Pascale, c'est facile. D'abord, tu dois fixer la date.

PASCALE D'accord... samedi quatorze, ça va?

JEAN-CLAUDE Oui. Après, tu dois demander la permission à tes parents, bien sûr.

PASCALE Je suis sûre qu'ils seront d'accord. Mais je leur demanderai ce soir.

JEAN-CLAUDE Bon. Si tu veux, moi, je peux envoyer les invitations.

PASCALE Vraiment? C'est gentil!

JEAN-CLAUDE Pour le reste... euh... , il faut surtout penser à choisir de la bonne musique. Si tu veux que tout le monde danse, c'est vachement important!

PASCALE Mais je n'ai pas beaucoup de disques, moi.

JEAN-CLAUDE C'est pas grave. Je peux apporter mes CD, et je choisirai la musique. D'accord?

PASCALE D'accord.

JEAN-CLAUDE Ça va être une fête super, tu vas voir!

Answers to Activity 18
Pascale va fixer la date et demander la permission aux parents. Jean-Claude va envoyer les invitations et choisir la musique.

*T*roisième étape

25 Ecoute! p. 259

1. — Oh, Serge! Je voulais te dire... Je suis désolée pour hier soir. J'aurais dû te téléphoner.
   — Oh, t'en fais pas.
   — J'ai été privée de sortie, c'est pour ça que je ne suis pas venue à ta boum.

2. — Dis, Cécile...
   — Ouais?
   — Excuse-moi pour ce matin... Je n'aurais pas dû dire à tous tes copains que tu avais eu cinq en maths.
   — J'étais vraiment gênée, tu sais?
   — Tu ne m'en veux pas, dis?
   — Non... enfin, il n'y a pas de mal.

3. — Frédéric... à propos de ton Walkman®... C'est de ma faute. Je me suis disputé avec Roland, il m'a poussé, et j'ai cassé ton Walkman.
   — Quoi? T'exagères quand même! Tu aurais pu faire attention!
   — Oh, je suis vraiment désolé. Je t'en achèterai un autre si tu veux.

Answers to Activity 25
1. Unable to go to party because she was grounded; Apology accepted.
2. Told friends that Cécile got a five in math; Apology accepted.
3. Dropped and broke Frédéric's Walkman; He is reproached.

*M*ise en pratique

1 p. 264

1. Bonjour, je m'appelle Désiré. Je suis déprimé parce que mes parents m'ont privé de sortie. Je suis rentré trop tard vendredi soir, et maintenant, ils ne veulent plus me laisser sortir le soir. Ce n'est pas de ma faute. J'avais oublié ma montre! Qu'est-ce que je peux faire?

2. Bonjour, mon nom est Murielle. Je suis embêtée parce que j'ai eu une très mauvaise note à ma dernière interro d'anglais. Je sais que mes parents vont être fâchés. Mais j'avais oublié mon livre au lycée, et je n'ai pas pu étudier pour l'interro. Qu'est-ce que je pourrais faire?

3. Salut. Moi, c'est Jérôme! J'ai rencontré une fille super sympa au parc l'autre jour. Je sais qu'elle habite à côté de chez moi, mais je ne lui ai pas demandé son numéro de téléphone, et maintenant, je voudrais bien la revoir. Qu'est-ce que je peux faire?

4. Je m'appelle Eric. Je suis invité à une boum ce week-end, mais je ne sais pas si je devrais y aller. Tu vois, mon amie Julie est invitée aussi, et... ben... on s'est disputés, et on ne se parle plus depuis trois jours. Elle est sans doute encore fâchée contre moi. Qu'est-ce que tu me conseilles de faire?

Answers to Mise en pratique Activity 1
1. c 2. b 3. a 4. d

Chapitre 10 : Je peux te parler?
Projects

Une causerie télévisée
(Group Project)

ASSIGNMENT

Working in groups of six, students will create and video-tape a television talk show. They should include the following functions and structures from the chapter in their program and use object pronouns where appropriate.
• Sharing a confidence
• Asking for advice
• Giving advice
• Apologizing
• Accepting an apology
• Reproaching someone

MATERIALS

✂ **Students may need**
• Video camera
• Videocassette
• Computer-generated or hand-drawn banners or signs
• Costumes or props

SUGGESTED SEQUENCE

1. Each group decides on a name for the talk show and its topic. The topic should be one that involves the chapter outcomes, such as *asking for and giving advice* and *apologizing.*

2. Students assign roles within the group. There should be a host, a psychologist, and several panel members whose specific roles (mother and daughter or husband and wife, for example) will be determined by the content of the show.

3. The group outlines the program. The panel members must be free to interact with one another and to respond to questions from the audience. Therefore, an outline of what will be discussed should be prepared, rather than an actual script.

4. Students rehearse the discussion in the order established in the outline. They should practice incorporating the functions from the chapter and object pronouns where appropriate.

5. To enhance their presentations, the groups may decide to create a set for the show, use some props or costumes, or simply display a banner bearing the name of the show.

6. For the presentation, you might allow students to carry index cards with an outline of the show and possible questions and answers, but they should not read from the cards. The host should allow each person to speak and encourage interaction among the guests. The host should also elicit questions from the audience (the rest of the class). You might give audience members extra credit for asking appropriate questions. If possible, videotape the shows and then play them for the class. Have students provide constructive feedback.

7. If a video camera is not available, you might record the show on an audiocassette and play it for the class.

GRADING THE PROJECT

Each group should receive a collective grade based on content, accuracy of language, and creativity and overall presentation. Group members should receive individual grades based on comprehensibility, and effort and participation in the project. You might have the class suggest grades for the content and overall quality of the presentations. Each group might also grade its members on individual effort and participation. These suggestions could be used to facilitate your final grading decisions.

Suggested Point Distribution (total = 100 points)

Content (inclusion of functions) . . . . . 20 points

Language use. . . . . 20 points

Creativity/presentation . . . . 20 points

Comprehensibility . . . . 20 points

Effort/participation . . . . 20 points

Chapitre 10 : Je peux te parler?
Games

CARRES HOLLYWOODIENS

In this game, which is played like the game Hollywood Squares®, students will practice the functions and vocabulary from this chapter.

Preparation The day before playing the game, ask each student to prepare five true-false statements or multiple-choice questions based on what they've learned in the chapter. The questions might focus on vocabulary, grammar, or culture, and should be in French. For example, students might write:

1. **Vrai ou Faux? On sert des amuse-gueule après le dîner.**
2. **Quelle est la meilleure réponse à la question «Tu peux m'aider?»**
   a) **C'est de ma faute.**
   b) **Ça ne fait rien.**
   c) **Avec plaisir.**

Collect the questions. Then, prepare nine large cards. On one side, write large Xs, and on the other, write large Os.

Procedure Ask for nine volunteers to serve as panelists. Seat them in chairs at the front of the class in three rows of three to form a tic-tac-toe grid. Give one of the nine cards to each panelist, and then form two teams. To play the game, a contestant from one team chooses a panelist. Read a question for <u>the panelist</u> to answer. The panelist may choose to answer correctly or incorrectly. The contestant then either agrees or disagrees with the panelist's answer. If the contestant agrees with a correct answer or disagrees with an incorrect answer, the panelist holds up an X or O in the square for the contestant's team. However, if the contestant agrees with an incorrect answer or disagrees with a correct answer, the turn passes to the other team. Teams alternate trying to get an X or an O in a square. The first team to get three Xs or Os in a row diagonally, horizontally, or vertically wins.

Chapitre 10
Je peux te parler?
pp. 244–267

*U*sing the Chapter Opener

Motivating Activity

Call attention to the title **Je peux te parler?** Ask students to whom such a question might be addressed (point out the familiar pronoun **te**) and under what circumstances. Ask students if they have ever asked a friend for advice or help with a problem. Ask if they received good advice and if they followed it.

Photo Flash!

① Arlette and Pascale are talking at a café in Aix-en-Provence. Pascale is asking for advice. The French often go to cafés for conversation with friends as well as for something to eat or drink.

Teaching Suggestion

Call students' attention to the document in the lower left corner of this page. Ask them if they can guess what it is (an invitation) and for what occasion (a birthday party). Ask them to complete the part that is obscured by the pen. (**Si vous voulez faire la fête avec nous, venez!**)

CHAPITRE

10
Je peux te parler?

C'est
L'ANNIVERSAIRE
de *Manu* !
Si vous voulez faire l
es ven

① A ton avis, qu'est-ce que je dois faire?

🌐 Culture Note

Point out the beverages that Arlette and Pascale are drinking and ask students if they notice anything unusual about them. (There is no ice in the drinks.) In France, beverages are not usually served with ice (**avec glaçons**) unless it's requested. French people usually do not put ice in their drinks as is customary in the United States.

Language Note

Surprise-partie was a term widely used by young people in the 1960s to refer to a *party,* not a *surprise party,* as the term is used in the United States. Currently, French teenagers use **une boum** for *a party.* Adults commonly refer to an evening gathering as **une soirée.**

Whom do you go to for advice when you have a problem? When you need a favor? Friends can help you plan a party, then give advice if things don't go well. And if you should make a mistake, a friend is always ready to accept an apology and move on!

In this chapter you will learn

- to share a confidence; to ask for and give advice
- to ask for and grant a favor; to make excuses
- to apologize and accept an apology; to reproach someone

And you will

- listen to people planning a party and asking for advice
- read a survey about friendship
- write an advice column
- find out whom francophone teenagers are likely to confide in

② Je suis désolé. Tu ne m'en veux pas?

③ Tu pourrais venir déguisé?

deux cent quarante-cinq 245

Focusing on Outcomes

Have students look at the photos and say as much as they can about them in French. Then, say the English equivalent of a French caption and have students try to guess which photo it describes. Finally, have students read the chapter outcomes and tell how each photo relates to them. NOTE: You may want to use the video to support the objectives. The self-check activities in **Que sais-je?** on page 266 help students assess their achievement of the objectives.

Photo Flash!

② This photo shows a group of teenagers at a birthday party in Arles. It is very common for teenagers to organize parties at their homes, since teenagers under eighteen cannot drive cars to go out and celebrate. A fourteen-year-old may drive a moped, but teenagers find that this method of transportation is not very practical for going out in groups.

③ In this photo, Cédric is on the telephone with Pascale. Pay phones in France that accept coins are becoming increasingly rare. They are being replaced by public phones that accept only the **Télécarte**, a plastic card that is inserted into the telephone. The post office **(la poste)** and tobacco shops **(les tabacs)** sell **Télécartes. Télécartes** of 50 or 120 units may be purchased. Calls may be made from any pay phone to anywhere in the world. A local call uses one unit, and a long distance or international call uses several units, depending on the distance. A screen displays how many units remain on the **Télécarte** and how many are expiring as the caller talks.

Culture Note

The black olives, tomatoes, and garlic pictured on this page are essential ingredients of Provençal cuisine. The rich land, coupled with a warm climate, produces an abundance of olive trees, spices, and vegetables. Seafood from the Mediterranean coast also contributes to the typical menu. The tomato-based dishes flavored with olive oil, a variety of herbs and spices, and garlic are unique to Provence.

VIDEO PROGRAM
OR EXPANDED VIDEO
PROGRAM,
Videocassette 4
01:25–06:32

OR VIDEODISC PROGRAM,
VIDEODISC 5B

Search 1, Play To 9215

Video Synopsis

In this segment of the video, Pascale wants to give a party for her birthday and asks Arlette for advice on how to plan one. Arlette makes suggestions about giving a party and offers to help Pascale organize it. Pascale also tells her about the misunderstanding she had with Cédric. (See **Mise en train** for Chapter 9, pages 222–223.) Arlette advises Pascale to call Cédric and invite him. The next day, Arlette is looking for a present for Pascale when she runs into Antoine. She asks him for advice on a present for Pascale. Antoine suggests a CD or a poster. Antoine invites Arlette to go to a concert on Saturday, the same night as Pascale's party! Arlette doesn't know what to do.

Motivating Activity

Have students imagine they're giving a party. Ask them how they would organize it and what decisions they would have to make (where and when to have the party, whom to invite, what to serve, what activities to plan). Ask them what they would need to do if they were invited to a friend's birthday party (find out when and where it is, decide what to buy for a gift or what to bring, decide what to wear). List their answers on the board or on a transparency.

Mise en train

Arlette   Pascale   Antoine

Qu'est-ce que je dois faire?

Sometimes it helps to ask friends for advice when you have a problem. Scan the story to find out what kinds of problems Arlette, Pascale, and Antoine are discussing.

Ecoute, j'aimerais inviter des amis pour mon anniversaire. Qu'en penses-tu?

C'est une excellente idée! J'adore les fêtes.

Je n'ai jamais organisé de fête. Tu as des conseils?

D'abord, n'oublie pas d'envoyer des invitations. Ensuite, je te conseille d'acheter des assiettes en carton. C'est pratique. Tu n'as pas à faire la vaisselle. Et tu devrais demander à chacun d'apporter quelque chose.

C'est pas bête, ça...

Euh, je peux te parler?

Oui. Je t'écoute.

Est-ce que tu crois que je devrais inviter Cédric?

Bien sûr. Pourquoi pas?

Tu sais, on a eu une dispute. C'était tellement bête, un malentendu. Qu'est-ce que je dois faire?

C'est ridicule. Téléphone-lui et invite-le.

Tes conseils sont toujours bons!

Alors, qu'est-ce que tu vas mettre pour ta soirée?

Je n'ai pas encore réfléchi. Voyons, je ne sais pas quoi mettre.

246 *deux cent quarante-six*

CHAPITRE 10   Je peux te parler?

RESOURCES FOR MISE EN TRAIN

Textbook Audiocassette 5B/Audio CD 10
Practice and Activity Book, p. 109
Video Guide
　　Video Program
　　Expanded Video Program, Videocassette 4
Videodisc Guide
　　Videodisc Program, Videodisc 5B

Eh! Tu pourrais me prêter ta robe rose? Elle est superbe.

Je voudrais bien, mais je l'ai déchirée. Je suis désolée.

Ça ne fait rien.

Si tu veux, je peux te prêter ma jupe bleue plissée.

C'est mignon! Mais, qu'est-ce que je peux mettre avec?

Tu pourrais mettre un chemisier blanc.

Tu as toujours de bonnes idées!

Le lendemain, Arlette rencontre son copain Antoine en ville.

Je cherche un cadeau d'anniversaire pour Pascale. Je ne sais pas quoi lui offrir. Tu as une idée?

Tu devrais lui offrir un poster de Cézanne. Elle l'aime beaucoup.

Ça, c'est une idée! Je te remercie. Qu'est-ce que je ferais sans toi?

Offre-lui un CD. Elle adore la musique.

Non, je lui ai déjà offert un CD de Mylène Farmer l'année dernière.

Samedi soir.

Samedi! Aïe!

Qu'est-ce qu'il y a?

Je voudrais bien, mais je suis invitée à la fête de Pascale. Je lui ai promis de l'aider à organiser sa fête. Je ne sais pas quoi faire!

Ecoute, j'ai deux places pour aller au concert des Vagabonds. Tu veux venir avec moi?

Je veux bien. C'est quand?

MISE EN TRAIN

deux cent quarante-sept 247

Video Integration

- *Expanded Video Program,*
  Videocassette 4, 06:33–10:49
- *Videodisc Program,*
  Videodisc 5B

Search 9215, Play To 16935

You may choose to continue with **Qu'est-ce que je dois faire? (suite)** or wait until later in the chapter. When the story continues, Antoine urges Arlette to go with him to the concert, but Arlette doesn't want to disappoint Pascale. Later, Arlette sees Cédric, who is planning to invite Pascale to the same concert. Arlette advises him to call and invite Pascale right away, before she makes other plans. Arlette and Pascale are reluctant to tell each other that they would rather go to the concert than have the party. As they come to realize each other's true feelings, Antoine and Cédric show up, and all four are delighted.

Presentation

Have students read the questions in Activity 1 on page 248 before they view the video. Play the video, and then ask the questions in Activity 1. If students can't answer a question, play the corresponding part of the video again. Then, play the recording and have students follow along in their books. Next, have students make a list of the party preparations Arlette advises Pascale to make. Ask them if they do the same things when they're planning a party. Finally, form groups of three and have them practice reading the dialogue in the **Mise en train**. Volunteers may wish to read and act out the dialogue for the class.

Teaching Suggestion

For additional listening practice, read aloud the sentences of the **Mise en train** one at a time, replacing one word or expression from each by blowing a whistle or ringing a bell. Students try to guess which words are missing. You should try to choose omissions that can be easily guessed from the context.

Thinking Critically

Analyzing Ask students what advice Arlette gave Pascale concerning Cédric (to call him and to invite him to the party). Ask them if they agree with the advice and why or why not. Ask students what they would do in this situation.

Teaching Suggestions

2 Ask for three volunteers to make complete sentences, using each of the possible choices. For example, the first student says **Pascale n'a jamais organisé de fête,** the second student says **Pascale n'a jamais demandé de conseils,** and the third says **Pascale n'a jamais écouté de musique.** Then, ask the class **Qui a raison?**

3 Have students read additional quotes from the **Mise en train** to a partner, who will try to guess who said them. You might have students read their quotes to the class rather than work in pairs.

For Individual Needs

3 **Visual/Tactile Learners** Have students write several quotes from the **Mise en train** on index cards. Then, have students pass the cards to a partner, who will group them according to the person who made the statement: Arlette, Pascale, or Antoine.

For videodisc application, see *Videodisc Guide.*

Teaching Suggestion

4 Play the video, pausing each time a functional expression is used. Have students write down the number of the function as it is used. Students can also raise their hands to signal you to pause the video when they hear a function being used.

Thinking Critically

5 **Synthesizing** Poll the class to find out who would go to the concert and who would help Pascale with her party. Ask students to imagine the consequences of either decision for all of the characters involved.

248 **MISE EN TRAIN** **CHAPITRE 10**

---

1 Tu as compris? See answers below.

1. Why is Pascale having a party?
2. What advice does Arlette offer her?
3. What favor does Pascale ask? Does Arlette agree to help?
4. What does Arlette ask Antoine for advice about? What does he suggest?
5. What decision does Arlette have to make at the end of **Qu'est-ce que je dois faire?**

2 Complète les phrases

1. Pascale n'a jamais...
   a. organisé de fête.
   b. demandé de conseils.
   c. écouté de musique.
2. Pascale et Cédric...
   a. se sont réconciliés.
   b. se sont disputés.
   c. se sont rencontrés.
3. Pascale va mettre...
   a. une robe rose.
   b. une jupe bleue.
   c. un anorak vert.
4. Comme cadeau, Antoine suggère...
   a. du parfum.
   b. des fleurs.
   c. un poster.
5. Antoine invite Arlette à...
   a. une fête.
   b. un concert.
   c. faire les magasins.

3 Qui dit quoi?

Pascale   **Arlette**   **Antoine**

Arlette
Téléphone-lui et invite-le.

Arlette
Je ne sais pas quoi lui offrir. Tu as une idée?

Antoine
J'ai deux places pour aller au concert des Vagabonds.

Pascale
Tu devrais lui offrir un poster de Cézanne.

Arlette
Qu'est-ce que je ferais sans toi!

Pascale
Je devrais inviter Cédric?

Antoine

4 Cherche les expressions

What do the people in **Qu'est-ce que je dois faire?** say to . . . See answers below.

1. ask for advice?
2. share a confidence?
3. give advice?
4. ask for a favor?
5. invite someone?
6. make excuses?

5 Et maintenant, à toi

If you were Arlette, what decision would you make? Why?

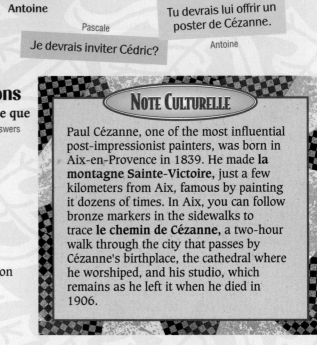

NOTE CULTURELLE

Paul Cézanne, one of the most influential post-impressionist painters, was born in Aix-en-Provence in 1839. He made **la montagne Sainte-Victoire,** just a few kilometers from Aix, famous by painting it dozens of times. In Aix, you can follow bronze markers in the sidewalks to trace **le chemin de Cézanne,** a two-hour walk through the city that passes by Cézanne's birthplace, the cathedral where he worshiped, and his studio, which remains as he left it when he died in 1906.

248 *deux cent quarante-huit*   CHAPITRE 10   Je peux te parler?

Answers

1 1. to celebrate her birthday
2. to send invitations, to buy paper plates, to ask each person to bring something
3. Pascale asks to borrow Arlette's pink dress; Yes, she helps by loaning Pascale her blue pleated skirt.
4. what to get Pascale for her birthday; a CD, a Cézanne poster
5. Arlette must decide whether to help organize Pascale's party or go to the concert with Antoine.

4 1. Tu as des conseils? Est-ce que tu crois que je devrais... ? Qu'est-ce que je dois faire? Tu as une idée?
2. ... je peux te parler?
3. N'oublie pas de... ; ... je te conseille de... ; Tu devrais... ; Téléphone-lui et invite-le; Tu pourrais... ; Offre-lui...
4. Tu pourrais... ?
5. Tu veux venir avec moi?
6. Je voudrais bien, mais...

PREMIERE ETAPE

Sharing a confidence; asking for and giving advice

QU'EN PENSES-TU?

Amitiés, amours, parents, études... Chaque semaine, posez votre question aux lecteurs.

VOICI LA QUESTION DE FERDINAND

(Aix-en-Provence)

J'ai un petit problème. Dans ma classe, il y a une fille que j'aime bien. Elle s'appelle Myriam. Elle est toujours avec ses copines et je ne sais pas comment l'aborder. Je suis bien embêté. J'ai l'impression qu'elle m'aime bien, mais je n'ose pas lui parler. Je suis très timide. Qu'est-ce que vous me conseillez? Aidez-moi!

ET VOICI LES RÉPONSES DE...

MATHILDE

(Pointe-à-Pitre, Guadeloupe)

A mon avis, tu devrais lui proposer d'aller au café après l'école. Parle-lui. Demande-lui si elle aime aller au cinéma. Ensuite, invite-la à voir un film. Si elle accepte, c'est parfait. Si elle refuse, tu devrais l'oublier.

FABIEN

(Biarritz, Pyrénées-Atlantiques)

Si tu n'oses pas lui parler, écris-lui un petit mot. Sois sincère. Peut-être qu'elle est timide, elle aussi. C'est une bonne façon de faire connaissance avec elle.

IRÈNE

(Dijon, Côte-d'Or)

Ce que tu devrais faire, c'est organiser une fête. Comme ça, tu as un prétexte pour l'inviter. Ensuite, ça va être plus facile de faire connaissance. Si tu ne sais pas quoi dire, tu peux l'inviter à danser!

LÉONARD

(Toulouse, Haute-Garonne)

A mon avis, tu devrais faire l'indifférent. Ne lui montre pas que tu es amoureux et fais semblant de t'intéresser à une de ses copines. Tu vas voir, elle va tout de suite te remarquer!

6 Les conseils

1. Quel est le problème de Ferdinand? *Il y a une fille qu'il aime bien, mais il est très timide et il n'ose pas lui parler.*
2. Quels conseils est-ce que chaque personne lui a donnés?
   a. Mathilde   b. Fabien   c. Irène   d. Léonard

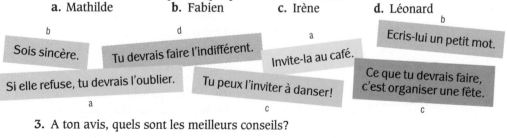

b Sois sincère.

d Tu devrais faire l'indifférent.

a Invite-la au café.

b Ecris-lui un petit mot.

a Si elle refuse, tu devrais l'oublier.

c Tu peux l'inviter à danser!

c Ce que tu devrais faire, c'est organiser une fête.

3. A ton avis, quels sont les meilleurs conseils?

PREMIERE ETAPE — *deux cent quarante-neuf* **249**

RESOURCES FOR PREMIERE ETAPE

Textbook Audiocassette 5B/Audio CD 10
Practice and Activity Book, pp. 110–112
Videodisc Guide
  Videodisc Program, Videodisc 5B

Chapter Teaching Resources, Book 3
• Teaching Transparency Master 10-1, pp. 63, 66
  Teaching Transparency 10-1
• Additional Listening Activities 10-1, 10-2, p. 67
  Audiocassette 10B/Audio CD 10
• Realia 10-1, pp. 71, 73
• Situation Cards 10-1, pp. 74–75
• Student Response Forms, pp. 76–78
• Quiz 10-1, pp. 79–80
  Audiocassette 8B/Audio CD 10

ᒍump Start!

Have students write two party preparations Arlette suggested to Pascale and two gift ideas that Antoine gave Arlette in the **Mise en train.**

MOTIVATE

Name some popular advice columns in newspapers or magazines *(Dear Abby, Ann Landers).* Ask students what kinds of problems people usually write about in these advice columns.

TEACH

Teaching Suggestion

Before students open their books, read aloud Ferdinand's letter. Ask students what the letter is about and to whom it might have been written. Then, ask them what advice they would give Ferdinand. Write down their suggestions on the board or on a transparency. Next, have them open their books and scan the responses to Ferdinand's letter to find the advice each person gives. Have students compare these to the advice they suggested.

◆ For Individual Needs

6 Visual/Auditory Learners Write each of the expressions on large strips of posterboard or construction paper. Then, write the names of the four teenagers who offered advice on the board. Show each piece of advice and read it aloud. Have a student tape the expression to the board under the appropriate name.

Language Note

Students may want to know the following vocabulary from **Qu'en penses-tu? Aborder** is a synonym for **approcher. Faire semblant** is an expression meaning *to pretend.*

Presentation

Comment dit-on... ? Have three volunteers rehearse the responses from **Comment dit-on... ?** Then, share your "confidences," beginning each one with a different expression, and have the three students respond as rehearsed. Do this several times and then circulate around the classroom, sharing the same or other confidences. Ask the volunteers to prompt students' responses, if necessary.

For Individual Needs

7 Slower Pace Before you play the recording, describe the situation in each of the pictures to the students and/or have students describe what they see.

7 Challenge Before students listen to the recording, have them talk about the pictures as much as possible in French. Then, play the recording and challenge students to find a variation of **Qu'est-ce que je peux faire?** (**Je peux peut-être faire quelque chose?**)

Presentation

Comment dit-on... ?
Describe several problems that would elicit the advice in **Comment dit-on... ?** (**Je me suis disputé(e) avec ma copine. Est-ce que je dois l'inviter à ma boum?**) Have students give advice from the list in their books.

For videodisc application, see *Videodisc Guide.*

COMMENT DIT-ON... ?
Sharing a confidence

To share a confidence:
Je ne sais pas quoi faire. *I don't know what to do.*
J'ai un problème.
Tu as une minute?
Je peux te parler?

To respond:
Qu'est-ce qu'il y a? *What's wrong?*
Qu'est-ce que je peux faire? *What can I do?*
Je t'écoute.

---

7 Ecoute!

Mohammed's friends all come to him with their problems. Choose the picture that illustrates each friend's problem. Then, imagine the dialogue about the remaining picture. 1. b 2. c 3. a

a.   b.   c.   d.

COMMENT DIT-ON... ?
Asking for and giving advice

To ask for advice:
A ton avis, qu'est-ce que je dois faire? *In your opinion, what should I do?*
Qu'est-ce que tu ferais, toi? *What would you do?*
Qu'est-ce que tu me conseilles?

To give advice:
Invite-le/-la/-les.
Invite him/her/them.
Parle-lui/-leur.
Talk to him/her/them.
Dis-lui/-leur que tu es fâché.
Tell him/her/them that . . .
Ecris-lui/-leur.
Write to him/her/them.
Explique-lui/-leur.
Explain to him/her/them.
Excuse-toi. *Apologize.*
Téléphone-lui/-leur.
Oublie-le/-la/-les.
Tu devrais lui écrire un petit mot.

Teaching Suggestion

7 Have students look at illustration **a.** Ask them how they can tell it's a French paper. (It's written on graph paper, and it has a grade of 10.) Ask them what kind of textbook is pictured in illustration **b** (a history book) and what Parisian monument is depicted on its cover (l'Arc de Triomphe).

Additional Practice

Ask questions, using direct and indirect objects. (**J'invite ma copine? J'écris à mes grands-parents?**) and have students respond, using object pronouns. (**Oui, invite-la! Oui, écris-leur!**) For visual learners, you might write the questions and answers on flashcards.

8 Les deux font la paire

Choisis la meilleure solution à chaque problème.   *Possible answers:*

1. J'ai cassé avec ma petite amie!   d
2. J'ai rencontré un garçon très sympa et je veux le revoir.   c
3. J'ai de mauvaises notes en maths et je ne comprends pas le prof.   g, h
4. J'ai été collé et mes parents m'ont privé de sortie. Mais ce n'était pas de ma faute!   a
5. Je suis tombé amoureux d'une fille qui habite à la Martinique.   h, d
6. Je me suis disputé avec ma sœur, et j'ai déchiré son autographe de Patrick Bruel.   f, g

a. Explique-leur.
b. Dis-lui bonjour.
c. Invite-le au cinéma.
d. Oublie-la!
e. Invite-les chez toi.
f. Excuse-toi!
g. Parle-lui.
h. Ecris-lui une lettre.

9 Jeu de conseils

Think of a problem and write it down on a piece of paper. Gather all the papers together and select one. After the problem is read aloud, each group has one minute to come up with as many solutions as possible. Then, select another problem. Which group has the most answers? The craziest? The worst advice?

VOCABULAIRE

lui expliquer ce qui s'est passé.

lui demander pardon.

lui offrir un cadeau.

lui dire que tu l'aimes.

te réconcilier avec elle.

téléphoner (à quelqu'un)   *to call (someone)*
s'excuser   *to apologize*
pardonner (à quelqu'un)   *to forgive (someone)*
écouter ce qu'il/elle dit   *to listen to what he/she says*

8 Slower Pace Have students copy the problems and write the appropriate advice next to each one. Then, have a student read the problems aloud and call on volunteers to offer the advice they chose. Encourage the student-teacher to praise the students who give the correct response. (**Très bien! Excellent! Bravo!**)

Teaching Suggestion

9 If students have difficulty thinking of a problem, you might bring in some advice columns from newspapers or magazines for them to use.

Presentation

Vocabulaire Use three stuffed animals or puppets to present the new vocabulary. Introduce **le garçon, sa petite amie,** and **son amie.** Demonstrate the conversation between **le garçon** and **son amie** and the advice she gives him. (**Tu devrais lui expliquer ce qui s'est passé.**) Act out the different scenes in which he follows her advice. (**Tu vois, j'étais privé de sortie, et c'est pour ça que je ne suis pas venu.**) Continue presenting the remaining expressions in this manner.

TPR Have partners act out the advice you give them. For example, if you say **Demande-lui pardon,** one partner might make an imploring gesture and facial expression. To show comprehension for **Réconcilie-toi avec ton ami(e),** students could shake hands. Students might say **Je t'aime** in response to **Dis-lui que tu l'aimes.**

For Individual Needs

10 Slower Pace Write the advice mentioned in the recording on the board or on a transparency in random order (see script on page 243C). Then, play the recording and have students number the advice in the order in which they hear it given.

Teaching Suggestion

11 Read aloud the four requests for advice, or have volunteers take turns reading them. For each one, have students read the options to themselves and write down the letter of their choice.

Presentation

Grammaire Give a pen to one student, saying **Tiens, je te donne un stylo,** and some pencils to two students, saying **Tenez, je vous donne des crayons.** Then, tell one student to give you a pen. (**Donne-moi un stylo.**) Ask **Tu me donnes un stylo?** and prompt **Oui, je vous donne un stylo.** With a student by your side, tell another to give both of you a pencil, saying **Donne-nous un crayon.** Then ask the student **Tu nous donnes un crayon?** and so on. Finally, ask students if you should do something and have them give you a positive or negative command, using the appropriate pronoun. (**Je mets le chapeau? Oui, mettez-le!**)

For Individual Needs

Visual Learners Show flashcards of questions containing object pronouns. (**Tu me parles?**) After students respond (**Oui, je vous parle**), show the answer you've written on the other side of the card.

---

10 Ecoute!

Lucie s'est disputée avec son copain Luc et elle demande des conseils à ses amis. Qu'est-ce que chaque personne lui conseille de faire? Qu'est-ce que toi, tu lui conseillerais de faire? Answers on p. 243C.

11 Un sondage

Lis ce sondage et choisis les conseils que tu donnerais à chaque personne. Puis, fais le sondage auprès de cinq camarades. Est-ce que vous êtes tous d'accord? Finalement, pense à deux autres conseils pour chaque problème.

DONNE TES CONSEILS!

1 Mon copain Thomas ne me parle plus. Qu'est-ce que tu me conseilles?
a. Oublie-le.
b. Ecris-lui un petit mot.
c. Téléphone-lui et demande-lui de t'expliquer pourquoi.

2 Je voudrais faire une fête pour mon anniversaire, mais je ne sais pas par où commencer. Tu as une idée?
a. Tu devrais envoyer des invitations, puis faire les courses. Et n'oublie pas de faire le ménage et de choisir la musique!
b. Tu devrais plutôt sortir seul(e). Tu seras plus tranquille.
c. C'est facile. Tu devrais téléphoner à tous tes amis. Ils pourraient t'aider.

3 Je vais faire une fête mais je ne sais pas si je dois inviter Pascale. On s'est disputés, mais c'était un malentendu. A ton avis, qu'est-ce que je dois faire?
a. Téléphone-lui et excuse-toi.
b. Téléphone-lui et invite-la à ta fête.
c. Oublie-la et amuse-toi bien!

4 Mes parents sont fâchés contre moi parce que j'ai cassé la chaîne stéréo. Qu'est-ce que je peux faire?
a. Achète-leur une autre chaîne.
b. Parle-leur et explique-leur ce qui s'est passé.
c. Fais la tête dans ta chambre. Ce n'est pas de ta faute!

---

*G*rammaire   Object pronouns and their placement

You've already seen the pronouns **le, la, l',** and **les** *(him, her, it, them)* and **lui** and **leur** *(to/for him/her/them).* Here are some new pronouns: **me** *(me, to/for me);* **te** *(you, to/for you);* **nous** *(us, to/for us);* **vous** *(you, to/for you).*

- These object pronouns usually come before the conjugated verb.
  Tu **me** parles?   Il **le** mettait tous les jours.
  Je **lui** ai parlé.   Ne **nous** parle plus!

- In affirmative commands, put all pronouns after the verb, connected with a hyphen. In this position, **me** and **te** change to **moi** and **toi.**
  Invite-**le!**   Parle-**moi!**   Excuse-**toi!**

- In a sentence with an infinitive, put the pronoun before the infinitive.
  Tu devrais **lui** parler.

CHAPITRE 10   Je peux te parler?

Additional Practice

Grammaire Prepare a set of index cards equal to the number of students in the class. On half of the cards, write questions (**Tu me pardonnes?**), and on the other half, write the responses to the questions. (**Oui, je te pardonne.**) Distribute one card to each student. Without showing their cards, students circulate around the room, trying to find the appropriate question or answer to match their card.

They should say whatever is on their card to every person they encounter. When they find a match, they read both the question and the answer to you. Continue until everyone has found a match. In large classes, you might make two identical sets of cards and have half of the students interact on one side of the room, and the other half on the other side of the room.

12 Un malentendu

Complète l'histoire de Van avec les pronoms qui conviennent.

Hier après-midi, j'ai vu ma copine Lien avec un autre garçon! Ils avaient l'air plutôt intimes. Et moi qui voulais __1__ inviter au cinéma! l'

Parle-lui!

J'étais vraiment fâché! J'ai téléphoné à Emmanuel qui __2__ m' a conseillé de __3__ lui parler.

Mais pourquoi?

Alors, je suis allé chez Lien. Je __4__ ai dit lui que c'était fini entre nous. Elle n'a pas compris. J'ai commencé à __5__ expliquer. lui

Enfin, devine qui est entré dans le salon! Le nouveau copain de Lien! Je ne pouvais pas __6__ croire! le

Je te présente mon cousin Tuan.

Oh! Je pensais que...

Quel imbécile! C'était le cousin de Lien! Je __7__ ai expliqué que je __8__ avais vus au café ensemble. 7. leur 8. les

Excuse-moi, Lien.

Alors, Lien a compris pourquoi j'étais fâché. Je __9__ ai lui demandé pardon. Elle __10__ a pardonné et elle a même dit qu'elle __11__ aimait malgré tout! 10. m' 11. m'

13 Pauvre Ferdinand!

Ferdinand, who wrote about his problem in **Qu'en penses-tu?** on page 249, explains his situation and asks a friend for advice. The friend offers him advice. Ferdinand reacts to the advice and decides with his friend what he'll do to solve his problem. Act this out with a partner. Then, reverse roles.

14 J'ai un problème...

Make up a problem you have about school, with your friends, or with your family. Tell a classmate about it. He or she sympathizes and offers advice. Take turns.

Tu te rappelles ?

You already know how to accept and refuse advice:

Non, je ne peux pas.
Pas question!
Non, je n'ai pas très envie.
Bonne idée!
Tu as (peut-être) raison.
C'est possible.
A mon avis, tu te trompes.

Teaching Suggestion

12 You might have students work in pairs to complete this activity. Then, write the sentences on a transparency and project them on the overhead. Ask volunteers to supply the correct pronouns, which another volunteer will write on the transparency.

Additional Practice

12 Ask the following questions to check comprehension:
1. **Quand est-ce que Van a vu Lien au café?** (hier après-midi)
2. **A qui est-ce que Van a téléphoné?** (à Emmanuel)
3. **Chez qui est-ce que Van est allé?** (chez Lien) **Pourquoi?** (pour lui dire que c'était fini entre eux)
4. **Qui est entré dans le salon?** (le nouveau copain de Lien) **C'était qui?** (le cousin de Lien)
5. **Est-ce que Lien a pardonné Van?** (oui)

Teaching Suggestion

Tu te rappelles? Review the expressions for *accepting and refusing advice* with students before they begin Activity 13.

CLOSE

To close this **étape**, use Activity 14. Have each student write his or her problem on a slip of paper. Collect and read them to yourself and put them in a box. Have students draw a slip of paper one at a time, read the problem aloud, and offer advice.

ASSESS

Quiz 10-1, *Chapter Teaching Resources, Book 3,* pp. 79–80

Assessment Items, Audiocassette 8B Audio CD 10

Performance Assessment

Write the following conversation stimulus on an index card.

A: Ask B for help with a problem. Describe the problem, listen to your partner's advice, and accept or refuse it.

B: Listen to A's problem and offer at least two pieces of advice.

Have two students at a time toss a coin to establish their roles. Have them read the card, collect their thoughts for one minute, and then act out the dialogue.

Write the following problems on the board and have students write advice for each one.
1. J'ai perdu mes devoirs pour mon cours d'anglais aujourd'hui.
2. J'ai deux rendez-vous pour le même soir.
3. Je suis trop timide pour inviter quelqu'un à sortir.
4. J'ai une interro en maths demain, mais j'ai oublié mon livre au lycée.

MOTIVATE

Ask students what favors they ask of their friends and what their friends ask of them. Ask them which favors they usually grant and which ones they refuse and why.

TEACH

Teaching Suggestion

Have partners read the letters to each other and answer the questions in Activity 15. To check reading comprehension, have students draw a grid consisting of three vertical and three horizontal columns. Have them label the vertical columns **Qu'est-ce qu'il/elle veut?/ Pourquoi?/Quand?** and the horizontal columns **Patrick, Hélène,** and **Danielle.** Then, have them fill in the grid with the information from the letters.

History Link

Around 1500 B.C. the Gauls migrated from the Rhine Valley to what is now France and northern Italy. The Romans began their conquest of Gaul in 123 B.C., which Julius Caesar concluded in 54 B.C. Throughout France, the Romans left vestiges of their sophisticated use of water in elaborate aqueduct and sewer systems and baths, such as in **Le parc des Thermes.**

DEUXIEME ETAPE

Asking for and granting a favor; making excuses

15 1. repairing his moped; Yes; She likes to work on motors, and she was planning on inviting Patrick to the movies anyway.
2. that Monique babysit for her; because she made a date with Patrick for the same time.
3. *Possible answer:* Hélène and Danielle are both planning to go out with Patrick the same afternoon.

Hélène,
Tu es libre demain après-midi? J'ai un grand service à te demander. Ma mobylette est en panne. J'ai passé le weekend à essayer de la réparer, mais tu sais la mécanique, c'est pas mon truc. Tu peux me donner un coup de main? Ça serait sympa de ta part.
Patrick

Cher Patrick,
Je n'ai rien à faire mercredi après-midi. À vrai dire, j'allais te demander si tu voulais aller au cinéma avec moi! Oui, je sais que toi et la mécanique, ça fait deux. Bien sûr que je peux t'aider à réparer ta mobylette; ça ne m'ennuie pas du tout. Tu sais que j'adore mettre le nez dans les moteurs! Et ensuite, si on a le temps, on pourrait aller au cinéma. Qu'est-ce que tu en dis?
Hélène

Très, très chère Monique,
J'ai rendez-vous avec Patrick au parc des Thermes demain après-midi. On va faire le tour des ruines. Enfin! Notre premier rendez-vous! J'étais tellement contente que j'ai complètement oublié que j'avais promis à Mme Dumont de garder ses enfants. Tu pourrais le faire à ma place? Les enfants sont mignons et c'est bien payé. Ça ne t'embête pas, dis? Dis-moi que c'est possible! Je t'aiderai à faire tous tes devoirs de maths jusqu'à la fin de l'année. Promis. Réponds-moi vite. Merci mille fois!
Danielle

NOTE CULTURELLE

Le parc des Thermes, where the Romans originally built their baths and where you can now see the remains of Roman villas, is one of many scenic meeting places in Aix-en-Provence. The thermal springs that first drew the Romans to the town in the first century B.C. still feed dozens of public fountains.

15 Tu as compris? See answers above.

1. What does Patrick need help with? Does Hélène agree to help him? Why or why not?
2. What favor is Danielle asking? Why?
3. What problem do you anticipate?

RESOURCES FOR DEUXIEME ETAPE

Textbook Audiocassette 5B/Audio CD 10
Practice and Activity Book, pp. 113–115
Videodisc Guide
   Videodisc Program, Videodisc 5B

Chapter Teaching Resources, Book 3
• Communicative Activity 10-1, pp. 59–60
• Teaching Transparency Master 10-2, pp. 64, 66
   Teaching Transparency 10-2
• Additional Listening Activities 10-3, 10-4, p. 68
   Audiocassette 10B/Audio CD 10
• Realia 10-2, pp. 72, 73
• Situation Cards 10-2, pp. 74–75
• Student Response Forms, pp. 76–78
• Quiz 10-2, pp. 81–82
   Audiocassette 8B/Audio CD 10

COMMENT DIT-ON... ?

Asking for and granting a favor; making excuses

To ask for a favor:

Tu peux m'aider? *Can you help me?*

Tu pourrais inviter Michel?

Ça t'ennuie de téléphoner à Léonard?
Would you mind . . . ?

Ça t'embête de ranger le salon?
Would you mind . . . ?

To make excuses:

Désolé(e).

J'ai quelque chose à faire. *I have something else to do.*

Je n'ai pas le temps. *I don't have time.*

Je suis très occupé(e). *I'm very busy.*

C'est impossible. *It's impossible.*

To grant a favor:

Avec plaisir. *With pleasure.*

Bien sûr.

Pas de problème. *No problem.*

Bien sûr que non. *Of course not.*

Pas du tout.

16 Ecoute!

Caroline is asking her family to help her get ready for her party tonight. Do they say they'll help or do they make excuses? Answers on p. 243C.

17 Tu peux m'aider?

How would you respond to the note from Danielle on page 254? Write a short note granting the favor or making an excuse.

VOCABULAIRE

Je voudrais faire une boum, mais je ne sais pas quoi faire.

C'est facile! Pour faire les préparatifs, tu dois...

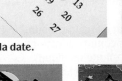

fixer la date.

demander la permission à tes parents.

envoyer les invitations.

choisir la musique.

préparer les amuse-gueule.

faire le ménage.

Presentation

Comment dit-on... ? On the board or on a transparency, label three columns *To ask for a favor, To make excuses,* and *To grant a favor.* Then, have students look at the letters on page 254 and tell which sentences illustrate these functions. Have a volunteer write the sentences in the appropriate columns as his or her classmates suggest them.

Teaching Suggestion

Write on the board the four expressions used *to ask a favor.* Have students use these expressions to ask you to do something for them. Either grant each favor or make an excuse, using the appropriate expressions. Do this several times. Then, ask students for favors and have them try to recall the expressions they heard you use.

 For videodisc application, see *Videodisc Guide.*

For Individual Needs

16 Challenge Have students listen to the recording again to identify the favors Caroline asks of her family members.

17 Slower Pace Have students work in small groups to answer one of the letters.

Presentation

Vocabulaire Tell students in French that you're planning a party. (**Je vais faire une boum.**) Then, tell and show them all of the preparations you will make, using props (a calendar, CDs, a feather duster) and gestures.

TPR Have students show their comprehension of the vocabulary by acting out the party preparations with props as you tell them what to do. (**D'abord, fixe la date. Puis, demande la permission à tes parents.**)

Teaching Suggestion

Vocabulaire Ask students if they have made these preparations. Tell them to answer yes and add details. If you ask **Tu as fixé la date?** a student might answer **Oui, c'est pour vendredi, le vingt-sept.**

18 Ecoute!

Pascale et Jean-Claude font des préparatifs pour la fête de Pascale. Qu'est-ce que Pascale va faire? Et Jean-Claude? Answers on p. 243D.

19 Tu devrais...

Patrick demande des conseils à Monique pour savoir comment organiser une boum. Qu'est-ce qu'elle lui conseille de faire? See answers below.

20 Quand tu fais une boum...

Réponds aux questions suivantes, puis pose ces questions à un(e) ami(e). Est-ce que vous faites les mêmes préparatifs? Fais la liste des réponses que vous avez en commun.

1. Quand tu veux faire une boum, est-ce que tu demandes la permission à tes parents?
2. Est-ce que tu envoies des invitations, ou est-ce que tu téléphones à tes copains?
3. Qui est-ce que tu invites?
4. Est-ce que tu fais le ménage avant ta boum?
5. Qu'est-ce que tu prépares comme amuse-gueule?
6. Qu'est-ce que tu choisis comme musique?
7. Qu'est-ce qu'on fait à tes fêtes préférées? On discute? On écoute de la musique? On regarde des vidéos?
8. A ta boum idéale...
   — qui sont les invités?   — quel groupe joue?   — qu'est-ce qu'on mange?

21 Jeu!

You're helping prepare for a French Club party at your house, and you need help. List four preparations from the **Vocabulaire** that you don't feel like doing and ask some classmates to do each chore. If the person you ask has the same chore on his or her list, he or she must refuse to do the favor for you. If the task isn't on his or her list, the person you ask must grant your favor. Write the name of the person who can do the task on your paper. The first person to find four different people to do the party preparations wins.

22 Range ton placard! See answers below.

You cleaned a lot of old things out of the closet before the party. Tell what you did with what you found.

—Mes baskets? Je les ai gardées!

le tee-shirt d'un ami
tes devoirs de 6ème
tes vieilles cassettes
le journal de ta sœur
ton vieux nounours
la photo de ton ex-petit(e) ami(e)
tes vieilles baskets
ton dernier bulletin scolaire

garder *(to keep)*
jeter *(to throw away)*
donner à...
écouter
mettre
lire
laver
déchirer

Note de Grammaire

When you use the direct object pronouns **le, la, l', les, me, te, nous,** or **vous** in the **passé composé,** the past participle agrees with the direct object pronoun. Add an **-e** if the pronoun is feminine, an **-s** if the pronoun is masculine and plural, and an **-es** if the pronoun is feminine and plural.

La poubelle? Je **l'**ai sorti**e.**
Les chiens? Je **les** ai promené**s.**
Il **nous** a oublié**(e)s.**
Mais, Cécile, il **t'**a invité**e!**

NOTE CULTURELLE

If you went to Provence, you would have the opportunity to try **provençale** cuisine. For an **amuse-gueule,** you might be served olives or **tapenade,** an aromatic paste of olives, garlic, and anchovies. At a dinner party, a typical **hors-d'œuvre** would be **pissaladière,** a type of pizza made with onions, anchovies, and olives. With fish, you would be likely to try **aïoli,** made of egg yolk, olive oil, and garlic. **Ratatouille** is a casserole of eggplant, tomatoes, zucchini, green peppers, and onions in a spicy tomato sauce. As you can tell, **provençale** cuisine uses a lot of garlic, olives, onions, tomatoes, and eggplant, all foods which grow well in the soil of Provence.

23 Un amuse-gueule

Get together with several friends to create a skit about making **pissaladière** for a party. One person should coordinate the effort, asking the others to do each task. Each person can play a different role: a kitchen whiz, a klutz, someone who always asks for advice, someone who does the opposite of what he or she is told, or other characters. Bring props to make your skit more interesting.

Pissaladière

125 grammes de farine
60 grammes de beurre
de l'eau, du sel
6 gros oignons, hachés
6 olives noires
4 filets d'anchois
2 cuillerées à soupe d'huile d'olive

1. Mélangez la farine, le beurre, l'eau et le sel pour faire une pâte.
2. Etendez la pâte sur un plat à four. Laissez reposer pendant vingt minutes.
3. Faites frire les oignons dans l'huile d'olive dans une poêle pendant vingt minutes.
4. Mettez la pâte au four pendant dix minutes.
5. Mettez les oignons, les olives et les anchois sur la pâte.
6. Mettez au four pendant 30 minutes.

DEUXIEME ETAPE *deux cent cinquante-sept* **257**

Possible answers

22 Le tee-shirt? Je l'ai donné à mon ami.
Mes devoirs de 6ème? Je les ai jetés.
Mes vieilles cassettes? Je les ai gardées.
Le journal de ma sœur? Je l'ai lu.
Mon vieux nounours? Je l'ai donné à mon frère.
La photo... ? Je l'ai déchirée.
Mes baskets? Je les ai lavées.
Mon dernier bulletin scolaire? Je l'ai jeté.

ASSESS

Quiz 10-2, *Chapter Teaching Resources, Book 3,* pp. 81–82

Assessment Items, Audiocassette 8B Audio CD 10

Performance Assessment

Have students imagine they're planning a party and write a letter asking a friend for help. They exchange letters and write a reply.

Teaching Suggestion

Note de grammaire Prepare one index card for each student. The right side of each card is used to ask a question, and the left side, to answer a question. To prepare the cards, lay them out side by side. Put a picture and a verb on the right side of a card (a picture of a trash can, **sortir**), and on the left side of the next card, put the same picture and verb, and so on. A student looks at the right side of his or her card and asks a question suggested by the picture and verb. (**Qui a sorti la poubelle?**) Whoever has the picture of the trash can on the left side of his or her card answers **Moi! Je l'ai sortie!** That student then asks a question based on the picture and verb on the right side of his or her card (**Qui a promené les chiens?**) and so on.

TPR **23** First say and act out the recipe directions, having students repeat after you and mimic your gestures. Then, call out the recipe directions (**Mélangez la farine...**), and have students act them out.

Family Link

Students might prepare the Pissaladière recipe at home with a family member.

CLOSE

To close this **étape,** write a request for a favor on an index card for each student. Have students stand in two lines facing one another. Each student reads the request aloud and the person opposite must respond within ten seconds. At your signal, the students in one line move down one, and the student at the end of the line moves to the front, so that each student is facing a new partner. Repeat the process until the original partners are opposite each other again.

Jump Start!

Have students answer these questions, using object pronouns and saying that they already did what was asked. (**Tu vas sortir la poubelle? Je l'ai déjà sortie.**) 1. **Tu vas passer l'aspirateur?** 2. **Tu vas choisir la musique?** 3. **Tu vas faire tes devoirs?** 4. **Tu vas téléphoner à ta copine?** 5. **Tu vas parler à tes parents?**

MOTIVATE

Ask students under what circumstances they would either accept an apology or reproach someone.

TEACH

Teaching Suggestion

24 Ask for volunteers to read the phone conversation aloud. Then, have partners read it aloud to each other and answer the questions.

Presentation

Comment dit-on... ? Write the functions on a transparency and the expressions on small strips of transparency. Read aloud each expression with appropriate intonation and gestures and have a student place the appropriate strip under the function it serves. Afterwards, hand back fake test papers with students' names on them. Intentionally bump people or return the wrong paper. Apologize and have students accept your apology. Then, tell students you didn't do something (**Je n'ai pas étudié.**) and have them tell you should or could have done it. (**Tu aurais dû étudier.**)

For videodisc application, see *Videodisc Guide.*

258   TROISIEME ETAPE

TROISIEME ETAPE

Apologizing and accepting an apology; reproaching someone

STEPHANE   Aurélie? Excuse-moi pour hier.

AURELIE   Pourquoi?

STEPHANE   Je suis vraiment désolé. Je voulais aller à ta boum, mais...

AURELIE   Mais c'est pas grave.

STEPHANE   Je sais que j'aurais dû te téléphoner. Tu ne m'en veux pas?

AURELIE   Mais non. T'en fais pas. Isabelle m'a dit que tu ne venais pas.

STEPHANE   Isabelle? Ouf, ça me rassure!

AURELIE   Bon, alors, ça sera pour la prochaine fois.

24 La boum manquée

1. Why did Stéphane call Aurélie?   to apologize for missing her party
2. Why is he worried?   He is afraid that Aurélie is mad at him for missing her party.
3. Why isn't she mad?   Isabelle had told her that Stéphane wasn't coming.

COMMENT DIT-ON... ?
Apologizing and accepting an apology; reproaching someone

To apologize:

C'est de ma faute. *It's my fault.*
Excuse-moi. *Forgive me.*
Désolé(e).
Tu ne m'en veux pas? *No hard feelings?*
J'aurais dû vous téléphoner. *I should have . . .*
J'aurais pu attendre dix minutes de plus. *I could have . . .*

To accept an apology:

Ça ne fait rien. *It doesn't matter.*
C'est pas grave.
Il n'y a pas de mal. *No harm done.*
T'en fais pas.
Je ne t'en veux pas. *No hard feelings.*

To reproach someone:

Tu aurais pu m'écouter.
You could have . . .
Tu aurais dû leur téléphoner.
You should have . . .

RESOURCES FOR TROISIEME ETAPE

Textbook Audiocassette 5B/Audio CD 10
Practice and Activity Book, pp. 116–118
Video Guide
  Video Program
  Expanded Video Program, Videocassette 4
Videodisc Guide
  Videodisc Program, Videodisc 5B

Chapter Teaching Resources, Book 3
• Communicative Activity 10-2, pp. 61–62
• Teaching Transparency Master 10-3, pp. 65, 66
  Teaching Transparency 10-3
• Additional Listening Activities 10-5, 10-6, p. 69
  Audiocassette 10B/Audio CD 10
• Realia 10-2, pp. 72, 73
• Situation Cards 10-3, pp. 74, 75
• Student Response Forms, pp. 76–78
• Quiz 10-3, pp. 83–84
  Audiocassette 8B/Audio CD 10

25 Ecoute!

Listen to the following conversations you overhear in the hall. Why is each person apologizing? Does the other person accept the apology or reproach him or her?

Answers on p. 243D.

Answers on p. 243D.

A la française

You can use **Pardon** or **Excuse(z)-moi** to apologize politely in most situations. If you feel really sorry about something you did, however, use **Désolé(e)** or **Je regrette.**

---

26 Qu'est-ce qu'ils disent? Possible answers.

1. Pardon./Ça ne fait rien.

2. Désolé!/Tu aurais dû téléphoner.

3. Je regrette!/T'en fais pas.

27 Tu aurais pu...

Tu aurais pu...

Dis à René ce qu'il aurait pu faire au lieu de faire la sieste cet après-midi. Fais-lui des reproches en utilisant ces images.

1. promener le chien.

2. faire tes devoirs.

3. faire du jogging.

4. me téléphoner.

5. faire la vaisselle.

Note de Grammaire

Remember that when a conjugated verb is followed by an infinitive, all object pronouns come before the infinitive:

—J'ai invité les voisins.
—Tu n'aurais pas dû **les** inviter.
—Je n'ai pas parlé à Lucien.
—Tu aurais dû **lui** parler.

TROISIEME ETAPE

deux cent cinquante-neuf **259**

Teaching Suggestion

Prepare flashcards on which are written the first sentences of various two-line dialogues (see **Note de grammaire** on this page). After students read the question and respond orally, show the other side of the card on which you've written the response to help visual learners. Afterwards, read the question and response to help auditory learners.

For Individual Needs

25 Challenge Play the recording again and have students tell what each person is apologizing for.

25 Auditory Learners Have students copy all the expressions from **Comment dit-on... ?** on page 258. As they listen to the recording, have them place a check mark next to an expression when they hear it. Ask them which of the expressions they heard twice (**Désolé.** and **J'aurais dû...**) and which were not used at all (**Tu ne m'en veux pas? J'aurais pu... ; Ça ne fait rien. C'est pas grave. Je ne t'en veux pas. Tu aurais dû...**).

26 Slower Pace Have students say as much as they can in French about the illustrations before they tell what the people are saying. Have students imagine who the people are, where they are, and what is happening.

27 Slower Pace Have students first name activities that the photos suggest.

Challenge/Auditory Learners Call out the first sentence of a dialogue similar to the ones in the **Note de grammaire** (**J'ai oublié mes devoirs.**) and have students respond. (**Tu n'aurais pas dû les oublier.**)

Visual/Tactile Learners Write several dialogues (see Challenge/Auditory Learners above) on paper divided into squares, with one word written in each square. Photocopy one page for every three students, cut apart the words, and distribute them to groups of three. Have students use the words to form several two-line dialogues.

Teaching Suggestion

28 For listening practice, read the letter aloud to students who listen with their books closed. Ask them to listen carefully and identify as many things as they can that Denis did wrong. They might jot these down in French or in English as they listen.

Additional Practice

28 Have students write a letter explaining what an imaginary friend did wrong in a certain situation, using the letter in the activity as a model. Then, have a partner read and respond to the letter.

 Portfolio

29 **Oral** This activity is appropriate for students' oral portfolios.

 Mon journal

30 For an additional journal entry suggestion for Chapter 10, see *Practice and Activity Book,* page 154.

 Portfolio

31 **Written** This activity is appropriate for students' written portfolios. For portfolio suggestions, see *Assessment Guide,* page 23.

CLOSE

To close this **étape,** have pairs of students choose one of the following situations to act out. **1. Tu arrives au cinéma en retard et ton ami(e) est fâché(e).** **2. Tu renverses ton coca sur la personne à côté de toi au café.** **3. Dans le couloir, tu marches sur les pieds de quelqu'un.** **4. Une personne cherche sa lentille de contact par terre. Tu passes par là et tu l'écrases.** **5. Deux personnes se bousculent dans le couloir, et tous leurs livres tombent par terre.**

28 Une catastrophe

Your friend Denis is upset because he did everything wrong last night. Read his note and answer it. Reproach him by telling what he could have or should have done instead.

> Tu aurais pu faire tes devoirs. Et tu n'aurais pas dû sortir...

29 Jeu de rôle

Avec un(e) camarade, choisissez une des scènes suivantes et jouez-la. Tu vas t'excuser et ton/ta camarade va te pardonner ou te faire un reproche. Puis, choisissez une autre scène et inversez les rôles.

1. Tu as perdu le livre de maths de ton ami(e).
2. Tu rentres chez toi à minuit et ton père (ta mère) n'est pas content(e)!
3. Tu as oublié de rendre le CD que ton ami(e) t'a prêté.
4. Tu n'es pas allé(e) à la boum de ton ami(e) parce que tu étais privé(e) de sortie.

30 Mon journal

In your journal, describe what happened the last time you had a misunderstanding or a disagreement with someone. Write about everything that happened and how you resolved it.

31 A nos lecteurs/lectrices...

Create an advice column for a magazine. Invent several "problems" and write responses to them. Be sure to take several different approaches in your responses—you can be comforting, matter-of-fact, reproachful, optimistic, or pessimistic. Use photos and art to make the column more eye-catching.

Hier soir, j'avais des devoirs à faire, mais je suis quand même sorti avec des copains. Je suis parti sans avertir mes parents – j'ai oublié de leur dire à quelle heure j'allais rentrer. En route, j'ai vu Caroline, une amie de ma copine Elodie. Je lui ai parlé pendant quelques minutes. Donc, j'étais en retard pour le film et je n'ai pas pu trouver mes amis au ciné. J'ai décidé d'attendre la séance suivante. Le film était super, mais je suis rentré chez moi très tard. Mes parents étaient furieux et ils m'ont privé de sortie pendant deux semaines. Ensuite, le téléphone a sonné. C'était Elodie, ma copine, qui n'était pas contente parce qu'elle m'avait vu en tête-à-tête avec Caroline! Je lui ai dit que je ne savais pas de quoi elle parlait et de me rappeler plus tard. Tout le monde est fâché contre moi mais, en fait, je n'ai rien fait de mal!

Tu te rappelles?

You already know how to make excuses, and sometimes you have to use them in the past tense.

J'avais quelque chose à faire.
Je n'ai pas eu le temps.
J'étais très occupé(e).
Je voulais le faire, mais j'ai dû...

ASSESS

Quiz 10-3, *Chapter Teaching Resources, Book 3,* pp. 83–84

Assessment Items, Audiocassette 8B Audio CD 10

Performance Assessment

Use Activity 31 to assess students' performance for this **étape.** You might base students' written grades on content, accuracy, and creativity.

Panorama Culturel

Antoine • France

Anselme • Côte d'Ivoire

Céline • Viêt-nam

VIDEO PROGRAM OR EXPANDED VIDEO PROGRAM, Videocassette 4 10:50–13:49

OR **VIDEODISC PROGRAM,** Videodisc 5B

Search 16935, Play To 19080

What do you do when you have a problem? Whom do you talk to? We asked some French-speaking teenagers what they do when they have a problem. Here's what they told us.

Qu'est-ce que tu fais quand tu as un problème? Tu parles à qui?

«Quand j'ai des problèmes, en général je les garde pour moi. Mais, sinon, quand ça va pas du tout, j'en parle à une amie qui m'aide. C'est tout.»

—Antoine

«Au village, quand tu as un problème, quand tu as un malheur, c'est le malheur de tout le village. Personne ne peut passer au village sans te dire bonjour.»

—Anselme

«J'en parle souvent à ma mère. Même si c'est pas très bon, enfin. Tout le monde en parle... Le plus souvent, les filles en parlent à leurs amies et ne se confient pas tellement à leurs parents. Mais moi, c'est le contraire.»

—Céline

Qu'en penses-tu?

1. When you have a problem, how do you resolve it?
2. When you ask someone for help with a problem, what kind of help do you usually want? New ideas? Sympathy? Moral support? Advice? An honest opinion?
3. When your friends have problems, what do you do? How do you help them find a solution?

Teacher Notes

- See *Video Guide, Videodisc Guide,* and *Practice and Activity Book* for activities related to the **Panorama Culturel**.
- Remind students that cultural material may be included in the Chapter Quizzes and Test.
- The interviewees' language represents informal, unrehearsed speech. Occasionally, edits have been made for clarification.

Motivating Activity

Ask students what they do when they have a problem. Does the type of problem they have determine with whom they'll discuss it?

Presentation

Write the following on the board: 1. **Je parle à ma mère.** 2. **Je garde mes problèmes pour moi.** 3. **Tout le village m'aide.** 4. **Quelquefois, je parle à une amie qui m'aide.**

Have students view the video and arrange the paraphrased sentences according to who said them (Antoine, Anselme, Céline).

Teaching Suggestion

Have students write the name of the interviewee whose handling of a problem most closely resembles the way they would handle it.

Teaching Suggestion

After students view the video, distribute typed copies of the interviews in which you've replaced some words with blank spaces. Then, play the recording and have students try to fill in the blanks with the words they hear. As a variation of this activity, write the missing words at the bottom of the page in random order for students to choose from as they fill in the blanks.

Questions

1. Qui parle souvent à sa mère de ses problèmes? (Céline)
2. Qui garde ses problèmes pour lui? (Antoine)
3. Qui a tout un village pour l'aider avec ses problèmes? (Anselme)
4. D'après Céline, à qui est ce que les filles se confient, en général? (à leurs amies)

READING STRATEGY

Reading inductively

Teacher Note

For an additional reading, see *Practice and Activity Book,* page 119.

PREREADING
Activities A–D

Motivating Activity

Have students suggest several qualities they look for in a friend and compile a list on the board or on a transparency.

Building on Previous Skills

Remind students to try to guess the meaning of an unfamiliar word from the context of the sentence in which it appears. Emphasize the importance of their concentrating on what they <u>do</u> know rather than on what they don't know.

Teaching Suggestions

B. Ask students to justify their choice by citing language from the text.

D. You might want to help students understand the words **amitié** and **déçu** by asking them **Est-ce que l'amitié est importante pour vous?** and **Est-ce que vous avez déjà été déçus? Comment?**

Terms in Lisons!

Students may want to know the following additional vocabulary in order to take the quiz: **sacré** *(sacred);* **donner un coup de main** *(to give a hand);* **l'égoïsme** *(selfishness);* **l'espoir** *(hope);* **les soucis** *(problems).*

LISONS!

Avez-vous des trésors d'amitié à offrir?
Répondez sans attendre à ces 12 questions et vous le saurez...

ÊTES-VOUS UN BON COPAIN?

1	Certains héros n'ont pas d'ami. Parmi eux, vous préférez...	5	Vous attendez d'un vrai copain qu'il vous dise...	9	Entre amis, il est si bon de partager...
	a) Lucky Luke.		a) « Pas de problème, tu peux compter sur moi. »		a) Les confidences.
	b) Poil de Carotte.		b) « Si tu veux, je t'en fais cadeau. »		b) Les fous rires.
	c) Le Petit Prince.		c) « O.K., je ne le répéterai à personne. »		c) Les soucis.
2	Un copain, c'est un sacré compagnon...	6	L'obstacle le plus contraire à l'amitié, c'est...	10	Se fâcher avec son meilleur copain, c'est comme...
	a) Vous n'hésitez pas à lui donner un coup de main.		a) L'égoïsme.		a) Un coup de tonnerre.
	b) Vous trouvez sympa de prendre le train avec lui.		b) L'incompréhension.		b) La traversée d'un désert.
	c) Vous aimez vous amuser ensemble.		c) L'indifférence.		c) Un jour de pluie.
3	Quelle marque d'amitié vous plaît le plus?	7	Votre espoir en amitié serait...	11	L'amitié, c'est un précieux atout...
	a) Les sourires confiants.		a) Que l'on ne se dispute jamais.		a) Face aux difficultés.
	b) Les signes discrets de complicité.		b) De ne jamais être déçu.		b) Face à la solitude.
	c) Les grands gestes de bienvenue.		c) De ne jamais se perdre de vue.		c) Face à l'ennui.
4	Avec un ami, vous aimez avant tout...	8	Vous ne feriez jamais votre ami de quelqu'un qui...	12	Deux bons copains s'entendent comme...
	a) Avoir de longues discussions.		a) Vous critique tout le temps.		a) L'arbre et l'oiseau.
	b) Faire les quatre cents coups.		b) Veut prendre votre place.		b) Le soufflet et la forge.
	c) Rencontrer de nouvelles têtes.		c) Critique un de vos copains.		c) Parole et musique.

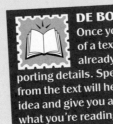

DE BONS CONSEILS
Once you get the gist or main idea of a text using strategies you've already learned, look for the supporting details. Specific facts and phrases from the text will help you flesh out the main idea and give you a more complete picture of what you're reading about.

A. What type of text is *Êtes-vous un bon copain?* How can you tell? See answers below.

B. Skim the title and the subtitle to get the gist. Are these questions about . . .
1. what kind of friend you value?
2. what kind of boyfriend or girlfriend you want?
3. what kind of friend you are?

C. Scan the text and use what you know about quizzes to answer the following questions. See answers below.
1. To whom are all twelve questions addressed?
2. What is the box labeled **Résultats** for? How can you tell?
3. What do the three paragraphs below the chart on page 263 describe?

D. To take the quiz, you'll need to know the following words:
amitié *friendship*
Lucky Luke *comic strip cowboy*

Culture Note

Self-tests such as this one are popular in French magazines for teenagers and in fashion or home magazines.

Possible answers

A self-quiz; the question at the top, numbered items, multiple choices for each item, a scoring grid

C 1. the reader **(vous)**
2. scoring the quiz; The grid shows numbers and letters that correspond to the numbers and letters of the quiz.
3. the type of friend you are according to your score on the quiz

ILLUSTRÉ PAR BLACHON
TEST DE GÉRARD TIXIER

R É S U L T A T S

Dans ce tableau, cochez, pour chaque question, la lettre qui correspond à votre réponse. Pour chaque ligne, comptez le nombre de cases cochées. (Quand la lettre est soulignée, comptez deux points.) Lisez le texte qui correspond à la ligne où vous avez le plus de points.

1	2	3	4	5	6	7	8	9	10	11	12	VOUS CHERCHEZ A ETRE :
b	b	<u>a</u>	b	c	<u>b</u>	c	b	a	a	b	b	c	Le meilleur copain
c	a	a	c	a	a	a	b	c	a	a	<u>b</u>	Le copain à toute épreuve
a	c	c	<u>b</u>	c	<u>b</u>	c	<u>c</u>	b	c	c	a	Le copain de la bande

LE MEILLEUR COPAIN

Vous n'accordez pas votre confiance tout de suite : il faut de la patience pour vous apprivoiser. Une atmosphère de complicité est nécessaire pour se confier à l'autre, et partager travail, inquiétudes, blagues et loisirs. Pour vous, l'amitié, c'est d'avoir des goûts communs, tout se dire, et s'estimer. Vous êtes un ami sûr, exigeant, et vous attendez la même chose de vos amis. Vous rêvez d'une amitié privilégiée, presque exclusive, qui défierait le temps.

LE COPAIN A TOUTE EPREUVE

Un bon copain doit faire ses preuves : être présent quand on a besoin de lui, démontrer, en toute occasion, son appui solidaire. En amitié, vous appréciez la spontanéité, la franchise, la générosité, la disponibilité. Vous n'aimez pas que l'on fasse les choses sans vous, qu'elles soient agréables ou difficiles. On peut compter sur vous pour sortir d'un mauvais pas... Pour vous, l'amitié, ça s'éprouve sur un terrain d'aventures!

LE COPAIN DE LA BANDE

Vous cultivez l'art de vous faire des copains. Vous aimez l'idée du groupe familier dans lequel chacun a sa personnalité, son surnom, ses manies et tient son rôle. Les amis de vos amis ont une chance de devenir vos amis. Ils aiment cette atmosphère cordiale où se partagent les éclats de rire, où les idées se bousculent, où les uns se chamaillent, tandis que les autres les réconcilient. Pour vous, l'amitié se partage à plusieurs, avec gaieté et esprit d'entraide.

Poil de Carotte *a boy who's always in trouble*
un sourire *a smile*
la complicité *sharing an understanding*
faire les quatre cents coups *to goof off, get into trouble*
déçu *disappointed*
les fous rires *uncontrollable laughter*
un coup de tonnerre *a clap of thunder*
un atout *an asset*
le soufflet et la forge *two things that are inseparable: the bellows and the fire*

E. Take the quiz. Then, copy the chart at the top of the right-hand page and score your quiz. In which category did you mark the most letters? Which type of friend are you?

F. Now that you have a general idea of what type of friend you are, look for specific details that define each of the three types of friends. On a separate sheet of paper, make three columns, one for each type of friend. Then, find four words or phrases to describe each type.   See answers below.

G. Interview a partner, asking him or her the 12 questions. Then, reverse roles. Do you both agree with the quiz's analysis of your partner's results? Which questions would you change? Together, make up your own **jeu-test** about friendship to give to the class. Be sure to include a scoring system!

deux cent soixante-trois **263**

Possible answers

F *Le meilleur copain:* atmosphère de complicité, goûts communs, tout se dire, ami sûr, amitié privilégiée, exclusive

Le copain à toute épreuve: présent quand on a besoin de lui, la spontanéité, la générosité, la franchise

Le copain de la bande: l'art de vous faire des copains, groupe familier, atmosphère cordiale, les éclats de rire, gaieté, esprit d'entraide

For Individual Needs

E., F. Slower Pace   You may want to have students work in pairs or small groups to help each other read and understand the quiz and do the follow-up activities.

POSTREADING
Activity G

Cooperative Learning

G. Have students work in groups to create the **jeu-test**. Assign a leader to head the discussion, a writer to record the items, one or two editors to proofread, and an artist to create the layout of the test.

Teaching Suggestion

G. Students might want to create a **jeu-test** about a different topic, such as **Etes-vous un(e) bon(ne) élève?**

Terms in Lisons!

Students might want to know the following vocabulary to help them read the results of the **jeu-test: cocher** *(to check);* **accorder** is a synonym for **donner; apprivoiser** *(to tame);* **partager** *(to share);* **des inquiétudes** *(worries);* **des blagues** *(jokes);* **des loisirs** *(free-time);* **des goûts** *(tastes);* **s'estimer** *(to value one another);* **défier** *(to defy);* **des preuves** *(proof);* **démontrer** *(to demonstrate);* **de l'appui** *(support);* **la franchise** *(frankness);* **la disponibilité** *(availability);* **un surnom** *(a nickname);* **les manies** *(peculiarities);* **se bousculer** *(to shake up);* **chamailler** *(to bicker);* **l'entraide** *(mutual aid).*

The **Mise en pratique** reviews and integrates all four skills and culture in preparation for the Chapter Test.

Teaching Suggestion

1 Before playing the recording, read the responses with the students. Ask them to what or to whom the pronouns refer. Have students try to guess what the callers' problems might be.

 **For Individual Needs**

1 Challenge Play the recording a second time, pausing after each caller to ask the following questions:
1. **Pourquoi est-que Désiré est déprimé? Pourquoi est-ce que ses parents sont fâchés? Pourquoi est-ce qu'il est rentré en retard?** 2. **Pourquoi est-ce que Murielle est embêtée? Pourquoi est-ce qu'elle a eu une mauvaise note?** 3. **Qui est-ce que Jérôme a rencontré? Où?** 4. **Où est-ce qu'Emile est invité? Pourquoi est-ce qu'il ne veut pas y aller?**

Thinking Critically

2 Synthesizing Distribute the following list of French proverbs and ask students which ones apply to each writer. Have students give reasons why they think a proverb applies to a certain writer.
Aide-toi, le ciel t'aidera.
  (Heaven helps those who help themselves.)
Avec des «si», on mettrait Paris en bouteille. *(If wishes were horses, beggars would ride.)*
Il faut battre le fer quand il est chaud. *(Strike while the iron is hot.)*
Qui ne dit mot consent.
  (Silence gives consent.)
Qui cherche trouve. *(He who seeks, finds.)*

MISE EN PRATIQUE

 1 Listen as several teenagers call in to a radio talk show for advice. Match the host's responses to the problems. What other advice would you give? **1.** c **2.** b **3.** a **4.** d

a. Tu devrais aller la chercher au parc.

b. D'abord, tu aurais dû étudier! Maintenant, tu devrais leur dire combien tu as eu à ton interro.

c. Explique-leur ce qui s'est passé.

d. C'est ridicule! Va à la fête et parle-lui.

PARLONS-EN!

OCCUPÉ	LA CHIPIE	IMPOSSIBLE

Je téléphone
Occupé
«Plus tard, peut-être»
Encore occupé
J'ai un problème
Je peux te parler?
«J'ai trente-six choses...
Désolé...
Occupé.»
Je dois te parler!
Mon copain
est occupé.
Que faire?
Tu peux t'occuper de moi?
 	
-- Pierre, Arles
	Ma petite sœur est une chipie
	Qui fait toujours des bêtises.
	Est-ce qu'on la punit?
	Mais non! Elle est «trop petite,
	    trop jeune», bien sûr!
	
	Hier, dans ma chambre
	Mon lieu sacré
	Elle a écouté ma musique à moi
	Pourquoi? Pour m'énerver.
	
	Mes CD partout, par terre,
	    une catastrophe,
	J'entre, incrédule, elle me sourit
	Je suis furieux, sans recours,
	Parce qu'elle sait qu'elle est
	    «trop petite».
	
	Que faire? Vraiment, que faire?
	Je suis tellement énervé
	Ce n'est pas juste, cette petite,
	    trop petite.
	Amis, avez-vous une idée?
	
	-- Jean-Paul, Avignon
		Je devrais l'oublier
		Le rayer de ma mémoire,
		Mais je pense toujours à lui
		Toute la journée, tous les
		    jours, tous les soirs.
		
		Sa nouvelle petite amie
		Est blonde, sympa, super.
		De l'avis de tout le monde,
		Ces deux-là, "Ils font la
		    paire!"
		
		Tout le monde me dit
		Que je dois le détester
		Mais je souffre, souffre tant
		Que je ne peux pas l'oublier.
		
		D'un regard je suis tombée
		    amoureuse
		Je l'aimais, je l'aime toujours.
		Je ne sais vraiment plus quoi
		    faire
		Pour oublier ce chagrin
		    d'amour.
		
		-- Félicité, Aix-en-Provence

See answers below.

2 **1.** What is the problem for the writer of **Occupé?** What does he want?

2. Look at **La chipie.** Who is **la chipie?** Why is she named this? How does the author of the poem feel?

3. Look through the poem **Impossible** to find words that you recognize. What is the poem about? Read the first line and the last two lines. What is Félicité's problem? What advice have her friends given her?

Language Note

You might call attention to the word **chipie,** which is slang for *vixen* or *little devil*.

Answers

2 1. He is trying to talk to his friend, who is always busy; He wants to talk to his friend about a problem.

2. **La chipie** is the author's little sister; She is named this because she is always getting into her brother's things; The author feels it is not fair that his sister can get away with mischief because she is little.

3. The poem is about a lost love; She can't forget about him even though he has a new girlfriend; Her friends say she should hate him.

3 Tu voudrais répondre à un de ces poèmes. Ecris à un des poètes pour lui donner des conseils. Tu pourrais même écrire un poème comme réponse!

4 You just got a call from a friend who is upset about a misunderstanding, but you can't leave until you clean the house. Look at the picture of the house and make a list of all that needs to be done. Then, call several friends to ask them to help you out as a favor. See answers below.

5 If you went to a restaurant in Provence, what local specialties could you order?
tapenade, pissaladière, ratatouille

6

JEU DE ROLE

Create a soap opera episode about a group of friends preparing a surprise party for a famous guest. Be sure to . . .

• decide whom to invite.
• ask for and give advice about the preparations.
• include some type of misunderstanding, like a lost invitation, an old grudge, or even a long-lost boyfriend or girlfriend who suddenly appears!

MISE EN PRATIQUE   *deux cent soixante-cinq* **265**

Possible answers
4 ranger la cuisine, faire la vaisselle, promener le chien, ranger le salon, passer l'aspirateur

Portfolio

3 Written You may wish to include the students' responses to the poems in their written portfolios. For portfolio information, see *Assessment Guide*, pages 2–13.

Teaching Suggestion

4 You might have students work with partners for a variation on this activity. One student describes what needs to be done according to his or her list of chores. The other student draws a quick sketch of what his or her partner describes. Students should check the sketches against the list to make sure they match. Then, have them switch roles, using a list that names the tasks in a different order.

Building on Previous Skills

5 You might have students enact a scene in a restaurant in Aix in which they order food and then pay the check.

Video Wrap-Up

• *VIDEO PROGRAM*
• *EXPANDED VIDEO PROGRAM*, Videocassette 4, 01:25–17:12
• *VIDEODISC PROGRAM*, Videodisc 5B

At this time, you might want to use the video resources for additional review and enrichment. See *Video Guide* or *Videodisc Guide* for suggestions regarding the following:
• **Qu'est-ce que je dois faire?** (Dramatic episode)
• **Panorama Culturel** (Interviews)
• **Vidéoclips** (Authentic footage)

QUE SAIS-JE?

This page is intended to help students prepare for the test. It is a brief checklist of the major points covered in the chapter. The students should be reminded that this is only a checklist and does not necessarily include everything that will appear on the test.

♜ Games

LÈVE-TOI! Prepare a stack of yellow and red cards and form two teams. Call out questions from **Que sais-je?** at random. Tell students to stand if they know the answer. The first person to stand is recognized and tries to answer. If the student gives an appropriate answer, his or her team scores a point. If not, repeat the question for the other team, and anyone may answer. When a student answers correctly one time, give him or her a yellow card. The second time a student answers correctly, he or she gets a red card and may no longer answer questions for the team. Students with red cards will help keep score, determine who stood first, and judge the accuracy of the answers. When all the questions have been answered, the team with the most points wins.

JE L'AI TROUVÉE Write the questions from **Que sais-je?** on one set of cards and the answers on another set. Tape the question cards on the board at random and put the answer cards in a bag. Then, form two teams. Have the first player from each team select one card from the bag, find the matching question on the board, and call out **Je l'ai trouvée!** The first player to find the correct question reads the question and the answer and wins a point for his or her team. Repeat the process with the remaining players.

Can you use what you've learned in the chapter?

Can you share a confidence? p. 250

Can you ask for and give advice? p. 250

1 How would you approach your friend if you had a problem?
Je peux te parler? Tu as une minute? J'ai un problème. Je ne sais pas quoi faire.

2 How would you respond if a friend approached you with a problem?
Qu'est-ce qu'il y a? Qu'est-ce que je peux faire? Je t'écoute.

3 How would you ask a friend for advice about doing better in one of your classes?   A ton avis, qu'est-ce que je dois faire? Qu'est-ce que tu ferais, toi? Qu'est-ce que tu me conseilles?

4 How would you advise your friend to. . .

1. apologize?   2. forgive her boyfriend?   3. telephone his parents?
   Excuse-toi.   Pardonne-lui.   Téléphone-leur.

Can you ask for a favor? p. 255

5 How would you ask a friend to do these tasks for you?   *Possible answers:*

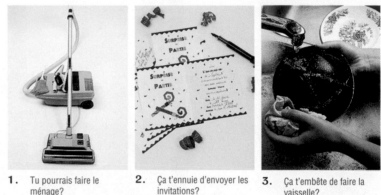

1. Tu pourrais faire le ménage?   2. Ça t'ennuie d'envoyer les invitations?   3. Ça t'embête de faire la vaisselle?

Can you grant a favor and make excuses? p. 255

6 How would you respond if your friend asked you for the following favors?   See answers below.

1. «Ça t'embête de téléphoner à Catherine?»
2. «Tu pourrais sortir la poubelle, s'il te plaît?»
3. «Ça t'ennuie de me prêter 200 F?»

Can you apologize and accept an apology? p. 258

7 How would you apologize to a friend with whom you had a misunderstanding?   *Possible answers:* C'est de ma faute. Excuse-moi. Désolé(e). Tu ne m'en veux pas? J'aurais dû... ; J'aurais pu...

8 How would you respond if your friend said . . .   See answers below.

1. «J'ai perdu ton livre. C'est de ma faute.»
2. «Je suis désolée de ne pas être venue à ta fête hier soir.»
3. «Tu ne m'en veux pas?»

Can you reproach someone? p. 258

9 How would you reproach a friend who was late meeting you at the movies?   Tu aurais pu... ; Tu aurais dû...

Possible answers
6 1. Bien sûr que non.
   2. Bien sûr. Pas de problème.
   3. Non, pas du tout.
8 1. Ça ne fait rien. C'est pas grave.
   2. Il n'y a pas de mal. T'en fais pas.
   3. Je ne t'en veux pas.

PREMIERE ETAPE

Sharing a confidence

Je ne sais pas quoi faire. *I don't know what to do.*

J'ai un problème. *I have a problem.*

Tu as une minute? *Do you have a minute?*

Je peux te parler? *Can I talk to you?*

Qu'est-ce qu'il y a? *What's wrong?*

Qu'est-ce que je peux faire? *What can I do?*

Je t'écoute. *I'm listening.*

Apologetic actions

un petit malentendu *a little misunderstanding*

expliquer ce qui s'est passé (à quelqu'un) *to explain what happened (to someone)*

demander pardon (à quelqu'un) *to ask (someone's) forgiveness*

se réconcilier (avec quelqu'un) *to make up (with someone)*

dire (à quelqu'un) que... *to tell (someone) that . . .*

téléphoner (à quelqu'un) *to call (someone)*

s'excuser *to apologize*

pardonner (à quelqu'un) *to forgive (someone)*

offrir (à quelqu'un) *to give (to someone)*

écouter ce qu'il/elle dit *to listen to what he/she says*

Asking for and giving advice

A ton avis, qu'est-ce que je dois faire? *In your opinion, what should I do?*

Qu'est-ce que tu ferais, toi? *What would you do?*

Qu'est-ce que tu me conseilles? *What do you think I should do?*

Invite-le/-la/-les. *Invite him/her/them.*

Parle-lui/-leur. *Talk to him/her/them.*

Dis-lui/-leur que... *Tell him/her/them that . . .*

Ecris-lui/-leur. *Write to him/her/them.*

Explique-lui/-leur. *Explain to him/her/them.*

Excuse-toi. *Apologize.*

Téléphone-lui/-leur. *Phone him/her/them.*

Oublie-le/-la/-les. *Forget him/her/them.*

Tu devrais... *You should . . .*

DEUXIEME ETAPE

Asking for and granting a favor; making excuses

Tu peux m'aider? *Can you help me?*

Tu pourrais... ? *Could you . . . ?*

Ça t'ennuie de... ? *Would you mind . . . ?*

Ça t'embête de... ? *Would you mind . . . ?*

Avec plaisir. *With pleasure.*

Bien sûr. *Of course.*

Pas du tout. *Not at all.*

Bien sûr que non. *Of course not.*

Pas de problème. *No problem.*

Désolé(e). *Sorry.*

J'ai quelque chose à faire. *I have something else to do.*

Je n'ai pas le temps. *I don't have time.*

Je suis très occupé(e). *I'm very busy.*

C'est impossible. *It's impossible.*

Party preparations

faire une boum *to give a party*

faire les préparatifs *to get ready*

demander la permission à tes parents *to ask your parents' permission*

fixer la date *to choose the date*

envoyer les invitations *to send the invitations*

choisir la musique *to choose the music*

préparer les amuse-gueule *to make party snacks*

faire le ménage *to do housework*

TROISIEME ETAPE

Apologizing and accepting an apology; reproaching someone

C'est de ma faute. *It's my fault.*

Excuse-moi. *Forgive me.*

Désolé(e). *I'm sorry.*

Tu ne m'en veux pas? *No hard feelings?*

J'aurais dû... *I should have . . .*

J'aurais pu.... *I could have . . .*

Ça ne fait rien. *It doesn't matter.*

C'est pas grave. *It's not serious.*

Il n'y a pas de mal. *No harm done.*

T'en fais pas. *Don't worry about it.*

Je ne t'en veux pas. *No hard feelings.*

Tu aurais pu... *You could have . . .*

Tu aurais dû... *You should have . . .*

♜ Game

DES TROUS To prepare for the game, form five teams and give a transparency to each one. Assign each team five vocabulary expressions and have them write a sentence with each one. Then, have them copy the sentences onto a transparency, leaving blank lines where the vocabulary items should appear. Collect the transparencies. To play the game, project the transparencies one at a time for thirty seconds each. Teams will write down the words they would use to fill in the blanks. They should sit out the round involving the transparency they created, so that each team will have four sets of answers. After you have shown the last transparency, have teams read their answers aloud and either verify or correct them. The team that filled in the most blanks correctly wins.

CHAPTER 10 ASSESSMENT

CHAPTER TEST

- *Chapter Teaching Resources, Book 3* pp. 85–90
- *Assessment Guide,* Speaking Test, p. 32
- *Assessment Items,* Audiocassette 8B Audio CD 10

TEST GENERATOR, CHAPTER 10

ALTERNATIVE ASSESSMENT

Performance Assessment

You might want to use the Jeu de rôle (p. 265) as a cumulative performance assessment activity.

📁 Portfolio Assessment

- **Written:** Activity 31, *Pupil's Edition,* p. 260
  Assessment Guide, p. 23
- **Oral:** Activity 29, *Pupil's Edition,* p. 260
  Assessment Guide, p. 23

♜ Game

CONCOURS DE VOCABULAIRE Write the six categories from the **Vocabulaire** on separate slips of paper and place them in a box. Form two teams. Have a player from one team draw a category from the box. Set a timer for 30 seconds or designate a timekeeper. Within 30 seconds, the player calls out as many words or expressions as possible that fit the category. Players must pronounce the words or expressions clearly in order to receive credit. Award one point for each correctly delivered expression. At the end of 30 seconds, the turn passes to another team.

Chapitre 11 : Chacun ses goûts
Chapter Overview

Mise en train pp. 270–272	Bientôt la Fête de la musique!	Practice and Activity Book, p. 121	Video Guide OR Videodisc Guide

	FUNCTIONS	GRAMMAR	CULTURE	RE-ENTRY
Première étape pp. 273–278	Identifying people and things, p. 273	• The verb **connaître**, p. 274 • **c'est** versus **il/elle est,** p. 275	**Panorama Culturel,** Musical tastes, p. 278	• Emphasizing likes and dislikes • Making and responding to suggestions
Deuxième étape pp. 279–283	Asking for and giving information, p. 280		• **Note Culturelle,** Movie theaters in France, p. 282 • **Rencontre Culturelle,** Using the **Minitel,** p. 283	
Troisième étape pp. 284–287	• Giving opinions, p. 284 • Summarizing, p. 286	The relative pronouns **qui** and **que,** p. 287		

Lisons! pp. 288–289	6 films qui ont fait date		Reading Strategy: Combining reading strategies

Review pp. 290–293	Mise en pratique, pp. 290–291	Que sais-je? p. 292	Vocabulaire, p. 293

Assessment Options	**Etape Quizzes**
	• *Chapter Teaching Resources, Book 3*
	  Première étape, Quiz 11-1, pp. 135–136
	  Deuxième étape, Quiz 11-2, pp. 137–138
	  Troisième étape, Quiz 11-3, pp. 139–140
	• *Assessment Items, Audiocassette 8B/Audio CD 11*
		Chapter Test
		• *Chapter Teaching Resources, Book 3,* pp. 141–146
		• *Assessment Guide,* Speaking Test, p. 33
		• *Assessment Items, Audiocassette 8B/Audio CD 11*
		
		Test Generator, Chapter 11

Video Program OR Expanded Video Program, Videocassette 4
OR Videodisc Program, Videodisc 6A

Textbook Audiocassette 6A/Audio CD 11

RESOURCES: Print

RESOURCES: Audiovisual

Textbook Audiocassette 6A/Audio CD 11

Practice and Activity Book, pp. 122–124
Chapter Teaching Resources, Book 3
• Teaching Transparency Master 11-1, pp. 119, 122 . . . . Teaching Transparency 11-1
• Additional Listening Activities 11-1, 11-2, p. 123 . . . . Additional Listening Activities, Audiocassette 10B/Audio CD 11
• Realia 11-1, pp. 127, 129
• Situation Cards 11-1, pp. 130–131
• Student Response Forms, pp. 132–134
• Quiz 11-1, pp. 135–136 . . . . Assessment Items, Audiocassette 8B/Audio CD 11
Video Guide. . . . . Video Program OR Expanded Video Program, Videocassette 4
Videodisc Guide. . . . . Videodisc Program, Videodisc 6A

Textbook Audiocassette 6A/Audio CD 11

Practice and Activity Book, pp. 125–127
Chapter Teaching Resources, Book 3
• Communicative Activity 11-1, pp. 115–116
• Teaching Transparency Master 11-2, pp. 120, 122 . . . . Teaching Transparency 11-2
• Additional Listening Activities 11-3, 11-4, p. 124 . . . . Additional Listening Activities, Audiocassette 10B/Audio CD 11
• Realia 11-2, pp. 128, 129
• Situation Cards 11-2, pp. 130–131
• Student Response Forms, pp. 132–134
• Quiz 11-2, pp. 137–138 . . . . Assessment Items, Audiocassette 8B/Audio CD 11
Videodisc Guide. . . . . Videodisc Program, Videodisc 6A

Textbook Audiocassette 6A/Audio CD 11

Practice and Activity Book, pp. 128–130
Chapter Teaching Resources, Book 3
• Communicative Activity 11-2, pp. 117–118
• Teaching Transparency Master 11-3, pp. 121, 122 . . . . Teaching Transparency 11-3
• Additional Listening Activities 11-5, 11-6, p. 125 . . . . Additional Listening Activities, Audiocassette 10B/Audio CD 11
• Realia 11-2, pp. 128, 129
• Situation Cards 11-3, pp. 130–131
• Student Response Forms, pp. 132–134
• Quiz 11-3, pp. 139–140 . . . . Assessment Items, Audiocassette 8B/Audio CD 11
Videodisc Guide. . . . . Videodisc Program, Videodisc 6A

Practice and Activity Book, p. 131

Video Guide. . . . . Video Program OR Expanded Video Program, Videocassette 4
Videodisc Guide. . . . . Videodisc Program, Videodisc 6A

Alternative Assessment
• Performance Assessment
 Première étape, p. 277
 Deuxième étape, p. 282
 Troisième étape, p. 287

• Portfolio Assessment
 Written: **Mise en pratique,** Activity 4, Pupil's Edition, p. 291
  Assessment Guide, p. 24
 Oral: Activity 24, Pupil's Edition, p. 282
  Assessment Guide, p. 24

Chapitre 11 : Chacun ses goûts
Textbook Listening Activities Scripts

For Student Response Forms, see *Chapter Teaching Resources, Book 3,* pp. 132–134.

Première étape

7 Ecoute! p. 274

ROMAIN Dis, Djé Djé, tu connais Vanessa Paradis?

DJE DJE Mais bien sûr! Tout le monde connaît. Je suis allé à son dernier concert. Elle est super!

ROMAIN Vraiment? Tu en as de la chance! Mais mon groupe préféré, c'est Zouk Machine. Tu connais?

DJE DJE Non, je ne connais pas. Ils sont d'où?

ROMAIN C'est un groupe antillais qui chante le zouk. J'adore danser le zouk, c'est sensas! Mais toi, tu préfères le pop, non? Tu connais Céline Dion?

DJE DJE Je connais, mais pas très bien. J'aime mieux Roch Voisine.

ROMAIN Ah, je parie que tu connais Patrick Bruel!

DJE DJE Mais bien sûr que je connais! J'ai tous ses albums, et j'ai vu son dernier film, *Profil bas!*

ROMAIN Super! Tu sais, je crois qu'il passe en concert mercredi soir.

Answers to Activity 7
Vanessa Paradis, Céline Dion, Patrick Bruel (Roch Voisine is also mentioned.)

12 Ecoute! p. 276

1. — Qu'est-ce qui te plaît comme musique, Arnaud?
   — Moi, j'aime bien le jazz.
   — Tu aimes la musique classique aussi?
   — Bof, pas tellement. Mais le blues, c'est génial!

2. — Et toi, Magali? Qu'est-ce que tu aimes comme musique?
   — Moi? Ben, ce que j'aime bien, c'est le rock. J'adore Jean-Jacques Goldman.
   — Tu écoutes autre chose?
   — Ça dépend. Parfois, j'écoute du reggae.

3. — Qu'est-ce que tu aimes comme musique, Thierry?
   — Moi, je suis plutôt du genre country ou rock. En général, j'aime bien la musique américaine.
   — Tu n'aimes pas le rap?
   — Bof, pas vraiment.

4. — Et toi, Elodie?
   — Moi, j'aime tout. J'écoute de la musique classique le matin, et du pop quand je fais mes devoirs.

5. — Et toi, Christian, tu aimes quel genre de musique?
   — Ben, ce que j'adore, c'est le rap. Je suis fou de MC Solaar, et j'ai plein de CD de rap!
   — C'est tout?
   — Non, j'écoute aussi du rock.

Answers to Activity 12
1. *Arnaud:* jazz, blues
2. *Magali:* rock, reggae
3. *Thierry:* country, rock, American music
4. *Elodie:* classical music, pop
5. *Christian:* rap, rock

Deuxième étape

19 Ecoute! p. 280

— J'ai envie d'aller au ciné ce soir. Qu'est-ce qui passe comme film?

— Attends... euh, il passe *Astérix chez les Bretons.*

— Bof, je n'aime pas tellement les dessins animés. Quoi d'autre?

— Bon... il passe *Le fugitif* et *Germinal.*

— *Germinal?* D'après le roman de Zola? C'est avec qui?

— C'est avec Gérard Depardieu et...

— Gérard Depardieu! C'est mon acteur préféré! Ça passe où?

— Partout! Ça passe au Gaumont Les Halles, au Quatorze Juillet, au Gaumont Alésia...

— Ben, Gaumont Les Halles, c'est le plus proche.

— Ça commence à dix-huit heures vingt et à vingt heures cinquante.

— Oh, zut! Il est déjà six heures! Dépêchons-nous!

Answers to Activity 19
1. b   2. c   3. b   4. a

22 Ecoute! p. 282

NADEGE Salut, Emile. Dis, j'ai bien envie de voir un film. Pas toi?

EMILE Si, c'est une bonne idée. Alors... *Zombie et le train fantôme,* ça te dit? C'est un bon film d'horreur.

NADEGE Pas question! C'est trop bizarre. Je préfère les films classiques.

EMILE Les films classiques... Tiens, j'ai une idée! Tu as envie de voir *Jules et Jim?* Il passe à l'UGC Biarritz.

NADEGE Non, ça ne me dit pas trop. Je l'ai déjà vu plusieurs fois.

EMILE Ben... *Monty Python sacré graal,* alors. C'est un film comique anglais. C'est vachement bien.

NADEGE Ben, comme tu veux. Vraiment, je n'ai pas de préférence.

EMILE Oh là là! Que tu es pénible! Bon, alors c'est moi qui décide! On va voir *Monty Python.* Allez, viens!

Answers to Activity 22
film d'horreur, film classique, film comique

Troisième étape

29 Ecoute! p. 285

LUC Dis donc, tu connais *Calvin et Hobbes?* Tu trouves pas ça génial, toi?

PERRINE Bof, ça ne casse pas des briques. Et puis, les histoires de tigre en peluche, c'est pas mon truc. Moi, je préfère la science-fiction. Tu connais *Daïren* par exemple?

LUC Non, qu'est-ce que ça raconte?

PERRINE Ça se passe au dix-septième millénaire, sur la planète Uyuni. Il y a plein de batailles inter-galactiques. On ne s'ennuie pas une seconde. Tu vas voir, c'est plein de rebondissements.

LUC Ah! C'est un peu comme *La guerre des étoiles,* non?

PERRINE Si tu veux. On appelle ça un «space opéra.»

LUC Dis donc, est-ce que tu as lu *La cantatrice chauve* pour le cours de français?

PERRINE Bien sûr. J'adore le théâtre. Et puis, c'est très drôle.

LUC Tu trouves? Moi, j'ai rien compris. Il n'y a pas d'histoire, et il n'y a même pas de cantatrice! A mon avis, c'est nul.

PERRINE Mais non! C'est parce que c'est absurde!

LUC C'est bien ce que je dis : c'est nul. Moi, de toute façon, je préfère les romans.

PERRINE Et bien moi, je pense que la science-fiction, c'est l'avenir de la littérature!

Answers to Activity 29

Luc aime *Calvin and Hobbes.* Perrine aime *Daïren, La cantatrice chauve.*

31 Ecoute! p. 285

1. — Bonjour, monsieur. Je cherche des romans de Simenon, s'il vous plaît.
   — Oui, les policiers sont tous au même endroit, sur ce rayon, et ils sont classés par auteur.
   — Merci.

2. — Je viens de voir le film *La reine Margot,* et je voudrais lire le livre maintenant. Où est-ce que je pourrais le trouver?
   — Dans les romans classiques. A Dumas.
   — Merci beaucoup, monsieur.

3. — Notre professeur de français prend sa retraite, et nous voudrions lui offrir les œuvres de Rimbaud. Elles se trouvent où, s'il vous plaît?
   — Toute la poésie est sur le mur de gauche.

4. — Bonjour, monsieur. Est-ce que vous pourriez m'aider, s'il vous plaît?
   — Oui?

— Je cherche *La Florentine* de Juliette... amie.
— C'est un roman policier?
— Non, c'est une histoire d'amour, je crois.
— Les romans d'amour sont au fond du magasin.
— Merci.

5. — Bonjour, monsieur. Je cherche la collection complète des œuvres de Tintin. C'est pour offrir.
   — Les bandes dessinées sont à l'entrée du magasin, juste derrière vous.
   — Merci, monsieur.

Answers to Activity 31

1. c   2. e   3. d   4. b   5. a

Mise en pratique

2 p. 290

MARTIN Bonsoir, mesdames et messieurs. Bienvenue à la Revue de Films avec Martin Blondeau et Janine Neuville.

JANINE Ce soir, nous parlerons du premier film du festival, *La Rue Cases-Nègres,* qui se passe dans les années trente à la Martinique.

MARTIN Ce film parle d'un jeune garçon, José Hassam, qui est élévé par sa grand-mère qui travaille dans les champs de canne à sucre.

JANINE La grand-mère rêve d'une meilleure vie pour José et l'encourage dans ses études pour qu'il ne soit pas condamné à travailler dans les champs de canne à sucre.

MARTIN José va souvent voir Monsieur Méduse, une sorte de père spirituel, qui lui parle de ses ancêtres en Afrique. Mais celui-ci finit par mourir dans les champs de canne à sucre. Enfin, José reçoit une bourse pour faire ses études à Fort-de-France et quitte la Rue Cases-Nègres pour aller vivre à la grande ville.

JANINE Une bonne fin pour un mauvais film.

MARTIN Moi, j'ai bien aimé ce petit film.

JANINE Moi, je l'ai trouvé trop long.

MARTIN En tout cas, c'est une belle histoire.

JANINE Mais non, c'est déprimant! Et on s'ennuie.

MARTIN Pas du tout! Je recommende ce film à tous ceux qui aiment les films classiques.

JANINE Et moi, si c'est le seul film qui passe!

Answers to Mise en pratique Activity 2

1. Martinique
2. A boy is raised by his grandmother, who encourages him to pursue a better life than that of a sugar cane worker.
3. *Martin:* good story; *Janine:* long, depressing, boring.

ojects

Couvert
(Individ

ASS ill design and make a book jacket for their
S book. The jacket will be designed as follows:
front cover: Illustration, title, and author
• Inside front flap: Summary of the book
• Inside back flap: Critical reviews and list of other works
  by the same author
• Back cover: Picture and description of the author
• Spine: Title and author

MATERIALS

✂ **Students may need**
• Construction or unlined paper
• Colored markers or pencils
• Scissors
• Tape or glue
• Typewriter or word processor
• Magazines or catalogues

SUGGESTED SEQUENCE

1. Have students choose a book they have read and
   enjoyed. If it's in English, they will need to translate the
   title into French. They should acquire a copy of the
   book to refresh their memory about the characters and
   the story. Have students research the author's background, residence, family, hobbies, and other works.

2. Students write the text for the book jacket, including a
   summary of the story for the inside front flap of the
   book jacket, a description of the author for the back

cover, and three favorable reviews and four French titles
of other works by the author for the inside back flap.
The summary should entice others to read the book
without revealing the ending of the story. Students
might exchange papers for peer editing. After making
corrections and recopying, students should hand in
these drafts for final corrections before they type them.
Allow students to write the text neatly if they don't
have access to a typewriter or a word processor. Indicate
errors by using symbols (see Chapter 5, page 111E).

3. While you correct the rough drafts, have students prepare the illustrations for their book jackets. They might
   want to use magazine or catalogue pictures to create a
   collage, or cut out letters to spell the title and the
   author's name.

4. After students have corrected their rough draft, they
   should type or write it, cut it out, and paste it in the
   proper places on the book jacket. You might want to display the finished jackets in the library.

GRADING THE PROJECT

Students should be graded on the content of the summary,
the accuracy of the language, the variety of vocabulary
used, creativity and effort, and the overall appearance of
the project.

Suggested Point Distribution (total = 100 points)

Content	20 points
Language use	20 points
Variety of vocabulary	20 points
Creativity/effort	20 points
Overall appearance	20 points

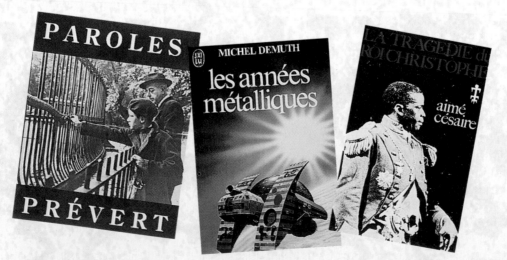

Chapitre 11 : Chacun ses goûts
♜ *Games*

FAIRE LA PAIRE

In this game, students will practice using relative pronouns.

Preparation The day before playing the game, have each student write three or four incomplete sentences about celebrities, musicians, books, or movies. The sentence starters should include the beginning of a relative clause. **(Mel Gibson est un acteur qui _____ .** *Thelma et Louise* **est un film que je _____ .)** Have students write the incomplete sentences on strips of paper. Collect and read them, choose some to use for the game, and put them in a box.

Procedure Have four contestants sit facing the class. The other students will be panelists. To play the game, a contestant draws an incomplete sentence from the box and reads it aloud. The contestant and all the panelists write the sentence starter and complete it as they wish. Then, the contestant reads aloud the complete sentence he or she wrote. Any panelist whose completed sentence matches the contestant's raises his or her hand. The contestant receives a point for every panelist's sentence that matches his or hers. Continue in this manner with the other three contestants. After several rounds, the contestant with the most points wins.

CHARADES

In this game, students will practice giving the French titles of movies, books, and songs.

Preparation
1. Write on separate index cards the French titles of several movies, books, and songs. (Songs: *An sèl zouk, Alouette, La vie en rose, La Marseillaise;* Books: *Daïren, Calvin et Hobbes, La cantatrice chauve, La leçon, Les années métalliques, Les misérables, Un amour de Swann, La belle histoire de Leuk-le-Lièvre;* Movies: *Notre-Dame de Paris, Au revoir les enfants, Le client, Trois hommes et un couffin, La belle et la bête, Cyrano de Bergerac, La rue Cases-Nègres, Le cercle des poètes disparus, Le grand bleu*)

2. Show a transparency of the entire list of movies, books, and songs that may appear in the game and have students repeat the titles after you before they begin to play the game.

3. Decide on a set of gestures to indicate the following clues: movie, book, song, number of words, short word, long word, first word, number of syllables, first syllable, and "sounds like." For example, to indicate that the title to be guessed is the title of a book, students might place their palms side by side, facing up.

Procedure To begin, have a student choose a card. The student tries to elicit each word in the title by using the gestures suggested above and any others. The other students try to guess the title, using French. Students may call out one word at a time, and the person giving the clues may indicate whether it's correct or incorrect. Ultimately, students must give the complete title in French, piecing together the correct words they've heard. The title does not have to be completely accurate, since students may not remember the exact wording, but it should be a close approximation. The person who guesses correctly gives the clues for the next title.

les films de science-fiction

les films d'amour

les films policiers

Star Trek®, terre inconnue

Carte verte

Le client

𝒰sing the Chapter Opener

Motivating Activity

Ask students to write down their favorite types of music (rock, country, rap), books, and movies (drama, horror, comedy). You might help them by writing categories on the board or on a transparency *(Movies: drama, science-fiction, romantic comedy).*

Photo Flash!

① A French movie theater typically displays large posters on its marquee. In this photo, the movies advertised are American films, which are very popular in France. Although the movie titles are sometimes in French, these movies could be showing either in **v.o. (version originale)** or in **v.f. (version française)** (see **Note Culturelle** on page 282).

Teaching Suggestion

Poll the class about their tastes in books, movies, and music. Then, ask students if they can guess the meaning of the title of the chapter, **Chacun ses goûts** *(To each his own).* If they can't guess the meaning, tell them that **goûts** is related to **déguster** (from Chapter 4) and means *tastes.* Then, ask them to try again. Ask students what they think Cédric is doing in Photo 3 and why? (He is demonstrating his personal preference for jazz.)

CHAPITRE

11
Chacun ses goûts

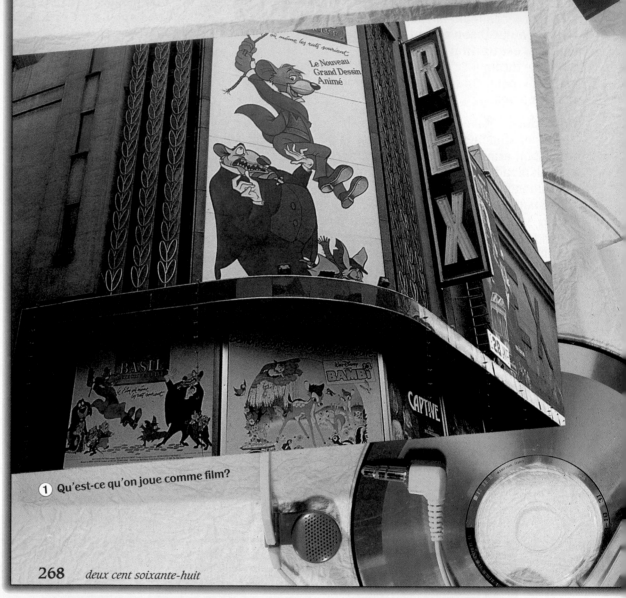

① Qu'est-ce qu'on joue comme film?

268 *deux cent soixante-huit*

Radio-Television-Film Link

During the Occupation and postwar era, French cinema focused on script and literary themes. During the postwar period of renewal, however, there emerged a new movement in film production called **la nouvelle vague,** or New Wave. The influential writings of Alexandre Astruc and André Bazin molded an entire generation of filmmakers. Astruc created the concept of the **caméra-stylo,** in which film became an audiovisual language, and the filmmaker, its writer. Bazin advocated rejecting mainstream cinematography in favor of hand-held cameras and elliptical or *invisible* editing. The New Wave was over by 1965, but certain directors of this movement continued to dominate French cinema well into the 1970s. French New Wave is one of few national movements that heavily influenced cinematic development world-wide.

What kind of music, movies, and books do you like? From rap to country, from action films to comedies, from poetry to spy novels, everyone has different tastes.

In this chapter you will learn

- to identify people and things
- to ask for and give information
- to give opinions; to summarize

And you will

- listen to people talk about the music that they like
- read book and movie reviews
- write a movie review
- find out about Minitel and music in francophone countries

② Tu connais Roch Voisine? C'est un chanteur canadien.

③ J'ai acheté un CD de Louis Armstrong. Il est génial!

Focusing on Outcomes

Have students describe each photo and replace the names in the captions with other names appropriate to their own interests. Then, have them read the chapter outcomes and match each one to a photo caption. NOTE: You may want to use the video to support the objectives. The self-check activities in **Que sais-je?** on page 292 help students assess their achievement of the objectives.

Photo Flash!

② Roch Voisine, a Canadian rock singer, is popular in France as well as in Canada.

③ In this photo, Cédric, Pascale, and Odile are at the **Place d'Albertas,** which is characteristic of eighteenth-century architecture. Aix-en-Provence is known for its many beautiful fountains, such as the one in the center of this square.

Architecture Link

Eighteenth-century architecture in France was characterized by the Baroque style, which emphasized movement and directionality and contrasted the static, defined shape of Renaissance architecture. Renaissance buildings were meant to be seen from all sides whereas Baroque buildings had a main viewpoint. Attention was generally focused on the entrance or the central pavilion.

Science Link

Point out the 3-D glasses on this page. To create the illusion of depth on a two-dimensional screen, two cameras are used to film the same scenes from two slightly different vantage points. Two projectors are used to project the film, each using a different polarized lens. The 3-D glasses have two different polarized lenses, thus only one of the projections reaches each eye.

Culture Note

Most French schools do not offer courses for learning to play a musical instrument. Students who wish to learn to play an instrument must take private lessons or classes at a club or community center. If a student has studied music before entering the **lycée,** he or she can choose a course of study that includes fine arts and musical instruction.

VIDEO PROGRAM
OR EXPANDED VIDEO
PROGRAM,
Videocassette 4
17:23–20:01

OR VIDEODISC PROGRAM,
VIDEODISC 6A

Search 1, Play To 4755

Video Synopsis

In this segment of the video, Cédric, Odile, and Pascale are talking about what to do during the **Fête de la musique** in Aix-en-Provence. A man who overhears them offers his copy of *Aix en musique,* a weekly guide to musical events. Pascale and Cédric are very enthusiastic about one of the groups listed, but Odile is not interested.

Motivating Activity

Ask students if they have ever been to a music festival or carnival. Did they go with a group of friends or family members? Did everyone want to do the same things? If students haven't been to a music festival, ask them to imagine what it would be like. Ask students what festival Pascale, Odile, and Cédric are talking about and what problem they have, judging from the photos.

Language Note

Call attention to the cobblestones on the ground where Cédric, Pascale, and Odile are standing in Photo 4. *Cobblestones* are called **des pavés,** *cobblestone streets* are **des rues pavées,** and *round cobblestones,* such as the ones pictured in the photos here, are called **des pavés ronds.**

Mise en train

Bientôt la Fête de la musique!

What kind of decision do you think Pascale, Cédric, and Odile are trying to make?

CHAPITRE 11   Chacun ses goûts

RESOURCES FOR MISE EN TRAIN
Textbook Audiocassette 6A/Audio CD 11
Practice and Activity Book, p. 121
Video Guide
    Video Program
    Expanded Video Program, Videocassette 4
Videodisc Guide
    Videodisc Program, Videodisc 6A

Language Note

Remind students why there is no accent on the entrance ticket that reads **ENTREE (entrée) POUR UNE PERSONNE.** (Accents are not obligatory on capital letters.)

Presentation

Have students view the video with their books closed. Afterwards, have them tell in French what they were able to understand about the story. Next, form four groups and have them read the **Mise en train.** Assign each group one of the following functions: 1) expressing your preference in music; 2) giving a favorable opinion; 3) giving an unfavorable opinion; and 4) telling about who is playing when and where. Have group members list the expressions they read that accomplish their assigned function and compile one list within their group. Finally, have a spokesperson from each group read the group's list to the class. Have the other students find and point to the expressions in **Bientôt la Fête de la musique!** as they hear them mentioned.

Group Work

Have groups of three write one-sentence captions for each of the photos, summarizing the action.

Thinking Critically

Drawing Inferences Ask students to infer from the conversation what *Aix en musique* is. Ask them what kind of information they would find in such a publication.

Culture Note

When traveling in France, you can find out what's going on in the town you're visiting by looking for entertainment guides at a **kiosk.** A **kiosk** is a newsstand that sells newspapers, magazines, and often postcards and candy, in addition to entertainment guides.

Video Integration

- **EXPANDED VIDEO PROGRAM,** *Videocassette 4*, 20:02–24:10
- **VIDEODISC PROGRAM,** *Videodisc 6A*

Search 4755, Play To 12195

You may choose to continue with **Bientôt la Fête de la musique! (suite)** or wait until later in the chapter. When the story continues, Pascale, Cédric, and Odile are still trying to decide which group to see, but they can't agree. They each make suggestions and give their opinions about the kind of music they like. A man appears, distributing programs for the festival, and Pascale, Cédric, and Odile ask him about the groups. They finally decide on a group to see. Next, we see them at the festival, listening to a group. Everyone seems satisfied!

Teaching Suggestions

2 Label four columns on the board **Cédric, Pascale, Odile,** and **le monsieur.** On separate strips of posterboard or construction paper, write the following sentences:

1. J'ai des courses à faire.
2. J'aimerais voir un concert de jazz.
3. J'ai envie d'aller voir un groupe de rock.
4. On pourrait voir l'Affaire Louis Trio.
5. Ce qui me plaît, c'est la musique classique.
6. Je n'aime pas tellement la musique rock.
7. Vous avez regardé *Aix en musique?*

Read aloud one sentence at a time and ask students which character in the **Mise en train** said it. Have a student tape the sentence to the board as his or her classmates suggest the correct column.

(*Answers:* 1. Cédric 2. Cédric 3. Pascale 4. Pascale 5. Odile 6. Odile 7. **le monsieur**)

3 Have students correct each false statement. You might have students work in pairs to write additional true-false statements based on the **Mise en train** and use them to quiz another pair of students.

Building on Previous Skills

4 Have partners suggest attending a certain concert and respond to the suggestion, using expressions they learned in Chapter 1: **Qu'est-ce qu'on fait? Si tu veux, on peut... ; On pourrait... ; Tu as envie de... ; Ça te dit de... ; D'accord. C'est une bonne idée. Je veux bien. Je ne peux pas. Ça ne me dit rien. Non, je préfère... ; Pas question!**

For videodisc application, see *Videodisc Guide.*

---

1 Tu as compris?

1. What event are the teenagers discussing? a music festival
2. What are they trying to decide? which type of musical group to see

They consult *Aix en musique.*

3. What do they do to help them decide?
4. What is the problem at the end of **Bientôt la Fête de la musique?** Odile doesn't like rock music, and she doesn't want to see l'Affaire Louis Trio.

2 Qu'est-ce qu'ils aiment comme musique?

Pascale
rock music

Odile
classical music

Cédric
jazz

3 Vrai ou faux?

1. Odile est libre pour la Fête de la musique. vrai
2. Pascale veut faire la fête sur le Cours Mirabeau. vrai
3. Cédric voudrait aller voir un groupe de blues. faux
4. Les jeunes achètent *Aix en musique.* faux
5. Ils décident d'aller voir l'Affaire Louis Trio. faux
6. Pascale n'est jamais contente. faux

4 Cherche les expressions

What do the people in **Bientôt la Fête de la musique!** say to . . .

1. make a suggestion?
2. emphasize what they like?
3. give unfavorable opinions?
4. give favorable opinions?
5. refuse a gift?
6. accept a gift?
7. express annoyance with someone?
See answers below.

NOTE CULTURELLE

La Fête de la musique is a world-renowned music festival that takes place on the first day of summer in France. Diverse performers share their music in the streets of every village and town. Spring and summer are the times for all sorts of festivals in every part of France. Probably the most famous festival of all is the Cannes Film Festival, where directors, producers, and stars from all over the world come to Cannes to show their new films and compete for awards.

5 Et maintenant, à toi

If you were helping these friends decide what to do, would you agree with Odile, Cédric, or Pascale, or would you make another suggestion?

Culture Note

The Cannes International Film Festival takes place every year for two weeks in May. It was held for the first time in 1939, but was interrupted by World War II and was not resumed until 1946. The **Palme d'or,** awarded at the festival, is one of the most important awards in the film industry. Another important award in the French film industry is the **César,** the equivalent of the American Oscar.

Answers

4 1. On pourrait faire...
2. Ce qui me plaît, moi, c'est la musique classique. J'adore!
3. Ça, c'est nul;... je n'aime pas tellement la musique rock; ... ça ne me dit rien.
4. C'est génial... ! Ça serait super! J'adore!
5. Mais, non. Il n'y a pas de raison.
6. C'est très gentil. Merci.
7. Oh, là là, ce que tu es pénible!

PREMIERE ETAPE

Identifying people and things

AIX - en - PROVENCE
Fête de la Musique
21 juin
Café Concert du Cours
Cours Mirabeau

17h - 18h30	**TRIO CLASSIQUE** Cantates de Bach
19h - 20h30	**Groupe MARACAS** Jazz Brésilien
21h - 22h30	**DIABOLO** Rock Blues

Toute la nuit
De nombreux autres groupes

Rap
Heavy Metal
Reggae
Zouk
Rock
Jazz
Funk
Soul
Blues

6 Tu as compris?

Quels genres de groupes est-ce qu'il y a? A quel concert est-ce que tu voudrais aller?
classical, jazz, rock, blues, rap, heavy metal, reggae, zouk, funk, soul

COMMENT DIT-ON... ?
Identifying people and things

To identify people and things:
Tu connais le groupe Maracas? *Are you familiar with . . . ?*
Bien sûr! C'est un groupe brésilien. *Of course! They are (He/She/It is) . . .*
Non, **je ne connais pas.** *I'm not familiar with them/him/her/it.*

RESOURCES FOR PREMIERE ETAPE

Textbook Audiocassette 6A/Audio CD 11
Practice and Activity Book, pp. 122–124
Video Guide
  Video Program
  Expanded Video Program, Videocassette 4
Videodisc Guide
  Videodisc Program, Videodisc 6A

Chapter Teaching Resources, Book 3
• Teaching Transparency Master 11-1, pp. 119, 122
  Teaching Transparency 11-1
• Additional Listening Activities 11-1, 11-2, p. 123
  Audiocassette 10B/Audio CD 11
• Realia 11-1, pp. 127, 129
• Situation Cards 11-1, pp. 130–131
• Student Response Forms, pp. 132–134
• Quiz 11-1, pp. 135–136
  Audiocassette 8B/Audio CD 11

Jump Start!

Distribute copies of the following scrambled conversation and have students rewrite it in a logical order.
— La musique classique? J'aime pas trop.
— Oh là là, ce que tu es pénible!
— Alors, qu'est-ce qu'on fait?
— Il y aura un concert de jazz au Parc des Thermes. Ça te dit d'y aller?
— Tiens, l'Affaire Louis Trio passe cet aprèm. C'est un groupe de rock.
— Qu'est-ce que tu veux faire aujourd'hui?
— Bof! Ça ne me dit rien. Je n'aime pas tellement le rock.
— Je n'aime pas tellement le jazz. Ce qui me plaît, c'est la musique classique.

MOTIVATE

Compile a list in English on the board or on a transparency of all the different types of music students can think of. Then, have them compare the list with the music in the program for the **Fête de la musique.**

TEACH

Presentation

Comment dit-on... ? Use the list that was suggested in the activity under Motivate to present these expressions. Have students suggest groups and musicians for each category of music in the list. Then, briefly explain the meaning of the verb **connaître** and ask students if they know the groups. (**Tu connais R.E.M.?**)

For videodisc application, see **Videodisc Guide.**

Teaching Suggestion

7 Play the recording a second time and have students write the names of the musicians in the word box in the order in which they occur in the recording. Afterwards, ask **Quand est-ce que Patrick Bruel passe en concert?**

Presentation

Note de grammaire Write the forms of the verb **connaître** and several subjects on the board or on a transparency in random order. Have students match the subjects with the verb forms. Then, ask students to make complete sentences, using the subjects and verbs and adding appropriate complements. You might have students ask one another if they are familiar with a place, a person, or a group, historical or contemporary.

Building on Previous Skills

8 If students don't know the teacher their partners mention, have them ask **Il/Elle est comment?** and have their partners describe the teacher. (**Il/Elle a les cheveux noirs. Il/Elle est de taille moyenne.**)

Presentation

Vocabulaire Gather pictures of singers and musicians from magazines, or have students bring them in. Show the pictures and identify the people in them. (**C'est Whitney Houston. C'est une chanteuse américaine.**) Write the titles of some songs on the board, such as *Alouette* and *This Land is Your Land* and identify them. (**C'est une chanson canadienne/ américaine.**)

---

7 Ecoute!

Romain and his friend Djé Djé, who is visiting from Côte d'Ivoire, are trying to decide which concert to go to during the **Fête de la musique.** Which singers and groups is Djé Djé familiar with?
Answers on p. 267C.

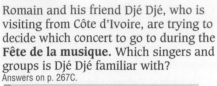

Patrick Bruel   Céline Dion
Zouk Machine   Vanessa Paradis

8 C'est qui?

Ecris le nom de trois de tes professeurs et demande à un(e) camarade s'il/elle les connaît. S'il/elle ne les connaît pas, explique-lui qui c'est.

—Tu connais M. Miller?
—Bien sûr! C'est un prof de maths. *ou* Non, c'est qui?
—C'est mon prof de maths.

Note de *Grammaire*

- **Connaître** is an irregular verb that means *to know, to be familiar with.*

Je conn**ais**
Tu conn**ais**
Il/Elle/On conn**aît** } la France.
Nous conn**aissons**
Vous conn**aissez**
Ils/Elles conn**aissent**

- The past participle of **connaître** is **connu.**

VOCABULAIRE

une chanteuse canadienne (un chanteur canadien)

un groupe antillais

une chanson américaine

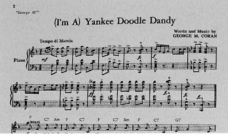

un musicien africain (une musicienne africaine)

Geography Link

Have students name songs and artists from several different countries or you might prepare a list in advance (Sade, Sting, Kassav', The Gipsy Kings, Céline Dion, *La vie en rose, An sèl zouk*). Mark all the countries on a world map with pins. Then, give students the French words for the nationalities represented. For additional countries, have students turn to the Supplementary Vocabulary on page 340.

Building on Previous Skills

Using the list of different countries and nationalities as suggested in the Geography Link, have students review adjective agreement as they identify each person or song listed. (*La vie en rose?* **C'est une chanson française.** Sting? **C'est un chanteur anglais.**)

9 C'est à qui?

Some of the performers for a benefit concert left their things backstage. What type of performer do the items belong to? See answers below.

1.

2.

3.

4.

—C'est à un musicien américain.

10 Tu les connais?

Tu connais les chanteurs, les groupes ou les chansons suivants? Identifie-les! See answers below.

1. Los Lobos
2. Zouk Machine
3. MC Solaar
4. *An sèl zouk*
5. Jean-Jacques Goldman
6. Céline Dion
7. *Alouette*
8. Whitney Houston
9. Savuka
10. Indochine

11 Qu'est-ce que tu voudrais écouter?

Complète la conversation entre Marc et Ali avec **c'est, il est** ou **elle est**.

MARC Dis, qu'est-ce que tu voudrais écouter comme musique? J'ai plein de CD!

ALI Euh... attends. Tu connais Jeanne Mas?

MARC Non, pas très bien. Qui c'est?

ALI ___1___ une chanteuse. Elle chante *En rouge et noir*.   C'est

MARC ___2___ française?   Elle est

ALI Non, je crois qu' ___3___ italienne.   elle est
En tout cas, c'est pas important.

MARC Tu connais Patricia Kaas?

ALI Mais bien sûr que je connais! Mais moi, je préfère Patrick Bruel. ___4___ un chanteur formidable et ___5___ acteur aussi!

MARC Oui, ___6___ super! J'ai son dernier CD. Tu veux l'écouter?   il est

4. C'est
5. il est

Note de *Grammaire*

- Notice that in French you can use **il est** or **c'est** to mean *he is,* and **elle est** or **c'est** to mean *she is,* depending on the situation.

- You can identify someone by profession or nationality using **il est/elle est** followed by a noun or adjective. In this case, you do not use an article before the noun:

  Roch Voisine **est** chanteur.
  Surya Bonaly? **Elle est** française.

- You can also begin with **c'est** followed by an article and a noun:

  Surya Bonaly? **C'est une Française.**

- Whenever you use <u>both</u> a noun and adjective, use **c'est.**

  Roch Voisine? **C'est un chanteur canadien.**

Presentation

Note de grammaire   Have the class name ten to fifteen celebrities and write their suggestions on the board. Then, have students choose five celebrities and write three sentences for each one, the first beginning with **Il/Elle est** to identify the celebrity's profession (**John Cleese? Il est acteur.**); the second with **C'est un(e)** to identify his or her nationality (**C'est un Anglais.**); and the third with **C'est un(e)**, combining the two previous sentences. (**C'est un acteur anglais.**)

Additional Practice

Gather pictures of celebrities from magazines and tape them to students' backs without their seeing them. Have students ask one another questions with **Il/Elle est** and **C'est un(e)** until they can identify the person taped to their back. (**C'est une femme? C'est une actrice? Elle est américaine?**) Students may only ask questions that can be answered with **Oui** or **Non.**

Teaching Suggestions

10 Have students ask their classmates if they know other musicians or songs. (**Tu connais Los Lobos, Simon?**)

11 Have partners do this activity and then practice the dialogue, substituting other musical artists.

For Individual Needs

11 Auditory Learners
Have students number a sheet of paper from 1–6. Read the dialogue aloud and whistle or ring a bell when you reach a numbered line. Have students write **c'est, il est,** or **elle est** to complete the dialogue.

Answers

9 1. C'est à un chanteur (une chanteuse) français(e).
 2. C'est à un musicien (une musicienne) africain(e).
 3. C'est à un groupe canadien.
 4. C'est à un chanteur (une chanteuse) antillais(e).

10 1. C'est un groupe américain.
 2. C'est un groupe antillais.
 3. C'est un chanteur français.
 4. C'est une chanson antillaise.
 5. C'est un chanteur français.
 6. C'est une chanteuse canadienne.
 7. C'est une chanson canadienne.
 8. C'est une chanteuse américaine.
 9. C'est un groupe africain.
 10. C'est un groupe français.

VOCABULAIRE

—Qu'est-ce qui te plaît comme musique?
—Ce qui me plaît, c'est...

la musique classique

le jazz

le rock

le rap

le blues

le country/le folk

le pop

le reggae

12 Ecoute!

Listen as Pascale asks her friends what music they like. What type(s) of music does each one like best? Answers on p. 267C.

13 Qu'est-ce qui vous plaît comme musique?

Comment est-ce que chaque personne répondrait à la question **Qu'est-ce qui vous plaît comme musique?**

Possible answers:

J'aime le country.

J'aime la musique classique.

Nous aimons le rock/la musique pop.

1.

2.

3.

14 Sondage

Demande à tes camarades ce qu'ils aiment comme musique. Quel genre de musique est le plus populaire? Le moins populaire?

15 Jeu

Draw a grid of nine squares, three across and three down. Write the name of one of your favorite groups, singers, musicians, or songs in each square. Find someone in your class who's familiar with one of the artists or songs in your grid. Have that person sign the appropriate box and write the type of music associated with the artist or song. The first person to get five different signatures that form an **X** or a **+** wins.

—Tu connais Bob Marley?
—Non. *ou* Oui, c'est un chanteur de reggae.
—Tu connais *The Dance*?
—Non. *ou* Oui, c'est une chanson de country.

16 Post-express

Write a response to one of the letters in **Post-Express**. Be sure to tell what types of music you like and don't like, which singers, groups, and musicians you listen to, and who each person is. Remember that French teenagers may not be familiar with the same music you are.

17 Bientôt la Fête de la musique!

With a friend, plan your own **Fête de la musique.** Make suggestions until you agree on several different groups to feature. You may want to mention specific songs or albums to support your suggestions.

Si tu as oublié making and responding to suggestions va à la page 209.

Tu te rappelles ?

You already know several expressions to emphasize your likes and dislikes:

Ce que j'aime bien, c'est...
Ce qui me plaît, c'est...
Ce que je préfère, c'est...
Ce que je n'aime pas, c'est...
Ce qui ne me plaît pas, c'est...

POST-EXPRESS

Tu cherches des amis, des disques, des posters? Cette rubrique est pour toi!

Recherche tout sur...

LE COUNTRY.
Je voudrais correspondre avec des F. de 13 à 15 ans. J'aime le country et je recherche des posters et des photos de musiciens et de chanteurs. J'aime aussi le rock et un peu le blues. Contre tout sur Roch Voisine, Vanessa Paradis et Paula Abdul.
Jérôme LEGER, 13 allée Paul Eluard, 44400 REZE.

LA MUSIQUE CLASSIQUE ET LE BLUES.
Je suis fan de Patrick Bruel et de Harry Connick Jr. Mais je recherche tout sur tout. Faites éclater ma boîte aux lettres! Réponse assurée à 100%! Florence PANIER, 200 rue de la Cité, 62370 SAINT FOLQUIN.

LE ROCK, LE POP.
Je m'appelle Damien. J'adore écrire, j'adore le sport, Elsa, le rock, et surtout les animaux, la nature... Je suis fan de Madonna et de toute la musique des U.S. Réponse assurée. A vos plumes!
Damien JARRE, 78 allée Bayard, 93190 LIVRY-GAGAN.

ASSESS

Quiz 11-1, *Chapter Teaching Resources, Book 3,* pp. 135–136

Assessment Items, Audiocassette 8B Audio CD 11

Performance Assessment

Have students pair off and imagine they are in a music store to buy a CD for a friend's birthday. The partners discuss three different CDs, mentioning where the artists are from and what type of music they play. The partners must finally decide what to buy for their friend, taking into account the friend's musical tastes. Have students perform the skits for the class.

Teaching Suggestion

14 When students finish their group poll, have them conduct a class poll. On the board, list the different types of music vertically, and the adverbs **beaucoup, un peu,** and **pas du tout,** horizontally. Have volunteers ask the class **Qui aime beaucoup la musique folk? Un peu? Pas du tout?** Have them count in French their classmates' raised hands and write the totals on the board. Afterwards, ask **Quel genre de musique est le plus populaire? Le moins populaire?**

Thinking Critically

16 Comparing and Contrasting Ask students what the teenagers who have written to **Post-Express** are looking for. What kind of magazine might this column have come from? Do American teen magazines feature this sort of column? If not, what kinds of columns do they feature?

Additional Practice

16 Ask questions about **Post-Express,** such as **Quel genre de musique est-ce que Jérôme aime? Qu'est-ce qu'il recherche? Quelle est l'adresse de Florence? Qu'est-ce que Damien aime faire?**

CLOSE

To close this **étape,** write on the board a numbered list of twenty musical groups or singers representing a variety of nationalities and types of music. On separate slips of paper, place the numbers 1–20 in a box. Have students draw a slip and tell whether they are familiar with the artist(s). If they are, they should identify the artist(s). If they aren't, they should draw again.

VIDEO PROGRAM
OR EXPANDED VIDEO
PROGRAM,
Videocassette 4
24:11–27:15

OR VIDEODISC PROGRAM,
Videodisc 6A

Search 12195, Play To 15870

Teacher Notes

- See *Video Guide, Videodisc Guide,* and *Practice and Activity Book* for activities related to the **Panorama Culturel.**
- Remind students that cultural material may be included in the Chapter Quizzes and Test.
- The interviewees' language represents informal, unrehearsed speech. Occasionally, edits have been made for clarification.

Motivating Activity

You might ask for volunteers to visit a music store, list as many nationalities as possible represented by the recordings in that store, and report back to class. Have students discuss music from different countries they are familiar with, telling whether they like it and why.

Presentation

Show the video and have students tell what they understood. Then, have students discuss the questions in **Qu'en penses-tu?** Finally, ask the **Questions** below to check for comprehension.

 Multicultural Link

Have students try to obtain a variety of recorded international music from the library, exchange students, acquaintances, or relatives.

PANORAMA CULTUREL

Marco • Québec

Flaure • Côte d'Ivoire

Catherine • Québec

We asked some francophone people what kind of music they like to listen to. Here's what they had to say.

Qu'est-ce que tu aimes comme musique?

«J'aime beaucoup le rock-n-roll. J'aime beaucoup les groupes comme U2, Duran [Duran], Bon Jovi. Maintenant, depuis quelques années, la musique française s'annonce beaucoup meilleure. On a maintenant de la bonne musique en français. Il y a de bons groupes qui sont sortis, comme Vilain Pingouin, mais la musique américaine est très populaire ici.»

—Marco

«La musique que j'aime, euh... J'aime à peu près toutes les musiques et puis, j'aime les musiques qui font danser, quoi.»

—Flaure

«J'ai bien des misères à classifier les sortes de musiques, mais je crois que j'aime le rock, le rock folk, le québécois. J'aime beaucoup de sortes de musiques.»

Qui est ton chanteur préféré?
«Mon chanteur préféré, j'en ai beaucoup. J'aime beaucoup Renaud mais j'aime aussi un groupe : Jethro Tull. J'aime Edie Brickell, Brenda Kane et des chanteurs des Etats-Unis, du Québec et de la France surtout.»

—Catherine

Qu'en penses-tu?

1. What kind of music do these people like? See answers below.
2. Which person shares your tastes in music?
3. What French musical artists have you heard?
4. Where can you go in your area to hear or buy music from foreign countries?

Questions

1. Quels sont les groupes préférés de Marco? (U2, Duran [Duran], Bon Jovi)
2. Quelle sorte de musique est-ce que Flaure aime? (toutes sortes de musique, surtout celles qui font danser)
3. Catherine préfère la musique qui vient de quels pays? (des Etats-Unis, du Québec, de la France)

Answers

1. Marco likes rock.
   Flaure likes all music, especially dance music.
   Catherine likes rock, folk-rock, and French-Canadian music.

DEUXIEME ETAPE

Asking for and giving information

DA ALADDIN. 1h30. Dessin animé américain en couleurs de John Musker, Ron Clements.
Au royaume d'Agrabah, un jeune homme débrouillard et effronté réussit à conquérir la jolie princesse grâce au tout-puissant Génie d'une lampe magique qui exauce pour lui trois souhaits. Des aventures extraordinaires et un festival de gags visuels et auditifs. 2 oscars 1993 : meilleure musique, meilleure chanson.
✦ **Club Gaumont Publicis Matignon 43 bis v.f.** ✦ **Denfert 82 v.f.** ✦ **Le Grand Pavois 94 v.f.** ✦ **Saint Lambert 96 v.f.**

PO LE FUGITIF. The fugitive. 2h10. Policier américain en couleurs de Andrew Davis avec Harrison Ford, Tommy Lee Jones, Jeroen Krabbé, Joe Pantoliano, Andreas Katsulas, Sela Ward.
Accusé à tort du meurtre de sa femme, condamné à mort, le docteur Richard Kimble réussit à s'enfuir et recherche -police aux trousses- l'assassin qu'il est seul à avoir vu... Inspiré de la célébrissime série télé avec David Janssen, un remake qui mêle habilement action, bravoure et suspense. ✦ **Le Grand Pavois 94 v.o.**

WS GERONIMO. An American legend. 1h55. Western américain en couleurs de Walter Hill avec Jason Patric, Wes Studi, Robert Duvall, Gene Hackman, Matt Damon.
En 1885, un seul guerrier, le célèbre chef apache Géronimo, tient tête à l'armée américaine qui veut parquer dans des réserves les dernières tribus indiennes. Toute la panoplie du western pour le portrait d'un rebelle devenu légende. ✦ **Saint Lambert 96 v.f.**

AV LES TROIS MOUSQUETAIRES. 1h45. Film d'aventures américain en couleurs de Stephen Herek avec Chris O'Donnell, Charlie Sheen, Kiefer Sutherland, Oliver Platt, Tim Curry, Rebecca de Mornay.
Arrivant de sa Gascogne natale, le jeune et fringant d'Artagnan rêve d'entrer dans la célèbre compagnie des mousquetaires du roi. Hélas ! Le fourbe Richelieu vient de la dissoudre... D'Artagnan, en compagnie d'Athos, Porthos et Aramis, saura néanmoins prouver son courage au cours d'une mission très périlleuse... Nouvelle version librement adaptée du roman d'Alexandre Dumas. ✦ **Le Grand Pavois 94 v.f.**

SF UNE BREVE HISTOIRE DU TEMPS. A brief history of time. 1992. 1h20. Film de science-fiction américain en couleurs de Errol Morris.
L'univers a-t-il eu un commencement? Le temps s'achèvera-t-il un jour ? Adapté du best-seller de Stephen Hawking, le réalisateur de «Dossier Adams» met en images des théories scientifiques au cours d'un voyage en compagnie d'un savant d'exception, que certains comparent à Einstein. ✦ **Denfert 82 v.o.**

DR UNE PURE FORMALITE. 1h45. Drame franco-italien en couleurs de Giuseppe Tornatore avec Gérard Depardieu, Roman Polanski, Sergio Rubini, Nicola Di Pinto.
Quelque part en Italie, dans un commissariat de police qui prend l'eau. Un commissaire féru de littérature, joue au chat et à la souris avec un écrivain célèbre, à qui il fait subir un interrogatoire. L'affrontement de deux grands acteurs pour un huis clos psychologique. ✦ **Le Saint-Germain-Des-Prés 36 v.o.** ✦ **Gaumont Les Halles 3** ✦ **Gaumont Opéra Impérial 7** ✦ **14 Juillet Hautefeuille 31** ✦ **Gaumont Ambassade 45** ✦ **La Bastille 71** ✦ **Escurial Panorama 77** ✦ **Gaumont Gobelins 78** ✦ **Gaumont Alésia 84** ✦ **Les 7 Parnassiens 90**

18 Si on allait au ciné?

Look at the movie listings and answer these questions.   See answers below.

1. What information is given in the first paragraph of every entry? How can you tell the type of film?
2. What information is given in the second paragraph of every entry?
3. What information is given at the end of each entry after the diamond symbol?
4. Which film(s) would you like to see or have you already seen?

DEUXIEME ETAPE   *deux cent soixante-dix-neuf* **279**

RESOURCES FOR DEUXIEME ETAPE

Textbook Audiocassette 6A/Audio CD 11
Practice and Activity Book, pp. 125–127
Videodisc Guide
  Videodisc Program, Videodisc 6A

Chapter Teaching Resources, Book 3
• Communicative Activity 11-1, pp. 115–116
• Teaching Transparency Master 11-2, pp. 120, 122
  Teaching Transparency 11-2
• Additional Listening Activities 11-3, 11-4, p. 124
  Audiocassette 10B/Audio CD 11
• Realia 11-2, pp. 128, 129
• Situation Cards 11-2, pp. 130–131
• Student Response Forms, pp. 132–134
• Quiz 11-2, pp. 137–138
  Audiocassette 8B/Audio CD 11

Jump Start!

Write the following paragraph on the board or on a transparency and have students complete the sentences with **Il est** or **C'est**.

  Tu connais le film *Madame Doubtfire*? _____, un film comique avec Robin Williams. Tu ne connais pas Robin Williams? _____ super, lui. _____ un acteur américain. _____ très drôle. Tu veux aller le voir? _____ un très bon film, je t'assure.

MOTIVATE

Have students list all the types of films they can think of (drama, comedy, horror, science-fiction, and so on). Ask which types of films they like and why. You might take a class poll to see which type is the most popular.

TEACH

Teaching Suggestion

Ask questions about the movie guide, such as the following: *Aladdin* a été fait en quelle année? (en 1993) Ça dure combien de temps? (1h30) Ce film a gagné combien d'Oscars? (deux) Dans quelles catégories? (musique et chanson) Ça passe dans combien de cinémas? (dans quatre cinémas) You might ask similar questions about the remaining movies in the guide.

Answers
18 1. type of film, title, year made, length, country of origin, color or black and white, director, principal actors; by the abbreviations in the black boxes before the title and in the description that follows
2. plot summary, description, any film prizes won
3. where the film is playing

DEUXIEME ETAPE   279

Presentation

Comment dit-on... ? Have students look at the movie listings on page 279. Then, ask questions about the films, using the expressions in **Comment dit-on... ?** Finally, distribute copies of movie listings from the newspaper and have partners ask each other about them, using the expressions in **Comment dit-on... ?**

For Individual Needs

19 Slower Pace Before playing the recording, read the suggested sentence completions with students. For each sentence, ask what the possible completions represent (1. movie titles; 2. actors; 3. movie theaters; 4. starting times). Then, ask them what information they will be listening for when they hear the conversation. (What is playing? Who is in a certain film? Where is it playing? What times are the feature presentations?)

20 Tactile/Visual Learners Have students write the sentences and questions on separate strips of paper, arrange them in logical order, and copy the dialogue on a sheet of paper before reading it aloud with a partner.

21 Challenge Have students choose a film from page 279 and give some information about it to a partner who will try to guess the title of the film.
— Ça dure 1h45. C'est avec Chris O'Donnell and Charlie Sheen.
— C'est *Les trois mousque-taires.*

COMMENT DIT-ON... ?
Asking for and giving information

To ask about films:
Qu'est-ce qu'on joue comme film?
What films are playing?
C'est avec qui?
Ça passe où?
Where is it playing?
Ça commence à quelle heure?

To respond:
On joue *Profil bas.*
. . . is showing.
C'est avec Patrick Bruel.
Ça passe au Gaumont.
It's playing at the . . .
A 18h30.

19 Ecoute!

Ecoute la conversation entre Béatrice et Fabien qui essaient de décider quel film aller voir. Puis, complète les phrases suivantes.

1. On joue...
   a. *Astérix chez les Bretons, Germinal, Jules et Jim.*
   b. *Astérix chez les Bretons, Le fugitif, Germinal.*
   c. *Astérix chez les Bretons, Profil bas, Germinal.*
2. *Germinal,* c'est avec...
   a. Patrick Bruel.
   b. Isabelle Adjani.
   c. Gérard Depardieu.
3. Ça passe au...
   a. Gaumont Gobelins, Gaumont Les Halles, 14 Juillet.
   b. Gaumont Les Halles, 14 Juillet, Gaumont Alésia.
   c. Gaumont Alésia, Gaumont Gobelins, UGC Georges V.
4. Ça commence à...
   a. 18h20 et à 20h50.
   b. 18h15 et à 19h50.
   c. 17h20 et à 20h30.

20 Méli-mélo! See answers below.

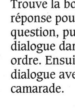

Trouve la bonne réponse pour chaque question, puis mets le dialogue dans le bon ordre. Ensuite, lis le dialogue avec un(e) camarade.

Ça passe où?
C'est avec qui?
Qu'est-ce qu'on joue comme film?
Ça commence à quelle heure?

Camille Claudel.
Euh... à 17h05 ou à 20h10.
Ça passe à l'UGC Triomphe et au Gaumont Opéra.
Gérard Depardieu et Isabelle Adjani.

21 Qu'est-ce qu'on joue comme film?

Choisis un des films de la page 279. Un(e) camarade va te demander quel film on joue, dans quels cinémas et qui sont les acteurs principaux. Ensuite, changez de rôles.

280   *deux cent quatre-vingts*   CHAPITRE 11   Chacun ses goûts

Possible answers
20 — Qu'est-ce qu'on joue comme film?
   — *Camille Claudel.*
   — C'est avec qui?
   — Gérard Depardieu et Isabelle Adjani.
   — Ça passe où?
   — Ça passe à l'UGC Triomphe et au Gaumont Opéra.
   — Ça commence à quelle heure?
   — Euh... à 17h05 ou à 20h10.

VOCABULAIRE

—Tu aimes quel **genre** de film?
—Moi, je préfère...

les westerns

les films comiques

les films d'horreur

Le train sifflera trois fois

Trois hommes et un couffin

Frankenstein

les films de science-fiction

les films d'amour

les films policiers

Star Trek ®, terre inconnue

Carte verte

Le client

les films classiques

les films d'aventures

les films d'action

La belle et la bête

Indiana Jones et la dernière croisade

Last action hero

DEUXIEME ETAPE

deux cent quatre-vingt-un **281**

CHAPITRE 11   DEUXIEME ETAPE   281

 Culture Note

In Paris, there are over 100 movie theaters and a choice of approximately 300 films to see every week. There are two main entertainment guides that feature movie listings: *Pariscope* and *L'Officiel des spectacles.* Movies are listed alphabetically, by genre, and by movie theater. There is also information about movie theaters outside of Paris in the suburbs (**en banlieue**). The guides also tell you which metro station is closest to the movie theater. In addition, these guides contain information about museum exhibitions, club happenings, cabaret shows, plays, sports activities, concerts, and much more.

Presentation

Vocabulaire Write the different film genres on the board. Photocopy and distribute the movie listings from a newspaper and ask which genre each film represents. (**C'est quel genre de film, ça?**) Write the titles of the movies under the appropriate categories as students suggest them. If a genre is not represented, ask students to name some films of that genre. Then, ask individuals **Tu aimes quel genre de film, toi?**

 For videodisc application, see *Videodisc Guide.*

Teaching Suggestion

Have partners ask each other about the films in the **Vocabulaire.** For each film, they should ask **Tu connais... ?** and **C'est avec qui?** Students might also identify the actors and actresses shown in the scenes here and give their nationalities. (**C'est Gary Cooper. C'est un acteur américain.**)

For Individual Needs

Challenge Ask students why they like a certain genre of film (**Pourquoi est-ce que tu aimes les films classiques?**) and have them answer in French.

Game

LES GENRES Form small groups and give each one a transparency. Then, call out a type of film (**les films comiques**). Groups have thirty seconds to list films of that genre. Call time and have each group count the number of films they listed. The group with the most films listed projects its transparency on the overhead.

For Individual Needs

22 Slower Pace Before you play the recording, give students the names of the films in the activity (see script on page 267C). Have students write them on a sheet of paper, and next to each one, its genre.

Teaching Suggestion

23 You might have students conduct a poll, using Activity 14 on page 277 as a model.

Building on Previous Skills

24 Encourage students to use the vocabulary they learned in the **Première étape** to identify the movies and actors in their discussions. (**Tu connais... ? Il est/Elle est... ; C'est un/C'est une...**)

Portfolio

24 Oral This activity is appropriate for students' oral portfolios. For portfolio suggestions, see *Assessment Guide,* page 24.

CLOSE

To close this **étape,** have students present the review they wrote for Activity 25 as if they were a TV film critic.

ASSESS

Quiz 11-2, *Chapter Teaching Resources, Book 3,* pp. 137–138

Assessment Items, Audiocassette 8B/Audio CD 11

Performance Assessment

Have students write and perform Activity 27 as a skit. They should discuss three different films, using the vocabulary and functional expressions from this **étape** to talk about when, where, and what types of films are showing.

---

22 Ecoute!

Ecoute Nadège et Emile qui essaient de décider quel film aller voir. Quels genres de films est-ce qu'Emile suggère?   Answers on p. 267C.

23 Le Hit-Parade

Fais une liste de tes dix films préférés. Ensuite, classe-les par genre. D'après ta liste, quel genre de films préfères-tu?

24 Ça te dit?

You're arranging a video night to show your favorite film. Invite several classmates to watch it with you. If they refuse or aren't familiar with the movie, tell them what kind of film it is and who's in it, and give them your opinion of it.

25 C'est toi, le critique

Ecris une critique de ton film préféré. N'oublie pas de préciser de quel genre de film il s'agit et qui sont le réalisateur *(director)* et les acteurs principaux, puis donne ton opinion sur le film.

26 Au Gaumont Alésia   See answers below.

a. Look at the first paragraph in the movie listings at the right. Find four types of information given.

b. Now look at the movie listings.
  1. How much is the full price for *L'enfant lion?* How much is the reduced price?
  2. Is *Aladdin* in French or in English?
  3. At the 2:00 P.M. showing of *Grosse fatigue,* what time does the feature film actually begin?
  4. Which of the movies listed here are French films?

27 Qu'est-ce qui passe au Gaumont?

Un(e) camarade et toi, vous avez envie de voir un film mercredi soir au Gaumont Alésia. Décidez ensemble quel film vous voulez voir et à quelle heure.

NOTE CULTURELLE

Before you go to the movies in France, check the local newspaper or movie guide. You'll notice that you can see many foreign films. Look for **v.o.** (**version originale**) to see a film in the original language with French subtitles, and **v.f.** (**version française**) to see a film dubbed in French. Look for ticket prices. Most theaters offer a discount (**tarif réduit**) for students and a lower ticket price for everyone on Mondays and/or Wednesdays. Check the time of the showing (**séance**), and be aware that there are 10–20 minutes of commercials before the movie actually starts.

---

84 GAUMONT ALESIA. 73, avenue du Général Leclerc. 43.27.84.50 36.65.75.14 M° Alésia. Perm de 14h à 24h. Pl : 43 et 42 F. Mer, tarif unique : 36 et 35 F ; Etud, CV : 36 et 35 F (Du Lun au Ven 18h) ; -12 ans : 30 F. Carte Gaumont : 5 places : 160 F (valables 2 mois, tlj à toutes les séances). Carte bleue acceptée. Rens : 3615 Gaumont. 1 salle équipée pour les malentendants.

L'incroyable voyage v.f. Dolby stéréo. Séances : 13h35, 15h45, 17h55, 20h05, 22h15. Film 10 mn après.

J'ai pas sommeil Dolby stéréo Séances : 13h35, 15h45, 17h55, 20h05, 22h15. Film 10 mn après.

L'enfant lion Dolby stéréo. (Pl : 48 et 37 F). Séances : 14h, 17h20, 21h. Film 25 mn après.

Aladdin v.f. Séances : Mer, Sam, Dim 13h25, 15h35. Film 15 mn après.

Une pure formalité Séances : Mer, Sam, Dim 17h50, 20h, 22h10 ; Jeu, Ven, Lun, Mar 13h30, 15h40, 17h50, 20h, 22h10. Film 15 mn après.

Le jardin secret v.f. Séances : 14h, 16h40, 19h20, 21h55. Film 20 mn après.

Madame Doubtfire v.f. Dolby stéréo. Séances : Mer, Sam, Dim 13h40, 15h30, 17h20. Film 20 mn après.

Les Aristochats v.f. Dolby stéréo Séances : Mer, Sam, Dim 19h15, 21h50. Jeu, Ven, Lun, Mar 13h55, 16h30, 19h15, 21h50. Film 15 mn après.

Salle Gaumontrama (Pl : 45 et 37 F):

Grosse fatigue Dolby stéréo. Séances : 14h, 16h, 18h, 20h, 22h. Film 20 mn après.

---

282 *deux cent quatre-vingt-deux*   CHAPITRE 11   Chacun ses goûts

---

Language Notes

- The **M** in the movie listing stands for **métro** and indicates the subway stop nearest the movie theater.
- **CV (Carte Vermeille)** is a senior-citizen discount card.
- **Tlj** means **tous les jours.**
- **Une carte bleue** is a debit card.
- **Les malentendants** are *the hard-of-hearing.*

Possible answers

26 a. address, phone number, métro stop, price, name of the theater

b. 1. 48 F; 37 F
   2. French
   3. 2:20
   4. *J'ai pas sommeil, La reine Margot, Une pure formalité, Grosse fatigue*

RENCONTRE CULTURELLE

Look at the Minitel screens below. What do you think Minitel is used for?

Qu'en penses-tu?

1. They provide information about movies, concerts, art expositions, museums, festivals, conferences, and other forms of entertainment.

1. What services are being offered on the Minitel screens above?

2. Are there similar information systems available in your area? What kinds of services are available through them?

Savais-tu que...?

Minitel is France's highly successful on-line information service. Subscribers gain access to Minitel from a computer terminal, and there is no installation fee for telephone subscribers. Numerous services are available. You can shop from your favorite catalogue, buy movie and concert tickets, make travel reservations, read magazine articles, or research colleges and technical schools. The most frequently used service is the electronic phone book, which allows you to look up any one of millions of subscribers.

Culture Note

One difference between **Minitel** and many American information systems is that the French customers don't need a modem or a computer to subscribe to the service. Small monitors that connect to the phone line are available for a modest fee, making Minitel easily accessible. As access to Internet becomes more widely available, students around the globe are able to gather information from anywhere in the world and to communicate with students in other countries. There are some excellent international services on Minitel for this purpose, such as **CGF (la classe globale francophone)**.

Jump Start!

Have students unscramble the following:
C'est avec qui?/*Le fugitif*/Ça passe où?/A 2h25 et à 5h10./Qu'est-ce qu'on joue comme film?/Aux Halles./Harrison Ford./Ça commence à quelle heure?

MOTIVATE

Ask students what makes a good book and what causes them to dislike a book.

TEACH

Presentation

Comment dit-on... ?
Gather several books. Label two columns on the board: *Favorable* and *Unfavorable*. Talk about a book, using the expressions in **Comment dit-on... ?** Write the book title in the appropriate column as you talk about it. Then, ask either-or questions about the books (*To Kill a Mockingbird*, **C'est un navet ou c'est une belle histoire?**), gesturing thumbs-up or thumbs-down. Next, on slips of paper, have students write the titles of their favorite and least favorite book and their opinions of these books, using the expressions in **Comment dit-on... ?** Collect the slips of paper and read them. (*Romeo and Juliette* **est une histoire passionnante.**) Ask students if they agree.

For videodisc application, see *Videodisc Guide*.

Answers

28 1. three; science fiction, comic strip, humorous/plays
2. absurdes, burlesque, dérisoire, comique
3. a battle in outer space
4. Calvin is dynamic, intrepid, intolerable. Hobbes is Calvin's sidekick: a stuffed tiger.

TROISIEME ETAPE

Giving opinions; summarizing

S. F.   **DAIREN**
Alain Paris (J'ai Lu).

S'appuyant sur des structures sociales très hiérarchisées, l'humanité du XVIIe millénaire pratique une politique galactique conquérante. Mais cette expansion musclée est freinée par la résistance des Zyis sur la planète Uyuni et par une légende, celle de la Terre mythique, qui prône l'entente entre toutes les races de l'univers. Daïren est un solide «Space Opera» relevé d'un zeste de mysticisme, qui a parfaitement assimilé les leçons de son glorieux modèle, la Guerre des étoiles.

Denis Guiot

B.D.   **CALVIN ET HOBBES**
Bill Waterson (Hachette)

Calvin, c'est le garçon dynamique, intrépide, insupportable. Hobbes, c'est son faire-valoir... un tigre en peluche! Waterson, un des plus célèbres dessinateurs de presse américain, utilise seulement deux à quatre images par gag. Un trait simple et nerveux, un humour sympathique. Voilà une B.D. bien agréable et une traduction excellente, puisqu'elle est due au scénariste Frank Reichert.

Yves Frémion

28   Tu as compris?   See answers below.

1. How many categories of books are presented? What are they?
2. Look at the review of *La leçon* and *La cantatrice chauve*. List the words that are used to describe the plot. How would you describe these works?
3. Scan the commentary on *Daïren* for cognates. What is this book about?
4. How does Yves Frémion describe the heroes of *Calvin et Hobbes*?

DECOUVRIR DES LIVRES POUR RIRE

LA LEÇON, LA CANTATRICE CHAUVE,
de Eugène Ionesco

Ionesco a composé la tragédie du langage. En rire majeur. Chez lui tout s'effondre : ses héros énoncent doctement des lieux communs éculés, entassent des axiomes absurdes dans leur conversation. Jusqu'au délire. De cette cacophonie burlesque naît l'image d'un monde en miettes, dérisoire et comique. (Folio.)

S.F.

COMMENT DIT-ON... ?
Giving opinions

Favorable:

C'est drôle/amusant. *It's funny.*
C'est une belle histoire.
It's a great story.
C'est plein de rebondissements.
It's full of plot twists.
Il y a du suspense. *It's suspenseful.*
On ne s'ennuie pas.
You're never bored.
C'est une histoire passionnante.
It's an exciting story.
Je te le/la recommande.
I recommend it.

Unfavorable:

C'est trop violent/long.
It's too violent/long.
C'est déprimant. *It's depressing.*
C'est bête. *It's stupid.*
C'est un navet. *It's a dud.*
C'est du n'importe quoi.
It's worthless.
Il n'y a pas d'histoire.
It has no plot.
C'est gentillet, sans plus.
It's cute (but that's all).
Ça casse pas des briques.
It's not earth-shattering.

284   *deux cent quatre-vingt-quatre*   CHAPITRE 11   Chacun ses goûts

---

RESOURCES FOR TROISIEME ETAPE

Textbook Audiocassette 6A/Audio CD 11
Practice and Activity Book, pp. 128–130
Videodisc Guide
    Videodisc Program, Videodisc 6A

Chapter Teaching Resources, Book 3
• Communicative Activity 11-2, pp. 117–118
• Teaching Transparency Master 11-3, pp. 121, 122
   Teaching Transparency 11-3
• Additional Listening Activities 11-5, 11-6, p. 125
   Audiocassette 10B/Audio CD 11
• Realia 11-2, pp. 128, 129
• Situation Cards 11-3, pp. 130–131
• Student Response Forms, pp. 132–134
• Quiz 11-3, pp. 139–140
   Audiocassette 8B/Audio CD 11

29 Ecoute!

Ecoute Luc et Perrine parler de *La cantatrice chauve*, *Daïren* et *Calvin et Hobbes*. Qu'est-ce que Luc aime? Et Perrine? Answers on p. 267D.

30 A mon avis

Fais une liste des trois derniers livres (ou pièces de théâtre) que tu as lus. Comment est-ce que tu les décrirais à un(e) ami(e)? Utilise les phrases du **Comment dit-on** à la page 284.

31 Ecoute!

Ecoute ces clients demander des livres au vendeur d'une librairie. Quel est le genre de chaque livre?

1. un roman de Simenon   c
2. *La reine Margot*   e
3. les œuvres de Rimbaud   d
4. *La Florentine*   b
5. les œuvres complètes de Tintin   a

    a. une B.D.
    b. un roman d'amour
    c. un polar
    d. un livre de poésie
    e. un classique

32 Une interview

Tu dois faire la critique d'un livre pour ton cours de français. Demande à un(e) camarade quel livre il/elle a lu récemment, de quel genre de livre il s'agit et son opinion sur ce livre.

—Qu'est-ce que tu as lu récemment?
—On a lu *Huckleberry Finn* pour le cours d'anglais.
—C'est quel genre de livre?
—C'est un classique.
—Tu as aimé?
—Oui, c'est une belle histoire et en plus, c'est très amusant.

VOCABULAIRE

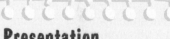

Ton livre préféré, c'est quel genre? C'est...

un roman policier (un polar)?

une autobiographie?

un roman d'amour?

un roman de science-fiction?

une bande dessinée (une B.D.)?

un livre de poésie?

un (roman) classique?

une pièce de théâtre?

Thinking Critically

Analyzing Ask students if they have ever seen a movie based on a book they've read. Ask which they generally prefer, the movie or the book, and why.

Culture Note

In francophone countries, as in the United States, comic books are not just for children. There are many **bandes dessinées** written for teenagers and adults. These comics often contain sophisticated humor and a complex story. It is not unusual for people to collect entire series of comic books; in fact, for some, it's a major hobby.

Teacher Note

Before presenting the **Vocabulaire**, do Activities 29 and 30. After the presentation, do Activities 31 and 32.

For Individual Needs

29 Kinesthetic Learners
Play the recording and have students signal thumbs-up when they hear a favorable opinion and thumbs down when they hear an unfavorable one. Then, play the recording a second time to complete the activity according to the directions.

Presentation

Vocabulaire Gather several books that fit the genres given in the **Vocabulaire**. Write the names of the different genres side-by-side across the board. Show each book, ask the students what kind of book it is (**C'est quel genre de livre?**), and place the book on the chalk ledge beneath the appropriate genre written on the board. Ask students if they have read the books, and if so, have them give their opinions of the books, using the expressions in **Comment dit-on... ?** on page 284.

For Individual Needs

31 Slower Pace Have students write the two lists of information in this activity side-by-side on a sheet of paper. As they listen to the recording, they should draw lines matching the books to the appropriate genres.

Teaching Suggestion

32 You might have volunteers present their conversations to the class as a skit in the form of a TV program that reviews books.

COMMENT DIT-ON… ?

Summarizing

To ask what something is about:
De quoi ça parle? *What's it about?*
Qu'est-ce que ça raconte? *What's the story?*

To tell what something's about:
Ça parle d'une femme qui devient actrice. *It's about . . .*
C'est l'histoire d'un chien qui cherche son père. *It's the story of . . .*

TROIS HOMMES ET UN COUFFIN   3
(FRANCE - 1985)
(couleurs)   1 h 40
Comédie de Coline Serreau
avec Roland Giraud, Michel Boujenah, André Dussollier

Jacques, Michel et Pierre sont des célibataires endurcis qui chérissent leur indépendance… jusqu'au jour où ils trouvent un bébé de six mois sur leur paillasson! Peu à peu, les trois hommes apprennent leur nouveau rôle de pères, pour le meilleur et pour le pire. Bientôt ils ne peuvent plus se passer de la petite Marie. Que feront-ils quand sa mère reviendra?

AU REVOIR LES ENFANTS   4
(FRANCE - 1987)
(couleurs)   1 h 42
Comédie dramatique de Louis Malle
avec Gaspard Manesse, Raphael Fejto

Pendant la Deuxième Guerre Mondiale, deux adolescents français se rencontrent et deviennent amis. Julien, le personnage principal, découvre l'absurdité du monde adulte à travers la triste histoire de son ami Jean qui est persécuté par les Allemands. Julien, enfant de bonne famille, et Jean, enfant prodige, vivent ensemble quelques aventures qu'on n'est pas près d'oublier.

NOTRE-DAME DE PARIS   2
(FRANCE-ITALIE - 1956)   **CINÉ CINÉMAS**
(couleurs)   1 h 40
Drame parisien de J. Delannoy d'après V. Hugo
avec G. Lollobrigida, A. Quinn, A. Cuny, R. Hirsch

C'est la fête des fous sur le parvis de Notre-Dame. Tout le monde y remarque Esmeralda, la danseuse gitane. Le capitaine Phœbus en tombe amoureux ainsi que Quasimodo, le bossu monstrueux qui habite la cathédrale. Mais le perfide Frollo a décidé d'enlever Esmeralda et est prêt à toutes les bassesses pour la conquérir.

L'ETERNEL RETOUR   1
(FRANCE - 1943)   **RTL**
(noir et blanc)   1 h 45
Drame de Jean Delannoy
avec J. Marais, M. Sologne, J. Murat, A. Rignault.

C'est le mythe de Tristan et Yseult revisité par Jean Delannoy, et par Jean Cocteau qui a signé le scénario. Les héros de la légende sont devenus Patrice et Nathalie, deux jeunes gens contemporains qui tombent amoureux l'un de l'autre sous l'effet d'un élixir magique qu'ils n'auraient jamais dû boire. Car Nathalie est mariée à l'oncle de Patrice.

33   De quoi ça parle?   See number placement above.

Lis les critiques des quatre films ci-dessus. Puis, lis les phrases suivantes et choisis le film qui correspond à chaque phrase.

1. C'est l'histoire de deux jeunes qui tombent amoureux.
2. Ce film parle de trois hommes qui tombent amoureux d'une danseuse gitane.
3. Ce film parle de trois hommes qui doivent s'occuper d'un bébé.
4. C'est l'histoire d'une amitié entre deux garçons.

When you summarize the plot of a book or movie, you use the present tense instead of the past tense, just as you do in English.
C'est l'histoire d'un jeune homme français qui veut être mousquetaire. Il va à Paris pour devenir mousquetaire du roi et en route, il prend part à trois duels.

Grammaire The relative pronouns qui and que

You can use clauses that begin with **qui** or **que** *(that, which, who, or whom)* to describe something or someone that's already been mentioned.

- **Qui** is the subject of a clause and is followed by a singular or plural verb, depending on the subject of the main clause that **qui** represents.

  C'est l'histoire d'un garçon **qui tombe** amoureux d'une fille.

  Ça parle de deux garçons **qui tombent** amoureux de la même fille.

- **Que (qu')** is the direct object of a clause. It's always followed by a subject and a verb.

  Il aime une fille **que sa mère déteste.**

  Le film **qu'elle a vu** était intéressant?

- When the **passé composé** follows **que**, the past participle always agrees with the noun **que** represents.

  La pièce que j'ai vue était amusante.

34 Qu'est-ce que tu as lu ce week-end?

Lisa read a good book this weekend, and she wrote about it for her French class. She could summarize her book even more smoothly by combining sentences, using **qui** or **que**. See if you can combine each group of sentences below into one sentence. You may have to add some words (like **mais** or **et**) or take away some words.   See answers below.

1. Ce week-end j'ai lu une B.D.
   J'ai adoré cette B.D.
2. C'est une des aventures de Tintin.
   Tintin est un personnage très connu en France.
3. C'est un reporter.
   Il vit des aventures pleines de suspense.
   Il voyage dans tous les pays du monde.
4. Il a deux très bons amis.
   Ils s'appellent Capitaine Haddock et Professeur Tournesol.
5. Dans cette histoire, Tintin découvre quelque chose.
   Le Professeur Tournesol a été kidnappé.
6. Tintin ne comprend pas bien pourquoi, mais il sait quelque chose.
   Le professeur travaillait sur un projet scientifique très important.
7. Tintin décide de partir à la recherche du Professeur Tournesol.
   Il a beaucoup d'estime pour son ami.
8. Lis cette bande dessinée si tu veux savoir la suite de cette aventure.
   Cette aventure, j'en suis sûre, te plaira beaucoup.

35 Devine!

Jot down a few sentences to summarize the last book you read. Then, give your group clues about the plot, the genre, and the characters. The person who correctly identifies the title takes the next turn.

36 Mon journal

Quel est le meilleur (ou le plus mauvais) livre que tu as lu? Résume l'histoire, décris les personnages principaux et explique pourquoi tu as aimé ou détesté ce livre.

TROISIEME ETAPE

deux cent quatre-vingt-sept **287**

Presentation

Grammaire Write two sentences on the board or on a transparency. Rewrite the sentences, joining them with **qui**. Do the same with two other sentences, joining them with **que**. Ask students what you did. Then, ask them why they think you used **qui** in one instance and **que** in the other. Point out that **qui** is used as the subject of a clause and is followed by a verb, and that **que** is the direct object of a clause. Finally, write other sentences, deleting the **qui** or **que**, and have students supply the relative pronouns. Point out that **qui** and **que** are used for both people and things.

Mon journal

36 For an additional journal entry suggestion for Chapter 11, see *Practice and Activity Book,* page 155.

CLOSE

To close this **étape**, write several well-known film and book titles on the board or on a transparency. Have students tell what kind of work it is, who the characters are, and what the plot is.

ASSESS

Quiz 11-3, *Chapter Teaching Resources, Book 3,* pp. 139–140

Assessment Items, Audiocassette 8B/Audio CD 11

Performance Assessment

Have students choose one film and one book and write a paragraph about each one. They should identify the genre, discuss the characters, and describe the plot.

Answers

34 1. Ce week-end, j'ai lu une B.D. que j'ai adorée.
2. C'est une des aventures de Tintin, qui est un personnage très connu en France.
3. C'est un reporter qui vit des aventures pleines de suspense et qui voyage dans tous les pays du monde.
4. Il a aussi deux très bons amis qui s'appellent Capitaine Haddock et Professeur Tournesol.
5. Dans cette histoire, Tintin découvre que le Professeur Tournesol a été kidnappé.

6. Tintin ne comprend pas bien pourquoi, mais il sait que le professeur travaillait sur un projet scientifique très important.
7. Tintin, qui a beaucoup d'estime pour son ami, décide de partir à la recherche du Professeur Tournesol.
8. Lis cette bande dessinée si tu veux savoir la suite de cette aventure qui, j'en suis sûre, te plaira beaucoup.

READING STRATEGY

Combining reading strategies

Teacher Note

For an additional reading, see *Practice and Activity Book,* page 131.

PREREADING

Motivating Activity

Ask students to name what they consider to be the most important, influential films in their lifetime and in the past. Have them give reasons for their selections.

READING
Activities A–E

Teaching Suggestions

•You might have students work in groups of three to find and discuss the answers to Activities A–E.

A. Have students research how the cinema was born in 1895. Have them also find out what the six other arts are if the cinema is considered to be the "seventh art."

Culture Note

France imports many more American films than the United States does French films. The French rarely produce high budget, high action films as Hollywood often does, so this may account for some of the appeal American films have for the French.

Cooperative Learning

B. You might have students work in groups of three to complete the exercise. Each student might be responsible for the information that follows one of the stars in each review.

LISONS!

o you enjoy the movies? **Le cinéma** is very popular in France.

> ### DE BONS CONSEILS
> Let's review some of the basic reading strategies you used in earlier chapters. In this reading, you will need to get oriented to the text, figure out its organization, and answer some questions to check your understanding of it.

A. Read the first and last sentences in the black box. What will the reading be about?
  1. special effects in films
  2. <u>some important films from the first 100 years of film-making</u>
  3. the history of filmmaking since 1895

B. Examine the organization of the text that deals with each of the eight films.
  1. What does the information following the first star tell you about the film?
     a. country of origin
     b. director
     c. date of film
     d. principal actors
     e. <u>all of the above</u>
  2. What do you find after the second star?
     a. a critique of the film
     b. <u>a summary of the plot</u>
     c. an interview with the star
  3. After the third star?
     a. <u>importance of the film in</u>

Le cinéma est né en 1895 : "le 7e art" s'apprête à fêter un siècle d'existence. En cent ans, que de progrès, que d'évolutions techniques, que de films ! Voici quelques-uns des films, qui, chacun à leur manière, ont marqué un tournant dans l'Histoire du cinéma.

6 FILMS QUI ONT FAIT DATE

2001, L'ODYSSEE DE L'ESPACE

★ Grande-Bretagne-Etats-Unis, 1968. De Stanley Kubrick. Avec Keir Dullea, Gary Lockwood.
★ Une tribu de singes découvre l'usage des armes. Quatre millions d'années plus tard, dans un vaisseau spatial, des hommes sont confrontés à l'ordinateur HAL.
★ Kubrick a réalisé une fable sur l'Homme face au progrès et à l'Univers. Ce film est aussi l'une des premières œuvres importantes en matière de science-fiction.

IL ETAIT UNE FOIS DANS L'OUEST

★ Italie, 1968. De Sergio Leone. Avec Henry Fonda, Charles Bronson.
★ Le film se passe dans l'Ouest américain, à la fin du siècle dernier. « Il était une fois dans l'Ouest est, sous le prétexte d'une histoire presque nulle, avec des personnages de convention, une tentative pour reconstruire l'Amérique de cette époque», explique le réalisateur italien Sergio Leone.
★ Jusqu'alors, les westerns étaient la chasse gardée des Américains. Sergio Leone renouvela complètement le genre, avec ce que l'on a appelé, le "western-spaghetti", une parodie du western classique. Avec des bons et des méchants. Mais sans réelle authenticité historique. Ce film, particulièrement célèbre pour la musique d'Ennio Morricone, fait partie d'une longue série, dont le premier, *Pour une poignée de dollars,* fut réalisé en 1964.

Radio-Television-Film Link

Most French films are not exported to the United States, but Hollywood will often remake a French film. Some examples of American remakes of French films are: *Cousins,* starring Ted Danson and Isabella Rossellini, from the French film *Cousin, Cousine; Three Men and a Baby,* with Ted Danson, Tom Selleck, and Steve Guttenberg, from *Trois hommes et un couffin (cradle); Paradise,* with Don Johnson and Melanie Griffith, from *Le grand chemin; Pure Luck,* starring Martin Short and Danny Glover, from *La chèvre; Sommersby* with Richard Gere and Jodie Foster, from *Le retour de Martin Guerre;* and *Nell,* starring Jodie Foster and Liam Neeson, from *L'enfant sauvage.*

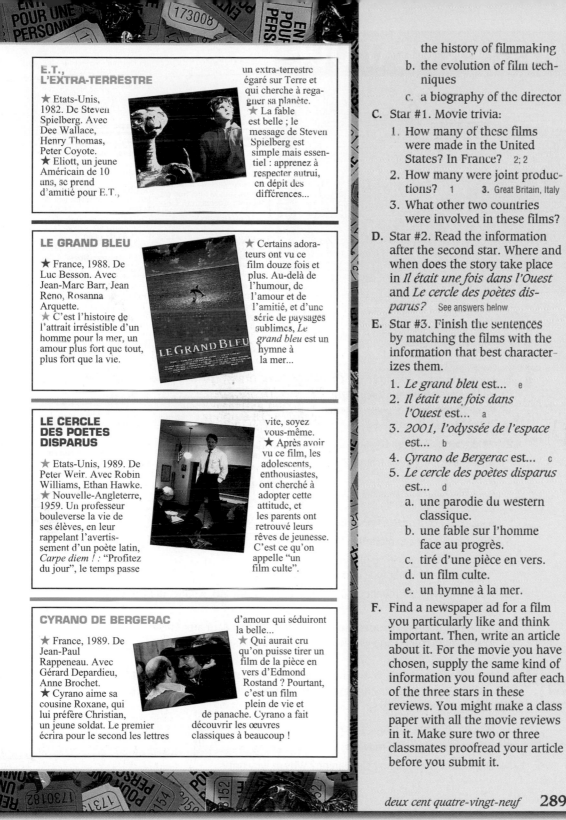

E.T., L'EXTRA-TERRESTRE

★ Etats-Unis, 1982. De Steven Spielberg. Avec Dee Wallace, Henry Thomas, Peter Coyote.
★ Eliott, un jeune Américain de 10 ans, se prend d'amitié pour E.T.,

un extra-terrestre égaré sur Terre et qui cherche à regagner sa planète.
★ La fable est belle ; le message de Steven Spielberg est simple mais essentiel : apprenez à respecter autrui, en dépit des différences...

LE GRAND BLEU

★ France, 1988. De Luc Besson. Avec Jean-Marc Barr, Jean Reno, Rosanna Arquette.
★ C'est l'histoire de l'attrait irrésistible d'un homme pour la mer, un amour plus fort que tout, plus fort que la vie.

★ Certains adorateurs ont vu ce film douze fois et plus. Au-delà de l'humour, de l'amour et de l'amitié, et d'une série de paysages sublimes, Le grand bleu est un hymne à la mer...

LE CERCLE DES POETES DISPARUS

★ Etats-Unis, 1989. De Peter Weir. Avec Robin Williams, Ethan Hawke.
★ Nouvelle-Angleterre, 1959. Un professeur bouleverse la vie de ses élèves, en leur rappelant l'avertissement d'un poète latin, Carpe diem ! : "Profitez du jour", le temps passe

vite, soyez vous-même.
★ Après avoir vu ce film, les adolescents, enthousiastes, ont cherché à adopter cette attitude, et les parents ont retrouvé leurs rêves de jeunesse. C'est ce qu'on appelle "un film culte".

CYRANO DE BERGERAC

★ France, 1989. De Jean-Paul Rappeneau. Avec Gérard Depardieu, Anne Brochet.
★ Cyrano aime sa cousine Roxane, qui lui préfère Christian, un jeune soldat. Le premier écrira pour le second les lettres

d'amour qui séduiront la belle...
★ Qui aurait cru qu'on puisse tirer un film de la pièce en vers d'Edmond Rostand ? Pourtant, c'est un film plein de vie et de panache. Cyrano a fait découvrir les œuvres classiques à beaucoup !

---

the history of filmmaking
  b. the evolution of film techniques
  c. a biography of the director

C. Star #1. Movie trivia:
  1. How many of these films were made in the United States? In France? 2; 2
  2. How many were joint productions? 1 **3.** Great Britain, Italy
  3. What other two countries were involved in these films?

D. Star #2. Read the information after the second star. Where and when does the story take place in *Il était une fois dans l'Ouest* and *Le cercle des poètes disparus?* See answers below

E. Star #3. Finish the sentences by matching the films with the information that best characterizes them.
  1. *Le grand bleu* est... e
  2. *Il était une fois dans l'Ouest* est... a
  3. *2001, l'odyssée de l'espace* est... b
  4. *Cyrano de Bergerac* est... c
  5. *Le cercle des poètes disparus* est... d
    a. une parodie du western classique.
    b. une fable sur l'homme face au progrès.
    c. tiré d'une pièce en vers.
    d. un film culte.
    e. un hymne à la mer.

F. Find a newspaper ad for a film you particularly like and think important. Then, write an article about it. For the movie you have chosen, supply the same kind of information you found after each of the three stars in these reviews. You might make a class paper with all the movie reviews in it. Make sure two or three classmates proofread your article before you submit it.

POSTREADING
Activity F

Thinking Critically

F. Analyzing Have students include in their article a justification of their opinion of the film they have chosen.

For Individual Needs

F. Slower Pace Have students limit the information that follows the second and third stars to one sentence.

F. Challenge Have pairs of students use the information in this activity to create and present a dialogue between film critics similar to the television program *At the Movies* with Siskel and Ebert.

Terms in Lisons!

Students might want to know the following vocabulary from the movie guides: *L'odyssée de l'espace:* **un singe** *(a monkey);* **un vaisseau spatial** *(a space ship);* **un œuvre** *(a work); Il était une fois dans l'Ouest:* **un siècle** *(a century);* **une tentative** *(an attempt);* **la chasse gardée** (literally *private hunting grounds*— here, *exclusive domain) E. T., L'extra-terrestre:* **égaré** *(lost);* **regagner** *(to get back to);* **autrui** *(others);* **en dépit de** *(in spite of); Le grand bleu:* **au-delà** *(beyond); Le cercle des poètes disparus;* **bouleverser** (figuratively, *to shake up);* **rappeler** *(to remind);* **l'avertissement** *(a warning); Cyrano de Bergerac:* **séduire** *(to seduce);* **Qui aurait cru... ?** *(Who would have believed . . . ?);* **une pièce en vers** *(a verse play);* **du panache** *(gallantry).*

Answers

D *Il était une fois dans l'Ouest:* in the western United States; at the end of the 19th century
Le cercle des poètes disparus: New England; in 1959

Culture Note

Students may have seen the comedy *Roxanne,* starring Steve Martin and Darryl Hannah. *Roxanne* is based on the French play *Cyrano de Bergerac* by Edmond Rostand (1897). *Roxanne* was released before the 1989 French film, *Cyrano de Bergerac,* with Gérard Depardieu and Anne Brochet. The stage production of the original *Cyrano de Bergerac* was popular in France long before the release of either movie.

MISE EN PRATIQUE

The **Mise en pratique** reviews and integrates all four skills and culture in preparation for the Chapter Test.

Teaching Suggestions

1 Ask the following questions about the **Guide de l'été:** Dans quelle ville est-ce qu'il y a un festival français de musique de films? (à Miramas) Quand est-ce qu'il y a de la danse à Aix-en-Provence? (du 14 au 28 juillet) Où est-ce qu'on peut voir de la danse en plein air? (à Carpentras) Quel est le numéro de téléphone du théâtre antique d'Orange? (90.51.89.58.)

1 You might have students do this activity with a partner. Have different pairs report to the class the answers they found for certain questions.

For Individual Needs

2 Challenge After students have listened to the recording and answered the activity questions, write the following questions on the board or on a transparency. Play the recording again and have students write their answers in French.

1. **En quelle année se passe ce film?** (dans les années trente)
2. **Qui a élevé José?** (sa grand-mère)
3. **Où est-ce que José travaille?** (dans les champs de canne à sucre)
4. **De quoi la grand-mère rêve-t-elle?** (d'une meilleure vie pour José)
5. **Qui est Monsieur Méduse?** (une sorte de père spirituel)
6. **Qu'est-ce qui arrive à Monsieur Méduse?** (Il finit par mourir dans les champs de canne à sucre.)
7. **Où est-ce que José fait ses études?** (à Fort-de-France)

Guide de l'été

Expositions
Concerts
Musees
Festivals

PROVENCE-CÔTE-D'AZUR

CINEMA

● **Miramas**

5 - 9 juillet
Festival français de musique de films. Projections de films et concerts de musique de films, sous la direction de Vladimir Cosma et Lalo Schiffrin.
℃ 91.42.18.18.

DANSE

● **Aix-en-Provence**

14 - 28 juillet
Aix en danse. Cours démonstrations, répétitions publiques, projets de rue et des spectacles assurés par nos jeunes chercheurs. Avec en prime : Alvin Ailey.
Espace Forbin, Cours Gambetta 13100 Aix-en-Provence.
℃ 42.63.06.75.

● **Avignon**

8 juillet - 2 août
Orientales. La danse moderne japonaise, Bill T. Jones et le ballet de l'opéra dansant Taylor, Robbins, Forsythe.
Divers lieux de la ville, 84000 Avignon.
34 ℃ 90.82.67.08.

● **Carpentras**

30 juillet
Ballet national de Marseille. Pour une seule soirée, Roland Petit propose une création sur une partition de Chabrier dont on célèbre le centième anniversaire de la mort.
Théâtre de plein air, place d'Inguimbert, 84200.
℃ 90.60.46.00.

● **Châteauvallon-Ollioules**

1er - 26 juillet
Trisha Brown, Caroline Carlson, plus un panorama de la nouvelle danse canadienne. Et le ballet de l'Opéra interprétant Tudor, Kylian, Mac Millan.
Théâtre national de la danse et de l'image, 83192.
℃ 94.24.11.76.

● **Orange**

20 et 24 août
Les grands classiques. *Le Lac des cygnes, Roméo et Juliette,* dansés avec ferveur par le ballet Kirov accompagné par son orchestre.
Théâtre antique, 84100.
℃ 90.51.89.58.

See answers below.

1 1. Look at these pages from the *Guide de l'été* on Provence-Côte d'Azur. What information is given for each event? Name four things.

2. Where would you go to see . . .
   a. a Canadian dance troupe?
   b. a Japanese dance?
   c. a Shakespeare play?
   d. the Kirov ballet?
   e. a concert of music from movies?

3. Which artists are exhibited in Provence in July?

4. Which musicians will be playing at Juan-les-Pins? What type of music do they play?

5. If you were in the Provence-Côte d'Azur area on July 26, what could you go to see?

6. If you had five days to spend in the Provence-Côte d'Azur area this summer, when would you go and which festivals would you see?

2 Listen as Martin and Janine, two radio film reviewers, give their opinions of *La rue Cases-Nègres,* which is playing at the **Festival français de musique de films.** Then, answer the questions. Answers on p. 267D.

1. Where does the film take place?
2. What happens in the movie?
3. Did Martin like the film? Did Janine? Why or why not?

CHAPITRE 11 Chacun ses goûts

Answers

1 1. *Possible answers:* city, date, description of event, artists involved, address, phone number

2. a. Châteauvallon-Ollioules
   b. Avignon
   c. Avignon
   d. Orange
   e. Miramas

3. Marc Chagall, Braque
4. Pat Metheny, Dee Dee Bridgewater, Gilberto Gil, Steve Grossman; jazz
5. Aix en danse, Orientales, Trisha Brown and Caroline Carlson, deux expositions de Marc Chagall, l'exposition de Braque, Festival international de jazz, Festival d'Avignon

EXPOSITIONS

● Nice

2 juillet - 30 octobre
**Marc Chagall, 1945-1985 :
les années méditerranéen-
nes.**
L'exposition est une
manière de saluer l'importance de la couleur dans
l'œuvre du maître.
*Musée national du mes-
sage biblique - Marc
Chagall. 36, avenue du
Docteur-Ménard, 06000
Nice.*
℡ **93.81.75.75.**

● Saint-Paul-de-Vence

2 juillet - 15 octobre
Braque : rétrospective.
Pour fêter son trentième
anniversaire, la Fondation
ne pouvait mieux choisir :
Braque, au travers de plus
de cent vingt œuvres.
*Fondation Maeght, 06570
Saint-Paul-de-Vence.*
℡ **93.32.81.63.**

● Vence

2 juillet - 30 octobre
**Marc Chagall, 1945-1985 :
les années méditerranéen-
nes.**

*Château de Villeneuve.
Fondation Émile Hugues.
3, place du Frêne, 06140
Vence.*
℡ **93.58.15.78.**

JAZZ

● Juan-les-Pins

19 - 27 juillet
**Festival international de jazz
d'Antibes-Juan-les-Pins.**
Pour sa trente-quatrième
édition, le célèbre festival
permettra de retrouver Pat
Metheny, Dee Dee
Bridgewater, Gilberto Gil,
Steve Grossman...
*Pinède Gould, 06160 Juan-
les-Pins.*
℡ **92.90.53.00.**

THEATRE

● Avignon

8 juillet - 1er août
Festival d'Avignon.
In ou off, c'est le roi des festivals, la fête totale du théâtre
avec ses beautés et ses
dérives. En officiel, on
pourra voir, entre autres,
l'*Andromaque* d'Euripide
monté par Jacques Lasalle et
le très remarquable *Henry VI*
de Shakespeare, que Start
Seide reprend ici après son
périple parisien.

PROVENCE-COTE-D'AZUR

35

3 a. Your group is in charge of
setting up an arts festival for
French teenagers visiting your
area this summer. Pick a
theme. Will you feature books
about your region? Your
favorite kind of music?
Adventure films? Plays by high
school students in your area?

b. Now make a list of what you'd
like to feature in your festival.
Then conduct a marketing poll
by asking other groups if
they're familiar with what
you've selected. If they're
familiar with something or
someone on your list, ask the
group's opinion. Keep track of
quotes you can use when you
advertise your festival.

4 Make a poster to advertise your
festival. Create a schedule like the
one for Provence-Côte d'Azur,
being sure to include the
performance dates, times, and
locations in town. Write a short
description of each event, and
decorate your poster with
magazine cutouts or art to make it
more appealing.

5 If you were in France, how could
you find information about
festivals going on in each area of
France? See answers below.

6 JEU DE ROLE

Make a radio or television advertisement about your festival to be
sent to France. Make sure you . . .
- give information about the events.
- identify the performers or features of your festival.
- use quotes that show how much people enjoy what you've
  chosen for your festival.

MISE EN PRATIQUE   *deux cent quatre-vingt-onze*   **291**

Possible answers
5 by logging onto **Minitel,** using guide books, or
looking in French newspapers

Language Note

Students might want to know the following
vocabulary words from the **Guide de l'été.**
Tell students that these words might change
meaning in another context: **une répétition**
(rehearsal); **assuré** *(presented);* **des chercheurs** *(students);* **en prime** *(in addition to);*
saluer *(to pay tribute to);* **des dérives**
(diversions); **un périple** *(trip).*

Teaching Suggestions

3 You might assign different
arts (books, movies, music,
films, plays) to different
groups.

4 Display the posters in a
prominent place in the school
to credit the creators of the
posters and to increase interest
in foreign language study.

◆ For Individual Needs

4 Slower Pace You might
want to give students the option
of working together in small
groups so that the requirements
of the project are broken down
into smaller tasks.

📁 Portfolio

4 Written This activity is
appropriate for students' written portfolios. For portfolio
suggestions, see *Assessment
Guide,* page 24.

📺 Video Wrap-Up

- *VIDEO PROGRAM*
- *EXPANDED VIDEO PROGRAM,*
  Videocassette 4, 17:23–29:12
- *VIDEODISC PROGRAM,*
  Videodisc 6A

At this time, you might want
to use the video resources for
additional review and enrich-
ment. See *Video Guide* or
Videodisc Guide for sugges-
tions regarding the following:
- **Bientôt la Fête de la
  musique!**
  (Dramatic episode)
- **Panorama Culturel**
  (Interviews)
- **Vidéoclips**
  (Authentic footage)

This page is intended to help students prepare for the test. It is a brief checklist of the major points covered in the chapter. The students should be reminded that this is only a checklist and does not necessarily include everything that will appear on the test.

For Individual Needs

Challenge Have pairs of students write and perform skits in which they include all of the information in **Que sais-je?** Have students imagine they are discussing what they are going to do for the evening. First, students will discuss going to concerts and talk about different singers, groups, and songs (#1 and #2). Then, they will discuss going to the movies and talk about the films that are playing (#3 and #4). Next, the partners will discuss going to a play and talk about plays, musicals, and plays based on novels (#5). Finally, students will interject opinions about certain films and books (#6 and #7) before agreeing on their plans. You might want to use this activity for oral assessment or as a chapter project.

Additional Practice

For additional listening, reading, and speaking practice, ask the following questions about the movie guide: **Quelle est l'adresse du cinéma?** (10, place Plumereau) **Combien coûte une place?** (38 francs) **Quels jours est-ce qu'il y a un tarif réduit?** (le mercredi et le lundi) **Combien coûte une place pour les moins de 26 ans?** (26 francs) *Aladdin* **est en version française ou en version originale?** (en version française) **A quelle heure commence la première séance pour** *Aladdin?* (à quinze heures trente) **Il y a combien de séances pour** *Les trois mousquetaires?* (quatre)

QUE SAIS-JE?

Can you use what you've learned in the chapter?

Can you identify people and things? p. 273

1 How would you ask a friend if she's familiar with your favorite singer? If she isn't, how would you identify the person?
Tu connais... ? C'est un/une...

2 How would you respond if someone asked you if you were familiar with . . . Bien sûr, c'est... ; Non, je ne connais pas.

1. *La vie en rose*?
2. Téléphone?
3. Jeanne Mas?
4. Kassav'?

Can you ask for and give information? p. 280

3 How would you ask a friend . . .
1. what movies are playing?
2. where a movie is playing?
3. who stars in a movie?
4. what time something starts?
See answers below.

4 According to this movie listing, how would you tell a friend what is playing tonight, where, and at what time?
See answers below.

Can you give opinions? p. 284

5 What's your opinion of . . .
1. the play, *Romeo and Juliet*?
2. romance novels?
3. westerns?
4. *To Kill a Mockingbird*?
5. classical music?
6. *La cantatrice chauve*?

6 What would you say about the last book you read that you liked? The last movie you saw that you didn't like?

Can you summarize? p. 286

7 How would you summarize the plot of . . .
1. your favorite film?
2. your favorite book?

> **LE PLUMEREAU** 10, place Plumereau. Pl : 38 F. Mer et Lun : 28 F ; -26 ans, 26 F. Séances sur réserv. Salle accessible aux handicapés.
>
> *Aladdin* v.f. 15h30 ; 17h30 ; 20h10
>
> *Beaucoup de bruit pour rien* v.o. Séances : 19h25 ; 21h40. Film 15 min après.
>
> *Les quatre cents coups* Dolby stéréo Séances : 14h15, 18h15, 21h25. Film 10 min après.
>
> *Les trois mousquetaires* v.f. Dolby stéréo. Séances : 14h ; 15h45 ; 18h30, 20h45. Film 15 min après.
>
> *Au revoir les enfants* Séances : 14h, 16h, 18h, 20h. Film 10 min après.

Answers
3 1. Qu'est-ce qu'on joue comme film?
2. Ça passe où?
3. C'est avec qui?
4. Ça commence à quelle heure?
4 *Possible answer:* Aladdin passe ce soir au Plumereau à quinze heures trente, à dix-sept heures trente et à vingt heures dix.

PREMIÈRE ÉTAPE

Identifying people and things

Tu connais... *Are you familiar with . . . ?*
Bien sûr. C'est... *Of course. They are (He/She/It is) . . .*
Je ne connais pas. *I'm not familiar with them/him/her/it.*

Music

une chanteuse (un chanteur) *singer*
un musicien (une musicienne) *musician*
un groupe *(music) group*
une chanson *song*
la musique classique *classical music*
le jazz *jazz*
le rock *rock*
le rap *rap*
le blues *blues*
le country/le folk *country/folk*
le pop *popular, mainstream music*
le reggae *reggae*

Adjectives

canadien(ne) *Canadian*
africain(e) *African*
antillais(e) *from the Antilles*
américain(e) *American*

DEUXIÈME ÉTAPE

Asking for and giving information

Qu'est-ce qu'on joue comme film? *What films are playing?*
On joue... *. . . is showing.*
Ça passe où? *Where is it playing?*
Ça passe à... *It's playing at . . .*
C'est avec qui? *Who's in it?*
C'est avec... *. . . is (are) in it.*

Ça commence à quelle heure? *What time does it start?*
A... *At . . .*

Types of films

un genre *a type (of film, literature, or music)*
un western *western*
un film comique *comedy*
un film d'horreur *horror movie*
un film de science-fiction *science-fiction movie*
un film d'amour *romantic movie*
un film policier *detective or mystery movie*
un film classique *classic movie*
un film d'aventures *adventure movie*
un film d'action *action movie*

TROISIÈME ÉTAPE

Giving opinions

C'est drôle/amusant. *It's funny.*
C'est une belle histoire. *It's a great story.*
C'est plein de rebondissements. *It's full of plot twists.*
Il y a du suspense. *It's suspenseful.*
On ne s'ennuie pas. *You're never bored.*
C'est une histoire passionnante. *It's an exciting story.*
Je te le/la recommande. *I recommend it.*
Il n'y a pas d'histoire. *It has no plot.*

Ça casse pas des briques. *It's not earth-shattering.*
C'est... *It's . . .*
   trop violent *too violent*
   trop long *too long*
   bête *stupid*
   un navet *a dud*
   du n'importe quoi *worthless*
   gentillet, sans plus *cute (but that's all)*
   déprimant *depressing*

Summarizing

De quoi ça parle? *What's it about?*
Qu'est-ce que ça raconte? *What's the story?*

Ça parle de... *It's about . . .*
C'est l'histoire de... *It's the story of . . .*

Types of books

un roman policier (un polar) *detective or mystery novel*
une (auto)biographie *(auto)biography*
une bande dessinée (une B.D.) *comic book*
un livre de poésie *book of poetry*
un roman d'amour *romance novel*
un roman de science-fiction *science-fiction novel*
un (roman) classique *classic*
une pièce de théâtre *play*

VOCABULAIRE
deux cent quatre-vingt-treize **293**

CHAPTER 11 ASSESSMENT

CHAPTER TEST
• *Chapter Teaching Resources, Book 3* pp. 141–146
• *Assessment Guide,* Speaking Test, p. 33
• *Assessment Items, Audiocassette 8B Audio CD 11*

TEST GENERATOR, CHAPTER 11

ALTERNATIVE ASSESSMENT
Performance Assessment
You might want to use the **Jeu de rôle** (p. 291) as a cumulative performance assessment activity.

Portfolio Assessment
• **Written: Mise en pratique,** Activity 4, *Pupil's Edition,* p. 291
   Assessment Guide, p. 24
• **Oral:** Activity 24, *Pupil's Edition,* p. 282
   Assessment Guide, p. 24

For Individual Needs

Tactile/Visual Learners Have students work in groups of six with two members working on the vocabulary of each **étape.** Students should write each vocabulary expression from their **étape** on separate index cards. For each card, they should prepare another card bearing a word, a name, or an expression that is associated with it. For example, in the **Première étape,** they might write **le rap** on one card and **MC Solaar** on another. In the **Deuxième étape,** have students also match questions (**Ça passe où?**) to answers (**Au Gaumont**). In the **Troisième étape,** students might name a type of film or book (**les films d'Alfred Hitchcock**) to fit the description. (**Il y a du suspense.**) Then, students shuffle the cards, exchange them with another group, and match the new cards they've been given.

Allez, viens au Québec!

pp. 294–323

EXPANDED VIDEO PROGRAM,
Videocassette 4
29:41–32:25

OR *VIDEODISC PROGRAM,*
Videodisc 6B

Search 1, Play To 4855

Motivating Activity

Have students share what they already know about Canada and the province of **Québec.** Have them suggest what the **Québécois** might do for fun and how they might travel through the province, especially during the winter. Then, have them compare their impressions with the photos on pages 294–297.

Background Information

The province of **Québec,** originally **la Nouvelle-France,** is the largest province in Canada. Explored first by Jacques Cartier in 1534, Quebec was later settled by fur traders, missionaries, and soldiers. Many towns in the province were originally fur trading posts, but as commerce developed and the demand for furs dropped, wood products gained prominence. More recently, mineral and hydroelectric resources have been exploited. The Québécois people and culture have been influenced by a variety of factors, including contact with the Amerindian population, the harsh winter climate, proximity to the St. Lawrence River and the sea, and their isolation as a French-speaking province.

CHAPITRE 12

Allez, viens au Québec!

Le mont Sainte-Anne

Geography Link

Le parc du mont Sainte-Anne, located 40 kilometers east of Quebec, was created in 1969 as a recreational area for the city. At the top of **le mont Sainte-Anne,** which is 320 meters high, there is a statue of Saint Anne, the mother of the Virgin Mary. The mountain offers excellent skiing and is even lit for nighttime skiing. From the summit, one can see the entire coastline along the baie de Percé (part of the Gulf of St. Lawrence), which includes the **Rocher Percé,** a large rock made of limestone. It is one of Canada's most famous natural phenomena.

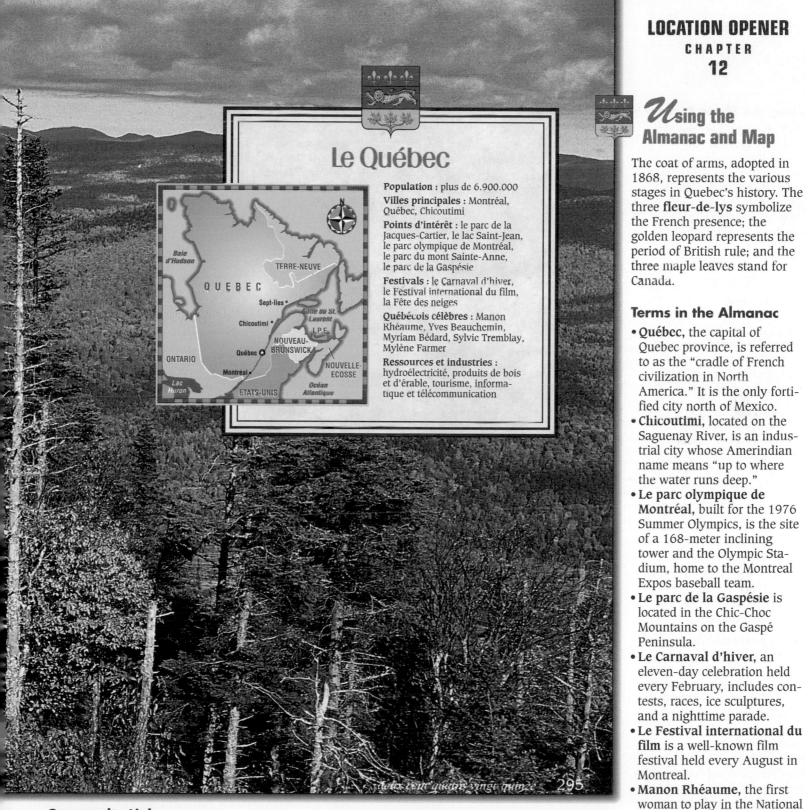

Le Québec

Population : plus de 6.900.000

Villes principales : Montréal, Québec, Chicoutimi

Points d'intérêt : le parc de la Jacques-Cartier, le lac Saint-Jean, le parc olympique de Montréal, le parc du mont Sainte-Anne, le parc de la Gaspésie

Festivals : le Carnaval d'hiver, le Festival international du film, la Fête des neiges

Québécois célèbres : Manon Rhéaume, Yves Beauchemin, Myriam Bédard, Sylvie Tremblay, Mylène Farmer

Ressources et industries : hydroélectricité, produits de bois et d'érable, tourisme, informatique et télécommunication

deux cent quatre-vingt-quinze 295

Geography Link

Le lac Saint-Jean serves as a basin into which all the area rivers flow, except the Saguenay, which is the only river that drains water from the lake.

Science Link

The Olympic **Vélodrome** has been converted into a **Biodôme,** which recreates four distinct North American ecosystems: a tropical rain forest, a polar habitat, the St. Lawrence River, and the Laurentian Forest.

Language Notes

- The name *Tremblay* in Quebec is a very common family name, similar to *Smith* in the United States.
- Much of the French engineering terminology related to hydroelectric power has been developed by the Québécois and is now used in France.

Using the Almanac and Map

The coat of arms, adopted in 1868, represents the various stages in Quebec's history. The three **fleur-de-lys** symbolize the French presence; the golden leopard represents the period of British rule; and the three maple leaves stand for Canada.

Terms in the Almanac

- **Québec,** the capital of Quebec province, is referred to as the "cradle of French civilization in North America." It is the only fortified city north of Mexico.
- **Chicoutimi,** located on the Saguenay River, is an industrial city whose Amerindian name means "up to where the water runs deep."
- **Le parc olympique de Montréal,** built for the 1976 Summer Olympics, is the site of a 168-meter inclining tower and the Olympic Stadium, home to the Montreal Expos baseball team.
- **Le parc de la Gaspésie** is located in the Chic-Choc Mountains on the Gaspé Peninsula.
- **Le Carnaval d'hiver,** an eleven-day celebration held every February, includes contests, races, ice sculptures, and a nighttime parade.
- **Le Festival international du film** is a well-known film festival held every August in Montreal.
- **Manon Rhéaume,** the first woman to play in the National Hockey League, was the goalie for the Tampa Bay Lightning.
- **Yves Beauchemin** is a Québécois novelist.
- **Myriam Bédard** is an Olympic gold-medal skier.
- **Sylvie Tremblay** and **Mylène Farmer** are popular Québécoise singers.

Using the Photo Essay

① **Vieux-Québec,** the old section of Quebec City, is known for its narrow streets and quaint cafés. The horse-drawn carriages (**calèches**), generally found in the Place d'Armes, provide a relaxing, informative tour of the city.

② **La rivière Saguenay,** which empties out of **le lac Saint-Jean,** is 155 kilometers long and navigable by ocean-going vessels to Chicoutimi. It has an average depth of 240 meters. **Le fjord Saguenay,** the world's southernmost fjord, and one of the longest, was made by glaciers.

③ **Les Laurentides,** among the world's oldest mountains, extend along the north side of the St. Lawrence from the Ottawa River to the Saguenay River. They are sprinkled with clear blue lakes, hills for skiing, and vast forests. This large region, which is accessible from both Montreal and Quebec City, is known as one of North America's largest ski areas. There are also opportunities for water sports, golf, tennis, and hiking.

④ **La péninsule de Gaspé** is where the explorer Jacques Cartier first landed. Because the peninsula's interior was so rugged, most of the inhabitants lived in small fishing villages scattered around the coast, and they were quite isolated from one another. Several English-speaking communities were established on the peninsula's south shore along the baie des Chaleurs.

Le Québec

La province du Québec a un statut très indépendant. Trois fois plus grande que la France, elle compte pourtant moins de huit millions d'habitants. La langue officielle est le français, mais pour le commerce, la plupart des Québécois doivent aussi parler anglais. Montréal est la ville qui a le plus grand nombre d'habitants bilingues du monde. Pourquoi est-ce qu'on parle français au Québec? Parce que ce sont les Français qui l'ont fondé. Jacques Cartier a exploré le fleuve Saint-Laurent en 1534 et Samuel de Champlain a fondé La Nouvelle-France en 1608.

① On peut visiter le Vieux-Québec dans une calèche traditionnelle.

② Les hautes falaises qui bordent la très large **rivière Saguenay** lui donnent un aspect de fjord norvégien.

③ On trouve la plus grande concentration de stations de ski d'Amérique du nord dans **les Laurentides.**

④ **La péninsule de Gaspé** est l'une des plus anciennes régions touristiques du Québec, avec ses forêts et sa belle côte sauvage.

Geography Links

② Beluga whales come to feed where the Saguenay's warmer river water empties into the colder waters of the St. Lawrence.

④ **La péninsule de Gaspé,** bounded by the St. Lawrence River and the baie des Chaleurs, is approximately 550 kilometers long and sparsely populated. The peninsula has two popular parks: the mountainous parc de la Gaspésie, and the parc national de Forillon, with its well-traveled hiking paths and abundant wildlife.

④ The **baie des Chaleurs** is a sheltered inlet that separates the Gaspé Peninsula from New Brunswick. As its name implies, the bay has relatively warm waters.

⑤ **Au bord du Saint-Laurent, Montréal** est la plus grande ville du Québec.

⑥ Au nord de la ville de Québec, **le parc de la Jacques-Cartier** offre une grande variété d'activités en pleine réserve naturelle.

⑦ **Les Inuits** sont un des peuples indigènes du Québec.

deux cent quatre-vingt-dix-sept 297

⑤ **Montréal**, Canada's second largest metropolitan area, is a multicultural island city. Despite the fact that Montreal is the largest French-speaking city outside of Paris, the majority of Montrealers speak both French and English, unlike the inhabitants of Quebec City, who are predominantly French-speakers. Montreal's flag reflects the city's cosmopolitan nature. The English rose, the Irish shamrock, the Scottish thistle, and the French **fleur-de-lys** each occupy a quarter of the flag. They are symbols of the four countries that influenced Montreal's development during the nineteenth century.

⑥ **Le parc de la Jacques-Cartier** is a paradise for sports enthusiasts. They can go down the river in rafts or kayaks, hike in the summer, and ski in the winter. The park is located in the highest part of the Laurentides and is one of 16 major parks in Quebec. It was begun by conservationists in order to protect the area from hydroelectric development. Naturalists regularly lead canoe trips, teaching visitors how the Montaignais Amerindians (part of the larger Algonquin community) traveled the rivière Jacques-Cartier.

⑦ **Les Inuits,** native Arctic inhabitants, were thought to be Asian hunters who migrated across the Bering Strait thousands of years ago. They are known as whale hunters, who developed the igloo for winter housing and live in tents made of hides in warmer weather.

Thinking Critically

Observing Ask students to look at the photos for examples of both ancient traditions and modern innovations.

Geography Link

⑤ **Montréal**, located downstream from where the rivière des Outaouais empties into the St. Lawrence, is truly surrounded by water. The St. Lawrence passes on the south side, and the rivière des Prairies separates it from Laval, a Montreal suburb. Laval is itself an island bounded by the rivière des Mille Iles on the north.

History Link

⑤ **Montréal** was known as **Hochelaga** by the Amerindians. **Ville-Marie de Montréal** was founded on an island in the St. Lawrence in 1642 and was settled by fur traders. Its later phenomenal growth was due to the development of the lumber and paper industries after fur trading declined. Montreal was occupied by Americans during the American Revolution, but after they failed to inspire the local people to revolt against the British, they withdrew.

Chapitre 12 : A la belle étoile
Chapter Overview

Mise en train pp. 300–302	Promenons-nous dans les bois	Practice and Activity Book, p. 133	Video Guide OR Videodisc Guide

	FUNCTIONS	GRAMMAR	CULTURE	RE-ENTRY
Première étape pp. 303–307	*Review* Asking for and giving information; giving directions, p. 304		**Note Culturelle, Le parc de la Jacques-Cartier,** p. 304	Pointing out where things are
Deuxième étape pp. 308–313	*Review* • Complaining; expressing discouragement and offering encouragement, p. 310 • Asking for and giving advice, p. 312	The verb **emporter,** p. 310	• Realia: **Bienvenue dans le parc de la Jacques-Cartier,** p. 311 • **Note Culturelle,** Ecology in Canada, p. 312 • **Panorama Culturel,** Endangered animals, p. 313	Clothing vocabulary
Troisième étape pp. 314–317	*Review* Relating a series of events; describing people and places, p. 314	The **passé composé** versus the **imparfait,** p. 315	**Rencontre Culturelle,** French-Canadian expressions, p. 317	

Lisons! pp. 318–319	A French travel brochure about trips to Canada	**Reading Strategy:** Summarizing

Review pp. 320–323	**Mise en pratique,** pp. 320–321	**Que sais-je?** p. 322	**Vocabulaire,** p. 323

Assessment Options	**Etape Quizzes** • *Chapter Teaching Resources, Book 3* **Première étape,** Quiz 12-1, pp. 191–192 **Deuxième étape,** Quiz 12-2, pp. 193–194 **Troisième étape,** Quiz 12-3, pp. 195–196 • *Assessment Items, Audiocassette 8B/Audio CD 12*	**Chapter Test** • *Chapter Teaching Resources, Book 3,* pp. 197–202 • *Assessment Guide, Speaking Test,* p. 33 • *Assessment Items, Audiocassette 8B/Audio CD 12* **Test Generator, Chapter 12**

Video Program OR Expanded Video Program, Videocassette 4 · Textbook Audiocassette 6B/Audio CD 12
OR Videodisc Program, Videodisc 6B

RESOURCES: Print	RESOURCES: Audiovisual

Textbook Audiocassette 6B/Audio CD 12

Practice and Activity Book, pp. 134–136
Chapter Teaching Resources, Book 3
• Teaching Transparency Master 12-1, pp. 175, 178 . . . . Teaching Transparency 12-1
• Additional Listening Activities 12-1, 12-2, p. 179 . . . . Additional Listening Activities, Audiocassette 10B/Audio CD 12
• Realia 12-1, pp. 183, 185
• Situation Cards 12-1, pp. 186–187
• Student Response Forms, pp. 188–190
• Quiz 12-1, pp. 191–192 . . . . Assessment Items, Audiocassette 8B/Audio CD 12
Videodisc Guide . . . . Videodisc Program, Videodisc 6B

Textbook Audiocassette 6B/Audio CD 12

Practice and Activity Book, pp. 137–139
Chapter Teaching Resources, Book 3
• Communicative Activity 12-1, pp. 171–172
• Teaching Transparency Master 12-2, pp. 176, 178 . . . . Teaching Transparency 12-2
• Additional Listening Activities 12-3, 12-4, p. 180 . . . . Additional Listening Activities, Audiocassette 10B/Audio CD 12
• Realia 12-2, pp. 184, 185
• Situation Cards 12-2, pp. 186–187
• Student Response Forms, pp. 188–190
• Quiz 12-2, pp. 193–194 . . . . Assessment Items, Audiocassette 8B/Audio CD 12
Video Guide . . . . Video Program OR Expanded Video Program, Videocassette 4
Videodisc Guide . . . . Videodisc Program, Videodisc 6B

Textbook Audiocassette 6B/Audio CD 12

Practice and Activity Book, pp. 140–142
Chapter Teaching Resources, Book 3
• Communicative Activity 12-2, pp. 173–174
• Teaching Transparency Master 12-3, pp. 177, 178 . . . . Teaching Transparency 12-3
• Additional Listening Activities 12-5, 12-6, p. 181 . . . . Additional Listening Activities, Audiocassette 10B/Audio CD 12
• Realia 12-2, pp. 184, 185
• Situation Cards 12-3, pp. 186–187
• Student Response Forms, pp. 188–190
• Quiz 12-3, pp. 195–196 . . . . Assessment Items, Audiocassette 8B/Audio CD 12
Videodisc Guide . . . . Videodisc Program, Videodisc 6B

Practice and Activity Book, p. 143

Video Guide . . . . Video Program OR Expanded Video Program, Videocassette 4
Videodisc Guide . . . . Videodisc Program, Videodisc 6B

Alternative Assessment
• Performance Assessment
  Première étape, p. 307
  Deuxième étape, p. 312
  Troisième étape, p. 316

• Portfolio Assessment
  Written: **Mise en pratique,** Activity 4, Pupil's Edition, p. 321
    Assessment Guide, p. 25
  Oral: **Mise en pratique,** Activity 2, Pupil's Edition, p. 321
    Assessment Guide, p. 25

Final Exam
• Assessment Guide, pp. 49–56
• Assessment Items,
  Audiocassette 8B
  Audio CD 12

Chapitre 12 : A la belle étoile
Textbook Listening Activities Scripts

For Student Response Forms, see *Chapter Teaching Resources, Book 3,* pp. 188–190.

Première étape

7 Ecoute! p. 304

1. Ça se trouve au bord du lac Saint-Jean, en face de la ville d'Alma.

2. Oui, c'est dans le nord du Québec, à l'est de Matane. C'est très beau, là-bas.

3. C'est pas loin d'ici. Vous allez à Thetford Mines, et c'est à l'est, au bord d'un très beau lac.

4. Oui, c'est un parc très célèbre. Ça se trouve au nord de Québec ville.

5. C'est assez loin. C'est une île dans l'Océan Atlantique. C'est dans le nord-est du Québec, près de Gaspé.

Answers to Activity 7
1. parc de la Pointe-Taillon
2. parc de la Gaspésie
3. parc de Frontenac
4. parc de la Jacques-Cartier
5. parc de l'Ile-Bonaventure-et-du-Rocher-Percé

10 Ecoute! p. 305

SON AMI	Alors, Francine, ce week-end au parc de la Jacques-Cartier, c'était comment?
FRANCINE	Super! On s'est vraiment bien amusés!
SON AMI	Ah, oui? Et qu'est-ce que vous avez fait?
FRANCINE	D'abord, on a fait une randonnée pédestre. On a vu un renard et plein d'orignaux. Je les ai même pris en photo.
SON AMI	Très bien. Comme ça, on pourra aussi les voir.
FRANCINE	Après ça, on avait faim, alors on a fait un pique-nique. Jérôme voulait donner à manger aux écureuils et aux canards, mais c'était interdit. Ensuite, on est allés nager dans la rivière. C'était génial! Et puis, on a fait du camping.
SON AMI	Est-ce que vous avez vu d'autres animaux?
FRANCINE	Ah! J'oubliais! Au retour, nous avons vu un ours énorme!

Answers to Activity 10
a fox, moose, squirrels, ducks, a bear

14 Ecoute! p. 307

1. Samedi, on s'est bien amusés! On a fait du canotage; c'était super! Mais on ne peut pas faire de la natation dans ce parc. Donc, on a fait du vélo de montagne. Et ensuite, on a fait de la voile. Après ça, on est revenus parce qu'on ne peut pas faire du camping dans ce parc.

2. Quel week-end! Tout a été de travers. On a fait du camping, bien sûr, mais il n'y avait pas grand-chose à faire comme sports. Tout le monde voulait faire du vélo de montagne, mais c'était impossible : interdit. Et le canotage, c'était impossible aussi! Enfin, on a fait une randonnée pédestre, et après, nous sommes allés à la pêche. Nous, les filles, on voulait se baigner, mais on ne peut pas là-bas! On n'a vraiment pas eu de chance!

3. On a passé un week-end très chouette. On est allés à la pêche, on a fait du vélo de montagne et on a vu une chute d'eau magnifique. En hiver, là-bas, on peut faire du ski alpin, mais en juillet, on a juste pu faire un pique-nique en plein air. Et puis après, on s'est reposés. Que la nature est belle!

Answers to Activity 14
1. canoeing, mountain biking, sailing
2. camping, hiking, fishing
3. fishing, mountain biking, picnic

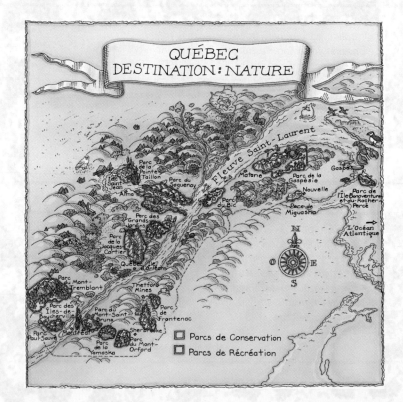

Deuxième étape

24 Ecoute! p. 311

1. — Mais qu'est-ce que tu fais, Elodie?
   — J'emporte des carottes pour les donner aux écureuils. Ils sont si mignons!
   — Mais tu ne dois pas nourrir les animaux! C'est interdit!
   — Vraiment? Ben, alors, je les mangerai.

2. — Romain! Arrête!
   — Mais qu'est-ce que tu as, toi, à crier comme ça?
   — Ne mutile pas les arbres! Tu devrais plutôt en prendre une photo pour en préserver le souvenir. Tiens, voilà mon appareil-photo.

3. — Tu ne vas pas jeter ces papiers, j'espère.
   — Mais... il n'y a pas de poubelle, Bénédicte. Qu'est-ce que je dois en faire?
   — Pourquoi tu ne les remportes pas avec toi? Tu peux les jeter plus tard. Il faut respecter la nature!

Answers to Activity 24
1. b   2. c   3. a

Troisième étape

29 Ecoute! p. 315

GUILLAUME   Qu'est-ce que tu as fait le week-end dernier?

SÉVERINE   Je suis allée camper au parc du Saguenay avec des amies. Nous sommes allées en voiture jusqu'au parc, puis nous avons marché.

GUILLAUME   Ah oui? Vous avez dû beaucoup vous amuser, surtout avec ce beau temps.

SÉVERINE   Oui, il faisait très beau, et nous avons pu faire du canotage, des randonnées...

GUILLAUME   Quelle chance! Ça doit être magnifique là-bas, surtout les fjords!

SÉVERINE   Oui, tu verras, j'ai pris beaucoup de photos. Le seul problème, c'était Monique.

GUILLAUME   Monique? Mais elle est super-sympa, non?

SÉVERINE   En général, oui, mais ce week-end, elle était de très mauvaise humeur. Elle se plaignait constamment. D'abord, elle avait mal aux pieds, ensuite, elle crevait de faim, après ça, son sac à dos était trop lourd. Et puis, elle ne voulait rien faire.

GUILLAUME   Alors, qu'est-ce que tu as fait?

SÉVERINE   Je lui ai parlé, et elle m'a expliqué ce qui s'était passé. C'était un malentendu avec son copain. Enfin, on s'est bien amusées.

Answers to Activity 29
1. Il faisait très beau.
2. Elles ont fait du canotage et des randonnées. Séverine a pris des photos.
3. Elle était de mauvaise humeur; Elle s'était disputée avec son copain.

Mise en pratique

3 p. 321

Vous aimez la pétanque, les jeux de fers et la danse? Ou peut-être préférez-vous simplement vous reposer au bord d'un lac? Il y en a pour tous les goûts chez nous! Alors, n'hésitez plus, venez donc passer vos vacances avec nous, et vous ne le regretterez pas. Situé rue Robitaille, à moins de dix minutes de l'autoroute des cantons de l'est, notre camping est un vrai paradis pour toute la famille.

Answers to Mise en pratique Activity 3
Camping Granby

Album de photo en vidéo
(Cooperative Learning Project)

ASSIGNMENT

Students will make a "photo album" of an imaginary camping trip in a public park. They will record the album on videocassette. The "photos," which students will create, will be mounted on construction paper with a caption below each one. Each group will make ten "photos" that they took on their camping trip showing where they went, what they took with them, what they did, what they saw, and how they felt at various times during the trip. They will write a caption to accompany each "photo," using the **passé composé,** the **imparfait,** and the vocabulary and functions from this chapter. The first "photo" in the album should show a map of the country and the park's location.

MATERIALS

✂ **Students may need**
- Research materials
- White construction paper
- Markers
- Magazines or catalogues
- Scissors
- Video camera
- Videocassette
- Overhead projector (see #8)

PREPARATION

Form groups of four. Assign a leader to organize and delegate research tasks. Designate a writer to assign and compile the research findings in French. Name a proofreader to assign group members to check for certain types of errors, and then to write the corrected text on the construction paper below the "photos." Select an art coordinator to draw the "photos" or choose them from magazines and arrange them. All group members will share in the oral presentation of the project.

SUGGESTED SEQUENCE

1. Each group will choose a national or regional park in any francophone country, department, or province as the site of their imaginary camping trip. You might reserve one or two class periods in the library and have the librarian select books on francophone countries, departments, or provinces for your use. You might remind students of the three parks they learned about in Côte d'Ivoire in Chapter 8: **le parc national du Banco, le parc national de Taï,** and **le parc national de la Comoë.**

2. Students should select or draw their "photos."

3. Students write a one- or two-sentence caption for each photo, proofread the text, and write the corrected text on the construction paper or below the "photos."

4. When the photos and captions are finished, students begin recording their "photo album" on videocassette.

5. To record the photos, tape one photo to the board or to the wall and focus the video camera only on the photo. Turn on the camera, have a student read the caption for that photo, and pause the camera. Follow the same procedure for each photo. The result is a series of pictures, similar to a slide show, with narration on videocassette.

6. While groups are videotaping their album, all other students will work quietly on their own.

7. Show the videocassette to the class and to other French classes.

8. If a video camera is not available for your use, have students make silhouettes from construction paper illustrating their camping trip to project on the overhead. The cutouts should be very simple shapes to illustrate the sentences. Instead of projecting the captions for everyone to see, have students read the captions to the class while they project their cutouts.

GRADING THE PROJECT

Each group should receive a collective grade based on content, accuracy of the language, and overall appearance of the project. Group members should receive individual grades based on comprehensibility, and effort and participation in the project. You might have the class evaluate the content and overall quality of the presentations.

Suggested Point Distribution (total = 100 points)

Content . . . . 20 points

Language use. . . . . 20 points

Overall appearance . . . . 20 points

Comprehensibility . . . . 20 points

Effort/participation . . . . 20 points

Chapitre 12 : A la belle étoile
♜ *Games*

PERIL

In this game, students will practice the vocabulary and expressions from this chapter and all previous chapters.

Preparation
(This game is similar to the game Jeopardy®.)

1. Draw a "Jeopardy" game board on a transparency: five columns with five squares in each. Write five categories across the top, such as *Animals, Camping, Complaining, Clothes,* and *Sports.*

2. In the squares, write numerical values from 100 in the first squares to 500 in the fifth squares.

3. For each square in each category, prepare one clue and answer relevant to the topic. Write the clues on a sheet of paper. Write the corresponding category and point value next to each clue. For example, for one of the squares in the *Clothes* category, you might write the clue **On la met autour du cou quand il fait froid** to elicit the answer **C'est une écharpe.**

4. The object of the game is to win the number of points in a square by giving the answer suggested by the clue.

5. Form three teams. Team members will take turns playing during a round. They may volunteer to participate, or you might draw names at random. If possible, obtain three buzzers or bells for three players (one from each team) to sound when they know the answer. Have a judge determine who was the first to sound the buzzer or bell.

6. Prepare several transparencies for different rounds. You might also want to have a *double* round and a *final* category (see explanations below).

Procedure

1. To begin, a player from one team chooses a category and a specific point value. **(Je voudrais** Complaining **pour 300, s'il vous plaît.)**

2. Read aloud the clue you prepared for that square. **(On dit ça quand on a été debout pendant toute la journée.)**

3. The player who sounds his or her buzzer or bell first may answer. **(J'ai mal aux pieds.)**

4. If the first contestant answers incorrectly, the others may sound their buzzer or bell to try to answer. If no contestant answers correctly, the last contestant to try to answer chooses the next category and point value.

5. The contestant who answers correctly earns the designated number of points and chooses another category and point value.

6. After several rounds, you might want to proceed to the *double* round in which each square is doubled in value. During this round, only the contestant who chooses the category and point value may try to answer. The other contestants may not try if he or she answers incorrectly.

7. In the *final* round, name one category. Contestants from each team secretly wager any number of points earned so far, based on how familiar they are with that category. They must write their wagers on index cards.

8. When the wagers have been made, give the clue. Students have one minute to write down their answer.

9. The team with the lowest number of points gives its answer first. If it's wrong, the number of points wagered is subtracted from the team's total. If the answer is correct, the number of points wagered is added to the previous total. The team with the most points at the end of the game wins.

Chapitre 12
A la belle étoile
pp. 298–323

𝒰sing the Chapter Opener

Motivating Activity

Ask students if they enjoy spending time outdoors, away from a city or town. What do they enjoy about nature? What kinds of activities do they like to do in the wilderness? What kinds of outdoor activities are available where they live? Which activities are not available? What are some of the disadvantages of spending time outdoors?

Teaching Suggestion

Show a map of Canada. Ask students why they think Canada would be a paradise for people who like the wilderness. (Much of the country is uninhabited and unspoiled.) Ask students to name states in the United States that might most closely resemble the Canadian wilderness (Alaska, Wyoming, Montana, Colorado).

Photo Flash!

① Paul, Denis, René, Michèle, and Francine stop during their hike to take in the beauty of the **parc de la Jacques-Cartier.** The park, located 40 kilometers north of Quebec City, is one of sixteen provincial parks in Quebec. It was created in 1981 in order to preserve the natural beauty of the area, which comprises 670 square kilometers. The leaves that obscure part of René's head are maple leaves. The maple tree is the Canadian national tree. The manufacturing of maple syrup is a major Canadian industry.

CHAPITRE
12
A la belle étoile

① Au Québec, il y a des forêts magnifiques!

298 *deux cent quatre-vingt-dix-huit*

Math Link

Have students convert the distance and area in the **Photo Flash!** from kilometers to miles. One kilometer equals 0.62 miles. To convert the distance from kilometers to miles, multiply the number of kilometers by 0.62. (The park is 24.8 miles north of Quebec.) You might also have students convert the distance between two cities in their area from miles to kilometers. One mile equals 1.609 kilometers. To convert miles to kilometers, multiply the number of miles by 1.609 (or divide the number of miles by 0.62).

Language Note

The article **la** is used in **parc de la Jacques-Cartier** because it refers to **la rivière Jacques-Cartier.**

What images come to mind when you think of the Canadian wilderness? Mountain streams, tall trees, cool lakes? Canada's many national parks and wildlife preserves are beautiful settings for hiking, canoeing, or just enjoying nature.

In this chapter you will review and practice

- asking for and giving information; giving directions
- complaining; expressing discouragement and offering encouragement; asking for and giving advice
- relating a series of events; describing people and places

And you will

- listen to tourist bureau directions to parks
- read about camping excursions you can take
- write a journal entry about a camping trip
- find out about endangered animals in francophone countries and become familiar with some French-Canadian expressions

Focusing on Outcomes

Help students recall some of the expressions they learned in previous chapters that accomplish the chapter outcomes. In Chapter 4, students learned *to ask for and give information* and *to give directions* (Où se trouve... ? Qu'est-ce qu'il y a à voir... ? Il y a... , se trouver, dans le nord, dans le sud, dans l'est, dans l'ouest). In Chapter 7, they learned *to complain* (Je ne me sens pas bien. J'ai mal partout!); *to express discouragement and offer encouragement* (Je n'en peux plus! Je craque! J'abandonne! Allez! Tu y es presque! Encore un effort! Courage!); and *to ask for and give advice* (Qu'est-ce que je dois faire? Tu dois... , Tu devrais... , Tu ferais bien de... , Tu n'as qu'à... , Pourquoi tu ne... pas... ?) In Chapters 1 and 4, students learned how *to relate a series of events* (d'abord, ensuite, puis, après ça, finalement, and enfin). In Chapter 8, they learned *to tell what things were like* (C'était... , Il y avait... , Il/Elle était...). Finally, have students match each photo caption with a chapter outcome. NOTE: You may want to use the video to support the objectives. The self-check activities in **Que sais-je?** on page 322 help students assess their achievement of the objectives.

② Aïe! J'ai mal aux pieds!

③ D'abord, on a fait une randonnée pédestre. C'était tellement beau là-bas!

Photo Flash!

② In this photo, Paul is tired, and his feet hurt from hiking. There are over 100 kilometers (or 62 miles) of hiking and biking trails in the **parc de la Jacques-Cartier.** You can choose from among sixteen different trails for a thirty-minute walk or an all-day hike.

Culture Note

The **parc de la Jacques-Cartier** is open from the end of May to mid-October. There are eleven semi-equipped or primitive camping sites in the park. Rock climbing, hiking, and mountain biking are available throughout the park season. Canoeing, kayaking, and mini-rafting are permitted on the river, and equipment can be rented. The Information Center offers guided nature activities, slide shows, lectures, and exhibits.

Photo Flash!

③ This photo shows one of several streams in the **parc de la Jacques-Cartier. La rivière Jacques-Cartier** is the major river running through the park. Fishing is allowed from May until September with a permit. The Information Center offers guided observations of salmon and trout during spawning season in mid-October.

**VIDEO PROGRAM
OR EXPANDED VIDEO
PROGRAM,**
Videocassette 4
32:26–40:26

OR VIDEODISC PROGRAM,
Videodisc 6B

Search 4855, Play To 19325

Video Synopsis

In this segment of the video, Francine, René, Paul, Michèle, and Denis are at a campground at the **parc de la Jacques-Cartier,** north of Quebec City. They set off on a hike, and after awhile, Paul starts complaining that his feet hurt. The others encourage him to continue. It begins to get dark, so they decide to take a shortcut. A little later, they realize they are lost!

Motivating Activity

Ask students if they have ever been camping. Ask for volunteers to share their experiences. Ask students what equipment would be essential to bring on a camping trip. Then, ask them the following questions and have them answer in French.

1. **Avez-vous déjà fait du camping? Où?**
2. **Qu'est-ce qu'on peut faire quand on fait du camping?**
3. **Qu'est-ce qu'on peut voir?**

Mise en train

Promenons-nous dans les bois

Have you ever been camping? What do you think happens to these campers?

Michèle Francine René
Mme Desrochers Paul Denis

Le matin, au camping du parc de la Jacques-Cartier. René, Francine, Michèle, Denis et Paul s'apprêtent à partir pour une randonnée. Les parents de Francine, M. et Mme Desrochers, vont rester au camping. René, lui, commence son journal.

*26 septembre.
8H15 - Tout le monde est prêt. On a l'eau, le pique-nique et des allumettes. Moi, j'ai mon appareil-photo. Mme Desrochers nous a donné une lampe de poche. A mon avis, ce n'est pas la peine. On va rentrer avant la nuit.*

Vous avez tout?

On devrait peut-être prendre une lampe de poche?

Oh, c'est pas la peine. On va rentrer avant la nuit.

La nuit tombe tôt. Je préférerais en avoir une.

Tiens, Francine. On ne sait jamais.

Bien. On y va?

On y va!

J'arrive!

Eh, vous avez vu! Superbe, non? Qu'en pensez-vous?

C'est magnifique.

Il doit y avoir des tas d'animaux. C'est idéal pour la chasse.

12H30 - Nous avons marché toute la matinée. Une balade superbe. C'est magnifique ici. C'est tellement calme et tellement beau. Il y a autant de bruit qu'à Québec, mais c'est le bruit de la nature: le chant des oiseaux, les coin-coin des canards... Et si on écoutait bien, on entendrait peut-être le grognement d'un ours!... A propos des animaux, Michèle et Denis se disputent... comme d'habitude.

300 *trois cents* CHAPITRE 12 A la belle étoile

RESOURCES FOR MISE EN TRAIN
Textbook Audiocassette 6B/Audio CD 12
Practice and Activity Book, p. 133
Video Guide
  Video Program
  Expanded Video Program, Videocassette 4
Videodisc Guide
  Videodisc Program, Videodisc 6B

Presentation

Have students view the video with their books closed and then summarize the story in English. Then, play the recording and have students read along as they listen. Ask the questions in Activity 1 on page 302. Next, form groups of six and have students read aloud the Mise en train, with each student assuming the role of one of the characters. Have four students each read one of the four journal entries. Finally, have students describe in one sentence what is happening in each photo.

For Individual Needs

Challenge Have students rewrite one of the journal entries from the point of view of a different character. Then, have volunteers read their revised journal entries aloud, and have the other students try to guess which character might have written it.

Kinesthetic Learners Have groups of six act out the dialogue in the Mise en train.

Thinking Critically

Synthesizing Ask students if they agree with Denis, who likes to hunt, or with Michèle, who is against hunting, and have them explain why.

Teacher Note

Call students' attention to the sign in Photo 5, indicating the name of the trail: **Le draveur nord.** Refer them to the **Note Culturelle** on page 304, which explains the significance of this name.

MISE EN TRAIN   *trois cent un*   **301**

 **Video Integration**

- **EXPANDED VIDEO PROGRAM,**
  Videocassette 4, 40:27–47:43
- **VIDEODISC PROGRAM,**
  Videodisc 6B

Search 19325, Play To 32430

You may choose to continue with **Promenons-nous dans les bois (suite)** or wait until later in the chapter. When the story continues, Francine and her friends decide to build a fire to stay warm. Denis leaves to go fishing and returns later with a small fish. A park ranger finds everyone seated around the fire and informs them that building fires and fishing without a permit are against park regulations! They're unaware that they are only a short distance from the campground, and the ranger leads them back, where they find Francine's parents anxiously waiting.

2 Auditory/Visual Learners Have students work in pairs. One student reads a sentence from the journal entries. The other student finds the appropriate journal entry and tells at what time René wrote that sentence.

3 Tactile Learners Have students write the characters' names on a sheet of paper and the sentences on small strips of paper. Have them place the sentences next to the name of the person who might have said them. Then, have them write additional clues to the characters' identities on strips of paper. Partners will place the strips next to the names of the appropriate people.

Teaching Suggestions

4 Once students have found the answers to this activity, have them call out one of the expressions at random and ask another student to name the function it accomplishes.

5 Have small groups write their own ending to the story. Then, you might play the *Expanded Video* or read aloud the synopsis of **Promenons-nous dans les bois (suite)** on page 301 so groups can compare their endings to what really happened.

For videodisc application, see *Videodisc Guide.*

Culture Note
Point out the Canadian coins pictured on this page. There are also five, ten, and twenty-five cent coins. The dollar is divided into 100 cents. Each bill denomination is a different color. The dollar coin is replacing the dollar bill, and the two-dollar bill is popular.

---

1 Tu as compris? See answers below.

1. Where are the young people?
2. What are they doing?
3. What do Michèle and Denis disagree about?
4. What happens at the end of **Promenons-nous dans les bois**?

2 Il est quelle heure?

At what time did René write the following in his journal?

1. *Ça y est! Nous sommes perdus!* à cinq heures vingt
2. *Mme Desrochers nous a donné une lampe de poche.* à huit heures quinze
3. *A propos des animaux, Michèle et Denis se disputent... comme d'habitude.* à midi et demi
4. *Il faudrait trouver une solution.* à cinq heures vingt
5. *Allons, faisons confiance à Francine!* à trois heures dix
6. *C'est tellement calme et tellement beau.* à midi et demi

3 Qui suis-je?

Michèle   **Denis**   **René**   **Francine**   **Paul**

Paul

Denis

René

Michèle

J'aime aller à la chasse.
Denis

J'ai faim.

J'écris dans mon journal.

Je suis embêtée.
Francine

Je veux prendre un raccourci.
Francine

Je suis ravi.
Denis

Je pense qu'on devrait préserver les animaux.

4 Cherche les expressions See answers below.

What do the people in **Promenons-nous dans les bois** say or write to . . .

1. ask for an opinion?
2. describe a place?
3. make a suggestion?
4. agree?
5. disagree?
6. ask for a suggestion?

5 Et maintenant, à toi

What do you think will happen next in the story? What would you do if you got lost while camping or hiking?

Answers

1 1. at Jacques-Cartier Park
2. preparing to go on a hike
3. whether people should hunt
4. The campers get lost.

4 1. Superbe, non? Qu'en pensez-vous?
2. C'est magnifique ici. C'est tellement calme. Tellement beau. Il y a autant de bruit qu'à Québec, mais c'est le bruit de la nature.

3. On devrait peut-être prendre une lampe de poche? On devrait peut-être prendre un raccourci? Si on marche... ?
4. Tu as raison. C'est une bonne idée.
5. Ce n'est pas peut-être une bonne idée. Ce n'est pas la peine.
6. Qu'est-ce que tu proposes?

PREMIERE ETAPE

Asking for and giving information; giving directions

QUÉBEC DESTINATION: NATURE

6 Destination nature

Possible answers:

1. What geographical features do you see on the map? What cities?
2. What animals would you expect to find in Quebec?
3. What types of parks can you find in Quebec?

1. the St. Lawrence river, lakes, mountains . . . ; Québec, Montréal, Alma, Matane . . .

whales, lobsters, geese, bears, deer . . .

recreational parks and nature preserves

RESOURCES FOR PREMIERE ETAPE

Textbook Audiocassette 6B/Audio CD 12
***Practice and Activity Book**, pp. 134–136*
Videodisc Guide
  Videodisc Program, Videodisc 6B

Chapter Teaching Resources, Book 3
• Teaching Transparency Master 12-1, pp. 175, 178
  Teaching Transparency 12-1
• Additional Listening Activities 12-1, 12-2, p. 179
  Audiocassette 10B/Audio CD 12
• Realia 12-1, pp. 183, 185
• Situation Cards 12-1, pp. 186–187
• Student Response Forms, pp. 188–190
• Quiz 12-1, pp. 191–192
  Audiocassette 8B/Audio CD 12

*J*ump Start!

Write the following descriptions on the board or on a transparency and have students match them with the characters from the **Mise en train**.
1. **Il adore l'aventure.** 2. **Ses parents vont s'inquiéter.**
3. **Elle n'est pas d'accord avec Denis.** 4. **Il n'est pas habitué aux longues marches.**
5. **Elle propose un raccourci.**
6. **Il écrit dans son journal.**
(*Answers:* 1. Denis 2. Francine 3. Michèle 4. Paul 5. Francine 6. René)

MOTIVATE

Have students look at the map of Quebec and compare it to their state or to another. How many parks are located near the Saint Lawrence River in Quebec? Do students know of another river near which several parks are located? What kinds of wild animals might they see in the parks in their area? Finally, ask students to recall the expressions for *asking for and giving directions* (**Où se trouve... ?, dans le nord, dans le sud, dans l'est, dans l'ouest**).

TEACH

Teaching Suggestions

• After students do Activity 6, ask questions about the map: **Combien de parcs voyez-vous? (seize) Il y a combien de villes sur cette carte? (huit) Comment s'appelle le lac qu'on voit sur la carte? (le lac Saint-Jean) Qu'est-ce qu'il y a au sud de la ville de Nouvelle? (le Parc de Miguasha)**
• For listening practice, make true-false statements about the locations of cities, lakes, and parks. (**Gaspé est à l'ouest de Matane. (faux) Le parc de Frontenac est au sud de Thetford Mines. (vrai)**)

Presentation

Comment dit-on... ? Point out a national park on a map of the United States. Describe the park and the surrounding area, using the expressions in **Comment dit-on... ?** Re-enter the vocabulary for nature and activities that students know (**les moustiques, une chute d'eau, une île, une rivière, la fôret, faire du vélo, aller à la pêche, faire du ski, faire de la natation, se promener**). Finally, point out another park and have students ask and tell about it.

◆ For Individual Needs

7 Slower Pace Have students find all the parks on the map on page 303. Ask them to tell in French where they are located in relation to each other, to cities, and to bodies of water. Then, play the recording.

Teaching Suggestion

8 To extend this activity, have students ask a partner to give the location of a well-known park in their area or in the United States. (**Où se trouve le Grand Canyon?**) Have them ask what there is to see or do there. (**Qu'est-ce qu'il y a à voir/faire là-bas?**)

Building on Previous Skills

8 Have students recall sports and nature vocabulary they've learned in previous chapters. Compile a list on the board and have students refer to it for this activity.

❓ COMMENT DIT-ON... ?
Asking for and giving information; giving directions

To ask for information:
Où se trouve le parc de la Jacques-Cartier?
Qu'est-ce qu'il y a à voir au parc?
Qu'est-ce qu'il y a à faire?

To give information:
Le parc **se trouve** près du lac Saint-Jean.
Il y a des forêts magnifiques et beaucoup d'animaux.
On peut faire des pique-niques, des safaris d'observation,...

To give directions:
C'est au nord/au sud/à l'est/à l'ouest de la ville de Québec.
It's to the north/south/east/west of . . .
C'est dans le nord/le sud/l'est/l'ouest du Québec. *It's in the northern/southern/eastern/western part of . . .*

7 Ecoute! Answers on p. 297C.

Stéphane est à Montréal. Il essaie de choisir quel parc il veut visiter. Ecoute les informations que l'office de tourisme lui donne et décide de quel parc on parle. Aide-toi du plan à la page 303.

8 C'est tellement beau!

Demande à ton/ta camarade où sont les parcs suivants et qu'est-ce qu'on peut y faire et y voir. Il/Elle va te répondre en s'aidant du plan à la page 303. Puis, changez de rôles.

NOTE CULTURELLE

There are many wilderness areas to visit in Quebec. **Le parc de la Jacques-Cartier** contains the southernmost tip of the band of boreal forest that circles the northern hemisphere from Quebec through Scandinavia and Siberia to Alaska. The park is named after Jacques Cartier, who claimed what is now Canada for the French crown in 1534. At the park you can follow the routes used by the **draveurs,** raftsmen who transported the trappers and lumberjacks who came to make their fortunes after Cartier mapped the area.

le parc du Mont-Tremblant

le parc du Saguenay

le parc de la Jacques-Cartier

Language Note

Remind students to use definite articles when naming countries and provinces, but not cities. Therefore, **du Québec** and **au Québec** refer to the province of Quebec, but **de Québec** and **à Québec** refer to Quebec City.

🌍 Culture Note

Le parc du Mont-Tremblant, created in 1894, is used throughout the year. The most popular winter activities include skiing, snowmobiling (**de la motoneige**), and snowshoeing. In the summer, camping and canoeing are popular. Moose hunting in season is permitted. There are twenty-two cottages available for rent, as well as primitive campgrounds at **lac Monroe, lac Chat,** and **lac Lajoie.**

9 On pourrait aller...

Ton ami(e) et toi, vous essayez de décider où vous voulez aller en vacances. Suggère un endroit et réponds aux questions de ton camarade qui te demande ce qu'il y a à voir et à faire là-bas. Puis, changez de rôles.

> au Québec   à Paris
> à Abidjan   en Touraine
> à la Martinique   en Provence

De bons conseils You've learned a lot of words and phrases. To review them, remember vocabulary in thematic groups. Think of a topic or situation that you've studied, such as making suggestions about what to see and do in Martinique. Then, list the vocabulary and phrases that you would need in that situation. Keep the lists you make and use them to study for your next test—and your final exam!

VOCABULAIRE

Qu'est-ce qu'on peut voir dans les parcs du Québec?

un orignal

un ours

un loup

un écureuil

un renard

un raton laveur

une mouffette

un canard

10 Ecoute!

Francine est revenue d'une excursion dans le parc de la Jacques-Cartier. Quels animaux est-ce qu'elle a vus? Answers on p. 297C.

PREMIERE ETAPE   *trois cent cinq*   305

Language Notes

• The following are common French idiomatic expressions involving animals: **vivre comme un ours** *(to live like a hermit)*; **vendre la peau de l'ours avant de l'avoir tué** *(to count your chickens before they're hatched)*; **avoir une faim de loup** *(to be hungry as a wolf)*; **avancer à pas de loup** *(to move stealthily)*; **Il faut hurler avec des loups** *(When in Rome, do as the Romans*

do); **être futé(e) comme un renard** *(to be sly as a fox)*; **un canard** *(a false rumor)*; **faire un froid de canard** *(to be freezing cold)*; **ne pas casser quatre pattes à un canard** *(not to be worth writing home about)*.

• **Mon petit canard** is a term of endearment that is often used with children.

• In French, a duck says «**Coin! Coin!**» not the English *"Quack! Quack!"*

Sidebar

PREMIERE ETAPE
CHAPITRE 12

Building on Previous Skills

9 Before they begin this activity, have students recall the expressions they learned in Chapter 8 for *making and responding to suggestions.* (**Si on allait... ? Si on visitait... ? D'accord. Bonne idée! Bof! Ça m'est égal. Non, je préfère... ; Non, je ne veux pas.**)

For Individual Needs

9 Slower Pace To prepare students for this activity, have them recall what there is to see and do in each of the places listed in the word box. Write these on the board for students to refer to as they decide where to go on vacation.

Presentation

Vocabulaire Gather or draw pictures of these animals. Show a picture, name the animal, and tell students a little about each one. (**Il est très féroce.**) Then, make animal noises or mime the actions of each animal and have students identify it.

TPR Name an animal and have students show their comprehension by making the appropriate animal call, by miming an action typical of that animal, or by going to the board and drawing it.

For Individual Needs

10 Tactile/Visual Learners Have students trace the photos in the **Vocabulaire** or draw quick sketches of each of the animals. Then, play the recording and have students put a check mark next to the pictures of the animals they hear mentioned.

Building on Previous Skills

11 Have students use their reading skills to guess from the context what **queue** and **museau** mean.

Additional Practice

11 To extend this activity, have students draw or gather pictures of the animals. Tape the pictures to students' backs without their seeing them. Have students ask each other yes-no questions until they can identify the animal taped to their back. (**Je suis rouge? J'ai une grande queue?**)

For videodisc application, see *Videodisc Guide*.

Teaching Suggestion

12 Have students imagine they are hosting a TV program as they conduct the interview. Volunteers might present their programs to the class.

Presentation

Vocabulaire Draw and number pictures of each activity on a transparency. Project the transparency, say the captions at random, and ask students to try to match each caption to the number of its corresponding picture. Then, ask questions, such as **Tu as déjà fait une randonnée en skis? Où est-ce qu'on peut faire du canotage?**

Teaching Suggestion

Compile a list of sports and activities from previous chapters. Have students compare the list to the activities in the chart. Then, ask questions about the chart, such as **Combien d'activités sont offertes à Yamaska? (sept) Est-ce qu'on peut manger dans un restaurant à Bic? (non)**

---

11 Qui suis-je? See answers below.

1. Je suis noir et blanc et j'ai une grande queue. Certains disent que je sens mauvais.
2. J'ai le museau et les oreilles pointus et une grande queue rousse. J'adore les poules!
3. Je suis gris et noir. J'ai une queue à rayures et je porte toujours un masque.
4. Je suis noir ou brun et les gens ont peur de moi parce que je suis grand et fort.
5. J'habite les lacs et les rivières. Les enfants adorent me donner à manger.

12 Et toi?

Réponds aux questions suivantes, puis interviewe un(e) camarade.

1. Quels animaux du **Vocabulaire** est-ce que tu as déjà vus?
2. Où est-ce que tu les as vus?
3. Est-ce que tu leur as donné à manger?
4. Quels animaux est-ce que tu n'as jamais vus?
5. Si tu pouvais être un de ces animaux, lequel choisirais-tu? Pourquoi?

VOCABULAIRE

Qu'est-ce qu'on peut faire au Québec? On peut...

faire du camping.

faire du canotage.

faire du vélo de montagne.

faire une randonnée en skis.

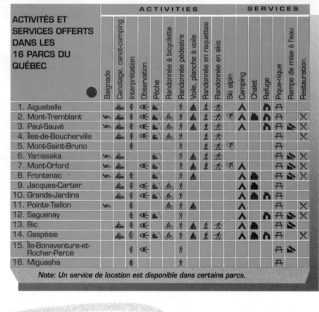

faire une randonnée en raquettes.

faire une randonnée pédestre.

Family Link

Have students show the chart to a family member. Have them ask the family member to try and guess what activities and services are offered at the parks based on the symbols and the French words.

Answers

11 1. une mouffette
2. un renard
3. un raton laveur
4. un ours
5. un canard

13 Vrai ou faux?

Regarde le tableau à la page 306 et décide si les phrases suivantes sont vraies ou fausses.

1. On peut se baigner au parc du Saguenay. faux
2. On peut faire du camping et du vélo de montagne au parc du Yamaska. faux 3. vrai
3. Au parc du Mont Tremblant, on peut faire une randonnée pédestre et aller à la pêche.
4. On peut faire une randonnée en raquettes au parc du Mont-Orford, mais on ne peut pas faire de canotage. faux
5. Au parc de la Gaspésie, on ne peut pas faire de ski alpin, mais on peut faire une randonnée en skis. vrai
6. Dans tous les parcs, il est possible de faire un pique-nique et une randonnée pédestre. vrai

14 Ecoute!

Ecoute ces personnes qui parlent de leurs week-ends. Fais une liste de ce que chaque groupe d'amis a fait. Answers on p. 297C.

15 Un week-end sportif

Des groupes de copains font du camping. Compare leurs activités. Qu'est-ce qu'ils font de semblable? Et de différent? See answers below.

Jules et Romain

Marie et Jeanne

16 Moi, j'aime bien...

Fais une liste des activités que tu aimerais pratiquer si tu allais au Québec. Quels sont les parcs qui offrent ces activités?

17 Si on allait... ?

En utilisant les listes que vous avez faites pour l'activité 16, choisissez un parc québécois où votre classe de français peut aller pour le voyage de fin d'année. Créez une publicité pour le parc pour persuader le reste de la classe d'y aller.

Answers
15 *Tous:* la pêche, une randonnée pédestre, un pique-nique; *Les garçons:* du canotage, des photos; *Les filles:* du vélo de montagne, de la natation

ASSESS

Quiz 12-1, *Chapter Teaching Resources, Book 3,* pp. 191–192

Assessment Items, Audiocassette 8B
Audio CD 12

Performance Assessment

Have students imagine they are on a camping trip and write a journal similar to the one René wrote in the **Mise en train.** Have them write about the park they're visiting, the activities they're doing or plan to do, and the animals they've seen. Students may wish to include their "journal entries" in their written portfolios.

Teaching Suggestion

13 Have pairs of students create additional true-false statements. Have them read the statements aloud or write and pass them to another pair of students to answer.

For Individual Needs

14 Challenge Have students listen a second time for what the groups were *not* able to do. Challenge the students to write in French the activities mentioned.
(Answers: 1. **de la natation, du camping** 2. **du vélo de montagne, du canotage, se baigner** 3. **du ski alpin**)

Additional Practice

15 As a homework assignment, have students imagine they went on a camping trip, and draw pictures of the activities they did and the animals they saw, or they may choose to cut them out of magazines or catalogues. In class, have students pass their drawings or pictures to a partner, who will tell or write what the classmate did and saw. (**Il/Elle a fait du vélo de montagne, et il/elle a vu un renard.**)

CLOSE

To close this **étape,** have students trace the map on page 303, including all the parks and towns. Then, have them choose four parks, four activities, and four animals and tell a partner where they went, what they did, and what they saw in each park. (**Je suis allé(e) au parc du Bic. Il se trouve au sud de Matane. Là, j'ai fait une randonnée pédestre, et j'y ai vu un orignal!**) The partner will sketch what the student did or saw next to the park mentioned on his or her map.

*J*ump Start!

Have students describe a national park in the United States. Have them give the location and tell about the activities they can do there and the animals they might see.

MOTIVATE

Have students suggest all the items they would need on a camping trip and justify their suggestions. Have a volunteer list the items on the board or on a transparency.

TEACH

Teaching Suggestion

Have students find a newspaper advertisement for a sporting goods store that pictures camping equipment. Have them write brief descriptions of the items in French and convert the prices to French francs. Have them tape or glue their French text over the English.

Math Link

Have students convert the prices in the *E. Leclerc* advertisement to American dollars. You can find the current rate of exchange in the business section of the newspaper. For additional practice, have students convert the American prices into Canadian dollars.

Language Note

Students might want to know the following vocabulary from the advertisement: **un anneau** *(ring)*; **une poignée** *(handle)*; **un moulinet** *(reel)*; **une cuillière** *(lure)*; **un gros carnassier** *(type of fish)*; **le garnissage** *(filling)*; **une cartouche** *(cartridge)*; **un cordon** *(cord)*; **un rabat** *(flap)*; **matelassé** *(quilted)*; **rembouré** *(padded)*; **lisse** *(smooth)*; **une armature** *(frame)*; **un arceau** *(arc)*; **un mât** *(pole)*; **l'acier** *(steel)* **zingué** *(zinc-coated)*.

DEUXIEME ETAPE

Complaining; expressing discouragement and offering encouragement; asking for and giving advice

E. LECLERC

46 F 90
Tue-insectes
4 W, 220 V.
Tube fluorescent.
Coloris noir.

36 F 95
Panoplie
Comprenant : 1 mini lancer téléscopique : Anneaux sur bridges. Poignée plastique antidérapante. Porte-moulinet à os plastique. 1 moulinet : métal. Bobine plastique. Frein avant garni. 1 cuillère type "Rublex" spéciale gros carnassier, dorée. 1 flotteur.

57 F 90
Sac de couchage
Nylon uni, transformable en couverture. Dimensions: 1,80 m x 75 cm. Doublé polyester coton. Garnissage 100 % polyester 200 g/m².

86 F 50
Lampe 80 watts sur cartouche "Beaux Jours"
Lampe camping fonctionnant avec une cartouche 200 grs modèle 880

68 F 00
Sac à dos
35 litres. Nylon 420 deniers. Fermeture : cordon bloqueur + rabat élastiqué - 1 boucle rapide. Bretelles matelassées, dos rembourré contact coton, 2 poches latérales zippées + 1 poche frontale zippée + 1 poche caméra fermeture velcro. Fond renforcé.

12 F 90
Tapis de sol lisse
Dimensions: 1,80 m x 50 cm x 8 mm. Utilisation: camping, gymnastique, plage. Coloris assortis. Mousse de polyéthylène.

245 F 00
Dôme avec avancée 3 places "KIWI I"
Grande avancée avec volet + fenêtres. Double toit nylon 70 deniers. Intérieur nylon taffetas. Tapis de sol polyéthylène. Armature: 2 arceaux en fibre de verre diam.: 7,9 mm, 2 mâts de relevée en acier zingué.

18 Tu as compris?

Regarde la publicité pour E. Leclerc et réponds aux questions suivantes.

1. Cette publicité est pour quelle sorte d'équipement? équipement de camping
2. Combien de poches a le sac à dos? Combien coûte-t-il? quatre; 68 F
3. Comment dit-on *sleeping bag* en français? Quelles sont les dimensions de celui sur la publicité? Combien coûte-t-il? sac de couchage; 1,80 m x 75 cm; 57F90
4. Comment est-ce qu'on peut utiliser le tapis de sol lisse? pour le camping, la gymnastique et la plage
5. Est-ce que la tente a des fenêtres? Elle peut loger combien de personnes? oui; trois

---

RESOURCES FOR DEUXIEME ETAPE

Textbook Audiocassette 6B/Audio CD 12
Practice and Activity Book, pp. 137–139
Video Guide
  Video Program
  Expanded Video Program, Videocassette 4
Videodisc Guide
  Videodisc Program, Videodisc 6B

Chapter Teaching Resources, Book 3
• Communicative Activity 12-1, pp. 171–172
• Teaching Transparency Master 12-2, pp. 176, 178
  Teaching Transparency 12-2
• Additional Listening Activities 12-3, 12-4, p. 180
  Audiocassette 10B/Audio CD 12
• Realia 12-2, pp. 184, 185
• Situation Cards 12-2, pp. 186–187
• Student Response Forms, pp. 188–190
• Quiz 12-2, pp. 193–194
  Audiocassette 8B/Audio CD 12

VOCABULAIRE

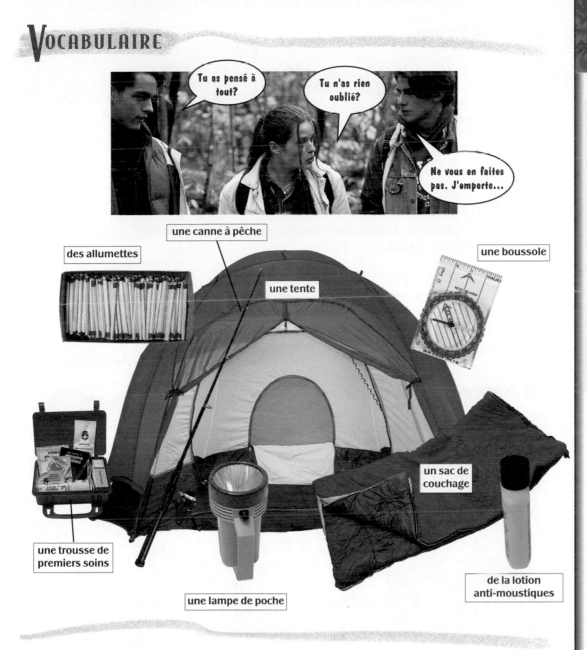

Tu as pensé à tout?

Tu n'as rien oublié?

Ne vous en faites pas. J'emporte...

une canne à pêche

des allumettes

une boussole

une tente

une trousse de premiers soins

un sac de couchage

de la lotion anti-moustiques

une lampe de poche

19 J'en ai besoin!

Si tu vas faire du camping, qu'est-ce qu'il faut que tu emportes pour...

5. une trousse de premiers soins

1. dormir? *un sac de couchage*
2. attraper des poissons? *une canne à pêche*
3. ne pas te perdre? *une boussole*
4. ne pas te faire piquer par les insectes?
   de la lotion anti-moustiques
5. soigner quelqu'un qui s'est fait mal?
6. bien voir la nuit? *une lampe de poche*
7. faire la cuisine? *des allumettes*

DEUXIEME ETAPE

trois cent neuf **309**

Language Notes

• You might caution students not to confuse **une boussole,** a directional compass, with **un compas,** a device for drawing circles.
• Call students' attention to the use of the word **trousse** in **une trousse de premiers soins.** Ask them if they know of another **trousse** *(a pencil case)* and what it might contain.
• In Canada, **la lotion anti-moustiques** is spelled with an -**s**, while in France, it is spelled without an -**s**.

20 N'oublie pas...

Ton ami(e) va aller faire du camping avec toi. Ecris-lui une lettre dans laquelle tu lui donnes des conseils sur ce qu'il/elle doit emporter et mettre.

Si tu as oublié **clothing vocabulary** va à la page 340.

Note de Grammaire

The verb **emporter** means *to take something with you.* It's a regular **-er** verb. You can use it to advise someone what to bring: **Emporte une boussole!**

COMMENT DIT-ON... ?
Complaining; expressing discouragement and offering encouragement

To complain:
Je crève de faim!
Je meurs de soif!
Je suis fatigué(e).
J'ai peur des loups!
I'm scared of . . . !

To express discouragement:
Je n'en peux plus!
J'abandonne!
Je craque!

To offer encouragement:
Courage!
Tu y es presque!
On y est presque!
Allez!

21 Qu'est-ce qu'ils disent?

1. Je suis fatiguée./Allez! On y est presque! 2. J'ai peur des ours! 3. Je meurs de soif! Je n'en peux plus.

22 Jeu de rôle

Ecris et joue une scène au sujet d'amis qui partent camper et qui se perdent. Parmi *(among)* tes amis, une personne est toujours en train de se plaindre *(complaining)*, une autre personne est découragée et elle a peur dans les bois, et la dernière personne essaie d'encourager les deux autres.

♟ **Game**

JE M'EN SOUVIENS! One student begins by saying **Je vais faire du camping. J'emporte une boussole.** The next student must repeat what was said and add another item. (**Je vais faire du camping. J'emporte une boussole et une tente.**) Continue in this manner until someone makes a mistake. The student who makes a mistake is out, but is then responsible for keeping track of what the players say. Start a new vocabulary round when someone makes a mistake, but the students who are out stay out. The winner is the last one remaining. You might also form small groups to play this game.

23 Au parc de la Jacques-Cartier

1. Look at the words in bold type at the top and bottom of the brochure. What is this brochure about? Who is it for?
2. If you were going to a state park, what things do you think would be forbidden? What would be encouraged?
3. According to the illustrations and text below each one, what are three things you shouldn't do at the **parc de la Jacques-Cartier**?
4. Read the brochure carefully to find two other things you shouldn't do, and two you should do.
   See answers below.

VOCABULAIRE

respecter la nature	*to respect nature*
jeter (remporter) les déchets	*to throw away (to take with you) your trash*
nourrir les animaux	*to feed the animals*
mutiler les arbres	*to deface the trees*
suivre les sentiers balisés	*to follow the marked trails*

24 Ecoute! 1. b 2. c 3. a

Ecoute Bénédicte et ses copains qui font une randonnée dans le parc. Choisis le dessin qui correspond à chaque conversation.

PARC DE LA JACQUES-CARTIER

BIENVENUE
DANS LE PARC DE LA JACQUES-CARTIER
«LA PROTECTION DU PARC, C'EST L'AFFAIRE DE TOUS»

Lorsque tu viens dans le parc, prends soin de:

- laisser chez toi les animaux domestiques
- garer ta voiture dans les aires de stationnement
- admirer les animaux sauvages sans les déranger ni tenter de les nourrir;
- jeter tes déchets dans les contenants prévus à cette fin;
- contempler les arbres, arbustes et autres plantes sans les prélever, ni les mutiler;
- ramener chez toi toute substance nocive tels savon, huile, combustible ou pesticide;
- éviter de peinturer, d'altérer ou de prélever les roches et autres formations naturelles

Québec ▪▪

a.

b.

c.

Answers

23 1. park rules; visitors
   2. Answers will vary.
   3. *Possible answers:* bring pets to the park, park your car outside of the parking lot, deface or remove rocks or other forms of nature
   4. *Shouldn't do:* bother or feed the animals, deface the trees or plants
      Should do: put litter in garbage cans, take with you any toxic substances, contemplate the trees and plants

Teaching Suggestion

You might have students create a public service announcement concerning appropriate behavior in national parks. You might use this as a chapter project.

Teaching Suggestion

23 After students do Activity 23, ask the following questions about the brochure: **Qu'est-ce qu'il faut laisser chez toi?** (les animaux domestiques) **Où est-ce que tu dois garer ta voiture?** (dans les aires de stationnement) **Qu'est-ce qu'il faut faire de tes déchets?** (les jeter dans les contenants prévus à cette fin) **Qu'est-ce qu'il faut ramener chez toi?** (toute substance nocive tels savon, huile, combustible ou pesticide) **Qu'est-ce qu'il faut éviter de faire?** (de peinturer, d'altérer ou de prélever les roches et autres formations naturelles)

Presentation

Vocabulaire Make drawings on the board to represent these activities, such as a tree with initials carved into it and a forest with marked trails. Then, tell students what one should or shouldn't do in the forest. **(Il faut respecter la nature. Il ne faut pas mutiler les arbres.)** Repeat the vocabulary and have students give a thumbs-up or a thumbs-down gesture to indicate whether one should or shouldn't do what you suggest.

For Individual Needs

24 Challenge Before you play the recording, have students tell as much as they can about the pictures in French. They should tell what the people are doing and then tell whether they should or shouldn't do it.

Presentation

Comment dit-on... ? Help students recall expressions from Chapter 7 *to give advice* (**Tu devrais...** , **Tu ferais bien de...** , **Evite de...** , **Tu ne devrais pas...**). Ask students what advice they would give a friend who eats a lot of junk food. Write the expressions on the board or on a transparency, and have students use them and the **Vocabulaire** on page 311 to give advice about appropriate behavior in parks. Then, have them use these expressions to give advice about school, table manners, and friendship.

Mon journal

27 For an additional journal entry suggestion for Chapter 12, see *Practice and Activity Book,* page 156.

CLOSE

To close this **étape,** have students present their posters from Activity 26 to the class. Have them explain the poster and read aloud the rules they've written.

ASSESS

Quiz 12-2, *Chapter Teaching Resources, Book 3,* pp. 193–194

Assessment Items, Audiocassette 8B/Audio CD 12

Performance Assessment

Have students create a phone conversation in which one friend announces that he or she is going camping, tells where he or she is going, and asks advice about what to bring on the trip. The other friend offers advice about what to bring and how to behave while in a park.

COMMENT DIT-ON... ?
Asking for and giving advice

To ask for advice:
  Qu'est-ce que je dois faire?

To give advice:
  Tu devrais respecter la nature.
  Tu ferais bien de suivre les sentiers balisés.
  Evite de nourrir les animaux.
  Tu ne devrais pas mutiler les arbres.

25 Qu'est-ce qu'ils font, ces enfants?!

Tu fais du camping avec un groupe d'enfants... mais ils font des bêtises. Qu'est-ce que tu leur conseilles?   See answers below.

26 Tu dois respecter les règles!

Fais un poster comme celui du parc de la Jacques-Cartier de la page 311. Ecris la liste des règles que l'on doit respecter dans un parc près de chez toi, dans ton école, dans ta classe ou dans ta chambre à la maison. Utilise des illustrations ou des extraits de magazines.

27 Mon journal

Est-ce que l'idée de faire du camping te plaît? Ecris ce que tu aimes et ce que tu n'aimes pas au sujet du camping.

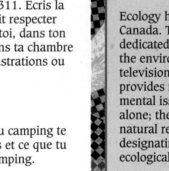

NOTE CULTURELLE

Ecology has been a growing concern in Canada. There are more than 500 groups dedicated to researching and protecting the environment in Canada alone. A television program, **La Semaine Verte,** provides regular updates on environmental issues. These groups don't work alone; the government seeks to protect the natural resources of Canada by designating areas as wildlife preserves, ecological reserves, and national parks.

Multicultural Link

Have students choose a country and research its ecological problems and programs that are in place to solve them.

Science Link

Have students ask their science teachers or do research to find out what technological advances are being made in the field of environmental preservation.

Possible answers

25 *(from left to right):* Tu ne devrais pas mutiler les arbres. Tu devrais utiliser de la lotion anti-moustiques. Evite de nourrir les animaux. Tu devrais respecter la nature. Tu devrais remporter les déchets. Tu ferais bien de suivre les sentiers balisés.

PANORAMA CULTUREL

Max • Martinique

Marius • Côte d'Ivoire

Mathieu • Québec

We asked some francophone people what they know about endangered animals in their areas. Here's what they had to say.

Quels sont les animaux en voie de disparition dans ta région?

«Il y en a beaucoup qui ont déjà complètement disparu, mais l'animal qui est en voie de disparition en ce moment, c'est l'iguane. Il en reste une dizaine d'unités. Ils sont au Fort Saint-Louis. Je crois que c'est plutôt ceux-là qui sont vraiment en voie de disparition.»

Qu'est-ce qu'on fait pour les protéger?

«J'ai l'impression qu'on ne s'en occupe pas beaucoup. Ils sont là. Ils sont livrés à eux-mêmes et je pense qu'ils vont disparaître dans très peu de temps.»

—Max

«Il y a des animaux en voie de disparition comme l'éléphant. L'éléphant en Côte d'Ivoire, il y en avait plein avant, mais maintenant ils commencent à disparaître et puis aussi il y a... il y a plein d'animaux. Je ne sais pas, hein... l'hippopotame, le crocodile et puis le singe et puis les jolis oiseaux, les petits oiseaux comme les grands. Bon, maintenant on n'en a pas trop. Pour les voir, il faut aller soit à l'intérieur du pays ou aller au zoo.»

—Marius

«Qui sont en voie de disparition? Dans le fleuve Saint-Laurent, ici, en bas du Québec, il y a les baleines. Il y a les bélugas qui sont en voie de disparition. A l'extérieur, il y en a plusieurs. Il y en a beaucoup qui ont déjà disparu aussi. Et puis, il y a beaucoup d'oiseaux aussi qui disparaissent, à cause des produits qu'on envoie dans l'environnement.»

Qu'est-ce qu'on fait pour les protéger?

«Le gouvernement, il pense, enfin ils veulent faire dépolluer le fleuve Saint-Laurent ici, mais ils [ne] font pas grand-chose.»

—Mathieu

Qu'en penses-tu?

1. Are there any endangered animals in your community? What endangered species have you read about or heard about in the news lately?
2. What is being done to protect endangered species? See answers below.

Possible answers

2. Wildlife protection groups have been formed to protect endangered species. They have proposed laws restricting hunting and urban development, enacted programs to reintroduce certain species where populations have been depleted, and educated the public on the importance of wildlife preservation.

Questions

1. En Martinique, où est-ce qu'on trouve des iguanes? (au fort Saint-Louis)
2. D'après Marius, où faut-il aller pour voir des animaux en Côte d'Ivoire? (soit à l'intérieur du pays, soit au zoo)
3. D'après Mathieu, pourquoi est-ce que les oiseaux disparaissent? (à cause des produits qu'on envoie dans l'environnement)
4. D'après lui, que fait le gouvernement? (pas grand-chose)

VIDEO PROGRAM OR EXPANDED VIDEO PROGRAM, Videocassette 4 47:44–52:02

OR VIDEODISC PROGRAM, Videodisc 6B

Search 32430, Play To 36485

Teacher Notes

- See *Video Guide*, *Videodisc Guide*, and *Practice and Activity Book* for activities related to the **Panorama Culturel**.
- Remind students that cultural material may be included in the Chapter Quizzes and Test.
- The interviewees' language represents informal, unrehearsed speech. Occasionally, edits have been made for clarification.

Presentation

Write on the board or on a transparency the following names of animals: **les orignaux, l'éléphant, le crocodile, l'iguane, les lions, les oiseaux, les orangs-outangs, les bélugas, le singe, les baleines, les ours, l'hippopotame, les perroquets, les poissons.**

Show the video and have students check off the animals they hear mentioned and tell where (country, department, or province) they are found. (*Answers:* l'éléphant, le crocodile, l'iguane, les oiseaux, le singe, les baleines (les bélugas), l'hippopotame; Martinique: l'iguane; Côte d'Ivoire: l'éléphant, l'hippopotame, le crocodile, le singe, les oiseaux; Québec: les baleines (les bélugas), les oiseaux)

*Relating a series of events;
describing people and places*

Jump Start!

Have students write three complaints a camper might make and an expression of encouragement in response to each one.

MOTIVATE

Ask students why it's difficult to follow a story told by a four year-old. Point out that learning to sequence events in a logical manner is an important skill that must be learned in your native language as well as any others you might study.

TEACH

Teaching Suggestion

28 Have students look at the journal entry again and find the words Sophie uses to indicate the order of the events of her trip (**d'abord, après ça, ensuite, enfin**).

Presentation

Comment dit-on... ? Ask students to recall the expressions in Chapters 1 and 4 to *relate a series of events* (**d'abord, ensuite, puis, après ça, finalement, enfin**), and the expressions in Chapter 8 *to tell what things were like* (**c'était, il y avait, il/elle était**). Then, tell a story, using the new expressions. As you tell it, have students raise their right hand when they hear an expression that relates a series of events, and raise their left hand when they hear an expression that describes people or places. Finally, have students tell each other what they did last night, sequencing and describing the events.

Lundi 12 septembre
Cher journal,   20h15
Me voici donc revenue de mon week-end de camping! Il faisait un temps horrible quand nous sommes partis, mais heureusement ça n'a pas duré. A midi, il faisait beau et chaud, un temps magnifique, surtout pour les randonnées. Alors, on s'est mis en route! D'abord, on a fait une randonnée super et Marc a pris des douzaines de photos. Il y avait une chute d'eau géniale ; il a pris une photo de moi devant. Nous avons même vu un ours! Après ça, on est allés se baigner dans la rivière. Ensuite, Julie est allée à la pêche, Marc est rentré au terrain de camping et moi, je suis restée nager. Malheureusement, les moustiques sont restés aussi! Ils m'ont piquée partout! Julie m'a prêté sa lotion anti-moustiques, mais c'était trop tard! Enfin, on a fait un pique-nique super. On a mangé les poissons que Julie avait attrapés. Quelle journée! Malgré les piqûres, c'était super-génial. Vive le camping!
                                                        Sophie

28 Tu as compris?

faire du camping

1. Où est-ce que Sophie et ses amis sont allés?
2. Quel temps faisait-il? Il faisait un temps horrible quand ils sont partis, mais à midi, il faisait beau et chaud.
3. Ils ont fait une randonnée. Ils ont pris des photos. Ils ont vu un ours. Ils sont allées se baigner. Julie est allée à la pêche. Sophie a nagé. Ils ont fait un pique-nique.
3. Qu'est-ce qu'ils ont fait là-bas?
4. Le week-end s'est bien passé? Oui. C'était super-génial.

✏ COMMENT DIT-ON... ?
Relating a series of events; describing people and places

To relate a series of events:
   D'abord, j'ai acheté des bottes et une casquette.
   Ensuite, je suis parti(e) au parc avec Francine et Denis.
   Après ça, on a fait une randonnée pédestre.
   Finalement, je me suis couché(e) très tôt.

To describe people and places:
   Il y avait beaucoup d'arbres et une chute d'eau.
   Paul **était** pénible parce qu'il **avait** faim.
   Francine **avait l'air** embêtée.
   Moi, j'**étais** ravi(e)!

314 *trois cent quatorze*   CHAPITRE 12   A la belle étoile

RESOURCES FOR TROISIEME ETAPE

Textbook Audiocassette 6B/Audio CD 12
Practice and Activity Book, pp. 140–142
Videodisc Guide
   Videodisc Program, Videodisc 6B

Chapter Teaching Resources, Book 3
• Communicative Activity 12-2, pp. 173–174
• Teaching Transparency Master 12-3, pp. 177, 178
   Teaching Transparency 12-3
• Additional Listening Activities 12-5, 12-6, p. 181
   Audiocassette 10B/Audio CD 12
• Realia 12-2, pp. 184, 185
• Situation Cards 12-3, pp. 186–187
• Student Response Forms, pp. 188–190
• Quiz 12-3, pp. 195–196
   Audiocassette 8B/Audio CD 12

29 Ecoute!

Séverine raconte son week-end au parc du Saguenay à son ami Guillaume. Ecoute, puis réponds aux questions. Answers on p. 297D.

1. Quel temps faisait-il?
2. Qu'est-ce qu'elles ont fait là-bas?
3. Est-ce que Monique était de bonne ou de mauvaise humeur? Pourquoi?

*G*rammaire The **passé composé** and the **imparfait**

- Remember that you use the **passé composé** to tell what happened in the past.
- When you use **être** as the helping verb, the past participle agrees with the subject.
- Words that often signal the **passé composé** are **un jour, une fois, soudain,** and the words you've learned to use to relate a series of events.
- You use the **imparfait** to describe what people or things were like; to describe repeated or habitual actions in the past, what used to happen; and to describe general conditions in the past, to tell what was going on.
- Words that often signal the **imparfait** are **toujours, d'habitude, souvent,** and **de temps en temps.**

30 Une histoire de fantômes

Francine raconte une histoire de fantômes à ses amis réunis autour d'un feu de camp. Complète son histoire en mettant les verbes au passé composé ou à l'imparfait. Est-ce que c'était un vrai fantôme? Qu'est-ce que c'était? See answers below.

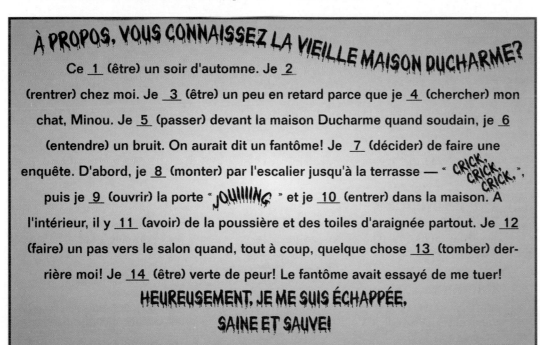

À PROPOS, VOUS CONNAISSEZ LA VIEILLE MAISON DUCHARME?

Ce __1__ (être) un soir d'automne. Je __2__ (rentrer) chez moi. Je __3__ (être) un peu en retard parce que je __4__ (chercher) mon chat, Minou. Je __5__ (passer) devant la maison Ducharme quand soudain, je __6__ (entendre) un bruit. On aurait dit un fantôme! Je __7__ (décider) de faire une enquête. D'abord, je __8__ (monter) par l'escalier jusqu'à la terrasse — " CRICK, CRICK, CRICK, " puis je __9__ (ouvrir) la porte " JOUIIIIING " et je __10__ (entrer) dans la maison. A l'intérieur, il y __11__ (avoir) de la poussière et des toiles d'araignée partout. Je __12__ (faire) un pas vers le salon quand, tout à coup, quelque chose __13__ (tomber) derrière moi! Je __14__ (être) verte de peur! Le fantôme avait essayé de me tuer!

HEUREUSEMENT, JE ME SUIS ÉCHAPPÉE, SAINE ET SAUVE!

TROISIEME ETAPE

trois cent quinze **315**

Presentation

Grammaire Ask students to recall what they know about the **passé composé** and the **imparfait.** Then, write the following paragraph on the board, underlining the **passé composé** and the **imparfait** verb forms in two different colors. Have students explain the tense of each verb.

Quand j'<u>étais</u> petit, d'habitude on <u>allait</u> à la plage. Mais une fois, on <u>est allés</u> camper. D'abord, on <u>a fait</u> une randonnée pédestre. Il <u>faisait</u> froid! J'<u>avais</u> très froid, et je <u>crevais</u> de faim. Après ça, on <u>a cuisiné</u> sur un feu de bois (heureusement). On <u>était</u> en train de dîner quand soudain, une mouffette <u>est entrée</u> dans notre tente! Mon père <u>avait</u> très peur! Finalement, la mouffette <u>est partie</u>, et tout le monde <u>était</u> content. C'<u>était</u> un week-end super!

Additional Practice

Distribute copies of the following paragraph and have students supply the correct verb forms.

Le week-end passé, je (j') ____ (faire) du vélo de montagne avec des copains. Ça (C') ____ (être) génial! Il ____ (faire) un temps superbe, et tout le monde ____ (être) de bonne humeur. Ça (C') ____ (être) dur, le vélo, mais on ____ (s'arrêter) souvent pour se reposer. Comme d'habitude, Jacques ____ (aller) moins vite que les autres, et en plus, il ____ (se perdre)! Heureusement, il nous ____ (retrouver). Tout est bien qui finit bien!

(Answers: ai fait, était, faisait, était, était, s'arrêtait, allait, s'est perdu, a retrouvés)

TROISIEME ETAPE

Answers

30 1. C'était
2. rentrais
3. j'étais
4. cherchais
5. passais
6. j'ai entendu
7. j'ai décidé

8. suis montée
9. j'ai ouvert
10. suis entrée
11. avait
12. j'ai fait
13. est tombé
14. j'étais

Teaching Suggestion

30 Write the activity on a transparency. After students have completed the activity, have a student come up to the overhead and write in the verb forms his or her classmates suggest. Have students explain why the **passé composé** or the **imparfait** is used in each case.

Teaching Suggestions

31 Before students begin this activity, make several statements describing these illustrations and have students write the letters of the illustrations you're describing. Then, have students think of expressions they might need to tell the story: *to get sprayed by a skunk* (**se faire arroser par une mouffette**); *to smell bad* (**sentir mauvais**).

32 You might refer students to the Supplementary Vocabulary on page 339 for outdoor activities.

Cooperative Learning

32 Have students form groups of three to peer-edit their papers. Have one person check spelling and accents, a second student check words that relate a series of events, and a third check the **passé composé** and the **imparfait**.

For videodisc application, see *Videodisc Guide*.

CLOSE

To close this **étape,** have students bring to class pictures of camping activities. Select four or five of them and have students tell a story, using the pictures in the order in which you display them.

ASSESS

Quiz 12-3, *Chapter Teaching Resources, Book 3,* pp. 195–196

Assessment Items, Audiocassette 8B/Audio CD 12

Performance Assessment

Display the pictures suggested for the Close activity and have students write a story, using any four they choose. Students should use the **passé composé,** the **imparfait,** and words that relate a series of events.

---

31 La journée de Pierre

Aujourd'hui, Pierre a fait une randonnée dans le parc. Mets ses activités en ordre et raconte sa journée. See answers below.

a.

b.

c.

d.

e.

f.

32 Quelle aventure!

Imagine que tu as passé le week-end avec un groupe d'amis dans un des parcs québécois. Décris le temps qu'il a fait là-bas, ce que tu as vu et ce que tout le monde a fait. Décris tes impressions de cette expérience dans la nature.

33 Raconte!

Maintenant pose des questions à ton ami(e) au sujet du week-end décrit dans l'activité 32. Demande-lui où il/elle est allé(e), avec qui, quel temps il a fait, comment était le parc, ce qu'il/elle a fait et si c'était bien. Changez de rôles.

Possible answers

31 e, a, f, d, c, b; Pierre est allé au parc. Il faisait beau, et il était très content. D'abord, il a fait une randonnée. Ensuite, il a fait un pique-nique. Un écureuil a mangé son sandwich, et il a vu une mouffette qui lui a fait une surprise! Pierre sentait mauvais, et il n'était pas très content. Alors, il s'est baigné dans la rivière. Finalement, il est rentré chez lui.

RENCONTRE CULTURELLE

If you visit Quebec, you might be surprised at some of the French-Canadian words and expressions you'll hear. See if you can match the French expressions on the left with their French-Canadian equivalents on the right.

1. maïs
2. dîner
3. stop
4. au revoir
5. boisson
6. pomme de terre
7. week-end
8. ça va
9. de rien
10. hot-dog

a. bonjour
b. breuvage
c. patate
d. bienvenue
e. fin de semaine
f. arrêt
g. souper
h. blé d'Inde
i. c'est correct
j. chien chaud

Qu'en penses-tu?

1. Which French expressions use English words? What do French Canadians use instead?   stop, week-end, hot-dog; arrêt, fin de semaine, chien chaud

2. Which French-Canadian expressions show the influence of North American culture?
bonjour *(used for "good-bye," lit., "good-day")*, **bienvenue** *(used for "you're welcome, lit., "welcome")*, and **patate** *(potato)*

Savais-tu que... ?

If you visit Quebec, some of the words and expressions you will hear may be different from those you would hear in many parts of France. Some words and expressions heard in Quebec were used only in certain regions of France and might not be used in France anymore. Other more modern expressions originated separately in France and Quebec. For example, in France, English words such as **hot-dog, week-end,** and **stop** are commonly used. In Quebec you are more likely to hear **chien chaud, fin de semaine,** and **arrêt.** Some expressions you will hear in Quebec reflect the influence of English, such as **bienvenue,** which literally means "welcome," and is used instead of **de rien** to mean "you're welcome."

(answers: 1 h, 2 g, 3 f, 4 a, 5 b, 6 c, 7 e, 8 i, 9 d, 10 j)

Language Note

Some French people might be surprised to hear **Bonjour, bienvenue!** when they leave a place of business in Quebec. In France, a merchant would say **Bonjour, bienvenue** to mean *Hello, welcome!* and **Merci, au revoir** to mean *Thank you, goodbye!* French-Canadians say **Bonjour** to mean *Have a nice day* and **bienvenue** to mean *You're welcome,* at the end of a business transaction after the customer has said **merci.**

Culture Note

In 1974, the Quebec National Assembly adopted French as the official language of the province. In 1976, the **Parti Québécois** won a majority of seats in the parliament. This separatist party submitted a referendum for popular vote to secede from the nation, but it was defeated. In 1994, for the first time since 1976, the separatist party, now called the **Bloc Québécois,** gained a majority of seats in the Quebec parliament.

READING STRATEGY
Summarizing

Teacher Note

For an additional reading, see *Practice and Activity Book*, page 143.

PREREADING
Activities A–B

Motivating Activity

Ask students what they would want to do if they had the opportunity to visit Quebec. Would they prefer to travel independently or with an organized group? What would they want to know before they left for Quebec? Would they camp out or stay in a hotel?

Culture Note

In the **parc de la Jacques-Cartier,** there are 132 species of birds and 23 species of mammals, including moose, black bear **(l'ours noir),** wolf, lynx **(le lynx),** raccoon, beaver **(le castor),** and **des cerfs de Virginie** (the Canadian expression for a type of hart — a member of the deer family).

READING
Activities C–D

For Individual Needs

C. Slower Pace Have students do this activity in pairs.

Terms in Lisons!

Students might want to know the following vocabulary: **côtoyer** *(to get next to);* **un élan** *(an elk);* **un feu de bois** *(a campfire);* **l'amorce** *(the beginning);* **des abris sous roches** *(rock shelters);* **des saumons** *(salmon);* **une clôture** *(closing);* **les assurances** *(insurance).*

LISONS!

DE BONS CONSEILS
Do you know someone who can't retell a story or describe an event without covering every detail, no matter how unimportant? You probably find yourself saying in frustration, "Just tell me in 25 words or less what happened!" What you want your friend to do is *to summarize,* to reduce a story to its most important elements. When you summarize, you leave out the unimportant details. A summary doesn't change a story, it simply reduces it to its essence. Summarizing is a good way to check your understanding of what you read.

A. Preview the text. Read the titles, headings, and subheadings. What kind of text is this?

   1. an article from a nature magazine
   2. <u>pages from a travel brochure</u>
   3. a journal entry by a naturalist

B. Skim for the gist. What's the point of this text?

   1. to describe a naturalist's journey through the wilderness
   2. to promote a novel called *The Call of the Wolf*
   3. <u>to describe travel packages available to French tourists</u>

C. Scan the text to answer these specific questions.   See answers below.

   1. What are three sports you can do at the **Centre de Vacances Edphy?**
   2. On which day of the **Circuit découverte** do tourists go back to Quebec?

318 *trois cent dix-huit*

L'APPEL DES LOUPS
CIRCUIT DÉCOUVERTE

Côtoyez la faune dans son habitat sauvage, au cœur de l'immense Parc de conservation de la rivière Jacques-Cartier. Explorez tous les aspects de la forêt québécoise: en randonnées pédestres, en canot et en survol par hélicoptère. Vivez un contact privilégié avec la nature, en suivant les guides naturalistes.

1er jour: Québec
Accueil à Québec. Installation à l'hôtel.

2e jour: Québec/Parc de la Jacques-Cartier
Transfert à l'auberge de la forêt Montmorency et rencontre avec les guides naturalistes. Dîner et logement.

3e jour: Parc de la Jacques-Cartier
Exploration de la flore de la forêt Montmorency. Découverte des chutes de la Rivière Noire. Départ pour le premier campement. Déjeuner au barrage Sautauriski. Premier contact avec le territoire sauvage et la faune du parc de conservation de la Jacques-Cartier: loups, lynx, castors, ours noirs, élans d'Amérique et autres animaux (23 espèces de mammifères et 132 espèces d'oiseaux). Arrivée au Lac des Alliés et montage du premier campement. Possibilité de pêche à la truite. Appel nocturne des loups.

4e jour: Parc de la Jacques-Cartier
Survol du territoire en hélicoptère. Accès au fond du Canyon de l'Équatèque et début de la randonnée de 11 km à pied le long de la rivière Jacques-Cartier. Repas au feu de bois. Soirée "légendes et chants folkloriques".

5e jour: Parc de la Jacques-Cartier
Initiation au canot de rivière. Amorce de la descente de la rivière Jacques-Cartier (30 km en deux jours). Petite excursion en montagne et découverte des abris sous roches. Poursuite de l'expédition jusqu'au camping du Héron.

6e jour: Parc de la Jacques-Cartier
Deuxième jour du parcours en canot (environ 15 km). Déjeuner au delta d'une rivière à saumons. Passage du rapide du draveur et de la Passe du loup. Visite du centre d'interprétation. Arrivée au camp en bois rond le Kernan. Soirée de clôture et fête.

7e jour: Parc de la Jacques-Cartier
Randonnée pédestre et interprétation. Découverte des cascades de la rivière-à-l'épaule. Retour vers Québec.

Départs garantis chaque samedi du début juin à la fin septembre (sauf en juillet).

Prix par personne : 4 410 F

Le prix comprend:
* Les transferts aller/retour Québec/Parc de la Jacques-Cartier.
* 1 nuit hôtel 1ère catégorie à Québec.
* 1 nuit à l'auberge de la forêt Montmorency.
* La pension complète du dîner jour 1 au déjeuner jour 7.
* Les services des guides naturalistes.
* Les équipements de transport sur le terrain, canots, tentes.
* Le survol en hélicoptère.
* Les taxes et services.

Le prix ne comprend pas:
* Le transport aérien Paris/Montréal/Paris.
* La taxe d'aéroport.
* Le sac de couchage.
* Les dépenses et assurances personnelles.

Science Link

Have students ask a science teacher or do research to find out about the boreal forest of the **parc de la Jacques-Cartier.** (The coniferous forest of the park is comprised of cone-bearing, needle-leaved pines, spruces, and furs. This is the characteristic vegetation of the boreal forest, which is the subpolar region between the colder tundra zone and the warmer temperate zone.)

Answers

C 1. *Possible answers:* tennis, judo, swimming, archery, canoeing, horseback riding, baseball, basketball, volleyball, handball
2. the seventh day
3. 325 F
4. b

SPECIAL ❧ JEUNES
HEBERGEMENT

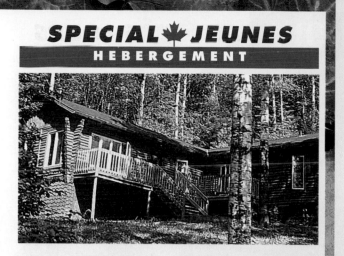

CENTRE DE VACANCES EDPHY INTERNATIONAL:
Unique en Amérique

A 80 km au nord de Mirabel, aux pieds de la chaîne de montagnes des Laurentides, c'est Edphy International, ses 590 acres de forêt, ses 3 lacs, la rivière du Nord et son parc récréo-sportif incomparable.

Activités proposées:

Sports individuels : tennis, judo, natation, tir à l'arc, canoë, équitation... Sports d'équipes : baseball, basket, volley, handball.
Atelier de cirque : trampoline, échasses, jonglerie, trapèze, acrobaties... Les événements spéciaux, olympiades, "beach party", festivals arts et culture.

Prix par personne:	
2 semaines	5200 F

Le prix comprend:

• L'hébergement, la pension complète, tout le programme d'activités multi sports/animation et l'encadrement, les taxes.

POHENEGAMOOK
Un environnement exceptionnel:

Pohénégamook Santé Plein Air est situé sur la berge est du lac Pohénégamook. Pohénégamook, en "montagnais" lieu d'hivernement, signifie également "endroit où il fait bon vivre". Le centre bénéficie d'un cadre naturel exceptionnel, d'un micro climat des

plus agréables, d'un rivage abritant plus de 750 chevreuils et d'une situation géographique peu commune, chevauchant les frontières de l'état du Maine, du nouveau Brunswick et du Québec. Une pléiade d'activités est offerte. Randonnées pédestres, observation de la faune, catamaran, voile, pêche, tir à l'arc, escalade, astronomie, pédalo, canot, baignade. (Les équipements nécessaires aux activités sont fournis gratuitement.)

Prix par personne et par jour:	
Prix enfant (jusqu'à dix-huit ans)	325 F
Prix adulte	450 F

Le prix comprend:

• L'hébergement, la pension complète, l'équipement et l'animation.

3. How much would a sixteen year-old traveler pay to stay one day at the **Pohénégamook Santé Plein Air?**

4. When can a traveler be guaranteed a departure for the trip to the Jacques-Cartier Park?

  a. Sundays from June to the end of September, including July

  b. Saturdays from June through September, except for July

  c. Saturdays only in July

D. Read the information in the box in the lower left corner of **l'Appel des Loups.** How does it relate to the rest of the text? If you were to pay the 4410 francs for the trip, what else would that price include? *See answers below.*

E. Which trip would you choose?

RAPPEL Before you summarize what you're reading, it helps to take notes. First, you need to be aware of the purpose of your summary. Next, go through the text and write down all the words and phrases you think are important and relevant to your purpose. Take notes only on that topic. Then, from the notes you've gathered, make your summary.

F. Summarize in one sentence the description of **Centre de Vacances Edphy International** and its activities. Do the same for the Pohénégamook resort in two sentences. *See answers below.*

G. Write a card to your pen pal in France in which you summarize your imaginary seven-day trip to the Jacques-Cartier Park. Use all the information you've read as the basis for your account. Don't bore your friend with every detail; choose only the five or six most important points of interest on your trip.

trois cent dix-neuf **319**

POSTREADING
Activities E–G

❖ For Individual Needs

F. Slower Pace Write a summary statement about the Centre Edphy and distribute it to partners. Have them decide which camp it describes. Then, have them write a summary statement about Pohénégamook, using your statement as a model.

📁 Portfolio

G. Written Students might include their card in their written portfolios. For portfolio information, see *Assessment Guide,* pages 2–13.

🤝 Cooperative Learning

Have students work in groups to write and design a travel brochure for a park or town in Quebec. Assign a leader to propose and delegate research topics, a writer to process the information and write the text, a proofreader to read the text and check for errors, another writer to type or write the text to be placed on the brochure, and an artist to draw or cut out the illustrations and arrange the art and text on the page. You might choose to use this activity as a chapter project.

Terms in Lisons!

Students might want to know the following vocabulary: **l'encadrement** *(training personnel);* **le tir à l'arc** *(archery);* **la berge/le rivage** *(the riverbank);* **abritant** *(sheltering);* **des chevreuils** *(a type of deer);* **chevauchant** *(overlapping);* **une pléiade** *(a group, more commonly used in Canada than in France).*

Answers

D It gives detailed information on what the price of the trip includes and does not include; transportation from Quebec to the park, lodging, meals from dinner the first day to lunch the last day, guides, equipment, helicopter trip, taxes and tips.

F *Possible answers:* The **Centre de Vacances Edphy International** is a vacation resort at the base of the Laurentides Mountains that offers many sports and recreational activities to its guests. The **Pohénégamook** is a lakeside resort that provides outdoor activities, which include hiking, wildlife observation, sailing, fishing, archery, climbing, astronomy, cycling, canoeing, and swimming.

MISE EN PRATIQUE

The **Mise en pratique** reviews and integrates all four skills and culture in preparation for the Chapter Test.

Teaching Suggestion

Ask the following questions about the advertisements: C'est quelle sorte de publicité? (pour des campings) Comment s'appellent les deux campings? (Parc Bromont et Camping Granby) Quelle est l'adresse du premier camping? (24, Lafontaine, C.P. 26) Qui est le propriétaire du deuxième camping? (André Rainville) Où se trouve le premier camping? (à trois kilomètres de Bromont) Quel est le numéro de téléphone du deuxième camping? (514–372–6639)

Language Note

Students might want to know the following vocabulary from the brochures: **le ski de fond** (cross-country skiing); **la location de roulotte** (trailer rental); **des glissades** (slides); **un marché aux puces** (flea market); **un ballon volant** (hot-air balloon); **un terrain de jeu** (playground); **une messe** (mass); **un matelas pneumatique** (inflatable mattress); **un égout** (sewer); **une laveuse/une sécheuse** (the Canadian terms for washer/dryer); **un dépanneur** (repairman).

Culture Note

La pétanque, also known as **le jeu de boules**, was introduced to the south of France by sailors of the Rhône River. It is played with heavy metal balls, roughly the size of oranges, and a smaller, wooden ball, called **un cochonnet** and is played on a flat, dirt surface. The object of the game is to throw the **cochonnet**, and then attempt to throw the other balls as close to it as possible.

320   *trois cent vingt*

CHAPITRE 12   A la belle étoile

Culture Note

Point out that telephone numbers in Quebec are organized numerically as they are in the United States. They have a three-digit area code, which is not necessary to dial if you are calling from the same area code, followed by a three-digit and a four-digit number. There is no set pattern for the way the numbers are read.

Language Note

The **C. P.** in the address of **Parc Bromont** stands for **casier postal** (similar to a **boîte postale**).

1 Look at the ads for the two campgrounds on page 320. In order to help you decide which one to go to, make a list of the things that are offered by both. Then, make separate lists of features that are unique to each campground. *See answers below.*

2 Now get together in a group to choose a campground. Suggest the campground that you prefer and try to persuade your friends to go there by telling what its advantages are, where it's located, and what there is to see and do there.

3 Listen to the following radio ad for a campground. Is this an ad for **Camping Granby** or **Parc Bromont?** *Answers on page 297D.*

4 You've been outvoted! Everyone else chose the campground that you like the least. Write a postcard home, telling what you did there and complaining about the things you didn't like.

5 Your friends decided to "rough it" on this camping trip, so you're off to the **parc de la Jacques-Cartier.** Before you go, read the **Conseils pratiques** of the lynx, the mascot of the park. *See answers below.*

1. When are you most likely to be bothered by insects at the park?
2. What should you do to protect yourself against bites?
3. **Non potable** means *not drinkable.* What water at the park is not drinkable?
4. What can you do to make the water drinkable?

6 What kind of comparisons can you make between the people and places you've learned about this year? Make a chart with **France, Martinique, Côte d'Ivoire, Quebec,** and **United States** in a column on the left. Across the top of the chart, write headings for six columns: **Location and Size, Language(s), History, Life for Teenagers, Leisure Activities,** and **Food.** Fill out the chart, using your book as a reference. Compare your chart with a partner's. What similarities and differences do you find among these cultures?

7

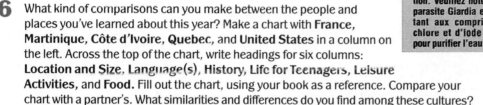
JEU DE ROLE

It's your job to convince a reluctant friend to come with you to the **parc de la Jacques-Cartier.** He or she has never been camping and is a bit fearful. You should tell your friend . . .

- what you know about the park's history,
- what there is to see and do at the park,
- what to bring, and
- what to do and what not to do at the park.

Conseils pratiques

Comme la période des insectes piqueurs s'étend de la mi-juin à la fin août, nous vous conseillons, pour un séjour agréable:
- d'apporter de l'huile à mouches;
- de porter des vêtements de couleur pâle;
- de ne pas consommer de bananes;
- d'éviter les produits parfumés.

Avertissement:

L'eau de surface (lacs, rivières et ruisseaux) est non potable et doit être bouillie pendant cinq minutes avant consommation. Veuillez noter que le parasite Giardia est résistant aux comprimés de chlore et d'iode utilisés pour purifier l'eau.

MISE EN PRATIQUE
CHAPITRE 12

📁 **Portfolio**

2 Oral This activity is appropriate for students' oral portfolios. For portfolio suggestions, see *Assessment Guide,* page 25.

✦ **For Individual Needs**

3 Slower Pace As students listen to the recording, have them place a check next to the features they hear mentioned on the lists they made in Activity 1.

4 Visual Learners Have students draw four illustrations depicting what they didn't like about the campground. For each illustration, they should write a one-sentence caption, using sequencing words and expressions for complaining. Students might draw their illustrations on paper or on a transparency, and then describe their trip to the class.

📁 **Portfolio**

4 Written This activity is appropriate for students' written portfolios. For portfolio suggestions, see *Assessment Guide,* page 25.

📺 **Video Wrap-Up**

- *VIDEO PROGRAM*
- *EXPANDED VIDEO PROGRAM,* Videocassette 4, 32:26–56:34
- *VIDEODISC PROGRAM,* Videodisc 6B

At this time, you might want to use the video resources for additional review and enrichment. See *Video Guide* or *Videodisc Guide* for suggestions regarding the following:

- **Promenons-nous dans les bois** (Dramatic episode)
- **Panorama Culturel** (Interviews)
- **Vidéoclips** (Authentic footage)

Answers

1 *Possible answers*
Both: camping familial, piscine/lac artificiel, glissade
Parc Bromont: golfe miniature, ski de fond, patinoire, location de roulotte, piste cyclable, factory outlets, marché aux puces
Camping Granby: tennis, croquet, pétanque, jeux de fers, ballon volant, terrain de jeux pour enfants, salle d'amusement, messe sur terrain, badminton, restaurant, laveuse, sécheuse

5 1. mid-June to the end of August
2. bring insect repellant, wear light-colored clothing, don't eat bananas, don't use perfumed products
3. water from rivers, lakes, streams
4. boil it for five minutes

This page is intended to help students prepare for the test. It is a brief checklist of the major points covered in the chapter. The students should be reminded that this is only a checklist and does not necessarily include everything that will appear on the test.

♜ Game

ALLEZ-Y! Form four teams and give a transparency and a transparency pen to each one. Then, make four sets of index cards, each set bearing the numbers 1-12 (48 cards total), and put the cards in a bag. Have one member from each team select four cards from the bag and place them face-down on his or her desk. Once all the teams have selected cards, call out **Allez-y!** and have them turn their cards over. Teams should then write on their transparency the answers to the questions from **Que sais-je?** that correspond to the numbers they drew. After two minutes, have students put down their pens. Have one member from each team bring their cards and transparency to the front. Show the cards and the transparency and have the class verify that the questions were answered correctly. Award one point for each correct answer. You might play for a certain number of rounds or points.

QUE SAIS-JE?

Can you ask for and give information, and give directions? p. 304

Can you complain and express discouragement? p. 310

Can you offer encouragement? p. 310

Can you ask for and give advice? p. 312

Can you relate a series of events and describe people and places? p. 314

Can you use what you've learned in this chapter?

1 How would you ask someone what there is to see and do in these places? How would you tell someone?

   1. in a Canadian park   2. in Abidjan   3. in your favorite city
Qu'est-ce qu'il y a à voir/faire... ? ; Il y a... ; On peut...

2 How would you ask where these places are? How would you tell where they are? See answers below.

   1. le parc de la Jacques-Cartier   2. la Côte d'Ivoire   3. la Martinique

3 What would you say if . . . See answers below.

   1. you were on a hike and just couldn't go on?
   2. you hadn't eaten since 5:00 this morning?
   3. you were afraid of a certain animal?

4 How would you encourage your friend to finish the hike?
Possible answers: Courage! Tu y es presque! On y est presque! Allez!

5 How would you ask someone for advice?
Qu'est-ce que je dois faire?

6 What would you advise a friend to pack for a camping trip . . .

   1. in the summer?   2. in the winter? See answers below.

7 What advice would you give a friend who . . . See answers below.

   1. is being bitten by mosquitos?
   2. is offering some potato chips to a squirrel?
   3. just threw the potato chip bag on the ground?

8 How would you say that you did these things in this order? See answers below.

9 How would you describe . . .

   1. the weather yesterday?   2. how you felt this morning?
   Hier, il faisait...   Ce matin, j'étais...

322   *trois cent vingt-deux*   CHAPITRE 12   A la belle étoile

Possible answers

2 Où se trouve...
  1. Il se trouve au nord de Québec.
  2. ... dans l'ouest de l'Afrique.
  3. ... au sud des Etats-Unis.

3 1. Je n'en peux plus! J'abandonne! Je craque!
  2. Je crève de faim!
  3. J'ai peur des... !

6 1. Tu devrais emporter un short, des lunettes de soleil, un maillot de bain, une tente, un sac de couchage, une boussole, une canne à pêche et de la lotion anti-moustiques.
  2. Tu ferais bien d'emporter un anorak, un pull, des bottes, des raquettes, des skis, une tente, un sac de couchage et une boussole.

7 1. Tu devrais mettre de la lotion anti-moustiques.
  2. Evite de nourrir les animaux.
  3. Tu devrais remporter les déchets.

8 D'abord, nous avons fait une randonnée pédestre. Ensuite, nous avons fait du canotage. Finalement, nous avons fait du vélo de montagne.

PREMIERE ETAPE

Asking for and giving information; giving directions

Où se trouve... ? *Where is ... located?*
Qu'est-ce qu'il y a à voir/faire... ? *What is there to see/do . . . ?*
... se trouve... *. . . is located . . .*
Il y a... *There is/are . . .*
On peut... *You can . . .*
C'est au nord/au sud/à l'est/à l'ouest de... *It's to the north/south/east/west of . . .*

C'est dans le nord/le sud/l'est/l'ouest de... *It's in the northern/southern/eastern/western part of . . .*

Animals

un orignal *moose*
un ours *bear*
un loup *wolf*
un écureuil *squirrel*
un renard *fox*
un raton laveur *raccoon*
une mouffette *skunk*
un canard *duck*

Outdoor activities

faire du camping *to go camping*
faire du canotage *to go canoeing*
faire du vélo de montagne *to go mountain-bike riding*
faire une randonnée pédestre *to go for a hike*
... en raquettes *. . . snow-shoeing*
... en skis *. . . cross-country skiing*

DEUXIEME ETAPE

Complaining; expressing discouragement and offering encouragement

Je crève de faim! *I'm dying of hunger!*
Je meurs de soif! *I'm dying of thirst!*
Je suis fatigué(e). *I'm tired.*
J'ai peur (de la, du, des)... *I'm scared (of) . . .*
Je n'en peux plus! *I just can't do any more!*
J'abandonne! *I'm giving up!*
Je craque! *I'm losing it!*
Courage! *Hang in there!*
Tu y es (On y est) presque! *You're (we're) almost there!*
Allez! *Come on!*

Asking for and giving advice

Qu'est-ce que je dois faire? *What should I do?*
Tu devrais... *You should . . .*
Tu ferais bien de... *You would do well to . . .*
Evite de... *Avoid . . .*
Tu ne devrais pas... *You shouldn't . . .*
respecter la nature *to respect nature*
jeter (remporter) les déchets *to throw away (to take with you) your trash*

nourrir les animaux *to feed the animals*
mutiler les arbres *to deface the trees*
suivre les sentiers balisés *to follow the marked trails*

Camping equipment

emporter *to bring (with you)*
une lampe de poche *flashlight*
une tente *tent*
un sac de couchage *sleeping bag*
une boussole *compass*
une trousse de premiers soins *first-aid kit*
une canne à pêche *fishing pole*
des allumettes *matches*
de la lotion anti-moustiques *insect repellent*

TROISIEME ETAPE

Relating a series of events; describing people and places

D'abord,... *First, . . .*

Ensuite,... *Then, . . .*
Après ça,... *After that, . . .*
Finalement,... *Finally, . . .*

Il y avait... *There was/were . . .*
Il était... *He was . . .*
Elle avait l'air... *She seemed . . .*
J'étais... *I was . . .*

♜ Game

CERCLE DES MOTS Have students make two identical sets of flashcards with French words or expressions on one side and the English equivalents on the other. Form two teams and have them each sit in a circle. Then, distribute one card to each student. One student begins by showing the English equivalent on his or her card to the teammate on his or her left. That student responds by giving the French expression. Then, he or she shows the English equivalent on his or her card to the student on his or her left. The first team to complete the circle wins.

CHAPTER 12 ASSESSMENT

CHAPTER TEST

- *Chapter Teaching Resources, Book 3* pp. 197–202
- *Assessment Guide,* Speaking Test, p. 33
- *Assessment Items,* Audiocassette 8B Audio CD 12

TEST GENERATOR, CHAPTER 12

ALTERNATIVE ASSESSMENT

Performance Assessment

You might want to use the **Jeu de rôle** (p. 321) as a cumulative performance assessment activity.

📁 Portfolio Assessment

- **Written: Mise en pratique,** Activity 4, *Pupil's Edition,* p. 321
  Assessment Guide, p. 25
- **Oral: Mise en pratique,** Activity 2, *Pupil's Edition,* p. 321
  Assessment Guide, p. 25

FINAL EXAM

- *Assessment Guide,* pp. 49–56
- *Assessment Items,* Audiocassette 8B Audio CD 12

♜ Game

CATÉGORIES This game practices the vocabulary and expressions from all the chapters. Type five games **(Jeux)** on one sheet of paper, each having five categories. For example, **Jeu #1** might have: 1. an animal; 2. an outdoor activity; 3. something you take camping; 4. complaining; 5. offering encouragement. Form groups of five and distribute a game sheet to each one. The groups try to give an answer for each category that no one else gives. For example, if for the first category, three teams name **un loup,** the fourth team names **un renard,** and the fifth team names **un ours,** only the fourth and fifth teams score a point. To start, each group uncovers **Jeu #1.** Players have three minutes to write something for each category. Call time and have each group name what they wrote for the first category. Tally the points and repeat for the other categories. Next, have students uncover and begin **Jeu #2,** and so on.

REFERENCE SECTION

SUMMARY OF FUNCTIONS

Function is another word for the way in which you use language for a specific purpose. When you find yourself in specific situations, such as in a restaurant, in a grocery store, or at school, you'll want to communicate with those around you. In order to communicate in French, you have to "function" in the language.

Each chapter in this book focuses on language functions. You can easily find them in boxes labeled **Comment dit-on... ?** The other features in the chapter—grammar, vocabulary, culture notes—support the functions you're learning.

Here is a list of the functions presented in this book and their French expressions. You'll need them in order to communicate in a wide range of situations. Following each function are the numbers of the level, the chapter, and page where the function was first introduced.

SOCIALIZING

Greeting people   **I Ch. 1, p. 22**

Bonjour.
Salut.

Saying goodbye   **I Ch. 1, p. 22**

Salut.   A bientôt.
Au revoir.   A demain.
A tout à l'heure.   Tchao.

Asking how people are   **I Ch. 1, p. 23**

(Comment) ça va?
Et toi?

Telling how you are   **I Ch. 1, p. 23**

Ça va.   Bof.
Super!   Pas mal.
Très bien.   Pas terrible.
Comme ci, comme ça.

Expressing thanks   **I Ch. 3, p. 82**

Merci.
A votre service.

Extending invitations   **I Ch. 6, p. 159**

Allons... !
Tu veux... ?
Tu viens?
On peut...

Accepting invitations   **I Ch. 6, p. 159**

Je veux bien.
Pourquoi pas?
D'accord.
Bonne idée.

Refusing invitations   **I Ch. 6, p. 159**

Désolé(e), je suis occupé(e).
Ça ne me dit rien.

J'ai des trucs à faire.
Desolé(e), je ne peux pas.

Identifying people   **I Ch. 7, p. 179**

C'est...
Ce sont...
Voici...
Voilà...

II Ch. 11, p. 273
Tu connais...
Bien sûr. C'est...
Je ne connais pas.

Introducing people   **I Ch. 7, p. 179**

C'est...
Je te/vous présente...
Très heureux (heureuse). (FORMAL)

Seeing someone off   **I Ch. 11, p. 296**

Bon voyage!   Amuse-toi bien!
Bonnes vacances!   Bonne chance!

Welcoming someone   **II Ch. 2, p. 33**

Bienvenue chez moi (chez nous).
Faites (Fais) comme chez vous (toi).
Vous avez (Tu as) fait bon voyage?

Responding to someone's welcome   **II Ch. 2, p. 33**

Merci.
C'est gentil de votre (ta) part.
Oui, excellent.
C'était fatigant!

Extending good wishes   **II Ch. 3, p. 71**

Bonne fête!
Joyeux (Bon) anniversaire!
Bonne fête de Hanukkah!
Joyeux Noël!
Bonne année!
Meilleurs vœux!

Félicitations!
Bon voyage!
Bonne route!
Bonne santé!

Congratulating someone II Ch. 5, p. 127

Félicitations!
Bravo!
Chapeau!

EXCHANGING INFORMATION

Asking someone's name and giving yours
I Ch. 1, p. 24

Tu t'appelles comment?
Je m'appelle...

Asking and giving someone else's name
I Ch. 1, p. 24

Il/Elle s'appelle comment?
Il/Elle s'appelle...

Asking someone's age and giving yours
I Ch. 1, p. 25

Tu as quel âge?
J'ai... ans.

Asking for information (about classes)
I Ch. 2, pp. 51, 54

Tu as quels cours... ?
Vous avez... ?
Tu as quoi... ?
Tu as... à quelle heure?

(places) II Ch. 4, p. 90

Où se trouve...?
Qu'est-ce qu'il y a...?
C'est comment?

II Ch. 12, p. 304
Où se trouve... ?
Qu'est-ce qu'il y a à voir... ?

(travel) II Ch. 6, p. 152

A quelle heure est-ce que le train (le car) pour...
  part?
De quel quai... ?
A quelle heure est-ce que vous ouvrez (fermez)?
Combien coûte... ?
  un aller-retour
  un aller simple
C'est combien, l'entrée?

(movies) II Ch. 11, p. 280

Qu'est-ce qu'on joue comme film?
Ça passe où?
C'est avec qui?
Ça commence à quelle heure?

Giving information
(about classes) I Ch. 2, pp. 51, 54

Nous avons...
J'ai...

Telling when you have class I Ch. 2, p. 54

à... heures
à... heures quinze
à... heures trente
à... heures quarante-cinq

Describing a place II Ch. 4, p. 90

dans le nord
dans le sud
dans l'est
dans l'ouest
plus grand(e) que
moins grand(e) que
charmant(e)
coloré(e)
vivant(e)

II Ch. 12, p. 314
Il y avait...
Il était...

Giving information
(travel) II Ch. 6, p. 152

Du quai...
Je voudrais...
Un..., s'il vous plaît.
... tickets, s'il vous plaît.

II Ch. 12, p. 304

...se trouve...
Il y a...
On peut...

(movies) II Ch. 11, p. 280

On joue...
Ça passe à...
C'est avec...
A...

Making requests I Ch. 3, p. 72

Tu as... ?
Vous avez... ?

Responding to requests I Ch. 3, p. 72

Voilà.
Je regrette.
Je n'ai pas de...

Asking others what they need
I Ch. 3, p. 74

Qu'est-ce qu'il te faut pour...
Qu'est-ce qu'il vous faut pour...

Expressing need I Ch. 8, p. 210

Qu'est-ce qu'il te faut?
Il me faut...

De quoi est-ce que tu as besoin?
J'ai besoin de...

Pas grand-chose.
Rien de spécial.

Expressing need *(shopping)* I Ch. 10, p. 265

Oui, il me faut...
Oui, vous avez... ?
Je cherche quelque chose pour...
J'aimerais... pour aller avec...
Non, merci, je regarde.

Getting someone's attention I Ch. 3, p. 82

Pardon
Excusez-moi.

I Ch. 5, p. 135

... s'il vous plaît.
Excusez-moi.
Monsieur!
Madame!
Mademoiselle!

Exchanging information *(leisure activities)*
I Ch. 4, p. 104

Qu'est-ce que tu fais comme sport?
Qu'est-ce que tu fais pour t'amuser?
Je fais...
Je ne fais pas de...
Je joue...

II Ch. 1, p. 12
Qu'est-ce que tu aimes faire?
Qu'est-ce que tu fais comme sport?
Qu'est-ce que tu aimes comme musique?
Quel est ton... préféré(e)?
Qui est ton... préféré(e)?

Ordering food and beverages I Ch. 5, p. 135

Vous avez choisi?
Vous prenez?
Je voudrais...
Je vais prendre..., s'il vous plaît.
Un sandwich, s'il vous plaît.
Donnez-moi..., s'il vous plaît.
Apportez-moi..., s'il vous plaît.
Vous avez... ?
Qu'est-ce que vous avez comme... ?

Paying the check I Ch. 5, p. 139

L'addition, s'il vous plaît.
Oui, tout de suite.
Un moment, s'il vous plaît.
Ça fait combien, s'il vous plaît?
Ça fait... francs.
C'est combien,... ?
C'est... francs.

Making plans I Ch. 6, p. 153

Qu'est- ce que tu vas faire... ?
Tu vas faire quoi... ?
Je vais...

Arranging to meet someone I Ch. 6, p. 163

Quand (ça)?	et demie
tout de suite	et quart
Où (ça)?	moins le quart
devant	moins cinq
au métro...	midi (et demi)
chez...	minuit (et demi)
dans...	vers
Avec qui?	On se retrouve...
A quelle heure?	Rendez-vous...
A cinq heures...	Entendu.

Describing and characterizing people I Ch. 7, p. 185

Il est comment?
Elle est comment?
Ils/Elles sont comment?
Il est...
Elle est...
Ils sont...

II Ch. 1, p. 10
avoir... ans
J'ai...
Il/Elle a...
Ils/Elles ont...
Je suis...
Il/Elle est...
Ils/Elles sont...

Describing people II Ch. 12, p. 314

Il avait...
Elle avait l'air...
J'étais...

Making a telephone call I Ch. 9, p. 244

Bonjour.
Je suis bien chez... ?
C'est...
(Est-ce que)... est là, s'il vous plaît?
(Est-ce que) je peux parler à... ?
Je peux laisser un message?
Vous pouvez lui dire que j'ai téléphoné?
Ça ne répond pas.
C'est occupé.

Answering a telephone call I Ch. 9, p. 244

Allô?
Bonjour.
Qui est à l'appareil?
Une seconde, s'il vous plaît.
D'accord.
Bien sûr.
Ne quittez pas.

Inquiring *(shopping)* I Ch. 10, p. 265

(Est-ce que) je peux vous aider?
Vous désirez?

Je peux l'(les) essayer?
Je peux essayer... ?
C'est combien,... ?
Ça fait combien?
Vous avez ça en... ?

Pointing out places and things   I Ch. 12, p. 317

Là, tu vois, c'est...
Regarde, voilà.
Ça, c'est...
Là, c'est...
Voici...

Asking for advice (directions)   I Ch. 12, p. 322

Comment est-ce qu'on y va?

Making suggestions   I Ch. 12, p. 322

On peut y aller...
On peut prendre...

Asking for directions   I Ch. 12, p. 327

Pardon,... , s'il vous plaît?
Pardon,... . Où est..., s'il vous plaît?
Pardon,... . Je cherche..., s'il vous plaît.

II Ch. 2, p. 45
Où est..., s'il vous plaît?

Giving directions   I Ch. 12, p. 327

Vous continuez jusqu'au prochain feu
  rouge.
Vous tournez...
Vous allez tout droit jusqu'à...
Vous prenez la rue..., puis traversez la rue...
Vous passez devant...
C'est tout de suite à...

II Ch. 2, p. 45
Traversez...
Prenez...
Puis, tournez à gauche dans/sur...
Allez (continuez) tout droit.
sur la droite (gauche)

II Ch. 12, p. 304
C'est au nord/au sud/à l'est/à l'ouest de...
C'est dans le nord/le sud/l'est/l'ouest de...

Inquiring about past events   I Ch. 9, p. 238

Qu'est-ce que tu as fait... ?
Tu es allé(e) où?
Et après?
Qu'est-ce qui s'est passé?

Inquiring about future plans   I Ch. 11, p. 289

Qu'est-ce que tu vas faire... ?
Où est-ce que tu vas aller... ?

Sharing future plans   I Ch. 11, p. 289

J'ai l'intention de...
Je vais...

Relating a series of events   II Ch. 1, p. 20

Qu'est-ce que tu vas faire... ?
D'abord, je vais...
Ensuite...,
Puis,...
Enfin,...

II Ch. 4, p. 99
Après ça...
Finalement...
Vers...

II Ch. 12, p. 314
D'abord,...
Ensuite,...
Puis...
Après ça,...
Finalement,...

Pointing out where things are
II Ch. 2, p. 39

Là, c'est...	en face de
A côté de...	à gauche de
Il y a...	à droite de
Ça, c'est...	près de

Making purchases   II Ch. 3, p. 58

Combien coûte(nt)... ?
Combien en voulez-vous?
Je vais en prendre...
Je vais (en) prendre...
Ça fait combien?

Asking what things were like   II Ch. 8, p. 198

C'était comment?
C'était tellement différent?

Describing what things were like
II Ch. 8, p. 198

C'était...
Il y avait...
La vie était plus... , moins...

Reminiscing   II Ch. 8, p. 201

Quand j'étais petit(e),...
Quand il/elle était petit(e),...
Quand j'avais... ans,...

Breaking some news   II Ch. 9, p. 232

Tu connais la nouvelle?
Tu ne devineras jamais ce qui s'est passé.
Tu sais qui...?
Tu sais ce que... ?
Devine qui...
Devine ce que...

Showing interest   II Ch. 9, p. 232

Raconte!
Aucune idée.
Dis vite!

Beginning a story   **II Ch. 9, p. 235**

A propos,...

Continuing a story   **II Ch. 9, p. 235**

Donc,...
Alors,...
Bref,...
C'est-à-dire que...
... quoi.
A ce moment-là,..
.... tu vois.

Ending a story   **II Ch. 9, p. 235**

Heureusement,...
Malheureusement,...
Finalement...

Summarizing   **II Ch. 11, p. 286**

De quoi ça parle?
Qu'est-ce que ça raconte?
Ça parle de...
C'est l'histoire de...

EXPRESSING FEELINGS AND EMOTIONS

Expressing likes and preferences about things
I Ch. 1, p. 26

J'aime (bien)...
J'aime mieux...
J'adore...
Je préfère...

I Ch. 5, p. 138
C'est...

Expressing dislikes about things   **I Ch. 1, p. 26**

Je n'aime pas...

I Ch. 5, p. 138
C'est...

Telling what you'd like and what you'd like to do
I Ch. 3, p. 77

Je voudrais...
Je voudrais acheter...

Telling how much you like or dislike something
I Ch. 4, p. 102

Beaucoup.
Pas beaucoup.
Pas tellement.
Pas du tout.
surtout

Inquiring about likes and dislikes   **I Ch. 5, p. 138**

Comment tu trouves ça?

Sharing confidences   **I Ch. 9, p. 247**

J'ai un petit problème.
Je peux te parler?
Tu as une minute?

II Ch. 10, p. 250
Je ne sais pas quoi faire.
J'ai un problème.
Tu as une minute?
Je peux te parler?
Qu'est-ce qu'il y a?
Je t'écoute.
Qu'est-ce que je peux faire?

Consoling others   **I Ch. 9, p. 247**

Ne t'en fais pas!
Je t'écoute.
Ça va aller mieux!
Qu'est-ce qu je peux faire?

II Ch. 5, p. 125
Ça va aller mieux.
T'en fais pas.
C'est pas grave.
Courage!

Hesitating   **I Ch. 10, p. 274**

Euh... J'hésite.
Je ne sais pas.
Il/Elle me plaît, mais il/elle est...

Making a decision   **I Ch. 10, p. 274**

Vous avez décidé de prendre... ?
Vous avez choisi?
Vous le/la/les prenez?
Je le/la/les prends.
Non, c'est trop cher.

Expressing indecision   **I Ch. 11, p. 289**

J'hésite.
Je ne sais pas.
Je n'en sais rien.
Je n'ai rien de prévu.

Expressing wishes   **I Ch. 11, p. 289**

J'ai envie de...
Je voudrais bien...

Asking how someone is feeling
II Ch. 2, p. 34

Pas trop fatigué(e)?
Vous n'avez pas (Tu n'as pas) faim?
Vous n'avez pas (Tu n'as pas) soif?

Telling how you are feeling   **II Ch. 2, p. 34**

Non, ça va.
Si, un peu.
Si, je suis crevé(e).
Si, j'ai très faim (soif)!
Si, je meurs de faim (soif)!

Accepting suggestions   I Ch. 4, p. 110

D'accord.   Allons-y!
Bonne idée.   Oui, c'est...

Turning down suggestions   I Ch. 4, p. 110

Non, c'est...
Ça ne me dit rien.
Désolé(e), mais je ne peux pas.

Responding to suggestions   II Ch. 1, p. 18

D'accord.
C'est une bonne (excellente) idée.
Je veux bien.
Je ne peux pas.
Ça ne me dit rien.
Non, je préfère...
Pas question!

II Ch. 8, p. 209
D'accord.
C'est une bonne idée.
Bof.
Ça m'est égal.
Non, je préfère...
Non, je ne veux pas.

Making excuses   I Ch. 5, p. 133

Désolé(e), j'ai des devoirs à faire.
J'ai des courses à faire.
J'ai des trucs à faire.
J'ai des tas de choses à faire.

II Ch. 5, p. 127
... , c'est pas mon fort.
J'a du mal à comprendre.
Je suis pas doué(e) pour...

II Ch. 10, p. 255
Désolé(e).
J'ai quelque chose à faire.
Je n'ai pas le temps.
Je suis très occupé(e).
C'est impossible.

Giving reasons   II Ch. 5, p. 127

Je suis assez bon (bonne) en...
C'est en... que je suis le/la meilleur(e).
... , c'est mon fort.

Making a recommendation   I Ch. 5, p. 133

Prends...

Asking for permission   I Ch. 7, p. 189

(Est-ce que) je peux... ?
Tu es d'accord?

Giving permission   I Ch. 7, p. 189

Oui, si tu veux.
Pourquoi pas?
Oui, bien sûr.
D'accord, si tu... d'abord...

Refusing permission   I Ch. 7, p. 189

Pas question!
Je ne suis pas d'accord.
Non, tu as... à...
Pas ce soir.

Making requests   I Ch. 8, p. 212

Tu peux aller faire les courses?
Tu me rapportes... ?

I Ch. 12, p. 320
Est-ce que tu peux... ?
Tu pourrais passer à... ?

Accepting requests   I Ch. 8, p. 212

Bon, d'accord.
Je veux bien.
J'y vais tout de suite.

I Ch. 12, p. 320
D'accord.
Je veux bien.
Si tu veux.

Declining requests   I Ch. 8, p. 212

Je ne peux pas maintenant.
Je regrette, mais je n'ai pas le temps.

I Ch. 12, p. 320
Désolé(e), mais je n'ai pas le temps.
J'ai des tas de choses (trucs) à faire.

Telling someone what to do   I Ch. 8, p. 212

Rapporte-moi...
Prends...
Achète(-moi)...
N'oublie pas.

Asking for food   II Ch. 3, p. 64

Je pourrais avoir... ?
Vous pourriez (tu pourrais) me passer... ?

Offering food   I Ch. 8, p. 219

Tu veux... ?   Tu prends... ?
Vous voulez... ?   Encore de... ?
Vous prenez... ?

II Ch. 3, p. 64
Voilà.
Vous voulez (tu veux)... ?
Encore... ?
Tenez (tiens).

Accepting food   I Ch. 8, p. 219

Oui, s'il vous (te) plaît.
Oui, avec plaisir.

II Ch. 3, p. 64
Oui, je veux bien.

Refusing food I Ch. 8, p. 219

Non, merci.
Non, merci. Je n'ai plus faim.
Je n'en veux plus.

II Ch. 3, p. 64
Merci, ça va.
Je n'ai plus faim (soif).

Asking for advice I Ch. 12, p. 322

Comment est-ce qu'on y va?

I Ch. 9, p. 247
A ton avis, qu'est-ce que je fais?
Qu'est-ce que tu me conseilles?

I Ch. 10, p. 264
Je ne sais pas quoi mettre pour...
Qu'est-ce que je mets?

II Ch. 3, p. 68
Tu as une idée de cadeau pour... ?
Qu'est-ce que je pourrais offrir à... ?
Bonne idée!

II Ch. 10, p. 250
A ton avis, qu'est-ce que je dois faire?
Qu'est-ce que tu ferais, toi?
Qu'est-ce que tu me conseilles?

II Ch. 12, p. 312
Qu'est-ce que je dois faire?

Giving advice I Ch. 9, p. 247

Oublie-le/-la/-les!
Téléphone-lui/-leur!
Tu devrais...
Pourquoi tu ne... pas?

I Ch. 10, p. 264
Pourquoi est-ce que tu ne mets pas... ?
Mets...

II Ch. 1, p. 15
Pense à prendre...
Prends...
N'oublie pas...

II Ch. 3, p. 68
Offre-lui (leur)...
Tu pourrais lui (leur) offrir...
...peut-être?

II Ch. 7, p. 173
Tu devrais...   Tu n'as qu'à...
Tu ferais bien de...   Pourquoi tu ne... pas... ?

II Ch. 10, p. 250
Oublie-le/-la/-les.   Explique-lui/-leur.
Invite-le/-la/-les.   Excuse-toi.
Parle-lui/-leur.   Téléphone-lui/-leur.
Dis-lui/-leur que...   Tu devrais...
Ecris-lui/-leur.

II Ch. 7, p. 178
Evite de...
Ne saute pas...
Tu ne devrais pas...

II Ch. 12, p. 312
Tu devrais...
Tu ferais bien de...
Evite de...
Tu ne devrais pas...

Accepting advice II Ch. 3, p. 68

Bonne idée!
C'est original.
Tu as raison...
D'accord.

II Ch. 7, p. 173
Tu as raison.
Bonne idée.
D'accord.

Rejecting advice II Ch. 3, p. 68

C'est trop cher.
C'est banal.
Ce n'est pas son style.
Il/Elle en a déjà un(e).

II Ch. 7, p. 173
Non, je n'ai pas très envie.
Je ne peux pas.
Ce n'est pas mon truc.
Non, je préfère...

Reminding I Ch. 11, p. 293

N'oublie pas...
Tu n'as pas oublié... ?
Tu ne peux pas partir sans...
Tu prends... ?

Reassuring I Ch. 11, p. 293

Ne t'en fais pas.
J'ai pensé à tout.
Je n'ai rien oublié.

II Ch. 8, p. 197
Tu vas t'y faire.
Fais-toi une raison.
Tu vas te plaire ici.
Tu vas voir que...

Asking a favor I Ch. 12, p. 320

Est-ce que tu peux... ?
(Est-ce que) tu pourrais me rendre un petit
    service?
Tu pourrais passer à... ?

Agreeing to a request I Ch. 12, p. 320

D'accord.
Je veux bien.
Si tu veux.

Refusing a request I Ch. 12, p. 320

Désolé(e), mais je n'ai pas le temps.
J'ai des tas de choses (trucs) à faire.
Non, je ne peux pas.

Reprimanding someone II Ch. 5, p. 127

C'est inadmissible.
Il faut mieux travailler en classe.
Il ne faut pas faire le clown en classe!
Ne recommence pas.

Justifying your recommendations II Ch. 7, p. 178

C'est bon pour toi.
C'est meilleur que...
Ça te fera du bien.

Advising against something II Ch. 7, p. 178

Evite de...
Ne saute pas...
Tu ne devrais pas...

Asking for a favor II Ch. 10, p. 255

Tu peux m'aider?
Tu pourrais...?
Ça t'ennuie de... ?
Ça t'embête de... ?

Granting a favor II Ch. 10, p. 255

Avec plaisir.
Bien sûr.
Pas du tout.
Bien sûr que non.
Pas de problème.

Apologizing II Ch. 10, p. 258

C'est de ma faute.   J'aurais dû...
Excuse-moi.   J'aurais pu...
Désolé(e).   Tu ne m'en veux pas?

Accepting an apology II Ch. 10, p. 258

Ça ne fait rien.
Je ne t'en veux pas.
Il n'y a pas de mal.

Reproaching someone II Ch. 10, p. 258

Tu aurais dû...
Tu aurais pu...

EXPRESSING ATTITUDES AND OPINIONS

Agreeing I Ch. 2, p. 50

Oui, beaucoup.
Moi aussi.
Moi non plus.

Disagreeing I Ch. 2, p. 50

Moi, non.
Non, pas trop.
Moi, si.

Asking for opinions I Ch. 2, p. 57

Comment tu trouves... ?
Comment tu trouves ça?

I Ch. 9, p. 237
Tu as passé un bon week-end?
Ça s'est bien passé?

I Ch. 10, p. 270
Comment tu trouves... ?
Ça me va?
Ça te (vous) plaît?
Tu aimes mieux... ou... ?

I Ch. 11, p. 297
Tu as passé un bon... ?
Ça s'est bien passé?
Tu t'es bien amusé(e)?

II Ch. 6, p. 144
C'était comment?
Ça t'a plu?
Tu t'es amusé(e)?

Expressing opinions I Ch. 2, p. 57

C'est...

I Ch. 9, p. 237
Oui, très chouette.
Oui, excellent.
Oui, très bon.
Oui, ça a été.
Oh, pas mal.
C'était épouvantable.
Très mal.

I Ch. 11, p. 297
Oui, très chouette.
C'était formidable!
Non, pas vraiment.
Oui, ça a été.
Oh, pas mal.
C'était épouvantable.
Je suis embêté(e).
C'était un véritable cauchemar!

Paying a compliment I Ch. 10, p. 270

C'est tout à fait ton style.
Ça te (vous) va très bien.
Ça va très bien avec...
Je le/la/les trouve...
sensas (sensationnel)
C'est parfait.

II Ch. 3, p. 64
C'est vraiment bon!
C'était délicieux!

II Ch. 2, p. 40
Il (Elle) est vraiment bien, ton (ta)...
Il (Elle) est cool, ton (ta)...
          beau (belle)
          génial(e)
          chouette

Responding to compliments   II Ch. 2, p. 40;
II Ch. 3, p. 64

    Ce n'est pas grand-chose.
    C'est gentil!
    Tu trouves?
    C'est vrai? (Vraiment?)

Criticizing   I Ch. 10, p. 270

    Ça ne te (vous) va pas du tout.
    Ça ne va pas du tout avec...
    Il/Elle est (Ils/Elles sont) trop...
    Je le/la/les trouve moche(s).

Emphasizing likes   II Ch. 4, p. 96

    Ce que j'aime bien, c'est...
    Ce que je préfère, c'est...
    Ce qui me plaît, c'est...

Emphasizing dislikes   II Ch. 4, p. 96

    Ce que je n'aime pas, c'est...
    Ce qui m'ennuie, c'est...
    Ce qui ne me plaît pas, c'est...

Expressing enthusiasm   II Ch. 6, p. 144

    C'était...
      magnifique.
      incroyable.
      superbe.
      sensas.
    Ça m'a beaucoup plu.
    Je me suis beaucoup amusé(e).

Expressing indifference   II Ch. 6, p. 144

    C'était...
      assez bien.
      comme ci, comme ça.
      pas mal.
    Mouais.
    Plus ou moins.

Expressing dissatisfaction   II Ch. 6, p. 144

    C'était...
      ennuyeux.

      mortel.
      nul.
      sinistre.
    Sûrement pas!
    Je me suis ennuyé(e).

*Wondering what happened and offering possible
explanations*   II Ch. 9, p. 228

    Je me demande...
    A mon avis,...
    Peut-être que...
    Je crois que...
    Je parie que...

Accepting explanations   II Ch. 9, p. 228

    Tu as peut-être raison.
    C'est possible.
    Ça se voit.
    Evidemment.

Rejecting explanations   II Ch. 9, p. 228

    A mon avis, tu te trompes.
    Ce n'est pas possible.
    Je ne crois pas.

Giving opinions   II Ch. 11, p. 284

    C'est drôle (amusant).
    C'est une belle histoire.
    C'est plein de rebondissements.
    Il y a du suspense.
    On ne s'ennuie pas.
    C'est une histoire passionnante.
    Je te le recommande.
    Il n'y a pas d'histoire.
    Ça casse pas des briques.
    C'est...
      trop violent.
      trop long.
      bête.
      un navet.
      du n'importe quoi.
      gentillet, sans plus.
      déprimant.

SI TU AS OUBLIE...

FAMILY AND PETS

le beau-père   *stepfather*
la belle-fille   *stepdaughter*
la belle-mère   *stepmother*
le cousin (la cousine)   *cousin*
le demi-frère   *half-brother/stepbrother*
la demi-sœur   *half-sister/stepsister*
l'enfant unique   *only child*
le frère   *brother*
la grand-mère   *grandmother*
le grand-père   *grandfather*
la mère   *mother*
l'oncle (m.)   *uncle*
le père   *father*
la sœur   *sister*
la tante   *aunt*
le canari   *canary*
le chat   *cat*
le chien   *dog*
le poisson   *fish*

CLOTHING AND COLORS

un blouson   *a jacket*
des boucles d'oreilles (f.)   *earrings*
un bracelet   *a bracelet*
un cardigan   *a sweater*
une casquette   *a cap*
une ceinture   *a belt*
un chapeau   *a hat*
des chaussettes (f.)   *socks*
des chaussures (f.)   *shoes*
une chemise   *a shirt (men's)*
un chemisier   *a shirt (women's)*
un collant   *hose*
une cravate   *a tie*
une jupe   *a skirt*
des lunettes de soleil (f.)   *sunglasses*
un maillot de bain   *a bathing suit*
un manteau   *a coat*
un pantalon   *a pair of pants*
une robe   *a dress*
des sandales (f.)   *sandals*
un short   *a pair of shorts*
un sweat-shirt   *a sweatshirt*
une veste   *a suit jacket, a blazer*
blanc(he)(s)   *white*
bleu(e)(s)   *blue*
gris(e)(s)   *grey*
jaune(s)   *yellow*
marron   *brown*
noir(e)(s)   *black*
orange   *orange*
rose(s)   *pink*
rouge(s)   *red*
vert(e)(s)   *green*
violet(te)(s)   *purple*

WEATHER AND SEASONS

Il fait beau.   *It's nice weather.*
Il fait chaud.   *It's hot.*
Il fait frais.   *It's cool.*
Il fait froid.   *It's cold.*
Il neige.   *It's snowing.*
Il pleut.   *It's raining.*
l'hiver   *the winter*
le printemps   *the spring*
l'été   *the summer*
l'automne   *the fall*

HOW TO TELL TIME

A quelle heure?   *At what time?*
à... heures   *at . . . o'clock*
à... heures quinze   *at . . . fifteen*
à... heures trente   *at . . . thirty*
à... heures quarante-cinq   *at . . . forty-five*
à... heures et demie   *at half past . . .*
à... heures et quart   *at quarter past . . .*
à... heures moins le quart   *at quarter to . . .*
à... heures moins cinq   *at five to . . .*
à midi   *at noon*
à minuit   *at midnight*
à midi (minuit) et demi.   *at half past noon (midnight).*

SPORTS

faire de l'aérobic   *to do aerobics*
faire de l'athlétisme   *to do track and field*
faire du jogging   *to jog*
faire de la natation   *to swim*
faire du patin à glace   *to ice-skate*
faire des photos   *to take pictures*
faire du roller en ligne   *to in-line skate*
faire du ski   *to ski*
faire du ski nautique   *to water ski*
faire du théâtre   *to do drama*
faire du vélo   *to bike*
faire de la vidéo   *to make videos*
jouer au base-ball   *to play baseball*
jouer au basket(-ball)   *to play basketball*
jouer au foot(ball)   *to play soccer*
jouer au football américain   *to play football*
jouer au golf   *to play golf*
jouer au hockey   *to play hockey*
jouer à des jeux vidéo   *to play video games*
jouer au tennis   *to play tennis*
jouer au volley(-ball)   *to play volleyball*

SUPPLEMENTARY VOCABULARY

This list presents additional vocabulary you may want to use when you're working on the activities in the textbook and workbook. If you can't find the words you need here, try the English-French and French-English vocabulary lists beginning on page 360.

ADJECTIVES

absurd *absurde*
agile *agile*
awesome (impressive) *impressionnant(e), imposant(e)*
boring *ennuyeux (ennuyeuse)*
chilly *froid(e); frais (fraîche)*
colorful (thing) *vif (vive);* (person) *pittoresque; coloré(e)*
despicable *abject(e); ignoble; méprisable*
eccentric *excentrique; original(e); bizarre*
horrifying *horrifiant(e)*
incredible *incroyable*
phenomenal *phénoménal(e)*

scandalous *scandaleux (scandaleuse)*
tasteless (flavor) *sans goût/insipide*
tasteless (remark) *de mauvais goût*
tasteful (remark, object) *de bon goût*
terrifying *terrifiant(e), épouvantable*
threatening *menaçant(e)*
tremendous (size) *énorme;* (excellent) *formidable; fantastique*
unbearable *insupportable*
unforgettable *inoubliable*
unique *unique*

ROOMS OF THE HOUSE AND FURNISHINGS

garage *le garage*
office *le bureau*
basement *la cave/le sous-sol*
attic *le grenier*
patio *la terrasse*
closet *le placard*
couch *le divan; le canapé*

easy chair *le fauteuil*
mirror *le miroir*
night stand *la table de nuit*
painting *le tableau*
refrigerator *le réfrigérateur (le frigo)*
oven *le four*
microwave *le micro-ondes*
dishwasher *le lave-vaisselle*
washing machine *le lave-linge, la machine à laver*
dryer *le sèche-linge*
wall-to-wall carpeting *la moquette*

SHOPS AND GIFTS

mall *le centre commercial*
jewelry shop *la bijouterie*
perfume shop *la parfumerie*
clothing store *la boutique de vêtements*
bookstore *la librairie*

music store *le disquaire*
jewelry *des bijoux*
ring *une bague*
watch *une montre*
necklace *un collier*
earrings *des boucles d'oreilles*
bracelet *un bracelet*
perfume *un parfum*
outfit (matching; women) *un ensemble*

DAILY ACTIVITIES

to wake up *se réveiller*
to get ready *se préparer*
to comb your hair *se peigner*

to fix your hair   *se coiffer*
to shave   *se raser*
to put on makeup   *se maquiller*
to put perfume on   *se parfumer*
to look at yourself in the mirror   *se regarder dans le miroir*
to hurry   *se dépêcher*
to shower   *se doucher, prendre une douche*

SCHOOL DAY ACTIVITIES

to get a good grade   *avoir une bonne note*
to see friends   *retrouver ses amis*
to have a substitute   *avoir un(e) remplaçant(e)*
to be quizzed   *être interrogé par le prof*
to win a game   *gagner un match*
to have an argument with a friend   *se disputer avec un copain*
to miss a class   *manquer un cours*
to be called to the principal's office   *être convoqué chez le proviseur*
to receive a warning   *recevoir un avertissement*

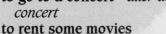

WEEKEND ACTIVITIES

to visit friends   *rendre visite à des amis*
to go to a concert   *aller au concert*
to rent some movies   *louer des vidéos*
to go to a party   *aller à une soirée/boum/fête*
to go to a botanical garden   *aller au jardin botanique*
to go to an art exhibit   *aller voir une exposition*
to go to a festival   *aller voir un festival*

ILLNESSES

to cough   *tousser*
bronchitis   *une bronchite*
tonsilitis   *une angine*
indigestion   *une indigestion*

sore neck   *un torticolis*
to be sick to your stomach   *avoir une crise de foie*

INJURIES

to have a bruise   *avoir un bleu*
to have a cut/wound   *avoir une coupure/plaie*
to strain a muscle   *se froisser un muscle*
to bump into   *se cogner contre*
to injure (something)   *se blesser (à la) (au)*

CHILDHOOD EVENTS, TOYS, AND GAMES

to get in trouble   *faire des bêtises*
to have slumber parties   *passer la nuit chez un copain (une copine)*
to jump chinese jump rope   *jouer à l'élastique*
to jump rope   *sauter à la corde*
to lose a tooth   *perdre une dent de lait*
to play blind man's bluff   *jouer à colin-maillard*
to play hopscotch   *jouer à la marelle*
to put one's tooth under one's pillow   *mettre sa dent sous l'oreiller*
run away   *faire une fugue*
to start school for the first time   *entrer à l'école*
to swing   *faire de la balançoire*
to wait for the Tooth Fairy   *attendre que la souris passe*

FAIRY TALES

Once upon a time . . .   *Il était une fois...*
bears   *des ours (m.)*
big bad wolf   *le grand méchant loup*
castle   *un château*
enchanted   *enchanté(e)*
fairy   *la fée*
golden hair   *des cheveux d'or*

king *le roi*
knight *le chevalier*
magic mirror *le miroir magique*
magician *le magicien*
poisoned apple *la pomme empoisonnée*
prince *le prince*
Prince Charming *le Prince Charmant*
princess *la princesse*
seven dwarves *les sept nains*
slipper *le soulier*
sword *l'épée*
queen *la reine*
wicked stepmother *la marâtre*
And they lived happily ever after. *Ils vécurent heureux et eurent beaucoup d'enfants.*

FRIENDSHIP

to be sorry *être désolé(e)*
to confide in someone *se confier à quelqu'un*
to feel guilty *se sentir coupable*

to get along with someone *s'entendre bien avec quelqu'un*
to help someone do something *aider quelqu'un à faire quelque chose*
to make friends *se faire des amis*
to meet after school *se retrouver après l'école*
to misunderstand *mal comprendre*
to take the first step *faire le premier pas*
to talk with friends *discuter avec des amis*

MORE MUSIC, MOVIES, BOOKS

latest (music) hits *les derniers tubes*
movie soundtrack *la bande originale d'un film*

music videos *les clips*
new wave *la new wave*
opera *l'opéra*

fantasy film *un film fantastique*
historic film *un film historique*
psychological drama *un drame psychologique*

war movie *un film de guerre*

biography *une biographie*
comedy *une comédie*
drama *un drame*
fable *une fable*
fairy tale *un conte de fée*
novel *un roman*
tragedy *une tragédie*

OUTDOOR ACTIVITIES

to climb mountains *faire de l'alpinisme*
to go rock-climbing *faire de l'escalade*
to go rafting *faire la descente d'une rivière*
to do archery *faire du tir à l'arc*
to go spelunking *faire de la spéléologie*
to go on a photo safari *aller faire un safari-photo*
to collect rocks *ramasser des pierres*
to collect butterflies *aller à la chasse aux papillons*
to pick wildflowers *cueillir des fleurs sauvages*
to collect wood *ramasser du bois*
to build a fire *faire un feu*
to sing around the campfire *chanter autour du feu de camp*

SUPPLEMENTARY VOCABULARY

trois cent trente-neuf **339**

GEOGRAPHICAL TERMS

THE CONTINENTS

Africa *l'Afrique* (f.)
Antarctica *l'Antarctique* (f.)
Asia *l'Asie* (f.)
Australia *l'Australie* (f.)
Europe *l'Europe* (f.)
North America *l'Amérique* (f.) *du Nord*
South America *l'Amérique* (f.) *du Sud*

COUNTRIES

Algeria *l'Algérie* (f.)
Argentina *l'Argentine* (f.)
Australia *l'Australie* (f.)
Austria *l'Autriche* (f.)
Belgium *la Belgique*
Brazil *le Brésil*
Canada *le Canada*
China *la Chine*
Egypt *l'Egypte* (f.)
England *l'Angleterre* (f.)
France *la France*
Germany *l'Allemagne* (f.)
Greece *la Grèce*
Holland *la Hollande*
India *l'Inde* (f.)
Ireland *l'Irlande* (f.)
Israel *Israël* (m.) (no article)
Italy *l'Italie* (f.)
Jamaica *la Jamaïque*
Japan *le Japon*
Jordan *la Jordanie*
Lebanon *le Liban*
Libya *la Libye*
Luxembourg *le Luxembourg*
Mexico *le Mexique*
Monaco *Monaco* (f.) *(no article)*
Morocco *le Maroc*
Netherlands *les Pays-Bas* (m.)
North Korea *la Corée du Nord*
Peru *le Pérou*
Philippines *les Philippines* (f.)
Poland *la Pologne*
Portugal *le Portugal*

the Republic of Côte d'Ivoire *la République de la Côte d'Ivoire*
Russia *la Russie*
Senegal *le Sénégal*
South Korea *la Corée du Sud*
Spain *l'Espagne* (f.)
Switzerland *la Suisse*
Syria *la Syrie*
Tunisia *la Tunisie*
Turkey *la Turquie*
United States *les Etats-Unis* (m.)
Vietnam *le Viêt-nam*

STATES

Alabama *l'Alabama* (m.)
Alaska *l'Alaska* (m.)
Arizona *l'Arizona* (m.)
Arkansas *l'Arkansas* (m.)
California *la Californie*
Colorado *le Colorado*
Connecticut *le Connecticut*
Delaware *le Delaware*
Florida *la Floride*
Georgia *la Géorgie*
Hawaii *Hawaii* (m.)
Idaho *l'Idaho* (m.)
Illinois *l'Illinois* (m.)
Indiana *l'Indiana* (m.)
Iowa *l'Iowa* (m.)
Kansas *le Kansas*
Kentucky *le Kentucky*
Louisiana *la Louisiane*
Maine *le Maine*
Maryland *le Maryland*
Massachusetts *le Massachusetts*
Michigan *le Michigan*
Minnesota *le Minnesota*
Mississippi *le Mississippi*
Missouri *le Missouri*
Montana *le Montana*
Nebraska *le Nebraska*
Nevada *le Nevada*
New Hampshire *le New Hampshire*
New Jersey *le New Jersey*
New Mexico *le Nouveau Mexique*
New York *l'état de New York*
North Carolina *la Caroline du Nord*

North Dakota   *le Dakota du Nord*
Ohio   *l'Ohio* (m.)
Oklahoma   *l'Oklahoma* (m.)
Oregon   *l'Oregon* (m.)
Pennsylvania   *la Pennsylvanie*
Rhode Island   *le Rhode Island*
South Carolina   *la Caroline du Sud*
South Dakota   *le Dakota du Sud*
Tennessee   *le Tennessee*
Texas   *le Texas*
Utah   *l'Utah*
Vermont   *le Vermont*
Virginia   *la Virginie*
Washington   *l'état de Washington*
West Virginia   *la Virginie de l'Ouest*
Wisconsin   *le Wisconsin*
Wyoming   *le Wyoming*

CITIES

Algiers   *Alger*
Brussels   *Bruxelles*
Cairo   *Le Caire*
Geneva   *Genève*
Lisbon   *Lisbonne*
London   *Londres*
Montreal   *Montréal*
Moscow   *Moscou*
New Orleans   *La Nouvelle-Orléans*
Quebec City   *Québec*
Tangier   *Tanger*
Venice   *Venise*
Vienna   *Vienne*

OTHER GEOGRAPHICAL TERMS

Alps   *les Alpes* (f.)
Atlantic Ocean   *l'Atlantique* (m.), *l'océan* (m.) *Atlantique*
border   *la frontière*
capital   *la capitale*
continent   *un continent*
country   *un pays*
English Channel   *la Manche*
hill   *une colline*
lake   *un lac*
latitude   *la latitude*
longitude   *la longitude*
Mediterranean Sea   *la mer Méditerranée*
mountain   *une montagne*
North Africa   *l'Afrique* (f.) *du Nord*
the North Pole   *le pôle Nord*
ocean   *l'océan* (m.)
Pacific Ocean   *le Pacifique, l'océan* (m.) *Pacifique*
plain   *une plaine*
Pyrenees   *les Pyrénées* (f.)
river   *une rivière, un fleuve*
sea   *la mer*
the South Pole   *le pôle Sud*
state   *un état*
valley   *une vallée*

trois cent quarante et un   341

NUMBERS

LES NOMBRES CARDINAUX

0	zéro	20	vingt	80	quatre-vingts
1	un	21	vingt et un(e)	81	quatre-vingt-un(e)
2	deux	22	vingt-deux	82	quatre-vingt-deux
3	trois	23	vingt-trois	90	quatre-vingt-dix
4	quatre	24	vingt-quatre	91	quatre-vingt-onze
5	cinq	25	vingt-cinq	92	quatre-vingt-douze
6	six	26	vingt-six	100	cent
7	sept	27	vingt-sept	101	cent un
8	huit	28	vingt-huit	200	deux cents
9	neuf	29	vingt-neuf	300	trois cents
10	dix	30	trente	800	huit cents
11	onze	31	trente et un(e)	900	neuf cents
12	douze	32	trente-deux	1.000	mille
13	treize	40	quarante	2.000	deux mille
14	quatorze	50	cinquante	3.000	trois mille
15	quinze	60	soixante	10.000	dix mille
16	seize	70	soixante-dix	19.000	dix-neuf mille
17	dix-sept	71	soixante et onze	40.000	quarante mille
18	dix-huit	72	soixante-douze	500.000	cinq cent mille
19	dix-neuf	73	soixante-treize	1.000.000	un million

- The word **et** is used only in 21, 31, 41, 51, 61, and 71.
- **Vingt (trente, quarante,** and so on) **et une** is used when the number refers to a feminine noun: **trente et une cassettes.**
- The **s** is dropped from **quatre-vingts** and is not added to multiples of **cent** when these numbers are followed by another number: **quatre-vingt-cinq; deux cents,** *but* **deux cent six.** The number **mille** never takes an **s: deux mille insectes.**
- **Un million** is followed by **de** + a noun: **un million de francs.**
- In writing numbers, a period is used in French where a comma is used in English.

LES NOMBRES ORDINAUX

1er, 1ère	premier, première	9^e	neuvième	17^e	dix-septième
2^e	deuxième	10^e	dixième	18^e	dix-huitième
3^e	troisième	11^e	onzième	19^e	dix-neuvième
4^e	quatrième	12^e	douzième	20^e	vingtième
5^e	cinquième	13^e	treizième	21^e	vingt et unième
6^e	sixième	14^e	quatorzième	22^e	vingt-deuxième
7^e	septième	15^e	quinzième	30^e	trentième
8^e	huitième	16^e	seizième	40^e	quarantième

PRONUNCIATION GUIDE

SOUND	LETTER COMBINATION	IPA SYMBOL	EXAMPLE
The sounds [y] and [u]	the letter **u** the letter combination **ou**	/y/ /u/	une nous
The nasal sound [ɑ̃]	the letter combination **an** the letter combination **am** the letter combination **en** the letter combination **em**	/ɑ̃/	anglais jambon comment temps
The vowel sounds [ø] and [œ]	the letter combination **eu** the letter combination **eu**	/ø/ /œ/	deux heure
The nasal sounds [ɔ̃], [ɛ̃], and [œ̃]	the letter combination **on** the letter combination **om** the letter combination **in** the letter combination **im** the letter combination **ain** the letter combination **aim** the letter combination **(i)en** the letter combination **un** the letter combination **um**	/ɔ̃/ /ɛ̃/ /œ̃/	pardon nombre cousin impossible copain faim bien lundi humble
The sounds [o] and [ɔ]	the letter combination **au** the letter combination **eau** the letter **ô** the letter **o**	/o/ /ɔ/	jaune beau rôle carotte
The vowel sounds [e] and [ɛ]	the letter combination **ez** the letter combination **er** the letter combination **ait** the letter combination **ais** the letter combination **ei** the letter **ê**	/e/ /ɛ/	apportez trouver fait français neige bête
The glides [j], [w], and [ɥ]	the letter **i** the letter combination **ill** the letter combination **oi** the letter combination **oui** the letter combination **ui**	/j/ /w/ /ɥ/	mieux maillot moi Louis huit
h, th, ch, and gn	the letter **h** the letter combination **th** the letter combination **ch** the letter combination **gn**	/'/ /t/ /ʃ/ /ɲ/	les halls théâtre chocolat oignon
The **r** sound	the letter **r**	/ʀ/	rouge vert

343

GRAMMAR SUMMARY

ARTICLES

SINGULAR		PLURAL	
MASCULINE	FEMININE	MASCULINE	FEMININE
un frère un ami	une sœur une amie	des frères des amis	des sœurs des amies
le frère l'ami	la sœur l'amie	les frères les amis	les sœurs les amies
ce frère cet ami	cette sœur cette amie	ces frères ces amis	ces sœurs ces amies

CONTRACTIONS WITH à AND de

à or de + article =	CONTRACTION
à + le =	au
à + la =	à la (no contraction)
à + l' =	à l' (no contraction)
à + les =	aux
de + le =	du
de + la =	de la (no contraction)
de + l' =	de l' (no contraction)
de + les =	des

ADJECTIVES: FORMATION OF FEMININE

	MASCULINE	FEMININE
Most adjectives (add -**e**)	Il est brun.	Elle est brune.
Most adjectives ending in -**é** (add -**e**)	Il est démodé.	Elle est démodée.
All adjectives ending in an unaccented -**e** (no change)	Il est jeune.	Elle est jeune.
Most adjectives ending in -**eux** (-**eux** → -**euse**)	Il est délicieux.	Elle est délicieuse.
All adjectives ending in -**ien** (-**ien** → -**ienne**)	Il est ivoirien.	Elle est ivoirienne.

ADJECTIVES AND NOUNS: FORMATION OF PLURAL

		MASCULINE	FEMININE
Most noun and adjective forms (add -**s**)	Singular Plural	un pantalon vert des pantalons verts	une jupe verte des jupes vertes
Most noun and masculine adjective forms ending in -**al** (-**al** → -**aux**)	Singular Plural	le sport principal les sports principaux	la rue principale les rues principales
All noun and masculine adjective forms ending in -**eau** (add -**x**)	Singular Plural	le nouveau manteau les nouveaux manteaux	la nouvelle robe les nouvelles robes
All noun and masculine adjective forms ending in -**s** (no change)	Singular Plural	un bus gris des bus gris	une maison grise des maisons grises
All masculine adjective forms ending in -**x** (no change)	Singular Plural	un garçon heureux des garçons heureux	une fille heureuse des filles heureuses

POSSESSIVE ADJECTIVES

SINGULAR		PLURAL		SINGULAR		PLURAL
MASCULINE	FEMININE	MASCULINE	FEMININE	MASCULINE	FEMININE	MASCULINE
mon frère mon ami ton ami son frère son ami	ma sœur mon amie ton amie sa sœur son amie	mes frères mes amis tes amis ses frères ses amis	mes sœurs mes amies tes amies ses sœurs ses amies	notre frère votre ami leur frère	notre sœur votre amie leur sœur	nos frères nos amis vos amis leurs frères leurs amis

PRONOUNS

INDEPENDENT PRONOUNS	SUBJECT PRONOUNS	DIRECT OBJECT PRONOUNS	INDIRECT OBJECT PRONOUNS	PRONOUN REPLACING à, dans, sur... + noun phrase	PRONOUN REPLACING de + noun phrase
moi toi lui elle soi nous vous eux elles	je (j') tu il elle on nous vous ils elles	me te le la nous vous les les	me te lui lui nous vous leur leur	y	en

INTERROGATIVE PRONOUNS

	PEOPLE	THINGS
SUBJECT OF VERB	qui qui est-ce qui	qu'est-ce qui
OBJECT OF VERB	qui qui est-ce que	que qu'est-ce que
OBJECT OF PREPOSITION	de qui à qui	de quoi à quoi

RELATIVE PRONOUNS

	Qui Subject of verb in clause	**Que** Object of verb in clause
PEOPLE	Laeticia parle avec une amie **qui** s'appelle Séverine.	Séverine sort avec un garçon **que** je ne connais pas.
PLACES	J'ai visité une ville **qui** est près de Strasbourg.	La ville **que** j'ai visitée était intéressante.
THINGS	C'est un poster **qui** vient des Etats-Unis.	C'est un poster **que** j'aime beaucoup.

REGULAR VERBS

	STEM	ENDING	STEM	ENDING	STEM	ENDING	STEM	ENDING
INFINITIVE	écouter		sortir		choisir		répondre	
PRESENT	écout	-e -es -e -ons -ez -ent	sor sort	-s -s -t -ons -ez -ent	chois	-is -is -it -issons -issez -issent	répond	-s -s — -ons -ez -ent
REQUESTS COMMANDS SUGGESTIONS	écout	-e -ons -ez	sor sort	-s -ons -ez	chois	-is -issons -issez	répond	-s -ons -ez

Verbs like sortir: dormir, partir
Verbs like choisir: finir, grandir, grossir, maigrir
Verbs like répondre: attendre, descendre, entendre, perdre, rendre, tondre

REGULAR VERBS: COMPOUND TENSES

		AUXILIARY		PAST PARTICIPLE	
PASSE COMPOSE	with avoir	ai as a	avons avez ont	aim chois répond	-é -i -u
	with être	suis es est	sommes êtes sont	arriv sort descend	-é(e)(s) -i(e)(s) -u(e)(s)

IMPERFECT (IMPARFAIT)

STEM	ENDING
Present tense **nous** form: habit**ons** finiss**ons** entend**ons**	-ais -ais -ait -ions -iez -aient

VERB CHARTS

VERBS WITH STEM AND SPELLING CHANGES

Verbs listed in this section are not irregular, but they do show some stem and spelling changes. The forms in which the changes occur are printed in **boldface** type.

Acheter *(to buy)*

Present	Imperfect	Commands
achète	achetais	
achètes	achetais	**achète**
achète	achetait	
achète	achetions	
achetons	achetiez	achetons
achètent	achetaient	achetez

Passé Composé: *Auxiliary:* avoir
Past Participle: acheté

Essayer *(to try)*

Present	Imperfect	Commands
essaie	essayais	
essaies	essayais	**essaie**
essaie	essayait	
essayons	essayions	essayons
essayez	essayiez	essayez
essaient	essayaient	

Passé Composé: *Auxiliary:* avoir
Past Participle: essayé

Appeler *(to call)*

Present	Imperfect	Commands
appelle	appelais	
appelles	appelais	**appelle**
appelle	appelait	
appelons	appelions	appelons
appelez	appeliez	appelez
appellent	appelaient	

Passé Composé: *Auxiliary:* avoir
Past Participle: appelé

Manger *(to eat)*

Present	Imperfect	Commands
mange	**mangeais**	
manges	**mangeais**	mange
mange	**mangeait**	
mangeons	mangions	**mangeons**
mangez	mangiez	mangez
mangent	**mangeaient**	

Passé Composé: *Auxiliary:* avoir
Past Participle: mangé

Commencer *(to start, to begin)*

Present	Imperfect	Commands
commence	**commençais**	
commences	**commençais**	commence
commence	**commençait**	
commençons	commencions	**commençons**
commencez,	commenciez	commencez
commencent	**commençaient**	

Passé Composé: *Auxiliary:* avoir
Past Participle: commencé

Préférer *(to prefer)*

Present	Imperfect	Commands
préfère	préférais	
préfères	préférais	**préfère**
préfère	préférait	
préférons	préférions	préférons
préférez	préfériez	préférez
préfèrent	préféraient	

Passé Composé *Auxiliary:* avoir
Past Participle: préféré

VERBS WITH IRREGULAR FORMS

Verbs listed in this section are those that do not follow the pattern of verbs like **aimer**, verbs like **choisir**, verbs like **sortir**, or verbs like **attendre**.

Aller *(to go)*

Present	Imperfect	Commands
vais	allais	
vas	allais	va
va	allait	
allons	allions	allons
allez	alliez	allez
vont	allaient	

Passé Composé: *Auxiliary:* être
                    Past Participle: allé

Connaître *(to know, to be acquainted with)*

Present	Imperfect	Commands
connais	connaissais	
connais	connaissais	connais
connaît	connaissait	
connaissons	connaissions	connaissons
connaissez	connaissiez	connaissez
connaissent	connaissaient	

Passé Composé: *Auxiliary:* avoir
                    Past Participle: connu

Avoir *(to have)*

Present	Imperfect	Commands
ai	avais	aie
as	avais	
a	avait	ayons
avons	avions	ayez
avez	aviez	
ont	avaient	

Passé Composé: *Auxiliary:* avoir
                    Past Participle: eu

Croire *(to believe)*

Present	Imperfect	Commands
crois	croyais	
crois	croyais	crois
croit	croyait	
croyons	croyions	croyons
croyez	croyiez	croyez
croient	croyaient	

Passé Composé: *Auxiliary:* avoir
                    Past Participle: cru

Boire *(to drink)*

Present	Imperfect	Commands
bois	buvais	
bois	buvais	bois
boit	buvait	
buvons	buvions	buvons
buvez	buviez	buvez
boivent	buvaient	

Passé Composé: *Auxiliary:* avoir
                    Past Participle: bu

Devoir *(to have to)*

Present	Imperfect	Commands
dois	devais	
dois	devais	dois
doit	devait	
devons	devions	devons
devez	deviez	devez
doivent	devaient	

Passé Composé: *Auxiliary:* avoir
                    Past Participle: dû

Conduire *(to drive)*

Present	Imperfect	Commands
conduis	conduisais	
conduis	conduisais	conduis
conduit	conduisait	
conduisons	conduisions	conduisons
conduisez	conduisiez	conduisez
conduisent	conduisaient	

Passé Composé: *Auxiliary:* avoir
                    Past Participle: conduit

Dire *(to say, tell)*

Present	Imperfect	Commands
dis	disais	
dis	disais	dis
dit	disait	
disons	disions	disons
dites	disiez	dites
disent	disaient	

Passé Composé: *Auxiliary:* avoir
                    Past Participle: dit

Ecrire *(to write)*

Present	Imperfect	Commands
écris	écrivais	
écris	écrivais	écris
écrit	écrivait	
écrivons	écrivions	écrivons
écrivez	écriviez	écrivez
écrivent	écrivaient	

Passé Composé: *Auxiliary:* avoir
                   Past Participle: écrit

Mettre *(to put, to put on)*

Present	Imperfect	Commands
mets	mettais	
mets	mettais	mets
met	mettait	
mettons	mettions	mettons
mettez	mettiez	mettez
mettent	mettaient	

Passé Composé: *Auxiliary:* avoir
                   Past Participle: mis

Etre *(to be)*

Present	Imperfect	Commands
suis	étais	
es	étais	sois
est	était	
sommes	étions	soyons
êtes	étiez	soyez
sont	étaient	

Passé Composé: *Auxiliary:* avoir
                   Past Participle: été

Ouvrir *(to open)*

Present	Imperfect	Commands
ouvre	ouvrais	
ouvres	ouvrais	ouvre
ouvre	ouvrait	
ouvrons	ouvrions	ouvrons
ouvrez	ouvriez	ouvrez
ouvrent	ouvraient	

Passé Composé: *Auxiliary:* avoir
                   Past Participle: ouvert

Faire *(to make, to do)*

Present	Imperfect	Commands
fais	faisais	
fais	faisais	fais
fait	faisait	
faisons	faisions	faisons
faites	faisiez	faites
font	faisaient	

Passé Composé: *Auxiliary:* avoir
                   Past Participle: fait

Pouvoir *(to be able, can)*

Present	Imperfect	Commands
peux	pouvais	
peux	pouvais	—
peut	pouvait	
pouvons	pouvions	—
pouvez	pouviez	—
peuvent	pouvaient	

Passé Composé: *Auxiliary:* avoir
                   Past Participle: pu

Lire *(to read)*

Present	Imperfect	Commands
lis	lisais	
lis	lisais	lis
lit	lisait	
lisons	lisions	lisons
lisez	lisiez	lisez
lisent	lisaient	

Passé Composé: *Auxiliary:* avoir
                   Past Participle: lu

Prendre *(to take)*

Present	Imperfect	Commands
prends	prenais	
prends	prenais	prends
prend	prenait	
prenons	prenions	prenons
prenez	preniez	prenez
prennent	prenaient	

Passé Composé: *Auxiliary:* avoir
                   Past Participle: pris

Savoir *(to know)*

Present	Imperfect	Commands
sais	savais	
sais	savais	sache
sait	savait	
savons	savions	sachons
savez	saviez	sachez
savent	savaient	

Passé Composé: *Auxiliary:* avoir
Past Participle: su

Voir *(to see)*

Present	Imperfect	Commands
vois	voyais	
vois	voyais	vois
voit	voyait	
voyons	voyions	voyons
voyez	voyiez	voyez
voient	voyaient	

Passé Composé: *Auxiliary:* avoir
Past Participle: vu

Venir *(to come)*

Present	Imperfect	Commands
viens	venais	
viens	venais	viens
vient	venait	
venons	venions	venons
venez	veniez	venez
viennent	venaient	

Passé Composé: *Auxiliary:* être
Past Participle: venu

Vouloir *(to want)*

Present	Imperfect	Commands
veux	voulais	
veux	voulais	veuille
veut	voulait	
voulons	voulions	
voulez	vouliez	veuillez
veulent	voulaient	

Passé Composé: *Auxiliary:* avoir
Past Participle: voulu

FRENCH-ENGLISH VOCABULARY

This list includes both active and passive vocabulary in this textbook. Active words and phrases are those listed in the **Vocabulaire** section at the end of each chapter. You are expected to know and be able to use active vocabulary. All entries in black heavy type in this list are active. All other words are passive. Passive vocabulary is for recognition only.

The number after each entry refers to the chapter where the word or phrase after each entry is introduced. Verbs are given in the infinitive. Phrases are alphabetized by the key word(s) in the phrase. Nouns are always given with an article. If it is not clear whether the noun is masculine or feminine, *m.* (masculine) or *f.* (feminine) follow the noun. An asterisk (*) before a word beginning with *h* indicates an aspirate *h*.

The following abbreviations are used in this vocabulary: pl. (plural), pp. (past participle), and inv. (invariable).

A

à *to, in (a city or place),* I, 11; **A...** *At . . . ,* II, 11; **à la** *to, at,* I, 6; **A bientôt.** *See you soon.* I, 1; **A côté de...** *Next to . . . ,* II, 2; **A demain.** *See you tomorrow.* I, 1; **à droite de** *to the right of,* II, 2; **à gauche de** *to the left of,* II, 2; **à l'autre bout** *at the other end,* II, 9; **à la mode** *in style,* I, 10; **A propos,...** *By the way, . . . ,* II, 9; **A quelle heure?** *At what time?* I, 6; **A tout à l'heure!** *See you later!* I, 1; **A votre service.** *At your service; You're welcome,* I, 3; **Tu n'as qu'à...** *All you have to do is . . . ,* II, 7

a: Il/Elle a... *He/She has . . . ,* II, 1

abandonne: J'abandonne. *I give up.* II, 7

les abdominaux (m.): **faire des abdominaux** *to do sit-ups,* II, 7

l' **accès** (m.) *access,* II, 2

l' **accident** (m.): **avoir un accident** *to have an accident,* II, 9

accord: D'accord. *OK.* I, 9; II, 7; **D'accord, si tu... d'abord.** *OK, if you . . . , first.* I, 7; **Bon, d'accord.** *Well, OK.* I, 8; **Je ne suis pas d'accord.** *I don't agree.* I, 7; **Tu es d'accord?** *Is that OK with you?* I, 7

accordons: accordons nos violons *let's come to an understanding,* II, 4

accueillant *welcoming,* II, 1

achetait: Si on achetait... ? *How about buying . . . ?* II, 8

achète: Achète (-moi)... *Buy me . . . ,* I, 8

acheter *to buy,* I, 9

l' **addition** (f.): **L'addition, s'il vous plaît.** *The check please.* I, 5

adore: J'adore... *I adore . . . ,* I, 1; *I love . . . ,* II, 1

l' **adresse** (f.) *skill,* II, 7

l' **aérobic: faire de l'aérobic** *to do aerobics,* I, 4; II, 7

africain(e) *African,* II, 11

l' **âge** (m.): **Tu as quel âge?** *How old are you?* I, 1

âgé(e) *older,* I, 7

ai: J'ai... *I have... ,* I, 2; II, 1

aider *to help,* II, 8; **(Est-ce que) je peux vous aider?** *May I help you?* I, 10; **Tu peux m'aider?** *Can you help me?* II, 10

l' **ail** (m.) *garlic,* II, 3

aime: Ce que j'aime bien, c'est... *What I like is . . . ,* II, 4; **Ce que je n'aime pas, c'est...** *What I don't like is . . . ,* II, 4; **J'aime bien...** *I like . . . ,* II, 1; **J'aime mieux...** *I prefer . . . ,* I, 1; II, 1; **Je n'aime pas...** *I don't like . . . ,* I, 1; II, 1; **Moi, j'aime (bien)...** *I (really) like . . . ,* I, 1

aimer *to like,* I, 1

aimerais: J'aimerais... pour aller avec... *I'd like . . . to go with . . . ,* I, 10

aimes: Qu'est-ce que tu aimes comme musique? *What music do you like?* II, 1; **Qu'est-ce que tu aimes faire?** *What do you like to do?* II, 1; **Tu aimes mieux... ou... ?** *Do*

you prefer . . . or . . . ? I, 10; **Tu aimes... ?** *Do you like . . . ?* I, 1

l' **air** (m.): **avoir l'air...** *to seem . . . ,* II, 9; **Ça n'a pas l'air d'aller.** *Something's wrong.* II, 5; **Elle avait l'air...** *She seemed . . . ,* II, 12; **Tu n'as pas l'air en forme.** *You don't seem too well.* II, 7

ajouter *to add,* II, 3

l' **algèbre** (f.) *algebra,* I, 2

allait: Si on allait... ? *How about going . . . ?* II, 4

allé: Je suis allé(e)... *I went . . .* I, 9; **Tu es allé(e) où?** *Where did you go?* I, 9

l' **allemand** (m.) *German (language),* I, 2

aller *to go,* I, 6; **l'aller-retour** (m.) *a round-trip ticket,* II, 6; **l'aller simple** (m.) *a one-way ticket,* II, 6; **aller à la pêche** *to go fishing,* II, 4; **Ça n'a pas l'air d'aller.** *Something's wrong.* II, 5; **Ça te dit d'aller... ?** *What do you think about going . . . ?* II, 4; **Ça va aller mieux!** *It's going to get better!* I, 9; II, 5; **On peut y aller...** *We can go there . . . ,* I, 12

les allergies (f.): **J'ai des allergies.** *I have allergies.* II, 7

allez: Allez! *Come on!* II, 7; **Allez (continuez) tout droit.** *Go (keep going) straight ahead.* II, 2; **Allez au tableau!** *Go to the blackboard!* I, 0

Allô? *Hello?* I, 9

allons: Allons... *Let's go . . . ,* I, 6; **Allons-y!** *Let's go!* I, 4

les allumettes (f.) *matches,* II, 12

l' allure (f.) *style, elegance*, II, 4
Alors,... *So . . .* , II, 9
amener: amener à ébullition
   bring to a boil, II, 3
américain(e) *American (adj.)*,
   II, 11
l' **ami(e)** *friend*, I, 1
l' **amitié** (f.) *friendship*, II, 10
amoureux (amoureuse) *in
   love*, II, 9; **tomber amoureux
   (-euse) (de quelqu'un)** *to
   fall in love (with someone)*, II, 9
amusant(e) *funny*, I, 7; II, 1;
   fun, II, 11
amuse: Amuse-toi bien! *Have
   fun!* I, 11
les **amuse-gueule** (m.): **préparer les
   amuse-gueule** *to make party
   snacks*, II, 10
**amusé: Je me suis beaucoup
   amusé(e).** *I had a lot of fun.*
   II, 6; **Tu t'es amusé(e)?** *Did
   you have fun?* II, 6; **Tu t'es
   bien amusé(e)?** *Did you have
   fun?* I, 11
**amuser: Qu'est-ce que tu fais
   pour t'amuser?** *What do you
   do to have fun?* I, 4; **s'amuser**
   to have fun, II, 4
les **ananas** (m.) *pineapple*, I, 8; II, 4
l' **anglais** (m.) *English*, I, 1
les **animaux** (m.).: **nourrir les animaux** *to feed the animals*, II,
   12
animé(e) *exciting*, II, 8
l' **année** (f.) *year*, II, 1; **Bonne
   année!** *Happy New Year!* II, 3
**anniversaire: Joyeux (Bon)
   anniversaire!** *Happy birthday!* II, 3
l' **anorak** (m.) *a ski jacket*, II, 1
ans: avoir... ans *to be . . . years
   old*, II, 1; **J'ai... ans.** *I am . . .
   years old.* I, 1; **Quand j'avais...
   ans,...** *When I was . . . years
   old, . . .* , II, 8
antillais(e) *from the Antilles*,
   II, 11
août *August*, I, 4
apercevoir (pp. aperçu) *to
   notice*, II, 8, 9
aplatir *to flatten*, II, 3
l' **appareil** (m.): **Qui est à l'appareil?** *Who's calling?* I, 9
l' **appareil-photo** (m.) *a camera*,
   I, 11; II, 1
appelle: Il/Elle s'appelle comment?
   What's his/her name? I, 1; **Il/
   Elle s'appelle...** *His/Her name
   is . . .* , I, 1; **Je m'appelle...** *My
   name is . . .* , I, 1
**appelles: Tu t'appelles com-
   ment?** *What's your name?* I, 1

apporter *to bring*, I, 9
**apportez: Apportez-moi... , s'il
   vous plaît.** *Please bring
   me . . .* I, 5
apprécier *to appreciate*, II, 1
l' **après-midi** *in the afternoon*, I,
   2; **après-midi libre** (m.) *afternoon off*, I, 2
après *after*, I, 9; **Après ça...** *After
   that . . .* , II, 4; **Après, je suis
   sorti(e).** *Afterwards, I went out.*
   I, 9; **Et après?** *And afterwards?*
   I, 9
les **arbres** (m.) *trees*, II, 12; **mutiler
   les arbres** *to deface the trees*,
   II, 12
l' **argent** (m.) *money*, I, 11
l' **armoire** (f.) *armoire/wardrobe*,
   II, 2
arracher *to grab, snatch*, II, 8
arrive: Qu'est-ce qui t'arrive?
   What's wrong? II, 5
arriver *to arrive*, II, 5
les **arts** (m.) **plastiques** *art class*,
   I, 2
as: Qu'est ce que tu as? *What's
   wrong?* , II, 7; **Tu as... ?** *Do you
   have . . . ?* I, 3; **Tu as... à quelle
   heure?** *At what time do you
   have . . . ?* I, 2
l' **ascenseur** (m.) *elevator*, II, 2
asseyez: Asseyez-vous! *Sit
   down!* I, 0
assez *sort of*, II, 9; **assez bien**
   OK, II, 6
**assister: assister à un spectacle
   son et lumière** *to attend a
   sound and light show*, II, 6
l' **athlétisme** (m.).: **faire de
   l'athlétisme** *to do track and
   field*, I, 4
attendre *to wait for*, I, 9
l' **attrait** (m.) *attraction*, II, 11
au *to, at*, I, 6; *to, in (before a
   masculine noun)*, I, 11; **Au
   revoir!** *Goodbye!* I, 1; **au
   métro...** *at the . . . metro stop*,
   I, 6
auberge: l'auberge de jeunesse
   youth hostel, II, 2
aucune: Aucune idée. *No idea.*
   II, 9
aujourd'hui *today*, I, 2
aurais: J'aurais dû... *I should
   have . . .* , II, 10; **J'aurais pu...**
   I could have . . . , II, 10; **Tu
   aurais dû...** *You should have
   . . .* , II, 10; **Tu aurais pu...**
   You could have . . . , II, 10
aussi *also*, I, 1; **Moi aussi.** *Me
   too.* I, 2
l' **automne** (m.) *autumn, fall*, I, 4;
   en automne *in the fall*, I, 4

aux *to, in (before a plural
   noun)*, I, 11
avais: Quand j'avais... ans,...
   When I was . . . years old, . . . ,
   II, 8
avait: Elle avait l'air... *She
   seemed . . .* , II, 12; **Il y avait...**
   There was/were . . . , II, 8
avec: avec moi *with me*, I, 6;
   Avec qui? *With whom?* I, 6;
   C'est avec qui? *Who's in it?*
   II, 11; **C'est avec...** *. . . is
   (are) in it.* II, 11
l' **avenir** (m.) *future*, II, 1
avez: Oui, vous avez... ? *Yes,
   do you have . . . ?* I, 10;
   **Qu'est-ce que vous avez
   comme... ?** *What kind of . . .
   do you have?* I, 5; **Vous
   avez... ?** *Do you have . . . ?*
   I, 2
l' **avion** (m.) *plane*, I, 12; **en
   avion** *by plane*, I, 12
avis: A mon avis,... *In my opinion, . . .* , II, 9; **A mon avis, tu
   te trompes.** *In my opinion,
   you're mistaken.* II, 9; **A ton
   avis, qu'est-ce que je dois
   faire?** *In your opinion, what
   should I do?* II, 10; **A ton avis,
   qu'est-ce que je fais?** *In your
   opinion, what do I do?* I, 9
les **avocats** (m.) *avocados*, I, 8
avoir *to have* I, 2 ; **avoir rendez-vous (avec quelqu'un)**
   to have a date (with someone),
   II, 9; **avoir des responsabilités**
   to have responsibilities, II, 8;
   avoir des soucis *to have worries*, II, 8; **avoir faim** *to be
   hungry*, I, 5; **avoir l'air...** *to
   seem . . .* , II, 9; **avoir soif** *to
   be thirsty*, I, 5; **avoir un accident** *to have an accident*, II,
   9; **avoir... ans** *to be . . . years
   old*, II, 1
avril *April*, I, 4

B

la **baguette** *long, thin loaf of bread*,
   II, 3
se **baigner** *to go swimming*, II, 4
le **bal** *dance, prom*, II, 1
le **balcon** *balcony*, II, 2
banal: C'est banal. *That's ordinary.* II, 3
les **bananes** (f.) *bananas*, I, 8
le **bananier** *banana tree*, II, 4
la **bande** *group of friends*, II, 10
la **bande dessinée (la B.D.)** *comic
   book* , II, 11

la banque *bank,* I, 12
barbant *boring,* I, 2
le base-ball *baseball,* I, 4; **jouer au base-ball** *to play baseball,* I, 4
le basket(-ball) *basketball,* I, 4; **jouer au basket-ball** *to play basketball,* I, 4
les baskets (f.) *a pair of sneakers,* I, 3; II, 1
le bateau *boat,* I, 12; **en bateau** *by boat,* I, 12; **faire du bateau** *to go sailing,* I, 11
le bâtiment *building,* II, 8
beau *handsome,* II, 1; **Il fait beau.** *It's nice weather.* I, 4
Beaucoup. *A lot.* I, 4; **Oui, beaucoup.** *Yes, very much.* I, 2; **Pas beaucoup.** *Not very much.* I, 4
beaux: beaux-arts *fine arts,* II, 2
belle *beautiful,* II, 1; **C'est une belle histoire.** *It's a great story.* II, 11
besoin: De quoi est-ce que tu as besoin? *What do you need?* I, 8; **J'ai besoin de...** *I need . . . ,* I, 8
la bête *beast, animal,* II, 6, 9; **bête** *stupid,* II, 1
les bêtises (f.): **faire des bêtises** *to do silly things,* II, 8
le beurre *butter,* I, 8; II, 3
la bibliothèque *library,* I, 6; II, 2
bien: bien se nourrir *eat well,* II, 7; **Ça te fera du bien.** *It'll do you good.* II, 7; **Il/Elle est vraiment bien, ton/ta...** *Your . . . is really great.* II, 2 ; **J'aime bien...** *I like . . . ,* II, 1; **J'en veux bien.** *I'd like some.* I, 8; **Je ne me sens pas bien.** *I don't feel well.* II, 7; **Je veux bien.** *Gladly.* I, 8; *I'd like to.* II, 1; *I'd really like to.* I, 6; **Moi, j'aime (bien)...** *I (really) like . . . ,* I, 1; **Très bien.** *Very well.* I, 1
Bien sûr. *Of course,* I, 3; II, 10; *Certainly,* I, 9; **Bien sûr que non.** *Of course not.* II, 10; **Bien sûr. C'est...** *Of course. They are (He/She is) . . . ,* II, 11; **Oui, bien sûr.** *Yes, of course.* I, 7
bientôt: A bientôt. *See you soon.* I, 1
Bienvenue chez moi (chez nous). *Welcome to my home (our home),* II, 2
le bifteck *steak,* I, 8; II, 3
le billet: billet d'avion *plane ticket,* I, 11; II, 1; **billet de train** *train ticket,* I, 11

la biographie *biography,* II, 11
la biologie *biology,* I, 2
la bise *kiss,* II, 1
blanc(he) *white,* I, 3
bleu(e) *blue,* I, 3; II, 1
le bleuet *blueberry,* II, 3
blond(e) *blond,* I, 7; II, 1
le blouson *a jacket,* I, 10
le blues *blues (music),* II, 11
le bœuf *beef,* II, 3
Bof! *(expression of indifference),* I, 1; II, 8
boire *to drink,* II, 3
le bois: en bois *made of wood,* II, 2
les boissons (f.): **Qu'est-ce que vous avez comme boissons?** *What do you have to drink?* I, 5
la boîte: **une boîte de** *a can of,* I, 8; **une boîte de chocolats** *box of chocolates,* II, 3
le bol *bowl,* II, 3
bon *good,* I, 5; **Bon voyage!** *Have a good trip!* I, 11; **Bon, d'accord.** *Well, OK.* I, 8; **C'est bon pour toi.** *It's good for you.* II, 7; **C'est vraiment bon!** *It's really good!* II, 3; **Oui, très bon.** *Yes, very good.* I, 9; **pas bon** *not very good,* I, 5; **Vous avez (Tu as) fait bon voyage?** *Did you have a good trip?* II, 2
bonne(s): Bonne chance! *Good luck!* I, 11; **Bonne fête!** *Happy holiday! (Happy saint's day!),* II, 3; **Bonne idée.** *Good idea.* I, 4; II, 3; **Bonnes vacances!** *Have a good vacation!* I, 11; **C'est une bonne (excellente) idée.** *That's a good (excellent) idea.,* II, 1; **de bonne humeur** *in a good mood,* II, 9
les bonbons (m.) *candies,* II, 3
le bonheur *happiness,* II, 1
Bonjour *Hello,* I, 1
bord: au bord de la mer *to/at the coast,* I, 11
les bottes (f.) *boots,* I, 10; II, 1
la boucherie *butcher shop,* II, 3
les boucles d'oreilles (f.) *earrings,* I, 10
la bougie *candle,* II, 3
la boulangerie *bakery,* I, 12; II, 3
la boum: aller à une boum *to go to a party,* I, 6; **faire une boum** *to give a party,* II, 10
la boussole *compass,* II, 12
bout: **à l'autre bout** *at the other end,* II, 9
la bouteille: **une bouteille de** *a bottle of,* I, 8
la boutique de cadeaux *gift shop,* II, 3
le bracelet *a bracelet,* I, 3

le bras: **J'ai mal au bras** *My arm hurts.* II, 7
brave *brave,* II, 1
Bravo! *Terrific!* II, 5
Bref,... *Anyway, . . . ,* II, 9
briques: Ça casse pas des briques. *It's not earth-shattering.* II, 11
brosser: se brosser les dents *to brush one's teeth,* II, 4
le bruit *noise,* II, 8, 12
brun(e) *brunette,* I, 7; *dark brown (hair),* II, 1
bruyant(e) *noisy,* II, 8
le bus: **en bus** *by bus,* I, 12; **rater le bus** *to miss the bus,* II, 5

C

ça: Ça fait combien? *How much does that make?* II, 3; **Ça fait combien, s'il vous plaît?** *How much is it, please?* I, 5; **Ça fait... francs.** *It's . . . francs.* I, 5; **Ça ne me dit rien.** *That doesn't interest me.,* II, 1; **Ça se voit.** *That's obvious.* II, 9; **Ça te dit d'aller... ?** *What do you think about going . . . ?* II, 4; **Ça te dit de... ?** *Does . . . sound good to you?* II, 1; **Ça va.** *Fine.* I, 1; **Ça, c'est...** *This is . . . ,* II, 2; **Comment ça s'est passé?** *How did it go?* II, 5; **Et après ça...** *And after that, . . . ,* I, 9; **Merci, ça va.** *No thank you, I've had enough.* II, 3; **Non, ça va.** *No, I'm fine.* II, 2; **Oui, ça a été.** *Yes, it was fine.* I, 9
les cacahuètes (f.) *peanuts,* II, 7
cacher *to hide,* II, 5
le cachot *a dungeon,* II, 6
le cadeau *gift,* I, 11; **Tu as une idée de cadeau pour... ?** *Have you got a gift idea for. . . ?* II, 3; **la boutique de cadeaux** *gift shop,* II, 3
le cadre (active vocabulary) *photo frame,* II, 3; (passive vocabulary) *setting, surroundings,* II, 6, 12; **un cadre rustique** *a country (rustic) atmosphere,* II, 1
le café *coffee, café,* I, 5
le cahier *notebook,* I, 3
la calculatrice *calculator,* I, 3
cambodgien *Cambodian* (adj), II, 1
camp: **ficher le camp** *to leave quickly, "scram,"* II, 5
la campagne: à la campagne *to/at the countryside,* I, 11

camping: faire du camping *to go camping,* I, 11; II, 12; **terrain de camping** *campground,* II, 2

canadien(ne) *Canadian,* II, 11

le canard *duck,* II, 12

le canari *canary,* I, 7

la canne à pêche *fishing pole,* II, 12

la cannelle *cinnamon,* II, 3

le canotage: faire du canotage *to go canoeing,* II, 12

la cantine: à la cantine *at the school cafeteria,* I, 9

la capitale *capital,* II, 4

le cardigan *sweater,* I, 10

les carottes (f.) *carrots,* I, 8

le carré d'agneau *rack of lamb,* II, 3

la carte *map,* I, 0; **La carte, s'il vous plaît.** *The menu, please.* I, 5

la case *box,* II, 10; *hut,* II, 11

la casquette *a cap,* I, 10

casse: Ça casse pas des briques. *It's not earth-shattering.* II, 11

casser (avec quelqu'un) *to break up (with someone),* II, 9; **se casser...** *to break one's ...,* II, 7

la cassette *cassette tape,* I, 3

la cathédrale *cathedral,* II, 2

le cauchemar: C'était un véritable cauchemar! *It was a real nightmare!* I, 11

ce *this; that,* I, 3; **Ce sont...** *These/those are . . . ,* I, 7

ce que: Ce que j'aime bien, c'est... *What I like is . . . ,* II, 4; **Ce que je n'aime pas, c'est...** *What I don't like is . . . ,* II, 4; **Ce que je préfère, c'est...** *What I prefer is . . . ,* II, 4; **Tu sais ce que... ?** *Do you know what . . . ?* II, 9

ce qui: Ce qui m'ennuie, c'est... *What bothers me is . . . ,* II, 4; **Ce qui me plaît, c'est...** *What I like is . . . ,* II, 4; **Ce qui ne me plaît pas, c'est...** *What I don't care for is . . . ,* II, 4

la ceinture *belt,* I, 10

le centre commercial *mall,* I, 6

les céréales (f.) *cereal,* II, 3

ces *these; those,* I, 3

c'est: C'est... *It's . . . ,* I, 2; II, 11; *This is . . . ,* I, 7; **C'est-à-dire que...** *That is, . . . ,* II, 9; **C'est comment?** *What's it like?* II, 4; **Ça, c'est...** *This is . . . ,* II, 2; **Non, c'est...** *No, it's . . . ,* I, 4; **Oui, c'est...** *Yes, it's . . . ,* I, 4

cet *this; that,* I, 3

C'était... *It was . . . ,* II, 6

cette *this; that,* I, 3

la chaîne stéréo *stereo,* II, 2

la chaise *chair,* I, 0

la chaleur *warmth,* II, 4

la chambre *bedroom,* I, 7; II, 2; **ranger ta chambre** *to pick up your room,* I, 7

les champignons (m.) *mushrooms,* I, 8

les champs (m.) **de canne à sucre** *sugarcane fields,* II, 4

la chance: Bonne chance! *Good luck!* I, 11; **C'est pas de chance, ça!** *Tough luck!* II, 5

la chanson *song,* II, 11

chanter *to sing,* I, 9

chanteur *(male) singer,* II, 11

chanteuse *(female) singer,* II, 11

le chapeau *hat,* I, 10; **Chapeau!** *Well done!* II, 5

la charcuterie *delicatessen,* II, 3

charmant(e) *charming,* II, 4

le chat *cat,* I, 7

châtain (inv.) *brown (hair),* II, 1

les châtelaines (f.) *ladies of the nobility,* II, 6

chaud: Il fait chaud. *It's hot.* I, 4

chauffer *to heat,* II, 3

les chaussettes (f.) *socks,* I, 10

les chaussures (f.) *shoes,* I, 10

la chemise *a shirt (men's),* I, 10

le chemisier *a shirt (women's),* I, 10

les chèques (m.) **de voyage** *traveler's checks,* II, 1

cher: C'est trop cher. *It's too expensive.* I, 10; II, 3

chercher *to look for,* I, 9

les cheveux (m.) *hair,* II, 1

la cheville: se fouler la cheville *to sprain one's ankle,* II, 7

le chèvre *goat cheese,* II, 3

chez... *to/at . . . 's house,* I, 6; **Bienvenue chez moi (chez nous).** *Welcome to my home (our home),* II, 2; **chez le disquaire** *at the record store,* I, 12; **Faites/Fais comme chez vous/toi.** *Make yourself at home.* II, 2; **Je suis bien chez... ?** *Is this . . . 's house?* I, 9

chic *chic,* I, 10

le chien *dog,* I, 7; **promener le chien** *to walk the dog,* I, 7

les chiffres (m.) *numbers,* II, 1

la chimie *chemistry,* I, 2

la chipie *rascal (for a girl only),* II, 10

le chocolat *chocolate,* I, 1; *hot chocolate,* I, 5

choisi: Vous avez choisi? *Have you decided?* I, 5

choisir *to choose, to pick,* I, 10; **choisir la musique** *to choose the music,* II, 10

la chorale *choir,* I, 2

chose: J'ai quelque chose à faire. *I have something else to do.* II, 10; **J'ai des tas de choses (trucs) à faire.** *I have lots of things to do.* I, 12; **Quelque chose ne va pas?** *Is something wrong?* II, 7

le chou *cabbage,* II, 3

chouette *very cool,* II, 2; **Oui, très chouette.** *Yes, very cool.* I, 9

la chute d'eau *waterfall,* II, 4

le cimetière *cemetery,* II, 2

le cinéma *the movies,* I, 1; *the movie theater,* I, 6

le circuit: faire un circuit des châteaux *to tour some châteaux,* II, 6

le classeur *loose-leaf binder,* I, 3

le clavecin *harpsicord,* II, 2

clignoter *to blink,* II, 9

climatisé *air-conditioned,* II, 2

le clocher *church tower,* II, 2

clown: Il ne faut pas faire le clown en classe! *You can't be goofing off in class!* II, 5

le coca *cola,* I, 5

cocher *to check off,* II, 10

le cocotier *coconut tree,* II, 4

le cœur: J'ai mal au cœur. *I'm sick to my stomach.* II, 7

coin: au coin de *on the corner of,* I, 12

le collant *hose,* I, 10

collé: être collé(e) *to have detention,* II, 5

le colombo de cabri *a type of spicy goat stew,* II, 3

colonie: en colonie de vacances *to/at a summer camp,* I, 11

coloré(e) *colorful,* II, 4

combien: C'est combien,... ? *How much is . . . ?* I, 5; **C'est combien?** *How much is it?* I, 3; **C'est combien, l'entrée?** *How much is the entrance fee?* II, 6; **Ça fait combien?** *How much is it?* I, 10; *How much does that make?* II, 3; **Ça fait combien, s'il vous plaît?** *How much is it, please?* I, 5; **Combien coûte(nt)... ?** *How much is (are)... ?* II, 3; **Combien en voulez-vous?** *How many (much) do you want?* II, 3

comme: Comme ci, comme ça. *So-so.* I, 1; II, 6; Qu'est-ce que tu fais comme sport? *What sports do you play?* I, 4; Qu'est-ce que vous avez comme... ? *What kind of . . . do you have?* I, 5

commence: Ça commence à quelle heure? *What time does it start?* II, 11

commencer *to begin, to start,* I, 9

comment *what,* I, 0; *how,* I, 1; (Comment) ça va? *How's it going?* I, 1; C'est comment? *What's it like?* II, 4; C'était comment? *How was it?* II, 6; *What was it like?* II, 8; Comment tu trouves... ? *What do you think of . . . ?* I, 2; Comment tu trouves ça? *What do you think of that/it?* I, 2 ; *How do you like it?* I, 5; Il/Elle est comment? *What is he/she like?* I, 7; Ils/Elles sont comment? *What are they like?* I, 7; Tu t'appelles comment? *What is your name?* I, 0

commenté: un circuit commenté *guided walk,* II, 2

la commode *chest of drawers,* II, 2

comprendre *to understand,* II, 5; J'ai du mal à comprendre *I have a hard time understanding.* II, 5

compris: Tu as compris? *Did you understand?,* II, 1

concassé *crushed,* II, 3

les concerts (m.) *concerts,* I, 1

le concombre *cucumber,* II, 3

condition: se mettre en condition *to get into shape,* II, 7

conduire: conduire une voiture *to drive a car,* II, 8

se confier à *to confide in,* II, 10

la confiserie *candy shop,* II, 3

la confiture *jam,* I, 8

connais: Je ne connais pas. *I'm not familiar with them (him/her).* II, 11; Tu connais la nouvelle? *Did you hear the latest?* II, 9; Tu connais... *Are you familiar with . . . ?* II, 11

connaissance: faire la connaissance de *to make someone's acquaintance,* II, 10

conseilles: Qu'est-ce que tu me conseilles? *What do you advise me to do?* I, 9; *What do you think I should do?* II, 10

consommer: consommer trop de sucre *to eat too much sugar,* II, 7

continuez: Vous continuez jusqu'au prochain feu rouge. *You keep going until the next light.* I, 12

contre *against,* II, 2

cool *cool,* I, 2; Il/Elle est cool, ton/ta... *Your . . . is cool.* II, 2

côté: à côté de *next to,* I, 12; II, 2

coton: en coton *cotton,* I, 10

le cou: J'ai mal au cou *My neck hurts.* II, 7

la couche *layer,* II, 3

se coucher *to go to bed,* II, 4

coule: J'ai le nez qui coule. *I've got a runny nose.* II, 7

le country *country (music),* II, 11

le coup *strike, blow, hit,* II, 7, 9; un coup de main *a helping hand,* II, 10

coupé *cut,* II, 3

coupe: ça coupe l'appétit *it spoils your appetite,* II, 3

se couper: se couper le doigt *to cut one's finger,* II, 7

la cour *court (of a king or queen),* II, 6

Courage! *Hang in there!* II, 5

le coureur *runner,* II, 4

le cours *course,* I, 2; cours de développement personnel et social (DPS) *health,* I, 2; Tu as quels cours... ? *What classes do you have . . . ?* I, 2

les courses (f.): Tu peux aller faire les courses? *Can you do the shopping?* I, 8

court(e) *short* (objects), I, 10; II, 1

le cousin *male cousin,* I, 7

la cousine *female cousin,* I, 7

coûte: Combien coûte(nt)... ? *How much is (are)... ?* II, 3

craque: Je craque! *I'm losing it!* II, 7

la cravate *tie,* I, 10

le crayon *pencil,* I, 3

la crème: crème fraîche *a type of thick, sour, heavy cream,* II, 3; de la crème contre les insectes *insect repellent,* II, 12

la crémerie *dairy,* II, 3

creuser *to dig,* II, 8

crève: Je crève de faim! *I'm dying of hunger!* II, 12

crevé: Si, je suis crevé(e). *Yes, I'm exhausted.* II, 2

les crevettes (f.) *shrimp,* II, 3

crier *to yell, scream,* II, 5

croire *to believe,* II, 6, 9

crois: Je crois que... *I think that . . . ,* II, 9; Je ne crois pas. *I don't think so.* II, 9

les croissants (m.) *croissants,* II, 3

le croque-monsieur *toasted cheese and ham sandwich,* I, 5

la cuillerée: cuillerée à soupe *tablespoonful,* II, 3; cuillerée à thé *teaspoonful,* II, 3

le cuir: en cuir *leather,* I, 10

cuire *to cook, bake,* II, 3

la cuisine *kitchen,* II, 2

D

d'abord: D'abord,... *First, . . . ,* II, 1; D'abord, j'ai fait... *First, I did . . . ,* I, 9

d'accord: D'accord. *OK.* I, 4; II, 1; D'accord, si tu... d'abord... *OK, if you . . . , first.* I, 7; Je ne suis pas d'accord. *I don't agree.* I, 7; Tu es d'accord? *Is that OK with you?* I, 7

d'habitude *usually,* I, 4

dangereux (dangereuse) *dangerous,* II, 8

dans *in,* I, 6

la danse *dance,* I, 2

danser *to dance,* I, 1; danser le zouk *to dance the zouk,* II, 4

la daube de lapin *rabbit stew,* II, 3

de *of,* I, 0; de l' *some,* I, 8; de la *some,* I, 8; de taille moyenne *of medium height,* II, 1; Je n'ai pas de... *I don't have . . . ,* I, 3; Je ne fais pas de... *I don't play/do . . . ,* I, 4

débarrasser la table *to clear the table,* I, 7

debout *standing up,* II, 5

décembre *December,* I, 4

les déchets (m.): jeter (remporter) les déchets *to throw away (to take with you) your trash,* II, 12

déchirer *to rip,* II, 5

décidé: Vous avez décidé de prendre... ? *Have you decided to take . . . ?* I, 10

la découverte *discovery,* II, 6

découvrir *to discover,* II, 2

la défaite *defeat,* II, 7

dégoûtant *gross,* I, 5

déguster *to taste, enjoy,* II, 4

déjà *already,* I, 9; Il/Elle en a déjà un(e). *He/She already has one (of them).* II, 3

le déjeuner *lunch,* I, 2; déjeuner *to have lunch,* I, 9

délicieux (délicieuse) *delicious,* I, 5; C'était délicieux! *That was delicious!* II, 3

deltaplane: faire du deltaplane *to hang glide,* II, 4

demain *tomorrow,* I, 2; A demain. *See you tomorrow.* I, 1

demande: Je me demande... *I wonder* . . . , II, 9

demander: demander la permission à tes parents *to ask your parents' permission,* II, 10; **demander pardon à (quelqu'un)** *to ask (someone's) forgiveness,* II, 10

demi: et demi *half past (after midi and minuit),* I, 6

demie: et demie *half past,* I, 6

démodé(e) *old-fashioned,* I, 10

les dents (f.): **J'ai mal aux dents** *My teeth hurt.* II, 7

déposer *to deposit,* I, 12

déprimant *depressing,* II, 11

déprimé(e) *depressed,* II, 9

se **dérouler** *to take place,* II, 4

derrière *behind,* I, 12

des *some,* I, 3

descendre *to go down,* II, 6

désirez: Vous désirez? *What would you like?* I, 10

Désolé(e). *Sorry.* I, 5; II, 10

le dessert *dessert,* II, 3

devant *in front of,* I, 6

devenir *to become,* II, 6

devine: Devine ce que... *Guess what* . . . , II, 9; **Devine qui...** *Guess who* . . . , II, 9

devineras: Tu ne devineras jamais ce qui s'est passé. *You'll never guess what happened.* II, 9

les devoirs (m.) *homework,* I, 2; **faire ses devoirs** *to do homework,* I, 7

devrais: Tu devrais... *You should* . . . , I, 9; II, 7; **Tu ne devrais pas...** *You shouldn't* . . . , II, 7

le dictionnaire *dictionary,* I, 3

difficile *hard,* I, 2

le dimanche *on Sundays,* I, 2

le dîner *dinner,* I, 8; **dîner** *to have dinner,* I, 9

dingue *crazy,* II, 9

dire *to say, tell,* I, 9; **dire à (quelqu'un) que...** *to tell (someone) that* . . . , II, 10; **Vous pouvez lui dire que j'ai téléphoné?** *Can you tell her/him that I called?* I, 9

dis: Dis vite! *Let's hear it!* II, 9; **Dis-lui/-leur que...** *Tell him/her/them that* . . . , II, 10

disponible *available,* II, 2

se **disputer (avec quelqu'un)** *to have an argument (with someone),* II, 9

le disquaire: chez le disquaire *at the record store,* I, 12

le disque compact/un CD *compact disc/CD,* I, 3

dit: Ça ne me dit rien. *That doesn't interest me.* I, 4; II, 1; **Ça te dit d'aller... ?** *What do you think about going* . . . ? II, 4; **Ça te dit de... ?** *Does . . . sound good to you?* II, 1; **écouter ce qu'il/elle dit** *to listen to what he/she says,* II, 10; **il dit** *he says,* II, 5

la diversité *diversity,* II, 2

le doigt: se couper le doigt *to cut one's finger,* II, 7

dois: Qu'est-ce que je dois... What should I... ? II, 1; **A ton avis, qu'est-ce que je dois faire?** *In your opinion, what should I do?* II, 10

doit: On doit. *Everyone should* . . . , II, 7

Donc,... *Therefore,* . . . , II, 9

donner: donner à manger aux animaux *to feed the animals,* II, 6

donnez: Donnez-moi... , s'il vous plaît. *Please give me . . .* I, 5

dorer *to brown,* II, 3

dormi: J'ai mal dormi. *I didn't sleep well.* II, 7

dormir *to sleep,* I, 1

le dos: J'ai mal au dos *My back hurts.* II, 7

la douceur *sweetness,* II, 4

doux (douce) *mild,* II, 1

la douzaine: une douzaine de *a dozen,* I, 8

le droit *the right to do something,* II, 8

droite: à droite *to the right,* I, 12; **à droite de** *to the right of,* II, 2; **sur la droite** *on the right,* II, 2

drôle: C'est drôle (amusant). *It's funny.* II, 11

du *some,* I, 8

dû (pp. of devoir): **J'aurais dû...** *I should have* . . . , II, 10; **Tu aurais dû...** *You should have* . . . , II, 10

dur *hard,* II, 3; *tough, difficult,* II, 4

E

l' eau (f.) *water,* I, 5; **l'eau minérale** *mineral water,* I, 5; **la chute d'eau** *waterfall,* II, 4

ébullition: amener à ébullition *bring to a boil,* II, 3

les échanges (m.): **échanges franco-américains** *Franco-American exchange programs,* II, 1

l' écharpe (f.) *scarf,* I, 10; II, 1

l' école (f.) *school,* I, 1

écoute: Je t'écoute. *I'm listening.* I, 9; II, 10

écouter: écouter ce qu'il/elle dit *to listen to what he/she says,* II, 10; **écouter de la musique** *to listen to music,* I, 1

Ecoutez! *Listen!* I, 0

l' écran (m.) *screen,* II, 1

écrasé *crushed,* II, 3

écris: Ecris-lui/leur. *Write him/her/them.* II, 10

s' **écrouler** *to collapse, fall down,* II, 5

l' écureuil (m.) *squirrel,* II, 12

l' éducation (f.) **physique et sportive (EPS)** *physical education,* I, 2

effort: Encore un effort! *One more try!* II, 7

l' église (f.) *church,* II, 2

l' élève (m./f.) *student,* I, 2

embêtant(e) *annoying,* I, 7; II, 1

embête: Ça t'embête de... ? *Would you mind . . . ?* II, 10

emmener *to take (someone) along,* II, 8

emporter *to bring (with you),* II, 12

emprunter *borrow,* I, 12

en *some, of it, of them, any, none,* I, 8; *to, in (before a feminine noun),* I, 11; **Combien en voulez-vous?** *How many (much) do you want?* II, 3; **en coton** *cotton,* I, 10; **en cuir** *leather,* I, 10; **en face de** *across from,* II, 2; **en jean** *denim,* I, 10; **Il/Elle en a déjà un(e).** *He/She already has one (of them).* II, 3; **Je n'en peux plus!** *I just can't do any more!* II, 7; **Je n'en veux plus.** *I don't want anymore,* I, 8; **Je ne t'en veux pas.** *No hard feelings.* II, 10; **J'en veux bien.** *I'd like some.* I, 8; **Je vais (en) prendre...** *I'll take* . . . , II, 3; **T'en fais pas.** *Don't worry.* II, 5; **Tu n'as pas l'air en forme.** *You don't seem too well.* II, 7; **Tu ne m'en veux pas?** *No hard feelings?* II, 10; **Vous avez ça en... ?** *Do you have that in . . . ? (size, fabric, color),* I, 10

encore: Encore de... ? *More . . . ?* I, 8; **Encore un effort!** *One more try!* II, 7; **Encore... ?** *Some more . . . ?* II, 3

énervé(e) *annoyed*, II, 9
Enfin,... *Finally, . . .* , II, 1; **Enfin, je suis allé(e)...** *Finally, I went . . .* , I, 9
ennuie: **Ça t'ennuie de... ?** *Would you mind . . . ?* II, 10; **Ce qui m'ennuie, c'est...** *What bothers me is . . .* , II, 4; **On ne s'ennuie pas.** *You're never bored.* II, 11
ennuyé: **Je me suis ennuyé(e).** *I was bored.* II, 6
ennuyer *to bother*, II, 8
ennuyeux (ennuyeuse) *boring*, II, 6; **C'était ennuyeux.** *It was boring*, I, 5
Ensuite,... *Next, . . .* , II, 1; *Then, . . .* , II, 12
entendre: **entendre le réveil** *to hear the alarm clock*, II, 5
Entendu. *OK.* I, 6
s' entraîner à... *to train for (a sport)*, II, 7
entre *between*, I, 12
l' entrée (f.) *first course*, II, 3; *entrance fee*, II, 6; **C'est combien, l'entrée?** *How much is the entrance fee?* II, 6
entrer *to enter*, II, 6
l' enveloppe (f.) *envelope*, I, 12
envie: **J'ai envie de...** *I feel like . . .* , 11; **Non, je n'ai pas très envie.** *No, I don't feel like it.* II, 7; **Tu as envie de... ?** *Do you feel like . . . ?* II, 1
envoyer: **envoyer des lettres** *to send letters*, I, 12; **envoyer les invitations** *to send the invitations*, II, 10
l' épicerie (f.) *(a small) grocery store*, I, 12
épouser *to marry*, II, 8
épouvantable: **avoir une journée épouvantable** *to have a horrible day*, II, 5; **C'était épouvantable.** *It was horrible.* I, 11; II, 9
épreuve: **à toute épreuve** *solid, unfailing*, II, 10
l' équilibre (m.) *balance*, II, 7
équitation: **faire de l'équitation** *to go horseback riding*, I, 1
les escargots (m.) *snails*, I, 1; II, 3
l' espagnol (m.) *Spanish*, I, 2
essayer: **Je peux essayer... ?** *Can I try on . . . ?* I, 10; **Je peux l'(les) essayer?** *Can I try it (them) on ?* I, 10
Est-ce que *(Introduces a yes-or-no question)*, I, 4; **(Est-ce que) je peux... ?** *May I . . . ?*

I, 7
l' est: **dans l'est** *in the east*, II, 4; **C'est à l'est de...** *It's to the east of . . .* , II, 12
est: **Ça s'est très bien passé!** *It went really well!* II, 5; **Comment ça s'est passé?** *How did it go?* II, 5; **Il/Elle est...** *He/She is . . .* , I, 7; II, 1
et *and*, I, 1; **Et après ça...** *And after that, . . .* , I, 9; **Et toi? And you?** I, 1
les étagères (f.) *shelves*, II, 2
étais: **J'étais...** *I was . . .* , II, 12
était: **C'était comment?** *What was it like?* II, 8; **C'était tellement différent?** *Was it really so different?* II, 8
l' été (m.) *summer*, I, 4; **en été** *in the summer*, I, 4
été (pp. of être): **Oui, ça a été.** *Yes, it was fine.* I, 9
l' étoile (f.) *star*, II, 4, 9
étonné(e) *surprised*, II, 9
étonnerait: **Ça m'étonnerait!** *That would surprise me.* II, 6
étranger: **à l'étranger** *abroad*, II, 1
être *to be*, I, 7; **être collé(e)** *to have detention*, II, 5; **être en train de** *to be in the process of (doing something)*, II, 9
l' étude (f.) *study hall*, I, 2
étudier *to study*, I, 1
Evidemment. *Obviously.* II, 9
évite: **Evite/Evitez de...** *Avoid . . .* , II, 7
les examens (m.) *exams, tests*, I, 1; **passer un examen** *to take a test*, I, 9
excellent *excellent*, I, 5; **Oui, excellent.** *Yes, excellent.* I, 9; II, 2
excuse: **Excuse-moi.** *Forgive me.* II, 10; **Excuse-toi.** *Apologize.* II, 10
s' excuser *to apologize*, II, 10
excusez: **Excusez-moi.** *Excuse me.* I, 3
l' exercice: **faire de l'exercice** *to exercise*, II, 7
explique: **Explique-lui/-leur.** *Explain to him/her/them.* II, 10
expliquer: **expliquer ce qui s'est passé (à quelqu'un)** *to explain what happened (to someone)*, II, 10

F

face: **en face de** *across from*, I, 12; II, 2

fâché(e) *angry*, II, 9
facile *easy*, I, 2
la façon *way*, II, 1
la faïence *glazed pottery*, II, 2
la faim: **avoir faim** *to be hungry*, I, 5; **Je n'ai plus faim.** *I'm not hungry anymore.* II, 3; **Si, j'ai très faim!** *Yes, I'm very hungry.* II, 2; **Vous n'avez pas (Tu n'as pas) faim?** *Aren't you hungry?* II, 2
faire *to do, to make, to play*, I, 4; **faire la connaissance de** *to make someone's acquaintance*, II, 10; **faire la tête** *to sulk*, II, 9; **faire les préparatifs** *to get ready*, II, 10; **faire semblant de** *to pretend to (do something)*, II, 10; **Fais-toi une raison.** *Make the best of it.* II, 8; **Faites/Fais comme chez vous (toi).** *Make yourself at home.* II, 2; **J'ai des courses à faire.** *I have errands to do.* I, 5; **J'ai des tas de choses à faire.** *I have lots of things to do.* I, 5; **J'ai des trucs à faire.** *I have some things to do.* I, 5; **Je ne sais pas quoi faire.** *I don't know what to do.* II, 10; **Qu'est-ce qu'on peut faire?** *What can we do?* II, 4; **Qu'est-ce que je dois faire?** *What should I do?* II, 12; **Qu'est-ce que tu aimes faire?** *What do you like to do?* II, 1; **Qu'est-ce que tu vas faire... ?** *What are you going to do . . . ?* I, 6; **se faire mal à...** *to hurt one's . . .* , II, 7; **Tu peux aller faire les courses?** *Can you do the shopping?* I, 8; **Tu vas faire quoi... ?** *What are you going to do . . . ?* I, 6; **Tu vas t'y faire.** *You'll get used to it.* II, 8
fais: **A ton avis, qu'est-ce que je fais?** *In your opinion, what do I do?* I, 9; **Fais-toi une raison.** *Make the best of it.* II, 8; **Ne t'en fais pas!** *Don't worry!* I, 9; **Faites (Fais) comme chez vous (toi).** *Make yourself at home.* II, 2; **Je fais...** *I play/do . . .* , I, 4; **Ne t'en fais pas.** *Don't worry.* I, 11; **Qu'est-ce que tu fais comme sport?** *What sports do you play?* II, 1; **Qu'est-ce que tu fais pour t'amuser?** *What do you do to have fun?* I, 4; **Qu'est-ce que tu fais quand... ?** *What do you do*

FRENCH-ENGLISH VOCABULARY

when . . . ? I, 4; **T'en fais pas.** *Don't worry.* II, 5

fait (pp. of faire) *done, made,* I, 9; **Ça fait combien?** *How much does that make?* II, 3; **Ça ne fait rien.** *It doesn't matter.* II, 10; **D'abord, j'ai fait...** *First, I did . . . ,* I, 9; **Il fait beau.** *It's nice weather.* I, 4; **Il fait frais.** *It's cool.* I, 4; **Il fait froid.** *It's cold.* I, 4; **Il fait chaud.** *It's hot.* I, 4; **Qu'est-ce qu'on fait?** *What should we do?* II, 1; **Qu'est-ce que tu as fait... ?** *What did you do . . . ?* I, 9

faites: Faites/Fais comme chez vous/toi. *Make yourself at home.* II, 2

la farine *flour,* I, 8

fatigant: C'était fatigant! *It was tiring!* II, 2

fatigué: Je suis fatigué(e) *I'm tired.* II, 12; **Pas trop fatigué(e)?** *(You're) not too tired?* II, 2

faut: Il faut mieux travailler en classe. *You have to do better in class.* II, 5; **Il me faut...** *I need . . . ,* I, 3; **Il ne faut pas faire le clown en classe!** *You can't be goofing off in class!* II, 5; **Oui, il me faut...** *Yes, I need . . . ,* I, 10; **Qu'est-ce qu'il te faut pour... ?** *What do you need for . . . ? (informal),* I, 3; **Qu'est-ce qu'il vous faut pour... ?** *What do you need for . . . ? (formal),* I, 3

la faute: C'est de ma faute. *It's my fault.* II, 10

les féculents (m.) *carbohydrates,* II, 7

Félicitations! *Congratulations!* II, 3

la fenêtre *window,* I, 0

fera: Ça te fera du bien. *It'll do you good.* II, 7

ferais: Qu'est-ce que tu ferais, toi? *What would you do?* II, 10; **Tu ferais bien de...** *You would do well to . . . ,* II, 7

fermez: A quelle heure est-ce que vous fermez? *When do you close?* II, 6; **Fermez la porte.** *Close the door.* I, 0

la fête: Bonne fête! *Happy holiday! (Happy saint's day!),* II, 3; **Bonne fête de Hanoukka!** *Happy Hanukkah!* II, 3; **la fête des Mères** *Mother's Day,* II, 3;

la fête des Pères *Father's Day,* II, 3

le feu *flame* (heat), II, 3

la feuille: une feuille de papier *a sheet of paper,* I, 0

février *February,* I, 4

ficher: ficher le camp *to leave quickly, "scram,"* II, 5

le film *movie,* I, 6; **film classique** *classic movie,* II, 11; **film comique** *comedy,* II, 11; **film d'action** *action movie,* II, 11; **film d'amour** *romantic movie,* II, 11; **film d'aventures** *adventure movie,* II, 11; **film d'horreur** *horror movie,* II, 11; **film de science-fiction** *science-fiction movie,* II, 11; **film policier** *detective or mystery movie,* II, 11; **voir un film** *to see a movie,* I, 6

Finalement... *Finally . . . ,* II, 4

fixer: fixer la date *to choose the date,* II, 10

le fleuriste *florist's shop,* II, 3

les fleurs (f.) *flowers,* II, 3

la fois: une fois par semaine *once a week,* I, 4

fondu *melted,* II, 3

le foot(ball) *soccer,* I, 1; **le football américain** *football,* I, 4

la forêt *forest,* I, 11; **en forêt** *to the forest,* I, 11; **la forêt tropicale** *tropical rainforest,* II, 4

la forme: Tu n'as pas l'air en forme. *You don't seem too well.* II, 7

formidable: C'était formidable! *It was great!* I, 11

fort(e) *strong,* I, 7; II, 1; **C'est pas mon fort.** *It's not my strong point.* II, 5; **C'est mon fort.** *It's my strong point.* II, 5

la fosse *grave,* II, 8

le foulard *scarf,* II, 3

se fouler: se fouler la cheville *to sprain one's ankle,* II, 7

le four *oven,* II, 3; **au four** *baked,* II, 3

fous: plus on est de fous, plus on rit *the more the merrier,* II, 3

frais: Il fait frais. *It's cool.* I, 4

les fraises (f.) *strawberries,* I, 8

le franc *(the French monetary unit),* I, 3; **C'est... francs.** *It's . . . francs.* I, 5

le français *French* (language), I, 1

français(e) *French* (adj), II, 1

frapper *to knock,* II, 2

le frère *brother,* I, 7

les frites (f.) *French fries,* I, 1

froid: Il fait froid. *It's cold.* I, 4

le fromage *cheese,* I, 5; II, 3

les fruits de mer (m.) *seafood,* II, 3

furieux (furieuse) *furious,* II, 9

G

gagner *to win, to earn,* I, 9

les gants (m.) *a pair of gloves,* II, 1

le garçon *boy,* I, 0

garder ta petite sœur *to look after your little sister,* I, 7

la gare *train station ,* II, 2

garni *garnished,* II, 3

le gâteau *cake,* I, 8

gauche: à gauche *to the left,* I, 12; **à gauche de** *to the left of,* II, 2; **sur la gauche** *on the left,* II, 2

gêné(e) *embarrassed,* II, 9

génial(e) *great,* I, 2; II, 2

gentil (gentille) *nice,* I, 7; II, 1; **C'est gentil de votre (ta) part.** *That's so nice of you.* II, 2; **C'est gentil!** *That's nice of you.* II, 2

gentillet: gentillet, sans plus *cute (but that's all),* II, 11

la géographie *geography,* I, 2

la géométrie *geometry,* I, 2

la glace *ice cream,* I, 1; **faire du patin à glace** *to ice-skate,* I, 4

glacé *iced,* II, 3

le golf *golf,* I, 4

les gombos (m.) *okra,* I, 8

la gomme *eraser,* I, 3

la gorge: J'ai mal à la gorge *I have a sore throat.* II, 7

gourmand(e) *someone who loves to eat,* II, 1

la gousse d'ail *clove of garlic,* II, 3

le goûter *afternoon snack,* I, 8

la goutte *drop,* II, 8

les goyaves (f.) *guavas,* I, 8

la grammaire *grammar,* II, 1

grand(e) *tall,* I, 7; II, 1; *big,* I, 10; II, 1; **moins grand(e) que** *smaller than . . . ,* II, 4; **plus grand(e) que** *bigger than . . . ,* II, 4

grand-chose: Ce n'est pas grand-chose. *It's nothing special.* II, 3; **Pas grand-chose.** *Not much.* I, 6

la grand-mère *grandmother,* I, 7

le grand-père *grandfather,* I, 7

grandir *to grow,* I, 10

grasses: des matières grasses *fat,* II, 7

gratuit *free,* II, 1

grave: C'est pas grave. *It's not serious.* II, 5

grec *Greek* (adj), II, 1

grignoter: grignoter entre les

repas *to snack between meals,* II, 7

grillé *grilled,* II, 3

la grippe: J'ai la grippe. *I've got the flu.* II, 7

gris(e) *grey,* I, 3

gros (grosse) *fat,* I, 7

grossir *to gain weight,* I, 10

le groupe *(music) group,* II, 11

guidée: une visite guidée *a guided tour,* II, 6

la gymnastique: faire de la gymnastique *to do gymnastics,* II, 7

H

s' habiller *to get dressed,* II, 4

habitude: d'habitude *usually,* I, 4

haché *chopped,* II, 3

*les hamburgers (m.) *hamburgers,* I, 1

*les haricots (m.) *beans,* I, 8; les haricots verts (m.) *green beans,* I, 8

l' hébergement (m.) *lodging,* II, 6, 12

hésite: Euh... J'hésite. *Oh, I'm not sure.* I, 10; J'hésite. *I'm not sure.* I, 11

l' heure (f.): A quelle heure? *At what time?* I, 6; A tout à l'heure! *See you later!* I, 1; Tu as... à quelle heure? *At what time do you have . . . ?* I, 2

heures: à... heures *at . . . o'clock,* I, 2; à... heures quarante-cinq *at . . . forty-five,* I, 2; à... heures quinze *at . . . fifteen,* I, 2; à... heures trente *at . . . thirty,* I, 2

Heureusement,... *Fortunately, . . . ,* II, 9

heureux: Très heureux (heureuse). *Pleased to meet you.* I, 7

l' histoire (f.) *history,* I, 2; C'est l'histoire de... *It's the story of . . . ,* II, 11; C'est une belle histoire. *It's a great story.* II, 11; C'est une histoire passionnante. *It's an exciting story.* II, 11; Il n'y a pas d'histoire. *It has no plot.* II, 11

l' hiver (m.) *winter,* I, 4; en hiver *in the winter,* I, 4

*le hockey *hockey,* I, 4; jouer au hockey *to play hockey,* I, 4

horrible *terrible,* I, 10

hors: hors du feu *away from the flame,* II, 3

*le hot-dog *hot dog,* I, 5

l' huile (f.) *oil,* II, 3

les huîtres (f.) *oysters,* II, 3

l' humeur (f): de mauvaise humeur *in a bad mood,* II, 9; de bonne humeur *in a good mood,* II, 9

I

l' idée (f.): Bonne idée! *Good idea!* II, 3; C'est une bonne (excellente) idée. *That's a good (excellent) idea.* II, 1; Tu as une idée de cadeau pour... ? *Have you got a gift idea for . . . ?* II, 3

l' île (f.) *island,* II, 4

il y a: Il y a... *There is/are . . . ,* II, 12; Il n'y a pas de mal. *No harm done.* II, 10

il y avait: Il y avait... *There was/were . . . ,* II, 12

imperméable *a raincoat,* II, 1

importe: du n'importe quoi *worthless,* II, 11; ; N'importe quoi! *That's ridiculous!* II, 6

impossible: C'est impossible. *It's impossible.* II, 10

inadmissible: C'est inadmissible. *That's not acceptable.* II, 5

incroyable *incredible,* II, 6; C'était incroyable! *It was amazing/unbelievably bad!* II, 5

indien *Indian* (adj), II, 1

indonésien *Indonesian* (adj), II, 1

l' informatique *computer science,* I, 2

inquiet (inquiète) *worried,* II, 9

intelligent(e) *smart,* I, 7; II, 1

intention: J'ai l'intention de... *I intend to . . . ,* 11

intéressant *interesting,* I, 2

l' intérieur (m.) *interior,* II, 2

l' interro (f.) *quiz,* I, 9

les invitations (f.): envoyer les invitations *to send the invitations,* II, 10

invite: Invite-le/-la/-les. *Invite him/her/them.* II, 10

J

jamais: ne... jamais *never,* I, 4

la jambe: J'ai mal à la jambe *My leg hurts.* II, 7

le jambon *ham,* I, 5; II, 3

janvier *January,* I, 4

le jardin *yard,* II, 2

jaune *yellow,* I, 3

le jazz *jazz,* II, 11

je *I,* I, 1

le jean *(a pair of) jeans,* I, 3; II, 1; en jean *denim,* I, 10

jeter: jeter (remporter) les déchets *to throw away (to take with you) your trash,* II, 12

le jeu *game,* II, 1

le jeudi *on Thursdays,* I, 2

jeune *young,* I, 7; II, 1

la jeunesse: l'auberge de jeunesse *youth hostel,* II, 2

les jeux (m.): jouer à des jeux vidéo *to play video games,* I, 4

la Joconde *the Mona Lisa,* II, 1

le jogging: faire du jogging *to jog,* I, 4

la joie *joy,* II, 1

jouait: Si on jouait... ? *How about playing . . . ?* II, 8

joue: Je joue... *I play . . . ,* I, 4; On joue... *. . . is showing.* II, 11; Qu'est-ce qu'on joue comme film? *What films are playing?* II, 11

jouer *to play,* I, 4; jouer à... *to play . . . (a game),* I, 4

jour: C'est pas mon jour! *It's just not my day!* II, 5

la journée: avoir une journée épouvantable *to have a horrible day,* II, 5; Comment s'est passée ta journée (hier)? *How was your day (yesterday)?* II, 5; Quelle journée! *What a bad day!* II, 5;

joyeux: Joyeux (Bon) anniversaire! *Happy birthday!* II, 3; Joyeux Noël! *Merry Christmas!* II, 3

juillet *July,* I, 4

juin *June,* I, 4

la jupe *a skirt,* I, 10

le jus: le jus d'orange *orange juice,* I, 5; le jus de pomme *apple juice,* I, 5

jusqu'à: Vous allez tout droit jusqu'à... *You go straight ahead until you get to . . . ,* 12

K

le kilo: un kilo de *a kilogram of,* I, 8

L

là: -là *there (noun suffix),* I, 3; (Est-ce que)... est là, s'il vous plaît? *Is . . . , there, please?* I, 9; Là, c'est... *Here (There) is . . . ,* II, 2 laisser *to permit,* II, 6, 8 *to leave,* II, 12; **Je peux laisser un message?** *Can I leave a message?* I, 9

le lait *milk,* I, 8; II, 3

la laitue *lettuce,* II, 3

la lampe *lamp,* II, 2; **la lampe de poche** *flashlight,* II, 12

le lapin chasseur *rabbit in tomato-mushroom sauce,* II, 3

large *baggy,* I, 10

le latin *Latin (language),* I, 2

laver *to wash,* I, 7; **laver la voiture** *to wash the car,* I, 7; **se laver** *to wash oneself,* II, 4

les légumes (m.) *vegetables,* II, 7

leur(s) *their,* I, 7; leur *(indirect object) to them,* I, 9

se lever *to get up,* II, 4

levez: **Levez la main!** *Raise your hand!* I, 0; **Levez-vous!** *Stand up!* I, 0

libanais *Lebanese (adj),* II, 1

la librairie *bookstore,* I, 12

les lieux (m.) *places,* II, 1

la limonade *lemon soda,* I, 5

lire *to read,* I, 1

le lit *bed,* II, 2

le litre: **un litre de** *a liter of,* I, 8

la livre: **une livre de** *a pound of,* I, 8

le livre *book,* I, 3; **le livre de poésie** *book of poetry,* II, 11

le logement *lodging,* II, 2

loin: **loin de** *far from,* I, 12

long (longue) *long,* II, 1; **trop long** *too long,* II, 11

la lotion: **la lotion anti-moustiques** *insect repellent,* II, 12

louer *to rent,* II, 6

le loup *wolf,* II, 12

lu *(pp. of lire) read,* I, 9

lui *to him, to her,* I, 9

la lumière *light,* II, 6, 9

le lundi *on Mondays,* I, 2

les lunettes de soleil (f.) *sunglasses,* I, 10

le lycée *high school,* II, 2

M

ma *my,* I, 7

madame (Mme) *ma'am; Mrs,* I, 1; **Madame!** *Waitress!* I, 5

mademoiselle (Mlle) *miss; Miss,* I, 1; **Mademoiselle!** *Waitress!* I, 5

les magasins (m.) *stores,* I, 1; **faire les magasins** *to go shopping,* I, 1; **un grand magasin** *department store,* II, 3

le magazine *magazine,* I, 3

le magnétoscope *videocassette recorder, VCR,* I, 0

magnifique *beautiful,* II, 6

mai *May,* I, 4

maigrir *to lose weight,* I, 10

le maillot de bain *a bathing suit,* I, 10

la main *hand,* I, 0; **J'ai mal à la main** *My hand hurts.* II, 7; **se serrer la main** *to shake hands,* II, 8; **un coup de main** *a helping hand,* II, 10

mais *but,* I, 1

le maïs *corn,* I, 8

la Maison des Jeunes et de la culture (MJC) *the recreation center,* I, 6

mal: **Il n'y a pas de mal.** *No harm done.* II, 10; **J'ai mal...** *My . . . hurts.* II, 7, **J'ai mal à la gorge.** *I have a sore throat.* II, 7; **J'ai mal à la jambe.** *My leg hurts.* II, 7; **J'ai mal à la main.** *My hand hurts.* II, 7; **J'ai mal à la tête.** *My head hurts.* II, 7; **J'ai mal au bras.** *My arm hurts.* II, 7; **J'ai mal au cœur.** *I'm sick to my stomach.* II, 7; **J'ai mal au cou.** *My neck hurts.* II, 7; **J'ai mal au dos.** *My back hurts.* II, 7; **J'ai mal au ventre.** *My stomach hurts.* II, 7; **J'ai mal aux dents (f).** *My teeth hurt.* II, 7; **J'ai mal à l'oreille (f).** *My ear hurts.* II, 7; **J'ai mal au pied.** *My foot hurts.* II, 7; **J'ai mal dormi.** *I didn't sleep well.* II, 7; **J'ai mal partout!** *I hurt all over!* II, 7; **mal à l'aise** *uncomfortable,* II, 9; **pas mal** *not bad,* I, 1; *all right,* II, 6; **se faire mal à...** *to hurt one's . . . ,* II, 7; **Très mal.** *Very badly.* I, 9

malade: **Je suis malade.** *I'm sick.* II, 7

le malentendu: **un petit malentendu** *a little misunderstanding,* II, 10

malgré *in spite of,* II, 5

Malheureusement,... *Unfortunately, . . . ,* II, 9

les mandarines (f.) *mandarin oranges,* II, 3

manger *to eat,* I, 6; II, 7; **donner à manger aux animaux** *to feed the animals,* II, 6

les mangues (f.) *mangoes,* I, 8

manque: **... me manque.** *I miss . . . (singular subject),* II, 8; **Ce qui me manque, c'est...** *What I miss is . . . ,* II, 8

manquent: **... me manquent.** *I miss . . . (plural subject),* II, 8

le manteau *coat,* I, 10

le maquis *popular Ivorian outdoor restaurant,* II, 8

marche: **rater une marche** *to miss a step,* II, 5

le mardi *on Tuesdays,* I, 2

marocain *Moroccan (adj),* II, 1

la maroquinerie *leather-goods shop,* II, 3

marron *brown,* I, 3; II, 1

le marron *a chestnut,* II, 3

mars *March,* I, 4

le masque *a mask,* II, 8

le match: **regarder un match** *to watch a game (on TV),* I, 6; **voir un match** *to see a game (in person),* I, 6

les maths (f.) *math,* I, 1

les matières grasses (f.) *fat,* II, 7

le matin *in the morning,* I, 2

mauvais(e): **Oh, pas mauvais.** *Oh, not bad.* I, 9; **Très mauvais.** *Very bad.* I, 9; **avoir une mauvaise note** *to get a bad grade,* II, 5; **de mauvaise humeur** *in a bad mood,* II, 9

méchant(e) *mean,* I, 7; II, 1

les médicaments (m.) *medicine,* I, 12

meilleur(s): **C'est meilleur que...** *It's better than . . . ,* II, 7; **Meilleurs vœux!** *Best wishes!* II, 3; **C'est en... que je suis le/la meilleur(e).** *I'm best in . . . ,* II, 5

mélanger *to mix,* II, 3

même *same,* II, 9; **le/la même** *the same,* II, 9

le ménage: **faire le ménage** *to do housework,* I, 1; II, 10

la méprise *mistake, error,* II, 1

la mer *sea,* II, 4; **au bord de la mer** *to/at the coast,* I, 11

merci: **Merci.** *Thank you,* I, 3; II, 2; **Merci, ça va.** *No thank you, I've had enough.* II, 3; **Non, merci.** *No, thank you.* I, 8

le mercredi *on Wednesdays,* I, 2

la mère *mother,* I, 7

mes *my,* I, 7

le métro: **au métro...** *at the . . . metro stop,* I, 6; **en métro** *by subway,* I, 12

mets: **Mets...** *Wear . . . ,* I, 10

mettre *to put, to put on, to wear,* I, 10; **Je ne sais pas quoi mettre pour...** *I don't know what to wear for . . . ;* **mettre: mets: Qu'est-ce que je mets?** *What shall I wear?* I, 10; **se mettre en condition** *to get into shape,* II, 7

meublé *furnished,* II, 2

meurs: Je meurs de soif! *I'm dying of thirst!* II, 12; **Si, je meurs de faim/soif!** *Yes, I'm dying of hunger/thirst!* II, 2

mexicain *Mexican (adj),* II, 1

midi *noon,* I, 6

mieux: Ça va aller mieux! *It's going to get better!* I, 9; *It'll get better.* II, 5; **J'aime mieux...** *I prefer . . . ,* I, 1; II, 1; **Tu aimes mieux... ou... ?** *Do you prefer . . . or . . . ?* I, 10

mignon(ne) *cute,* I, 7; II, 1

le mille-feuille *layered pastry,* II, 3

mince *slender,* I, 7

minuit *midnight,* I, 6

la minute: Tu as une minute? *Do you have a minute?* I, 9; II, 10

le mobilier *furniture,* II, 2

moche: Je le/la/les trouve moche(s). *I think it's (they're) really tacky.* I, 10

la mode *fashion,* II, 3; **à la mode** *in style,* I, 10

moi: Moi, non. *I don't.* I, 2

moins: La vie était ... moins... *Life was . . . , less . . . ,* II, 8; **moins cinq** *five to,* I, 6; **moins grand(e) que** *smaller than . . . ,* II, 4; **moins le quart** *quarter to,* I, 6; **Plus ou moins.** *More or less.* II, 6

moitié: la moitié de *half of,* II, 3

moment: A ce moment-là,... *At that point, . . . ,* II, 9; **Un moment, s'il vous plaît.** *One moment, please.* I, 5

mon *my,* I, 7

monsieur (M.) *sir; Mr.* I, 1; **Monsieur!** *Waiter!* I, 5

la montagne *mountain,* I, 11; **à la montagne** *to/at the mountains,* I, 11; **faire du vélo de montagne** *to go mountain-bike riding,* II, 12; **les montagnes russes** *the roller coaster,* II, 6

monter *to go up,* II, 6; **monter dans une tour** *to go up in a tower,* II, 6

la montre *watch,* I, 3

montrer *to show,* I, 9

le morceau: un morceau de *a piece of,* I, 8

mortel (mortelle) *deadly dull,* II, 6

la mosquée *mosque,* II, 8

Mouais. *Yeah.* II, 6

la mouffette *skunk,* II, 12

mourir *to die,* II, 6

le moustique *mosquito,* II, 4

le mouton *mutton,* II, 3

le moyen *means, way to do something,* II, 8

le Moyen Age *Middle Ages,* II, 6

moyenne: de taille moyenne *of medium height,* II, 1

le mur *wall,* II, 5

la musculation: faire de la musculation *to lift weights,* II, 7

le musée *museum,* I, 6; II, 2

le musicien (la musicienne) *a musician,* II, 11

la musique *music,* I, 2; **la musique classique** *classical music,* II, 11; **écouter de la musique** *to listen to music,* I, 1; **Qu'est-ce que tu aimes comme musique?** *What music do you like?* II, 1

mutiler: mutiler les arbres *to deface the trees,* II, 12

N

nager *to swim,* I, 1

naître *to be born,* II, 6

la natation: faire de la natation *to swim,* I, 4

nautique: faire du ski nautique *to water-ski,* I, 4

le navet: C'est un navet. *It's a dud.* II, 11

ne: ne... jamais *never,* I, 4; **ne... pas encore** *not yet,* I, 9; **ne... pas** *not,* I, 1; **Pourquoi tu ne... pas... ?** *Why don't you . . . ?* II, 7; **Tu n'as qu'à...** *All you have to do is . . . ,* II, 7

neige: Il neige. *It's snowing.* I, 4

le nez: J'ai le nez qui coule. *I've got a runny nose.* II, 7

le Noël: Joyeux Noël! *Merry Christmas!* II, 3

noir(e) *black,* I, 3; II, 1

les noix de coco (f.) *coconuts,* I, 8

le nom *(last) name,* II, 1

non *no,* I, 1; **Moi, non.** *I don't.* I, 2; **Moi non plus.** *Neither do I.* I, 2; **Non, pas trop.** *No, not too much.* I, 2

le nord: dans le nord *in the north,* II, 4; **C'est au nord de...** *It's to the north of . . . ,* II, 12

nos *our,* I, 7

la note: avoir une mauvaise note *to get a bad grade,* II, 5

notre *our,* I, 7

nourrir: nourrir les animaux *to feed the animals,* II, 12; **bien se nourrir** *eat well,* II, 7

nouveau *new,* II, 2

nouvelle *new,* II, 2; **Tu connais la nouvelle?** *Did you hear the latest?* II, 9

novembre *November,* I, 4

nul (nulle) *useless,* I, 2; *lame,* II, 6; *worthless,* II, 8

nullement *not at all,* II, 9

O

l' occasion (f.) *chance,* II, 1

occupé: C'est occupé. *It's busy.* I, 9; **Désolé(e), je suis occupé(e).** *Sorry, I'm busy.* I, 6; **Je suis très occupé(e).** *I'm very busy.* II, 10

s' occuper de *to take care of someone or something,* II, 10

octobre *October,* I, 4

l' œil (m.) *(pl. les yeux) eye,* II, 1; **Mon œil!** *Yeah, right!* II, 6

les œillets (m.) *carnations,* II, 3

œufs (m.) *eggs,* I, 8; II, 3

l' oeuvre (f.) *work, piece of art,* II, 11

l' office de tourisme (m.) *tourist information office,* II, 2

offre: Offre-lui (-leur)... *Give him/her (them) . . . ,* II, 3

offrir (à quelqu'un) *to give (to someone),* II, 10; **Qu'est-ce que je pourrais offrir à... ?** *What could I give to . . . ?* II, 3; **Tu pourrais lui (leur) offrir...** *You could give him/her (them) . . . ,* II, 3

oh: Oh là là! *Oh no!* II, 5; **Oh, pas mauvais.** *Oh, not bad.* I, 9

l' ombre (f.) *shade,* II, 1

on: On... ? *How about . . . ?* I, 4; **On fait du ski?** *How about skiing?* I, 5; **On joue au baseball?** *How about playing baseball?* I, 5; **On pourrait...** *We could . . . ,* II, 1; **On va au café?** *Shall we go to the café?* I, 5

l' oncle (m.) *uncle,* I, 7

orange (inv.) *orange (color),* I, 3; **les oranges (f.)** *oranges,* I, 8

l' ordinateur (m.) *computer,* I, 3

l' oreille (f.) *ear,* II, 7; **J'ai mal à l'oreille** *My ear hurts.* II, 7

original: C'est original. *That's unique .* II, 3

l' orignal (m.) *moose,* II, 12

où: Où (ça)? *Where?* I, 6; **Où est-ce que tu vas aller... ?** *Where are you going to go . . . ?* I, 11; **Où est... s'il vous plaît?** *Where is . . . , please?* II, 2; **Où se trouve... ?** *Where is . . . ?* II, 4; **Tu es**

allé(e) où? *Where did you go?* I, 9

oublie: N'oublie pas... *Don't forget . . .* , I, 8; II, 1; **Oublie-le/-la/-les!** *Forget him/her/them!* I, 9; II, 10

oublié: Je n'ai rien oublié. *I didn't forget anything.* I, 11; **Tu n'as pas oublié... ?** *You didn't forget . . . ?* I, 11

oublier *to forget,* I, 9

l' ouest: dans l'ouest *in the west,* II, 4; **C'est à l'ouest de...** *It's to the west of . . .* , II, 12

oui *yes,* I, 1

l' ours (m.) *bear,* II, 12

ouvert *open,* II, 1

ouvrez: A quelle heure est-ce que vous ouvrez? *When do you open?* II, 6; **Ouvrez vos livres à la page...** *Open your books to page . . .* , I, 0

P

la page *page,* I, 0

le pagne *a piece of Ivorian cloth,* II, 8

le pain *bread,* I, 8; II, 3; **le pain au chocolat** *croissant with a chocolate filling,* II, 3

le palmier *palm tree,* II, 4

les paniers (m.) *baskets,* II, 8

la panne: tomber en panne *to break down,* II, 9

le pantalon *a pair of pants,* I, 10

les papayes (f.) *papayas,* I, 8

la papeterie *stationery store,* I, 12

le papier *paper,* I, 0

le paquet: un paquet de *a carton/box of,* I, 8

le parc *park,* I, 6; II, 2; **visiter un parc d'attractions** *to visit an amusement park,* II, 6

pardon: Pardon *Pardon me,* I, 3; **demander pardon à (quelqu'un)** *to ask (someone's) forgiveness,* II, 10; **Pardon, madame. ... s'il vous plaît?** *Excuse me, ma'am . . . please?* I, 12; **Pardon, mademoiselle. Où est... s'il vous plaît?** *Excuse me, miss. Where is . . . please?* I, 12; **Pardon, monsieur. Je cherche... s'il vous plaît.** *Excuse me, sir. I'm looking for . . . please.* I, 12

pardonner à (quelqu'un) *to forgive (someone),* II, 10

parfait: C'est parfait. *It's perfect.* I, 10

parie: Je parie que... *I bet that . . .* , II, 9

parle: Ça parle de... *It's about . . .* , II, 11; **De quoi ça parle?** *What's it about?* II, 11; **Parle-lui/-leur.** *Talk to him/her/them.* II, 10

parlé: Nous avons parlé. *We talked.* I, 9

parler *to talk, to speak,* I, 1; **(Est-ce que) je peux parler à... ?** *Could I speak to . . . ?* I, 9; **Je peux te parler?** *Can I talk to you?* I, 9; II, 10; **parler au téléphone** *to talk on the phone,* I, 1

part: A quelle heure est-ce que le train (le car) pour... part? *What time does the train (the bus) for . . . leave?* II, 6; **C'est gentil de votre (ta) part.** *That's so nice of you.* II, 2

partager *to share,* II, 7

partenaire (m./f.) *partner,* II, 1

partir *to leave,* I, 11; II, 6; **Tu ne peux pas partir sans...** *You can't leave without . . .* , 11

partout: J'ai mal partout! *I hurt all over!* II, 7

pas: Il/Elle ne va pas du tout avec... *It doesn't go at all with . . .* , I, 10; *Out of the question!* I, 7; **Pas du tout.** *Not at all.* II, 10; **Pas mal.** *Not bad.* I, 1; **Pas moi.** *Not me.* I, 2; **Pas question!** *No way!,* II, 1; **Pas terrible.** *Not so great.* I, 1; **pas super** *not so hot,* I, 2

passe: Ça passe à... *It's playing at . . .* , II, 11; **Ça passe où?** *Where is that playing?* II, 11; **Qu'est-ce qui se passe?** *What's going on?* II, 5

passé: Ça s'est bien passé? *Did it go well?* I, 11; **Ça s'est très bien passé!** *It went really well!* II, 5; **Comment ça s'est passé?** *How did it go?* II, 5; **expliquer ce qui s'est passé (à quelqu'un)** *to explain what happened (to someone),* II, 10; **J'ai passé une journée épouvantable!** *I had a terrible day!* II, 5; **Qu'est-ce qui s'est passé?** *What happened?* I, 9; **Tu as passé un bon week-end?** *Did you have a good weekend?* I, 9; **Tu as passé un bon... ?** *Did you have a good . . . ?* I, 11

passer: passer un examen *to take a test,* I, 9; **Tu pourrais passer à... ?** *Could you go by . . . ?* I, 12

passez: Vous passez devant... *You'll pass . . .* , 12

le passeport *passport,* I, 11; II, 1

passionnant(e) *fascinating,* I, 2; **C'est une histoire passionnante.** *It's an exciting story.* II, 11

le pâté *paté,* II, 3

les pâtes (f.) *pasta,* II, 7

le patin: faire du patin à glace *to ice skate,* I, 4

la pâtisserie *pastry,* I, 12; *pastry shop,* I, 12; II, 3

pauvre: Pauvre vieux/vieille! *You poor thing!* II, 5

le pays *country,* II, 6

la pêche: aller à la pêche *to go fishing,* I, 4

les pêches (f.) *peaches,* I, 8

pêcheurs: village de pêcheurs *fishing village,* II, 4

pédestre: faire une randonnée pédestre *to go for a hike,* II, 12

la peinture *painting,* II, 2

pendant: pendant ce temps *meanwhile,* II, 1

la pendule *clock,* II, 9

pénible *a pain in the neck,* I, 7

pense: Pense à prendre... *Remember to take . . .* , II, 1

pensé: J'ai pensé à tout. *I've thought of everything.* I, 11

la pension *meals,* II, 12

perdre *to lose,* II, 5; **se perdre** *to get lost,* II, 9

le père *father,* I, 7

la permission: demander la permission à tes parents *to ask your parents' permission,* II, 10

le petit déjeuner *breakfast,* I, 8

petit(e) *short (height),* I, 7; II, 1; *small,* I, 10; II, 1; **petit à petit** *little by little,* II, 3; **Quand il/elle était petit(e),...** *When he/she was little, . . .* , II, 8; **Quand j'étais petit(e),...** *When I was little, . . .* , II, 8

les petits pois (m.) *peas,* I, 8

peu: Si, un peu. *Yes, a little.* II, 2

la peur: J'ai peur (de la, du, des)... *I'm scared (of) . . .* , II, 12

peut: On peut... *We can . . .* , II, 4; *You can . . .* , II, 12; **Qu'est-ce qu'on peut faire?** *What can we do?* II, 4; **Si tu veux, on peut...** *If you like, we can . . .* , II, 1

peut-être *maybe,* II, 3; **Tu as peut-être raison.** *Maybe you're right.* II, 9

peux: (Est-ce que) je peux... ? *May I . . . , ?* I, 7; **Est-ce que tu peux... ?** *Can you . . . ?*

I, 12; **Je n'en peux plus!** *I just can't do any more!* II, 7; **Je ne peux pas maintenant.** *I can't right now.* I, 8; **Je ne peux pas.** *I can't.* II, 1; **Je peux te parler?** *Can I talk to you?* II, 10; **Non, je ne peux pas.** *No, I can't.* I, 12; **Qu'est-ce que je peux faire?** *What can I do?* I, 9; **Tu peux m'aider?** *Can you help me?* II, 10

la pharmacie *drugstore,* I, 12
les photos: faire des photos *to take pictures,* I, 4
la physique *physics,* I, 2
la pièce *room* (of a house), II, 2; *play* (theatrical), I, 6; **voir une pièce** *to see a play,* I, 6; **une pièce** (d'or ou d'argent) *coin,* II, 4
le pied *foot,* I, 12; **à pied** *on foot,* I, 12; **J'ai mal au pied.** *My foot hurts.* II, 7
piétonnier *pedestrian* (adj.), II, 2
le pique-nique: faire un pique-nique *to have a picnic,* I, 6; II, 6
la piscine *swimming pool,* I, 6; II, 2
la pizza *pizza,* I, 1
la plage *beach,* I, 1; II, 4
plaire: Tu vas te plaire ici. *You're going to like it here.* II, 8
plaisantes: Tu plaisantes! *You're joking!* II, 6
plaisir: Avec plaisir. *With pleasure.* II, 10; **Oui, avec plaisir.** *Yes, with pleasure.* I, 8
plaît: Il/Elle me plaît, mais c'est cher. *I like it, but it's expensive.* I, 10; **Il/Elle te/vous plaît?** *Do you like it?* I, 10; **Ce qui me plaît, c'est...** *What I like is . . . ,* II, 4; **Ce qui ne me plaît pas, c'est...** *What I don't care for is . . . ,* II, 4; **s'il vous/te plaît** *please,* I, 3; **Un... s'il vous plaît.** *A . . . , please.* II, 6
planche: faire de la planche à voile *to go windsurfing,* I, 11; II, 4
le plat principal *main course,* II, 3
plein: C'est plein de rebondissements. *It's full of plot twists.* II, 11; **plein tarif** *full admission price,* II, 2
pleurer *to cry,* II, 6
pleut: Il pleut. *It's raining.* I, 4
plongée: faire de la plongée avec un tuba *to snorkel,* II, 4; **faire de la plongée sous-marine** *to scuba dive,* II, 4
plu (pp. of plaire): **Ça m'a beau-**

coup plu. *I really liked it.* II, 6; **Ça t'a plu?** *Did you like it?* II, 6
plus: Je n'ai plus faim/soif. *I'm not hungry/thirsty anymore.* II, 3; **Je n'en peux plus!** *I just can't do any more!* II, 7; **Je n'en veux plus.** *I don't want anymore,* I, 8; **La vie était plus...** *Life was more . . . ,* II, 8; **Moi non plus.** *Neither do I.* I, 2; **Non, merci. Je n'ai plus faim.** *No thanks. I'm not hungry anymore.* I, 8; **plus grand(e) que** *bigger than . . . ,* II, 4; **plus on est de fous, plus on rit** *the more the merrier,* II, 3; **Plus ou moins.** *More or less.* II, 6
plutôt *rather,* II, 9
la poêle *frying pan,* II, 3
les poires (f.) *pears,* I, 8
le poisson *fish,* I, 7; II, 3
la poissonnerie *fish shop,* II, 3
les pommes (f.) *apples,* I, 8
les pommes de terre (f.) *potatoes,* I, 8
les pompes (f.): **faire des pompes** *to do push-ups,* II, 7
le pop *popular, mainstream music,* II, 11
le porc *pork,* I, 8
la porte *door,* I, 0
le portefeuille *wallet,* I, 3; II, 3
porter *to wear,* I, 10
poser (un problème, une question) *to present or ask,* II, 5
possible: C'est possible. *That's possible.* II, 9; **Ce n'est pas possible.** *That's not possible.* II, 9; **Pas possible!** *No way!* II, 6
la poste *post office,* I, 12; II, 2
le poster *poster,* I, 3; II, 2
la poterie *pottery,* II, 8
la poubelle *trashcan,* I, 7; **sortir la poubelle** *to take out the trash,* I, 7
les poules (f.) *chickens,* I, 8
le poulet *chicken,* I, 8; II, 3
pour: Qu'est-ce qu'il te faut pour... ? *What do you need for . . . ? (informal),* I, 3; **Qu'est-ce que tu fais pour t'amuser?** *What do you do to have fun?* I, 4
pourquoi: Pourquoi est-ce que tu ne mets pas... ? *Why don't you wear . . . ? ,* I, 10; **Pourquoi pas?** *Why not?* I, 6; **Pourquoi tu ne... pas?** *Why don't you . . . ?* I, 9; II, 7
pourrais: Je pourrais avoir...? *May I have some . . . ?* II, 3;

Qu'est-ce que je pourrais offrir à... ? *What could I give to . . . ?* II, 3; **Tu pourrais... ?** *Could you . . . ?* II, 10; **Tu pourrais lui (leur) offrir...** *You could give him/her (them) . . . ,* II, 3; **Tu pourrais passer à... ?** *Could you go by . . . ?* I, 12
pourrait: On pourrait... *We could . . . ,* II, 1
pourriez: Vous pourriez (tu pourrais) me passer... *Would you pass . . . ,* II, 3
pouvoir *to be able to, can,* I, 8
pratiquer *to practice,* II, 1
préfère: Ce que je préfère, c'est... *What I prefer is . . . ,* II, 4; **Je préfère** *I prefer,* I, 1; II, 1; **Non, je préfère...** *No, I'd rather . . . ,* II, 1
préféré: Quel est ton... préféré(e)? *What is your favorite . . . ?* II, 1; **Qui est ton... préféré(e)?** *Who is your favorite . . . ?* II, 1
le premier étage *second floor,* II, 2
prendre *to take or to have (food or drink),* I, 5; **avoir (prendre) rendez-vous (avec quelqu'un)** *to have (make) a date (with someone),* II, 9; **Je vais (en) prendre...** *I'll take . . . ,* II, 3; **Je vais prendre... , s'il vous plaît.** *I'll have . . . , please.* I, 5; *I'm going to have . . . , please.* I, 5; **On peut prendre...** *We can take . . . ,* 12; **Pense à prendre...** *Remember to take . . . ,* II, 1; **Prends...** *Take . . . ,* II, 1; **Vous avez décidé de prendre... ?** *Have you decided to take . . . ?* I, 10
prends: Prends... *Get . . . ,* I, 8; **Prends/Prenez...** *Have . . . ,* I, 5; **Je le/la/les prends.** *I'll take it/them.* I, 10; **Tu prends... ?** *Are you taking . . . ?* I, 11; *Will you have . . . , ?* I, 8
prenez: Prenez... *Take . . . ,* II, 2; **Prenez une feuille de papier.** *Take out a sheet of paper.* I, 0; **Vous le/la/les prenez?** *Are you going to take it/them?* I, 10; **Vous prenez?** *What are you having?* I, 5; **Vous prenez... ?** *Will you have . . . , ?* I, 8; **Prenez la rue... , puis traversez la rue...** *Take . . . Street, then cross . . . Street,* I, 12
le prénom *first name,* II, 1
les préparatifs (m.): **faire les préparatifs** *to get ready,* II, 10

préparer: préparer les amuse-gueule *to make party snacks,* II, 10

près: près de *close to,* I, 12; *near,* II, 2

présente: Je te/vous présente... *I'd like you to meet . . .* I, 7

presque: Tu y es (On y est) presque! *You're (we're) almost there!* II, 7

pressé(e) *in a hurry,* II, 7

prévu: Je n'ai rien de prévu. *I don't have any plans.* I, 11

le printemps *spring,* I, 4; **au printemps** *in the spring,* I, 4

pris (pp. of prendre) *took,* I, 9

privé: être privé(e) de sortie *to be "grounded,"* II, 9

le problème: J'ai un petit problème. *I've got a problem.* I, 9; **J'ai un problème.** *I have a problem.* II, 10; **Pas de problème.** *No problem.* II, 10

prochain: Vous continuez jusqu'au prochain feu rouge. *You keep going until the next light.* I, 12

proche *nearby,* II, 1; *close,* II, 5

le professeur (le prof) *teacher,* I, 2

profiter *to take advantage of,* II, 1

le projet *projects, plans,* II, 1

la promenade: faire une promenade *to go for a walk,* I, 6

promener: promener le chien *to walk the dog,* I, 7; **promener** *to go for a walk,* II, 4

promouvoir *to promote,* II, 2

propos: A propos,... *By the way, . . . ,* II, 9

propre *(one's) own,* II, 1; **propre** *clean,* II, 8

pu (pp. of pouvoir): **J'aurais pu...** *I could have . . . ,* II, 10; **Tu aurais pu...** *You could have . . . ,* II, 10

la publicité *advertisement,* II, 3

puis: Puis,... *Then, . . . ,* II, 1; **Puis, tournez à gauche dans/sur...** *Then, turn left on . . . ,* II, 2; **Prenez la rue... , puis traversez la rue...** *Take . . . Street, then cross . . . Street,* I, 12

le pull(-over) *a pullover sweater,* I, 3; II, 1

Q

qu'est-ce que: Qu'est ce que tu as? *What's wrong? ,* II, 7; **Qu'est-ce qu'il y a... ?** *What is there . . . ?* II, 4; **Qu'est-ce**

qu'il y a? *What's wrong?* II, 10; **Qu'est-ce qu'on fait?** *What should we do?* II, 1; **Qu'est-ce qu'on peut faire?** *What can we do?* II, 4; **Qu'est-ce que je peux faire?** *What can I do?* I, 9; II, 10; **Qu'est-ce que tu aimes faire?** *What do you like to do?* II, 1; **Qu'est-ce que tu as fait... ?** *What did you do . . . ?* I, 9; **Qu'est-ce que tu fais... ?** *What do you do . . . ?* I, 4; **Qu'est-ce que tu fais quand... ?** *What do you do when . . . ?* I, 4; **Qu'est-ce que tu vas faire... ?** *What are you going to do . . . ?* I, 6; **Qu'est-ce que vous avez comme... ?** *What kind of . . . do you have?* I, 5

qu'est-ce qui: Qu'est-ce qui s'est passé? *What happened?* I, 9; **Qu'est-ce qui se passe?** *What's going on?* II, 5; **Qu'est-ce qui t'arrive?** *What's wrong?* II, 5

le quai: De quel quai... ? *From which platform . . . ?* II, 6; **Du quai...** *From platform . . . ,* II, 6

quand: Quand (ça)? *When?* I, 6

quant: quant à *with respect to,* II, 1

quart: et quart *quarter past,* I, 6; **moins le quart** *quarter to,* I, 6

quel(s): Quel est ton... préféré? *What is your favorite . . . ?* II, 1; **Quel week-end formidable!** *What a great weekend!* II, 5; **Quel week-end!** *What a bad weekend!* II, 5; **Tu as quel âge?** *How old are you?* I, 1; **Tu as quels cours... ?** *What classes do you have . . . ?* I, 2

quelle: Quelle journée formidable! *What a great day!* II, 5; **Quelle journée!** *What a bad day!* II, 5; **Tu as... à quelle heure?** *At what time do you have . . . ?* I, 2

quelqu'un *someone,* II, 3

quelque chose: J'ai quelque chose à faire. *I have something else to do.* II, 10; **Je cherche quelque chose pour...** *I'm looking for something for . . . ,* I, 10; **Quelque chose ne va pas?** *Is something wrong?* II, 7

quelquefois *sometimes,* I, 4

question: Pas question! *No way!,* II, 1; *Out of the question!* I, 7

qui: Avec qui? *With whom?* I, 6; **Qui est ton/ta... préféré(e)?** *Who is your favorite . . . ?* II, 1

quittez: Ne quittez pas. *Hold on.* I, 9

quoi: ... quoi. *. . . you know.* II, 9; **Je ne sais pas quoi faire.** *I don't know what to do.* II, 10; **Je ne sais pas quoi mettre pour...** *I don't know what to wear for . . . ,* I, 10; **N'importe quoi!** *That's ridiculous!* II, 6; **Tu as quoi... ?** *What do you have . . . ?* I, 2

R

le raccourci *short cut,* II, 12

raconte: Raconte! *Tell me!* II, 5; **Qu'est-ce que ça raconte?** *What's the story?* II, 11

raconter *to tell (a story),* II, 1

la radio *radio,* I, 3

le raisin *grapes,* I, 8

raison: Fais-toi une raison. *Make the best of it.* II, 8; **Tu as raison...** *You're right . . . ,* II, 3

rajouter *to add,* II, 7

le ramasseur de balle *ballboy,* II, 8

le randonnée: faire de la randonnée *to go hiking,* I, 11; **faire une randonnée en raquettes** *to go snow-shoeing,* II, 12; **faire une randonnée en skis** *to go cross-country skiing,* II, 12; **faire une randonnée pédestre** *to go for a hike,* II, 12

le rang *row,* II, 3

ranger: ranger ta chambre *to pick up your room,* I, 7

le rap *rap (music),* II, 11

râpé *grated,* II, 3

raplapla: Je suis tout raplapla. *I'm wiped out.* II, 7

rappeler: Vous pouvez rappeler plus tard? *Can you call back later?* I, 9

rapporte: Rapporte-moi... *Bring me back . . . ,* I, 8

rapportes: Tu me rapportes... ? *Will you bring me . . . , ?* I, 8

les raquettes (f.): **faire une randonnée en raquettes** *to go snow-shoeing,* II, 12

rater: rater le bus *to miss the bus,* I, 9; II, 5; **rater un examen** *to fail a test,* I, 9; **rater une marche** *to miss a step,* II, 5

le raton laveur *raccoon,* II, 12

les rebondissements (m.): **C'est plein de rebondissements.** *It's full of plot twists.* II, 11 recevoir: recevoir le bulletin trimestriel *to receive one's report card*, II, 5

recommande: Je te le recommande. *I recommend it.* II, 11

recommence: Ne recommence pas. *Don't do it again.* II, 5

réconcilier: se réconcilier avec (quelqu'un) *to make up (with someone)*, II, 10

la récréation *break*, I, 2

réduit *reduced*, II, 2

le regard *look, glance*, II, 10

regarde: Non, merci, je regarde. *No, thanks, I'm just looking.* I, 10; Regarde, c'est... *Look, here's (there's) (it's) . . . ,* I, 12

regarder *to watch, to look at,* I, 1; regarder la télé(vision) *to watch TV,* I, 1; regarder un match *to watch a game (on TV),* I, 6

regardez: Regardez la carte! *Look at the map!* I, 0

le régent (la régente) *the regent; someone who rules in place of the king or queen,* II, 6

le reggae *reggae music,* II, 11

le régime: suivre un régime trop strict *follow a diet that's too strict.* II, 7

la règle *ruler,* I, 3; les règles *rules,* II, 7

regrette: Je regrette. *Sorry,* I, 3; Je regrette... *I miss . . . ,* II, 8; Je regrette, mais je n'ai pas le temps. *I'm sorry, but I don't have time.* I, 8

la reine *the queen,* II, 6

relaxant(e) *relaxing,* II, 8

la religieuse *cream puff pastry ,* II, 3

le renard *fox,* II, 12

rencontrer *to meet,* I, 9; II, 9

rendez-vous: avoir (prendre) rendez-vous (avec quelqu'un) *to have (make) a date (with someone),* II, 9; Rendez-vous... *We'll meet . . .* I, 6

rendre *to return something,* I, 12; rendre les examens *to return tests,* II, 5

rentrer *to go back (home),* II, 6

renverser *to knock over, spill,* II, 5

répartir *to spread evenly,* II, 3

le repas *meal,* II, 7; sauter un repas *to skip a meal,* II, 7

répéter *to rehearse, to practice,* I, 9

répétez: Répétez! *Repeat!* I, 0

répond: Ça ne répond pas.

There's no answer. I, 9

répondre *to answer,* I, 9

respecter: respecter la nature *to respect nature,* II, 12

les responsabilités (f.): avoir des responsabilités *to have responsibilities,* II, 8

ressuciter *to bring back to life,* II, 8

le restaurant *the restaurant,* I, 6

rester *to stay,* II, 6

rétablissement: Bon rétablissement! *Get well soon!* II, 3

retirer: retirer de l'argent (m.) *withdraw money,* I, 12

retourner *to return,* II, 6

rétro (inv.) *style of the Forties or Fifties,* I, 10

retrouve: Bon, on se retrouve... *We'll meet . . .* I, 6

le rêve *dream,* II, 1

réveil: entendre le réveil *to hear the alarm clock,* II, 5

revenir *to come back,* II, 6; faire revenir dans le beurre *to sauté in butter,* II, 3

le rez-de-chaussée *first (ground) floor,* II, 2

le rhume: J'ai un rhume. *I've got a cold.* II, 7

rien: Ça ne fait rien. *It doesn't matter.* II, 10; Ça ne me dit rien. *That doesn't interest me.* I, 4; Je n'ai rien oublié. *I didn't forget anything.* I, 11; Rien de spécial. *Nothing special.* I, 6

le riz *rice,* I, 8

la robe *a dress,* I, 10

le rock *rock,* II, 11

le roi *the king,* II, 6

le roller: faire du roller en ligne *to in-line skate,* I, 4

le roman *novel,* I, 3; le roman classique *classic (novel),* II, 11; le roman d'amour *romance novel,* II, 11; le roman de science-fiction *science-fiction novel,* II, 11; le roman policier (le polar) *detective or mystery novel,* II, 11

rose *pink,* I, 3

le rôti de bœuf *roast beef,* II, 3

roue: la grande roue *the ferris wheel,* II, 6

rouge *red,* I, 3

rousse (roux) *red-headed,* I, 7

route: Bonne route! *Have a good (car) trip!* , II, 3

roux *red-headed,* I, 7; II, 1

russe *Russian* (adj), II, 1; les montagnes russes *roller coaster,* II, 6

S

sa *his, her,* I, 7

le sable *sand,* II, 4

le sac (à dos) *bag; backpack,* I, 3; le sac à main *purse,* II, 3; le sac de couchage *sleeping bag,* II, 12

le sachet *small bag,* II, 3

sais: Je n'en sais rien. *I have no idea.* I, 11; Je ne sais pas quoi faire. *I don't know what to do.* II, 10; Je ne sais pas. *I don't know.* I, 10; Tu sais ce que... ? *Do you know what . . . ?* II, 9; Tu sais qui... ? *Do you know who . . . ?* II, 9

la salade *salad, lettuce,* I, 8

sale *dirty,* II, 8

saler *to salt,* II, 3

la salle à manger *dining room,* II, 2; la salle de bains *bathroom,* II, 2

le salon *living room,* II, 2

saluer *to greet,* II, 8

Salut! *Hi! or Goodbye!* I, 1

le samedi *on Saturdays,* I, 2

les sandales (f.) *sandals,* I, 10

le sandwich *sandwich,* I, 5

la santé *health,* II, 7

le saucisson *salami,* I, 5; II, 3

sauf *except,* II, 2

saupoudrer *to sprinkle (with),* II, 3

saute: Ne saute pas... *Don't skip . . . ,* II, 7

sauter: sauter un repas *to skip a meal,* II, 7

sauver *to save,* II, 5

les sciences (f.) naturelles *natural science ,* I, 2

sec (sèche) *dry, dried,* II, 7

la seconde: Une seconde, s'il vous plaît. *One second, please.* I, 9

le séjour *visit, stay,* II, 1

le sel *salt,* II, 7

la semaine *week,* I, 4; une fois par semaine *once a week,* I, 4

semblant: faire semblant de *to pretend to (do something),* II, 10

sens: Je ne me sens pas bien. *I don't feel well.* II, 7

sensas (sensationnel) *fantastic,* I, 10; *sensational,* II, 6

les sentiers (m.): suivre les sentiers balisés *to follow the marked trails,* II, 12

septembre *September,* I, 4

serré(e) *tight,* I, 10

se serrer: serrer la main *to shake hands,* II, 8

service: A votre service. *At your service; You're welcome,* I, 3

ses *his, her,* I, 7
seul(e) *only one,* II, 4
le short *(a pair of) shorts,* I, 3
si: Moi, si. *I do.* I, 2; **Si on achetait... ?** *How about buying . . . ?* II, 8; **Si on allait... ?** *How about going . . . ?* II, 4; **Si on jouait... ?** *How about playing . . . ?* II, 8; **Si on visitait... ?** *How about visiting . . . ?* II, 8; **Si tu veux, on peut...** *If you like, we can . . . ,* II, 1
le siècle *century,* II, 6
la sieste: faire la sieste *to take a nap,* II, 8
s'il vous/te plaît *please,* I, 5
simple *simple,* II, 8
sinistre *awful,* II, 6
le ski *skiing,* I, 1; **faire du ski** *to ski,* I, 4; **faire du ski nautique** *to water-ski,* I, 4
les skis (m.): faire une randonnée en skis *to go cross-country skiing,* II, 12
la sœur *sister,* I, 7
la soif: avoir soif *to be thirsty,* I, 5; **Je n'ai plus soif.** *I'm not thirsty anymore.* II, 3; **Si, j'ai très soif!** *Yes, I'm very thirsty.* II, 2; **Vous n'avez pas (Tu n'as pas) soif?** *Aren't you thirsty?* II, 2
le soir *evening; in the evening,* I, 4; **Pas ce soir.** *Not tonight.* I, 7
son *his, her,* I, 7
le sondage *poll,* II, 1
sont: Ce sont... *These/those are . . . ,* I, 7; **Ils/Elles sont...** *They're . . . ,* I, 7; II, 1
la sortie *dismissal,* I, 2; **être privé(e) de sortie** *to be "grounded,"* II, 9
sortir *to go out,* II, 6; **sortir avec les copains** *to go out with friends,* I, 1; **sortir la poubelle** *to take out the trash,* I, 7
les soucis (m.): avoir des soucis *to have worries,* II, 8
sous-marine: faire de la plongée sous-marine *to scuba dive,* II, 4
souvent *often,* I, 4
spécial: Rien de spécial. *Nothing special.* I, 6
le spectacle: assister à un spectacle son et lumière *to attend a sound and light show,* II, 6
le sport *sports,* I, 1; *gym class,* I, 2; **faire du sport** *to play sports,* I, 1; **Qu'est-ce que tu fais comme sport?** *What sports do you play?* I, 4
le stade *the stadium,* I, 6
le steak-frites *steak and French fries,* I, 5
le style: C'est tout à fait ton style. *It looks great on you!* I, 10; **Ce n'est pas son style.** *That's not his/her style.* II, 3
le stylo *pen,* I, 3
le sud: dans le sud *in the south,* II, 4; **C'est au sud de...** *It's to the south of . . . ,* II, 12
suite: C'est tout de suite à... *It's right there on the . . . ,* I, 12; **J'y vais tout de suite.** *I'll go right away.* I, 8; **tout de suite** *right away,* I, 6
suivre *to follow,* II, 7; **suivre les sentiers balisés** *to follow the marked trails,* II, 12; **suivre un régime trop strict** *to follow a diet that's too strict,* II, 7
super (adj.) *super,* I, 2; **(adv.)** *really, ultra-,* II, 9; **Super!** *Great!* I, 1; **pas super** *not so hot,* I, 2
superbe *great,* II, 6
sur: sur la droite/gauche *on the right/left,* II, 2
sûr: Bien sûr. *Of course.* II, 10; **Bien sûr. C'est...** *Of course. They are (He/She is) . . . ,* II, 11
sûrement: Sûrement pas! *Definitely not!* II, 6
surprenant *surprising,* II, 2
surtout *especially,* I, 1
le surveillant *university student who supervises younger students at school,* II, 5
le suspense: Il y a du suspense. *It's suspenseful.* II, 11
le sweat(-shirt) *a sweatshirt,* I, 3; II, 1
sympa (abbrev. of sympathique) *nice,* I, 7; II, 1
sympathique *nice,* I, 7

T

ta *your,* I, 7
le tableau *blackboard,* I, 0
le taille-crayon *pencil sharpener,* I, 3
le tam-tam *an African drum,* II, 8
la tante *aunt,* I, 7
le tapis *rug,* II, 2
les tapisseries (f.) *tapestries,* II, 2
taquiner *to tease,* II, 8
tard *late,* II, 4
le tarif *admission price,* II, 2
la tarte *pie,* I, 8; **la tarte aux pommes** *apple tart,* II, 3

la tartine *bread, butter, and jam,* II, 3
tas: J'ai des tas de choses à faire. *I have lots of things to do.* I, 5
tasse *cup,* II, 3
taxi: en taxi *by taxi,* I, 12
Tchao! *Bye!* I, 1
le tee shirt *T-shirt,* II, 1
la télé(vision) *television, TV,* I, 1; **regarder la télé(vision)** *to watch TV,* I, 1
le téléphone *telephone,* I, 1; **parler au téléphone** *to talk on the phone,* I, 1; **Téléphone-lui/-leur!** *Call him/her/them!* I, 9; **Phone him/her/them.** II, 10
téléphoner à (quelqu'un) *to call (someone),* II, 10
tellement: C'était tellement différent? *Was it really so different?* II, 8; **Pas tellement.** *Not too much.* I, 4
temps: de temps en temps *from time to time,* I, 4; **Je suis désolé(e), mais je n'ai pas le temps.** *Sorry, but I don't have time.* I, 12; **Je n'ai pas le temps.** *I don't have time.* II, 10
Tenez. *Here you are.* II, 3
le tennis *tennis,* I, 4
la tente *tent,* II, 12
la tenue *outfit,* II, 1
le terrain de camping *campground,* II, 2
la terrasse *terrace,* II, 2
terrible: Pas terrible. *Not so great.* I, 1
tes *your,* I, 7
la tête *head,* II, 7; **J'ai mal à la tête** *My head hurts.* II, 7; **faire la tête** *to sulk,* II, 9
thaïlandais *Thai (adj),* II, 1
le thé *tea,* II, 3
le théâtre *theater,* I, 6; II, 2; **faire du théâtre** *to do drama,* I, 4
les tickets (m.): Trois tickets, s'il vous plaît. *Three (entrance) tickets, please.* II, 6
Tiens. *Here you are.* II, 3
le timbre *stamp,* I, 12
timide *shy,* I, 7
le tissu *fabric, cloth,* II, 8
toi *you,* I, 1; **Et toi?** *And you?* I, 1
les toilettes (les W.-C.) (f.) *toilet, restroom,* II, 2
les tomates (f.) *tomatoes,* I, 8
tomber *to fall,* II, 5; **tomber amoureux (-euse) (de quelqu'un)** *to fall in love (with someone),* II, 9; **tomber en panne** *to break down,* II, 9

ton *your,* I, 7
tôt *early,* II, 4
la tour *tower,* II, 6
le tour: faire un tour sur la grande roue *to take a ride on the ferris wheel,* II, 6; **faire un tour sur les montagnes russes** *to take a ride on the roller coaster,* II, 6
tournez: Puis, tournez à gauche dans/sur... *Then, turn left on . . . ,* II, 2; **Vous tournez... ** *You turn . . . ,* I, 12
le tournoi de joute *jousting tournament,* II, 6
tout: A tout à l'heure! *See you later!* I, 1; **Allez (continuez) tout droit.** *Go (keep going) straight ahead.* II, 2; **C'est tout à fait ton style.** *It looks great on you!* I, 10; **C'est tout de suite à...** *It's right there on the . . . ,* I, 12; **J'ai pensé à tout.** *I've thought of everything.* I, 11; **J'y vais tout de suite.** *I'll go right away.* I, 8; **Pas du tout.** *Not at all.* I, 4; II, 10; **Tout a été de travers!** *Everything went wrong!* II, 5; **tout de suite** *right away,* I, 5; **Vous allez tout droit jusqu'à...** *You go straight ahead until you get to . . . ,* 12
toute: à toute épreuve *solid, unfailing,* II, 10
le train *train,* I, 12; **en train** *by train,* I, 12; **être en train de** *to be in the process of (doing something),* II, 9
la tranche: une tranche de *a slice of,* I, 8
tranquille *calm,* II, 8
travailler *to work,* I, 9; **Il faut mieux travailler en classe.** *You have to do better in class.* II, 5
les travaux (m.) **pratiques** *lab,* I, 2
travers: Tout a été de travers! *Everything went wrong!* II, 5
Traversez... *Cross . . . ,* II, 2
très: Très bien. *Very well.* I, 1; **Ça s'est très bien passé!** *It went really well!* II, 5
trompes: A mon avis, tu te trompes. *In my opinion, you're mistaken.* II, 9
trop *too (much),* I, 10; **C'est trop cher.** *It's too expensive.* I, 10; II, 3; **Non, pas trop.** *No, not too much.* I, 2
la trousse *pencil case,* I, 3; **la trousse de premiers soins** *first-aid kit,* II, 12

trouve: Je le/la/les trouve... *I think it's/they're . . . ,* I, 10; **Où se trouve... ?** *Where is . . . ?* II, 4
trouver *to find,* I, 9
trouves: Comment tu trouves... ? *How do you like . . . ?* I, 10; *What do you think of . . . ?* I, 2; **Tu trouves?** *Do you think so?* II, 2;
truc(s): Ce n'est pas mon truc. *It's not my thing.* II, 7; **J'ai des tas de choses (trucs) à faire.** *I have lots of things to do.* I, 12; **J'ai des trucs à faire.** *I have some things to do.* I, 5
tu *you,* I, 0

U

un *a; an,* I, 3
une *a; an,* I, 3

V

Ça me va? *Does it suit me?* I, 10; **Ça ne te/vous va pas du tout.** *That doesn't look good on you.* I, 10; **Ça te/vous va très bien.** *That suits you really well.* I, 10; **Ça va.** *Fine.* I, 1; **Ça va aller mieux.** *It'll get better.* II, 5; **Ça va très bien avec...** *It goes very well with . . . ,* I, 10; **Comment est-ce qu'on y va?** *How can we get there?* I, 12; **Quelque chose ne va pas?** *Is something wrong?* II, 7
les vacances (f.) *vacation,* I, 1; **Bonnes vacances!** *Have a good vacation!* I, 11; **Comment se sont passées tes vacances?** *How was your vacation?* II, 5; **en colonie de vacances** *to/at a summer camp,* I, 11; **en vacances** *on vacation,* I, 4
vachement *really,* II, 9
vais: D'abord, je vais... *First, I'm going to . . . ,* II, 1; **Je vais...** *I'm going . . .* I, 6; *I'm going to . . . ,* I, 11; **Je vais (en) prendre...** *I'll take . . . ,* II, 3
la vaisselle: faire la vaisselle *to do the dishes,* I, 7
la valise *suitcase,* I, 11
vas: Qu'est-ce que tu vas faire... ? *What are you going to do . . . ?* II, 1
le vase *vase,* II, 3
le vélo *bike,* I, 1; **à vélo** *by bike,* I, 12; **faire du vélo** *to bike,* I, 4; **faire du vélo de montagne**

to go mountain-bike riding, II, 12
le vendredi *on Fridays,* I, 2
venir *to come,* II, 6
le ventre: J'ai mal au ventre *My stomach hurts.* II, 7
véritable: C'était un véritable cauchemar! *It was a real nightmare!* I, 11
le verre *glass,* II, 2
vers *around,* I, 6; **Vers... ** *About (a certain time) . . . ,* II, 4
verser *to pour,* II, 3
vert(e) *green,* I, 3; II, 1
la veste *a suit jacket, a blazer,* I, 10
veux: J'en veux bien. *I'd like some.* I, 8; **Je ne t'en veux pas.** *No hard feelings.* II, 10; **Je veux bien.** *Gladly,* I, 12; *I'd like to.* II, 1; *I'd really like to.* I, 6; **Non, je ne veux pas.** *No, I don't want to.* II, 8; **Oui, je veux bien.** *Yes, I would.* II, 3; **Oui, si tu veux.** *Yes, if you want to.* I, 7; **Si tu veux, on peut...** *If you like, we can . . . ,* II, 1; **Tu ne m'en veux pas?** *No hard feelings?* II, 10; **Tu veux... ?** *Do you want . . . ?* I, 6; II, 3
la viande *meat,* I, 8
la vidéo: faire de la vidéo *to make videos,* I, 4; **jouer à des jeux vidéo** *to play video games,* I, 4
la vidéocassette *videotape,* I, 3
la vie *life,* II, 8; **La vie était plus... moins...** *Life was more . . . , less . . . ,* II, 8
vieille: Pauvre vieille! *You poor thing!* II, 5
viens: Tu viens? *Will you come?* I, 6
vietnamien *Vietnamese* (adj), II, 1
vieux: Pauvre vieux! *You poor thing!* II, 5
le village de pêcheurs *fishing village,* II, 4
la ville *city,* II, 2
violent: trop violent *too violent,* II, 11
violet(te) *purple,* I, 3
violons: accordons nos violons *let's come to an understanding,* II, 4
visitait: Si on visitait... ? *How about visiting . . . ?* II, 8
la visite: une visite guidée *a guided tour,* II, 6
visiter *to visit (a place),* I, 9; II, 6
vite: Dis vite! *Let's hear it!* II, 9
le vitrail (pl. -aux) *stained glass,* II, 2

les vitrines (f.): faire les vitrines *to window-shop*, I, 6
vivant(e) *lively*, II, 4
vivre *to live*, II, 4
vœux: Meilleurs vœux! *Best wishes!* II, 3; une carte de vœux *greeting card*, II, 3
Voici... *This is* . . . , I, 7
voilà: Voilà. *Here it is.* II, 3; *Here*, I, 3; Voilà... *There's* . . . , I, 7
voile: faire de la planche à voile *to go windsurfing*, I, 11; faire de la voile *to go sailing*, I, 11
voir *to see*, I, 6; Qu'est-ce qu'il y a à voir... *What is there to see* . . . ? II, 12; Tu vas voir que... *You'll see that* . . . , II, 8; voir un film *to see a movie*, I, 6; voir un match *to see a game (in person)*, I, 6; voir une pièce *to see a play*, I, 6
vois: ... tu vois. . . . *you see.* II, 9
voit: Ça se voit. *That's obvious.* II, 9
la voiture *car*, I, 7; en voiture *by car*, I, 12; laver la voiture *to wash the car*, I, 7
la volaille *poultry*, II, 3
le volcan *volcano*, II, 4

le volley(-ball) *volleyball*, I, 4; jouer au volley-ball *to play volleyball*, I, 4
vos *your*, I, 7
votre *your*, I, 7
voudrais: Je voudrais acheter... *I'd like to buy* . . . , I, 3; Je voudrais bien... *I'd really like to* . . . , 11; Je voudrais... *I'd like* . . . , I, 3; II, 6
voulez: Vous voulez... ? *Do you want* . . . , ? I, 8; II, 3
vouloir *to want*, I, 6
vous *you*, I, 0
voyage: Bon voyage! *Have a good trip! (by plane, ship)*, I, 11; II, 3; Vous avez (Tu as) fait bon voyage? *Did you have a good trip?* II, 2
voyager *to travel*, I, 1
vrai: C'est pas vrai! *You're kidding!* I, 6; C'est vrai? *Really?* II, 2
vraiment: Vraiment? *Really?* II, 2; C'est vraiment bon! *It's really good!* II, 3; Il/Elle est vraiment bien, ton/ta... *Your* . . . *is really great.* II, 2 ; Non, pas vraiment. *No, not really.* I, 11
vu (pp. of voir) *seen*, I, 9
vue *with a view of*, II, 2

W

le week end *weekend; on weekends*, I, 4; ce week-end *this weekend*, I, 6; Comment s'est passé ton week-end? *How was your weekend?* II, 5
le western *western (movie)*, II, 11

Y

y *there*, I, 12; Allons-y! *Let's go!* I, 4; Comment est-ce qu'on y va? *How can we get there?* I, 12; Il y avait... *There were* . . . , II, 8; Je n'y comprends rien. *I don't understand anything about it.* II, 5; On peut y aller... *We can go there* . . . , 12; Tu vas t'y faire. *You'll get used to it.* II, 8
le yaourt *yogurt*, I, 8
les yeux (m.) *eyes*, II, 1

Z

zéro *a waste of time*, I, 2
le zoo *the zoo*, I, 6; II, 6
zouk: danser le zouk *to dance the zouk*, II, 4
Zut! *Darn!*, I, 3

ENGLISH-FRENCH VOCABULARY

In this vocabulary, the English definitions of all active French words in the book have been listed, followed by the French. The numbers after each entry refer to the level and chapter where the word or phrase first appears, or where it becomes an active vocabulary word. It is important to use a French word in its correct context. The use of a word can be checked easily by referring to the unit where it appears.

French words and phrases are presented in the same way as in the French-English vocabulary.

A

a *un, une,* I, 3
about: about (a certain time) . . . *Vers...* , II, 4; **It's about** . . . *Ça parle de...* , II, 11; **What's it about?** *De quoi ça parle?* II, 11
acceptable: That's not acceptable. *C'est inadmissible.* II, 5
accident: to have an accident *avoir un accident,* II, 9
across: across from *en face de,* I, 12; II, 2
action: action movie *un film d'action,* II, 11
adventure: adventure movie *un film d'aventures,* II, 11
advise: What do you advise me to do? *Qu'est-ce que tu me conseilles?* I, 9
aerobics: to do aerobics *faire de l'aérobic,* I, 4; II, 7
African *africain(e),* II, 11
after: And after that, . . . *Et après ça...* , I, 9; II, 4
afternoon: afternoon off *l'après-midi libre,* I, 2; **in the afternoon** *l'après-midi,* I, 2
afterwards: Afterwards, I went out. *Après, je suis sorti(e),* I, 9; **And afterwards?** *Et après?* I, 9
again: Don't do it again! *Ne recommence pas!* II, 5
agree: I don't agree. *Je ne suis pas d'accord.* I, 7
ahead: Go (keep going) straight ahead. *Allez (continuez) tout droit.* II, 2
alarm: to hear the alarm clock *entendre le réveil,* II, 5
algebra *l'algèbre* (f.), I, 2
all: All you have to do is . . . *Tu n'as qu'à...* , II, 7; **Not at all.** *Pas du tout.* I, 4; II, 10; **I hurt all over!** *J'ai mal partout!* II, 7; **all right** *pas mal,* II, 6
allergies: I have allergies. *J'ai des allergies.* II, 7
almost: You're (We're) almost there!

Tu y es (On y est) presque! II, 7
already *déjà,* I, 9
also *aussi,* I, 1
am: I am . . . *Je suis...* , II, 1
amazing: It was amazing! *C'était incroyable!* II, 5
American *américain(e),* II, 11
amusement park *un parc d'attractions,* II, 6
an *un, une,* I, 3
and *et,* I, 1
angry *fâché(e),* II, 9
ankle: to sprain one's ankle *se fouler la cheville,* II, 7
annoyed *énervé(e),* II, 9
annoying *embêtant(e),* I, 7; II, 1
answer *répondre,* I, 9; **There's no answer.** *Ça ne répond pas.* I, 9
any (of it) *en,* I, 8
any more: I don't want any more *Je n'en veux plus.* I, 8; **I just can't do any more!** *Je n'en peux plus!* II, 7
anymore: I'm not hungry/thirsty anymore. *Je n'ai plus faim/soif.* II, 3
anything: I didn't forget anything. *Je n'ai rien oublié.* I, 11
Anyway, . . . *Bref,...* , II, 9
apologize *s'excuser,* II, 10; **Apologize.** *Excuse-toi.* II, 10
apple: apples *les pommes* (f.), I, 8; **apple juice** *le jus de pomme,* I, 5; **apple tart** *la tarte aux pommes,* II, 3
April *avril,* I, 4
argument: to have an argument (with someone) *se disputer (avec quelqu'un),* II, 9
arm *le bras,* II, 7
armoire *l'armoire* (f.), II, 2
around *vers,* II, 4
arrive *arriver,* II, 5
art class *les arts* (m.) *plastiques,* I, 2
ask: to ask (someone's) forgiveness *demander pardon à (quelqu'un),* II, 10; **to ask your parents' permission** *demander la permission à tes parents,* II, 10
at *à,* I, 6, II, 2; **at** . . . **fifteen** *à...*

heures quinze, I, 2; **at** . . . **forty-five** *à... heures quarante-cinq,* I, 2; **at** . . . **'s house** *chez...* , I, 6; **At that point,** . . . *A ce moment-là,...* , II, 9; **at the record store** *chez le disquaire,* I, 12; **At what time?** *A quelle heure?* I, 6
attend: to attend a sound and light show *assister à un spectacle son et lumière,* II, 6
August *août,* I, 4
aunt *la tante,* I, 7
avocados *les avocats* (m.), I, 8
Avoid . . . *Evitez de...* , II, 7; *Evite de...* , II, 12
away: Yes, right away. *Oui, tout de suite.* I, 5
awful *sinistre,* II, 6

B

back *le dos,* II, 7
back: come back *revenir,* II, 6; **go back (home)** *rentrer,* II, 6
backpack *le sac à dos,* I, 3
bad: *mauvais,* I, 9 **It was unbelievably bad!** *C'était incroyable!* II, 5; **not bad** *pas mal,* I, 2; **Oh, not bad.** *Oh, pas mauvais.* I, 9; **Very bad.** *Très mauvais.* I, 9; **What a bad day!** *Quelle journée!* II, 5; **What a bad weekend!** *Quel weekend!* II, 5
bag *le sac,* I, 3
baggy *large,* I, 10
bakery *la boulangerie,* I, 12; II, 3
balcony *le balcon,* II, 2
banana tree *un bananier,* II, 4
bananas *les bananes* (f.), I, 8
bank *la banque,* I, 12
baseball *le base-ball,* I, 4; **to play baseball** *jouer au base-ball,* I, 4
basketball *le basket(-ball),* I, 4; **to play basketball** *jouer au basket(-ball),* I, 4
baskets *des paniers,* (m.) II, 8
bathing suit *le maillot de bain,* I, 10
bathroom *la salle de bains,* II, 2

be *être*, I, 7

be able to, can *pouvoir*, I, 8; **Can you . . . ?** *Est-ce que tu peux... ?*, I, 12; **I can't** *Je ne peux pas.*, II, 7

be in the process of (doing something) *être en train de (\ infinitive)*, II, 9

beach *la plage*, I, 1

beans *des haricots* (m.), I, 8

bear *un ours*, II, 12

beautiful *beau (belle) (bel)*, II, 2; *magnifique*, II, 6

become *devenir*, II, 6

bed *le lit*, II, 2; **to go to bed** *se coucher*, II, 4

bedroom *la chambre*, II, 2

begin *commencer*, I, 9

behind *derrière*, I, 12

belt *la ceinture*, I, 10

best: **Best wishes!** *Meilleurs vœux!* II, 3; **Make the best of it.** *Fais-toi une raison.* II, 8

bet: **I bet that . . .** *Je parie que...*, II, 9

better: **It'll get better.** *Ça va aller mieux.* II, 5; **It's better than . . .** *C'est meilleur que...*, II, 7; **You have to do better in class.** *Il faut mieux travailler en classe.* II, 5

between *entre*, I, 12

big *grand(e)*, I, 10, II, 1

bigger: **bigger than . . .** *plus grand(e) que*, II, 4

bike *le vélo, faire du vélo*, I, 4; **by bike** *à vélo*, I, 12

biking *le vélo*, I, 1

binder: **loose-leaf binder** *le classeur*, I, 3

biography *la biographie*, II, 11

biology *la biologie*, I, 2

birthday: **Happy birthday!** *Joyeux (Bon) anniversaire!* II, 3

black *noir(e)*, I, 3; **black hair** *les cheveux noirs*, II, 1

blackboard *le tableau*, I, 0; **blackboard: Go to the blackboard!** *Allez au tableau!*, I, 0

blazer *la veste*, I, 10

blond *blond(e)*, I, 7; **blond hair** *les cheveux blonds*, II, 1

blue *bleu(e)*, I, 3

blues music *le blues*, II, 11

boat *le bateau*, I, 12; **by boat** *en bateau*, I, 12

book *le livre*, I, 0

bookstore *la librairie*, I, 12

boots *les bottes* (f.), I, 10, II, 1

bored: **I was bored.** *Je me suis ennuyé(e).* II, 6; **You're never bored.** *On ne s'ennuie pas.* II, 11

boring *barbant*, I, 2; *ennuyeux (ennuyeuse)*, II, 6; **It was boring.** *C'était ennuyeux.* I, 5

born: **be born** *naître*, II, 6

borrow *emprunter*, I, 12

bother *ennuyer*, II, 8; **What bothers me is . . .** *Ce qui m'ennuie, c'est...*, II, 4

bottle: **a bottle of** *une bouteille de*, I, 8

box: **a carton/box of** *un paquet de*, I, 8

boy *le garçon*, I, 0

bracelet *le bracelet*, I, 3

brave *brave*, II, 1

bread *le pain*, I, 8; II, 3

break *la récréation*, I, 2; **break down** *tomber en panne*, II, 9; **break up (with someone)** *casser (avec quelqu'un)*, II, 9; **to break one's . . .** *se casser...*, II, 7

breakfast *le petit déjeuner*, I, 8

bring *apporter*, I, 9; **Bring me back . . .** *Rapporte-moi...*, I, 8; **Please bring me . . .** *Apportez-moi... , s'il vous plaît.* I, 5; **to bring (with you)** *emporter*, II, 12; **Will you bring me . . . ?** *Tu me rapportes... ?* I, 8

brother *le frère*, I, 7

brown *marron*, I, 3; **brown hair** *les cheveux châtain*, II, 1; **dark brown hair** *les cheveux bruns*, II, 1

brunette *brun(e)*, I, 7

brush: **to brush one's teeth** *se brosser les dents*, II, 4

bus: **by bus** *en bus*, I, 12; **miss the bus** *rater le bus*, II, 5

busy: **I'm very busy.** *Je suis très occupé(e).* II, 10; **It's busy.** *C'est occupé.* I, 9; **Sorry, I'm busy.** *Désolé(e), je suis occupé(e).* I, 6

but *mais*, I, 1

butcher shop *la boucherie*, II, 3

butter *le beurre*, I, 8; II, 3

buy *acheter*, I, 9; **Buy me . . .** *Achète(-moi)...*, I, 8; **How about buying . . . ?** *Si on achetait... ?* II, 8

by: **By the way, . . .** *A propos,...*, II, 9

Bye! *Tchao!* I, 1

C

cafeteria: **at the school cafeteria** *à la cantine*, I, 9

cake *le gâteau*, I, 8

calculator *la calculatrice*, I, 3

call (someone) *téléphoner à (quelqu'un)*, II, 10; **Call him/her/them!** *Téléphone-lui/-leur!* I, 9; **Can you call back later?** *Vous pouvez rappeler plus tard?* I, 9; **Then I called . . .** *Ensuite, j'ai téléphoné à...*, I, 9

calling: **Who's calling?** *Qui est à l'appareil?* I, 9

calm *tranquille*, II, 8

camera *l'appareil-photo* (m.), I, 11; II, 1

camp: **to/at a summer camp** *en colonie de vacances*, I, 11

campground *le terrain de camping*, II, 2

camping: **to go camping** *faire du camping*, I, 11

can (to be able to) *pouvoir*, I, 8; **Can you do the shopping?** *Tu peux aller faire les courses?* I, 8; **Can I try on . . . ?** *Je peux essayer... ?* I, 10; **Can you . . . ?** *Est-ce que tu peux... ?* I, 12; **Can I talk to you?** *Je peux te parler?* II, 10; **If you like, we can . . .** *Si tu veux, on peut...*, II, 1; **We can . . .** *On peut...*, II, 4; **What can I do?** *Qu'est-ce que je peux faire?* II, 10; **What can we do?** *Qu'est-ce qu'on peut faire?* II, 4

can: **a can of** *une boîte de*, I, 8

can't: **I can't.** *Je ne peux pas.* II, 1; **I can't right now.** *Je ne peux pas maintenant.* I, 8

Canadian *canadien(ne)*, II, 11

canary *le canari*, I, 7

candies *les bonbons*, II, 3

candy shop *la confiserie*, II, 3

canoe: **to go canoeing** *faire du canotage*, II, 12

cap *la casquette*, I, 10

capital *la capitale*, II, 4

car *la voiture*, I, 7; **by car** *en voiture*, I, 12; **to wash the car** *laver la voiture*, I, 7

care: **What I don't care for is . . .** *Ce qui ne me plaît pas, c'est...*, II, 4

carrots *les carottes* (f.), I, 8

carton: **a carton/box of** *un paquet de*, I, 8

cassette tape *la cassette*, I, 3

cat *le chat*, I, 7

cathedral *la cathédrale*, II, 2

CD (compact disc) *le disque compact/le CD*, I, 3

cereal *les céréales*, II, 3

Certainly. *Bien sûr.* I, 9

chair *la chaise*, I, 0

charming *charmant(e)*, II, 4

check: **The check, please.** *L'addition, s'il vous plaît.* I, 5; **traveler's checks** *les chèques* (m.) *de voyage*, II, 1

cheese *le fromage*, I, 5, II, 3; **toasted cheese and ham sandwich** *le croque-monsieur*, I, 5

chemistry *la chimie*, I, 2

chest: **chest of drawers** *la commode*, II, 2

chic *chic*, I, 10

chicken *le poulet*, II, 3; chicken meat *du poulet*, I, 8; live chickens *les poules*, I, 8

chocolate *le chocolat*, I, 1; box of chocolates *la boîte de chocolats*, II, 3

choir *la chorale*, I, 2

choose *choisir*, I, 10; to choose the date *fixer la date*, II, 10; to choose the music *choisir la musique*, II, 10;

Christmas: Merry Christmas! *Joyeux Noël!* II, 3

church *l'église* (f.), II, 2

class: What classes do you have . . . ? *Tu as quels cours... ?* I, 2

classic book *un (roman) classique*, II, 11; classic movie *un film classique*, II, 11

classical: classical music *la musique classique*, II, 11

clean *propre*, II, 8; to clean house *faire le ménage*, I, 7

clear the table *débarrasser la table*, I, 7

clock: to hear the alarm clock *entendre le réveil*, II, 5

close to *près de*, I, 12

close: Close the door! *Fermez la porte!*, I, 0; When do you close? *A quelle heure est-ce que vous fermez?* II, 6

cloth *le tissu*, II, 8

coast: to/at the coast *au bord de la mer*, I, 11

coat *le manteau*, I, 10

coconut tree *un cocotier*, II, 4

coconuts *les noix de coco* (f.), I, 8

coffee *le café*, I, 5

cola *le coca*, I, 5

cold: I've got a cold. *J'ai un rhume.* II, 7; It's cold. *Il fait froid.*

colorful *coloré(e)*, II, 4

come *venir*, II, 6; Come on! *Allez!* II, 7; Will you come? *Tu viens?* I, 6

come back *revenir*, II, 6

comedy (film) *un film comique*, II, 11

comic book *une bande dessinée (une B. D.)*, II, 11

compact disc/CD *le disque compact/le CD*, I, 3

compass *la boussole*, II, 12

computer *l'ordinateur* (m.), I, 3

computer science *l'informatique*, I, 2

concerts *les concerts* (m.), I, 1

Congratulations! *Félicitations!* II, 3

cool *cool*, I, 2; very cool *chouette*, II, 2; Your . . . is cool. *Il (Elle) est cool, ton (ta)... ,* II, 2; It's cool (outside). *Il fait frais.* I, 4

corn *du maïs*, I, 8

corner: on the corner of *au coin de*, I, 12

cotton: in cotton *en coton*, I, 10

could: Could you . . . ? *Tu pourrais...?* II, 10; Could you do me a favor? *(Est-ce que) tu pourrais me rendre un petit service?* I, 12; Could you go by . . . ? *Tu pourrais passer à... ?* I, 12; I could have . . . *J'aurais pu... ,* II, 10; We could . . . *On pourrait... ,* II, 1; You could give him/her (them) . . . *Tu pourrais lui (leur) offrir... ,* II, 3; You could have . . . *Tu aurais pu... ,* II, 10

country, folk music *le country/le folk*, II, 11

country: to/at the countryside *à la campagne*, I, 11

course *le cours*, I, 2; first course of a meal *l'entrée*, II, 3; main course of a meal *le plat principal*, II, 3; Of course. *Bien sûr.* I, 3; Of course not. *Bien sûr que non.* II, 10

cousin *le cousin (la cousine)*, I, 7

cream puff pastry *la religieuse*, II, 3

croissant *le croissant*, II, 3; croissant with a chocolate filling *le pain au chocolat*, II, 3

cross-country: to go cross-country skiing *faire une randonnée en skis*, II, 12

cross: Cross . . . *Traversez... ,* II, 2

cut: to cut one's finger *se couper le doigt*, II, 7

cute *mignon (mignonne)*, I, 7, II, 1

cute: cute (but that's all) *gentillet, sans plus*, II, 11

D

dairy *la crémerie*, II, 3

dance (verb) *danser*, I, 1; (noun) *la danse*, I, 2; to dance the zouk *danser le zouk*, II, 4

dangerous *dangereux (dangereuse)*, II, 8

Darn! *Zut!* I, 3

date: to have (make) a date (with someone) *avoir (prendre) rendez-vous (avec quelqu'un)*, II, 9

day: I had a terrible day! *J'ai passé une journée épouvantable!* II, 5; It's just not my day! *C'est pas mon jour!* II, 5; What a bad day! *Quelle journée!* II, 5

deadly dull *mortel (mortelle)*, II, 6

December *décembre*, I, 4

decided: Have you decided to take . . . ? *Vous avez décidé de prendre... ?* I, 10; Have you decided? *Vous avez choisi?* I, 5

deface: to deface the trees *mutiler les arbres*, II, 12

Definitely not! *Sûrement pas!* II, 6

delicatessen *la charcuterie*, II, 3

delicious *délicieux (délicieuse)*, I, 5; That was delicious! *C'était délicieux!* II, 3

denim: in denim *en jean*, I, 10

deposit *déposer*, I, 12

depressed *déprimé(e)*, II, 9

depressing *déprimant*, II, 11

dessert *le dessert*, II, 3

detective: detective or mystery movie *un film policier*, II, 11; detective or mystery novel *un roman policier (un polar)*, II, 11

detention: to have detention *être collé(e)*, II, 5

dictionary *le dictionnaire*, I, 3

die *mourir*, II, 6

diet: follow a diet that's too strict. *suivre un régime trop strict*, II, 7

different: Was it really so different? *C'était tellement différent?* II, 8

dining room *la salle à manger*, II, 2

dinner *le dîner*, I, 8; to have dinner *dîner*, I, 9

dirty *sale*, II, 8

dishes: to do the dishes *faire la vaisselle*, I, 7

dismissal (when school gets out) *la sortie*, I, 2

do *faire*, I, 4; All you have to do is . . . *Tu n'as qu'à... ,* II, 7; Don't do it again. *Ne recommence pas.* II, 5; I don't know what to do. *Je ne sais pas quoi faire.* II, 10; I don't play/do . . . *Je ne fais pas de... ,* I, 4; I have errands to do. *J'ai des courses à faire.* I, 5; I just can't do any more! *Je n'en peux plus!* II, 7; I play/do . . . *Je fais... ,* I, 4; In your opinion, what do I do? *A ton avis, qu'est-ce que je fais?* I, 9; It'll do you good. *Ça te fera du bien.* II, 7; to do homework *faire les devoirs*, I, 7; to do the dishes *faire la vaisselle*, I, 7; What are you going to do . . . ? *Qu'est-ce que tu vas faire...* ? I, 6, II, 1; What are you going to do . . . ? *Tu vas faire quoi... ?* I, 6; What can I do? *Qu'est-ce que je peux faire?* I, 9; What can we do? *Qu'est-ce qu'on peut faire?* II, 4; What did you do . . . ? *Qu'est-ce que tu as fait... ?* I, 9; What do you advise me to do? *Qu'est-ce que tu me conseilles?* I, 9; What do you do . . . *Qu'est-ce que tu fais... ,* I, 4; What do you do when . . . *Qu'est-ce que tu fais quand... ,* I, 4; What do you like to do? *Qu'est-ce que tu aimes faire?* II, 1; What should we do? *Qu'est-ce qu'on fait?* II, 1

dog *le chien,* I, 7
dog: to walk the dog *promener le
  chien,* I, 7
done *fait (pp. of faire),* I, 9
door *la porte,* I, 0
down: go down *descendre,* II, 6
dozen. a dozen *une douzaine de,* I, 8
drama: to do drama *faire du
  théâtre,* I, 4
drawers: chest of drawers *la commode,* II, 2
dress *la robe,* I, 10
dressed: to get dressed *s'habiller,*
  II, 4
drink: What do you have to drink?
  *Qu'est-ce que vous avez comme
  boissons?* I, 5
drive: to drive a car *conduire une
  voiture,* II, 8
drugstore *la pharmacie,* I, 12
drum (from Africa) *un tam-tam,*
  II, 8
duck *un canard,* II, 12
dud: It's a dud. *C'est un navet,* II, 11
dying: I'm dying of hunger! *Je crève
  de faim!* II, 12; I'm dying of thirst!
  Je meurs de soif! II, 12

E

early *tôt,* II, 4
earrings *les boucles d'oreilles* (f.), I,
  10
ear *l'oreille* (f.), II, 7; my ear hurts
  j'ai mal à l'oreille. II, 7
earth-shattering: It's not earth-shattering. *Ça casse pas des briques.*
  II, 11
east: in the east *dans l'est,* II, 4; It's
  to the east of . . . *C'est à l'est
  de... ,* II, 12
easy *facile,* I, 2
eat *manger,* I, 6, II, 7; to eat too
  much sugar *consommer trop de
  sucre,* II, 7; someone who loves to
  eat *gourmand(e),* II, 1; to eat well
  bien se nourrir, II, 7
eggs *les œufs* (m.), I, 8, II, 3
else: I have something else to do.
  J'ai quelque chose à faire. II, 10
embarrassed *gêné(e),* II, 9
English *l'anglais* (m.), I, 1
enjoy *déguster,* II, 4
enter *entrer,* II, 6
entrance: How much is the entrance
  fee? *C'est combien, l'entrée?*
  II, 6
envelope *l'enveloppe* (f.), I, 12
eraser *la gomme,* I, 3
especially *surtout,* I, 1
evening: in the evening *le soir,* I, 2
everyone: Everyone should . . . *On
  doit.* II, 7

everything: Everything went wrong!
  Tout a été de travers! II, 5; I've
  thought of everything. *J'ai pensé
  à tout.* I, 11
exams *les examens* (m.), I, 1
excellent *excellent,* I, 5, II, 2
exciting: It's an exciting story. *C'est
  une histoire passionnante.* II, 11
excuse: Excuse me. *Excusez-moi.* I,
  3; Excuse me, . . . , please?
  Pardon,... , s'il vous plaît? I, 12;
  Excuse me, sir. I'm looking for . . .
  Pardon, monsieur. Je cherche... , I, 12
exercise *faire de l'exercice,* II, 7
exhausted: Yes, I'm exhausted. *Si,
  je suis crevé(e),* II, 2
expensive: It's too expensive. *C'est
  trop cher.* II, 3
explain: Explain to him/her/them.
  Explique-lui/leur. II, 10; to explain
  what happened (to someone)
  *expliquer ce qui s'est passé (à
  quelqu'un),* II, 10
eyes *les yeux* (m.), II, 1

F

fabric *le tissu,* II, 8
fail: to fail a test *rater un examen,*
  I, 9
fall: in the fall *en automne,* I, 4
fall: *tomber,* II, 5, to fall in love
  (with someone) *tomber amou-
  reux(-euse) (de quelqu'un),* II, 9
familiar: Are you familiar with . . . ?
  Tu connais... , II, 11; I'm not familiar with them (him/her). *Je ne
  connais pas.* II, 11
fantastic *sensas (sensationnel),* I,
  10; II, 6
far from *loin de,* I, 12
fascinating *passionnant,* I, 2
fat (adjective) *gros (grosse),* I, 7;
  (noun) *les matières grasses,* II, 7
father *le père,* I, 7
fault: It's my fault. *C'est de ma
  faute.* II, 10
favor: Could you do me a favor?
  *(Est-ce que) tu pourrais me rendre
  un petit service?* I, 12
favorite: What is your favorite . . . ?
  Quel(le) est ton/ta... préféré(e)? II,
  1; Who is your favorite . . . ? *Qui
  est ton/ta... préféré(e)?* II, 1
February *février,* I, 4
fee: How much is the entrance fee?
  C'est combien, l'entrée? II, 6
feed: to feed the animals *donner à
  manger aux animaux,* II, 6; *nourrir
  les animaux,* II, 12
feel: Do you feel like . . . ? *Tu as
  envie de... ?* II, 1; I don't feel well.

Je ne me sens pas bien. II, 7; I feel
  like . . . *J'ai envie de... ,* I, 11; No,
  I don't feel like it. *Non, je n'ai pas
  très envie.* II, 7
feelings: No hard feelings. *Je ne
  t'en veux pas.* II, 10; No hard feelings? *Tu ne m'en veux pas?* II, 10
ferris wheel *la grande roue,* II, 6
film: What films are playing?
  Qu'est-ce qu'on joue comme film?
  II, 11
finally: Finally, . . . *Enfin,... ,* II, 1,
  Finalement... , II, 4
find *trouver,* I, 9
fine: Fine. *Ça va.* I, 1; Yes, it was
  fine. *Oui, ça a été.* I, 9
first-aid kit *la trousse de premiers
  soins,* II, 12
first: *d'abord... ,* I, 7, II, 1
fish *le poisson,* I, 7; II, 3
fish shop *la poissonnerie,* II, 3
fishing: to go fishing *aller à la
  pêche,* II, 4; fishing pole *une
  canne à pêche,* II, 12; fishing village *un village de pêcheurs,* II, 4
flashlight *une lampe de poche,* II, 12
floor: first (ground) floor *le rez-de-
  chaussée,* II, 2; second floor *le
  premier étage,* II, 2
florist's shop *le fleuriste,* II, 3
flour *la farine,* I, 8
flu: I've got the flu. *J'ai la grippe.*
  II, 7
folk (music) *le folk*
follow: to follow a diet that's too
  strict *suivre un régime trop strict,*
  II, 7; to follow the marked trails
  suivre les sentiers balisés, II, 12
foot: *le pied,* II, 7; on foot *à pied,* I,
  12; My foot hurts. *J'ai mal au
  pied.* II, 7
football: to play football *jouer au
  football américain,* I, 4
for: It's good for you. *C'est bon pour
  toi.* II, 7
forest: to the forest *en forêt,* I, 11
forget *oublier,* I, 9; Don't forget.
  N'oublie pas. I, 8, II, 1; Forget
  him/her/them! *Oublie-le/-la/-les!*
  I, 9; II, 10; I didn't forget anything.
  Je n'ai rien oublié. I, 11; You didn't
  forget your . . . ? *Tu n'as pas
  oublié... ?* I, 11
forgive: Forgive me. *Excuse-moi.* II,
  10; forgive (someone) *pardonner
  à (quelqu'un),* II, 10
forgiveness: to ask (someone's) forgiveness *demander pardon à
  (quelqu'un),* II, 10
Fortunately, . . . *Heureusement,... ,*
  II, 9
fox *un renard,* II, 12
frame: photo frame *le cadre,* II, 3

franc (the French monetary unit) *le franc*, I, 3

French *le français*, I, 1; French fries *les frites* (f.), I, 1

Friday: on Fridays *le vendredi*, I, 2

friend *l'ami(e)*, I, 1

friends: to go out with friends *sortir avec les copains*, I, 1

from: From platform . . . *Du quai... ,* II, 6

front: in front of *devant*, I, 6

fun *amusant(e)*, II, 8 to have fun *s'amuser*, II, 4; Did you have fun? *Tu t'es amusé(e)?* I, 11; II, 6; Have fun! *Amuse-toi bien!* I, 11; I had a lot of fun. *Je me suis beaucoup amusé(e).* II, 6; What do you do to have fun? *Qu'est-ce que tu fais pour t'amuser?* I, 4

funny *amusant(e)*, I, 7, II, 1; It's funny. *C'est drôle (amusant).* II, 11

furious *furieux (furieuse)*, II, 9

G

gain: to gain weight *grossir*, I, 10

game: to watch a game (on TV) *regarder un match*, I, 6

geography *la géographie*, I, 2

geometry *la géométrie*, I, 2

German *l'allemand* (m.), I, 2

get: Get . . . *Prends... ,* I, 8; to get up *se lever*, II, 4; You'll get used to it. *Tu vas t'y faire.* II, 8; Get well soon! *Bon rétablissement!* II, 3; How can we get there? *Comment est-ce qu'on y va?* I, 12; It'll get better. *Ça va aller mieux.* II, 5; to get a bad grade *avoir une mauvaise note*, II, 5; to get lost *se perdre*, II, 9; to get ready *faire les préparatifs*, II, 10

gift *le cadeau*, I, 11; gift shop *la boutique de cadeaux*, II, 3; Have you got a gift idea for. . . ? *Tu as une idée de cadeau pour... ?* II, 3

give *offrir (à quelqu'un)*, II, 10; Give him/her (them) . . . *Offre-lui (leur) ... ,* II, 3; Please give me . . . *Donnez-moi... , s'il vous plaît.* I, 5; What could I give to . . . ? *Qu'est-ce que je pourrais offrir à... ?* II, 3; You could give him/her (them) . . . *Tu pourrais lui (leur) offrir... ,* II, 3; I'm giving up. *J'abandonne.* II, 7

Gladly. *Je veux bien.* I, 8

gloves: pair of gloves *les gants* (m.), II, 1

go *aller*, I, 6; to go back (home) *rentrer*, II, 6; to go down *descendre*, II, 6; to go out *sortir*, II, 6; to go up *monter*, II, 6; Go to the

blackboard! *Allez au tableau!*, I, 0; Could you go by . . . ? *; Tu pourrais passer à... ?* I, 12; Go straight ahead. *Allez tout droit*, II, 2; How did it go? *Comment ça s'est passé?* II, 5; Let's go . . . *Allons... ,* I, 6; It doesn't go at all with . . . *Il/Elle ne va pas du tout avec... ,* I, 10; It goes very well with . . . *Ça va très bien avec... ,* I, 10; to go for a walk *faire une promenade*, I, 6; I'd like . . . to go with . . . *J'aimerais... pour aller avec... ,* I, 10; We can go there . . . *On peut y aller... ,* I, 12; What are you going to do . . . ? *Qu'est-ce que tu vas faire... ?* I, 6; II, 1; *Tu vas faire quoi... ?* I, 6; Where are you going to go . . . ? *Où est-ce que tu vas aller... ?* I, 11; Where did you go? *Tu es allé(e) où?* I, 9; First, I'm going to . . . *D'abord, je vais... ,* II, 1; How about going . . . ? *Si on allait... ?* II, 4; How's it going? *(Comment) ça va?* I, 1; I'm going . . . *Je vais... ,* I, 6; I'm going to . . . *Je vais... ,* I, 11; I'm going to have . . . , please. *Je vais prendre... , s'il vous plaît.* I, 5; What do you think about going . . . ? *Ça te dit d'aller... ?* II, 4; You're going to like it here. *Tu vas te plaire ici.* II, 8; You keep going until the next light. *Vous continuez jusqu'au prochain feu rouge.* I, 12

golf: to play golf *jouer au golf*, I, 4

good *bon(ne)*, I, 5; Did you have a good . . . ? *Tu as passé un bon... ?* I, 11; Did you have a good trip? *Vous avez (Tu as) fait bon voyage?* II, 2; Good idea! *Bonne idée!* II, 3, 7; It'll do you good. *Ça te fera du bien.* II, 7; It's good for you. *C'est bon pour toi.* II, 7; It's really good! *C'est vraiment bon!* II, 3; not very good *pas bon*, I, 5; That's a good (excellent) idea. *C'est une bonne (excellente) idée.* II, 1; Yes, very good. *Oui, très bon.* I, 9; Goodbye! *Au revoir!, Salut!* I, 1

goof: You can't be goofing off in class! *Il ne faut pas faire le clown en classe!* II, 5

grade: to get a bad grade *avoir une mauvaise note*, II, 5

grandfather *le grand-père*, I, 7

grandmother *la grand-mère*, I, 7

grapes *les raisins* (m.), I, 8

great *génial(e)*, I, 2; II, 2; *superbe*, II, 6; Great! *Super!* I, 1; It was great! *C'était formidable!* I, 11; Not so great. *Pas terrible.* I, 1;

What a great day ! *Quelle journée formidable!* II, 5; What a great weekend! *Quel week-end formidable!* II, 5; Your . . . is really great. *Il (Elle) est vraiment bien, ton (ta)... ,* II, 2

green *vert(e)*, I, 3; green beans *les haricots verts* (m.), I, 8

grey *gris(e)*, I, 3

grocery store *l'épicerie* (f.), I, 12

gross *dégoûtant*, I, 5

grounded: to be "grounded" *être privé(e) de sortie*, II, 9

group *un groupe*, II, 11

grow up *grandir*, I, 10

guavas *les goyaves* (f.), I, 8

guess: Guess what . . . *Devine ce que... ,* II, 9; Guess who . . . *Devine qui... ,* II, 9; You'll never guess what happened. *Tu ne devineras jamais ce qui s'est passé.* II, 9

guided: to take a guided tour *faire une visite guidée*, II, 6

gym *le sport*, I, 2

gymnastics: to do gymnastics *faire de la gymnastique*, II, 7

H

hair *les cheveux* (m.), II, 1; black hair *les cheveux noirs*, II, 1; blond hair *les cheveux blonds*, II, 1; brown hair *les cheveux châtain*, II, 1; dark brown hair *les cheveux bruns*, II, 1; long hair *les cheveux longs*, II, 1; red hair *les cheveux roux*, II, 1; short hair *les cheveux courts*, II, 1

half: half past *et demie*, I, 6; (after midi and minuit) *et demi*, I, 6

ham *le jambon*, I, 5; toasted cheese and ham sandwich *le croque-monsieur*, I, 5

hamburgers *les hamburgers* (m.), I, 1

hand *la main*, I, 0

handsome (beautiful) *beau (belle) (bel)*, II, 1

hang glide *faire du deltaplane*, II, 4

hang: Hang in there! *Courage!* II, 5

Hanukkah: Happy Hanukkah! *Bonne fête de Hanoukka!* II, 3

happen: What happened? *Qu'est-ce qui s'est passé?* I, 9; to explain what happened (to someone) *expliquer ce qui s'est passé (à quelqu'un)*, II, 10; You'll never guess what happened. *Tu ne devineras jamais ce qui s'est passé.* II, 9

happy: Happy birthday! *Joyeux (Bon) anniversaire!* II, 3; Happy

Hanukkah! *Bonne fête de Hanoukka!* II, 3; **Happy holiday! (Happy saint's day!)** *Bonne fête!* II, 3; **Happy New Year!** *Bonne année!* II, 3

hard *difficile,* I, 2; **No hard feelings.** *Je ne t'en veux pas.* II, 10; **No hard feelings?** *Tu ne m'en veux pas?* II, 10

harm: No harm done. *Il n'y a pas de mal.* II, 10

has: He/She has . . . *Il/Elle a... ,* II, 1

hat *le chapeau,* I, 10

have *avoir,* I, 2; **to take or to have (food, drink)** *prendre,* I, 5; **to have fun** *s'amuser,* II, 4; **to have to: All you have to do is . . .** *Tu n'as qu'à... ,* II, 7; **You have to do better in class.** *Il faut mieux travailler en classe.* II, 5; **Do you have that in . . . ? (size, fabric, color)** *Vous avez ça en... ?* I, 10; **Have a good trip! (by car)** *Bonne route!;* **(by plane, ship)** *Bon voyage!* II, 3; **I have some things to do.** *J'ai des trucs à faire.* I, 5; **I'll have/I'm going to have . . . , please.** *Je vais prendre... , s'il vous plaît.* I, 5; **May I have some . . . ?** *Je pourrais avoir... ?* II, 3; **to have an accident** *avoir un accident,* II, 9; **to have an argument (with someone)** *se disputer (avec quelqu'un),* II, 9; **What classes do you have . . . ?** *Tu as quels cours... ?* I, 2; **What do you have . . . ?** *Tu as quoi... ?* I, 2; **What kind of . . . do you have?** *Qu'est-ce que vous avez comme... ?* I, 5

head *la tête,* II, 7

health *le cours de développement personnel et social (DPS),* I, 2

hear: Did you hear the latest? *Tu connais la nouvelle?* II, 9; **Let's hear it!** *Dis vite!* II, 9; **to hear the alarm clock** *entendre le réveil,* II, 5

height: of medium height *de taille moyenne,* II, 1

Hello *Bonjour,* I, 1; **Hello? (on the phone)** *Allô?* I, 9

help *aider,* II, 8

help: Can you help me? *Tu peux m'aider?* II, 10; **May I help you?** *(Est-ce que) je peux vous aider?* I, 10

her *la,* I, 9; **her...** *son/sa/ses,* I, 7; **to her** *lui,* I, 9

here: Here. *Voilà.* I, 3; **Here (There) is . . .** *Là, c'est... ,* II, 2; **Here it is.** *Voilà.* II, 3; **Here you are.** *Tenez (tiens).* II, 3

Hi! *Salut!* I, 1

high school *le lycée,* II, 2

hike: to go for a hike *faire une ran-*

donnée pédestre, II, 12; **to go hiking** *faire de la randonnée,* I, 11

him *le,* I, 9; **to him** *lui,* I, 9

his *son/sa/ses,* I, 7

history *l'histoire* (f.), I, 2

hockey *le hockey,* I, 4; **to play hockey** *jouer au hockey,* I, 4

Hold on. *Ne quittez pas.* I, 9

holiday: Happy holiday! (Happy saint's day!) *Bonne fête!* II, 3

home: Make yourself at home. *Faites (Fais) comme chez vous (toi),* II, 2; **Welcome to my home (our home)** *Bienvenue chez moi (chez nous),* II, 2

homework *les devoirs,* I, 2; **to do homework** *faire les devoirs,* I, 7

horrible: It was horrible. *C'était épouvantable.* I, 9; **to have a horrible day** *avoir une journée épouvantable,* II, 5

horror movie *un film d'horreur,* II, 11

horseback: to go horseback riding *faire de l'équitation,* I, 1

hose *le collant,* I, 10

hostel: youth hostel *l'auberge* (f.) *de jeunesse,* II, 2

hot: hot chocolate *le chocolat,* I, 5; **hot dog** *le hot-dog,* I, 5; **It's hot (outside).** *Il fait chaud.* I, 4; **not so hot** *pas super,* I, 2

house: Is this . . . 's house? *Je suis bien chez... ?* I, 9; **to clean house** *faire le ménage,* I, 7; **to/at . . . 's** *chez... ,* I, 11

housework: to do housework *faire le ménage,* I, 1

how: How did it go? *Comment ça s'est passé?* II, 5; **How do you like it?** *Comment tu trouves ça?* I, 5; **How old are you?** *Tu as quel âge?* I, 1; **How was it?** *C'était comment?* II, 6; **How was your day (yesterday)?** *Comment s'est passée ta journée (hier)?* II, 5; **How was your vacation?** *Comment se sont passées tes vacances?* II, 5; **How was your weekend?** *Comment s'est passé ton week-end?* II, 5; **How's it going?** *(Comment) ça va?* I, 1

how about: How about . . . ? *On... ?* I, 4; **How about buying . . . ?** *Si on achetait... ?* II, 8; **How about going . . . ?** *Si on allait... ?* II, 4; **How about playing . . . ?** *Si on jouait... ?* II, 8; **How about playing baseball?** *On joue au baseball?* I, 5; **How about skiing?** *On fait du ski?* I, 5; **How about visiting . . . ?** *Si on visitait... ?* II, 8;

how much: How much is . . . ? *C'est combien,... ?* I, 3; *Combien coûte... ?*

II, 3; **How much are . . . ?** *Combien coûtent... ?* II, 3; **How much does that make?** *Ça fait combien?* I, 5; **How many (much) do you want?** *Combien en voulez-vous?* II, 3

hunger: I'm dying of hunger! *Je crève de faim!* II, 12; *Je meurs de faim!* II, 2

hungry: to be hungry *avoir faim,* I, 5; **Aren't you hungry?** *Vous n'avez pas (Tu n'as pas) faim?* II, 2; **He was hungry.** *Il avait faim.* II, 12; **I'm not hungry anymore.** *Non, merci. Je n'ai plus faim.* I, 8; **I'm very hungry.** *J'ai très faim!* II, 2

hurt: I hurt all over! *J'ai mal partout!* II, 7

hurt: My . . . hurts. *J'ai mal à... ,* II, 7; **to hurt one's . . .** *se faire mal à... ,* II, 7

I

I *je,* I, 1; **I do.** *Moi, si.* I, 2; **I don't.** *Moi, non.* I, 2

ice cream *la glace,* I, 1

ice-skate *faire du patin à glace,* I, 4

idea: Good idea. *Bonne idée.* I, 4; **That's a good (excellent) idea.** *C'est une bonne (excellente) idée.* II, 1; **I have no idea.** *Je n'en sais rien.* I, 11; **No idea.** *Aucune idée.* II, 9

if *si,* I, 7; **OK, if you . . . first.** *D'accord, si tu... d'abord.* I, 7

impossible: It's impossible. *C'est impossible.* II, 10

in *dans,* I, 6; **(a city or place)** *à,* I, 11; **(before a feminine noun)** *en,* I, 11; **(before a masculine noun)** *au,* I, 11; **(before a plural noun)** *aux,* I, 11; **in front of** *devant,* I, 6; **in the afternoon** *l'après-midi,* I, 2; **in the evening** *le soir,* I, 2; **in the morning** *le matin,* I, 2; **. . . is (are) in it.** *C'est avec... ,* II, 11; **Who's in it?** *C'est avec qui?* II, 11

incredible *incroyable,* II, 6

indifference: (expression of indifference) *Bof!* I, 1

insect repellent *de la lotion anti-moustiques,* II, 12

intend: I intend to . . . *J'ai l'intention de... ,* I, 11

interest: That doesn't interest me. *Ça ne me dit rien.* I, 4

interesting *intéressant,* I, 2

invite: Invite him/her/them. *Invite-le/-la/-les.* II, 10

island *l'île* (f.), II, 4

it *le, la,* I, 9
it's: It's . . . *C'est... ,* I, 2; **It's . . . francs.** *Ça fait... francs.* I, 5

J

jacket *le blouson,* I, 10; **ski jacket** *l'anorak (m.),* II, 1
jam *de la confiture,* I, 8
January *janvier,* I, 4
jazz *le jazz,* II, 11
jeans *le jean,* I, 3, II, 1
jog *faire du jogging,* I, 4
joking: You're joking! *Tu plaisantes!* II, 6
July *juillet,* I, 4
June *juin,* I, 4

K

kidding: You're kidding! *C'est pas vrai!* II, 6
kilogram: a kilogram of *un kilo de,* I, 8
kind: What kind of . . . do you have? *Qu'est-ce que vous avez comme... ?* I, 5
kitchen *la cuisine,* II, 2
know: . . . , you know. *... , quoi.* II, 9; **Do you know what . . . ?** *Tu sais ce que... ?* II, 9; **Do you know who . . . ?** *Tu sais qui... ?* II, 9; **I don't know what to do.** *Je ne sais pas quoi faire.* II, 10; **I don't know.** *Je ne sais pas.* I, 10

L

lab *les travaux (m.) pratiques,* I, 2
lame *nul (nulle),* II, 6
lamp *la lampe,* II, 2
late *tard,* II, 4
later: Can you call back later? *Vous pouvez rappeler plus tard?* I, 9; **See you later!** *A tout à l'heure!* I, 1
latest: Did you hear the latest? *Tu connais la nouvelle?* II, 9
Latin *le latin,* I, 2
leather: in leather *en cuir,* I, 10
leather-goods shop *la maroquinerie,* II, 3
leave *partir,* I, 11; **Can I leave a message?** *Je peux laisser un message?* I, 9; **leave: You can't leave without . . .** *Tu ne peux pas partir sans... ,* I, 11
left: to the left *à gauche,* I, 12; **on the left** *sur la gauche;* **to the left of** *à gauche de,* II, 2
leg *la jambe,* II, 7
lemon soda *la limonade,* I, 5
less: Life was more . . . , less . . . *La*

vie était plus... moins... , II, 8; **More or less.** *Plus ou moins.* II, 6
let's: Let's go! *Allons-y!* I, 4; **Let's hear it!** *Dis vite!* II, 9
letter: to send letters *envoyer des lettres,* I, 12
library *la bibliothèque,* I, 6
life *la vie,* II, 8
lift: to lift weights *faire de la musculation,* II, 7
like *aimer,* I, 1; **Did you like it?** *Ça t'a plu?* II, 6; **Do you like . . . ?** *Tu aimes... ?* I, 1; **Do you like it?** *Il/Elle te/vous plaît?* I, 10; **How do you like . . . ?** *Comment tu trouves... ?* I, 10; **How do you like it?** *Comment tu trouves ça?* I, 5; **I (really) like...** *Moi, j'aime (bien)... ,* I, 1; **I don't like...** *Je n'aime pas... ,* I, 1; **I like . . .** *J'aime bien... ,* II, 1; **I like it, but it's expensive.** *Il/Elle me plaît, mais c'est cher.* I, 10; **I'd like . . .** *Je voudrais... ,* I, 3; **I'd like . . . to go with . . .** *J'aimerais... pour aller avec... ,* I, 10; **I'd like to.** *Je veux bien.* II, 1; **I'd really like to.** *Je veux bien.* I, 6; **If you like, . . .** *Si tu veux,... ,* II, 1; **What are they like?** *Ils sont comment?* I, 7; **What do you like to do?** *Qu'est-ce que tu aimes faire?* II, 1; **What I don't like is . . .** *Ce que je n'aime pas, c'est... ,* II, 4; **What I like is . . .** *Ce que j'aime bien, c'est... ,* II, 4; *Ce qui me plaît, c'est... ,* II, 4; **What is he/she like?** *Il /Elle est comment?* I, 7; **What music do you like?** *Qu'est-ce que tu aimes comme musique?* II, 1; **What was it like?** *C'était comment?* II, 8; **You're going to like it here.** *Tu vas te plaire ici.* II, 8; **I really liked it.** *Ça m'a beaucoup plu.* II, 6
listen: to listen to music *écouter de la musique,* I, 1; **Listen!** *Ecoutez!,* I, 0; **to listen to what he/she says** *écouter ce qu'il/elle dit,* II, 10; **I'm listening.** *Je t'écoute.* I, 9
liter: a liter of *un litre de,* I, 8
little: When he/she was little, . . . *Quand il/elle était petit(e),... ,* II, 8; **When I was little, . . .** *Quand j'étais petit(e),... ,* II, 8; **Yes, a little.** *Si, un peu.* II, 2
lively *vivant(e),* II, 4
living room *le salon,* II, 2
located: . . . is located . . . *... se trouve... ?* II, 12; **Where is . . . located?** *Où se trouve... ?* II, 12
long *long (longue),* II, 11; **long hair** *les cheveux longs,* II, 1
look: to look for *chercher,* I, 9; **Look**

at the map! *Regardez la carte!,* I, 0; **Look, here's (there's) (it's) . . .** *Regarde, c'est... ,* I, 12; **That doesn't look good on you.** *Ça ne te (vous) va pas du tout.* I, 10; **to look after someone** *garder ,* I, 7; **I'm looking for something for . . .** *Je cherche quelque chose pour... ,* I, 10; **No, thanks, I'm just looking.** *Non, merci, je regarde.* I, 10; **It looks great on you!** *C'est tout à fait ton style.* I, 10
lose *perdre,* II, 5; **I'm losing it!** *Je craque!* II, 7; **to lose weight** *maigrir,* I, 10
lost: to get lost *se perdre,* II, 9
lot: A lot. *Beaucoup.* I, 4; **I had a lot of fun.** *Je me suis beaucoup amusé(e).* II, 6
lots: I have lots of things to do. *J'ai des tas de choses (trucs) à faire.* I, 12
love: I love . . . *J'adore... ,* II, 1; **in love** *amoureux (amoureuse),* II, 9; **to fall in love (with someone)** *tomber amoureux(-euse) (de quelqu'un),* II, 9
luck: Good luck! *Bonne chance!* I, 11; **Tough luck!** *C'est pas de chance, ça!* II, 5
lunch *le déjeuner,* I, 2; **to have lunch** *déjeuner,* I, 9

M

ma'am *madame (Mme),* I, 1
magazine *le magazine,* I, 3
make *faire,* I, 4; **make up (with someone)** *se réconcilier (avec quelqu'un),* II, 10; **How much does that make?** *Ça fait combien?* II, 3; **Make the best of it.** *Fais-toi une raison.* II, 8; **to make a date (with someone)** *prendre rendez-vous (avec quelqu'un),* II, 9
mall *le centre commercial,* I, 6
mangoes *les mangues (f.),* I, 8
many: How many (much) do you want? *Combien en voulez-vous?* II, 3
map *la carte,* I, 0
March *mars,* I, 4
mask *le masque,* II, 8
matches *les allumettes* (f.), II, 12
math *les maths* (f.), I, 1
matter: It doesn't matter. *Ça ne fait rien.* II, 10
May *mai,* I, 4
may: May I . . . ? *(Est-ce que) je peux... ?* I, 7; **May I have some . . . ?** *Je pourrais avoir... ?* II, 3; **May I help you?** *(Est-ce que) je peux vous aider?* I, 10

maybe *peut-être,* II, 3; **Maybe . . .** *Peut-être que... ,* II, 9; **Maybe you're right.** *Tu as peut-être raison.* II, 9

meal *un repas,* II, 7

mean *méchant(e),* I, 7

meat *la viande,* I, 8

medicine *les médicaments* (m.), I, 12

meet *rencontrer,* I, 9; **I'd like you to meet . . .** *Je te (vous) présente... ,* I, 7; **Pleased to meet you.** *Très heureux (heureuse).* I, 7; **We'll meet . . .** *Bon, on se retrouve... ,* I, 6; *Rendez-vous... ,* I, 6

menu: The menu, please. *La carte, s'il vous plaît.* I, 5

merry: Merry Christmas! *Joyeux Noël!* II, 3

message: Can I leave a message? *Je peux laisser un message?* I, 9

metro: at the . . . metro stop *au métro... ,* I, 6

midnight *minuit,* I, 6

milk *le lait,* I, 8; II, 3

mind: Would you mind . . . ? *Ça t'embête de... ?* II, 10; *Ça t'ennuie de... ?* II, 10

mineral water *l'eau minérale* (f.), I, 5

minute: Do you have a minute? *Tu as une minute?* I, 9

miss (Miss) *mademoiselle (Mlle),* I, 1

miss: I miss . . . *Je regrette... ,* II, 8; **I miss . . .** *(plural subject)* *...me manquent.* II, 8; *(singular subject)* *...me manque.* II, 8; **to miss the bus** *rater le bus,* II, 5; **What I miss is . . .** *Ce qui me manque, c'est... ,* II, 8

mistaken: In my opinion, you're mistaken. *A mon avis, tu te trompes.* II, 9

misunderstanding: a little misunderstanding *un petit malentendu,* II, 10

moment: One moment, please. *Un moment, s'il vous plaît.* I, 5

Monday *lundi,* I, 2; **on Mondays** *le lundi,* I, 2

money *l'argent,* I, 11

mood: in a bad/good mood *de mauvaise/bonne humeur,* II, 9

moose *l'orignal,* II, 12

more: More . . . ? *Encore de... ?* I, 8; **I just can't do any more!** *Je n'en peux plus!* II, 7; **Life was more . . . , less . . .** *La vie était plus... moins... ,* II, 8; **More or less.** *Plus ou moins.* II, 6; **One more try!** *Encore un effort!* II, 7; **Some more . . . ?** *Encore... ?* II, 3

morning: in the morning *le matin,* I, 2

mosque *une mosquée,* II, 8

mosquito *un moustique,* II, 4

mother *la mère,* I, 7

mountain: to go mountain-bike riding *faire du vélo de montagne,* II, 12; **to/at the mountains** *à la montagne,* I, 11

movie: movie theater *le cinéma,* I, 6; **the movies** *le cinéma,* I, 1

Mr. *monsieur (M.),* I, 1

Mrs. *madame (Mme),* I, 1

much: How much is (are) . . . ? *Combien coûte(nt)... ?* II, 3; **How much is . . . ?** *C'est combien,... ?* I, 3; **How much is it, please?** *Ça fait combien, s'il vous plaît?* I, 5; **How much is the entrance fee?** *C'est combien, l'entrée?* II, 6; **No, not too much.** *Non, pas trop.* I, 2; **Not much.** *Pas grand-chose.* I, 6; **Not too much.** *Pas tellement.* I, 4; **Not very much.** *Pas beaucoup.* I, 4; **Yes, very much.** *Oui, beaucoup.* I, 2

museum *le musée,* I, 6

mushrooms *les champignons* (m.), I, 8

music *la musique,* I, 2; **music group** *le groupe,* II, 11; **classical music** *la musique classique,* II, 11; **What music do you like?** *Qu'est-ce que tu aimes comme musique?* II, 1

musician *un musicien(ne),* II, 11

my *mon/ma/mes,* I, 7; **It's just not my day!** *C'est pas mon jour!* II, 5

mystery: detective or mystery movie *un film policier,* II, 11

N

name: His/Her name is... *Il/Elle s'appelle... ,* I, 1; **My name is...** *Je m'appelle... ,* I, 1; **What's your name?** *Tu t'appelles comment?* I, 1

nap: to take a nap *faire la sieste,* II, 8

natural science *les sciences* (f.) *naturelles,* I, 2

near *près de,* II, 2

neck *le cou,* II, 7; **a pain in the neck** *pénible,* I, 7

need: I need . . . *Il me faut... ,* I, 3; *J'ai besoin de... ,* I, 8; **What do you need for . . . ?** *(formal)* *Qu'est-ce qu'il vous faut pour... ,* I, 3; **What do you need for . . . ?** *(informal)* *Qu'est-ce qu'il te faut pour... ?* I, 3; **What do you need?** *De quoi est-ce que tu as besoin?* I, 8; *Qu'est-ce qu'il te faut?* I, 8; **Yes, I need . . .** *Oui, il me faut... ,* I, 10

neither: Neither do I. *Moi non plus.* I, 2

never *ne... jamais,* I, 4

new *nouveau (nouvelle) (nouvel),* II, 2

new: Happy New Year! *Bonne année!* II, 3

next to *à côté de,* I, 12; II, 2

next: Next, . . . *Ensuite,... ,* II, 1

nice *gentil (gentille),* I, 7; II, 1; *sympa, sympathique,* I, 7; II, 1; **It's nice weather.** *Il fait beau.* I, 4; **That's nice of you.** *C'est gentil!* II, 2; **That's so nice of you.** *C'est gentil de votre (ta) part,* II, 2

nightmare: It was a real nightmare! *C'était un véritable cauchemar!* I, 11

no *non,* I, 1; **No way!** *Pas question!* II, 1

noisy *bruyant(e),* II, 8

none (of it) *en,* I, 8

noon *midi,* I, 6

north: in the north *dans le nord,* II, 4; **It's to the north of . . .** *C'est au nord de... ,* II, 12

nose: I've got a runny nose. *J'ai le nez qui coule.* II, 7

not: Definitely not! *Sûrement pas!* II, 6; **Not at all.** *Pas du tout.* I, 4, II, 10; **Oh, not bad.** *Oh, pas mauvais.* I, 9; **Not me.** *Pas moi.* I, 2; **not so great** *pas terrible,* I, 5; **not very good** *pas bon,* I, 5; **not yet** *ne... pas encore,* I, 9

notebook *le cahier,* I, 0

nothing: It's nothing special. *Ce n'est pas grand-chose.* II, 3; **Nothing special.** *Rien de spécial.* I, 6

novel *le roman,* I, 3

November *novembre,* I, 4

O

o'clock: at . . . o'clock *à... heures,* I, 2

obvious: That's obvious. *Ça se voit.* II, 9

obviously *évidemment,* II, 9

October *octobre,* I, 4

of *de,* I, 0; **Of course.** *Bien sûr.* I, 3, II, 10; **Of course not.** *Bien sûr que non.* II, 10; **of it** *en,* I, 8; **of them** *en,* I, 8

off: afternoon off *l'après-midi libre,* I, 2

often *souvent,* I, 4

oh: Oh no! *Oh là là!* II, 5

OK. *D'accord.* I, 4, II, 1; **OK.** *Entendu.* I, 6; **Is that OK with you?** *Tu es d'accord?* I, 7; **It was OK.** *C'était assez bien,* II, 6; **No, I'm okay.** *Non, ça va,* II, 2; **Well, OK.**

Bon, d'accord. I, 8; **Yes, it was OK.** *Oui, ça a été.* I, 9

okra *du gombo,* I, 8

old-fashioned *démodé(e),* I, 10

old: How old are you? *Tu as quel âge?* I, 1; **to be . . . years old** *avoir... ans,* II, 1; **When I was . . . years old, . . .** *Quand j'avais... ans,... ,* II, 8

older *âgé(e),* I, 7

on: Can I try on . . . ? *Je peux essayer... ?* I, 10; **on foot** *à pied,* I, 12; **on the right (left)** *sur la droite (gauche),* II, 2

one-way: a one-way ticket *un aller simple,* II, 6

one: He/She already has one (of them). *Il/Elle en a déjà un(e).* II, 3

open: Open your books to page . . . *Ouvrez vos livres à la page... ,* I, 0; **When do you open?** *A quelle heure est-ce que vous ouvrez?* II, 6

opinion: In my opinion, you're mistaken. *A mon avis, tu te trompes.* II, 9; **In your opinion, what do I do?** *A ton avis, qu'est-ce que je fais?* I, 9; **In your opinion, what should I do?** *A ton avis, qu'est-ce que je dois faire?* II, 10

orange *orange,* I, 3; **orange juice** *le jus d'orange,* I, 5; **oranges** *les oranges* (f.), I, 8

ordinary: That's ordinary. *C'est banal.* II, 3

our *notre/nos,* I, 7

out: go out *sortir,* II, 6; **Out of the question!** *Pas question!* I, 7

oysters *les huîtres,* II, 3

P

page *la page,* I, 0

pain: a pain *pénible,* II, 1

pair: (a pair of) jeans *un jean,* I, 3; **(a pair of) shorts** *un short,* I, 3; **(pair of) boots** *les bottes* (f.), II, 1; **(pair of) gloves** *les gants* (m.), II, 1; **(pair of) pants** *un pantalon,* I, 10; **(pair of) sneakers** *les baskets* (f.), II, 1

palm tree *un palmier,* II, 4

papayas *les papayes* (f.), I, 8

paper *le papier,* I, 0; **sheets of paper** *les feuilles* (f.) *de papier,* I, 3

pardon: Pardon me. *Pardon,* I, 3

park *le parc,* I, 6; II, 2

party: to give a party *faire une boum,* II, 10; **to go to a party** *aller à une boum,* I, 6

pass: Would you pass . . . *Vous pourriez (tu pourrais) me passer... ,* II, 3; **You'll pass . . .** *Vous passez devant... ,* I, 12

passport *le passeport,* I, 11; II, 1

pasta *des pâtes,* II, 7

pastry *la pâtisserie,* I, 12

pastry shop *la pâtisserie;* I, 12; II, 3

paté *le pâté,* II, 3

peaches *les pêches* (f.), I, 8

pears *les poires* (f.), I, 8

peas *les petits pois* (m.), I, 8

pen *le stylo,* I, 0

pencil *le crayon,* I, 3; **pencil case** *la trousse,* I, 3; **pencil sharpener** *le taille-crayon,* I, 3

perfect: It's perfect. *C'est parfait.* I, 10

permission: to ask your parents' permission *demander la permission à tes parents,* II, 10

phone: Phone him/her/them. *Téléphone-lui/-leur.* II, 10; **to talk on the phone** *parler au téléphone,* I, 1

photo: photo frame *le cadre,* II, 3

physical education *l'éducation* (f.) *physique et sportive (EPS),* I, 2

physics *la physique,* I, 2

pick *choisir,* I, 10; **to pick up your room** *ranger ta chambre,* I, 7

picnic: to have a picnic *faire un pique-nique,* I, 6; II, 6

picture: to take pictures *faire des photos,* I, 4

pie *la tarte,* I, 8; II, 3

piece: a piece of *un morceau de,* I, 8

pineapple *un ananas,* I, 8; II, 4

pink *rose,* I, 3

pizza *la pizza,* I, 1

plane ticket *le billet d'avion,* I, 11

plane *l'avion* (m.), I, 12; **by plane** *en avion,* I, 12

plans: I don't have any plans. *Je n'ai rien de prévu.* I, 11

platform: From which platform . . . ? *De quel quai... ?* II, 6; **From platform . . .** *Du quai... ,* II, 6

play *faire,* I, 4; *jouer,* I, 4; **play (theatrical)** *la pièce,* I, 6; **to see a play** *voir une pièce,* I, 6; **How about playing . . . ?** *Si on jouait... ?* II, 8; **I don't play/do . . .** *Je ne fais pas de... ,* I, 4; **to play (a game)** *jouer à... ,* I, 4; **to play sports** *faire du sport,* I, 1; **What sports do you play?** *Qu'est-ce que tu fais comme sport?* I, 4; II, 1

playing: It's playing at . . . *Ça passe à... ,* II, 11; **What films are playing?** *Qu'est-ce qu'on joue comme film?* II, 11; **Where is that playing?** *Ça passe où?* II, 11

please *s'il vous (te) plaît,* I, 3

pleased: Pleased to meet you. *Très heureux (heureuse).* I, 7

pleasure: With pleasure. *Avec plaisir.* I, 8; II, 10

plot: It has no plot. *Il n'y a pas d'histoire.* II, 11; **It's full of plot twists.** *C'est plein de rebondissements.* II, 11

poetry: book of poetry *un livre de poésie,* II, 11

point: At that point, . . . *A ce moment-là,... ,* II, 9

pool *la piscine,* II, 2

poor: You poor thing! *Pauvre vieux (vieille)!* II, 5

pop: popular, mainstream music *le pop,* II, 11

pork *du porc,* I, 8

possible: That's not possible. *Ce n'est pas possible.* II, 9; **That's possible.** *C'est possible.* II, 9

post office *la poste,* I, 12; II, 2

poster *le poster,* I, 0; II, 2

potatoes *les pommes de terre* (f.), I, 8

pottery *la poterie,* II, 8

pound: a pound of *une livre de,* I, 8

practice *répéter,* I, 9

prefer: Do you prefer . . . or . . . ? *Tu aimes mieux... ou... ?* I, 10; **I prefer** *Je préfère,* I, 1; II, 1; *J'aime mieux... ,* I, 1; II, 1; **No, I prefer . . .** *Non, je préfère... ,* II, 7; **What I prefer is . . .** *Ce que je préfère, c'est... ,* II, 4

problem: I have a problem. *J'ai un (petit) problème.* I, 9; I, 10; **No problem.** *Pas de problème.* II, 10

process: to be in the process of (doing something) *être en train de,* II, 9

pullover (sweater) *le pull-over,* I, 3

purple *violet(te),* I, 3

purse *le sac à main,* II, 3

push-ups: to do push-ups *faire des pompes,* II, 7

put *mettre,* I, 10

put on (clothing) *mettre,* I, 10

Q

quarter: quarter past *et quart,* I, 6; **quarter to** *moins le quart,* I, 6

question: Out of the question! *Pas question!* I, 7

quiz *l'interro* (f.), I, 9

R

raccoon *un raton laveur,* II, 12

radio *la radio,* I, 3

rain: It's raining. *Il pleut.* I, 4

raincoat *l'imperméable* (m.), II, 1

rainforest: tropical rainforest *la forêt tropicale,* II, 4 raise: **Raise your hand!** *Levez la main!*, I, 0

rap *le rap*, II, 11

rather *plutôt*, II, 9; **No, I'd rather...** *Non, je préfère...*, II, 1

read *lire*, I, 1

read *lu (pp. of lire)*, I, 9

ready: to get ready *faire les préparatifs*, II, 10

really: I (really) like... *Moi, j'aime (bien)...*, I, 1; **I really liked it.** *Ça m'a beaucoup plu.* II, 6; **I'd really like to...** *Je voudrais bien...*, I, 11; **I'd really like to.** *Je veux bien.* I, 6; **No, not really.** *Non, pas vraiment.* I, 11; **Really?** *C'est vrai? (Vraiment?)*, II, 2; **Was it really so different?** *C'était tellement différent?* II, 8; **Your... is really great.** *Il (Elle) est vraiment bien, ton (ta)...*, 2; **really** *vachement*, II, 9; **really, ultra-** *super*, II, 9

receive: to receive one's report card *recevoir le bulletin trimestriel*, II, 5

recommend: I recommend it. *Je te le recommande.* II, 11

record: at the record store *chez le disquaire*, I, 12

recreation center *la Maison des Jeunes et de la culture (MJC)*, I, 6

red: *rouge*, I, 3; **red hair** *les cheveux roux*, II, 1; **red-headed** *roux (rousse)*, I, 7

reggae music *le reggae*, II, 11

rehearse *répéter*, I, 9

relaxing *relaxant(e)*, II, 8

remember: Remember to take... *Pense à prendre...*, II, 1

repeat: Repeat! *Répétez!*, I, 0

report card: to receive one's report card *recevoir le bulletin trimestriel*, II, 5

respect: to respect nature *respecter la nature*, II, 12

responsibilities: to have responsibilities *avoir des responsabilités*, II, 8

restaurant *le restaurant*, I, 6

restroom: toilet, restroom *les toilettes (les W.-C.)*, II, 2

return *retourner*, II, 6; **to return something** *rendre*, I, 12; **to return tests** *rendre les examens*, II, 5

rice *du riz*, I, 8

ride: to go horseback riding *faire de l'équitation*, I, 1; **to take a ride on the ferris wheel** *faire un tour sur la grande roue*, II, 6; **to take a ride on the roller coaster** *faire un tour sur les montagnes russes*, II, 6

ridiculous: That's ridiculous! *N'importe quoi!* II, 6

riding: to go horseback riding *faire de l'équitation*, I, 1

right: I can't right now. *Je ne peux pas maintenant.* I, 8; **I'll go right away.** *J'y vais tout de suite.* I, 8; **right away** *tout de suite*, I, 6; **It's right there on the...** *C'est tout de suite à...*, I, 12; **on the right** *sur la droite*, II, 2; **to the right** *à droite*, I, 12; **to the right of** *à droite de*, II, 2; **Yeah, right!** *Mon œil!* II, 6 **You're right...** *Tu as raison...*, II, 3

rip *déchirer*, II, 5

rock (music) *le rock*, II, 11

roller coaster *les montagnes russes*, II, 6

romance novel *un roman d'amour*, II, 11

romantic: romantic movie *un film d'amour*, II, 11

room (of a house) *la pièce*, II, 2

room: to pick up your room *ranger ta chambre*, I, 7

round-trip: a round-trip ticket *un aller-retour*, II, 6

rug *le tapis*, II, 2

ruler *la règle*, I, 3

runny: I've got a runny nose. *J'ai le nez qui coule.* II, 7

S

sailing: to go sailing *faire de la voile, faire du bateau*, I, 11

salad *de la salade*, I, 8

salami *le saucisson*, I, 5

salt *le sel*, II, 7

sand *le sable*, II, 4

sandals *les sandales (f.)*, I, 10

sandwich *le sandwich*, I, 5

Saturday: on Saturdays *le samedi*, I, 2

scared: I'm scared (of)... *J'ai peur (de la, du, des)...*, II, 12

scarf (for outdoor wear) *l'écharpe*, I, 10 (dressy) *le foulard*, II, 3

school *l'école (f.)*, I, 1

school: high school *le lycée*, II, 2

science fiction: novel *un roman de science-fiction*, II, 11; **movie** *un film de science-fiction*, II, 11

scuba dive *faire de la plongée sous-marine*, II, 4

sea *la mer*, II, 4

second: One second, please. *Une seconde, s'il vous plaît.* I, 9

see *voir*, I, 6, **... you see.** *... tu vois.* II, 9; **See you later!** *À tout à l'heure!* I, 1; **See you soon.** *À bientôt.* I, 1; **See you tomorrow.** *À demain.* I, 1; **to see a game (in person)** *voir un match*, I, 6; **to see a movie** *voir un film*, I, 6; **to see a**

play *voir une pièce*, I, 6; **What is there to see...?** *Qu'est-ce qu'il y a à voir...?* II, 12; **You'll see that...** *Tu vas voir que...*, II, 8

seem: to seem *avoir l'air*, II, 9; **You don't seem too well.** *Tu n'as pas l'air en forme.* II, 7; **She seemed...** *Elle avait l'air...*, II, 12

seen *vu (pp. of voir)*, I, 9

send: to send letters *envoyer des lettres*, I, 12; **to send the invitations** *envoyer les invitations*, II, 10

sensational *sensas*, II, 6

September *septembre*, I, 4

serious: It's not serious. *C'est pas grave.* II, 5

service: At your service; You're welcome. *À votre service.* I, 3

shall: Shall we go to the café? *On va au café?* I, 5

shape: to get into shape *se mettre en condition*, II, 7

sheet: a sheet of paper *la feuille de papier*, I, 0

shelves *les étagères*, II, 2

shirt (men's) *la chemise*, I, 10; **shirt (women's)** *le chemisier*, I, 10

shoes *les chaussures (f.)*, I, 10

shop: to go shopping *faire les magasins*, I, 1; **to window-shop** *faire les vitrines*, I, 6

shopping: Can you do the shopping? *Tu peux aller faire les courses?* I, 8

short (height) *petit(e)*, I, 7; **(length)** *court(e)*, I, 10; **short hair** *les cheveux courts*, II, 1

shorts: (a pair of) shorts *le short*, I, 3; II, 1

should: Everyone should... *On doit.* II, 7; **I should have...** *J'aurais dû...*, II, 10; **In your opinion, what should I do?** *À ton avis, qu'est-ce que je dois faire?* II, 10; **What do you think I should do?** *Qu'est-ce que tu me conseilles?* II, 10; **What should I...?** *Qu'est-ce que je dois...?* II, 1; **What should we do?** *Qu'est-ce qu'on fait?* II, 1; **You should...** *Tu devrais...*, I, 9; II, 7; **You should have...** *Tu aurais dû...*, II, 10

shouldn't: You shouldn't... *Tu ne devrais pas...*, II, 7

show (verb) *montrer*, I, 9; **sound and light show** *un spectacle son et lumière*, II, 6

showing: ... is showing. *On joue...*, II, 11

shrimp *les crevettes*, II, 3

shy *timide*, I, 7

sick: I'm sick to my stomach. *J'ai mal au cœur.* II, 7; **I'm sick.** *Je suis malade.* II, 7

silly: to do silly things *faire des bêtises*, II, 8
simple *simple*, II, 8
sing *chanter*, I, 9
singer *une chanteuse (un chanteur)*, II, 11
sir *monsieur (M.)*, I, 1
sister *la sœur*, I, 7
sit-ups: to do sit-ups *faire des abdominaux*, II, 7
sit: Sit down! *Asseyez-vous!*, I, 0
skate: to ice-skate *faire du patin à glace*, I, 4; to in-line skate *faire du roller en ligne*, I, 4
ski *faire du ski*, I, 4; to water-ski *faire du ski nautique*, I, 4; ski jacket *l'anorak* (m.), II, 1
skiing *le ski*, I, 1
skip: Don't skip . . . *Ne saute pas...*, II, 7; skipping a meal *sauter un repas*, II, 7
skirt *la jupe*, I, 10
skunk *une mouffette*, II, 12
sleep *dormir*, I, 1; I didn't sleep well. *J'ai mal dormi.* II, 7
sleeping bag *un sac de couchage*, II, 12
slender *mince*, I, 7
slice: a slice of *une tranche de*, I, 8
small, short *petit(e)*, I, 10; II, 1
smaller: smaller than . . . *moins grand(e) que...*, II, 4
smart *intelligent(e)*, I, 7; II, 1
snack: afternoon snack *le goûter*, I, 8; snacking between meals *grignoter entre les repas*, II, 7; party snacks *les amuse-gueule* (m.), II, 10
snails *les escargots* (m.), I, 1; II, 3
sneakers *les baskets* (f.), I, 3; II, 1
snorkel *faire de la plongée avec un tuba*, II, 4
snow: It's snowing. *Il neige.* I, 4; to go snow-shoeing *faire une randonnée en raquettes*, II, 12
So . . . *Alors,...*, II, 9; so-so *comme ci, comme ça*, I, 1; II, 6; not so great *pas terrible*, I, 5
soccer *le football*, I, 1; to play soccer *jouer au foot(ball)*, I, 4
socks *les chaussettes* (f.), I, 10
some *du, de la, de l', des*, I, 8; I'd like some. *J'en veux bien.* I, 8; Some more . . . ? *Encore... ?* II, 3; some (of it) *en*, I, 8; II, 3
sometimes *quelquefois*, I, 4
song *une chanson*, II, 11
soon: See you soon. *A bientôt.* I, 1
Sorry. *Je regrette.* I, 3; *Désolé(e).* I, 5; II, 10
sort of *assez*, II, 9
sound: Does . . . sound good to you? *Ça te dit de... ?* II, 1; sound and

light show *un spectacle son et lumière*, II, 6
south: in the south *dans le sud*, II, 4; It's to the south of . . . *C'est au sud de...*, II, 12
Spanish *l'espagnol* (m.), I, 2
speak: Could I speak to . . . ? *(Est-ce que) je peux parler à... ?* I, 9
special: It's nothing special. *Ce n'est pas grand-chose.* II, 3; Nothing special. *Rien de spécial.* I, 6
sports *le sport*, I, 1; to play sports *faire du sport*, I, 1; What sports do you play? *Qu'est-ce que tu fais comme sport?* I, 4; II, 1
sprain: to sprain one's ankle *se fouler la cheville*, II, 7
spring: in the spring *au printemps*, I, 4
squirrel *un écureuil*, II, 12
stadium *le stade*, I, 6
stamp *le timbre*, I, 12
stand: Stand up! *Levez-vous!*, I, 0
start *commencer*, I, 9; What time does it start? *Ça commence à quelle heure?* II, 11
stationery store *la papeterie*, I, 12
stay *rester*, II, 6
steak *le bifteck*, I, 8; II, 3
steak and French fries *le steak-frites*, I, 5
step: to miss a step *rater une marche*, II, 5
stereo *la chaîne stéréo*, II, 2
stomach *le ventre*, II, 7; I'm sick to my stomach. *J'ai mal au cœur.* II, 7
stop: at the metro stop *au métro*, I, 6
stores *les magasins* (m.), I, 1
story: It's a great story. *C'est une belle histoire.* II, 11; It's the story of . . . *C'est l'histoire de...*, II, 11; What's the story? *Qu'est-ce que ça raconte?* II, 11
straight ahead: You go straight ahead until you get to . . . *Vous allez tout droit jusqu'à...*, I, 12; Go (keep going) straight ahead. *Allez (continuez) tout droit*, II, 2
strawberries *les fraises* (f.), I, 8
street: You take . . . Street, then . . . Street. *Prenez la rue..., puis traversez la rue...*, I, 12
strict: to follow a diet that's too strict. *suivre un régime trop strict*, II, 7
strong *fort(e)*, I, 7; II, 1
strong: It's not my strong point. *Ce n'est pas mon fort.* II, 5
student *l'élève* (m./f.), I, 2
study *étudier*, I, 1
study hall *l'étude*, I, 2
stupid *bête*, II, 1

style: in style *à la mode*, I, 10; That's not his/her style. *Ce n'est pas son style.* II, 3; style of the Forties or Fifties *rétro* (inv.), I, 10
subway: by subway *en métro*, I, 12
sugar: sugarcane fields *des champs de canne à sucre*, II, 4
suit jacket, blazer *la veste*, I, 10
suit: Does it suit me? *Ça me va?* I, 10; That suits you really well. *Ça te (vous) va très bien.* I, 10
suitcase *la valise*, I, 11
sulk *faire la tête*, II, 9
summer: in the summer *en été*, I, 4
Sunday: on Sundays *le dimanche*, I, 2
sunglasses *les lunettes* (f.) *de soleil*, I, 10
super *super*, I, 2
sure: Oh, I'm not sure. *Euh... J'hésite.* I, 10
surprise: That would surprise me. *Ça m'étonnerait!* II, 6
surprised *étonné(e)*, II, 9
suspenseful: It's suspenseful. *Il y a du suspense.* II, 11
sweater *le cardigan*, I, 10; *le pull*, I, 10
sweatshirt *le sweat*, II, 1
swim *nager*, I, 1; *faire de la natation*, I, 4; to go swimming *se baigner*, II, 4
swimming pool *la piscine*, I, 6

T

T-shirt *le tee-shirt*, I, 3; II, 1
table: to clear the table *débarrasser la table*, I, 7
tacky: I think it's (they're) really tacky. *Je le/la/les trouve moche(s).* I, 10
take out: Take out a sheet of paper. *Prenez une feuille de papier.* I, 0; to take out the trash *sortir la poubelle*, I, 7
take *prendre*, I, 5; Are you going to take it/them? *Vous le/la/les prenez?* I, 10; Have you decided to take . . . ? *Vous avez décidé de prendre... ?* I, 10; I'll take . . . *Je vais (en) prendre...*, II, 3; I'll take . . . (of them). *Je vais en prendre...*, II, 3; I'll take it/them. *Je le/la/les prends.* I, 10; Remember to take . . . *Pense à prendre...*, II, 1; Take . . . *Prends..., Prenez...*, II, 2; to take pictures *faire des photos*, I, 4; We can take . . . *On peut prendre...*, I, 12; You take . . . Street, then . . . Street. *Prenez la rue..., puis traversez la rue...*, I, 12

taken *pris (pp. of prendre)*, I, 9
taking: Are you taking . . . ? *Tu prends... ?* I, 11
talk: Can I talk to you? *Je peux te parler?* I, 9; II, 10; **Talk to him/her/them.** *Parle-lui/leur.* II, 10; to talk on the phone *parler au téléphone*, I, 1
talked: We talked. *Nous avons parlé.* I, 9
tall *grand(e)*, I, 7; II, 1
tart: apple tart *la tarte aux pommes*, II, 3
taste *déguster*, II, 4
taxi: by taxi *en taxi*, I, 12
teacher *le professeur*, I, 0
tease *taquiner*, II, 8
teeth *les dents* (f.), II, 7
television *la télévision*, I, 0
tell: Can you tell her/ him that I called? *Vous pouvez lui dire que j'ai téléphoné?* I, 9; **Tell him/her/them that . . .** *Dis-lui/-leur que... ,* II, 10; **Tell me!** *Raconte!* II, 5; to tell (someone) that . . . *dire à (quelqu'un) que... ,* II, 10
tennis: to play tennis *jouer au tennis*, I, 4
tent *une tente*, II, 12
terrible *horrible*, I, 10; **I had a terrible day!** *J'ai passé une journée horrible!* II, 5
Terrific! *Bravo!* II, 5
tests *les examens* (m.), I, 1; **to take a test** *passer un examen*, I, 9
than: bigger than . . . *plus grand(e) que... ,* II, 4; It's better than . . . *C'est meilleur que... ,* II, 7; smaller than . . . *moins grand(e) que... ,* II, 4
thanks: Thank you. *Merci, I, 3,* II, 2; No, thank you. *Non, merci.* I, 8; Yes, thank you. *Oui, s'il vous (te) plaît.* I, 8; No thank you, I've had enough. *Merci, ça va.* II, 3; No thanks. I'm not hungry anymore. *Non, merci. Je n'ai plus faim.* I, 8
that *ce, cet, cette,* I, 3; **That is, . . .** *C'est-à-dire que... ,* II, 9; **This/That is . . .** *Ça, c'est... ,* I, 12
theater *le théâtre,* I, 6, II, 2
their *leur/leurs,* I, 7
them *les,* I, 9, *leur,* I, 9
then: Then I called . . . *Ensuite, j'ai téléphoné à... ,* I, 9; II, 1 Then, . . . *Puis,... ,* II, 1
there *-là (noun suffix),* I, 3; *y,* I, 12; **Here (There) is . . .** *Là, c'est... ,* II, 2; **Is . . . there, please?** *(Est-ce que)... est là, s'il vous plaît?* I, 9; **There is . . .** *Il y a... ,* II, 2; **There's . . .** *Voilà... ,* I, 7; **You're almost there!** *Tu y es presque!* II, 7

Therefore, . . . *Donc,... ,* II, 9
these *ces,* I, 3; **These/Those are . . .** *Ce sont... ,* I, 7
thing: It's not my thing. *Ce n'est pas mon truc.* II, 7; I have lots of things to do. *J'ai des tas de choses à faire.* I, 5; I have some things to do. *J'ai des trucs à faire.* I, 5
think: Do you think so? *Tu trouves?* II, 2; I don't think so. *Je ne crois pas.* II, 9; I think it's/they're . . . *Je le/la/les trouve... ,* I, 10; I think that . . . *Je crois que... ,* II, 9; What do you think about going . . . ? *Ça te dit d'aller... ?* II, 4; What do you think I should do? *Qu'est-ce que tu me conseilles?* II, 10; What do you think of . . . ? *Comment tu trouves... ?* I, 2; What do you think of that/it? *Comment tu trouves ça?* I, 2
thirst: I'm dying of thirst! *Je meurs de soif!* II, 2
thirsty: Aren't you thirsty? *Vous n'avez pas (Tu n'as pas) soif?* II, 2; I'm not hungry/thirsty anymore. *Je n'ai plus faim/soif.* II, 3; to be thirsty *avoir soif,* I, 5
this *ce, cet, cette,* I, 3; This is . . . *C'est... ,* I, 7; This is . . . *Voici... ,* I, 7; This/That is . . . *Ça, c'est... ,* I, 12
those *ces,* I, 3; These (those) are . . . *Ce sont... ,* I, 7
thought: I've thought of everything. *J'ai pensé à tout.* I, 11
throat *la gorge,* II, 7
throw: to throw away (to take with you) your trash *jeter (remporter) les déchets,* II, 12
Thursday: on Thursdays *le jeudi,* I, 2
ticket: plane ticket *le billet d'avion,* I, 11; II, 1; Three (entrance) tickets, please. *Trois tickets, s'il vous plaît.* II, 6; train ticket *le billet de train,* I, 11
tie *la cravate,* I, 10
tight *serré(e),* I, 10
time: a waste of time *zéro,* I, 2; At what time do you have . . . ? *Tu as... à quelle heure?* I, 2; At what time? *A quelle heure?* I, 6; from time to time *de temps en temps,* I, 4; I don't have time. *Je n'ai pas le temps.* II, 10; What time does it start? *Ça commence à quelle heure?* II, 11; What time does the train (the bus) for . . . leave? *A quelle heure est-ce que le train (le car) pour... part?* II, 6
tired: (You're) not too tired? *Pas trop fatigué(e)?* II, 2; I'm tired. *Je suis fatigué(e).* II, 12

tiring: It was tiring! *C'était fatigant!* II, 2
to: *à la, au,* I, 6; (a city or place) *à,* I, 11; (before a feminine noun) *en,* I, 11; (before a masculine noun) *au,* I, 11; (before a plural noun) *aux,* I, 11
today *aujourd'hui,* I, 2
toilet: toilet, restroom *les toilettes (les W.-C.),* II, 2
tomatoes *les tomates* (f.), I, 8
tomorrow *demain,* I, 2; See you tomorrow. *A demain.* I, 1
tonight: Not tonight. *Pas ce soir.* I, 7
too: It's too expensive. *C'est trop cher.* I, 10; II, 3; Me too. *Moi aussi.* I, 2; No, not too much. *Non, pas trop.* I, 2; Not too much. *Pas tellement.* I, 4; too violent *trop violent,* II, 11
tough: Tough luck! *C'est pas de chance, ça!* II, 5
tour: to take a guided tour *faire une visite guidée,* II, 6; to tour some châteaux *faire un circuit des châteaux,* II, 6
tourist: tourist information office *l'office de tourisme,* II, 2
tower: to go up in a tower *monter dans une tour,* II, 6
track: to do track and field *faire de l'athlétisme,* I, 4
trails: to follow the marked trails *suivre les sentiers balisés,* II, 12
train for (a sport) *s'entraîner à... ,* II, 7
train: by train *en train,* I, 12; train station *la gare,* II, 2; train ticket *le billet de train,* I, 11
trash: to take out the trash *sortir la poubelle,* I, 7
trashcan *la poubelle,* I, 7
travel *voyager,* I, 1
trip: Did you have a good trip? *Vous avez (Tu as) fait bon voyage?* II, 2; Have a good (car) trip! *Bonne route!* II, 3; Have a good trip! (by plane, ship) *Bon voyage!* II, 3
tropical rainforest *la forêt tropicale,* II, 4
try: Can I try it (them) on ? *Je peux l'(les) essayer?* I, 10; One more try! *Encore un effort!* II, 7
Tuesdays: on Tuesdays *le mardi,* I, 2
turn: Then, turn left on . . . *Puis, tournez à gauche dans... ,* II, 2; You turn . . . *Vous tournez... ,* I, 12
TV: to watch TV *regarder la télé(vision),* I, 1
twists: It's full of plot twists. *C'est plein de rebondissements.* II, 11

U

uncle *l'oncle* (m.), I, 7
uncomfortable *mal à l'aise*, II, 9
Unfortunately, . . . *Malheureusement,... ,* II, 9
unique: That's unique. *C'est original.* II, 3
up: go up *monter*, II, 6
used: You'll get used to it. *Tu vas t'y faire.* II, 8
useless *nul*, I, 2
usually *d'habitude*, I, 4

V

vacation *les vacances* (f.), I, 1; **Have a good vacation!** *Bonnes vacances!* I, 11; **on vacation** *en vacances*, I, 4
vase *le vase*, II, 3
VCR (videocassette recorder) *le magnétoscope*, I, 0
vegetables *des légumes*, II, 7
very: not very good *pas bon*, I, 5; **very cool** *chouette*, II, 2; **Yes, very much.** *Oui, beaucoup.* I, 2
video: to make videos *faire de la vidéo*, I, 4; **video games** *faire des jeux vidéo*, I, 4
videocassette recorder, VCR *le magnétoscope*, I, 0
videotape *la vidéocassette*, I, 3
village: fishing village *un village de pêcheurs*, II, 4
violent *violent*, II, 11
visit *visiter*, I, 9; II, 6; **How about visiting . . . ?** *Si on visitait... ?* II, 8
volcano *le volcan*, II, 4
volleyball: to play volleyball *jouer au volley(-ball)*, I, 4

W

wait for *attendre*, I, 9
Waiter! *Monsieur!* I, 5
Waitress! *Madame!* I, 5, *Mademoiselle!* I, 5
walk: to go for a walk *faire une promenade*, I, 6, *se promener*, II, 4; **to walk the dog** *promener le chien*, I, 7
wallet *le portefeuille*, I, 3; II, 3
want *vouloir*, I, 6; **No, I don't want to.** *Non, je ne veux pas.* II, 8; **Do you want . . . ?** *Tu veux... ?* I, 6; II, 3; **Do you want . . . ?** *Vous voulez... ?* I, 8; II, 3; **Yes, if you want to.** *Oui, si tu veux.* I, 7
wardrobe: armoire/wardrobe *l'armoire* (f.), II, 2

wash: to wash oneself *se laver*, II, 4; **to wash the car** *laver la voiture*, I, 7
waste: a waste of time *zéro*, I, 2
watch *la montre*, I, 3; **to watch a game (on TV)** *regarder un match*, I, 6; **to watch TV** *regarder la télé(vision)*, I, 1
water: to water-ski *faire du ski nautique*, I, 4
waterfall *une chute d'eau*, II, 4
way: No way! *Pas question!* II, 1; *Pas possible!* II, 6
wear *mettre, porter*, I, 10; **I don't know what to wear for . . .** *Je ne sais pas quoi mettre pour... ,* I, 10; **Wear . . .** *Mets... ,* I, 10; **What shall I wear?** *Qu'est-ce que je mets?* I, 10; **Why don't you wear . . . ?** *Pourquoi est-ce que tu ne mets pas... ?* I, 10
Wednesday: on Wednesdays *le mercredi*, I, 2
weekend: Did you have a good weekend? *Tu as passé un bon week-end?* I, 9; **on weekends** *le week-end*, I, 4; **this weekend** *ce week-end*, I, 6; **What a bad weekend!** *Quel week-end!* II, 5
welcome: At your service; You're welcome. *A votre service.* I, 3; **Welcome to my home (our home)** *Bienvenue chez moi (chez nous),* II, 2
well: Did it go well? *Ça s'est bien passé?* I, 11; **Get well soon!** *Bon rétablissement!* II, 3; **I don't feel well.** *Je ne me sens pas bien.* II, 7; **It went really well!** *Ça s'est très bien passé!* II, 5; **Very well.** *Très bien.* I, 1; **Well done!** *Chapeau!* II, 5; **You don't seem too well.** *Tu n'as pas l'air en forme.* II, 7; **You would do well to . . .** *Tu ferais bien de... ,* II, 7
west: in the west *dans l'ouest*, II, 4; **It's to the west of . . .** *C'est à l'ouest de... ,* II, 12
western (film) *un western*, II, 11
what *comment*, I, 0; **I don't know what to do.** *Je ne sais pas quoi faire.* II, 10; **What are you going to do . . . ?** *Qu'est-ce que tu vas faire... ?* I, 6; **What are you going to do . . . ?** *Tu vas faire quoi... ?* I, 6; **What bothers me is . . .** *Ce qui m'ennuie, c'est... ,* II, 4; **What can we do?** *Qu'est-ce qu'on peut faire?* II, 4; **What do you have to drink?** *Qu'est-ce que vous avez comme boissons?* I, 5; **What do you need for . . . ?** (formal) *Qu'est-ce qu'il vous faut pour... ?* I, 3; **What do**

you need for . . . ? (informal) *Qu'est-ce qu'il te faut pour... ?* I, 3; **What do you think of . . . ?** *Comment tu trouves... ?* I, 2; **What do you think of that/it?** *Comment tu trouves ça?* I, 2; **What I don't like is . . .** *Ce que je n'aime pas, c'est... ,* II, 4; **What I like is . . .** *Ce qui me plaît, c'est... ,* II, 4; **What is there . . . ?** *Qu'est-ce qu'il y a... ?* II, 4; **What is your name?** *Tu t'appelles comment?,* I, 0; **What kind of . . . do you have?** *Qu'est-ce que vous avez comme... ?* I, 5; **What's his/her name?** *Il/Elle s'appelle comment?* I, 1; **What's it like?** *C'est comment?* II, 4
when: When? *Quand (ça)?* I, 6; **When do you open (close)?** *A quelle heure est-ce que vous ouvrez (fermez)?* II, 6
where *où*, I, 6 **Where did you go?** *Tu es allé(e) où?* I, 9; **Where is . . . , please?** *Où est... , s'il vous plaît?* II, 2
which: From which platform . . . ? *De quel quai... ?* II, 6
white *blanc(he)*, I, 3
who: Who's calling? *Qui est à l'appareil?* I, 9
whom: With whom? *Avec qui?* I, 6
why: Why don't you . . . ? *Pourquoi tu ne... pas?* I, 9; II, 7; **Why not?** *Pourquoi pas?* I, 6
win *gagner*, I, 9
window *la fenêtre*, I, 0; **to window-shop** *faire les vitrines*, I, 6
windsurfing: to go windsurfing *faire de la planche à voile*, I, 11; II, 4
winter: in the winter *en hiver*, I, 4
wiped out: I'm wiped out. *Je suis tout raplapla.* II, 7
wishes: Best wishes! *Meilleurs vœux!* II, 3
with: with me *avec moi*, I, 6; **With whom?** *Avec qui?* I, 6
withdraw: to withdraw money *retirer de l'argent* (m.), I, 12
without: You can't leave without . . . *Tu ne peux pas partir sans... ,* I, 11
wolf *un loup*, II, 12
wonder: I wonder . . . *Je me demande... ,* II, 9
work *travailler*, I, 9
worried *inquiet (inquiète)*, II, 9
worries: to have worries *avoir des soucis*, II, 8
worry: Don't worry! *Ne t'en fais pas!* I, 9; *T'en fais pas.* II, 5
worthless *nul (nulle)*, II, 8; **It's worthless** *C'est du n'importe quoi,* II, 11

would: What would you do?
Qu'est-ce que tu ferais, toi? II, 10;
Would you mind . . . ? *Ça t'em-bête de... ?* II, 10; *Ça t'ennuie de... ?* II, 10; **Would you pass . . .** *Vous pourriez (tu pourrais) me passer... ,* II, 3; **Yes, I would.** *Oui, je veux bien.* II, 3; **You would do well to . . .** *Tu ferais bien de... ,* II, 7
would like: **I'd like to buy . . .** *Je voudrais acheter... ,* I, 3;
write: **Write him/her/them.** *Ecris-lui/leur.* II, 10
wrong: **Everything went wrong!** *Tout a été de travers!* II, 5; **Is something wrong?** *Quelque chose ne va pas?* II, 7; **You look like something's wrong.** *Ça n'a pas l'air d'aller.* II, 5; **What's wrong?** *Qu'est-ce qui t'arrive?* II, 5; *Qu'est ce que tu as?* II, 7; *Qu'est-ce qu'il y a?* II, 10

Y

yard *le jardin,* II, 2
Yeah. *Mouais.* II, 6
yeah: **Yeah, right!** *Mon œil!* II, 6
year: **I am . . . years old.** *J'ai ... ans.* I, 1; **When I was . . . years old, . . .** *Quand j'avais... ans,... ,* II, 8
yellow *jaune,* I, 3
yes *oui,* I, 1

yet: **not yet** *ne... pas encore,* I, 9
yogurt *du yaourt,* I, 8
you *tu, vous,* I, 0; **And you?** *Et toi?* I, 1
young *jeune,* I, 7, II, 1
your *ton/ta/tes/votre/vos,* I, 7

Z

zoo *le zoo,* I, 6, II, 6

GRAMMAR INDEX

A

à: Contractions with **à**, p. 44

adjective: Adjective agreement, p. 11; Irregular adjectives, pp. 11 and 39; The use of **de** before a plural adjective and a noun, p. 88

air: **avoir l'air** + adjective, p. 227

aller: The future with **aller**, p. 21

articles: Partitive articles, p. 65

avoir: **avoir l'air** + adjective, p. 227

C

c'est: **il/elle est** vs. **c'est**, p. 275

c'était, p. 144

commands: Imperatives, p. 15

connaître, p. 274

contractions: Contractions with **à**, p. 44; with **de**, p. 39

D

de: The use of **de** before a plural adjective and a noun, p. 88; Contractions with **de**, p. 39

E

elle: **il/elle est** vs. **c'est**, p. 275

emporter, p. 310

en: The object pronoun **en**, p. 58; The pronoun **en** with activities, p. 172

est: **il/elle est** vs. **c'est**, p. 275

était, p. 144

être: The **passé composé** with **être**, pp. 124 and 147

être en train de: The **passé composé** and the **imparfait** with interrupted actions, p. 237

F

future tense: The future with **aller**, p. 21

I

il: **il/elle est** vs. **c'est**, p. 275

imparfait: Formation of the **imparfait**, pp. 199 and 202; Making suggestions with **si on** + the **imparfait**, p. 209; The **passé composé** and the **imparfait**, pp. 233 and 315; The **passé composé** and the **imparfait** with interrupted actions, p. 237

imperatives, p. 15

indirect object: The indirect object pronouns **lui** and **leur**, p. 68

infinitive: Object pronouns before an infinitive, p. 259

irregular: Irregular adjectives, pp. 11 and 39

L

leur: The indirect object pronouns **lui** and **leur**, p. 68

lui: The indirect object pronouns **lui** and **leur**, p. 68

O

object pronouns: The pronoun **en**, p. 58; Direct object pronouns with the **passé composé**, p. 257; Object pronouns before an infinitive, p. 259; Placement of object pronouns, p. 252

ouvrir, p. 153

P

partitive articles, p. 65

passé composé: The **passé composé** with avoir, p. 120; Direct object pronouns with the **passé composé**, p. 257; The **passé composé** with **être**, pp. 124 and 147; Reflexive verbs in the **passé composé**, pp. 124 and 168; The **passé composé** and the **imparfait**, pp. 233 and 315; The **passé composé** and the **imparfait** with interrupted actions, p. 237

present tense: The present tense of reflexive verbs, p. 100

Q

que: The relative pronouns **qui** and **que**, p. 287

questions: Formal and informal phrasing of questions, p. 152

qui: The relative pronouns **qui** and **que**, p. 287

R

S

ACKNOWLEDGMENTS (continued from ii)

Camping Granby: Advertisement, "Camping Granby," from *Camping/Caravaning '93.*

Casterman: Cover of *Les aventures de Tintin : Le Secret de la Licorne* by Hergé. Copyright © 1947, 1974 by Casterman.

Centre Équilibre Santé les Quatre-Temps: Cover of brochure, *Centre Équilibre Santé Les Quatre-Temps.*

City Lights Books and Photo Izis Bidermanas: Cover of *Paroles: Selected Poems* by Jacques Prévert, translated by Lawrence Ferlinghetti. Translation copyright © 1958 by Lawrence Ferlinghetti.

COFIROUTE: Excerpt from map of Touraine from *Guide des autoroutes,* 18th edition.

Comité Français d'Education Pour la Santé: "Vive l'eau" from *Les Secrets de la Forme-Guides Pratiques,* no. 14. From the poster "Code des enfants pour les enfants," edited and distributed by CFES-2, rue August Comte-92170 Vanves.

Contrex: Photograph from "Vive l'eau" from *Les Secrets de la Forme—Guides Pratiques,* no. 14.

Domaine des Arpents Verts: Advertisement, "Domaine des Arpents Verts," from *Camping/Caravaning '93.*

EDICEF: "78. Les questions difficiles (suite)" and cover from *La Belle Histoire de Leuk-le-Lièvre* by Léopold Sédar Senghor and Abdoulaye Sadji. Copyright © 1953 by Librairie Hachette.

Editions Gallimard: Cover and text from *La cantatrice chauve* by Eugène Ionesco. Copyright © 1954 by Editions Gallimard. Cover of *La cantatrice chauve suivi de La leçon* by Eugene Ionesco. Copyright © 1954 by Editions Gallimard. "Le cancre" and "Page d'écriture" from *Paroles* by Jacques Prévert. Copyright © 1980 by Editions Gallimard. Cover of *Un amour de Swann* by Marcel Proust. Copyright © 1954 by Editions Gallimard.

Editions J'ai Lu: Cover of *Les années métalliques* by Michel Demuth. Copyright © 1977 by Éditions Robert Laffont, S.A. Cover of *Daïren* by Alain Paris.

Editions J. M. Fuzeau: Cover of "Lycée Alfred Kastler: Carnet de Correspondance."

EF Foundation: From "Votre année en High School aux USA" from *Une année scolaire à l'étranger,* 1993–94.

Grand Teint, Gonfreville, Ivory Coast: Portion of cloth manufactured by Grand Teint.

Groupement E. Leclerc: Photographs and text of camping equipment and logo from *Bientôt les vacances,* June 9–19, 1993. Nine photographs of fruits and vegetables and logo from *Grande Fraicheur à petits prix,* October 13–23, 1993.

Gymnase Club: Schedule of activities for October 1993 for Gymnase Club.

Hachette Filipacchi Presse: From "Secret de Beauté : Claudia Schiffer" by Caroline Corvaisier from *OK Podium!* Copyright © by Hachette Filipacchi Presse.

La Cave: Advertisement, "La Cave," from *Chartres : Ville d'Art.*

La Napolitaine-Pizzeria: Advertisement, "La Napolitaine-Pizzeria."

La Passacaille: Advertisement, "La Passacaille," from *Chartres : Ville d'Art.*

Le Chêne Fleuri: Advertisement, "Le Chêne Fleuri," from *Chartres : Ville d'Art.*

Le Figaro: From "Theatre: Avignon" from "Provence-Côte-d'Azur" from *Le Figaro Magazine: Guide de l'été,* June 25, 1994. Copyright © 1994 by Le Figaro.

Le P'tit Morard: Advertisement, "Le P'tit Morard," from *Chartres : Ville d'Art.*

Le Temple d'Angkor: Advertisement, "Le Temple d'Angkor," from *Chartres : Ville d'Art.*

Les Baladins du Comte de Taillebourg Mairie: Advertisement, "Taillebourg: 'Le génie du château'" from *Évasions,* no. 49, August 1993.

Librairie des Champs-Élysées: Cover of *Mort sur le Nil* by Agatha Christie, translated by Louis Postif. Copyright © 1948 by Agatha Christie Librairie des Champs-Élysées.

Ministère de la Culture et de la Francophonie: "Les exclus du loisir" from *Francoscopie 1993* by Gérard Mermet.

Ministère de l'environnement et de la Faune: "Conseils pratiques" with illustration and "Bienvenue dans le Parc de la Jacques-Cartier" with illustrations from *Parc de la Jacques-Cartier.* Chart, "Activités et services offerts dans les 16 parcs du Québec" from *Destination Nature: Les Parcs du Québec.*

Office de Tourisme de Chartres: Map of Chartres from *Chartres: Ville d'Art.* "Le Centre International du Vitrail," "Le Maison Picassiette," "Le Musée des Beaux Arts," and "Les Tours de la Cathédrale" from *Passeport Culturel pour Chartres,* 1992. Copyright © 1992 by the Office de Tourisme de Chartres.

Office de Tourisme de Fontainebleau: "Renseignements Pratiques" from *Fontainebleau.*

Office Départemental du Tourisme de la Martinique: From "Calendrier des Evénements" from *Tourist Magazine.*

Pariscope: une semaine de Paris: "Aladdin," "Le Fugitif," "Geronimo," "les Trois Mouquetaires," "Une breve histoire du temps," and "Une pure formalite" from *Pariscope: une semaine de Paris,* no. 1357, May 25–31, 1994, pages 82, 87, 88, 90, 95, 97, 138, 139. Copyright © 1994 by Pariscope.

Parc Bromont: Advertisement, "Parc Bromont," from *Camping/Caravaning '93.*

Pocket: Cover of *L'enfant noir* by Camara Laye. Copyright © 1953 by Librairie Plon.

Présence Africaine: Cover of *La tragédie du Roi Christophe* by Aimé Césaire. Copyright © 1963 by Présence Africaine.

PROMOTRAIN: Advertisement, "Une promenade insolite, sans fatigue," from *Chartres : Ville d'Art.*

Rainbow Symphony, Inc: Portion of "The Original Lazer Viewers™ 3-D Fireworks Glasses."

Daho Malick Raoul: Adaptation of "Un Jeune Ivoirien s'en Souvient" by Hoba Raoul from *Le Miroir d'Abidjan,* no. 001, page 3.

Scoop: Adaptation of Table of Contents from *Paris Match,* no. 2342, April 14, 1994. Copyright © 1994 by Scoop.

Services Touristiques de Touraine: From "Circuits d'une demi-journée," from "Circuits d'une journée," and from "Spectacles son et lumière" from *Châteaux de la Loire : Circuits en autocars au départ de TOURS du 10 AVRIL au 30 SEPTEMBRE 1993.*

SNCF: Direction Grandes Lignes: SNCF train schedule.

Sony Music France: Cover and side 2 of CD from *Tékit izi* by Kassav'. Copyright © 1992 by Sony Music Entertainment (France) S.A./Saligna Production.

Sony Tunes: Lyrics from "An Sèl Zouk" from *Tékit izi* by Kassav'. Copyright © 1992 by Sony Music Entertainment (France) S.A./Saligna Production.

Spiral SARL: Advertisements, "Saran: A la recherche de la lumière" and "Valençay : La 'belle', dans le parc aux daims," from *Évasions*, no. 49, August 1993.

STS Student Travel Schools AB: Photographs: "La fête de la 'Graduation'..." and "Participez au bal..." and photographs and text: "Guillaume Fabry" and "Sonia Gabor" from *Une année scolaire aux USA 1993/1994*. Copyright © 1993 by STS Student Travel Schools AB.

Télé Câble: "L'Eternel retour," and "Notre-Dame de Paris" from "Films de mars: le choix de Cinémaniac" from *Télé Câble*, no. 2, March 1993. Copyright © 1993 by Télé Câble.

Télé 7 Jours: From television program schedule for Wednesday (Mercredi), August 18 from *Télé 7 Jours*, no. 1733, pp. 80, 82, and 84, August 14, 1993. Copyright © 1993 by Télé 7 Jours.

Vacances Air Canada: "L'appel des loups" and "Spécial jeunes" from *Vacances Air Canada: brochure été 1994*. Copyright © 1994 by Air Canada.

PHOTOGRAPHY CREDITS

Abbreviations used: (t) top, (c) center, (b) bottom, (l) left, (r) right, (bckgd) background.

FRONT COVER: (t), Tony Freeman/PhotoEdit; (b), Robert Fried Photography. **BACK COVER:** (t), Nabil Zorkot/ProFoto; (b), SuperStock. **FRONT AND BACK COVER BACKGROUND:** © MICHELIN Map No. 989, 1994 edition. Permission No. 94-522. **FRONT AND BACK COVER COLLAGE:** HRW Photo by Andrew Yates.

Chapter Opener Photographs: Scott Van Osdol.

All Photographs HRW Photos by Marty Granger/Edge Productions except:

TABLE OF CONTENTS: Page v(cl), v(cr), HRW Photo by Scott Van Osdol; v(bc), v(br), HRW Photo by Sam Dudgeon; vi(tc), vi(c), vi(bc), HRW Photo by Scott Van Osdol; vi(tr), vi(cl), vi(bl), HRW Photo by Scott Van Osdol; vii(t) vii(b), HRW Photo by Scott Van Osdol; vii(cl), viii(tl), viii(cl), viii(cr), HRW Photo by Sam Dudgeon; viii(tr), viii(bl), ix(tl), ix(cl), ix(bc), HRW Photo by Scott Van Osdol; ix(tr), ix(bl), HRW Photo by Sam Dudgeon; x(tc), HRW Photo by Scott Van Osdol; x(cr), HRW Photo by Sam Dudgeon; x(cl), x(bc), x(br), Harbrace Photo by Mark Antman; xi(tl), Burke/Triolo Photographic Studio; xi(tc), xi(cl), xi(bl), xi(br), HRW Photo by Scott Van Osdol; xi(c), xi(cr), HRW Photo by Sam Dudgeon; xii(tl) Louis Boireau, xii(br) HRW Photo by Louis Boireau/Edge Productions xii(tc), HRW Photo by Scott Van Osdol; xii(tr), xii(cl), xii(bl), HRW Photo by Sam Dudgeon; xiii(tl), xiii(cr), HRW Photo by Scott Van Osdol; xiii(bc), HRW Photo by Sam Dudgeon; xiii(br), HRW Photo by Patrice Maurin; xiv(tr), xiv(br), HRW Photo by Sam Dudgeon; xiv(bc), HRW Photo by Scott Van Osdol; xv(tl), xv(tr), xv(cl), xv(bl), xv(br), HRW Photo by Sam Dudgeon; xv(cr), HRW Photo by Scott Van Osdol; xvi(tc), xvi(bc), HRW Photo by Scott Van Osdol; xvi(cl), xvi(cr), xvi(bl) SuperStock, xvi(br), HRW Photo by Sam Dudgeon.

UNIT ONE: Page xxiv-1(c), Phillipe Chardon/Option Photo; 2(t), Bill Wassman/The Stock Market; 2(c), George Seurat, French, 1859-1891, A Sunday on La Grande Jatte - 1884, oil on canvas, 1884-86, 207.6 x 308 cm, Helen Birch Bartlett Memorial Collection, 1926.224; 2(b), S. Kanno/FPG International; 3(t), Steve Elmore/Tony Stone Images, Inc.; 3(cl), Marc Deville/Gamma Liaison; 3(bc), Brigitte Perigois/Option Photo; 3(br), J. Reznicki/The Stock Market. **Chapter One:** Page 5(b), 6(bl), HRW Photo by Sam Dudgeon; 9(l), Walter Chandoha; 9(c), HRW Photo by May Polycarpe; 10(l), Banaroch/Sipa Press; 10(r), Toussaint/Sipa Press; 10(cl), Philippe Denis/Sipa Press; 10(cr), Sebastien Raymond/Sipa Press; 12(t), HRW Photo by Russell Dian; 13, Mark Antman/The Image Works; 14(both), HRW Photo by Sam Dudgeon; 16(l), Serge Coté/L'Imagier; 16(r), HBJ Photo by Capretz; 17(l), HRW Photo by Louis Boireau/Edge Productions; 19(t), Ulrike Welsch/PhotoEdit; 19(b), Emmanuel Rongieras d'Usseau; 21(r), Ken Sax/Shooting Star; 22(b), HRW Photo; 24(b), HRW Photo by Stan Rappaport; 26(l), HRW Photo by Russell Dian; 26(r), Tony Freeman/PhotoEdit; 26(c), HRW Photo by Henry Friedman. **Chapter Two:** Page 30(br), HRW Photo by Sam Dudgeon; 34(l), Chapman/IPA/The Image Works; 34(cr), R. Lucas/The Image Works; 34(r), 35(r), HRW Photo by Sam Dudgeon; 35(c), Michelle Bridwell/Frontera Fotos; 36(r), HRW Photo by Sam Dudgeon; 38(tl), HRW Photo; 38(tc), HRW Photo by Sam Dudgeon; 38(cr), Gill C. Kenny/The Image Bank; 43(tl), HRW Photo by John Langford; 43(cl), HBJ Photo by Oscar Buitrago; 43(c), IPA/The Image Works; 50(l), HRW Photo by Sam Dudgeon; 50(r), Michelle Bridwell/Fronteras Fotos; 50(c), UPI Photo/UPI/Bettmann. **Chapter Three:** Page 53(all), Mark Antman/The Image Works; 63(t), HRW Photo by Sam Dudgeon; 63(c), HRW Photo by Cooke Photographic; 70(l), HRW Photo by Sam Dudgeon; 72, Jacques Charmoz/Artist Rights Society; 74(c), HRW Photo by Sam Dudgeon; 74(b), Amy Reichman/Envision; 76(all), HRW Photo by Sam Dudgeon

UNIT TWO: Chapter Four: Page 85(t), HRW Photo by Russell Dian; 86(cr), Pamela Pate; 87(b), The Bettmann Archive; 89(cl), Robert Rattner; 90(l) HRW Photo by Louis Boireau/Edge Productions; 91(l), HRW Photo/Edge Productions; 92(b), Allan A. Philiba; 93 (top row), (1, 3), Robert Fried; (2) Allan A. Philiba; (center row), (2), Kit Kittle/Viesti Associates; (bottom row), (1), Robert Fried; 97(all), Joe Viesti/Viesti Associates; 101(l), HBJ Photo by Capretz; 101(r), Allan A. Philiba; 102, HRW Photo by Sam Dudgeon; 103(both), HRW Photo by Sam Dudgeon; 104(tl), Robert Fried; 104(tr), Allan A. Philiba; 104(cl), Pamela Pate.

UNIT THREE: Page 108-109(c), 110(tl), Four By Five, Inc.; 110(tr), Dennis Hallinan/FPG International; 110(cr), E. Scorcelletti/Gamma Liaison; 110(bl), 110(bc), SuperStock; 111(t), S. Vidler/SuperStock; 111(cl), Culver Pictures, Inc.; 111(br), Giraudon/Art Resource, New York. **Chapter Five:** Page 113(t), HRW Photo by Sam Dudgeon; 113(b), David Young-Wolff/PhotoEdit; 115(both), 122, HRW Photo by Sam Dudgeon; 123, HRW Photo by Scott Van Osdol; 125(r), 125(c), HRW Photo by Sam Dudgeon; 127, HRW Photo by Scott Van Osdol. **Chapter Six:** Page 141(t), T. Mogi/Superstock; 141(c), Paul Barton/The Stock Market; 142(tl), Robert Fried/Stock Boston; 142(tc), Jose Carrillo/PhotoEdit; 142(tr), W. Bertsch/PhotoEdit; 142(center row), (1) Owen Franken/Stock Boston; (2) Michael Melford/The Image Bank; (4), The Image Bank; 142(bl), Robert Fried; 142(bc), H. Kanus/Superstock; 142(br), Adam Woolfitt/Woodfin Camp & Associates; 145(b), HRW Photo by Scott Van Osdol; 149(c), Culver Pictures, Inc.; 149(cr), The Image Works Archive; 149(b), The Bettmann Archive; 156(inset), E. Scorcelletti/Liaison International; 156(c), Stephen Studd/Tony Stone Images; 157(t), Culver Pictures, Inc.; 158(r), Tony Freeman/PhotoEdit. **Chapter Seven:** Page 160(c), Tony Freeman/PhotoEdit; 161(t), Burke/Triolo Photographic Studio; 171(c), Richard Hutchings/PhotoEdit; 171(bl), Tony Freeman/PhotoEdit; 171(bc), Robert Fried;

ILLUSTRATION AND CARTOGRAPHY CREDITS